T0387784

The Palgrave Handbook of Teacher Education in Central and Eastern Europe

Marta Kowalczuk-Walędziak
Roza A. Valeeva • Marija Sablić
Ian Menter
Editors

The Palgrave Handbook of Teacher Education in Central and Eastern Europe

palgrave
macmillan

Editors
Marta Kowalczuk-Walędziak
University of Białystok
Białystok, Poland

Roza A. Valeeva
Kazan Federal University
Kazan, Russia

Marija Sablić
Josip Juraj Strossmayer University of Osijek
Osijek, Croatia

Ian Menter
University of Oxford
Oxford, UK

ISBN 978-3-031-09514-6   ISBN 978-3-031-09515-3 (eBook)
https://doi.org/10.1007/978-3-031-09515-3

This Palgrave Macmillan imprint is published by the registered company Springer Nature Switzerland AG.
The registered company address is: Gewerbestrasse 11, 6330 Cham, Switzerland

Foreword

At its core, education has no boundaries—teacher education too. Over the past few decades, teacher education programmes have become an increasingly important facet of our contemporary societies here in Europe, as we move towards ever more globalised and digitised communities of teaching and learning. Indeed, this culture shift has accelerated exponentially in the past year alone as the teaching community has found innovative ways to respond to the challenges of the Covid-19 pandemic by migrating online and, in doing so, upholding students' right to an education in the face of sudden school closures and physical distancing.

Schools are vital pillars for our societies' futures. But without well-educated and well-resourced teachers, a school is just an empty building—or series of Zoom rooms—because it is these teachers who are able to design learning environments where pupils can actually create the future through the development of new knowledge, new skills, and new competences. However, these processes of educating and resourcing teachers are highly politicised. Against these backdrops, this book focuses on Central and Eastern Europe, the part of the European continent most commonly overlooked in discussions around teacher education. Thus, taking the fall of the Soviet Union in 1989 as its starting point, it charts the roads travelled by educators in this part of the world over the past three decades. A rich array of insights from teams of authors across 21 countries—from Estonia in the north to North Macedonia in the south, from Russia in the east to Poland in the west—offer the reader stimulating analyses and inspiring solutions to education problems, often carried out with great courage and energy despite the socio-political difficulties of their original context. From these generous examples, teacher educators, wherever they are in the world, can find encouragement as they outline and design new solutions for the problems they face in their own teacher education systems.

The Association for Teacher Education in Europe (ATEE) strongly supports this critical cultural movement, committed to enshrining and promoting the importance of education and, consequently, of teacher education. The UN *2030 Agenda for Sustainable Development* calls for ensuring 'inclusive and equitable quality education and promot[ing] lifelong learning opportunities for all'. This book is a great example of just that: its ultimate purpose is to continue the task—already long begun in Central and Eastern Europe—of building inclusive education and creating opportunities for everybody, via the vital work of teacher educators and teachers.

Brussels, Belgium   Davide Parmigiani
October 25, 2020

Acknowledgements

The editors would like to acknowledge the Faculty of Education at the University of Białystok (Poland) for their financial support of this project. We would also like to sincerely thank Aileen McKay for her invaluable linguistic and editorial support with this handbook.

Contents

Part I   Introduction   1

1   **Setting the Scene: The Changing Contexts of Teacher
     Education in Central and Eastern Europe and Beyond**   3
     *Marta Kowalczuk-Walędziak, Ian Menter, Marija Sablić,
     and Roza A. Valeeva*

Part II   The Visegrad Countries   25

2   **Teacher Education in the Czech Republic: Recent
     Developments and Future Prospects**   27
     Karolina Duschinská and Miroslava Černochová

3   **Teacher Education in Hungary: Between Autonomy and
     Control**   53
     Erika Kopp and Orsolya Kálmán

4   **Teacher Education in Poland: Contested Terrains Between
     Policy and Practice**   83
     *Alicja Korzeniecka-Bondar, Marta Kowalczuk-Walędziak, and
     Hanna Kędzierska*

5   **Teacher Education in Slovakia: Recent Joys and Challenges
     for the Future**   109
     Daniela Bačová and Zdenka Gadušová

Part III   The Balkans   135

 6   Teacher Education in Albania: Reforms and Future
     Developments   137
     Nikoleta Mita and Livia Nano

 7   Teacher Education in Bosnia and Herzegovina: The Most
     Significant Changes in Recent Decades for the Initial
     Education and Professional Development of Teachers   159
     *Irma Čehić, Sanela Merjem Rustempašić, Jasmina Bećirović-
     Karabegović, and Izela Habul-Šabanović*

 8   Teacher Education in Croatia: Reforms and Challenges   181
     Marija Sablić, Alma Škugor, and Marija Lesandrić

 9   Teacher Education in the Republic of Serbia: Challenges,
     Possibilities, and Directions for Development   201
     *Olivera Gajić, Svetlana Španović, Biljana Lungulov, and
     Branka Radulović*

10   Teacher Education in Kosovo: Responding to a Challenging
     Local Context and Converging Towards Good International
     Practices   225
     Blerim Saqipi

11   Teacher Education in North Macedonia: Reforms,
     Standardisation, and Creating Communities of Lifelong
     Learners   243
     Majda Joshevska and James M. Underwood

12   Teacher Education in Slovenia: Between the Past, the Present,
     and the Future   269
     Mojca Peček

13   Teacher Education in Montenegro: The Current State,
     Challenges, and Future Perspectives   295
     Dijana Vučković, Veselin Mićanović, and Tatjana Novović

14 The Professionalisation of Teaching Careers in Romania: Transition Processes from Pre-university Education to Higher Education   331
Romita Iucu, Anca Nedelcu, and Mirabela Amarandei

15 Teacher Education in Bulgaria: The Last Three Decades   355
Viara Todorova Gyurova

Part IV   The Baltics   377

16 Teacher Education in Lithuania: Striving for Professionalism   379
Aušra Rutkienė and Lina Kaminskienė

17 Teacher Education in Latvia: Educating Teachers to Become Global Citizens   395
Mārīte Kravale-Pauliņa, Dzintra Iliško, Eridiana Oļehnoviča, Ilona Fjodorova, and Inga Belousa

18 Teacher Education in Estonia: From the Soviet School System to One of the Best in Europe According to PISA Results   433
Katrin Poom-Valickis and Eve Eisenschmidt

Part V   Eastern Europe   453

19 Teacher Education in Russia: The Current State and Development Prospects   455
Roza A. Valeeva and Aydar Kalimullin

20 Teacher Education and Professional Development in the Republic of Belarus: 1990–2020 Overview and Future Prospects   481
Maria Zhigalova

21 Teacher Education in the Republic of Moldova: Past and Present Trends   505
Larisa Kobylyanskaya

**22   Teacher Education in Ukraine: Surfing the Third Wave of
      Change**   527
      Olena Shyyan and Roman Shyyan

Part VI   Conclusion   553

**23   Teacher Education in Central and Eastern Europe: Emerging
      Themes and Potential Future Trajectories**   555
      *Ian Menter, Marta Kowalczuk-Walędziak, Roza A. Valeeva, and
      Marija Sablić*

Index   571

Editors and Contributors

About the Editors

Marta Kowalczuk-Walędziak is Vice-dean for International Co-operation and an assistant professor at the University of Białystok, Poland, and a visiting professor at Daugavpils University, Latvia. She served as a member of the Administrative Council of the Association for Teacher Education in Europe (ATEE), 2018–2021.

Ian Menter is Emeritus Professor of Teacher Education at the University of Oxford, UK. He has been the president of both the Scottish and British Educational Research Associations.

Marija Sablić is Associate Professor and the chair of postgraduate doctoral studies in Pedagogy and Contemporary School Culture at the J.J. Strossmayer University, Faculty of Humanities and Social Sciences, Croatia. She served as a member of the Administrative Council of the Association for Teacher Education in Europe (ATEE), 2015–2021. She is a member of the Editorial Board of the *European Journal of Teacher Education*.

Roza A. Valeeva is Professor, DSc, of Pedagogic Sciences, and the head of the Pedagogy Department in the Institute of Psychology and Education, Kazan Federal University, Russia. She is also the president of Janusz Korczak Society, Russia, and general secretary of the International Korczak Association (IKA). She is the national representative of the International Study Association on Teachers and Teaching (ISATT), and editor in chief of the journal *Education and Self Development*.

List of Contributors

Mirabela Amarandei University of Bucharest, Bucharest, Romania

Daniela Bačová University of Bolton, Bolton, UK

Jasmina Bećirović-Karabegović University of Sarajevo, Sarajevo, Bosnia and Herzegovina

Inga Belousa University of Latvia, Riga, Latvia

Irma Čehić University of Sarajevo, Sarajevo, Bosnia and Herzegovina

Miroslava Černochová Charles University, Prague, Czech Republic

Karolina Duschinská Charles University, Prague, Czech Republic

Eve Eisenschmidt Tallinn University, Tallinn, Estonia

Ilona Fjodorova Center of Sustainable Education, Daugavpils University, Daugavpils, Latvia

Zdenka Gadušová University of Constantine the Philosopher, Nitra, Slovakia

Olivera Gajić University of Novi Sad, Novi Sad, Serbia

Viara Todorova Gyurova Sofia University St. Kliment Ohridski, Sofia, Bulgaria

Izela Habul-Šabanović University of Sarajevo, Sarajevo, Bosnia and Herzegovina

Dzintra Iliško Center of Sustainable Education, Daugavpils University, Daugavpils, Latvia

Romita Iucu University of Bucharest, Bucharest, Romania

Majda Joshevska Foundation for Education and Cultural Initiatives Step by Step, Skopje, Macedonia

Aydar Kalimullin Kazan Federal University, Kazan, Russia

Orsolya Kálmán Eötvös Loránd University, Budapest, Hungary

Lina Kaminskienė Vytautas Magnus University, Kaunas, Lithuania

Hanna Kędzierska University of Warmia and Mazury, Olsztyn, Poland

Larisa Kobylyanskaya Slavic University of the Republic of Moldova, Chisinau, Republic of Moldova

Erika Kopp Eötvös Loránd University, Budapest, Hungary

Alicja Korzeniecka-Bondar University of Białystok, Białystok, Poland

Marta Kowalczuk-Walędziak University of Białystok, Białystok, Poland

Mārīte Kravale-Pauliņa Center of Sustainable Education, Daugavpils University, Daugavpils, Latvia

Marija Lesandrić Josip Juraj Strossmayer University of Osijek, Osijek, Croatia

Biljana Lungulov University of Novi Sad, Novi Sad, Serbia

Ian Menter University of Oxford, Oxford, UK

Veselin Mićanović University of Montenegro, Podgorica, Montenegro

Nikoleta Mita University of Tirana, Tirana, Albania

Livia Nano University of Tirana, Tirana, Albania

Anca Nedelcu University of Bucharest, Bucharest, Romania

Tatjana Novović University of Montenegro, Podgorica, Montenegro

Eridiana Oļehnoviča Center of Sustainable Education, Daugavpils University, Daugavpils, Latvia

Mojca Peček University of Ljubljana, Ljubljana, Slovenia

Katrin Poom-Valickis Tallinn University, Tallinn, Estonia

Branka Radulović University of Novi Sad, Novi Sad, Serbia

Sanela Merjem Rustempašić University of Sarajevo, Sarajevo, Bosnia and Herzegovina

Aušra Rutkienė Vytautas Magnus University, Kaunas, Lithuania

Marija Sablić Josip Juraj Strossmayer University of Osijek, Osijek, Croatia

Blerim Saqipi University of Prishtina, Prishtina, Kosovo

Olena Shyyan Lviv Regional In-service Teacher Training Institute, Lviv, Ukraine

Roman Shyyan Institute of Education Content Modernization, Kyiv, Ukraine

Alma Škugor Josip Juraj Strossmayer University of Osijek, Osijek, Croatia

Svetlana Španović University of Novi Sad, Novi Sad, Serbia

James M. Underwood University of Northampton, Northampton, UK

Roza A. Valeeva Kazan Federal University, Kazan, Russia

Dijana Vučković University of Montenegro, Podgorica, Montenegro

Maria Zhigalova Brest State Technical University, Brest, Belarus

List of Figures

Fig. 3.1   The relationship between public education system stages and the required teacher qualifications   55

Fig. 3.2   ITE programmes in Hungary (In the brackets first showed the credits of the subject fields, second the credits of teacher' preparation)   66

Fig. 3.3   Teachers' career model   72

Fig. 8.1   Education system in Croatia   183

Fig. 12.1   Structure of the education system in the Republic of Slovenia (2019)   273

Fig. 12.2   The structure of the teacher education in Slovenia (Peček and Lesar 2011)   281

Fig. 14.1   An updated model of the European Teacher Education Area—ETEA, based on Iucu (2009)   334

Fig. 14.2   The evolution of pre-university teachers' numbers, based on the *Report on the State of pre-university education in Romania*   337

Fig. 16.1   Number of teachers and number of students in pre-school, primary, and secondary education (2014–2019) (Statistics Lithuania 2020)   381

Fig. 17.1   Stakeholder grouping according to their interest and involvement in GCE   416

Fig. 18.1   Three phases in teacher education   438

List of Tables

Table 3.1   Comparison of teacher education in EU documents
             (Symeonidis 2019) and in Hungary   64
Table 6.1   General data on students and teachers (MOESY 2019)   142
Table 6.2   Registered students in HEIs according to study fields (MOESY
             2019)   143
Table 7.1   Quantitative analysis of the representation of first-cycle courses   171
Table 10.1   Summary of the University of Prishtina's current primary
             teacher education curriculum   232
Table 13.1   Strategic goals, 2016   300
Table 13.2   Faculties for teacher education   301
Table 13.3   Subject percentages in class teacher and pre-school teacher
             education plans in the 1990s and early 2000s   302
Table 13.4   Subject percentages in initial teacher education plans in the
             1990s until 2007   303
Table 13.5   Subject percentages in class and pre-school teacher education
             plans from 2007 to 2016/2017   307
Table 13.6   Subject percentages in subject teacher education plans from
             2007 to 2016/2017   308
Table 13.7   Enrolment into education programmes for teachers in
             Montenegro (bachelor's studies)   316
Table 18.1   Teachers' education by school level   439

Part I

Introduction

1

Setting the Scene: The Changing Contexts of Teacher Education in Central and Eastern Europe and Beyond

Marta Kowalczuk-Walędziak, Ian Menter, Marija Sablić, and Roza A. Valeeva

Introduction

Over the last few decades, ensuring the quality of teacher education (TE) has been positioned as a vital goal at the forefront of education policies and reforms in many countries around the world (e.g., Darling-Hammond and Bransford 2005; Flores 2016; Darling-Hammond 2017). This particular focus on teacher education is supported by a plethora of research, indicating that TE has the power to generate highly beneficial outcomes for students, schools, national education systems, and for society as a whole (Hattie 2009; Hargreaves and Fullan 2012). Of course, this kind of influence is not as straightforward as we might expect, as the process of training teachers is

M. Kowalczuk-Walędziak (✉)
University of Białystok, Białystok, Poland
e-mail: m.kowalczuk@uwb.edu.pl

I. Menter
University of Oxford, Oxford, UK

M. Sablić
Josip Juraj Strossmayer University of Osijek, Osijek, Croatia

R. A. Valeeva
Kazan Federal University, Kazan, Russia

© The Author(s), under exclusive license to Springer Nature Switzerland AG 2023
M. Kowalczuk-Walędziak et al. (eds.), *The Palgrave Handbook of Teacher Education in Central and Eastern Europe*, https://doi.org/10.1007/978-3-031-09515-3_1

embedded in broader political, economic, and cultural contexts in which education is viewed as a public good, as well as a matter of state responsibility and control (Saha and Dworkin 2009; Menashy 2009; Menter et al. 2017). At present, efforts to explore new teacher education and professional development pathways in Central and Eastern Europe (CEE) are driven by a particular intensity born from the profoundly complex political, socio-economic, cultural, and education transformations of recent times. Indeed, since the end of the communist era, the teaching profession in this part of Europe has been considered a vital tool for transforming society towards consolidating democracy and advancing socio-economic development (Silova 2009; Valeeva and Gafurov 2017). This comes as no surprise, as teacher education programmes have the unique potential to deliver graduates who, by providing high-quality education in their schools, impart knowledge and skills to students so that they in turn can make a difference in their local and national communities. Based on these premises, from the very beginning of CEE's post-communist transformation processes, teacher education has often been a target for reforms and modernisations (Silova 2009). However, we must ask critical questions regarding whether all of these many reforms have been complementary and mutually reinforcing, or contradictory and inhibiting—and to what extent they have meaningfully affected (future) teachers' knowledge and capacities to cope efficiently with the intersecting challenges facing schools in this twenty-first-century reality. Furthermore, we can ask whether or not these reforms were based on robust research evidence, or on modern ideologies rooted in the politics of capitalism, neo-liberalism, and globalisation (Tatto and Menter 2019).

In recent years, there have been several attempts to address some of these questions; however, the majority of such reports, policy documents, and research studies were carried out in select countries or groups of countries in the CEE region (e.g., Godonń et al. 2004; Duda and Clifford-Amos 2011; Silova 2011; Duda et al. 2013; Hálasz 2015; Corner 2017). Therefore, to date, there appears to be no book written in English which comprehensively maps teacher education across the whole CEE region in terms of recent and current legislative, policy, and institutional developments. This handbook therefore bridges this gap by expanding our knowledge base of teacher education policies and practices into new territory, spanning 21 CEE countries with far-reaching and in-depth overviews.

More specifically, this handbook pursues three interrelated objectives. Firstly, it conveys teacher education trajectories over the last three decades reaching from the Balkans, through the Visegrad Group, to Eastern Europe, and up to the Baltic states. Secondly, it provides an analysis of teacher education reform trends, as well as their effects on the structure and organisation of teacher education provision. Thirdly, by critically examining these issues from different perspectives, the book opens up new horizons for re-thinking teacher education policies and practices in CEE, in response to the risks and opportunities generated by globalisation.

How Did This Book Come into Being?

Truthfully, we have long thought of creating this book. So much of the existing literature on the topic of teacher education in Europe is dominated by western European countries and perspectives, often assumed as a proxy for the whole continent (Silova et al. 2020). However, living, researching, and teaching in Central and Eastern Europe, we were highly aware of our region's own history—how it differs from the rest of the continent, but also how it presents unique sets of both problems and opportunities. Although, as noted above, CEE teacher education has been a focus of some studies published so far, most of these efforts generally frame education trends in our part of the world as being 'in transformation' as a default (Kürti and Skalník 2009). In 2021, we think that this lens is outdated and assumes an (unspoken) narrative whereby western European countries are setting the pace and eastern European countries can only ever be slow to catch up. Therefore this book does not seek to prove the worthiness of eastern European teacher education systems against the metric of western European teacher education systems, but rather offers an alternative, more balanced perspective completely—one where CEE countries are presented on their own terms, in their own voices.

As such, from the very beginning, our aim as editors was to build a picture of teacher education in CEE over the last three decades from insiders' perspectives, as a means of challenging how so many of the internationally renowned studies on TE produced and carried out in these countries, perhaps rather ironically, depend predominantly on western theories for their frameworks. Over time, this amounts to a dismissal of research studies and theoretical approaches constructed by CEE scholars themselves (Kürti and Skalník 2009). Our belief in the particular value of these perspectives is embedded in the fact that this geo-political positionality may afford the researcher more nuanced insight and awareness not necessarily readily accessible to outsiders (Kürti and Skalník 2009). Therefore, we invited contributors with extensive knowledge and research experience in the field of teacher education living and working in the very geo-political contexts which they investigate. It was important for us that most of the chapter authors were involved in making education transformations happen—that is, they have been or are actively involved in planning and implementing changes as university or faculty leaders, members of national associations, members of governing or decision-making bodies, teacher educators, or teachers. From these positions of lived experience, they are able to provide richly factual and first-hand perspectives and insights, ranging from the local to the national (Kürti and Skalník 2009).

At the same time, we were fully aware of the dangers of relying exclusively on insiders' perspectives with national borders as the default dividing lines, especially in the current context of rising nationalism and populism across the continent, and indeed in many other parts of the world (Kürti and Skalník 2009). Therefore, as editors, we ensured that these researchers, having spent many years striving to understand precise phenomena in their own countries, received our guidance in order to avoid the over-provision of hyper-detailed, location-specific knowledge with which readers from and in other places cannot do much in practice. Furthermore, structuring our text around singular national positions would have run the risk of overlooking alternative or opposing analyses, or producing oversimplifications caused by the 'we-all-know' syndrome (Kürti and Skalník 2009) which assumes all readers know what the writer themself already knows. Thus, to avoid these dangers of monolithic, national narratives, the teams of authors consist of researchers belonging to different generations and educational backgrounds, or even, as is the case with the North Macedonia and Slovakia chapters, researchers who live and work in other countries. Furthermore, we have organised our editorial team so that while three members come from CEE countries—Poland, Russia, and Croatia respectively—one comes from western Europe, England.

Both the editorial team and the authors were brought together by their active membership in the Association for Teacher Education in Europe (ATEE): a network that has been involved in research and policy analysis in the field of teacher education in Europe (and beyond) for many decades. The association has significantly increased its involvement with CEE countries over the past few years through various initiatives (e.g., conferences and workshops) with the goal of facilitating a better understanding of the trends, challenges, and future prospects for teacher education in this part of Europe. Indeed, several recent ATEE conferences have been organised in CEE countries (namely, Poland, Romania, Croatia, Latvia, and Lithuania) where the issues and problems in teacher education across the region have been intensively discussed. Building on this foundational network, this handbook expands the association's knowledge base by re-examining and re-interpreting the evolution of knowledge, research traditions, and policies in teacher education from the early 1990s onwards from primarily first-hand perspectives.

In order to support the processes of drafting the chapters in this handbook, we created opportunities for the authors and editors to connect and exchange the ideas they generated within their own national and regional contexts with international colleagues and peers. The first such event was a European Parliament seminar in 2019, where authors from Poland, Hungary, Russia, and Albania presented selected issues from their draft chapters to wider audiences, providing excellent grounds for cross-border dialogue (Kowalczuk-Walędziak and Parmigiani 2020). From 2019 onwards, the International Forum on Teacher Education (IFTE), organised by Kazan Federal University (Russia), has been a key meeting point for our team to have discussions and report progress on chapter-writing.

What Does the Modern Central and Eastern Europe Landscape Look Like?

To begin, it would be very misleading to see this region as one single block, whether historically, culturally, or geo-politically (Eberhardt 2003). Indeed, as Barwiński (2019, p. 151) states: '[t]here is no consensus concerning the clear delimitation of the regions, with differences in political and cultural, as well as geographical, historical or civilisational criteria'. Therefore, for the purposes of this work, we have been pragmatic and identified 21 countries that exist independently in the present day.

Politically, all were subjected to some form of communist or socialist government before the 1990s (Glenny 1993). However, we have not included Germany, although of course the eastern part of the present-day federal republic was under communist government until 1989. We have organised these 21 nations into four groups.

* All four countries of the Visegrad Group, that is, the Czech Republic, Hungary, Poland, and Slovakia, were under the strict influence of the Soviet Union until the late 1980s, with the Czech and Slovak nations being one as Czechoslovakia. In all of these countries, however, there had been movements towards democratisation at various points since WWII, but full formal independence was only established in the Soviet Union's Perestroika reform period of the late 1980s and since the fall of the Berlin Wall in 1989 (Garton Ash 1990).
* The Balkans group includes seven countries that were part of former Yugoslavia: Bosnia and Herzegovina, Croatia, Kosovo, Serbia, North

Macedonia, Slovenia, and Montenegro. Several of these states had endured destruction during the 1980s and 1990s as the Yugoslavian state started to break up (Glenny 1992). Albania is also included in this Balkan group, as it was a fiercely self-contained communist state for many years under Enver Hoxha, influenced by Russia, Cuba, and China. The other Balkan states included here are Bulgaria and Romania, again, countries that had existed for many years in their own right, but in the twentieth century were very much under Soviet influence.

* The trio of Baltic republics, Lithuania, Estonia, and Latvia, achieved—or re-achieved—their independence from the Soviet Union in the early 1990s (Lieven 1999).

* Lastly, the eastern European nations are Russia, Belarus, Moldova, and Ukraine—each of which had been part of the Union of Soviet and Socialist Republics (USSR) for almost 95 years. Russia is now a federation encompassing many territories, but is still by far the largest nation covered in this work.

Even this apparently simple outline of these geo-political groups shows how truly complex the history of this region is and how varied their paths towards present-day independence have been. Therefore, this fundamental complexity must always be taken into account when trying to reach any general conclusions concerning the various factors influencing and impacting teacher education reform processes and outcomes in the region.

The collapse of the Soviet system—with its communist misrule and rigid ideology—in the early 1990s was the starting point of radical education changes for many CEE countries, taking place in parallel to major political and economic transformations. Newly gained independence; democratisation of politics and societies; decentralisation; privatisation and marketisation; the liberalisation of the economy; and increased freedom of movement and diversification of ethnicities and religions all had a profound influence on the region's education systems in terms of structure, curriculum, textbooks, examination and assessment systems, and infrastructure (Webster et al. 2011). By way of mapping these relationships between politics and education, Cerych (1997, p. 76) identified the four-level impact of these wider socio-political transformations on education in CEE:

* the depoliticisation of education—namely, the end of strict political ideological control over the education system;
* the breaking down of the state monopoly in education by allowing private and denominational schools to be established;

* the recognition of the right of pupils (and/or their parents and guardians) to choose an educational path according to their abilities and interests;
* and the decentralisation of the management and administration of the education system, including devolving powers to schools and local and/or regional authorities.

The effectiveness of these changes required a restoration of past (i.e., pre-communist) teacher education patterns and structures, shaped towards adapting and assimilating into alternative (mainly western European) trends. In 1999, most CEE countries joined the Bologna Process (with a few exceptions: Russia, joining in 2003; Moldova and Ukraine, joining in 2005; and, more recently, Belarus, joining in 2015). The signing of the Bologna Declaration was a crucial step in initiating a process of profound and large-scale higher education reforms towards building the European Higher Education Area. These include, for example, the adoption of a three-cycle structure of higher education (i.e., bachelor's, master's, and doctoral degree programmes), implementing quality assurance standards, and the European credit transfer and accumulation system (ECTS) for higher education. With most teacher education systems having adapted to the Bologna cycles in the early 2000s (Symeonidis 2021), there was a shift towards 'universitisation' (Zgaga 2013) in teacher education, with programmes offered mainly at higher education institutions; teaching qualifications raised to the level of higher education and entailing a research-based component; and establishing curricula based on learning outcomes (stipulated in accordance with level and field).

However, while such frameworks of teacher education reform may appear to be similar in this introductory overview, it should not be assumed that all CEE countries automatically underwent a similar course of transformation in reality (Silova and Steiner-Khamsi 2008). Instead, we want to stress that many governments in these countries have introduced their own policy documents regulating teacher education strategies in terms of, for example, teacher certification, professional standards for teachers, and the minimum requirements for becoming a teacher. This 'nationalisation' of teacher education policies has led to significant differences in strategies, practices, models, and approaches across the whole region (Zgaga 2006; Symeonidis 2021).

Which Unified Analytical Framework Is Best for Understanding Teacher Education Across Central and Eastern Europe?

As outlined above, CEE is a definitively diverse region of peoples, cultures, and education systems, meaning that finding a common analytical framework for tracing teacher education trajectories across such pluralistic and complex contexts was a real challenge—although not an impossible one.

Our starting point for this work was a shared view that teacher education is a fundamentally broad process that occurs over the course of teachers' professional lifespans (Menter et al. 2017; Kowalczuk-Walędziak et al. 2020). On a theoretical and methodological basis, we believe that teacher education and professional learning is a continuum: from initial/pre-service teacher education, through induction, and onwards to ongoing professional development. Therefore, the term 'teacher education' as used in this handbook involves both initial teacher preparation and continuing professional development. This broad conceptualisation not only adds richness to our examination of teacher education processes in CEE, but also allows us to encompass the real multiplicity and diversity of teacher education pathways across the 21 countries.

Now that 30 years have passed since the collapse of the communist regime, it is important to empower ourselves and each other with the knowledge of how the past can and does shape the present and future of teacher education. As mentioned earlier, we do realise that the notions of 'transition' and 'transformation' seem to be the dominant, and often automatic, analytical lenses framing discussions of education systems in CEE (e.g., McLeish 2003; Silova and Steiner-Khamsi 2008; Henesova 2016). While it is certainly true that some of the countries in this part of the world are undergoing significant and profound change that seems to position them as lagging 'behind' western Europe—for instance, still adjusting some laws to align with European Union standards—these are not adequate grounds for framing the entire region as being in the throes of radical transition. Although the ripple effects of the communist era are still felt today across the education systems of many CEE countries (Mincu 2016), it is a political system best and most accurately understood as firmly relegated to the past, rather than how these communities organise and run themselves in the present day. Now, this clear distinction between lingering patterns and fundamental structure provides a clear lens for in-depth studies which truly reflect the current reality of CEE, opening up new possibilities for articulating and addressing relevant questions, in order to investigate recent developments and potential future directions in the field of teacher education.

Nonetheless, our analytical framework employs historical lenses in every chapter of this book for at least three reasons. Firstly, they contribute to understanding the current situation of teacher education in each setting: indeed, 'it is hardly possible to understand a present-day issue without a sound knowledge of its background development' (O'Donoghue 1993, p. 26 cited in O'Donoghue et al. 2017, p. 11–12). Secondly, an application of historical background is what allows us to locate teacher education processes within their broader cultural, economic, and social contexts and, therefore, allow for the construction of macro-micro linkages across time and place (Placier et al. 2016). Thirdly, it is only with historical knowledge that we can critically examine the extent to which present government-issued reforms are dependent on the rebranding of ineffectual, past reforms or on the creation of innovative, new reforms responsive to the actual needs of students and teachers.

In our age of globalisation, the relationship between national and international teacher education developments must be considered (Menter 2018). Although we recognise that teacher education processes depend on the laws, policies, and knowledge and research traditions of each country, as well as the CEE region as a whole, we must also remember that these processes are pressurised by the uniformity of so-called international agendas—for example, neo-liberal competitions for 'best' student outcomes and standardisation of teaching competences—regarding what is deemed to be important in educating twenty-first-century teachers. Simultaneously, however, carefully adopted globalisation processes do have the potential to serve as 'a source of modification, to varying degrees, of the long trajectories of education policy unique to each national context' (Maroy et al. 2017, p. 101), that is to say offering inspiration, guidance, and motivation. To accommodate these coexisting tensions, the framework within which we undertook this multi-setting inquiry employs a vernacular globalisation perspective (Rizvi and Lingard 2010; Menter 2019), drawing on both international and local literature, knowledge, and experience, in order to better understand how CEE countries have reconciled global neo-liberal pressures with their national identities, values, and practices of education.

Against this backdrop, we asked the chapter authors to use a common analytical framework covering four broad themes:

* the wider context of political, societal, and educational transformations over the last three decades in their country;

* the logic, forces, successes, and challenges underpinning the reformation of teacher education since the fall of communism (i.e., how did global trends in education shape teacher education rhetoric and reforms in their national context? To what extent, and in what ways, are international trends in teacher education understood and reflected in their national teacher education systems?);
* the current landscape of initial teacher education (i.e., pathways to teaching, selection, and recruitment processes) and continuing professional development (i.e., organisation, structure, providers, and financing);
* some recommendations and potential directions for the future development of teacher education in an increasingly globalised and capitalist world.

To collect knowledge on the above themes we charged authors to draw from existing research studies, reports, policy documents, and legal acts produced both in their own national contexts and at an international level. Our hope is that these collectively comprehensive analyses of such a wealth of secondary sources may encourage other scholars to design valuable research studies for fresh primary data collection.

However, we would like to add here that we did not pressure our authors to stick rigidly to the framework we outlined; rather we invited them to adopt their own approaches, simply taking the framework as a starting point. Therefore, it is not surprising that there is an appropriately rich diversity of interpretations within these pages. For example, several authors adopted a chronological approach to outlining the historical development of teacher education in their national contexts (e.g., Slovakia, the Czech Republic, Ukraine, and Poland). Other authors highlighted important current issues related to teacher education in their countries, such as global competences and international communities of practice, making them a focal point for their reflections on our proposed themes (e.g., Latvia, Romania, and North Macedonia). Other authors still centred on one of the themes we proposed, such as the impact of international measures on the development of teacher education in their national context, and organised the other three themes around it (e.g., Estonia). This wide range of approaches and perspectives enriches the whole handbook, as such diversity validates and contributes to ongoing dialogues around the 'enduring themes' underpinning contemporary teacher education previously identified by Ian Menter (2019):

* 'professionalisation' and 'universitisation';
* the relationships between research, policy, and practice;
* partnership between schools and the higher education sector;

* power and control;
* the rise of 'standards';
* the impact of performativity and accountability;
* and the impact of digitisation.

Indeed, these vital themes are addressed—whether explicitly or implicitly—by all the authors of the following chapters, thus clarifying their importance in the processes of building and developing a constructive and fruitful future for teacher education in this part of Europe.

What Is the Structure of This Handbook?

As mentioned earlier, we have organised the 21 CEE countries covered in this book into four geo-political groups—the Visegrad countries, the Balkans, the Baltic states, and eastern Europe. We are starting here, in Part I, Chap. 1, with an outline of the journey we will take together through CEE.

Part II: The Visegrad Countries

The second part of the handbook covers contributions from: the Czech Republic (Chap. 2), Hungary (Chap. 3), Poland (Chap. 4), and Slovakia (Chap. 5).

In Chap. 2 on the Czech Republic, Karolina Duschinská and Miroslava Černochová observe how, after the Velvet Revolution of 1989 and the subsequent division of Czechoslovakia into two nations, the key goal of the new state reforms was to develop a democratic administration that would respect human rights, as well as restore private property and a market economy. Under this new ideology, a number of education reforms—including in teacher education—were executed. This was a four-phase process, comprising the following periods: directly post-1989, from the mid-1990s onwards, from 2003 onwards, and from 2017 onwards. Despite some positive changes throughout these periods, Duschinská and Černochová also highlight a number of challenges that teaching professionals in the Czech Republic still face today: including low prestige and salaries, low investment in education, lack of career prospects, and lack of professional support.

In Chap. 3 on Hungary, Erika Kopp and Orsolya Kálmán analyse the two waves of teacher education reforms (the 2005 Bologna reform and the 2013 restoration of the previously undivided initial teacher education programme for subject teachers), concluding that the reform processes are built on structural and content-focused changes, and, to a lesser extent, are related to changes in learning processes and student-centred approaches. Furthermore, the authors highlight that reform and turbulent change have been a dominant characteristic of initial teacher education in this country, not offset by long-lasting, strategic implementation and evaluation. They also call for nuanced reforms based on in-depth consultation, and giving full consideration to the interests, realities, and perspectives of the different actors directly involved.

In Chap. 4 Alicja Korzeniecka-Bondar, Marta Kowalczuk-Walędziak, and Hanna Kędzierska highlight the complexity of the (lack of) intersections between teacher education policy and practice in post-independence Poland (1989) as shaped by the socio-economic forces of communism, neo-liberalism, and capitalism. Looking to the future, the most important recommendations for developing teacher education in Poland are to break the political character of education reforms and, instead, to focus more on teachers' needs and expectations, as well as to think long-term about modernising the education process as a whole.

In Chap. 5 Daniela Bačová and Zdenka Gadušová outline the development of Slovakia's teacher education policies over the last three decades in two broad periods. The first spans from 1990 to 2004, when Slovakia joined the EU. The second encompasses the subsequent period of decisive changes in teacher education brought about by the Bologna Process; the introduction of key legislation, including acts that defined the roles, responsibilities, and status of teachers across all education sectors; as well as school and national curriculum reforms. Both of these periods are explored at three levels by the authors, that is: the macro-, meso-, and micro-level.

Part III: The Balkans

This part of the handbook encompasses 10 chapters written by scholars from: Albania (Chap. 6), Bosnia and Herzegovina (Chap. 7), Croatia (Chap. 8), the Republic of Serbia (Chap. 9), Kosovo (Chap. 10), North Macedonia (Chap. 11), Slovenia (Chap. 12), Montenegro (Chap. 13), Romania (Chap. 14), and Bulgaria (Chap. 15).

Chapter 6 on Albania by Nikoleta Mita and Livia Nano explains that improving the social status of the teaching profession has been the main focus of teacher education reforms in their country for many years. The government's decision to include teaching on their list of regulated professions in 2010 was crucial in this regard. Beyond this, a number of new laws and regulations were created in order to establish new programmes, criteria, required credits, and a liberalised market for teacher training (in accordance with the Bologna Process). However, despite these positive changes, teacher education in Albania still faces many challenges, including: the absence of comprehensive policy to support the development of the teaching profession; excessive government involvement in the modernisation of teacher education; and an inadequate mentoring system for teachers and prospective teachers.

Irma Čehić, Sanela Rustempašić, Jasmina Bećirović-Karabegović, and Izela Habul-Šabanović begin Chap. 7 on Bosnia and Herzegovina by arguing that the development of teacher education in line with the Bologna Process has not been harmonious—rather, there are numerous inconsistencies in legislative, policy, and institutional developments across the country. This is particularly evident in terms of teacher education certification and curricula (especially the number and scope of general and professional subjects available), as well as the providers of teacher development programmes. Therefore, the authors recognise the urgent need to rethink current policies in order to unify legislation, as well as to develop teacher competency standards and enhance the quality of teaching in the future.

In Chap. 8 Marija Sablić, Alma Škugor, and Marija Lesandrić find that teacher education modernisation processes in Croatia have been guided by three, sometimes contradictory, rationales: cultural and historical values, national identity, and 'European' standards. Their detailed analysis of existing pre-service and in-service teacher education programmes reveals a combination of international and local influences. Furthermore, they highlight that even though many recent changes have improved the quality of teacher education and professional development, Croatia should nonetheless renew its teacher education strategy by offering new forms of cooperation between schools, universities, authorities, and extracurricular agencies.

Changes to Serbia's teacher education system, as Olivera Gajić, Svetlana Španović, Biljana Lungulov, and Branka Radulović note in Chap. 9, began with the signing of the Bologna Declaration in 2003—setting out to synchronise their national objectives and curricula with the declaration's principles; defining standards of teacher competences; and rendering participation in professional development compulsory. However, the majority of these reforms were introduced in a top-down manner, without consultation with teachers: who are, as a result, now the executors of reforms rather than their co-creators. The authors conclude that further development of teacher education in the Republic of Serbia requires the introduction of a coherent information system and framework for closely monitoring reform.

Writing about Kosovo, in Chap. 10 Blerim Saqipi highlights how teacher education has been at the forefront of the country's education reform debate to date, addressing the core problems of weak professionalism and poor quality teaching. The author notes that teacher education reforms over the last two decades have been characterised by increasing qualification requirements for teachers, with a view to enhancing professionalism, with mixed success. This reform approach was closely linked with the adoption of policies from recognised good practice models in other countries.

In Chap. 11 Majda Joshevska and James Underwood identify two main waves of teacher education reforms affected by the political transitions and corresponding turbulence as North Macedonia became a democratic country. The first wave was the implementation of the Bologna higher education reforms (from 2003 onwards), aimed at increasing the transparency and quality of the education system, as well as international academic mobility. The second wave was the introduction of a nine-year primary education programme with the ultimate goal of improving students' education outcomes. While these reforms have certainly improved the social status of teachers and the teaching profession, they have arguably done less for improving the quality of initial teacher education and professional development.

Chapter 12 on Slovenia by Mojca Peček notes that when the country's independence was won in 1991, the key focus for education policy was on the immediate changes required for adapting to the new economic and political structure (as well as international trends). This entailed creating the conditions required to improve the quality of research and teacher education programmes. However, prior to this, in 1987, the first cohort of students enrolled in full higher education programmes; then, in 2009, the implementation of the new Bologna study programmes began. Currently, teachers can also acquire their degree through subject-specific courses from one of Slovenia's three public universities. All of these changes, as Peček argues, have created starkly different working conditions for faculty of education academic staff, necessitating adaptation on their part: namely, they have been forced to attain doctoral degrees as quickly as possible and to secure the new accreditation required for working at a university.

Dijana Vučković, Veselin Mićanović, and Tatjana Novović begin Chap. 13 by explaining that Montenegro's teacher education was delivered via two kinds of programmes up until the 1990s: four-year university programmes for the education of class teachers and subject teachers, and two-year college programmes for the education of pre-school teachers. After the signing of the Bologna Declaration in 2003 and three (re)accreditation processes, there remained a great difference between the education of class and pre-school teachers, on the one hand, and subject teachers on the other. The authors conclude that the education of future teachers faces challenges and dilemmas, in particular: a lack of orientation towards teacher competences (in the education of subject teachers); discrepancies between teacher education programmes; and insufficient commitment to research.

In Romania, in recent years, one of the main problems regarding the training of both higher education teaching staff and school teachers has been the separation of the two systems, severing the connections and exchanges in their mutual training and professionalisation, as Romita Iucu, Anca Nedelcu, and Mirabela Amarandei explain in Chap. 14. Therefore, the authors propose a system for initial and ongoing professional formation with the goal of facilitating well-balanced careers in which individual motivation plays an essential role. This system is based on accommodating institutional idiosyncrasies and upholding the principles of new pedagogies, including: modular learning, problem-based learning, flipped classrooms, collaborative online learning, education-research interaction, critical thinking skills, and learning analytics.

Chapter 15 on Bulgaria by Viara Gyurova outlines the clash between the national and European or international factors affecting the development of teacher education, since winning independence from the Ottoman Empire in 1908. The author presents a detailed analysis of four-factor groupings—political, economic, social, and technological—and their role in shaping the current landscape of teacher education in Bulgaria. This analysis reveals that these factors have led to many positive changes in the quality of teacher education and professional development, through: the introduction of a three-degree system; expanding the internationalisation of teacher education; and implementing professional standards in teacher education programmes. However, Bulgaria still faces many challenges in the field of teacher education, and therefore future policies and modernisation efforts should be created collaboratively with its main stakeholders (i.e., teachers) and continuously grounded in these six principles: planning, initiating, controlling, supporting, informing, and evaluating.

Part IV: The Baltics

The fourth part of our handbook platforms contributors from the three Baltic republics: Lithuania (Chap. 16), Latvia (Chap. 17), and Estonia (Chap. 18).

In Chap. 16 on Lithuania, Aušra Rutkienė and Lina Kaminskienė outline how, after the country gained its independence in 1990, the education system was rebuilt around four core principles: humanism, democracy, commitment to Lithuanian culture and plurality, and renewal. Subsequent reformation efforts were designed to open up alternative routes towards a teaching qualification and to make teacher professional development an ongoing process throughout an active professional life—starting from a pedagogical traineeship and progressing into horizontal and vertical career trajectories. Despite some successes in these reformation processes, the country still faces challenges in the field of teacher education, namely: the lack of highly qualified teachers in some regions; insufficiently child-centred practices (specifically, failing to accommodate different learning needs); the low social status of the profession; the dominance of frontal teaching methods; and limited innovations in the field as a whole.

In Chap. 17 Mārīte Kravale-Pauliņa, Dzintra Iliško, Eridiana Oļehnoviča, Ilona Fjodorova, and Inga Belousa initially paint a general picture of teacher education in Latvia over the last 30 years. They then go on to provide a contextual reflection on the process and experience of moving from an emphasis on the national context (in terms of education content, values, and development) to the integration of global citizenship competences into the teacher education curriculum. The authors conclude that the introduction of global citizenship competences in teacher education ultimately marks a turning point for teacher education in Latvia.

In Chap. 18 Katrin Poom-Valickis and Eve Eisenschmidt divide post-Soviet education reforms in Estonia into three periods: firstly, reforms between the mid-1980s and mid-1990s; secondly, reforms between 1995 and 2004; and, thirdly, reforms from 2004 onwards. Based on detailed analysis of changes through these decades, the authors identify some milestones in the modernisation of teacher education, yielding successful Programme for International Student Assessment (PISA) results. These include: introducing national professional teaching standards; enhancing the social status of the teaching profession; treating teacher education as a continuum (starting with initial teacher education, continuing with the induction year, and feeding into continuous professional learning); consulting teachers; and locating the heads of schools as key actors in the process.

Part V: Eastern Europe

The fifth part of the handbook includes chapters from authors who come from four eastern European countries: Russia (Chap. 19), Belarus (Chap. 20), Moldova (Chap. 21), and Ukraine (Chap. 22).

In Chap. 19 Roza A. Valeeva and Aydar Kalimullin argue that teacher education in Russia is in a transitional state: shifting from the traditional Soviet model to training teachers in non-pedagogical universities (i.e., the model now adopted by most countries in the region). Many policy initiatives have been implemented since the 1990s with the aim of bringing teacher education in line with the latest achievements in pedagogical theory and practice. The authors divide the modernisation of teacher education in Russia into the following areas: optimising the structure and organisation of vocational teacher training; improving the content and form of teacher training; and scientific and educational support for updating teacher education. In the context of teacher education reforms in Russia, openness, self-organisation, self-determination, and self-development are becoming essential characteristics.

In the case of Belarus, as Maria Zhigalova notes in Chap. 20, after the collapse of the USSR and the formation of the independent Republic of Belarus in 1991, the government paid particular attention to the modernisation of teacher training, viewing this as the key to increasing the quality of the education system, as well as building Belarus' human potential more broadly. Reform processes have intensified in the last five years by setting new goals for teacher education, as well as pursuing some modernisation strategies and moving to adopt more research-based, active, collective learning. Furthermore, the plans also outline the transition to a cluster model of teacher development, ensuring the integration of psychological and pedagogical science and optimising effective educational practice—as well as increasing the resources allocated to the national education system and boosting the prestige of the teaching profession.

In Chap. 21 Larisa Kobylyanskaya finds that the process of reforming teacher education in the Republic of Moldova has been an important task over the last three decades—with the main purpose of dismantling the communist ideologies underpinning education and science. After the signing of the Bologna Declaration in 2005, the modernisation of teacher education sped up significantly, specifically in terms of institutional structure, curricula, and assessment and examinations. However, the author highlights that, despite the steps taken to reform teacher education in the Republic of Moldova, there are still unresolved problems: the incompatibility of the teacher training system with UNESCO provisions and European standards; the lack of an external accreditation system for pedagogical institutions; the discrepancy between the supply and demand of teachers in the labour market; and the lack of student mobility.

In Chap. 22 Olena Shyyan and Roman Shyyan argue that after Ukraine won its independence in 1991, the development of the country's own education policy and higher education system began under an inherited Soviet system that could not respond adequately to rapid global changes and emerging national policy. During the first wave of transformations (directly post-independence), a number of initiatives took place in the higher education sector—in particular, introducing the Ukrainian government's 1999 *Convention on the Recognition of Qualifications concerning Higher Education in the European Region*. Joining the Bologna Process in 2005 was a major further step towards integration within the European Higher Education Area. Thus commenced a new phase of modernising teacher education in Ukraine, before further opportunities for change came with the Euromaidan revolution in 2014 and the adoption of the new *Law on Education* by the Verkhovna Rada in 2017. This move centred the main aim of solving problems in the education system—outdated didactics; teachers' low social status and pay; lack of motivation for professional growth, and so on—and shifting Ukrainian education towards social equality and cohesion, economic development, and competition.

The handbook concludes with Part VI, collectively authored by the editorial team—Ian Menter, Marta Kowalczuk-Walędziak, Roza A. Valeeva, and Marija Sablić—who offer a synthesising review in Chap. 23 of what has gone before in the country-specific chapters. After providing an overview of the past, present, and future of teacher education across CEE, we then draw out eight major themes that emerge from these accounts. We are not claiming that these themes are unique to CEE countries, but we do suggest that together they provide a characterisation of the changes and developments that have been occurring across this very complex and fascinating region of the world in recent years.

As can be seen from the above brief summaries of the chapters, each one offers a profound and invaluable reading of the highs, lows, hopes, and problems defining teacher education in the authors' countries and communities. Therefore, we would like to thank all of the authors for their engagement, passion, extensive knowledge, and research skills, keeping to deadlines, as well as patience in responding to comments from our reviewers and language editor. Such a working atmosphere led not only to fascinating chapters, but also, ultimately, allowed us to build a new community of responsible and committed researchers in a European space. Step by step, email by email, we have been developing personal and professional relationships imbued with mutual solidarity, support, and concern for each other—especially during the pandemic. Furthermore, the work in this book reminds us (and hopefully our readers) that people working in harmony and focused on a set of mutual objectives are the backbone in (re)building a strong and cohesive Europe.

Taking our team of Editors and Authors as an example, we can say that through dialogue, collaboration, constructive feedback, and free exchange (and confrontation!) between various opinions on the teacher education systems in our countries, we are able to collaboratively express our investment in the future of Europe, which—we think—is largely determined by the quality of teachers' education and development. It is teachers who have a great (perhaps even the greatest) influence on the intellectual capacities, the form, and the functioning of our future societies (Kowalczuk-Walędziak and Parmigiani 2020). What the teacher says or does in the classroom shapes students' knowledge, beliefs, attitudes, emotions, future interests, choices, and passions.

To sum up, this handbook provides a vibrant and unique picture of teacher education systems across 21 diverse CEE settings by highlighting fascinating commonalities and differences; tensions between local and global influences on contemporary policy and practice; and many other surprising insights. However, we do hope that this handbook will be of interest not only to CEE scholars, students, policy-makers, and practitioners, but also to their peers and colleagues across a wide range of geo-political and development contexts. Our goal is for this text to serve as a source of new knowledge and understanding regarding contemporary issues and trends in teacher education, as well as a stimulus for articulating further questions through critical thinking, comparison, and contrast.

References

Barwiński, M. (2019). Geographical, historical and political conditions of ongoing and potential ethnic conflicts in Central and Eastern Europe. *European Spatial Research and Policy*, 26(1), 149–173.

Cerych, L. (1997). Educational reforms in Central and Eastern Europe: Processes and outcomes. *European Journal of Education*, 32(1), 75–96.

Corner, T. (Ed.). (2017). *Education in the European Union: Post-2003 member states.* London: Bloomsbury.

Darling-Hammond, L., and J. Bransford (Eds.). (2005). *Preparing teachers for a changing world. What teachers should learn and able to do?* San Francisco, CA: Jossey-Bass.

Darling-Hammond, L. (2017). Teacher education around the world: What can we learn from international practice? *European Journal of Teacher Education*, 40(3), 291–309.

Duda, A., and T. Clifford-Amos. (2011). *Study on teacher education for primary and secondary education in six countries of the eastern partnership: Armenia, Azerbaijan,*

Belarus, Georgia, Moldova and Ukraine. Final report. Brussels: European Commission, Directorate-General for Education and Culture.

Duda, A., M. Golubeva, and T. Clifford-Amos. (2013). *Teacher education and training in the Western Balkans. Final synthesis report.* Brussels: European Commission, Directorate-General for Education and Culture.

Eberhardt, P. (2003). *Ethnic groups and populations changes in the twentieth-century in Central-Eastern Europe. History, data and analysis.* New York and London: Routledge, Taylor & Francis Group.

Flores, M. A. (2016). Teacher education curriculum. In: J. Loughran and M. L. Hamilton (Eds.), *International handbook of teacher education* (pp. 187–230). Dordrecht: Springer Press.

Garton Ash, T. (1990). *We the People.* London: Granta Books.

Glenny, M. (1992). *The fall of Yugoslavia.* London: Penguin.

Glenny, M. (1993). *The rebirth of history.* London: Penguin.

Godoń, R., P. Jucevičienė, and Z. Kodelja. (2004). Philosophy of education in post-Soviet societies of Eastern Europe: Poland, Lithuania and Slovenia. *Comparative Education,* 40(4), 559–569.

Hálasz, G. (2015). Education and social transformation in Central and Eastern Europe. *European Journal of Education,* 50(3), 350–371.

Hargreaves, A., and M. Fullan. (2012). *Professional capital: Transforming teaching in every school.* New York, NY: Teachers College Press.

Hattie, J. (2009). *Visible learning: A synthesis of over 800 meta-analyses relating to achievement.* London: Routledge.

Henesova, D. (2016). *Teachers under the microscope: A review of research on teachers in a post-communist region.* AuthorHouse.

Kowalczuk-Walędziak, M., A. Lopes, J. Underwood, L. Daniela, and O. Clipa. (2020). Meaningful time for professional growth or a waste of time? A study in five countries on teachers' experiences within master's dissertation/thesis work. *Teaching Education,* 31(4), 459–479.

Kowalczuk-Walędziak, M., and D. Parmigiani. (2020). Introduction. Teacher education in Central and Eastern Europe: Issues, policies, practices. *Eastern European Journal of Transnational Relations,* 4(1), 7–12. Retrieved from http://eejtr.uwb.edu.pl/article/view/437.

Kürti, L., and P. Skalník. (2009). Introduction. Postsocialist Europe and the anthropological perspective from home. In: L. Kürti and P. Skalník (Eds.), *Postsocialist Europe. Anthropological perspectives from home* (pp. 1–28). Berghahn Books.

Lieven, A. (1999). *The Baltic revolution.* Harvard: Yale University Press.

Maroy, C., X. Pons, and C. Dupuy. (2017). Vernacular globalisations: Neo-statist accountability policies in France and Quebec education. *Journal of Education Policy,* 32(1), 100–122.

McLeish, A. E. (2003). Post-totalitarian educational transition: To change a label is easy, but to effect a comprehensive change in practice represents a far greater challenge. *European Journal of Education,* 38(2), 163–175.

Menashy, F. (2009). Education as a global public good: The applicability and implications of a framework. *Globalisation, Societies and Education*, 7(3), 307–320.

Menter, I., R. Valeeva, and A. Kalimullin. (2017). A Tale of two countries—Forty years on politics and teacher education in Russia and England. *European Journal of Teacher Education*, 40(5), 616–629.

Menter, I. (2018). Defining teachers' professional knowledge: The interaction of global and national influences. *Education and Self-Development*, 13(1), 32–42.

Menter, I. (2019). The interaction of global and national influences. In: M. T. Tatto and I. Menter (Eds.), *Knowledge, policy and practice in teacher education: A cross-national study* (268–279). London: Bloomsbury.

Mincu, M. E. (2016). Communist education as modernisation strategy? The swings of the globalisation pendulum in Eastern Europe (1947–1989). *History of Education*, 45(3), 319–334.

O'Donoghue, T. A. (1993). Clio and the curriculum: History and true professional. *Australian Journal of Teacher Education*, 18(1). https://doi.org/10.14221/ajte.1993v18n1.4

O'Donoghue, T., J. Harford, and T. O'Doherty. (2017). *Teacher preparation in Ireland. History, policy and future directions*. Bingley: Emerald.

Placier, P. L., M. Letseka, J. Seroto, J. Loh, C. Montecinos, N. Vásquez, and K. Tirri. (2016). The history of initial teacher preparation in international contexts. In: J. Loughran and M. Hamilton (Eds.), *International handbook of teacher education* (pp. 23–68). Springer.

Rizvi, F., and B. Lingard. (2010). *Globalizing education policy*. London: Routledge.

Saha, L. J., and A. G. Dworkin. (2009). Introduction: New perspectives on teachers and teaching. In: L. J. Saha, and A. G. Dworkin (Eds.), *International handbook of research on teachers and teaching* (pp. 3–11). Dordrecht: Springer Press.

Silova, I., and G. Steiner-Khamsi. (2008). Introduction: Unwrapping the post-socialist reform package. In: I. Silova and G. Steiner-Khamsi (Eds.), *How NGOs react. Globalization and education reform in the Caucasus, Central Asia and Mongolia* (pp. 1–42). Bloomfield, CT: Kumarian Press.

Silova, I. (2009). Varieties of educational transformation: The post-socialist states of Central/Southeastern Europe and the Former Soviet Union. In: R. Cowen and A. M. Kazamias (Eds.), *International handbook of comparative education* (pp. 295–320). Dordrecht: Springer Press.

Silova, I. (2011). Education and post-socialist transformations in Central Asia: Exploring margins and marginalities. In: I. Silova (Ed.), *Globalization on the margins: Education and post-socialist transformations in Central Asia* (pp. 1–23). Charlotte, NC: Information Age Publishing.

Silova, I., J. Rappleye, and Y. You (Eds.). (2020). Beyond the western horizon in educational research: Towards a deeper dialogue about our interdependent futures [special issue]. *ECNU Review of Education*, 3(2), 1–179.

Symeonidis, V. (2021). *Europeanisation in teacher education: A comparative case study of teacher education policies and practices*. Oxon, New York: Routledge.

Tatto, M. T., and I. Menter. (2019). Understanding teacher education policy and practice cross-nationally. In: M. T. Tato and I. Menter (Eds.), *Knowledge, policy and practice in teacher education. A cross-national study* (pp. 3–8). London: Bloomsbury Academic.

Webster, C., I. Silova, A. Moyer, and S. Mcallister. (2011). Leading in the age of post-socialist education transformations: Examining sustainability of teacher education reform in Latvia. *Journal of Educational Change*, 12(3), 347–370.

Valeeva, R. A., and I. R. Gafurov. (2017). Initial teacher education in Russia: Connecting theory, practice and research. *European Journal of Teacher Education*, 40(3), 342–360.

Zgaga, P. (2006). *Looking out: The Bologna Process in a global setting. On the 'External dimension' of the Bologna Process.* Oslo: Norwegian Ministry of Education and Research.

Zgaga, P. (2013). The future of European teacher education in the heavy seas of higher education. *Teacher Development*, 17(3), 347–361.

Part II

The Visegrad Countries

2

Teacher Education in the Czech Republic: Recent Developments and Future Prospects

Karolina Duschinská and Miroslava Černochová

Introduction

This chapter focuses on issues related to initial teacher education and professional development in the Czech Republic. In addition to international research, surveys, and reports, it incorporates original research published in Czech education journals or in professional publications that could be used as a source for teachers' self-reflection, for institutions providing teacher education, and for education policy experts.

In this mapping endeavour, the historical and political context are a crucial starting point. Shortly after the Second World War—in 1946—a law was passed in Czechoslovakia, based upon which pedagogical faculties were established and primary and secondary school teachers were required to be educated at universities. In 1948, the Communists took power, and communist ideology governed the administration of all sectors, including education. Under the Education Act of 1948, for the first time in the history of Czechoslovak education, a unified state school system was established and common education goals were introduced. The basic education of all young people was declared compulsory up to the age of 15. Education at primary and secondary schools, as well as universities, was provided free of charge in public education institutions. Great emphasis was placed on teachers having

K. Duschinská (✉) • M. Černochová
Charles University, Prague, Czech Republic
e-mail: karolina.duschinska@pedf.cuni.cz

a Marxist-Leninist political orientation and making a singular commitment to that worldview. Decades later, as a result of the social and political changes brought about by the Velvet Revolution of November 1989 which saw the end of one-party Communist rule in Czechoslovakia, the country's education policy, including teacher education, had to change.

This chapter deals with both key issues of the past thirty years and perspectives for future development. What have been the most important changes since the dissolution of one-party communism? What was the subsequent transition process like? What did it achieve? What new and emerging circumstances did the system of teacher training and in-service teacher education need to encompass? After so many years, what problems do teacher education and training—including the system of teacher professional development—in the Czech Republic still face? Prior to November 1989, most people in then Czechoslovakia did not expect that the political situation could change, essentially from one day to the next: indeed, they did not imagine that major systemic changes in education could or would be implemented rapidly. Arguably, this is a period of transition which can be characterised by many expectations, much inexperience, great opportunities, and a real diversity of interest groups. Freedom and democracy came at an unexpected speed and, even now, many are still learning how to deal with it.

Context of Teacher Education

Over the past three decades, the Czech Republic has gone from a totalitarian political system and centrally planned state economy to a democratic administration that respects human rights, restores private property, and runs a market economy. The course of historical events leading to this radical change was rapid. After the Velvet Revolution (1989), Czechoslovakia returned to a liberal democracy, then, after the division with Slovakia in 1993, the Czech Republic was founded. Since 1995, the Czech Republic has been a member of the OECD and, since 1999, a member of NATO. In turn, all of these changes have also affected the education sector (Greger and Walterová 2007), but since the Czech Republic already had a relatively long tradition of higher education for teachers, a renewed system of teacher education could be developed on this solid basis.

In 1946, soon after the end of World War II, faculties of education were established as part of public universities in Czechoslovakia. For more information on the history of teacher education in the Czech lands (i.e. Bohemia, Moravia, and Czech Silesia—the three historical regions which formed the

Czech part of Czechoslovakia from 1918), see Novotná (2019). Since the post-war period, primary and secondary school teachers have been university qualified. Before 1989, there was a relatively dense network of teacher education institutions which still exists today, however, prior to the Velvet Revolution, the whole education system had been under the exclusive control of a central power. The totalitarian regime used teachers as its servants (Moree 2013), with the Communist Party of Czechoslovakia influencing the admissions process for applicants to teacher education studies by checking their political 'reliability'. All faculties of education were obliged to have the same study programmes and uniform syllabi: the content and organisational structure of teacher education was centrally co-ordinated, and the state final exams included one on Marxism-Leninism. Fundamentally, the teaching of general didactics was based on the work of socialist educators (e.g. V. V. Davydov, L. V. Zankov, P. J. Galperin), with the teaching of subject didactics developed in collaboration with scientists from socialist countries. Communist resolutions were also strictly applied to the daily life and work taking place in teacher education faculties.

In terms of school education, the most important success following November 1989 was the disappearance of communist ideology, combined with the new possibility of freedom of expression and opinion during a time of rapid political, economic, and social changes. Other important reforms were also addressed in the areas of foreign policy, corporate governance, and legislation, so it should be noted that education was not at the centre of political priorities. Indeed, since 1989, a total of 19 ministers from six different political parties have held the Minister of Education post, making it impossible to maintain continuity and often negatively influencing the speed of and approach to solving problems in the field of education, including teacher education.

After 1989, private and church schools at all levels of education were gradually established. Nonetheless, the majority of pupils and students today are educated in public institutions: currently, 91.5% of kindergartens, 93.7% of primary schools, and 83.9% of secondary vocational schools are in the public domain. In addition, some pupils are educated at home, which is referred to as 'home education'.

One significant problem facing the Czech education sector is its financing. The OECD (2019a, p. 3) reported that:

[e]expenditure on educational institutions in the Czech Republic is lower than on average across the OECD. Total (public and private) expenditure on primary

to tertiary education as a percentage of gross domestic product (GDP) was 3.5% in 2016, well below the OECD average of 5.0%.

Within this comparatively low level of public spending on education, teachers' salaries are among the lowest across OECD countries and consistently below those of tertiary-educated adults at all levels of education (OECD 2019a, p. 3).

The several stages of the development of education in the Czech Republic after 1989 are described by Greger and Walterová (2007) as being crucial for the new shape of the sector, including teacher education. Deconstruction—the first phase of education transformation—lasted only a few months following the political upheaval of November 1989, and was characterised as a period of annulation or correction (Greger and Walterová 2007, p. 15) The second phase (1991–2000) in this transformation was termed 'partial stabilisation' and was characterised by 'gradual, partial legislative, organisational and pedagogical measures' (Greger and Walterová 2007, p. 16). The third and most recent phase lasted from 2005 onwards: that is, the 'period of implementation' of the systemic reform for which the previous reconstruction phase had laid the groundwork. Kotásek et al. (2004, p. 4) specify:

> [i]n the first stage of the transformation, and even later, there was no doubt that most efforts were necessary and fruitful. The trend of 'negating the past and restoring the "status quo ante"' was pursued—particularly in political and academic circles—with the lack of profound knowledge of West-European and global developments in education policies and without a constructive view of the long-term prospects of the development of democratic schooling.

The understandable consequence of such profound upheaval has, in some ways, been the abolition of functional best practices and the overall instability of the system.

With the fall of the communist regime, the Czech Republic's universities were liberated: overnight, all subjects and exams related to communist ideology disappeared from study programmes, including in teacher education. People who, after 1968, had had to leave universities for political reasons could return to academic life at last—they were rehabilitated and many of them went on to significantly influence the further development of Czech education. Professor Radim Palouš—who, as a student in 1945, joined the Prague Revolt as a member of the Czech resistance, and was banned from teaching in 1959—became the first rector of Charles University after the Velvet Revolution. Another very important personality who underwent rehabilitation, regaining his official status as a professor post-regime, was the prominent mathematician and philosopher, Professor Petr Vopěnka, who eventually became Minister of Education (1990–1992). Professor Jiří Kotásek was another a rehabilitated academic, who became Dean of the Faculty of Education at Charles University and led the team that developed the 2001 education development strategies in the National Programme for the Development of the Education System (designated as a White Paper), one of the major milestones in supporting the democratisation of education and pupil-centred approaches to teaching.

In terms of access to higher education courses, those offered at public and state institutions are free of charge, with the exception of administration fees and fees for extending the duration of study beyond a set limit. Over the last three decades, the demographic characteristics of applicants for teacher education courses have partially changed: for instance, now, applicants older than high school graduates, who, for a variety of reasons, did not have the opportunity to study at university pre-1989, have since begun studying at teacher education faculties.

Teacher Education Reforms in the Last Three Decades in Light of Global Trends

Teacher education reform in the Czech Republic was motivated by national trends in social and education reform. With the democratisation of the early 1990s came the topic of democratic citizenship, the opening of private and alternative schools, and the replacement of compulsory Russian language studies with English. These new topics and new school subjects led to a huge need for teacher retraining through both continuing professional development and initial teacher education. Since the mid-1990s, the Czech Republic has been actively involved in large-scale international measures of education success (i.e. TIMSS, PISA, PIRLS, TALIS), thus bringing a global dimension to the nation's education sphere. In this opening up of the Czech Republic's education sector, one of the major milestones was, as mentioned above, the National Programme for the Development of the Education System (Kotásek et al. 2001), which was designed to support democratisation in education, as well as pupil-centred approaches to teaching. As of 2003, all schools are legal entities in their own right, and school heads are fully responsible for the quality of the educational process within their institution—indeed, as is common practice in Europe (Shewbridge et al. 2016), the Czech Republic's School Act

(Zákon č. 561/2004 Sb.) declared the authority of the school curriculum. The Central Educational Programme was replaced by the Framework Educational Plans, the launch of key competences, and a cross-cutting accent on current issues in society. Further, these new focuses, in combination with global trends in environmental education, multiculturalism, and ICT required a fundamental shift in teachers' thinking and professional skills. In fact, teachers became curriculum designers, a new role which made new demands on initial and continuing teacher education. Following these significant changes in the early 2000s, 2017 brought a focus on equity and inclusive approaches in education. Thus, in summary, over the past 30 years, teachers in the Czech Republic have been under constant pressure from waves of reforms. The following is an analysis of the impacts of selected global trends.

Democratic Citizenship

The changes in teacher education after 1989 took place in a society that sought to return to democracy—characterised by a movement from non-freedom to relative freedom, across the areas of institutions, course content, and staff. Indeed, teachers of all grades are important stakeholders in the teaching of democratic citizenship (Dvořáková et al. 2001), therefore it is logical that this requirement was reflected in the post-regime transformation of teacher education. In the Czech Republic today, citizenship education is established as a compulsory part of the curriculum for both primary and secondary education.

Cross-curricular subjects in the Framework Education Programme (FEP) explore problems of the contemporary world, and have become a significant, even indispensable, part of elementary education. These subjects create opportunities for pupils' individual engagement, as well as mutual cooperation and development of their character, primarily in terms of attitudes and values. For instance, the cross-curricular subject, Civic Education for Democracy, is of an interdisciplinary and multicultural nature. Generally, it comprises a synthesis of values—namely justice, tolerance, and responsibility—as well as, specifically, developing critical thinking, an awareness of rights and obligations, and an understanding of the democratic social order and democratic methods for resolving problems and conflicts. Civic Education for Democracy should provide the pupil with a basic level of citizenship literacy, that is, the ability to orient themselves within the intricacies, problems, and conflicts of an open, democratic, and pluralistic society. In order to facilitate this new type of learning, the country's teacher education faculties underwent a completely new conceptualisation and course content-creation process in the fields of civic education—furthermore, points of interconnection with other fields (e.g. history and ethics) had to be created. Truly, the Civic Education for Democracy course is not an isolated unit designed to serve a singular ideology, but a tool for critically thinking about people, science, and active citizenship.

Internationalisation

After November 1989, the state borders opened. The citizens of Czechoslovakia could travel 'freely' all over the world, and people from different continents began to visit Czechoslovakia. Czechoslovakia became, for example, a hub for international conferences about education, with one of them being the ATEE conference in 1994. This new geographical freedom meant that academic staff involved in teacher education and research focused on education could embark upon professional cooperation with experts from other countries, and deliver lectures at foreign universities.

The Bologna Declaration (1999) contained a list of priorities, including (1) the implementation of a unified and comprehensive framework for obtaining academic degrees; (2) the introduction of a structured study system, divided into comparable degrees (bachelor's, master's, and doctoral); (3) the introduction of the European Credit Transfer System (ECTS) and the issuing of diploma supplements; (4) promoting the mobility of students and teachers; and (5) the development of European cooperation in quality assurance.

As a result of the Bologna Process, the five-year master's programme in teacher education was transformed into a bachelor's plus corresponding master's degree, with the exception of the primary school teacher education programme (see also Novotná 2019). This shift has been strongly criticised in the Czech Republic, with academics, in particular, accepting it much less than students (Bendl et al. 2013). Some experts consider the split 'destructive' to the continuity of learning the subject, didactics, and reflexive practices (Minaříková et al. 2015). This change does, however, allow more graduates of non-teaching bachelor's programmes to choose teaching for their subsequent master's degree.

Since the mid-1990s, the Czech Republic has been actively involved in large-scale international studies (TIMSS since 1995, PISA since 2000, PIRLS since 2011, TALIS since 2012, and ICILS since 2013), each of which have brought an international and global dimension to the education environment. Information and data from these comparative research surveys compensate somewhat for the lack of national-level data collection about the state of education in the Czech Republic, yielding results which assist in revealing the weaknesses of the education system. They prompt and direct consideration of factors which have a decisive influence on pupils' success in the subjects they study. The results of these comparative studies are discussed not only at the level of education management, but also in teacher education faculties themselves.

The Czech Republic was also involved in a large-scale international survey, Second Information Technology in Education Study (SITES), focused on the role of ICT in teaching and learning in mathematics and science classrooms. On a practical level, it examined how teachers and students used ICT; the student-to-computer ratio used for instruction; and the extent to which schools had access to the internet for instructional purposes. On a pedagogical level, SITES investigated the extent to which certain pedagogical practices considered conducive to the development of twenty-first-century skills were present, plus the extent to which ICT contributed to changes in approaches to pedagogy.

Beyond these large-scale assessments, international cooperation via teacher education institutions has an impact on teacher education in the Czech Republic in multiple ways. Indeed, at faculties of education, international cooperation takes place both within the framework of participation in joint study programmes and within the framework of various international projects. For instance, the Erasmus Mundus MA/Mgr in Special Education Needs (EM SEN) created as a Master's Course funded by the European Commission's Erasmus Mundus Programme (EMP) to challenge and educate students in inclusive policy and practice in education (Grinbergs and Jones 2013) was an example of cooperation via joint study programmes, instigated by the Charles University Faculty of Education, then acting in collaboration with the universities of Roehampton (England) and Oslo (Norway). This joint degree programme was open to students and academics from the European Union and third countries with a professional focus on the education of people with special educational needs. Unfortunately, however, the cooperation of Czech faculties of teacher education with foreign universities on joint degree programmes is complicated owing to differences in national systems and structures of teacher education, as well as the respective regulations and requirements for the cross-border accreditation of study programmes.

The involvement of Czech faculties of education in international projects contributes not only to improving teacher education; innovation in educational content, standards for the teaching profession, and teacher competences, as well as reflection on teacher educators' work, but also to the presentation and sharing of research findings. Faculties of teacher education in the Czech Republic have gained extensive experience with various EU projects since 1989—namely, TEMPUS, PHARE, ERASMUS+, 5FP, 6FP or 7FP, and Horizon2020. For example, the TEMPUS project of the 1990s focused on student teachers working in the areas of Informatics and ICT, within which the sub-project AQUA brought new teaching methods for teacher education to ICT, Chemistry, and Biology. The Czech Republic was also involved in the 5FP School+ project, the aim of which was to develop and verify an e-learning platform.

While the results of international cooperation are reflected in the teaching of student teachers, the results of these projects are seldom sufficiently implemented at the national level. Therefore, it would be strategically important for the Ministry of Education, Youth and Sport (MoEYS; Ministerstvo školství, mládeže a tělovýchovy [MŠMT]) in Czech to become more interested in how to exploit such opportune educational strategies, then prioritise the results and recommendations generated by international projects, in order to support their sustainability at a national level.

Active involvement in international associations or networks also has great importance for teacher education institutions. As already mentioned, the Czech Republic is represented in the ATEE through the Charles University Faculty of Education, a faculty which is also an institutional member of the Children's Identity & Citizenship European Association (CiCea). Furthermore, the Czech Republic is involved in the European Literacy Policy Network (ELINET) and is a member of the European Educational Research Association (EERA) through the Czech Educational Research Association (ČAPV).

Although the above networks are primarily for qualified teachers, the opportunities for student teachers in the field of international cooperation are extensive too. For example, student teachers may apply to the ERASMUS+ mobility scheme for several reasons: firstly, to improve in a foreign language (e.g. English, German, or French) or to learn another foreign language (e.g. Italian or Portuguese); secondly, to gain deeper knowledge in a field (e.g. in psychology at top universities in the Netherlands or Belgium, or in history at top universities in France or Poland); and, thirdly, to become acquainted with institutions where interesting approaches to the studied area or to the field of didactics are being developed (e.g. in Spain or Italy).

Student teacher mobility contributes to what may be termed 'intercultural teacher competence'. Following their return from studying abroad, many student teachers from the Czech Republic talk openly about their new awareness of current social problems and patterns, such as protest strikes, environmental movements, immigration policy, and how different countries accept immigrants. During internships in foreign schools, these student teachers are also likely to encounter the fact that it is common for children from different countries to be together in the same classroom environments—not only in Europe, but also in Africa and Asia. Through their time abroad, they also have the unique opportunity to explore the importance of foreign language competences, located within the real-time contexts of various phenomena, history, culture, and life in the EU or further afield. This need for Czech students to create international networks extends beyond term-time commitments, with some Czech student teachers being aware of the need to know a foreign language well. As such, student teachers—not only of foreign languages, but also of History, Mathematics, Biology, and the Czech language—go to summer language schools in, for example, Germany, Austria, Russia, and England. During their study abroad, student teachers are able to establish contacts with young people and proactively become part of international communities. These communities are also created and strengthened through student teachers' collaboration with their peers in other countries: for example, the collaborative project between Charles University and the University of Michigan-Flint (USA), 'How I am becoming a teacher' enhanced student teachers' collaborative and conceptual learning through a photography and animation project done in pairs, with the outcome of creating a visual representation of their education journeys.

Elsewhere, consideration is already being given to how EU programmes could contribute to the education of 'European teachers' (see Simões et al. 2018). This idea has not yet been discussed in the Czech Republic, where, so far, ERASMUS mobility is generally seen as an opportunity to improve language skills, to gain valuable life experience (e.g. to become more independent, to get to know European culture, to understand what the EU is, etc.), or to learn how to implement newly acquired pedagogical knowledge into the Czech setting, including the practice of institutions and associations, upon return from abroad. Currently, Czech schools are already very active in terms of international cooperation, as evidenced by the number of applications for international projects within ERASMUS+. It is therefore necessary to start preparing student teachers for long-term international cooperation during their studies. For example, at the Charles University Faculty of Education, the newly accredited MA study programme for IT teachers has succeeded in including the optional subject, collaborative internet projects in education, in which student teachers will focus on models of international cooperation in educational practice in schools—such an example could pave the way towards other initiatives which share the goal of producing internationally minded teachers.

Emphasis on Competences, Rather than Knowledge

Changes in education in connection with changes in society post-1989 were reflected in, among other places, curricular reforms. However, teachers have had difficulty accepting them. This may be because they have not been invited to contribute to reform preparation, or because reforms have not been sufficiently explained to them. Nonetheless, the success of reforms always depends on whether or not they are positively accepted by their implementers—in this case, teachers. While, since the 1990s, curricular policy in Western countries has again been influenced by the idea of centralisation, Czech curricular policy has striven to move away from a centrally planned curriculum and towards a school-based curriculum. The core of this reform lies in the transition to a two-level system of curricular documents: the state-level curriculum (Framework Education Programmes, i.e. FEPs) and the school-level curriculum (School Education Programmes, i.e. SEPs) (Mináříková et al. 2015, p. 381). The school-level curriculum means that schools develop their own programmes, in accordance with corresponding FEPs. Curricular reform based on the principle of FEPs was well-intentioned—aiming to create suitable conditions to improve the quality of instruction—but met with misunderstanding in school practice and with conflicting responses among education experts.

Curricular reform was expected to lead to the teacher's role being extended to encompass 'curricular activity', meaning that the teacher would become a creator of the curriculum. A key piece of extensive and very thorough research, A Quality School *(Kvalitní škola)* was carried out in 2011 on the basis of a set of single-case studies across various fields of education; a questionnaire survey; interviews with teachers, principals, and SEP co-ordinators; and observations and analysis of video recordings of teaching (Píšová et al. 2011, p. 12; p. 277). The research concluded that: (i) the impact of curricular reform on actual teaching is relatively small; (ii) curricular reform has provided stimuli for thinking about teaching and learning in schools; (iii) in many schools, the creation of SEPs has been an opportunity for collaboration and teamwork among teachers; (iv) teachers prefer to teach what they want and know, rather than what they are obliged to; (v) it is a question of what role language plays, respectively the languages used by the FEP in working with the objectives and content and used by teachers in the creation of the SEP; (vi) teachers deal more with pupils' activities in terms of content than with the 'well-defined objectives'; and (vii) there are differences between teachers in terms of which teaching methods they use in implementing SEPs. With regards to this final point, some teachers choose traditional approaches (e.g. in chemistry education), while others pursue more innovative approaches (e.g. in geography, mathematics, or art education, etc.). One of the subjects from the study, D. Dvořák called what is happening in connection with curricular reform in school practice 'curricular DIY' (Píšová et al. 2011, p. 283), and Štech (2013) speaks about 'evidence-less curriculum reform', both of which capture the piecemeal nature of this aspect of the reforms in practice. Indeed, Píšová et al. (2011, p. 283) concluded that 'curriculum development is, to certain extent, a specialised and demanding activity [such that] it is not reasonable to fully delegate it to ordinary teachers'. Despite this gap between reform stipulations and teachers' realities, the FEP emphasis on key competences and expected outcomes have robustly reinforced the message that targets are an essential component of the curriculum, communicating the idea that course content is then understood only as a means to achieve the set of expected outcomes.

In summary, formal research, as well as discussions with teachers and principals, on the implementation of curricular reform have shown that said reform has not been unequivocally or easily accepted: in fact, over the course of time, an increasing tendency towards resistance has become apparent (Pešková et al. 2019). Currently, the National Institute for Education is working on a revision of the national curricula. The task is to clearly determine the scope and content of education as the common basis for the individual development of each pupil. The intended changes should help better achieve required learning outcomes, and allow enough time to acquire and consolidate the necessary knowledge and skills, as well as to develop creativity.

ICT, Digital Technology, and Teacher Education

After 1989, the market opened up and computers from foreign companies were imported into the Czech Republic. In schools, correspondingly, technology enthusiasts soon started using computers in their teaching, and teacher training faculties also began to equip themselves with computer technology and the available software. All student teachers also became acquainted with the use of computers, initially in subjects such as Technical Instructional Tools or Educational Technology, and later in compulsory subjects as a part of general basic studies at university. In the 90s, and also at the beginning of the millennium, these courses were very popular—students discovered the world of the internet through their institutions, as most of them could not buy a computer with an internet connection due to the cost. In this way, the faculties contributed to the computer literacy development of student teachers.

The effectiveness of this teaching, as well as the motivation for student teachers to learn with a computer, increased when it became more affordable to buy a home computer and, later, an internet connection.

In the years from 2000 to 2006, the MEYS implemented a national Governmental Information Policy in Education project (i.e. Státní informační politika ve vzdělávání, abbreviated as SIPVZ) aiming to ensure the availability of digital technologies (i.e. infrastructure) to all people in education (both in schools and life-long learning) and create a basic framework for digital technology integration into teaching. Emphasis was placed on the role of trained teachers. The SIPVZ focused on the information literacy of teachers at four levels, that is, basic, intermediate, advanced, and highly specialised; the development of learning object repository; and the infrastructure development of schools, including their connection to the internet.

> In the Czech Republic under the decision of the MoEYS in 2005, ICT education became a compulsory subject at all levels of school education (from primary to lower and upper secondary schools) due to the introduction of the Framework Educational Programmes (FEPs) into schools. Nonetheless, teaching ICT subjects has focused mainly on developing users' skills in order to be able to work with computers, to use the internet, to search for information, and to work with commonly available computer applications. (Černochová and Novotná 2020)

Currently, ICT and Informatics teachers are educated at faculties of education and in some professional faculties (like the Faculty of Informatics at Masaryk University, and the Faculty of Maths and Physics at Charles University), so that they can provide teaching for the compulsory subject of ICT in primary and secondary schools.

The MoEYS, through the Czech School Inspectorate (ČŠI), evaluates the level of technical equipment available in schools; its usage in particular subjects of the school curriculum; numbers of teachers who use computer technology in their pedagogical work; whether or not primary and secondary school teachers improve their digital competency; whether or not ICT or Informatics is taught by qualified teachers; and so on. Schools in the Czech Republic have long struggled with a lack of qualified IT teachers in schools. ICT or Informatics is regularly taught by teachers who have not studied these subjects themselves.

> In Czech schools, the use of desktop computers (PCs) and laptops is clearly prevalent. A low proportion of BYOD implementation into schools is related to

a lack of appropriate infrastructure in schools and to a lack of capacity to administer and manage ICT resources. (ČŠI 2017, p. 19; cited in Černochová and Novotná 2020)

Only 52% of teachers are qualified for teaching informatics and computing in small basic schools, 43% in big basic schools, and about 80% in secondary schools and tertiary professional schools. (ČŠI 2017, p. 3)

The current reform of ICT education in primary, and lower and upper secondary school curricula is currently being completed. The subject will be renamed 'Informatics and ICT', and its content will be selected topics from the fields of informatics or computer science, with the addition of some themes about digital technologies. Pupils' activities will be focused on computational thinking development—that is, programming, algorithms, and robotics, among other things. More broadly, pupils' digital literacy is also to be developed by teachers of other subjects (e.g. Mathematics, History, Music, etc.). The Czech Republic uses the concept of digital literacy accepted by EU countries, based on the DigComp 2.0 scheme, as its measure (Vuorikari et al. 2016).

This curricular reform follows the Strategy for Digital Education (*Strategie digitálního vzdělávání*) in which the development of pupils' and teachers' computational thinking is one of the core priorities. Faculties of education will provide compulsory subject courses in teacher education for primary education and ICT or Informatics, through which student teachers will be introduced to the basics of informatics and methodological approaches to pupils' computational thinking development. In addition, a support system for teachers and schools (i.e. a network of teaching method cabinets) will be established on a national level to uphold teachers in their professional practice.

Equity and Inclusion

The Czech Republic has made reducing inequality in the education system one of its key priorities in the Education Policy Strategy for 2020 (MŠMT 2014). Czech authorities and policy-makers aim to focus on equal access to education, as well as to ensure that students' personal or social circumstances do not hinder their educational achievement. At present, in the Czech Republic the impact of students' socio-economic background on individual educational attainment at the age of 15 is below the OECD average (OECD 2019b, p. 161). On the other hand, differences in reading performance between schools within the Czech Republic are higher than the OECD average and appear to be largely explained by schools' socio-economic characteristics.

The Czech government has introduced multiple policies to support students, particularly those who might be at risk of factors outwith their control impacting their performance in school. An emphasis on early care has led to the introduction of a compulsory final year of kindergarten and the extension of compulsory schooling to ten years (i.e. when the child is approximately 16 years of age). Furthermore, the amendment of the Education Act—effective from 2016—guarantees the right for children to access supportive measures. These measures should fit the particular needs of children and pupils who experience social disadvantages, who come from minoritised cultural backgrounds, or who have disabilities and additional support needs (including being extraordinarily talented).

The education community in the Czech Republic was aware of the changes needed in pre-service teacher education in order to prepare future teachers to meet the needs of all students. This is considered to be one of the key prerequisites for making inclusive education a reality for mainstream schools (Strnadová and Hájková 2012). The consequence for teacher education is the introduction of inclusive didactics as a compulsory curricular component, and faculties of education are open to students with special educational needs who receive individual support on their own journey to becoming teachers.

Main Characteristics of the Existing National Initial Teacher Education System

Most teachers must obtain a master's degree during their five years of study— lower and upper secondary teachers must complete bachelor's and master's degrees, and primary school teachers must complete a five-year master's degree (and an alternative pathway to the teaching profession is the acquisition of vocational higher education and subsequent pedagogical studies). Initial teacher education programmes consist of an academic component and a practical component. Recently, there have been changes in the accreditation process, which has refined the curricula of teacher education programmes and delegated the accreditation process to universities. The National Accreditation Office of Higher Education Institutions (hereinafter referred to as the 'Accreditation Office') is an independent body established under the Higher Education Act (Zákon č. 111/1998 Sb., amended in 2016) and decides on the accreditation of both study programmes and institutions. Teacher training programmes are subject to the approval of the MoEYS and follow binding structure guidelines. The principles underpinning the new standards for teacher education programmes are set out in the MoEYS Framework Requirements for Teacher Education Programmes.

General training now consists of general and school pedagogy; pedagogical and school psychology; general didactics; inclusive didactics; ICT; and, optionally, Ethics, Sociology, and other subjects. For primary school teachers, there is a minimum of 78 ECTS for general preparation; a minimum of 150 ECTS for the study of the subject, including didactics of subjects; and a minimum of 30 ECTS (i.e. 900 hours) for reflective practice, all completed within an undivided five-year master's degree programme (300 ECTS). For secondary school teachers, there is a minimum of 60 ECTS for general preparation (of which 24 ECTS are for subject didactics); 150 ECTS for subject knowledge; and a minimum of 24 ECTS (720 hours) for reflective practice—all completed within a three-year bachelor's programme (180 ECTS) plus a two-year follow-up master's programme (120 ECTS).

The accreditation system has changed several times in recent years: these changes demand a great deal of work and bring an administrative burden for academics. Going forwards, we hope that the system now established will remain for some time, allowing us to focus primarily on ensuring and developing the quality of teaching. In turn, the development of teacher education faculties is driven by research and innovation. University education is traditionally, naturally, linked to pedagogical research (Svatoš 2013), and large-scale grant research projects are aimed at improving the teaching profession (e.g. the interdisciplinary grant, *The teaching profession in changing educational requirements 2007–2014*). Indeed, there is much pressure on those working in the field of research to produce professional articles and monographs. By contrast, exerting actual influence on pedagogical practice via research is very minimally supported on a practical level, for example, authorship of textbooks and university scripts do not count as research, often leading to the separation of research findings from teaching practice. That said, one positive sign is that professional-pedagogical journals have recently been focusing on publishing empirical studies born from action research, and many contemporary researchers are directly involved in educational activities, both within and outwith universities.

Current innovations in university teacher education are largely implemented according to project priorities set out in EU calls, and some recent projects illustrate the thematic focus of the priorities very well. Firstly, community practice *(Společenství praxe)* is focused on *the* development of key competences within subject didactics, cross-cutting topics, and interdisciplinary relationships. The aim is to develop the competences of teachers from teacher education faculties and early years education schools (ISCED 0–3) through community practice. Community practice is a regular and long-term cooperation, based on the principles of action research, in order to develop the skills of both groups of actors and develop a more comprehensive elaboration upon the educational strategies set for individual subjects and via cross-cutting themes.

Secondly, supporting undergraduate education *(Pregraduální vzdělávání I. a II.)* has upheld the project goals in several areas. The first is improving the quality of future teachers' practical training, namely by: increasing the quality of student pedagogical practices; offering education aimed at developing the mentoring and reflective skills of university and faculty teachers; and the networking of faculty schools. The second is to increase the competences of future teachers in terms of inclusive education for children and pupils. The third is to improve the quality of university teachers' work, through: supporting the development of didactic competences; supporting beginning university teachers; increasing the pedagogical competences of university teachers, in order to allow them to provide descriptive feedback to their students; and supporting the development of professional competences of academic staff, specifically in terms of preparation for the conferment/appointment procedure. The overall approach across these three areas is focused on the development of the personal and social competences of students—future teachers—by linking theory and practical teaching, particularly with regards to the context of inclusion; the practical use of innovative approaches in teaching students; and the involvement of practising teachers from kindergarten, primary, and secondary in educating student teachers.

Thirdly, some projects support the use of technology and the implementation of research activities in undergraduate education, namely via: preparing innovative educational materials and courses; creating and running didactic innovation centres; and supporting research activities. Through the PRIM project (Podpora rozvíjení informatického myšlení, translated to English as Support of development of computational thinking), all pedagogical faculties incorporate thinking and concepts from the field of informatics into the education of future teachers, including kindergarten teachers, such as preparing for the deployment of robotics in schools. Furthermore, through the DG project (Podpora rozvoje digitální gramotnosti, translated to English as Support for the development of digital literacy), all pedagogical faculties will employ digital literacy in the education of future teachers and subject didactics across curricular areas. Trained teachers will develop the digital literacy of pupils across the country.

In summary, project calls enable significant innovation in university education. Faculties are autonomous but, at the same time, almost all innovate in line with EU proposals out of financial need for the corresponding investment in Czech schools. On the other hand, project calls of this sort also present a significant problem and administrative burden for both state administrative staff and university academic staff. Furthermore, the impact and sustainability of short-term projects is questionable, given that continuity of work and systematic problem-solving are difficult to achieve under the pressure of externally set goals. While a great benefit of these projects is that the country's faculties cooperate with each other, it might well be argued that university teachers themselves should be paid for carrying out such innovations by default, since it is ultimately academic work.

Characteristics of Existing National Teacher Professional Development Systems

After obtaining a master's degree, student teachers are fully qualified to teach. According to Act on Education Staff (Zákon č. 563/2004 Sb.), all teaching professionals are obliged to attend professional development activities and are allowed to use up to 12 working days for professional development per school year. The types of professional development vary, covering courses, peer observations, seminars, qualification programmes, and so on. According to TALIS, attending courses and seminars is one of the most popular types of professional development for teachers across the OECD, and, in the Czech Republic, 84% of teachers participate in this kind of training. Across OECD countries, three areas have been identified where teachers say they need more training: developing advanced ICT skills; teaching in a multicultural/multilingual environment; and teaching students with special needs. Within this, teachers in the Czech Republic have expressed, in particular, a comparatively higher need for preparation for teaching students with special educational needs (OECD 2019c, p. 172).

Additionally, supporting newly qualified teachers is crucial for their survival and professional success. The Czech education system does not offer any official induction programme for fully qualified first-year teachers; some schools do, on the other hand, provide their own induction programme. Indeed, according to TALIS (2018), 57% of teachers in the Czech Republic (with 42% being the OECD average) report having participated in some kind of formal or informal induction when they joined their current school.

However, only 26% of novice teachers (i.e. those with up to five years of experience) in the Czech Republic have an assigned mentor (with 22% being the OECD average), which is not sufficient since school principals generally consider mentoring to be important for teachers' work and students' performance. Other research studies point to a lack of effective support for beginning teachers to help them cope with the introductory period in the profession—showing that it is perceived as functional by only about 10% of beginning teachers, and that, in many cases, it is missing or still formally set up, and thus about a third of new teachers are considering leaving their roles (Hanušová et al. 2017; Vítečková 2018).

In the Czech Republic, headteachers are responsible for staff development and training. The offer of continuous professional development (CPD) education programmes is a rich system, yet somewhat confusing and lacking in quality assurance. In addition to the publicly-funded National Pedagogical Institute, CPD is also provided by many external private and non-governmental providers. In-service teacher education varies greatly between schools, due to their high degree of autonomy: some schools might only approach CPD formally, whereas some exemplify good practice in professional learning communities.

Tensions and Challenges in Transforming the Teacher Education System in the Czech Republic

Tensions in the teacher education system reflect tensions in the education sector more broadly. Despite the positive changes in education policy, legislation, governance, funding regulation, curriculum, and teacher professionalism, as well as the development of support structures, there are still hurdles to overcome, such as a lack of mechanism management and monitoring in the sector. These problems are not new: in 2007, Greger and Walterová wrote that a lack of political consensus had been a challenge for 12 years, and their observations are still relevant today. As outlined in this chapter, better support for teachers, reducing inequalities, and improving governance were three strategic priorities for Czech education policy up to 2020. However, in practice, it remains a challenge for the teaching profession to attract the most talented students. Some students choose teacher education as a second choice, probably due to systemic problems in the education sector: low professional prestige and salaries; low state investment in education; lack of career prospects;

and lack of professional support. Two years ago, the authorities prepared a highly-anticipated career system, but there was insufficient political support for its implementation.

Although future teachers are educated in modern approaches to teaching, unfortunately, when faced with the reality of school practice and, sometimes, conservative school environments, they either retreat from teaching or leave the profession altogether. The subjectively-perceived professional competence of in-service teachers in inspiring and facilitating the active involvement of pupils in teaching is currently below the EU average and is still, despite improvements made since 2013, among the very lowest included in the TALIS survey (Boudová et al. 2019, pp. 8–9). In terms of tackling some of these shortcomings, roundtables with teachers and principals have resulted in recommendations regarding strengthening undergraduate preparation, especially in terms of subject didactics; the ability to work with curricular documents; improving the results of weaker pupils; and methods for working in heterogeneous classes. Additionally, practitioners themselves call for support in developing skills for cooperation with other teachers, teaching assistants, and other supportive professions; skills for recognising psychosocial problems (e.g. family, housing, etc.) and solving them within the school; and skills for working with pupils' parents and legal guardians. The newly accredited study programmes of pedagogical faculties acknowledge these elements.

Strategy 2030+ places a great emphasis on preparing Czech education for 'pervasive digitisation' associated with a 'fundamental technological transformation of the economy' (Veselý et al. 2019, p. 11). Indeed, in the Czech Republic routine skills are expected to be replaceable within five years with 1.3 million employees and within 15 years with 2.2 million employees (Ministry of Industry and Trade 2019). Correspondingly, the need to adapt education to new socio-economic trends is also reflected in other strategic documents outwith the field of education, such as the *National Strategy for the Development of Artificial Intelligence* (*Národní strategie umělé inteligence v České republice*) proposed by the Ministry of Industry and Trade (Veselý et al. 2019, p. 12). However, the implementation of these visions, which have been formulated independently by several ministries, supposes close cooperation between these ministries and education institutions—yet, in actuality, such plans necessitate clarification and media coverage for citizens, including in terms of their implementation in the field of education, such as via teacher training. Who will be responsible for their fulfilment? Who will prepare teacher educators to realise these visions?

Suggestions for the Future Development of Teacher Education in the Czech Republic

Consultations with the OECD review team found that training graduates in practical teaching skills is a key issue for the future development of teacher education. In more specific terms, closer collaboration with schools; encouraging active student learning; responding to future challenges; developing ICT; supporting inclusive education; and involving professionals—while maintaining a high level of theoretical studies—can all serve as means of achieving this. These recommendations are also in accord with the student voice, which has been louder of late. The other aspect of the future development of teacher education is the support and development of teacher educators themselves. Currently, participation in research activities and the writing of articles are included in the evaluation of academic staff, therefore, going forwards, there needs to be emphasis and recognition of the importance of high-quality teaching; writing textbooks and methodological materials; promoting pedagogical competences; and reducing administrative burdens. Furthermore, investing in modern learning approaches, like tandem teaching, as well as allocating more funding to teacher education, are key factors for future development.

In more depth, guidelines for the future development of teacher education in the Czech Republic can be outlined in several directions. First of all, at a national level, a system of methodical cabinets, that is, structured, supportive professional communities of teachers, for specific education areas will be created (e.g. the Methodical Cabinet for Mathematics Education). Methodical cabinet activities would be based on the professional support system model, feeding into methodical cabinets at a regional level. The aim is to overcome ineffective professional support of teachers through in-service professional teacher development. The starting point is 'the belief that teacher education should be systemically conceptually clarified at the national level in its entirety' (Slavík et al. 2019, p. 4), as well as in relation to the relevant theoretical background and subject didactics.

Second of all, the system-level approach to improving teacher education will be based on the concept of the professionalisation continuum (Stuchlíková and Janík 2017), in which four stages are defined: (1) acquiring quality applicants for teaching—diagnostics of study and professional prerequisites; (2) initial teacher education; (3) induction into the teaching profession; and (4) in-service training and teacher professional development. The individual stages of this continuum should be interconnected and facilitated to an appropriate standard. Based on the systemic connection between universities (i.e. teacher training and subject didactics) and the terrain of practice (i.e. schools and in-service teachers), a mutual partnership between schools and research should be developed. In order to strengthen the work of teacher educators and researchers, both practice and theory should be equally represented across all four stages of the continuum: the two facets should not be separated, but interconnected and collaborative—with theory helping teachers to understand their professional practice more deeply and reflexively, and professional practice informing the agendas of theory and research.

Lastly, by way of conclusion, we have devised priority recommendations for the future development of teacher education in the Czech Republic, drawing from the approved document of *Strategy 2030+* (MŠMT 2020). In order to prepare graduates for the increasing demands of the profession, initial teacher education institutions need to offer a clear competency model for student teachers (i.e. outlining exactly what graduates of the programme will know and be able to do upon completion of their studies). Simultaneously, stakeholders should plan how to link this preparatory education period more robustly with the two-year adaptation period at the beginning of in-service teaching.

Changes of undergraduate education through appropriate changes in university funding models should be promoted. In particular, it is a matter of limiting project funding and taking due account of the cost of the desired form of study. The result will be larger share of individual work with the student, larger share of reflected internships, and so on. It is also desirable to encourage pedagogical research carried out at faculties which train teachers.

Spanning their careers, meaningful and lasting professional development for present and future teachers in the Czech Republic will require systemic changes. Initial teacher education can lay the foundations for teaching quality, but creating fully-prepared professionals is neither realistic nor desirable. Rather, an important step in improving the quality of the education provided to pupils is to ensure that teachers themselves can continue to grow and develop as learners—from their very first days in class and onwards throughout their careers (OECD 2017). Teachers in the early years of their careers are vulnerable to dropping out, hence, improving the induction system should be a priority: reducing direct or indirect pedagogical activities (in the school); increasing intensive mentoring; and evaluating the adaptation procedures, all serve the aim of reducing the burden on teachers at every stage of their career.

Longer term, the vision of schools as learning communities is essential. Teachers, across the OECD (OECD 2019c), report that professional development based on collaboration and collaborative approaches to teaching is among the most impactful for them. However, only 45% of teachers in the Czech Republic participate in training based on peer learning and coaching: this share should increase, as facilitating mutual learning and support within and between school pedagogical teams is the way forwards.

On the whole, such a system of ongoing education could fulfil the educational needs of the school, teachers, principals, and other pedagogical staff to a greater extent. Professional development may include intervision (i.e. a mutual activity between a small group of professionals who have a common professional context, with an emphasis on multilateral exchange, see Willems et al. 2000), supervision, and the analysis of implemented teaching—all facilitated via the offer of high-quality methodological materials, the use of communication technologies, and implemented in cooperation with methodical cabinets, universities, and other schools.

Ultimately, we perceive it to be a good sign that, in recent years, Czech education policy representatives have begun to openly name the situation in education and to offer solutions. It is clearly documented that investments in improving the quality of teachers' work, in the sense of achieving better academic results for pupils, are an investment with a very high return, quite literally, in that they lead to a very significant increase in economic growth (e.g. Krajčová et al. 2019). The quality of teachers' work is gradually becoming a political priority, and this gives us hope for the future of teacher education in the Czech Republic.

Acknowledgements This chapter is a result of the COOPERATIO *General Education and Pedagogy* research (2022–2026) funded by Charles University.

The authors would like to thank Dr. Glynn Kirkham for his kind consultation in the process of creating this chapter.

References

Bendl, S., H. Voňková, and M. Zvírotský. (2013). Impact of the Bologna Process two-cycle implementation on teacher education in the Czech Republic. *Pedagogická orientace, 23*(6), 767–785.

Boudová, S., V. Šťastný, and J. Basl. (2019). *Národní zpráva. Mezinárodní šetření TALIS 2018.* Praha: Česká školní inspekce. Retrieved from https://www.csicr.cz/Prave-menu/Mezinarodni-setreni/TALIS/Narodni-zpravy/Mezinarodni-setreni-TALIS-2018-Narodni-zprava.

Černochová, M., and J. Novotná. (2020). *Report on ICT in education in the Czech Republic.* In: L. Dejian, H. Ronghuai, L. Bojan, Z. Haijun, and Z. Nikola (Eds.),

Comparative analysis of ICT in education between China and Central and Eastern European Countries (pp. 107–131). Singapore: Springer Verlag.

Dvořáková, M., M. Dopita, H. Grecmanová, and N. D. Wright (Eds.). (2001). *Nové horizonty výchovy k občanství: kurikulum kurzu pro studenty vysokých škol.* Olomouc: Univerzita Palackého.

ČŠI. (2017). *Využívání digitálních technologií v mateřských, základních, středních a vyšších odborných školách. Tématická zpráva* [Use of digital technologies in kindergartens, basic, secondary and higher professional schools. Thematic report]. Prague: Česká školní inspekce.

Greger, D., and E. Walterová. (2007). In pursuit of educational change: Transformation of education in the Czech Republic. *Orbis Scholae,* 1(2), 11–44.

Grinbergs, C. J., and H. Jones. (2013). Erasmus Mundus SEN: The inclusive scholarship program? *International Journal of Inclusive Education,* 17(4), 349–363.

Hanušová, S., M. Píšová, …., S. Ježek. (2017). *Chtějí zůstat, nebo odejít? Začínající učitelé v českých základních školách.* Brno: Masarykova univerzita.

Kotásek, J., D. Greger, and I. Procházková. (2004). *Demand for schooling in the Czech Republic (Country Report for OECD).* Paris: OECD Publishing. Retrieved from: http://www.oecd.org/dataoecd/38/37/33707802.pdf.

Kotásek, J. et al. (2001). *Národní program rozvoje vzdělávání v České republice. Bílá kniha.* Praha: Tauris.

Krajčová, J., D. Münich, and T. Protivínský. (2019). *Kvalita práce učitelů, vzdělanost, ekonomický růst a prosperita České republiky.* Praha: IDEA CERGE-EI.

Minaříková, E., M. Píšová, and T. Janík. (2015). Using video in teacher education: An example from the Czech Republic. In: L. Orland-Barak and Ch. Craig (Eds.), *International teacher education: Promising pedagogies (Part B)* (pp. 379–400) Bingley: Emerald.

Moree, D. (2013). Teachers and school culture in the Czech Republic before and after 1989. *The Curriculum Journal,* 24(4), 586–608.

MŠMT (2014). *Strategie vzdělávací politiky České republiky do roku 2020.* Retrieved from http://www.msmt.cz/vzdelavani/skolstvi-v-cr/strategie-vzdelavaaci-politiky-2020.

MŠMT (2020). *Strategy for the Education Policy of the Czech Republic up to 2030+.* Retrieved from http://www.msmt.cz/vzdelavani/skolstvi-v-cr/strategie-2030.

Národní strategie umělé intelligence v České republice. MPO, květen 2019.

Novotná, J. (2019). Learning to teach in the Czech Republic: Reviewing policy and research trends. In: M. T. Tatto and I. Menter (Eds.), *Knowledge, policy and practice in teacher education: A cross-national study.* London: Bloomsbury.

OECD. (2017). *Do new teachers feel prepared for teaching? Teaching in Focus,* No. 17. Paris: OECD Publishing. Retrieved from https://doi.org/10.1787/980bf07d-en.

OECD. (2019a). *Education at a glance, the Czech Republic.* Retrieved from http://www.oecd.org/education/education-at-a-glance/EAG2019_CN_CZE.pdf.

OECD. (2019b). *Education at a Glance 2019: OECD indicators.* Paris: OECD Publishing. Retrieved from http://www.oecd.org/education/education-at-a-glance/.

OECD. (2019c). *TALIS 2018 Results (Volume I): Teachers and School Leaders as Lifelong Learners*, TALIS. Paris: OECD Publishing. Retrieved from https://doi.org/10.1787/1d0bc92a-en.

Pešková, K., M. Spurná, and P. Knecht. (2019). Teachers' acceptance of curriculum reform in the Czech Republic: One decade later. *Inceps Journal*, 9(2), 73–97.

Píšová, M., K. Kostková, and T. Janík (Eds.). (2011). *Kurikulární reforma na gymnáziích. Případové studie tvorby kurikula.* VÚP: Praha.

Shewbridge, C. et al. (2016). *OECD reviews of school resources: Czech Republic 2016*, OECD Reviews of School Resources. Paris: OECD Publishing. Retrieved from https://doi.org/10.1787/9789264262379-en.

Simões, A., M. Lourenço, and N. Costa (Eds.). (2018). *Teacher education policy and practice in Europe: Challenges and opportunities.* London: Routledge.

Slavík, J. et al. (2019). *Osnova modelu systému profesní podpory pro jednotlivé metodické kabinety.* Materiál—kód WBS: 4.3.1. Praha: SYPO.

Štech, S. (2013). Když je kurikulární reforma evidence-less. *Pedagogická orientace*, 23(5), 615–633.

Strnadová, I., and V. Hájková. (2012). Striving for inclusive education in the Czech Republic. *Intervention in School and Clinic,* 47(5), 307–311.

Stuchlíková, I., and T. Janík. (2017). Rámcová koncepce přípravy učitelů základních a středních škol aneb o hledání a nacházení konsensu mezi aktéry. *Pedagogická orientace*, 27(1), 242–265.

Svatoš, T. (2013). A student teacher on the pathway to teaching profession: Reviewing research and proposing a model. *Pedagogická orientace,* 23(6), 786–809.

Veselý, A., J. Fischе, M. Jabůrková, M. Pospíšil D. Prokop, R. Sáblík, I. Stuchlíková, S. Štech. (2019). *Hlavní směry vzdělávací politiky ČR do roku 2030+.* Pracovní verze ze dne 31.10. 2019 určená k diskusi.

Vítečková, M. (2018). *Začínající učitel: jeho potřeby a uvádění do praxe.* Brno: Paido.

Vuorikari, R., Y. Puni, S. G. Carretero, and G. van den Brand. (2016). *DigComp 2.0: The digital competence framework for citizens. Update phase 1: The conceptual reference model.* Luxembourg: Publication Office of the European Union.

Willems, G. M., J. H. J. Stakenborg, and W. Veugelers. (2000). *Trends in Dutch teacher education.* Leuven: Garant.

Zákon č. 563/2004 Sb. Zákon o pedagogických pracovnících. [Act No. 563/2004 Collection of Law, on Pedagogical Staff].

Zákon č. 561/2004 Sb. Zákon o předškolním, základním, středním, vyšším odborném a jiném vzdělávání (Školský zákon) [Act No. 561/2004 Collection of Law, on Pre-school, Basic, Secondary, Tertiary Professional and Other Education (the Education Act)].

Zákon č. 111/1998 Sb. Zákon o vysokých školách. [Act No. 111/1998 Coll. Higher Education Act].

3

Teacher Education in Hungary: Between Autonomy and Control

Erika Kopp and Orsolya Kálmán

Context of Teacher Education

> For him who flies above it, a map is all he sees,
> this living scape of being but symbols and degrees;
> the reader of the map lines has neither known nor felt
> the place where the great Mihály Vörösmarty dwelt;
> what's hidden in the map? Yes, barracks, mills and arms,
> but for me crickets, oxen, steeples, quiet farms.
> Miklós Radnóti, 'I know not what…'. (Radnóti 2000, p. 96)

Miklós Radnóti was one of Hungary's most insightful poets of the twentieth century, who, in the face of Nazi fascism, crafted words urging his readers to understand the world around them from new perspectives—in this case, from above, from a distant perspective. Hungary is a country in Central Europe, with a population of 10 million and has been a member of the European Union since 2004. Students are enrolled in the public education system between the ages of three and 18, with education being compulsory until the age of 16. In the 2018/2019 school year, 1,669,000 students (85.8% of the population aged three to 22) were in full-time education in public and higher education (Statistics Hungary 2019).

E. Kopp (✉) • O. Kálmán
Eötvös Loránd University, Budapest, Hungary
e-mail: kopp.erika@ppk.elte.hu

© The Author(s), under exclusive license to Springer Nature Switzerland AG 2023
M. Kowalczuk-Walędziak et al. (eds.), *The Palgrave Handbook of Teacher Education in Central and Eastern Europe*, https://doi.org/10.1007/978-3-031-09515-3_3

Due to Hungary's falling birth rate, the number of students in the public education system is constantly decreasing, although the decline has been slowing since 2014. Parallel, in the public education system, the proportion of pupils with special education needs (SEN) and from low-income families constantly increases (Hermann et al. 2019). According to Programme for International Student Assessment (PISA) reports, the performance of Hungarian students is below the Organisation for Economic Co-operation and Development (OECD) average in all areas. Among the participating countries, Hungary belongs to the group in which family background variables explain student performance significantly more than is the case for the OECD average. National and international performance measures show significant differences between pupils at school level, but they are more homogeneous within schools. In the EU context, the Hungarian education system shows the greatest socio-economic and regional inequalities among students (Hermann et al. 2019).

In Hungary teachers' wages, according to OECD and Eurostat data, are generally below 60% of other groups with the same qualifications. Within this, the salaries of early-stage nursery and secondary teachers were the lowest among the surveyed countries. Low salary contributes significantly to the feminisation of the teaching profession: more than 80% of teachers are women. Teachers' shortages are constantly increasing, with one factor being the proximity to retirement of the existing teaching cohort: nearly 30% of those who currently work in the system are expected to retire in five to 10 years (European Commission 2017; OECD 2019). After describing the context, we turn to the presentation of the system. The following simplified Fig. 3.1 illustrates the relationship between the public education system and the teacher education system.

However, what historical, social, and economic factors influence the data and structures presented above? Indeed, such factors are always difficult to summarise due to the fundamental complexity of how they influence teacher education (Mason 2008; Cochran-Smith et al. 2014; Burns and Köstler 2016; Kauko et al. 2018). This complexity is increased by the fact that teacher training is a lifelong learning process, in which teacher education and continuing education represent different stages of a unified, ongoing process (OECD 2011; Caena 2014). Furthermore, teacher education exists at the intersection of public education and higher education (HE), which means that both systems affect how teacher education operates.

In this chapter, the complex factors that fundamentally influence Hungarian teacher education are viewed and interpreted through the lens of the major socio-political changes in the image of the country's teaching profession in

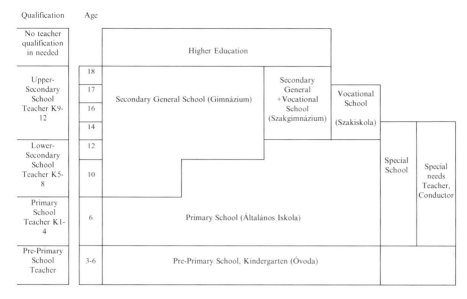

Fig. 3.1 The relationship between public education system stages and the required teacher qualifications

modern history (Németh 2009; Guerriero 2017). Our premise is that the status of the teaching profession, in turn, defines the social status of educators, therefore, decisively influencing teacher education and professional development. Based on this premise, this chapter will examine key elements of the profession along with two main issues: firstly, how and to what extent is a teacher's work viewed as a complex profession that requires high-quality professional knowledge and competences, and, secondly, to what extent are teachers autonomous? (Normand et al. 2019).

Historical Development of Hungarian Education: The Position of Teachers and the Historical Roots of Teacher Education

Hungary is located in Central Europe and its 'intermediate' position between the East and West of the continent has played a decisive role in its history (Szűcs 1981; Németh 2005a; Körösényi et al. 2007). This geopolitical position has directly influenced the development of Hungary's education system and theory of education—in particular, historically under the dominance of continental (i.e. German/Austrian) influence, but the Soviet cultures of teacher education theory and policy made an impact as well (Németh 2005b).

The Hungarian education system has traditionally followed the Austro-German model: where the typical school system consisted of four years of elementary education, followed by secondary education. Still, despite the continuous development of this system, the real expansion of Hungary's own education system began during the period between the two world wars (Németh 2012). The central curriculum closely regulated the content of education being provided in the nation's schools and a system of inspection was established for supervising teachers' work. Despite this centralised management on a national level, many actors were able to become education providers (e.g. church and state), which promoted school diversity. Characteristics of the German model of governance and regulation can be clearly identified, both in terms of content regulation and the control of the system (Németh 2005a).

The first official institutions of teacher education in Hungary were established during the Austro-Hungarian monarchy of the eighteenth century, with a view to modernising society (Gyáni and Kövér 2006). The education system of this period separated different socio-economic groups, and this separation also appeared in teachers' career paths and teacher education. At this time, there were two separate forms of teacher training in Hungary: one by way of a seminary (i.e. school of theology) for teaching at elementary schools, and the other by way of academic training for positions at secondary schools. The above-mentioned societal separation also appeared in the names given to the two professional groups: only the secondary school teacher was called *tanár* (teacher), while the primary school teacher was named *tanító* (educator). Indeed, this segregation created different statuses in terms of income and social prestige (Németh 2012): while primary school teaching was essentially an occupation afforded low prestige and only semi-professional status, the secondary school teacher belonged to one of Hungary's most prestigious professions (Sáska 2015).

The Soviet occupation of the country in 1945 brought radical changes to this linear development process. Between 1946 and 1989, Hungary existed under the Soviet communist dictatorship. One of the first steps following the takeover by the communist party was the radical transformation of education because it was a strategic sector of citizen control for communist governance. During this Sovietisation, the state became the only education provider. The school system was completely redesigned, the curriculum was centralised, and external evaluation was implemented. Along with these structural changes within the school system, the system itself became a major tool for social restructuring. During this period, there was an unprecedented expansion of formal education in Hungary, first in primary education and then in secondary education.

Correspondingly, teachers' societal positions and teacher education went through comprehensive reforms. The growing number of students necessitated an increase in the number of teachers, but the already low salaries of teachers were pushed down during the price and wage reform of the early 1950s. As a result of the central wage reform, teachers' salaries were barely higher than the salaries of so-called 'unskilled' workers and agricultural workers (Lannert 2010; Polónyi 2015). Consequently, the gap between the two separate social classes of teachers did narrow, while the prestige of the teaching profession as a whole deteriorated. However, this economic devaluing of teachers' labour did not lead to a significant shortage of teachers, as a large, new cohort of female workers entered the teaching profession (Polónyi 2015). This is when the significant feminisation of teaching began, a trend which is still prevalent in Hungary today.

A subsequent important change in the teaching profession came in the 1970s and 1980s when the education of primary school teachers and pre-primary school teachers was moved from upper secondary school to college level—in 1974 for the former and 1983 for the latter. However, all these changes were not accompanied by the consolidation of possible training pathways in teacher education, thus maintaining separate training programmes for teachers working at different levels of the school system (Hunyady 2004; Németh 2007; Baska and Hegedűs 2015). Now, it can be generally concluded that the development of Hungary's education system follows global development trends on a regulatory level, albeit with some delay, with stops and setbacks found on a national level as a result of radical changes in Hungary's political environment.

In summary, the evolution of teacher education and education as a whole in Hungary can be characterised as follows: (1) politics has a powerful impact on education; (2) the teaching profession has traditionally been characterised by strong central regulation and control; (3) the teaching profession comprises segregated groups which are distinct from each other in terms of training, socio-economic privilege, and career paths; (4) the autonomy of the teaching profession is weak; and (5) the prestige of the teaching profession as a whole is declining, and has been since Sovietisation.

Major Changes in Hungary's Education System Over the Last Three Decades

In 1989, after the collapse of the Soviet regime, Hungary became a democratic country. The subsequent main socio-economic changes can be summarised as follows: after a very rapid period of marketisation, a fundamentally capitalist economic system emerged, in which the role of the state in the distribution of resources has remained significant. Since then, material inequalities have increased radically, not only between regions but also within regions. In turn, these inequalities have affected students' and teachers' living and working conditions and are reflected in national performance indicators (Halász and Lannert 2003). Simultaneously, birth rates have continued to fall (Körösényi et al. 2007). Over the past decade, such unfavourable demographic trends in Hungary have been further reinforced by the migration of citizens seeking job and education opportunities in other EU countries. As a result of these socio-economic shifts, the number of students in Hungary is constantly decreasing (Kolosi and Sági 1997; Halász and Lannert 2003).

Since 1989, the field of education policy has also changed radically. Completely new actors (e.g. churches, associations, companies) have appeared, generating new forms of interaction between them and fundamentally transforming the power balance and dynamics on a policy level. Churches and private companies have emerged as education providers, and advocacy and professional consultation forums have been launched, including the Rectors' Conference which plays a crucial role in higher education reforms, including teacher education reforms (Halász 2011a). Nonetheless, like before, political actors have continued to play a decisive role in education policy, divided along political lines. This divergence in education policy did not occur immediately after the official change in political system, from a regime to a democracy, but at the beginning of the millennium, splitting opinion into two main positions: one advocating for strong state intervention and central management, as opposed to school autonomy and local focus; and the other advocating for integration and inclusive schools, as opposed to the segregation and separation of disadvantaged pupils, for instance, Roma students or students with learning difficulties (Halász 2017).

The end of the communist regime also had a profound effect on the organisation of the education system. As a result of rapid reforms, the highly centralised education system gave way to a diverse and decentralised system, characterised by the following features. First of all, the role of the state as the sole provider of education was diminished, and school maintenance fell under the jurisdiction of local government, with the church and private stakeholders emerging in the same capacity. Additionally, newly established or transformed institutions were reorganised: six-grade and eight-grade secondary schools appeared, while a form of the eight-grade elementary school still existed. The centralised, prescriptive curriculum was replaced by the National Core Curriculum, which prescribed about 50% of the school curriculum while a curriculum devised by the school defined the rest. Compulsory enrolment and attendance at district schools was replaced by a free choice of schools. Lastly, the formal external evaluation of schools was abolished and the government began to develop a national competence measurement system (Halász 1998; Halász and Lannert 2003; Halász 2011a).

Simultaneously, the higher education system also went through significant structural changes, with many having a decisive impact on teacher education. As with primary and secondary education, new providers appeared in higher education, the same as above. Additionally, quality management systems were launched: the Hungarian Accreditation Committee was established, and internal quality management systems were introduced. Then, in 2005. the Hungarian higher education system became part of the Bologna Process (Halász 2009; Kováts 2010; Szolár 2010; Halász 2012).

Despite the democratisation in terms of the structure and content of Hungary's education, many elements of the old system have remained intact. These shortcomings have led to long-term problems. Firstly, public and HE financing is fundamentally disordered, leading to a significant negative discrepancy between teachers' salaries in Hungary and teachers' salaries in other European countries, contributing to the low societal prestige of teachers, a workforce shortage, and the extreme feminisation of the profession. Secondly, Hungary's school system does not have a clear structure: different types of schools coexist, overlapping in terms of activity. Indeed, this lack of structure coupled with free school choice has resulted in an increase in the proportion of pupils struggling to perform in the upper level of primary schools. Thirdly, despite efforts to strengthen school integration, students' social background inequalities between schools have been continuously increasing. Lastly, while formal, quality control systems have been introduced, for example in the case of school pedagogical programmes and the system used for evaluating textbooks, a lack of appropriate evaluation systems has led to a deterioration in the quality of teaching (Halász and Lannert 2003; Balázs et al. 2011).

The 2010 election dramatically changed the socio-political environment within which the Hungarian education system operates. The right-wing conservative party, Fidesz, gained a two-thirds majority that enabled them, as the ruling party, to carry out comprehensive reforms which restructured almost every element of the political system, including the constitution and the electoral system. The government also implemented a fundamental education reform, the Public Education Act of 2011, with the following main elements. Firstly, the state has become the key player in education provision once again, taking over from the municipalities. Secondly, the government has transformed the role of the national core curriculum into a prescriptive curriculum that covers 90% of school education content. Thirdly, textbook publishing has been made a state monopoly. Fourthly, inspection has been re-introduced for the evaluation of schools. Lastly, the teaching career path has been defined in levels, and progression is based on external, individual evaluation by the inspectorate. These decisions have re-centralised the public education system and entrenched the hierarchy between actors. The new system has significantly reduced the professional autonomy of schools and teachers and failed to solve some of the pressing issues facing the education sector: teacher shortage, an ageing workforce of teachers, and the deterioration in the quality of education by international measures (Balázs et al. 2011; Halász 2011b).

National centralisation efforts have also appeared in Hungary's higher education policy. The first step was to abolish the Bologna-type, divided teacher education, in 2011, and to re-establish the undivided form from the pre-Bologna period. Higher education institutions have lost their economic independence due to the financial management of universities by government-appointed chancellors: indeed, currently, Hungarian institutions have the lowest financial autonomy in the EU, according to Kováts' recent evaluation (2015). Most recently, the April 2017 amendment of the Higher Education Act has raised further concerns regarding academic freedom for teachers and educators in Hungary (EUA 2017).

Teacher Education Reforms Over the Last Three Decades in the Context of Global Trends

In the most recent decades of global educational policy discourse, the economic approach has been strengthened (Gitlin and Smyth 1988; Tenorth 2014), with the effectiveness of education systems measured by their contribution to national economic growth (as measured by gross domestic product) and market competitiveness (Venger et al. 2012). Within the economy-focussed framework, the quality of teachers has been identified as a key factor impacting the effectiveness of education systems (OECD 2011; Creemers and Kyriakidēs 2012; Halász 2013; Kyriakides et al. 2010). This ideology has influenced the professional understanding of teachers' quality, professionalisation, and learning, as well as the developments and interventions in teacher education policy (Tatto 2006). However, this over-simplified relationship implying that teachers' quality (e.g. competences, professional knowledge) directly determines quality in teaching that leads to better learning outcomes has been criticised in recent research (Darling-Hammond and Bransford 2005; Kauko et al. 2018). Furthermore, the need for a values-based approach to teacher education, rather than an economic-focussed approach, has been raised by researchers such as Biesta (2009, 2019). The aforementioned approaches have also shaped Hungarian public discourse, for example, the discussion on how teachers' work should be assessed (Rapos and Kopp 2015).

If teachers do matter to such a great extent (OECD 2011), then the quality of teacher education should also be given a central role in ongoing discourses on education, particularly because research shows that student performance correlates to teacher quality (Burroughs et al. 2019). So, the main question for teacher education now is how the quality of teachers can be ensured. Indeed, in modern global trends, two relevant approaches can be identified: one that strengthens teachers' professionalisation by focusing on their professional autonomy, professional development, and learning, and another that highlights the accountability of teacher education to the public.

The focus on effectiveness and professionalisation of teachers has strengthened the current evidence-based (or evidence-informed) approach in European education policy on the one hand, and the integrated teacher education policy from initial teacher education to continuous professional development on the other. However, despite this progress, one of the major challenges remaining is how to integrate research-based knowledge into practice or, in other words, how knowledge production, mediation, and application can be linked more effectively (Guerriero 2017). Seeking to overcome this challenge, a comprehensive and robust system for supporting teacher education is needed, rooted in policy that builds on hard instruments, such as regulation, as well as soft ones, such as enhancing cooperation between stakeholders (Darling-Hammond and Bransford 2005).

The influence of global trends on Hungarian teacher education can be seen from different points of view. Some researchers argue that European policies are mainly 'downloaded' onto the Hungarian context (e.g. Halász 2017), while others emphasise that it is not a one-way process (e.g. Ozga et al. 2011; Prøitz 2015) in that global trends are formed by local traditions, that is, a complex adaptation process which is also influenced by both the education policy elites and the social needs of the country (Németh 2005a; Grek et al. 2009). Global and European trends—such as the Bologna Process, the European Qualification Framework, teacher competences and standards, the induction period for graduate student teachers and newly qualified teachers, and the teacher career model (initiated in 2013)—were all introduced in Hungarian higher and teacher education. However, these rapid, often parallel, changes, as well as subsequent revocations (e.g. the new undivided initial teacher education programme which will be mentioned later in this chapter), have taken place without substantial evaluation of their impact. This turbulence and scant discussion of the impact and quality of teacher education has caused tensions and incongruences between the different parts of teacher education, impeding a harmonious and all-embracing strategy towards future teacher education (Symeonidis 2019).

Changes in Hungarian teacher education have usually begun with initial teacher education (ITE), as the research on teachers' learning first of all has an impact on the designing of ITE programmes. Teachers' competences; facilitating and assessing learning with a portfolio; and the concept of continuous professional development (CPD) were also first developed and introduced into ITE programmes (Falus 2006). Teacher educators as researchers endeavoured to implement their own research findings and to translate international trends for the Hungarian context. Additionally, the Hungarian Association for Teacher Educators has had a great impact on professional work and knowledge exchange. Organising the Teacher Education Academy (2006) and the renewed version of the *Hungarian Journal of Teacher Education* (2003) have also strengthened the professional knowledge and discourse on Hungarian TE (Hadar and Brody 2017). In 2006, teachers' competences were first developed for secondary school teachers' ITE programmes by the country's community of teacher educators, after which this competence framework was also included in the regulation of teachers' qualifications (see the Ministerial Decree 15/2006 regarding the requirements of TE qualifications, plus its amendment in EMMI 2013), and later became the basis for the teachers' career model.

In terms of its positive impact, the competence framework certainly reinforced the importance of teachers' pedagogical knowledge as a quality indicator within teacher education (Guerriero 2017; Ulferts 2019) by defining the main competence areas (Ministerial Decree 15/2006):

1. Development of pupil/student personality;
2. Assisting and developing the establishment of learning groups and communities;
3. Planning the pedagogical process;
4. Development of literacy and skills of pupils/students applying disciplinary knowledge;
5. Development of the competences laying the foundations for lifelong learning;
6. Organisation and facilitation of the learning process;
7. Application of the numerous tools of pedagogical evaluation;
8. Cooperation and communication among professionals;
9. Self-instruction and teaching; dedication to further professional development.

Furthermore, this competence framework took the first step towards an integrated TE framework: firstly, it was a common requirement for all subject student teachers and within the CPD system, and, secondly, it helped to integrate the quality expectations placed upon teachers across all fields. In practical terms, this means that while in ITE there are separate routes for kindergarten, primary, secondary, and special education needs (SEN) teachers, in CPD (induction period included) all teachers are met with almost the same competence requirements. Still, some criticisms can be raised here, as teachers were not actively involved in the framework-building process, which in practice, led to their resistance, although research findings show that, by and large, they do agree with the competence framework (Kotschy 2006). The language of competence framework was general which may have helped its professional acceptance, also it was efficiently shaping curriculum design in ITE. However, regarding the career model, teacher standards were, at least at first, too detailed and not easily assessed. Lastly, a great shortcoming of the competence framework is that it has not been able to adequately frame one of the biggest issues of education quality in Hungary: namely, the challenge of inequalities. A summary of the main trends in integrated teacher education—from ITE through induction to CPD—in the European Union and Hungary is offered in Table 3.1.

Regarding the balance between the professional autonomy of (individual) teachers and the macro-level accountability of teacher education, the following crucial features can be highlighted. The main requirements of Hungary's ITE programmes were regulated by the state but, within that, pedagogical approaches were open to be defined by institutions, which led to the emergence of reflective and research-based approaches to teacher education (Menter et al. 2010). However, quality development has not been linked to ITE programmes because quality assurance and accreditation are carried out at an institutional level.

As seen above, the relationships in Hungary between TE policy, research on TE, and professional practice itself can be characterised as turbulent and incoherent, weakening the emergence of evidence-informed policy. While some interweaving between the three different strands can be identified over the past three decades, they are now further apart from each other than they were at the beginning of the 1990s after the collapse of the dictatorship. Positive examples of collaboration can be connected to the competence framework, practice orientation in ITE, the introduction of the induction period, and continuous professional development. However, even these areas remain problematic. For example, despite the fact that the integrated system of TE was initiated and supported by researchers and policymakers (Kotschy 2006;

Table 3.1 Comparison of teacher education in EU documents (Symeonidis 2019) and in Hungary

	EU documents (Symeonidis 2019)	Hungary
Initial TE	programme development (balance between knowledge and skills; new contents)	TE as mainly structural reform; developments in TE (portfolio evaluation; practice)
	selection; recruitment	entrance exam; student-teacher scholarship named after Klebelsberg
	partnership in programme development with stakeholders	informal or project-based
Induction	partnership with the novice teacher; adequate financial and time resources; support system	one-year practicum; two-year induction period; mentoring process
Continuous professional development	stakeholder collaboration; support structures; career paths; competence levels	teacher career model connected with external evaluation and appraisal
Teacher competence frameworks	learning outcome-based; agency, empowerment, and responsibility of teaching staff	learning outcome-based TE programmes, teacher appraisal system based on teacher competence framework
Role of teacher educators	competence framework; collaboration between stakeholders	informal and non-formal learning as a teacher educator

Rapos and Kopp 2016; Stéger 2019), the term 'CPD' has not been included in formal regulation because, in practice, it is still hard to understand, and validate, the informal means of CPD. The growing misalignment between policy, research, and practice can be also attributed to typical Hungarian implementation strategies that still focus almost exclusively on top-down regulatory decisions. Also, in terms of evidence-informed policy, the recent lack of usable data on TE is a serious cause for concern as it impedes analysis and evaluation of trends in Hungary's TE (Hajdu et al. 2018).

Main Characteristics of Initial Teacher Education

Reforms and turbulent changes, as outlined above as one of the main characteristics of initial teacher education in Hungary, have not been followed by long-lasting strategic implementation and evaluation. So, to understand the existing system of ITE, consideration must be given to at least the last two waves of top-down transformation: namely the Bologna reform in 2005, and the restoration of the previous undivided ITE programme for subject teachers in 2013 (Stéger and Greguss 2014). These three broad dimensions can be used for summarising the main features of ITE: (a) ITE as a system, (b) ITE as a programme, and (c) ITE as a professional learning process.

ITE as a System

In the Hungarian system, ITE belongs to the jurisdiction of higher education, meaning that pre-service teachers can study either at colleges or universities and receive a higher education degree (see Fig. 3.1). Only those educators who work in day-care centres with children under the age of three do not need to have a higher education degree. However, in 2009 a new bachelor's programme—Infant and Early Childhood Educators—was introduced as a new option.

For Hungarian higher education institutions, ITE is a highly relevant field: 41 of the 65 institutions offer some form of ITE, including vocational teacher education programmes (Eurydice 2019). Teacher educators who work in HE are instructed to follow academic career requirements, that is, primarily focussing on their quality as researchers, not as teachers. As such, TE can play a crucial role in innovating educational practice in HE, given that the diffusion of education innovation is highest among larger, more scientifically-focussed universities, where teacher education can enhance the culture of innovation (Horváth 2016).

The scale of ITE offered in Hungary's higher education institutions differs widely. Those institutions where the initial subject teacher education programme is offered in at least two subject fields have had to establish a Teacher Education Centre (TEC) (Act on National Higher Education 2011). The primary tasks of these centres as separate units within the university are the alignment and coordination of professional tasks such as content and structure of subject teacher education; as well as the operative procedures of ITE, such as organising entrance and final exams, school placements, evaluation of student teachers' progress, and tracking graduates' careers. These TECs function in diverse ways and occupy various positions within their broader institutional structures. To some extent, they lack operative competences, experience of delivering public education, and, sometimes, are overburdened—especially when they take on the responsibility of the theoretical parts of ITE (Csapó et al. 2015). These centres work in partnership with the basic and partner ITE schools which helped in building networks between practice schools and universities (Stéger and Greguss 2014).

ITE as a Programme in Higher Education

In Hungary, the state strongly regulates the structure and learning outcomes of teacher education, as well as the percentages of the course content taken from specific fields (e.g. 130 credits for each subject of upper secondary school teachers but only 100 credits for lower secondary school teachers) (Fig. 3.2). ITE programmes are established nationally, approved and accredited by the Hungarian Accreditation Committee.

In recent decades, the structure of ITE programmes for kindergarten, special education needs, conductive, and primary education have remained the same, but for subject teachers, a dramatic change occurred with the CCIV. Act on National Higher Education in 2011. The initial education of infant and early childhood educators, and kindergarten teachers, is now provided as a three-year bachelor's programme, with that of primary school teachers and special needs educators as a four-year one. The programme for all subject teachers between 2006 and 2013 was offered at master's level as a two-and-a-half-year programme after graduating in at least one subject field at bachelor's

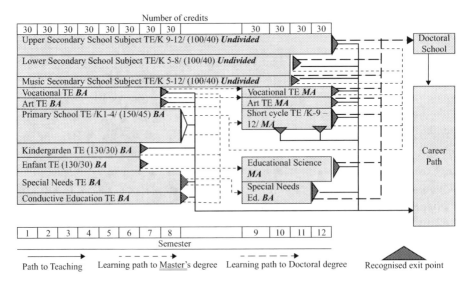

Fig. 3.2 ITE programmes in Hungary (In the brackets first showed the credits of the subject fields, second the credits of teacher' preparation)

level (i.e. the consecutive system). This Bologna-type ITE programme demonstrated a high commitment to teacher education as a profession and not as
a scientific, discipline-focussed education.

However, in 2013, ITE in Hungary was reorganised as an undivided, long-
cycle programme that lasts five years for K5–8 teachers and six years for
K9–12 teachers. This new structure increased the length of the ITE programme from five and a half to six years, which mainly derives from the prolonged school placement at the end of the course. Also, it separated the
preparation of lower and upper secondary school teachers in the subject field
but not in the pedagogical-psychological study area. As explained above, this
segregation goes back to the system which existed before the Bologna Process
and is highly criticised because it strengthens the different social and professional prestige of teachers teaching in primary (K1–8) and secondary schools
(K9–12), as well as widens the socio-economic gap between primary teachers
(K1–8) and secondary teachers. Furthermore, such a divide in professional
status underestimates the pedagogical and pedagogical content knowledge of
all teachers (Shulman 1986), as well as going against the international trends
of teacher professionalism focussing on teachers' competences and professional knowledge instead of subject knowledge (Stéger and Greguss 2014).
Although two routes exist for upper and lower secondary school teachers, in
practice, 75% of student teachers in Hungary choose to study for six years, so
even financially it is not worth organising different types of routes (Stéger
2019). ITE programmes prepare student teachers for two subject areas in 11
types of combinations (e.g. math and physics), reducing the possible combinations of subject areas compared to the Bologna-type system where 125
types of combinations existed, and helping to better respond to the expectations of schools.

So-called short cycle subject teacher education programmes were introduced with the 8/2013 Decree on requirements for teachers. These new routes
made ITE programmes more flexible, and provided easier access for graduates
with a qualification in a disciplinary field—or for those who already had a
bachelor's degree, master's subject teaching qualification, or primary teaching
qualification, then applied for a new teaching qualification. However, in practice, the number of applicants who are now choosing these routes is small and
decreasing (Stéger 2019), therefore meaning that the current teacher shortage
cannot be solved only via these new paths to TE. There is a real problem in
that no other type of access is supported: the field of teacher education does
not offer easy access to applicants from other professional fields (e.g. for engineers to become STEM teachers).

Hungarian ITE has a separate system for kindergarten and primary teachers on the one hand, and subject teachers for K5–12 on the other. The only transition from kindergarten, special needs education, and K1–4 ITE programmes to a scientific career path is the master's programme in Educational Science, but this does not qualify candidates to teach in upper grades. In addition, special needs educators with a bachelor's degree can proceed their studies directly on the same field at master's level for one and a half years. K1–4 teachers can apply for a shorter four- or five-semester subject teacher education programme. Doctoral programmes are open to teachers with an MA teacher certification: they may obtain a PhD in subject-specific or education science doctoral programmes. Overall, the transition points within Hungarian ITE are still quite inflexible.

In Hungary, all higher education programmes have been built upon the intended learning outcomes regulated at the national level since 2017. Subject teacher education programmes have had a longer tradition in competence-based education because, from 2006, a teacher's competence list was identified as the main requirement. The outcome requirements of initial subject teacher education have remained almost the same since 2006, but the proportions of courses allocated to specific fields have changed to a greater extent. This change can be said to have led to the misalignment of the programme, namely, in the form of excessive learning outcomes which cannot be implemented within the reduced proportions of pedagogical-psychological and subject teaching preparation (Rapos and Kopp 2015; Stéger 2019). Furthermore, another tension can be identified between the intended learning outcomes of the kindergarten and primary teachers' bachelor's programme and the subject teachers' master's programme—the developed competences do not differ between the two as much as the typical disparity outlined between the sixth and seventh levels of the European Qualification Framework. Also, despite the differences in learning outcomes of ITE programmes, after graduation teachers will be evaluated by the same standards of the teacher career model.

At present, the subject teacher programme consists of two subject fields and the teacher preparation part. Pre-service teachers for lower secondary earn 100 ECTS for each subject field, while those training to teach upper secondary earn 130 ECTS. The teacher's preparation covers pedagogical-psychological content, subject teaching, and school practice, which altogether make up 100 ECTS. The new undivided teacher education programme has changed as follows. Firstly, the proportion of subject fields has increased, while the proportion of pedagogical-psychological studies has decreased—both of which shifts are in contradiction with European trends (Stéger and Greguss 2014). Besides, the emphasis on subject teaching (which is included in teacher's preparation) has not increased, which raises the question of how student teachers' pedagogical content knowledge can be effectively developed (Stéger 2019). Secondly, subject teaching and school practice have gained more credits, with increased school practice strengthening the characteristics of competence-based education and practice orientation. However, school placements are organised in the last year of the programme, a choice criticised by experts because it does not help the ongoing competence development of student teachers, or the integration of theoretical and practical knowledge (Rapos and Kopp 2015; Stéger 2019). In 2021 it looks that school practice will be reorganised and divided for the whole TE programme from the first year till the end—as the education policy has also started to support this idea.

These changes mainly stem from ideological concerns, rather than scrutiny of the effectiveness of the different ITE programmes (Hunyady 2010). Unfortunately, on the one hand, these unfounded changes increase uncertainty within the system; on the other hand, they do not result in real transformation because the actors of the system adapt to the changes on the surface only.

ITE as Student Teachers' Professional Learning Process

A study by Paksi et al. (2015) showed that, in Hungary, three times more female candidates were applying to teacher education than male candidates. According to their findings, other demographics less frequently opting for teacher education included those students whose parents had a higher educational qualification themselves, those living in better financial circumstances, and students with better formal measures of academic achievement. Other studies have also shown negative self-selection in Hungarian teacher education based on the achievement of applicants (e.g. Veroszta 2015). Furthermore, 2018 applicants from the new undivided system of TE gained fewer points on the entrance exams compared to students from the other undivided programmes (Polónyi 2019). Thus, it can be said that if the 2013 teachers' career model had any positive impact on the prestige of the teaching profession, it had all but vanished for 2018 TE applicants (Polónyi 2019; Stéger 2019).

The ITE entrance exam in Hungary has two parts: one relies on points from matriculation exams plus the grades students gain in the last two years of their secondary education, and the other requirement is an aptitude test. In kindergarten and primary school teaching programmes, a special selection process was established in the late 1990s. In these early stages, it involved a more complex examination of applicants' commitment and preparedness; nowadays, the exam has a narrower focus on applicants' physical, verbal, and musical aptitude. In the undivided initial teacher education programme, an oral aptitude exam was introduced in the 2013/2014 academic year. In this process, applicants are asked about their personal motivations, career plan, communication competences, and beliefs about education. A Hungarian review of international practice and development projects was conducted (e.g. Falus 2011) before introducing the aptitude exam, but the results have not influenced practice, meaning that the aptitude exam still only consists of an unstructured oral discussion between a committee of teacher educators and the applicant. The validity and reliability of this new oral aptitude exam are highly debated within the Hungarian professional community (Stéger 2019). Indeed, applicants themselves are not satisfied with it: when surveyed, only 20% of students thought that the procedure was appropriate for filtering out those who are 'incapable' of becoming a teacher (Kállai and Szemerszki 2015).

A new Klebelsberg Training Scholarship was established in 2014 (52/2013 (II.25.) Governmental Decree), funding the best and most committed student teachers, in order to retain them in the teaching profession after graduation. Issued to 2582 students by 2019, the main targets of the scholarship are where the teacher shortage is most pronounced: for example, in STEM disciplines and in the countryside. Scholarship holders are employed by one of three schools of their choice, and must work as a teacher for at least the same amount of time as they received the scholarship.

In ITE for secondary school teachers, the development of student teachers' competences is supported by reflective learning practices throughout university courses and the school placement, as well as preparing a portfolio, which is part of the final exam (Rapos and Kopp 2015). However, the length of time elapsed between courses on general education, which are mainly at the beginning of the undivided ITE programme, and actual teaching practice, which mainly takes place at the end of the programme, has damaged the cohesion of ITE as a whole. In terms of the quantity of student teachers' learning, the undivided programme tends to put a heavier burden on student teachers but not the other ITE programmes. While students in higher education spend an average of 33 hours per week on their studies, that is, contact hours plus independent learning, students in the field of teacher education spend an average of less than 30.7 hours per week on their studies. On the other hand, those students on the undivided programmes (mainly in medical and subject teacher education programmes) study for an average of 44.3 hours per week (Hámori 2018).

All in all, students from the field of teacher education report feeling well prepared for Hungarian labour market expectations, with 69% of those surveyed by Hámori (2018) evaluating such preparation offered through their ITE as 'good', as well as rating this aspect of their education as being second-highest in value (after theological study area). However, the number of students undertaking a teacher's degree has decreased in recent years. While 9480 students received a degree for K-12 education in 2005, in 2016 that number almost halved with n=4932 (Polónyi 2019). Additionally, the dropout rate of student teachers is currently quite high, sitting at an average of 20–25%—with the dropout rate for STEM teachers sitting above average (Stéger 2019).

Main Characteristics of Professional Development

In Hungary, the system of teachers' professional development is traditionally based on formal courses—but the overall concept of teachers' lifelong learning, as well as the development of ITE, induction, and CPD along the same principles have been growing since the 1990s. Since 1997, teachers have been required to participate in in-service teacher education, amounting to 120-hour learning obligation every seven years. There are multiple ways to fulfil this obligation: (1) attending an accredited in-service teacher education programme; (2) obtaining a new higher education degree; (3) participating in school development projects; and (4) participating in ICT or foreign language training. Formal in-service TE programmes are organised by higher education institutions, pedagogical institutes, and private contractors, and must be accredited by the National Education Office. Although the system of in-service TE has long been in place in Hungary, it has always struggled with issues related to quality. Firstly, in many cases, training programmes are too general and not concretely linked to local problems or developments in schools; secondly, teachers' CPD continues to be based on formal, individual learning, so the acquired knowledge cannot be easily integrated into school activities (Liskó and Fehérvári 2008; Lannert 2010); and, thirdly, for a significant number of teachers, fulfilling the training obligation is simply a formal task and is not based on their own conscious career planning (Kálmán and Rapos 2018).

In 2013, the introduction of the teaching career model radically changed the professional development of teachers in Hungary. The career model is aligned with the new system of complex external evaluation of institutions,

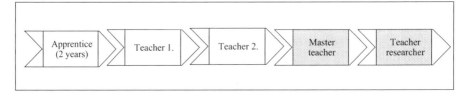

Fig. 3.3 Teachers' career model

leaders, and educators, in which supervision by the inspectorate plays a crucial role. This system has implemented a five-grade career path for teachers, where the first three levels are required and the second two are optional (Fig. 3.3).

After completing the initial two years of the internship period and successfully passing the qualification exam, teachers enter the 'Teacher 1' level. In order to advance to the 'Teacher 2' level, teachers must have an additional six years of teaching experience: teachers can voluntarily apply for this qualification after six years, with the procedure becoming obligatory after nine.

The evaluation process is the same across the first three levels: a qualification committee evaluates the teacher's competences, based on lesson observations and a portfolio, which they defend in an examination. One of the important requirements for evaluation at each stage is the participation in continuous professional development. The areas of competences included in the assessment are the same as those covered in ITE, however, the indicators are much more detailed. The same indicators are applied for each of the first three levels in the career model, with incrementally increasing thresholds to be achieved. Beyond this, the 'Master teacher' grade requires 14 years of experience plus an additional professional exam, and the 'research teacher' grade also requires 14 years of professional experience plus a PhD. These last two levels are voluntary and primarily based on teachers' planned professional activities concerning professional development, innovation, research, and knowledge-sharing (Kotschy 2014; Oktatási Hivatal 2019; Szivák and Pesti 2020).

The external evaluation of teachers in Hungary has decreased the professional autonomy of schools to a great extent. Indeed, a 2016 qualitative study by Vámos et al. showed that even the most innovative teachers in the Hungarian education system experience a low level of decision-making power (Fehérvári et al. 2016; Fullan and Hargreaves 2012). Furthermore, this focus on individual teachers within the accountability system has correspondingly strengthened the focus on individual learning, detracting from professional learning communities which, as research shows, are actually the more effective means of professional learning (e.g. Caena 2011, 2014; Cordingley 2015; Cordingley et al. 2015).

These recent changes in education policy were introduced without professional or societal consultation, but were accompanied by an intensive public debate that was focused on the wage compensation linked to the career model. As such, in the public debate, the model was not framed in terms of CPD, but to the time of advancement and increase in wages at each level. Other major focuses of these debates included criticism of how the new evaluation system places excessive administrative tasks on institutions and teachers, as well as being left without an adequate system to support the evaluation process. Additionally, the evaluation criteria were criticised as inadequate for assessing the effectiveness of education and the quality of teachers' work, a problem confounded by how the external evaluation of teachers is separated from internal institutional evaluation. Lastly, many of those who spoke up noted how the introduction of the model was a radical, sudden change, instead of incremental. To date, these discussions have not been satisfactorily concluded, which indicates that the reform has failed to resonate with a significant proportion of Hungary's teachers.

Challenges and Further Directions for Teacher Education in Hungary

The previous sections have described in detail how the socio-political background of teacher education in Hungary has changed historically; how the teacher education system has evolved into its modern form; and what problems and difficulties can be identified in the system today. Mainly aligned with European trends at structural and regulatory levels, the integrated teacher education system—that is, ITE, induction, and in-service training—is now established in Hungary. However, at the implementation level, several shortcomings can be identified.

Based on the original questions from the start of the chapter, this section will summarise the most important challenges currently facing teacher education in Hungary, and offer some critical suggestions for addressing them effectively. Although each problem is summed up somewhat separately for the sake of readability, it is necessary to emphasise here, once again, the extremely complex and intersecting natures of these challenges and problems—this means that, in turn, viable solutions can only be formulated in an equally complex way, in order to have a comprehensive impact on the teacher education system as a whole.

Firstly, consideration must be given to the loss of professional autonomy at all levels of the system: indeed, as shown above, centralisation has been a major endeavour in education policy over the last decade. Within this, weakening professional autonomy can be identified not only at the level of individual teachers, but also at the level of institutions (i.e. schools and universities) and processes (i.e. curriculum regulation, financing, and evaluation). Regarding the former, the fading image of the teacher as an autonomous professional also affects recruitment and retirement—too often creative, innovative applicants do not choose the teaching profession, or, if they do, they may leave it. Simultaneously, the possibility of autonomous, collaborative professional decision-making in the field is reduced, or even made impossible, by centralisation. On each of these levels, the erosion of professional autonomy damages Hungary's education system.

Secondly, teacher education and the teaching profession face challenges on the level of professionalisation. The current teacher shortage threatens the long-term viability of the entire education system. Thus, the greatest danger for the profession is that the qualification requirements may be lowered with a view to alleviating the teacher shortage, but, in reality, this would further diminish the prestige of the teaching profession and the quality of teaching delivered. The present minimised autonomy of different actors in the system mean that policy decisions dictate how these processes will evolve in the future. Indeed, many reforms have taken place in recent years with the aim of strengthening professionalisation. However, the weighting currently given to pedagogical content is not sufficient. In particular, the preparation for teaching marginalised students is inadequate, while the proportion of such students in Hungary's school system is increasing. In order to attract the best students to the profession and to select suitable prospective teachers, a scholarship system and an admission system were introduced in 2013, but did not meet expectations. As a result, the number of applicants for teacher training has increased, but not to a desired or necessary extent, and dropout rates within TE programmes remain significant. At present, however, there is a reduction in the amounts of available data and research on teachers and teacher education across the board; parallel with this, on a cultural level, the importance of data-driven decision-making in education policy is decreasing. This fundamental lack of knowledge compromises and curtails the professional capacity of teacher education in Hungary today.

As mentioned above, there is a pressing need to articulate potential solutions to these problems on a policy level, as that is where most of the autonomy regarding teacher education in Hungary is currently held, and would have a decisive impact on the teacher education system. The seriousness of the problems outlined here show that there is an urgent need for complex reforms based on robust consultation that comprehensively accounts for the interests, realities, and views of the various actors. As such, there must be access to and generation of current and nuanced data; support for research in the field of teacher education; and participation in international assessments of teacher education, all tailored to the specific needs of schools across the country. A one-size-fits-all approach does not work—for example, in schools in economically underprivileged areas, where teachers are facing poverty and high student dropout rates, the uniform external teacher evaluation system is too far from their reality.

Indeed, a multi-faceted approach is needed in order to attract the best students to the teaching profession and to reduce the number of teachers leaving the profession. Reforming some parts of the system is not enough: without legitimately elevating the autonomy of teachers and schools, raising teachers' salaries, and investing in the image of the teaching profession, these types of reforms will never bring about the necessary changes. As a pathway towards this type of system-level transformation, a shift away from initiating changes exclusively via regulatory processes must take place, with 'softer' methods due more attention. Concretely, this could be achieved by enhancing knowledge-sharing and collaboration between actors, or by applying more varied, flexible, and long-lasting strategies for the implementation and evaluation of any interventions. Ultimately, looking forward, professionalisation in Hungary's teacher education can only be strengthened by a renewed commitment to a rich support system of student teachers, in-service teachers, the teaching community, and schools.

References

EMMI rendelet a tanári felkészítés közös követelményeiről és az egyes tanárszakok képzési és kimeneti követelményeiről [Decree on common requirements for Teacher Education and subject-specific teacher education requirements]. (2013). (EMMI) 8 (Hung.).

Act on National Higher Education, Pub. L. No. CCIV. (2011). Retrieved from https://www.mab.hu/wp-content/uploads/Nftv_angol_2Sept2016_EMMI-forditas.pdf.

Balázs, É., M. Kocsis, and I. Vágó. (2011). *Jelentés a magyar közoktatásról 2010* [Hungarian Public Education Report 2010]. Oktatáskutató és Fejlesztő Intézet. Retrieved from http://www.ofi.hu/kiadvanyaink/jelentes-2010/19-minoseg.

Baska G., and J. Hegedűs. (2015). *A magyarországi pedagógusképzés története a recepciós hatások tükrében* (A pedagógusképzés megújítása) [History of teacher education in Hungary in the light of Reception (Renewal of teacher education)]. ELTE.

Biesta, G. (2009). Good education in an age of measurement: On the need to reconnect with the question of purpose in education. *Educational Assessment, Evaluation and Accountability*, 21(1), 33–46.

Biesta, G. (2019). Reclaiming teaching for teacher education: Towards a spiral curriculum. *Beijing International Review of Education*, 1(2–3), 259–272.

Burns, T., and F. Köstler. (2016). *Governing education in a complex world.* Paris: OECD Publishing.

Burroughs, N., J. Gardner, Y. Lee, S. Guo, I. Touitou, K. Jansen, and W. Schmidt (Eds.). (2019). *A review of the literature on teacher effectiveness and student outcomes.* Springer International Publishing.

Caena, F. (2011). *Literature review teachers' core competences: requirements and development. European Commission Thematic Working Group 'Professional Development of Teachers'.* Retrieved from https://ec.europa.eu/assets/eac/education/expertsgroups/2011-2013/teacher/teacher-competences_en.pdf.

Caena, F. (2014). Teacher competence frameworks in Europe: Policy-as-discourse and policy-as-practice. *European Journal of Education*, 49(3), 311–331.

Cochran-Smith, M., F. Ell, L. Ludlow, L. Grudnoff, and G. Aitken. (2014). The challenge and promise of complexity theory for teacher education research. *Teachers College Record*, 39.

Cordingley, P. (2015). The contribution of research to teachers' professional learning and development. *Oxford Review of Education*, 41(2), 234–252.

Cordingley, P., S. Higgins, T. Greany, N. Buckler, D. Coles-Jordan, B. Crisp, L. Saunders, and R. Coe. (2015). *Developing great teaching: Lessons from the international reviews into effective professional development. Teacher Development Trust.* Retrieved from https://tdtrust.org/wp-content/uploads/2015/10/DGT-Fullreport.pdf.

Creemers, B. P. M., and L. Kyriakidēs. (2012). *Improving quality in education: Dynamic approaches to school improvement.* Routledge.

Csapó, B., L. Bodorkós, and E. Bús. (2015). *A tanárképző központok működési standardjainak és akkreditációs szempontjainak kialakítása* [Operational standards and accreditation of teacher education centers]. TÁMOP-4.1.2.B.2-13/1-2013-0010 project. Retrieved from http://ofi.hu/sites/default/files/attachments/a_tanarkepzo_kozpontok_mukodesi_standardjainak_es_akkreditacios_szempontjainak_kialakitasa.pdf.

Darling-Hammond, L., and J. Bransford. (2005). The design of teacher education programs. In: L. Darling-Hammond and J. Bransford (Eds.), *Preparing teachers for a changing world* (pp. 390–441). Jossey-Bass.

EUA. (2017). *Annual report 2017.* European University Association. Retrieved from https://www.eua.eu/downloads/content/eua-2017-annual-report.pdf.

European Commission. (2017). *Magyarország. Eurydice—European Commission*. Retrieved from https://eacea.ec.europa.eu/national-policies/eurydice/content/hungary_hu.

Eurydice. (2019). *National Education Systems - Hungary Overview*. European Commission/EACEA/Eurydice. Retrieved from https://eacea.ec.europa.eu/.

Falus, I. (Ed.). (2011). *Tanári pályaalkalmasság—kompetenciák—sztenderdek: Nemzetközi áttekintés* [Teacher aptitude—competencies—standards: International overview]. Eszterházy Károly Főiskola.

Falus, I. (2006). *A tanári tevékenység és a pedagógusképzés új útjai* [Teaching activities and new ways of teacher education]. Budapest: Gondolat Kiadó.

Fehérvári, A., I. Nahalka, O. Kálmán, E. Kopp, J. Szivák, S. Lénárd, N. Rapos, J. Sipos, É. Verderber, and Á. Vámos. (2016). *Tanuló pedagógusok és az iskola szakmai tőkéje* [Teachers' learning and professional capital of the school]. (Á. Vámos, Ed). ELTE Eötvös Kiadó. Retrieved from http://www.eltereader.hu/media/2017/05/Vamos_Agnes_Tanulo_pedagogusok_READER.pdf.

Fullan, M., and J. Hargreaves. (2012). *Professional capital*. Routledge.

Gitlin, A., and J. Smyth. (1988). 'Dominant' view of teacher evaluation and appraisal: An international perspective. *Journal of Education for Teaching*, 14(3), 237–257.

Grek, S., M. Lawn, B. Lingard, J. Ozga, R. Rinne, C. Segerholm, and H. Simola. (2009). National policy brokering and the construction of the European Education Space in England, Sweden, Finland and Scotland. *Comparative Education*, 45(1), 5–21.

Guerriero, S. (Ed.). (2017). *Pedagogical knowledge and the changing nature of the teaching profession*. Paris: OECD Publishing.

Gyáni, G., and G. Kövér. (2006). *Magyarország társadalomtörténete a reformkortól a második világháborúig* [The social history of Hungary from the reform age to the Second World War]. Budapest: Osiris.

Hadar, L. L., and D. L. Brody. (2017). Professional learning and development of teacher educators. In. Clandinin, D. J. & Husu, J. (Eds.), *The SAGE handbook of research on teacher education* (pp. 1049–1064). SAGE Publication.

Hajdu, T., Z. Hermann, D. Horn, and J. Varga. (2018). *A közoktatás indikátorrendszere, 2017* [Indicators of Hungarian public education 2017]. Magyar Tudományos Akadémia Közgazdaság- és Regionális Tudományi Kutatóközpont Közgazdaságtudományi Intézet. Retrieved from http://mek.oszk.hu/17900/17966.

Halász, G. (2011a). *Az oktatáspolitika két évtizede Magyarországon: 1990–2010* [Two decades of education policy in Hungary: 1990–2010]. (manuscript) http://halaszg.elte.hu/download/Policy_kotet.pdf.

Halász, G. (1998). Policy reform, decentralisation and privatisation in elementary and secondary education in Hungary. In: P. Beredsford-Hill (Ed.), *Education and privatisation in Eastern Europe and the Baltic Republics* (pp. 61–72). Oxford: Oxford Studies in Comparative Education.

Halász, G. (2009). A felsőoktatás globális trendjei és szakpolitikai válaszok az OECD országokban [Global trends and policy responses in higher education in OECD countries]. In: Gy. Drótos (Ed.), *Felsőoktatás-menedzsment* [Management of higher education] (pp. 13–30). Budapest: Aula.

Halász, G. (2011b). *Javaslat a nemzeti oktatási innovációs rendszer fejlesztésének stratégiájára* [Proposal for the development strategy of the Hungarian national educational innovation system]. Budapest: Oktatáskutató és Fejlesztő Intézet.

Halász, G. (2012). Finanszírozási reformok a felsőoktatásban [Financial reforms in Higher Education]. In: J. Temesi (Ed.), *Felsőoktatás-finanszírozás* [Funding for higher education] (pp. 11–66). Budapest: Aula.

Halász, G. (2013). Az oktatáskutatás globális trendjei [Global trends of educational research]. *Neveléstudomány*, 1(1–2), 64–90. Retrieved from http://nevelestudomany.elte.hu/downloads/2013/nevelestudomany_2013_1_64-90.pdf.

Halász, G. (2017). The spread of the learning outcomes approaches across countries, sub-systems and levels: A special focus on teacher education. *European Journal of Education*, 52(1), 80–91.

Halász, G., and J. Lannert (Eds.). (2003). *Jelentés a 84agyar közoktatásról 2003* [Hungarian public education report 2003]. Budapest: Oktatáskutató Intézet.

Hámori, Á. (2018). A tanulási intenzitás és a megtérülés képzési területi mintázatai [Patterns of learning intensity and return by field of higher education]. In: Á. Hámori (Ed.), *Erőforrások, eredmények és élmények a felsőoktatásban. Az EUROSTUDENT VI nemzetközi hallgatói kutatás magyarországi eredményei* [Resources, achievements and experiences in higher education. Results of the EUROSTUDENT VI international student survey in Hungary] (pp. 63–77). Budapest: Oktatási Hivatal.

Hermann, Z., T. Hajdu, D. Horn, and J. Varga. (2019). *A közoktatás indikátorrendszere 2019* [Indicators of Hungarian public education 2019]. Hungarian Academy of Sciences Centre of Excellence Centre for Economic and Regional Studies. Retrieved from https://www.mtakti.hu/wp-content/uploads/2020/01/A_kozoktatas_indikatorrendszere_2019.pdf.

Horváth L. (2016). *Az oktatási innovációk terjedési modelljeinek bemutatása* [Educational innovation diffusion models]. ELTE-PPK NI. Retrieved from https://ppk.elte.hu/file/innova_2-2.pdf.

Hunyady, G. (2004). A hazai főiskolai szintű tanár-, tanító-, és óvóképzés pedagógiai programjai [Pedagogical programs of Hungarian kindergarten teacher and primary school teacher education colleges]. *Pedagógusképzés*, 2(1), 3–9.

Hunyady, G. (2010). Bologna és a tanárképzés [Bologna and teacher education]. *Felsőoktatási Műhely*, 3(2), 101–106.

Kállai, G., and M. Szemerszki. (2015). Pedagógushallgatók a képzés elején [Teacher students at the beginning of their teacher education]. *Educatio*, 24(1), 123–128.

Kálmán, O., and N. Rapos. (2018). Teachers' experiences and perceptions about professional development and their innovative practices. *Hungarian Educational Research Journal (HERJ)*, 8(3), 43–61.

Kauko, J., R. Rinne, and T. Takala. (Ed.). (2018). *Politics of quality in education: A comparative study of Brazil, China and Russia*. Routledge.

Kolosi, T., and M. Sági. (1997). Strukturális változás és egyenlőtlenség [Structural change and inequality]. *Társadalom és gazdaság*, 19(2), 9–30.

Körösényi, A., C. Tòth, and G. Török. (2007). *A magyar politikai rendszer* [Hungarian political system]. Osiris.

Kotschy, B. (2006). A kompetencia alapú tanárképzés képzési követelményei a munkáltatók szemével. *Társadalom és Gazdaság*, 28(2), 225–242.

Kotschy, B. (2014). A pedagógiai munka értékelése—a pedagógusok minősítése [Evaluation of teachers work—teacher assesment]. *Könyv és nevelés*, 16(4), 102–110.

Kováts, G. (2010). *Felsőoktatás-irányítás és finanszírozás: nemzetközi trendek és hazai gyakorlat* [Governance and financing of higher education: international trends and Hungarian practice]. Budapest: OFI.

Kováts, G. (2015). *Recent developments in the autonomy and governance of higher education institutions in Hungary: The introduction of the chancellor system*. Paper presented at the Central European Higher Education Cooperation Conference, Corvinus University, Budapest, Hungary.

Központi Statisztikai Hivatal [Hungarian Central Statistical Office]. (2019). Statistics Hungary, *Oktatási adatok 2019/20 [Educational data 2019/20]*. https://www.ksh.hu/.

Kyriakides, L., B. Creemers, P. Antoniou, and D. Demetriou. (2010). A synthesis of studies searching for school factors: Implications for theory and research. *British Educational Research Journal*, 36(5), 807–830. https://doi.org/10.1080/01411920903165603.

Lannert, J. (2010). *Pedagógus 2010 kutatás*. [Teacher research 2010] Tarki-Tudok. Retrieved from http://www.t-tudok.hu/file/tanulmanyok/v_nemzetkozi_lj.pdf.

Liskó, I., and A. Fehérvári. (2008). *Hatásvizsgálat: A HEFOP által támogatott integrációs program keretében szervezett pedagógus-továbbképzésekről* [Impacts of in-service teacher trainings organized in the framework of the HEFOP project]. Budapest. Oktatáskutató és Fejlesztő Intézet.

Mason, M. (Ed.). (2008). *Complexity theory and the philosophy of education*. Wiley-Blackwell.

Menter, I., M. Hulme, D. Elliot, and J. Lewin. (2010). Literature review on teacher education in the 21st century. Glasgow: University of Glasgow. Retrieved from https://www2.gov.scot/Resource/Doc/325663/0105011.pdf.

Németh, A. (2005a). A magyar pedagógus professzió kialakulásának előtörténete—A 18. Században és a 19. Század első felében [The development of the teaching profession in Hungary—the 18th century and the first half of the 19th century]. *Pedagógusképzés*, 3(1), 17–32.

Németh, A. (2005b). A modern magyar iskolarendszer kialakulása a nemzetközi intézményfejlődési és recepciós folyamatok tükrében [Development of the modern Hungarian school system in the light of international institutional development and reception trends]. *Iskolakultúra*, 15(9), 50–70.

Németh, A. (2007). A modern középiskolai tanári és tanítói szakmai tudástartalmak kibontakozásának történeti folyamatai [Historical processes of the development of the professional knowledge contents of modern primary and secondary school teachers]. *Pedagógusképzés*, 5(1–2), 5–26.

Németh, A. (2009). A magyar középiskolai tanárképzés és szakmai professzió kialakulása a 18–20. Században [The development of the Hungarian secondary school teacher education and the profession in the 18–20. Century]. *Educatio*, 18(3), 279–290.

Németh, A. (2012). *Magyar pedagógusképzés és pedagógus szakmai tudásformák I. 1775–1945* [Hungarian teacher education and the knowledge of teachers I. 1775–1945]. ELTE Eötvös Kiadó.

Normand, R., M. Liu, L. M. Carvalho, D. A. Oliveira, and L. LeVasseur (Eds.). (2019). *Education policies and the restructuring of the educational profession*. Singapore: Springer.

OECD. (2011). *Building a high-quality teaching profession*. OECD Publishing. Retrieved from https://www2.ed.gov/about/inits/ed/internationaled/background.pdf.

OECD. (2019). *Hungary—OECD*. Retrieved from https://www.oecd.org/hungary/.

Oktatási Hivatal. (2019). *Pedagógus minősítés* [Teacher qualification]. Retrieved from https://www.oktatas.hu/kozneveles/pedagogusminosites/jogszabalyi_hatter.

Ozga, J., P. Dahler-Larsen, C. Segerholm, and H. Simola. (2011). *Fabricating quality in Education: Data and governance in Europe*. Oxon, New York: Routledge.

Paksi, B., Zs. Veroszta, A. Schmidt, A. Magi, A. Vörös, V. Endrődi-Kovács, and K. Felvinczi. (2015). *Pedagógus—pálya—motiváció. Egy kutatás eredményei* [Teacher—profession—motivation. Research results]. Budapest: Oktatási Hivatal.

Polónyi, I. (2019). Az életpályamodell bevezetése után. Bevezetés—elemzések és adatok [After the Introducing the Teachers' Career Model. Introduction—analysis and data]. *Új Pedagógiai Szemle*, 69(5–6), 115–129.

Polónyi, I. (2015). Pedagógusbérek—Mindig lent? [Are teachers' salaries always low?] *Educatio*, 24(1), 30–46.

Prøitz, T. S. (2015). Uploading, downloading and uploading again—concepts for policy integration in education research. *Nordic Journal of Studies in Educational Policy*, 2015(1), 27015.

Radnóti, M. (2000). Foamy sky: The major poems of Miklós Radnóti (Z. Ozsváth & F. Turner, Trans.; Bilingual edition). Budapest: Corvina.

Rapos, N., and E. Kopp (Eds.). (2015). *A tanárképzés megújítása—2015* [Renewal of Teacher Education—2015]. ELTE Eötvös Kiadó.

Rapos, N., and E. Kopp. (2016). Szükséges-e/lehetséges-e a pedagógusképzés újabb átalakítása? *Pedagógusképzés*, 15(1–4), 49–59.

Sáska, G. (2015). Az elmúlt két évtized pedagógusképzési reformküzdelmei, kreditekben elbeszélve [Reforms in teacher education over the last two decades, focusing on the credit system]. *Magyar Tudomány*, 176(7), 819–827.

Shulman, L. S. (1986). Those who understand: Knowledge growth in teaching. *Educational Researcher*, 15(2), 4–14.

Stéger, C. (2019, January 26). *A tanári életpálya képzési szakaszának fejlesztéséről* [Development of preservice teacher education] [Presentation]. Teacher Education Academy, Association of Hungarian Teacher Educators, Budapest.

Stéger, C., and A. C. Greguss. (2014). *State of play in teacher education in Hungary after the Bologna reforms*. Eötvös University Press: Eötvös Loránd University.

Symeonidis, V. (2019). Teacher competence frameworks in Hungary: A case study on the continuum of teacher learning. *European Journal of Education*, 54(3), 400–412.

Szivák, J., and C. Pesti. (2020). *A pedagógusprofesszió hazai megújításának esélyei a mesterpedagógus programok tükrében* [Renewal of the teaching profession in Hungary in the light of the Master Teacher Programs]. L'Hamattan.

Szolár, É. (2010). A felsőoktatás reformja és a Bologna-folyamat Magyarországon [Higher education reform and the Bologna Process in Hungary]. *Magyar Pedagógia*, 110(3), 239–263.

Szűcs, J. (1981). Vázlat Európa három történeti régiójáról [A sketch about Europe's three historical regions]. *Történelmi Szemle*, 24(3), 313–359.

Tatto, M. T. (2006). Education reform and the global regulation of teachers' education, development and work: A cross-cultural analysis. *International Journal of Educational Research*, 45(4–5), 231–241.

Tenorth, H.-E. (2014). Evidenzbasierte Bildungsforschung vs. Pädagogik als Kulturwissenschaft-über einen neuerlichen Paradigmenstreit in der wissenschaftlichen Pädagogik [Evidence-based educational research versus pedagogy as a cultural science—a new paradigm debate in academic pedagogy]. *Neveléstudomány*, 2(3), 5–21.

Ulferts, H. (2019). *The relevance of general pedagogical knowledge for successful teaching: Systematic review and meta-analysis of the international evidence from primary to tertiary education*. OECD Education Working Papers, No. 212. Paris: OECD Publishing.

Venger, A., M. Novelli, and H. K. Altinyelken (Ed.). (2012). *Global education policy and international development: New agendas, issues and Policies*. New York: Continuum.

Veroszta, Zs. (2015). Pályakép és szelekció a pedagóguspálya választásában [Career image and selection in teacher career choice]. *Educatio*, 24(1), 47–62.

4

Teacher Education in Poland: Contested Terrains Between Policy and Practice

Alicja Korzeniecka-Bondar, Marta Kowalczuk-Walędziak, and Hanna Kędzierska

Introduction

Teacher education in Poland has been (and still is) subject to the great interest of policymakers and politicians, seeking to infiltrate the curricula in order to mould teachers into advocates of their politics and ideologies among students, that is, future citizens. This influence was particularly intense during the Soviet period (up to the 1990s) when the communist party turned special attention to teacher education, in order to establish total control over the education system and society as a whole (Hejnicka-Bezwińska 2015). However, paradoxically given the supposed trajectory towards 'freedom' post-communism, 30 years later, the situation seems to remain quite similar: indeed, post-1990s governments, under the umbrella of 'democratisation', have established a strong grip on teacher education through a combination of the professional standards and competences demanded of all teachers, namely in that they are expected to prepare students to live and work in a global market economy. As Gawlicz and Starnawski (2018, p. 387), argue:

A. Korzeniecka-Bondar (✉) • M. Kowalczuk-Walędziak
University of Białystok, Białystok, Poland
e-mail: alibon@uwb.edu.pl

H. Kędzierska
University of Warmia and Mazury, Olsztyn, Poland

© The Author(s), under exclusive license to Springer Nature Switzerland AG 2023   **83**
M. Kowalczuk-Walędziak et al. (eds.), *The Palgrave Handbook of Teacher Education in Central and Eastern Europe*, https://doi.org/10.1007/978-3-031-09515-3_4

[t]he sphere of education can be perceived simultaneously as an object and as a vehicle of change: a field to be adjusted to fit post-transition realities (requirements of neoliberal policies, dynamics of public sphere, integration with European Union (EU) structures, etc.) as well as a promoter of societies' readiness for their self-conversion: casting off the 'old' and taking up 'new' assumptions of what is proper, rational, and desirable in the collective, individual, public, and private lives of a country's population.

Although this entanglement of teacher education in politics is typical for many countries across the world (Biesta et al. 2020), in Poland these already contested terrains are further destabilised by the myth of the so-called balance between school autonomy and government control (Osiecka-Chojnacka 2010). Indeed, using Simkins' (1997 cited in Higham and Earley 2013, p. 704) terminology, while the operational power (i.e. 'how' the service is to be provided and resourced) has been increasingly transferred into the hands of school leaders in recent years, the criteria power (i.e. aims and purposes of the service) has been drawn much more firmly into central government, thus away from teachers themselves.

The aim of this chapter is to analyse the major shifts in teacher education policies and practices in Poland over the last three decades and, based on this analysis, to provide recommendations for the further development of teacher education in this country, and perhaps beyond. The chapter begins by outlining the major socio-educational transformations in Poland after the fall of communism. In light of these changes, the legal, organisational, and institutional reconstructions in the field are overviewed, followed by a discussion of the tensions, challenges, and paradoxes that have accompanied them. The paper concludes with some potential trajectories and key insights into the changes needed in order to locate students and their teachers at the heart of future education policy reforms.

Shifting Sands: Poland's Socio-educational Landscape over the Past 30 Years

The development of education in Poland after regaining full independence from communist control in 1989 mirrors the country's wider socio-economic landscape, closely following the timeline of major political transformations. Before 1989, the dominating party had full control over all education institutions, including those that educated prospective teachers. The deepening economic crisis in Poland—combined with empty communist promises of increased living standards, wealth, and social benefits for everyone, such as healthcare and housing—contributed to the growing frustration and irritation felt among many Poles, thus rousing the desire for change among them (Giza-Poleszczuk et al. 2000). The post-independence process of change in the education system was initiated, as in other areas of social life, from the Polish Round Table Talks, that is the negotiations between the then communist government and the opposition. During these talks, different stakeholders worked in small groups to discuss social and political issues such as environmental protection, mining, youth, science, education, and technological progress, among others.

Following the fruitful outcomes of these roundtable talks, the Polish education system underwent two main reform strategies between 1989 and 1991: bottom-up and top-down. The bottom-up reforms were the result of pedagogical innovation from individual teachers, researchers, social activists, parents, and associations. This type of reform consisted of introducing alternative education solutions to the school system (e.g. teachers creating their own programmes based on the principles of, for instance, Waldorf's pedagogy). On the other hand, top-down reforms were initiated by the first Minister of Education in the Third Republic of Poland, Henryk Samsonowicz, including key reforms aimed at the gradual delegating of school affairs to local authorities (Śliwerski 1999). While the goal of these reforms was commendable, achieving them in practice was laborious and lengthy due to the necessity of 'adapting the centralised and monopolised education system of the [...] socialist state to the requirements of the emerging parliamentary democracy' (Majewski 1996, p. 198). As such, enacting the reforms required: (1) the development of new education law in line with democratic principles; (2) movement away from a centralised (governmental) formulation of education policies, plans, and curricula; (3) the development of new school curricula without political indoctrination (4) an increase in public financial investment in the sector; and (5) changes in the existing staff working in schools (including leadership staff). This process of adaptation concluded with the Polish parliament passing the new *Act on the Education System of 7 September 1991*. The act contained a number of provisions indicating the opening of Polish education law to the political rules governing in other democratic countries, including: (1) founding education on universal values, including Polish cultural traditions; (2) recognising the co-responsibility of the state and local governments for financing, organising, and supervising education; (3) recognising the supportive role of the family in educating children and young people, plus the right of parents to have a say in the material delivered in schools; (4) granting all citizens the right to participate in educational initiatives; (5)

increasing the role of school headteachers, pedagogical councils, and social bodies in school management (e.g. via student governments, parents' councils, and school councils); and (6) linking education law with legal acts in other fields (Majewski 1996, p. 198).

Although not all the above objectives were fully realised, a major achievement during this period was the abolition of the state's monopoly in the running and management of schools. In practice, this means that since then schools have been run by state administration units, local governments, or social or religious organisations (Majewski 1996, pp. 202–203). In addition, this is the point when Poland's teachers were given full autonomy over the development and selection of curricula, textbooks, and teaching resources (Szyszka 2010).

However, the most significant changes in the education system came a few years later, in 1999, when the new Ministry of National Education reform came into force (Act of 25 July 1998 amending the School Education Act, *Journal of Laws 1998*, No. 117, item 759; No. 162, item 1126). This reform aimed to improve the quality of education offered in school, as well as equalise educational opportunities and, consequently, to increase the schooling rate at secondary and higher levels. The major changes introduced covered the following areas: (1) the structure of the school system (i.e. implementing 6-year primary school, 3-year lower secondary school (*gimnazjum*), and 3-year upper secondary school cycles, plus vocational schools); (2) the principles of educational institution management and financing (e.g. merging schools with high per-pupil costs); (3) curricula (i.e. in terms of education goals, the tasks of the school, and the content of syllabi); and (4) the examination system (i.e. introducing an external system of examinations at the end of each stage of education, carried out by central and district examination commissions) (Zahorska 2009; Wiśniewski and Zahorska 2020).

During this time of profound change, attention was also paid to improving the quality of teaching, teacher education, and teacher professional development. In 2000, a four-level system of teachers' career progression was introduced (Kowalczuk-Walędziak 2021). Pursuant to this system, entrants to the profession began as trainee teachers (the first grade) and undertook a probationary period lasting one school year, before being promoted to the rank of a contracted teacher (the second grade). Then, teachers could become an appointed teacher (the third grade) and, beyond that, a certified teacher (the fourth grade). This system was intended as a motivational mechanism that would encourage teachers to invest in their professional development (Wiłkomirska 2005; Wiłkomirska and Zielińska 2013) and—as a consequence—to improve the quality of their work, as well as guarantee employment stability for appointed and certified teachers. Progressing through the professional positions was also linked to a pay rise: a certified teacher was guaranteed a rate amounting to 225% of the trainee teacher's salary (Zahorska 2009). However, on 1 September 2022 the Ministry of Education and Science changed this career progression system once more, reducing the number of stages to only two: i.e. appointed teacher and certified teacher. The outcomes of this later reform are yet to play out.

The results of the significant 1999 reform are held in mixed regard by scholars, students, parents, and representatives of local school authorities (Putkiewicz et al. 1999; Konarzewski 2004; Wiśniewski and Zahorska 2020). On the one hand, this reform led to an increase in the numbers of students continuing their education at secondary and tertiary levels, as well as an improvement in PISA scores. On the other hand, this reform was to some extent an '[i]mitation […] of educational policy models developed originally in the West' (Gawlicz and Starnawski 2018, p. 387), meaning that they were not designed with the Central and Eastern European (or Polish) context in mind. Furthermore, all of these transformations were implemented in a great hurry, without taking into account research knowledge and teachers' voices, an omission which negatively affected the quality of the new curricula and textbooks, and led to miscalculation of teachers' salaries, as well as the bureaucratisation of the teacher professional development model.

In 2017, after the victory of the right-wing nationalist, conservative political Law and Justice Party in the parliamentary elections, another radical reform of the Polish education system took place (Dorczak 2019). This reform was preceded by a short public consultation with various education stakeholders on the planned directions of changes in education policy and the objectives of the reformation processes. The fundamental change resulting from this reform is the new (and current) structure of the school system, that is primary school has been extended to last eight years; lower secondary school has been abolished; general secondary school has been extended to four years; vocational secondary school has been extended to five years; and first-degree (three-year) and second-degree (two-year) sectoral vocational schools have been established. Exams have been introduced at the end of primary school: in Polish, a foreign language, mathematics, as well as one chosen subject. The results from these exams then form the basis for the pupil's success in applying to their chosen secondary school. A new core curriculum, plus new textbooks and teaching resources for each subject, are gradually being introduced in all types of schools, based on the ruling party's publicised values, including, for example, 'self-sacrifice', 'cooperation', 'solidarity', 'altruism', 'patriotism', and 'respect for tradition'.

The results of this reform, as was the case with the 1999 reform, are highly controversial and politically driven—resulting in a wave of protests—and only pretend to enter into cooperation with teachers, trade unions, or other education stakeholders (Dorczak 2019). In real terms, the abolition of the *gimnasjum* led directly to many teachers losing their jobs. In addition, this reform further highlighted the existing gap between education policy and practice in Poland, as outlined in the introduction to this chapter. In fact, reform projects over the last three decades have been constructed in a top-down manner and were to be implemented by teachers who were neither their co-creators nor sufficiently prepared for their implementation (Gajdzica 2006, 2013). Indeed, as Śliwerski (2013, p. 305) notes, education at this time was:

> treated as a POLITICAL GOOD, not a GENERAL GOOD. From 1992 onwards, politicians who successively took power in the Ministry of National Education appropriated Polish education to achieve particular political goals of the party or coalition that brought them to power […] education turned out to be a bargaining chip for political party and trade union battles.

As such, these political influences were also highly evident in the transformation of the teacher education field, as further discussed in the subsequent section.

Initial Teacher Education in Post-1989 Poland: Towards Increasing Standardisation and Accountability

As with the other elements of the education system described above, reforming teacher education after 1989 was not an easy task—largely due to the stubborn remnants of the communist system, which had led to the complete subordination of teachers to the ruling party and state under the regime. Firstly, the communist regime gradually reduced the research-based, academic model of teacher training to a narrowly focused, craft knowledge-based education. Secondly, a formal legacy of communism in Poland is the 1982 Teachers' Charter (Act of 26 January 1982—Karta Nauczyciela [The Teacher Charter with further amendments), the first education law passed by the government after the introduction of martial law. Although this document has since been subject to numerous—and more or less extensive—amendments, it is still in force today, defining who can become a teacher and setting out the rules for this professional group. Thirdly, communism led to a regression in the level of teachers' qualifications: there was no long-term school staff policy under the regime. Between 1976 and 1980 Poland had a glut of teachers, to which the government responded by introducing enrolment quotas for teacher education studies in order to prevent unemployment in the sector. However, paradoxically, this measure created a serious national teacher shortage. At this time, teachers were trained in two-year post-secondary courses, but it was not uncommon for people without a high school diploma or any teaching qualifications to work in a school. Ultimately, these remnants of the communist system influenced the direction of post-1989 reforms in Poland's teacher education system (Majewski 1996).

To address the above disadvantages, upon regaining full independence Poland's Ministry of Education drew up an ambitious programme to ensure that all teachers would have a university degree by 1998. Subsequently, an enormous number of teachers enrolled to complete their qualifications and obtain the newly required master's degree; however, the country's universities and teacher training colleges were unable to meet this sudden increase in demand, therefore private universities offering pedagogical courses for teachers filled the deficit (Majewski 1996). Since the early 1990s, teacher education in Poland has taken place across a variety of higher education institutions, namely: universities, higher pedagogical schools, and teacher training colleges (Bogaj et al. 1994). Since 1992, the latter two have been operating under the supervision of universities, enabling teachers to continue their education up to a master's degree. The three-year college programme was tailored to student teachers and teachers working in kindergartens, primary schools, and other educational institutions, resulting in a bachelor's degree awarded by the university with which the college had signed a cooperation agreement (Jung-Miklaszewska 2003; Kautz 2011).

Since 1990, the Minister of Higher Education has defined, by regulation, the guidelines universities must meet in order to establish and operate courses of study, as well as the standards for initial teacher training. From this point onwards, both the Act on Higher Education and the standards for teacher education were amended four times. The first education law in post-communist Poland (passed on the 12 September 1990, article 4a.) defined teacher education standards in terms of: (1) the profile of the graduate; (2) the subjects included in pedagogical education; (3) the preparation of the graduate in two specialities, IC technology, and a foreign language; (4) the duration and type of internships; and (5) curriculum content and required skills (Act of 12 September 1990 on Higher Education (Journal of Laws No. 65, item 385, as amended).

However, these standards for teacher education announced in 1990 were not enacted until 2003 (MENiS 2003, *Journal of Laws 2003* No. 170, item 1655) due to consecutive Polish governments failing to make education a consistent priority. In line with these standards, higher education institutions could educate teachers within the frameworks of higher vocational studies, master's studies, and postgraduate studies. Across all three, preparation for the teaching profession included the following interlinked aspects: (1) subject education, that is, for conducting educational activities in a specific subject area; (2) teacher training (330 hours), that is, for carrying out general teaching and caring tasks; and (3) pedagogical practice (at least 150 hours), that is, developing professional skills, plus understanding the organisation of schools and institutions (MENiS 2003, *Journal of Laws 2003* No. 170, item 1655).

One year later, in 2004, new standards for teacher education were defined (MENiS 2004, *Journal of Laws 2004* No. 207, item 2110), allowing teachers to train to teach two subjects rather than one—for example, kindergarten and elementary education, with an additional specialisation in a foreign language. In this case, teacher education for the first subject was realised in accordance with the requirements stipulated in the teaching standards for that particular field. Teacher education for the second subject was implemented within the scope of preparing teachers in accordance with the core curriculum of preschool or general education, as appropriate (i.e. at least 400 hours). Beyond this, the condensed, part-time training of teachers could also take place via evening and extramural sessions—respectively covering at least 80% and 60% of the number of full-time classes, while maintaining the curriculum content.

Further amendments to the standards of initial teacher education were made in 2012 and 2019 respectively. The 2012 standards (MNiSW 2012, *Journal of Laws 2012*, item 131) included:

1. a description of educational outcomes, in terms of:

   (a) substantive and methodological knowledge,
   (b) pedagogical and psychological knowledge, including preparation for working with students who have special educational needs,
   (c) use of technologies,
   (d) knowledge of a foreign language;

2. a description of the organisation of the teaching process;
3. a description of teaching modules (along with a description of the educational content of individual subjects, including internships);
4. a description of the organisation of internships.

Notably, these 2012 standards use the language of 'learning outcomes' (i.e. defined as the level of knowledge, skills, and competences of a graduate), ECTS points, and the division of studies into first-cycle, second-cycle, and long-cycle programmes. This framing proves the strong influence of the Bologna system on the teacher education system in Poland, in particular the linking of learning outcomes with the integrated qualification system for any given level of education (i.e. the Bologna ISCED 6 and 7). Preparation for teaching in kindergartens and elementary schools was covered by first-cycle studies in pedagogy (or other studies preparing teachers to work in elementary education). Substantive preparation for subject-specific teaching in elementary schools, lower secondary schools, upper secondary schools, and vocational schools was covered by second-cycle and long-cycle master's studies in the field of study appropriate for the taught subject.

The 2019 Regulation of the Minister of Science and Higher Education (MNiSW 2019, *Journal of Laws 2019*, item 1450) contains three annexes specifying the standards for the teaching profession, covering: teachers; preschool and elementary school teachers; and special education teachers, speech therapists, and support teachers. Consequently, the qualifications for preschool, elementary, and special education teaching can only be acquired via long-cycle, five-year master's programmes.

On an organisational level, the 2019 standards specify that teacher education includes content preparation and pedagogical preparation—in particular, the organisation of the learning process (e.g. minimum number of class hours, groups of subjects in which specific learning outcomes are achieved, and number of European Credit Transfer System points (ECTS) and both general and specific learning outcomes (i.e. the scope of knowledge, skills, and social competences of the graduate), as well as their verification. The standards also clarify the requirements for internships (e.g. the internship should be closely linked to the course of study for the subject); the infrastructure (e.g. schools and other institutions where internships are undertaken should enable the full achievement of the expected learning outcomes); and staff necessary for conducting the teaching process (e.g. academic teachers should have practical and/or research experience in the field relevant to their courses). Teacher education can only be provided by an institution that is authorised to award a doctoral degree in the discipline to which the field of study is assigned (Act of 3 July 2018—Provisions introducing the Law on Higher Education and Science, *Journal of Laws 2018*, item 1669, article 206. 1)—as such providing an opportunity to closely link contemporary teacher education with scientific research.

A teaching qualification—according to the 2019 standards—may also be obtained via postgraduate studies, with the exception of pre-school and elementary school education. The standards clearly specify that postgraduate studies should be of a duration not less than three semesters and allow the candidate to achieve the same learning outcomes as in the full study programme. Furthermore, preparation for the teaching profession provided as part of a postgraduate teaching programme should be carried out by staff enrolled in training teachers in universities at bachelor's or master's level.

Despite the numerous pathways towards entering the teaching profession, the most widespread model of initial teacher education is still the concurrent model. In this model, the pedagogical preparation component is provided from the beginning of the teacher's studies, together with general education and/or education in their taught subject area/s.

All teachers in Poland are required to have preparation in a given subject (e.g. biology and mathematics) and pedagogical training (i.e. teaching methods, psychology, and pedagogy) (*Regulation of the Ministry of National Education of 1 August 2017 on the specific qualifications required from teachers*) (*Journal of Laws 2020*, item 1289). However, these qualifications differ depending on the type of school where the teacher will be employed. Teachers employed in pre-primary and primary schools are required to have, as a minimum qualification, a bachelor's degree, whereas teachers employed in lower-secondary and upper-secondary schools (as well as basic vocational schools) are required to hold a minimum of a master's degree or equivalent. Since 2018, all candidates who would like to work as pre-school or elementary school teachers have needed to complete a five-year, long-cycle master's programme.

The right to work as a teacher in Poland involves the recognition of professional qualifications—and people who have appropriate teaching qualifications and experience acquired in the EU member states may also apply for recognition of their qualifications in Polish education settings (Dwojewski 2015). Pursuant to the *Teachers' Charter*, a person may work as a teacher if:

- they have completed a course of higher education which includes the appropriate pedagogical preparation, or they have completed education at a teacher training centre;
- they observe basic moral principles;
- they possess the good health required for the profession.

In addition, employment contracts for teachers are generally offered if the school is able to employ them full-time for an indefinite period of time, and if the person:

1. has Polish citizenship (this does not apply to citizens of the European Union, the Swiss Confederation, or a member state of the European Free Trade Association (EFTA)—all three of which are party to the European Economic Area);
2. has a full legal capacity to act and enjoys civil rights;
3. is not subject to an ongoing criminal proceeding in a case concerning an intentional indictable offence or a disciplinary proceeding;
4. has not been convicted with a valid court decision for an intentional offence or an intentional tax offence
      (4a) has not been subject to a valid disciplinary punishment in the 3 years before the beginning of the employment contract;
5. has the qualifications necessary for the position.

Continuing Professional Development: A Story on the Margins of the Career Progression System

The continuing professional development (CPD) of teachers in the Polish context most commonly refers to the career progression system (Wiłkomirska and Zielińska 2013; Kowalczuk-Walędziak 2021). Since September 2018, all teachers in Poland have had a statutory obligation to undertake professional development—in accordance with the needs of their school, and with the goal of improving the knowledge and skills connected with their performed work (Act of January 26th 1982—Karta Nauczyciela [The Teachers' Charter with further amendments, Journal of Laws of 2019, item 2215 and of 2021, item 4). However, although up until this point in-service training had not been compulsory, nonetheless teachers were obliged to expand their knowledge and skills. The need for professional development had been set out by key education regulations and documents, for example, the Teachers' Charter mentions several times that the teacher should pursue their full personal development in accordance with their school's needs. Furthermore, professional development is also an important element in evaluating a teacher's work and achieving the successive stages of their career progression.

In-service training in Poland is provided along two paths, namely: complementary education (that enables teachers to obtain higher or additional qualifications) and staff development (that allows teachers to develop or improve their subject knowledge and skills) (Madalińska-Michalak 2017, p. 90). The network of staff development in Poland is relatively well developed and covers the following (Norkowska 2018):

1. the activity of in-service training institutions for teachers:

   – central/national institutions
   – regional institutions
   – local institutions
   – non-public in-service training institutions;

2. methodological consultancy

   – assistance to teachers in planning
   – organising and testing the effects of the teaching and educational process
   – developing, choosing, and adapting the curriculum;

3. school-based training aimed at the shared learning process of the teaching staff in areas significant for the school/institution;
4. self-educational activities not highlighted in legal regulations, including:

   – reading professional literature, such as journals
   – using profession-specific websites
   – watching educational programmes
   – attending exhibitions
   – exchanging knowledge and experiences with peers
   – collaborating with universities, educational institutions, employers, and so on.

The national institution supporting teachers' professional development in Poland is the Centre of Education Development (Ośrodek Rozwoju Edukacji). It offers teachers from all across the country opportunities to participate in seminars and conferences, which may be organised in cooperation with foreign institutions. At regional and local levels, the Regional Centres of Teaching Methodology, as well as smaller public and non-public institutions, offer teachers a wide range of courses, trainings, and seminars (Madalińska-Michalak 2017). At the last count (September 2016), there were 425 active in-service teacher training institutions in Poland.

Legal regulations also specify the level of expenditure for complementary education and staff development. According to the Teachers' Charter, the budgets of school governing bodies should include funds for subsidising in-service teacher training, including professional courses to the value of 0.8% of the annual funds allocated for teachers' personal remunerations (Act of January 26th 1982—Karta Nauczyciela [The Teachers' Charter with further amendments], *Journal of Laws of 2019*, item 2215). Additionally, a separate regulation specifies the forms of teachers' professional development and the kinds of connected expenditures which can be financed with these resources, as well as detailed criteria for the granting of these funds (MEN 2019).

Although much attention has been given to the restructuring of and investment in in-service training for teachers in Poland over the past three decades, surprisingly, there is a lack of studies on teachers' own experiences of professional development. While the available studies mainly refer to teachers' measurable career progression, less attention has been given to their first-hand perception and experience of in-service training, as well as its impact on their practice (Kowalczuk-Walędziak 2021). Broadly speaking, existing research shows that Polish teachers declare a readiness to take part in various forms of professional development, such as courses, workshops, seminars, conferences, or doing research (Wiłkomirska and Zielińska 2013; OECD 2014; Wiłkomirska 2017), but that they assess this impact on their everyday practice as modest (Fazlagić 2012). Furthermore, some scholars point out that teacher professional development culture in Poland is mainly driven by the bureaucratic trappings of the official career progression trajectory (e.g. Wiłkomirska and Zielińska 2013; Fazlagić and Erkol 2015). This means that teachers participate in professional development activities not so much out of an internal feeling or sense of need, but rather to fulfil the statutory requirements for their career progression. However, as highlighted by Fazlagić and Erkol (2015, p. 545), '[t]he real problem is that the formal criteria are not a measure of genuine professionalism', meaning that '[t]he criteria which a teacher must meet to be promoted are overly focused on meeting bureaucratic standards'—ultimately at the expense of developing truly independent and critically thinking teachers (Kowalczuk-Walędziak 2021, pp. 61–62).

Tensions, Challenges, and Paradoxes in Reforming Teacher Education over the Last Three Decades

The post-1989 education landscape in Poland was characterised by the search for a model of teacher education adequate for meeting the new challenges of a democratic society recovering from a dictatorial regime (Rutkowiak 1986; Kwiatkowska 1988; Lewowicki 1990; Gołębniak 1998; Mizerek 1999, 2000). As the country re-established its own mechanisms of education, the need to depart from instrumental education focused on fluency in controlling the educational process or shaping teachers' qualities and skills was stressed. Instead, the need for a thorough theoretical, methodological, and axiological education was emphasised, within which teachers' knowledge and values were considered as a necessary condition for their proper functioning. A lively discussion on teacher education has continued into the twenty-first century (e.g. Kwieciński 2000; Palka 2003; Wiłkomirska 2005; Lewowicki 2007; Kwiatkowska 2008; Szempruch 2013). However, the adoption of successive legal guidelines and standards in the field has slowed down the processes of reflecting critically and searching for a concept of teacher education that truly meets the requirements of the contemporary, changing, and uncertain world we live in—creating tensions, challenges, and paradoxes in Poland's teacher education reform, as will be explored below.

The state of teacher education in Poland today is shaped by the standards envisioned by those in government, specifically as recommended by the minister responsible for higher education. This top-down approach indicates, on the one hand, the governments' desire to improve the quality of teacher education, but, on the other hand, the limited autonomy of universities in the creation of educational concepts and the implementation of the teacher education process—thus suggesting that the contemporary authorities aspire to control the field of education themselves (Czerepaniak-Walczak 2012, 2013). In this vein, it is critical to note the dramatic increase in attention paid to the organisation of the education sector (including the specifics of learning outcomes) by the Polish government over the last two decades. Government standards presently stipulate the guidelines for teacher education in great detail—having devoted just four pages to these concerns in 2003, this rose to nine in 2004, 22 in 2012, and 129 in 2019. Along a similar trajectory, the number of learning outcomes named by the government numbered 14 in 2003, 28 in 2004, 49 in 2012, and 1137 in 2019 (Atroszko 2020). This ever-increasing detail and accelerating complexity of standards makes it difficult to develop study programmes that meaningfully include all of the demanded elements in practice (Krause 2015; Szyling 2016). Indeed, standards have become a simplistic tool with which to measure the quality of education for future teachers, rather than facilitate an in-depth and nuanced approach to gauge and improve the quality of study programmes. This discrepancy is also the case in many other countries, where 'teacher education has been caught up in the same logic of measurement, competition, and control' (Biesta et al. 2020, p. 455). This signals the need to urgently re-think what exactly we mean by 'teacher education quality' beyond our national boundaries—is it a neoliberal measure of passes and fails, or a reflection of humanistic values such as passion, empathy, and collaboration?

As was mentioned above, preparation for the teaching profession in Poland today, as stipulated in the current government-issued standards (2019), includes both substantive preparation and pedagogical preparation. The latter consists of firstly, psychological and pedagogical preparation, and, secondly, didactic preparation (which, in turn, consists of: the fundamentals of didactics, vocal training, and didactic preparation for teaching a subject). Yet, while these standards place much emphasis on the teacher's practical and methodological skills, they lack the philosophical, historical, and theoretical context of the broader educational concept being implemented. As such, it is worth considering what implications this isolation has for the development of future teachers. Indeed, such a rigid conceptualisation of teacher education is far from that of the reflective practitioner well-equipped and ready to handle the fundamental multi-dimensionality and fluidity of the profession. Reducing the highly nuanced nature of the education process to repetitive, methodologically 'correct' activities may give rise to a false sense of ease among students seeking to enter the profession, rooted in an unwarranted conviction that a one-dimensional, step-by-step approach to teaching is sufficient—whereby undertaking studies simply provides a pre-made package of reliable ways of acting, rather than exposing them to and supporting them in navigating the dilemmas and complexities of the teacher's role (Mockler 2011).

The present standards do speak of the potential to include local issues in the nation's curriculum; however, this is only an illusion given that the study programme is already overflowing with compulsory content, to which it is not possible to add any further topics within the available number of hours in the study plan. In reality, as regards the existing study plans, the only element that individual universities may decide for themselves is whether the programmes they offer will have a practical or general academic profile.

At present, ministerial guidelines do not enshrine any obligation to conduct the selection of candidates for teacher education studies through, for instance, entrance examinations or interviews. Instead, the admissions criteria are regulated by the training institutions themselves, based mainly on grades achieved in the secondary school leaving examination. However, despite this lack of a formal entry process, access to teacher education studies is not without restriction (Eurydice 2009). Higher education institutions are obliged to calculate the number of students to be enrolled, derived from the student-to-staff ratio of 13:1. This ratio is assumed by the Ministry of Science and Higher Education to be the most important entry mechanism as regards higher education—indeed, this ratio is also the basis it uses for calculating its public spending in the sector (Lewicki 2018, p. 175).

The absence of any rigorous qualitative entry procedure designed to identify those individuals best suited to a career in teaching means that, among those choosing to study on a teacher education course, are people who are not wholly or sustainably motivated to pursue the demands and challenges of the job, instead making their career choice on the basis of, for instance, a childhood memory or by chance (Dróżka and Madalińska-Michalak 2016). In turn, this lack of open communication around entry to the teaching profession leads to low levels of candidate motivation and a lack of identification with the teaching profession. In turn once again, such feelings of displacement and dissatisfaction among some students put a burden on teacher educators to devote enormous amounts of energy to motivating and inspiring them to become good teachers.

Given these tensions and discrepancies, those presently seeking to advance Poland's teacher education field must ask some important questions: what is the status of the teacher educator's profession and what are the competences required for their work today? According to legal requirements, Poland's teacher educators are selected in line with their previous education and/or research attainments, forming a highly heterogeneous group—in terms of qualifications held, place of work, personal development path both within and outside the university, teaching practice, and so on—hence, with such a diversity of experiences and needs, it is difficult to define the requirements for a high quality teacher educator and common principles for supporting teacher educators in the challenges of their work.

To sum up, contemporary teacher education in Poland can be understood as the outcome of a clash between many factors:

1. socio-cultural and political transformations bringing about radical changes in the education system (namely in the form of governmental control);
2. various concepts of teacher education:

   – coming from the West,
   – imposed by regulations set by those in power,
   – re-constructed from the past,
   – developed autonomously in educational practice;

3. the still deeply rooted socialist mentality, for instance in terms of hierarchical social relationships and a highly bureaucratic approach to decision-making in the field of education (Koczanowicz 2008).

Therefore, Poland's teacher education field seems to be in a dynamic and constant cycle of review and change. These transformations can be described in terms of a shift from isolation and reduction (i.e. as enforced by the communist authorities prior to the fall of the Soviet Union) to an opening up towards a diversity of approaches to teacher education—although while keeping the practice of teacher education strictly within the framework of the current minister's standards and guidelines. Nevertheless, despite this attachment to standardisation, the direction of change unfolding now—increasing the quality of teacher education—raises hopes for improving the quality of education of future citizens, in turn, thus strengthening the well-being and intellectual character of Polish society of today.

What Next? Suggestions and Recommendations for Further Development

As this chapter has demonstrated, teacher education in Poland has been and is characterised by two key features: firstly, near-constant change—resulting from global, national, and local transformations—and, secondly, the political imposition of policies, reforms, and regulations in the field. These dual influences have and continue to bring about particular consequences: contradictions within transformations in the field of teacher education, and the ideological character of such changes—all with a limited connection to robust research knowledge. As mentioned previously, education is not currently perceived by Poland's politicians as a common good or a process requiring long-term thinking; rather it simply serves as a bargaining chip in subsequent elections, transformed according to the election manifesto of the ruling parties. Indeed, as Śliwerski (2009, p. 19) argues, 'what one has shortened, another has lengthened, what one has enriched, another has diminished by the same amount, what one has broken with, another, as if in opposition, has established, and so on'. This present approach of supposed public consultations, which, in fact, took place before some of the reforms analysed in this chapter, amount to little more than official documents used as false proof of cooperation between the authorities and stakeholders. Instead, their outcomes should be implemented in education policy. Therefore, we want to argue here that it is worth striving for the full depoliticisation of the teacher education system, instead building fruitful, sustainable, and dialogue-based relationships between politicians, researchers, and professionals (Helgetun and Menter 2022).

Another important issue in the further development of teacher education in Poland is how to ensure that it prepares future teachers with in-depth, reflective understandings of the specifics and challenges of contemporary times. Existing international studies show that focusing solely on 'efficacy, efficiency and meeting imposed standards' (Biesta et al. 2020, p. 458) is an insufficient strategy for training high quality teachers (Mockler and Stacey 2021), meaning that there is an urgent need to use research results in the process of planning and designing changes in the field (Ion and Iucu 2015; Kowalczuk-Walędziak et al. 2020). On this note, it is worth taking stock of the fact that while there are numerous small-scale studies on different aspects of contemporary teachers' work in Poland, there is a lack of comprehensive, non-political research on teacher education in terms of the specifics, challenges, and desired directions of changes. Therefore, in order to enrich the existing body of knowledge, there is a need to plan, design, and carry out more independent, large-scale, comparative studies that exist in close dialogue with the day-to-day work and voices of teachers and other education professionals.

In terms of entry into initial teacher education, there is a real need to analyse prospective students' personal and professional expectations, as well their predisposition to work with children and adolescents—all of which then should be taken into account in developing criteria for recruiting the best candidates to the teaching profession. Such requirements at the university recruitment stage would create a chance of recruiting those future professionals who have the greatest potential for doing valuable work in schools (Madalińska-Michalak 2017, p. 97). From a longer-term perspective, this type of threshold would provide an opportunity to increase the prestige of the teacher's job: concretely, the selection of the best candidates for the profession should be paired with an increase in teachers' salaries. Currently, according to the OECD's *Education at a glance* report (OECD 2020), teachers in Poland earn below the average teacher salary of the EU23 (i.e. the 23 EU countries in the OECD)—in practical terms, this means that many teachers pursue 'patch-work careers' (Kędzierska 2012), combining school work with other paid activities in order to meet the cost of living (Korzeniecka-Bondar 2018).

As for teachers' professional development, offerings should more closely meet their needs and respond to their personal motivations and goals, not only the formal bureaucratic requirements of the career progression system and the needs of their schools. For this purpose, the expectations and prefer-ences of teachers concerning their own professional development should be systematically studied, and taken into account in the planning of teacher pro-fessional development paths. It is also necessary to build the vision of profes-sional development as a joined-up, lifelong process—not simply 'event to event'—but pro-actively providing 'specific, concrete, and practical ideas that directly relate to the day-to-day operation of their classrooms' (Guskey 2002, p. 382).

Furthermore, going forwards, it is worth undertaking a wider debate on the professionalism and the quality of teacher educator work in Poland. Although Polish education law specifies the criteria for the evaluation of the scientific and didactic activities carried out by academic teachers working in universi-ties and other higher education institutions the qualifications and compe-tences required specifically for teacher educators have not been developed yet. In addition, the universities do not monitor how teacher educators employ their research-based knowledge in their practice, to what extent they know and understand the challenges of teaching in modern schools, as well as whether or not their own research career path is combined with participation in the practice of teacher education. There is no national policy or research regarding the status and professional experiences of teacher educators. Therefore, as some scholars suggest (e.g. Madalińska-Michalak 2011; Szplit 2019), greater policy and research efforts are needed in order to further define and regulate the status of teacher educators in Poland and the competences required for their role, as well as to identify their own professional develop-ment needs and expectations.

Summing up, we consider the matters indicated above as key, priority issues to be addressed in the coming years. However, what needs to be done—and what can already be done—is to work on excluding education from the influ-ence of the agendas of the current authorities, and instead work on changing pre-service and in-service teacher education in partnership with the teaching community (i.e. teacher educators, student teachers, teachers, and head teachers).

Conclusion

Over the last three decades, Polish education and the teacher education system have travelled a long road of transformation from post-communist, state-subordinated systems to solutions founded in the order of a democratic society. The dynamics of these transformations reflect the difficulties in building a new social and educational order from the ground up. Indeed, a significant part of these problems has its roots in the past—the greatest among them being the lingering conviction that education is a tool for achieving the goals of politicians and parties. Another barrier to the creation of a responsible education policy and training of teaching staff was the fulfilment of the Bologna Declaration (The Bologna Declaration 1999) provisions: although introduced in order to reduce the gap between Polish and European education, they were never designed with Central and Eastern Europe at their core, meaning that they were not an automatic fit for these cultures and systems. Simultaneously, the massification of teacher education—resulting from, among other things, the introduction of three-stage academic education in the absence of adequate financial and human resource support from public universities—led to the establishment of private higher education institutions offering training for teachers and other education professionals and, consequently, to a huge variation in the quality of teacher education between different institutions. It is worth noting that until 2002, when the State Accreditation Commission began its work, the state did not take a systematic interest in the actual quality of teacher education.

The issues facing contemporary teachers in Poland are no longer purely local (to the country, let alone any particular region or school). Teachers in many different parts of the world are experiencing similar challenges as they learn how to teach, for example, in our increasingly digitised lives, as well as through the profound socio-economic upheaval of a global pandemic. Similar challenges are also emerging for teacher educators, as they search for ways to prepare teachers for these contemporary realities. Therefore, there is a need to seek a balance between international or continent-wide policies and initiatives, and local, community-specific approaches to teacher education (Darling-Hammond and Lieberman 2012) that remain sensitive to historical, geographical, and political influences. Going forwards, Poland should create effective national teacher education policies in parallel with international and European teacher education policy, informed by existing research studies. This multifaceted approach brings with it the promise of a dynamic and responsive education culture that truly caters to the needs of modern Poland.

References

Act of 26 January 1982—Karta Nauczyciela [The Teachers' Charter with further amendments]. Retrieved from https://isap.sejm.gov.pl/isap.nsf/download.xsp/WDU19820030019/U/D19820019Lj.pdf.

Act of 12 September 1990 on Higher Education (Journal of Laws No. 65, item 385, as amended). Retrieved from http://isap.sejm.gov.pl/isap.nsf/DocDetails.xsp?id=wdu19900650385.

Act of 25 July 1998 amending the School Education Act (Journal of Laws 1998, No. 117, item 759). Retrieved from http://isap.sejm.gov.pl/isap.nsf/DocDetails.xsp?id=WDU19981170759.

Act of 3 July 2018—Provisions introducing the Law on Higher Education and Science; Journal of Law of 2018, item 1669). Retrieved from https://konstytuc-jadlanauki.gov.pl/content/uploads/2020/06/act-of-20-july-2018-the-law-on-higher-education-and-science.pdf.

Atroszko, B. (2020). Miejsce innowacyjności w standardach kształcenia nauczycieli [The place of innovation in teacher education standards]. *Forum Oświatowe*, 32(1), 113–126.

Biesta, G., K. Takayama, M. Kettle, and S. Heimans. (2020). Teacher education between principle, politics, and practice: A statement from the new editors of the Asia-Pacific Journal of Teacher Education. *Asia-Pacific Journal of Teacher Education*, 48(5), 455–459.

Bogaj, A., S. M. Kwiatkowski, and M. Szymański. (1994). *Rozwój oświaty w Polsce w latach 1992–1993. Raport dla Międzynarodowego Biura Oświaty w Genewie* [Educational development in Poland 1992–1993. Report for the International Bureau of Education in Geneva]. Warszawa.

The Bologna Declaration. (1999). Retrieved from http://www.ehca.info/media.ehea.info/file/Ministerial_conferences/02/8/1999_Bologna_Declaration_English_553028.pdf.

Czerepaniak-Walczak, M. (2012). Ile techne, ile praxis? W poszukiwaniu koncepcji praktyki jako elementu kształcenia nauczycielskiego profesjonalizmu [How much techne and how much praxis? In search of a concept of practice as an element of teacher professionalism training]. *Teraźniejszość—Człowiek—Edukacja*, 3(59), 7–22.

Czerepaniak-Walczak, M. (2013). Autonomia w kolorze sepii w inkrustowanej ramie KRK. O procedurach i treściach zmiany w edukacji akademickiej [Autonomy in sepia colour in the encrusted frame of the NQF. On the procedures and content of change in academic education]. In: M. Czerepaniak-Walczak (Ed.), *Fabryki dyplomów czy universitas? O "nadwiślańskiej" wersji przemian w edukacji akademick-iej* [Diploma factories or universitas? The 'Vistula' version of changes in higher education] (pp. 29–56). Kraków: Oficyna Wydawnicza "Impuls".

Darling-Hammond, L., and A. Lieberman. (2012). Teacher education around the World: What can we learn from international practice? In: L. Darling-Hammond and A. Lieberman (Eds.), *Teacher education around the world: Changing policies and practices* (pp. 151–169). London: Routledge.

Dorczak, R. (2019). *Wokół reformy edukacji z 2017. Krytyczna analiza dyskursu* [Around the 2017 education reform: A critical discourse analysis]. Kraków: Instytut Spraw Publicznych UJ. Retrieved from https://isp.uj.edu.pl/documents/2103800/139368467/Wokół+reformy+edukacji+z+2017+roku+–+Krytyczna+Analiza+Dyskursu/2150180a-0cb8-4da7-8495-765ebfff16d9.

Dróżka, W., and J. Madalińska-Michalak. (2016). Prospective teachers' motivations for choosing teaching as a career. *Kwartalnik Pedagogiczny*, 1(239), 83–101.

Dwojewski, D. (2015). *Zasady zatrudniania nauczycieli w szkołach i placówkach oświatowych* [Rules of Employing Teachers at Schools and Educational Institutions]. Retrieved from http://samorzad.infor.pl/temat_dnia/454585,Zasady-zatrudniania-nauczycieli-w-szkolach-i-placowkachoswiatowych.html.

Eurydice. (2009). *Key data on education in Europe*. Brussels: Education, Audiovisual and Culture Executive Agency. Retrieved from http://www.eurydice.org.

Fazlagić, J. (2012). Jakość szkoleń dla polskich nauczycieli [The quality of training for Polish teachers]. *E-mentor*, 4(46), 69–76.

Fazlagić, J., and A. Erkol. (2015). Knowledge mobilisation in the Polish education system. *Journal of Education for Teaching*, 41(5), 541–554.

Gajdzica, A. (2006). *Reforma oświaty a praktyka edukacji wczesnoszkolnej* [Education reform and early childhood education practice]. Katowice: Wydawnictwo Uniwersytetu Śląskiego.

Gajdzica, A. (2013). *Portret zbiorowy nauczycieli aktywnych. Między zaangażowaniem a oporem wobec zmian* [A collective portrait of active teachers. Between commitment and resistance to change]. Cieszyn—Toruń: Wydawnictwo Adam Marszałek.

Gawlicz, K., and M. Starnawski. (2018). Educational policies in Central and Eastern Europe: legacies of state socialism, modernisation aspirations and challenges of semi-peripheral contexts. *Policy Futures in Education*, 16(4), 385–397.

Giza-Poleszczuk, A., M. Marody, and A. Rychard. (2000). *Strategie i system: Polacy w obliczu zmiany społecznej* [Strategies and the system: Poles in the face of social change]. Warszawa: Instytut Filozofii i Socjologii PAN.

Gołębniak, B. D. (1998). *Zmiany edukacji nauczycieli. Wiedza—biegłość—refleksyjność* [Changes in teacher education. Knowledge—proficiency—reflexivity]. Toruń—Poznań: Edytor.

Guskey, T. R. (2002). Professional development and teacher change. *Teachers and Teaching: Theory and Practice*, 8(3), 381–391.

Hejnicka-Bezwińska, T. (2015). *Praktyka edukacyjna w warunkach zmiany kulturowej (w poszukiwaniu logiki zmian)* [Educational practice under cultural change (in search of a logic of change)]. Warszawa: PWN.

Helgetun, J. B., and I. Menter. (2022). From an age of measurement to an evidence era? Policy-making in teacher education in England. *Journal of Education Policy*, 37(1), 88–105.

Higham, R., and P. Earley. (2013). School autonomy and government control: School leaders' views on a changing policy landscape in England. *Educational Management Administration & Leadership*, 41(6), 701–717.

Ion G., and R. Iucu. (2015). Does research influence educational policy? The perspective of researchers and policy-makers in Romania. In: A. Curaj, L. Matei, R. Pricopie, J. Salmi, and P. Scott (Eds.), *The European Higher Education Area* (pp. 865–880). Springer, Cham.

Jung-Miklaszewska, J. (2003). System edukacji w Rzeczypospolitej polskiej. Szkoły i dyplomy [Education system in the Republic of Poland. Schools and diplomas]. Warszawa: Biuro Uznawalności Wykształcenia i Wymiany Międzynarodowej. Retrieved from http://www.wychmuz.pl/userfiles/Publikacje%20bezplatne/2003%20System%20edukacji%20w%20Rzeczypospolitej%20Polskiej.pdf.

Kautz, T. (2011). Przegląd systemu kształcenia nauczycieli w Polsce w latach 1945–2010 [A review of the teacher education system in Poland 1945–2010]. *Zeszyty Naukowe Akademii Marynarki Wojennej*, 2(185), 187–202.

Kędzierska, H. (2012). *Kariery zawodowe nauczycieli. Konteksty—wzory—pola dyskursu* [Teachers' careers. Contexts—patterns—fields of discourse]. Toruń: Wydawnictwo Adam Marszałek.

Koczanowicz, L. (2008). *Politics of time: Dynamics of identity in Post—communist Poland*. New York, Oxford: Berghahn Books.

Konarzewski K. (2004). *Reforma oświaty. Podstawa programowa i warunki kształcenia* [Educational reform. Core curriculum and educational conditions]. Warszawa: ISP.

Korzeniecka-Bondar, A. (2018). *Codzienny czas w szkole. Fenomenograficzne studium doświadczeń nauczycieli* [Everyday time at school. Phenomenographic study of teachers' experiences]. Kraków: Oficyna Wydawnicza "Impuls".

Kowalczuk-Walędziak, M. (2021). *Building a research-rich teaching profession. The promises and challenges of doctoral studies as a form of teacher professional development*. Berlin, Bern, Bruxelles, New York, Oxford, Warszawa, Wien: Peter Lang.

Kowalczuk-Walędziak, M., A. Lopes, J. Underwood, L. Daniela, and O. Clipa. (2020). Meaningful time for professional growth or a waste of time? A study in five countries on teachers' experiences within master's dissertation/thesis work. *Teaching Education*, 31(4), 459–479.

Krause, A. (2015). Kształcenie nauczycieli (wczesnej edukacji). Praktyczne konsekwencje niejasnych rozwiązań prawnych w świetle doświadczeń członka Polskiej Komisji Akredytacyjnej [Education of (early childhood education) teachers. The practical consequences of unclear legal solutions in the light of the experiences of a member of the Polish Accreditation Committee]. *Studia Pedagogiczne*, LXVIII, 51–62.

Kwiatkowska, H. (1988). *Nowa orientacja w kształceniu nauczycieli* [A new orientation in teacher education]. Warszawa: Państwowe Wydawnictwo Naukowe.

Kwiatkowska, H. (2008). *Pedeutologia* [Pedeutology]. Warszawa: Wydawnictwa Akademickie i Profesjonalne.

Kwieciński, Z. (2000). *Tropy—ślady—próby. Szkice z pedagogii pogranicza*. Poznań-Olsztyn: Wydawnictwo EDYTOR.

Lewicki, J. (2018). Nowy algorytm podziału dotacji podstawowej dla uczelni akademickich. Pierwsze skutki zmian i wstępne wnioski [A new algorithm for the distribution of the basic subsidy to academic institutions. First effects of the changes and preliminary conclusions]. *Nauka i Szkolnictwo Wyższe*, 2(52), 171–187.

Lewowicki, T. (1990). O dotychczasowych koncepcjach edukacji nauczycielskiej i potrzebie określania nowej koncepcji tej edukacji [On previous concepts of teacher education and the need to define a new concept of this education]. *Ruch Pedagogiczny*, 1–2.

Lewowicki, T. (2007). *Problemy kształcenia i pracy nauczycieli* [Problems of teacher education and work]. Warszawa—Radom: Instytut Technologii Eksploatacji—PIB.

Madalińska-Michalak, J. (2011). Teacher education in the context of improving quality in higher education in Poland. In: E. Eisenschmidt and E. Löfström (Eds.), *Developing quality cultures in teacher education: Expanding horizons in relation to quality assurance* (pp. 35–54). Tallinn: OU Vali Press.

Madalińska-Michalak, J. (2017). Teacher education in Poland: Towards teachers' career-long professional learning. In: B. Hudson (Ed.), *Overcoming fragmentation in teacher education policy and practice* (pp. 73–100). Cambridge: Cambridge University Press.

Majewski, S. (1996). Przemiany oświaty i wychowania w Polsce w latach 1989–1995 [Transformations of education in Poland in 1989–1995]. *Studia Pedagogiczne. Problemy Społeczne, Edukacyjne i Artystyczne*, 11, 189–214.

Ministry of National Education (MEN). (2019). Rozporządzenie Ministra Edukacji Narodowej z dnia 23 sierpnia 2019 r. w sprawie dofinansowania doskonalenia zawodowego nauczycieli, szczegółowych celów kształcenia branżowego oraz trybu i warunków kierowania nauczycieli na szkolenia branżowe (Dz. U. z 2019 r. poz. 1653). [Regulation of the Minister of National Education of 23 August 2019 on the financing of in-service training for teachers, detailed objectives of professional training for sectoral vocational schools, and the procedure and conditions for assigning teachers to sectoral professional training (Journal of Laws of 2019, item 1653)]. Retrieved from http://isap.sejm.gov.pl/isap.nsf/download.xsp/WDU20190001653/O/D20191653.pdf.

Ministry of National Education and Sport (MENiS). (2003). Rozporządzenie Ministra Edukacji Narodowej i Sportu z dnia 23 września 2003 r. w sprawie standardów kształcenia nauczycieli (Dz.U. 2003 nr 170 poz. 1655). [Regulation of the Minister of National Education and Sport of 23 September 2003 on standards for teacher education (Journal of Laws 2003 No. 170, item 1655)]. Retrieved from http://isap.sejm.gov.pl/isap.nsf/DocDetails.xsp?id=WDU20031701655.

Ministry of National Education and Sport (MENiS). (2004). Rozporządzenie Ministra Edukacji Narodowej i Sportu z dnia 7 września 2004 r. w sprawie standardów kształcenia nauczycieli (Dz.U. 2004 nr 207 poz. 2110). [Regulation of the Minister of National Education and Sport of 7 September 2004 on standards for teacher education (Journal of Laws 2004 No. 207, item 2110)]. Retrieved from http://isap.sejm.gov.pl/isap.nsf/DocDetails.xsp?id=WDU20042072110.

Ministry of Science and Higher Education (MNiSW). (2012). Rozporządzenie Ministra Nauki i Szkolnictwa Wyższego z dnia 17 stycznia 2012 r. w sprawie standardów kształcenia przygotowującego do wykonywania zawodu nauczyciela (Dz.U. 2012 poz. 131). [Regulation of the Minister of Science and Higher Education on standards for teacher preparation programmes (Journal of Laws 2012 item 131)]. Retrieved from http://isap.sejm.gov.pl/isap.nsf/DocDetails.xsp?id=WDU20120000131.

Ministry of Science and Higher Education (MNiSW). (2019). Rozporządzenie Ministra Nauki i Szkolnictwa Wyższego z dnia 25 lipca 2019 r. w sprawie standardu kształcenia przygotowującego do wykonywania zawodu nauczyciela. (Dz.U. 2019 poz. 1450). [Regulation of the Minister of Science and Higher Education on standards for teacher preparation programmes (Journal of Laws 2019 item 145)]. Retrieved from http://isap.sejm.gov.pl/isap.nsf/DocDetails.xsp?id=WDU20190001450.

Mizerek, H. (1999). *Dyskursy współczesnej edukacji nauczycielskiej. Między tradycjonalizmem a ponowoczesnością* [Discourses of contemporary teacher education. Between traditionalism and postmodernity]. Olsztyn: Uniwersytet Warmińsko-Mazurski.

Mizerek, H. (2000). Alternatywne sposoby myślenia o nauczycielu i jego edukacji: pytania do badaczy i edukatorów [Alternative ways of thinking about teachers and their education: questions for researchers and educators]. In: Z. Kwieciński (Ed.), *Alternatywy myślenia o/dla edukacji* [Alternatives for thinking about/for education] (pp. 329–346). Warszawa: IBE.

Mockler, N., and M. Stacey. (2021). Evidence of teaching practice in an age of accountability: when what can be counted isn't all that counts. *Oxford Review of Education*, 47 (2), 170–188.

Mockler, N. (2011). Beyond 'what works': Understanding teacher identity as a practical and political tool. *Teachers and Teaching Theory and Practice*, 17(5), 517–528.

Norkowska, E. (2018). Doskonalenie zawodowe nauczycieli [In-service training for teachers]. *Monitor Dyrektora Szkoły*, 9, 56–58.

OECD. (2014). *TALIS 2013 results. An international perspective on teaching and learning.* Paris: OECD Publishing.

OECD. (2020). *Education at a Glance 2020: OECD Indicators.* Paris: OECD Publishing.

Osiecka-Chojnacka, J. (2010). Rola centralnych władz oświatowych w reformowanym systemie oświatowym [The role of central education authorities in the reformed education system]. *Studia BAS*, 2(22), 9–40.

Palka, S. (2003). Pedeutologia w perspektywie badawczej pedagogiki [Pedeutology in the research perspective of general pedagogy]. In: D. Ekiert-Oldroyd (Ed.), *Problemy współczesnej pedeutologii. Teoria—praktyka—perspektywy* [Problems of contemporary pedeutology. Theory—practice—perspectives]. Katowice: Wydawnictwo Uniwersytetu Śląskiego.

Putkiewicz E., K. Siellawa-Kolbowska, A. Wiłkomirska, and M. Zahorska. (1999). *Nauczyciele wobec reformy edukacji* [Teachers towards education reform]. Warszawa: ISP.

Rutkowiak, J. (1986). Metodologiczna sytuacja pedagogiki a modele kształcenia nauczycieli [The methodological condition of pedagogy versus models of teacher education]. *Ruch Pedagogiczny*, 5–6.

Szempruch, J. (2013). *Pedeutologia. Studium teoretyczno-pragmatyczne* [Pedeutology. A theoretical and pragmatic study]. Kraków: Oficyna Wydawnicza "Impuls".

Szplit, A. (2019). *Od nowicjusza do eksperta. rozwój ekspertywności nauczycieli nauczycieli języków obcych* [From novice to expert. Developing the expertise of foreign language teacher educators]. Kielce: Wydawnictwo Uniwersytetu Jana Kochanowskiego.

Szyling, G. (2016). Koncepcja walidacji efektów uczenia się. Obszary pedagogicznych redukcji i ich (nie) zamierzonych skutków [The concept of validation of learning outcomes. Areas of pedagogical reductions and their (un)intended effects]. *Rocznik Andragogiczny*, 23, 169–189.

Szyszka, M. (2010). Edukacja w Polsce—konieczność reformy i nowe wyzwania [Education in Poland—the need for reform and new challenges]. *Roczniki Nauk Społecznych*, 2(38), 255–274.

Śliwerski, B. (1999). Remanent reformowania oświaty w III RP [A review of education reform in the 3rd Republic of Poland]. *Edukacja i Dialog*, 3, 30–36.

Śliwerski, B. (2009). *Problemy współczesnej edukacji. Dekonstrukcja polityki oświatowej III RP* [Problems of contemporary education. Deconstruction of the educational policy of the 3rd Republic of Poland]. Warszawa: Wydawnictwa Akademickie i Profesjonalne.

Śliwerski, B. (2013). *Diagnoza uspołecznienia publicznego szkolnictwa III RP w gorsecie centralizmu* [Diagnosis of the socialisation of public education in the Third Republic of Poland in the corset of centralism]. Oficyna Wydawnicza "Impuls": Kraków.

Wiłkomirska, A. (2005). *Ocena kształcenia nauczycieli w Polsce* [Evaluation of teacher education in Poland]. Warszawa: Instytut Spraw Publicznych.

Wiłkomirska, A., and A. Zielińska. (2013). *Ocena systemu awansu zawodowego nauczycieli w Polsce. Studium empiryczne* [Evaluation of professional promotion path for teachers in Poland. Empirical study]. Warszawa: Wydawnictwa Uniwersytetu Warszawskiego.

Wiłkomirska, A. (2017). Doskonalenie zawodowe nauczycieli a jakość pracy nauczycieli i szkoły [Teachers' professional development and the quality of teachers and schools' work] In: J. Madalińska-Michalak (Ed.), *O nową jakość edukacji nauczycieli* [Towards a new quality of teacher education] (pp. 225–245). Warszawa: Wydawnictwa Uniwersytetu Warszawskiego.

Wiśniewski J., and M. Zahorska. (2020). Reforming education in Poland. In: F. Reimers (Ed.), *Audacious education purposes* (pp. 181–208). Cham: Springer.

Zahorska, M. (2009). Sukcesy i porażki reformy edukacji [Successes and failures of education reform]. *Przegląd Socjologiczny*, 58(3), 119–142.

5

Teacher Education in Slovakia: Recent Joys and Challenges for the Future

Daniela Bačová and Zdenka Gadušová

Introduction

This chapter describes the development of teacher education (TE) in Slovakia over a period of 30 years, commencing in the early 1990s and concluding with the current challenges teacher education faces on its way towards further transformation. The macro-level analysis of TE in Slovakia points at tensions and contradictions in the legal framework that controls and directs teacher education. It evaluates the impact of the political decision to grant universities high levels of independence (see it in Act No. 131/2002), without making them accountable for the employability of their teaching graduates or for meeting the pedagogical demands of the school sector. The meso-level analysis reviews the structure and content of university-based teacher education, noting the challenges universities face, primarily from the perspective of inadequate allocation of teaching time for the student teachers at the university and funding for the teaching practice of student teachers. At the micro-level, the study describes teachers' responses to sudden societal changes after the fall of communism: namely, teachers' desire to enhance their professional skills through their individual agency, resulting in engagement with international

D. Bačová (✉)
University of Bolton, Bolton, UK
e-mail: d.bacova@bolton.ac.uk

Z. Gadušová
University of Constantine the Philosopher, Nitra, Slovakia

© The Author(s), under exclusive license to Springer Nature Switzerland AG 2023
M. Kowalczuk-Walędziak et al. (eds.), *The Palgrave Handbook of Teacher Education in Central and Eastern Europe*, https://doi.org/10.1007/978-3-031-09515-3_5

collaborative activities and projects. However, it also observes teachers' gradual dissatisfaction with and disengagement from their professional development, due to inappropriate and unsystematic changes in teaching policies which have failed to meaningfully address teachers' loss of social and economic status, starting from the middle of the twentieth century (Valica and Pavlov 2007). The study concludes with the identification of key challenges that teacher education faces in meeting the profound economic, social, and environmental changes currently underway, including the incorporation of information and communication technology (ICT) and greater integration of students with special needs (Hajdukova 2013; Hašková 2019; Hašková and Bitterova 2018).

Historical-Political Background

After 1989, Czechoslovakia commenced its political, economic, and cultural journey towards becoming a developed, Western-type parliamentary democracy (Kosová and Porubský 2007; Malová and Dolný 2016), a journey which has not been without challenges, tensions, or contradictions. In January 1993, Slovakia, a smaller geographical part of Czechoslovakia, became an independent state. In 2004, after a period of political struggle and international isolation, Slovakia joined the European Union in order to fulfil its dream of becoming 'an equal member of the family of European nations' (Malová and Dolný 2016, p. 302).

The difficult process of transition—from autocracy to democracy, from centrally planned economy to market economy, and the independent nation-state-building process after 1993—has had a profound effect on the attitudes and decisions of political elites regarding educational reforms. The leading political parties focused on the need to develop legislation and other aspects of a newly formed nation-state administration, while struggling to reverse an economic slowdown which was accompanied by 'murky privatisation' and high levels of political corruption (Malová 2017, p. 2). Educational policy, therefore, remained on the fringes of political interests, which impacted subsequent teacher education practices.

As numerous authors argue (Hroncová 1999; Kasáčová 2004; Kosová and Porubský 2011b; Porubský et al. 2014b; Hašková and Pisoňová 2019), radical economic, political, and social changes require the execution of a well thought through school reform, including teacher education reform. Such reform would need to be supported by a systematic analysis of the economic and cultural requirements of the country. It would also necessitate the dedication of all stakeholders engaged in the school sector at all levels, and inevitably require a cross-party political consensus regarding the aims of educational reform and strategies for its implementation. To date, despite a number of legislative and curricular initiatives, Slovakia's political elites have been unable to agree on a shared vision for the future of teacher education policy. Each successive minister of education has attempted to promote their own vision of reform: however, none of them were anchored in the specifics of the Slovak cultural and historical context, nor were their decisions based upon evidence from practice (Porubský et al. 2014a).

From a historical perspective, three main barriers have hindered effective school and teacher education reforms in Slovakia (Kosová and Porubský 2011a). The first is the result of a deep-rooted belief that education should be managed and controlled through centrally-formulated directives initiated by the state education department. Top-down management as national management strategy in the absence of democratic political traditions within Slovakia's historical development has led to the continuation of a culture that perceives teachers as 'officials' or 'administrators' expected to routinely implement new curricular reforms, while ignoring their personal and contextual needs or professional experience (Kosová and Porubský 2011a, p. 20). The implementation of change is therefore often initiated with insufficient pedagogical preparation or material support for teachers (Porubský et al. 2014a; Kubalíková and Kacian 2016).

Secondly, teaching and learning in Slovakia are traditionally based on the information transmission model of education (Kosová and Porubský 2011a; Kosová and Tomengová 2015), favouring the accumulation of encyclopaedic knowledge at the expense of creativity, critical evaluation, and application in practice. As such, the teacher is viewed as an 'executor' of the centrally approved and politically controlled curriculum without an autonomous professional status (Kosová and Porubský 2011a, p. 21). However, even when the government reconceptualised the professional role of teachers as 'co-creators' of the school curriculum (Act No. 245/2008), teachers generally perceived this change with a high level of scepticism and resistance towards another top-down initiative (Kosová and Porubský 2011a).

Thirdly, the social and personal value of education has been diminished to the level of other commodities: that is to say, society, parents, and learners themselves value education predominantly as a gateway to the job market (Gadušová et al. 2014a; Kubalíková and Kacian 2016). In addition, there seems to be an absence of any strong public pressure for an educational reform that would address the substantially decreased social and economic status of teachers. Furthermore, all existing and prospective reforms are hindered by 'a rather mixed political system in Slovakia' (Malová 2017, p. 10), with weakly-institutionalised and less stable political parties unable to develop a cross-party consensus on the longitudinal aims and principles of state-run public education, despite the governing parties' seeming willingness to implement wider EU educational directives (Kubalíková and Kacian 2016; Malová and Dolný 2016; Kneuer et al. 2018).

Teacher Education Reform

It is possible to discern a number of phases within teacher education reform in Slovakia. Covering the period from 1989 to 2009, Kosová and Porubský (2011b) identify four phases in the transformation of teacher education. The first phase spans Slovakia's coexistence with the Czech Republic from 1989 to 1992, in which both countries shared similar educational reforms, with this period of 'searching for new beginnings' (Kosová and Porubský 2011b, p. 45) lasting until 1996/1997, and featuring a rapid expansion in higher education institutions offering teacher education programmes. The second phase, from 1998 to 2004, was the period of the 'conceptualisation of teacher education' and marked the first significant effects of the Europeanisation of education in the structure of university education: the acceptance of the Bologna Process divided the structure of university-based teacher education into two distinct stages—a bachelor's and a master's award—which has had a detrimental impact on the promising attempts to reform initial teacher education (ITE) (Kosová et al. 2012). The ITE reform of the previous period aimed to strengthen the interconnectedness between pedagogical theory and its application in practice with emphasis on the gradual development of teacher's professional identity as a reflective practitioner. However, as Kosová et al. (2012) strongly argue, the two distinct stages of university teacher education weakened the position of subject didactics in the ITE curriculum and thus prevented a more integrated teacher education (see more in detail below).

The third phase covers approximately the period from 2005 to 2009, most notably two key educational policies that influenced teacher education, the National Curriculum reform (2008) and the Pedagogical and Professional Employees Act (Act No. 317/2009). The fourth phase, post-2009, is characterised by the need for a systematic, evidence-based educational policy reform that addresses the contradictions and tensions between the current ITE curriculum structure, in-service teachers' careers and education progress, as well as the needs of schools in a fast-changing contemporary society. However, the new Pedagogical and Professional Employees Act (Act No.138/2019), aimed at addressing irregularities and contradictions between the previous legislative framework and the reality of teachers' professional status, education, and career opportunities, seems—thus far—to have only served to fossilise existing problems.

1990–2004: The Drive for Innovation at the Micro-Level Challenged by the Drive to Maintain the Status Quo at the Macro-Level

The 1990s were characterised by a historically unprecedented rate of change in the education system, with teachers demonstrating high levels of enthusiasm and willingness to change their professional practice, but gradually stifled by increased political control and a lack of political effort to initiate a systemic reform (Kosová and Porubský 2007). After 1989, teacher education and training underwent a number of changes. Unfortunately, these were neither systematically planned nor strategically implemented in any way (Kosová and Porubský 2007). A number of factors are responsible for this situation: firstly, school reform lagged considerably behind economic reforms; secondly, the political elites disregarded educational policy that would interlink school reform with teacher education reform and harness teachers' willingness and desire to explore and implement innovative approaches in their professional practice; and thirdly, the university reform bills that granted universities autonomy enabled higher education institutions to structure teacher education programmes following their own needs and interests (Kosová and Porubský 2011a, b; Kosová and Tomengová 2015).

As Hargreaves and Shirley (2012, p. 49) argue, teachers' professional capital plays a decisive role in the successful implementation of any school reform, and includes 'assets among teachers […] that are developed, invested […] and circulated in order to produce a high yield […] in the quality of teaching and learning'. Professional capital is manifested through five forms of capital. To become agents of change, teachers should possess high levels of *human* capital (knowledge and skills developed via education and training), social capital (ability to work with others), *moral* capital (seeing oneself as responsible for others' well-being and development), *symbolic* capital (having the high status of a profession that attracts people to it), and *decisional* capital (being capable of solving complex problems over a sustained period of time) (Hargreaves and Shirley 2012).

In this historical review of teacher education in Slovakia, which is inevitably linked with educational reforms, it is possible to observe teachers' high levels of social and moral capital in their enthusiasm and willingness to engage in the transformation of their teaching practice during the last decade of the twentieth century. In addition, this rare moment of bottom-up pressure to reform originated from all stakeholders in education—educational experts, teacher educators, parents, and learners themselves—and seemed to win a positive response from the political leadership of the early 1990s. However, this opportunity has since been lost due to ad hoc educational reforms without any systematic analysis of the existing situation or consideration for teachers' moral and decisional capital (Kosová and Porubský 2007).

Political Discourse and Educational Changes

In the early 1990s, there was a societal paradigm shift regarding the aims and sociocultural value of education. The communist ideology which had been underpinning the content of curricula at all levels of education was legally removed by parliamentary acts immediately after the political changes (Kosová and Porubský 2007). A different ideological and philosophical discourse emerged in newly formulated governmental policy papers, in which the aims of the democratisation and humanisation of education were emphasised. In this context, education was seen as a means to accomplish radical social changes that would lead to the establishment of a pluralistic democracy. The new values of education were defined in the spirit of the Erasmian humanist tradition of education (Parrish 2010), in which pupils and students should be led to aspire to higher human values such as love, freedom, and solidarity. These humanist ideals of education, accentuating respect for an individual and their cognitive, emotional, and creative growth, stood in stark contrast to the preceding communist educational discourse.

During the 1990s, three different, though philosophically and ideologically interconnected, documents outlining a new direction for school and teacher education reforms were presented to the government. The first document, *Duch školy* (Turek 1990; *The Spirit of School*) formulated a strong belief in education as a means to achieve radical social, economic, and political change. The document made explicit references to UNESCO's recommendations on education and also outlined the profile of an ideal teacher, emphasising the personality of the teacher as virtuous, knowledgeable, and positive in attitude towards self-education. However, the message of the document was soon lost in the political turmoil of Czechoslovakia's separation into two independent states.

During this decade, two other aspirational concepts were outlined by leading educational experts and presented to the government as possible directions for decisive educational reform: *Constantine* and *Millennium*. In 1994, the Ministry of Education published the first in-depth, complex conception of education and training, '*Constantine: The national programme of education and training*' (Ministerstvo školstva a vedy 1994), outlining the aims, content, and structure of education and training in a similar philosophical vein to *The Spirit of School*. However, the concept was never seriously given life and was eventually succeeded four years later by '*Millennium: The new conception of the development of education and training within 10–15 years*' (Rodina a škola 2002), which the government accepted in 2001 as part of its new conception of education system reform. *Millennium* identified key changes to be addressed in the new educational reform, in particular reformulating the aims and content of the national curriculum, and explicitly defining humanistic principles that would underpin school reform. It again highlighted a need to change the structure and quality of teachers' professional identities in order to place more emphasis on their personal and professional development and growth. Furthermore, it demanded the creation of a professional framework for the recognition of teachers' career stages and called upon the government to address teachers' low social capital. Unfortunately, the concept followed the destiny of its two predecessors (OZPSAV SK 2013; Porubský et al. 2014b). A watered-down version was eventually accepted as part of the new school act, and national curriculum reform was agreed by the government in 2008 reform which was implemented into the education system in an abrupt manner without providing the necessary time, funding, or expertise. Traditionally, teachers had always been expected to implement the national curriculum developed by the National Institute for Education, and therefore did not possess adequate experience nor the requisite knowledge and skills for curriculum design. Indeed, the concepts of curriculum development, design, and innovation had not been part of the ITE curriculum, and therefore reports on teachers' willingness to engage with the changes and implement them in their classroom practice revealed rather disappointing findings (Porubský et al. 2014b, 2015; Butašová et al. 2017; Bockaničová et al. 2018).

Higher Education Institutions and Teacher Education

Teacher education in socialist Czechoslovakia followed the model of a higher education-based certification for primary and secondary teachers, while early years teachers were graduates from upper secondary schools and academies

(Petrová and Zápotočná 2018). Primary teacher education lasted for four years at the Faculties of Education. Lower and higher secondary teacher education entailed studying dual subject disciplines together alongside educational psychology and didactics for five years.

Changes in legislation (i.e. the Higher Education Act: 1990, amended in 1996 and the new act in 2002) enabled higher education institutions to gain autonomy as soon as the early 1990s. As a result, universities were able to open departments with new specialisations, equip laboratories to undertake research activities, and engage in international networks. The HEIs also embraced EU support programmes. For example, funding via PHARE (European Parliament 1998) and TEMPUS (European Commission 2014) programmes facilitated the exchange of knowledge, skills, and expertise among academics and university students, namely through the provision of mobility grants for collaborative education and research projects, international conferences, and language courses. Universities could also offer and some really did additional study programmes designed to meet the new national demand for teachers of foreign languages, brought about by changes in the national curriculum whereby learners were offered a choice of six foreign languages (English, French, German, Italian, Russian, and Spanish). Russian stopped being taught as the only compulsory and first foreign language and, through parental pressure, was substituted with English.

The growth of cross-border contacts increased the process of the Europeanisation and internationalisation of education (Dakowska and Harmsen 2015), further contributing to universities' transformations. Support from various international organisations (e.g. the British Council and the Fulbright Commission in Bratislava), charity organisations, and volunteers (e.g. Peace Corps, East European Partnership, and Education for Democracy) enhanced the flow of human capital, as many HE departments accommodated the visits of colleagues from Western European and American universities who contributed significantly to the currency of subject disciplines; supported innovation in subject curricula; exposed academics to alternative teaching methods; and improved their foreign language competences. The universities also received resources in the form of books and modern information and communication technology (Fonodová 1996; Pugsley and Kershaw 2015). This international support was particularly crucial during the 1990s when the country faced a serious economic downturn. The funding of education projects coming from mainly EU institutions became a significant source of supplementary budget for HEIs. While the education sector was severely underfunded on every level, against these odds, there was a rapid increase in the number of HE institutions (including private ones) and faculties, many of which began to offer teacher education programmes. For instance, there were only five HEIs offering teacher training programmes prior to 1989, but by 2004 there were nine such HEIs (Kosová et al. 2012).

The newly acquired independence of universities brought about a number of consequences for initial teacher education still visible today. Firstly, individual institutions could make their own decisions about the quality of ITE. Though the teacher education model continued to mirror the pre-1989 tradition, there was a rapid increase in institutions offering teacher education programmes structured around subject knowledge, with considerably less emphasis being placed upon practical aspects of teacher pedagogical knowledge, skills, and competences. Indeed, the recent body of research, *To dá rozum* (That makes sense 2016–2020), clearly demonstrates the prevailing practice of teaching via traditional methods of lecturing, with limited practical application of theory in classrooms.

Secondly, despite the fact that HEIs are required to accredit their ITE programmes via an education expert (usually a professor) and a subject-specific guarantor, there has been a tendency to undermine any legitimate need for the application of theory into practice. Due to funding limitations, for example, universities have restricted the provision of teaching practice for trainee teachers. Consequently, trainees are expected to organise teaching placements on their own. This has resulted in unsystematic, unstructured, and ad hoc arrangements with no appropriate mentoring support for trainees, who often contact their childhood school's teachers in order to conduct observations and lead classes there. By extension, unfortunately, it is all too possible at present to observe the direct consequences of the decision to emphasise subject knowledge at the expense of pedagogical expertise. As many researchers conclude, novice teachers consequently struggle with behaviour management and have a poor understanding of how to support learners with specific learning needs, as well as in formatively assessing learners, providing feedback, performing administrative tasks, and so on (Kosová and Tomengová 2015; Magová et al. 2016; Gadušová and Predanocyová 2018).

Thirdly, the status of pedagogy as a legitimate scientific subject was considerably undermined due to the socio-political, ideological role pedagogy played in the pre-1989 teacher education curriculum. The communist regime exploited pedagogy as a tool for its ideological control and indoctrination, which led directly to limited research into teacher education and other aspects of teaching and learning. This, as mentioned above, has also resulted in a weakened position of subject didactics: the focus is more on the theoretical knowledge base of trainees rather than on the actual application of theory in practice. Tandlichová (2008), for example, comments critically on the loss of foreign language didactics from the teacher education curriculum, highlighting the high levels of poorly qualified teachers teaching languages in primary, lower, and higher secondary schools as the outcome.

From the second half of the 1990s and onwards into the new millennium (1996–2004), a number of teacher training colleges (Faculties of Education) engaged in collaborative projects with their Czech counterparts, resulting in the development of a new, updated teacher education curriculum. The content of this curriculum was aimed at primary school teachers and was enriched with theories of teaching and learning; innovative and alternative teaching methods; child developmental psychology; and subject-related pedagogies. The aim was to develop a new professional identity of the teacher as a reflective practitioner (Kosová 2012; Kosová and Tomengová 2015), as opposed to the prevalent model of the teacher as an academic expert, as traditionally emphasised in programmes for secondary teachers of subjects in the humanities, social and natural sciences, and technology. Regrettably, these promising developments were abruptly interrupted by structural changes in the university systems following the requirements of the Bologna Process. Indeed, the directive to recognise two levels of higher education programmes—the bachelor's and master's—has had a detrimental effect on the quality of teacher education and training in Slovakia (Kosová 2012), and is still seen as one of the main barriers to transforming ITE into a more practice-based approach so as to adequately equip future teachers with the skills and competences to meet twenty-first-century challenges (Valica and Pavlov 2007; Schleicher 2015).

Teachers as Enthusiastic Agents of Change

The reluctance to consider the decreasing economic and social status of teachers—and the negation of educational reforms at the macro-level—can be viewed in stark contrast with 'innovation-eager' teachers at the micro-level (Porubský et al. 2014b). Teachers, determined to address the demand for pedagogical knowledge and transformation necessitated by the long-ignored need for educational reforms, began setting up professional organisations in their respective disciplines to enable national and international networking. As Kosová et al. (2012) rightly express, such a dynamic, bottom-up movement to promote educational reforms, including teacher education reforms, had not been evident at any stage in the history of Slovak schooling.

Even though some of Slovakia's professional organisations had ceased to exist by the end of the 1990s, many have adopted a charity status or live on through their most popular events still being regularly organised by enthusiastic teachers and teacher educators. For example, one such event that continues to thrive (more than 20 years since its inception) is a foreign language school theatre festival, a highly popular event managed by lecturers from Constantine the Philosopher University (UKF) in Nitra, and annually attended by around 200 performing pupils from primary and secondary schools across the region and abroad. The festival is the outcome of a project originally financed by the British Council in Bratislava in collaboration with the UKF to develop the subject didactics of English language teachers (Bačová 2021) and was part of the activities promoted within an active and lively organisation for teachers of English (Slovak Association of Teachers of English). Set up in 1992 and active until 2012, its members were teacher educators, and in- and pre-service English teachers working across all educational levels and provision types. The aim of the organisation was to explore and develop communicative and creative approaches for language teaching and learning—it provided a platform for teachers and academics to share experiences, examples of good practice, and innovative teaching methods, as well as participate in different projects and events.

Other organisations were established in different, less economically developed geographical regions of Slovakia in order to introduce alternative teaching methods into the schooling system, and to simultaneously enhance teachers' skills in these innovative approaches—offering short- and long-term courses to support teachers in pursuing their individual interests in specific pedagogical approaches. For instance, founded in 1992, Susan Kovalik's Association: Education for the Twenty-First Century (ASK n.d.), has been actively involved in in-service and pre-service teacher education, collaborating with regional teacher education centres and some universities, with a particular focus on developing teachers' understandings of the concept of an integrated thematic curriculum, and how to apply it in their practice. Similarly, the Association of Friends of Free Waldorf Schools (APSWŠ n.d.) set up regional centres for implementing innovative teaching and learning methods into the mainstream school system and, despite increased governmental efforts to halt free experimentation with particular teaching approaches, it remains active. The same is true of the Wide Open School organisation that has supported inclusion programmes for pupils from low socio-economic backgrounds and minoritised ethnic backgrounds (from Roma communities in particular), via developing training materials for teachers in the early years and primary sector (Škola dokorán—Wide Open School n.d.; Petrová and Zápotočná 2018). In a similar vein, the Association Orava (Združenie Orava 2019), established in 1994 as part of the Orava—IOWA project, has since grown and successfully established regional centres for facilitating the collaboration of professionals from a wide spectrum of educational institutions, to promote critical thinking and reading literacy in particular. Like the above-mentioned organisations, it has supported teachers' continuous professional development via workshops, conferences (e.g. *Innovations in School*), and online resources. However, increasing governmental control over teachers' involvement in their continuous professional development via independently organised, non-state-funded groups has gradually stifled teachers' enthusiasm and voluntary engagement in extracurricular and professional activities. As a result, by the beginning of the millennium, a number of teacher and parent-led educational initiatives ceased to exist under the burden of administrative requirements and increased school inspection (Kosová et al. 2012; Porubský et al. 2014b). The activity of enthusiastic and creative teachers has, to some extent, been refocused on engagement with a variety of European-funded projects (e.g. Erasmus+) which have enabled schools and teachers, particularly those fluent in a foreign language, to engage in collaborative partnerships with colleagues from schools in other European Union countries.

2004–2020: Key Legislative Frameworks Defining Teacher Professionalism and the Impact of the Bologna Process on Teacher Education

The ongoing reluctance of political elites to systematically address the professional status of teachers is evident in the fact that it took Parliament 20 years to clarify the role, responsibilities, career stages, and required qualifications of employees working in the school sector. The No. 317/2009 Coll., Pedagogical and Professional Employees Act (i.e. the 2009 Act) originally drew upon a research project led by a group of experts between 2002 and 2005 (Kosová 2012). The findings and recommendations were introduced to the government in 2007, and despite the fact that the project was widely reviewed positively in the academic and teaching community, it took a further two years for Parliament to formally accept it. Unfortunately, the actual legislative outcome created a much more restricted view on the legal status of educators; their professional roles; required qualifications; career progression routes; and a formalised credit system of professional development than the authors of the research project had suggested themselves. Though the Act emphasised teachers' autonomy in making decisions about their professional growth—following recommendations from the European Commission regarding the quality of teacher education (Commission of the European Communities 2007)—this has been restricted via the process of institutional accreditation.

Immediately after its publication, the Ministry of Education redefined the required qualifications for teachers and limited the choice of accredited institutions offering continuous professional development (CPD) courses. It also restricted the role of faculties of education in providing accredited teaching qualifications and CPD courses, in order to open the market to other providers. For instance, according to the Slovak Centre of Scientific and Technical Information Data (CVTI SR 2020), during the 2016/2017 academic year, there were a total of seven faculties of education at universities in Slovakia. However, up to 11 universities and 28 faculties trained a total of almost 15,000 future teachers—meaning that only 55% (8, 275 out of 14, 959) of future teachers were trained in faculties of education, while non-education faculties trained the other 45%. This situation, whereby almost half of Slovakia's future teachers are being trained outwith education-specific faculties, has raised serious concerns about the quality of such teacher education programmes due to the definitive lack of pedagogical knowledge, expertise, and practical experience of teaching staff in non-education faculties, as numerous studies have expressed (Pavlov 2013; Kosová and Tomengová 2015).

The 2009 Act was updated ten years later in an attempt to address some of its inconsistencies (Act No. 138/2019 Coll. on Pedagogical and Professional Employees, 2019). However, the new act has actually fossilised—and even exacerbated—the problems with continuous teacher education, thus has been strongly criticised by teachers across the board (Slovenská komora učiteľov 2012–2020). It maintains, for example, the conditions which enable teachers to teach up to 70% of their workload in subjects they are not qualified to teach, and has dismantled the system of lifelong learning (Slovenská komora učiteľov 2012–2020).

Initial Teacher Education After the Bologna Process

Slovakia became a signatory of the Bologna Process in 1999. The three-level framework of higher education was introduced by Act No. 131/2002 on Higher Education, which has subsequently shaped the structure of teacher education programmes since 2005 (László 2008). The university-based teacher education programme was divided into three levels and currently has the following structure: a three-year bachelor's degree, focusing on mastering theoretical subject knowledge, with some limited access to pedagogical disciplines and teaching practice; a master's degree, concentrating on mastering specialist subject-related disciplines, and pedagogical and subject didactics knowledge with their application in practice; and finally, the doctorate level, focusing on empirical educational research.

In general, Slovak educators believe that the adoption of the Bologna Process was 'a serious blow to the promising developments of teacher education programmes' (Kosová and Tomengová 2015, p. 39). While the central premise of the EU policy was to offer students mobility, study stays abroad, and recognition of their results (i.e. transcripts of records) in order to aid graduates in entering the job market after the completion of the bachelor's programme, teacher educators did not believe that a three-year programme would enable graduates to develop a robust knowledge base of their discipline(s), subject didactics, and their professional skills all at the same time. This fear was confirmed by the subsequent legislation (the 2009 Act), which provided bachelor's graduates with very limited opportunities for employment (László 2008). Furthermore, universities have also struggled to develop the content and structure of ITE study programmes in a manner that would meaningfully and sufficiently meet the needs of employers, schools, and candidates' diverse job profiles in the accepted two-level structure (Kosová et al. 2012). For example, from the point of view of primary school teacher education, the bachelor's programmes aim to prepare their candidates for such job roles as qualified nursery nurse and/or educator in an informal educational setting, but are simultaneously viewed as a precondition for progression to master's level for those candidates who wish to become qualified teachers in the primary sector. The master's level study programme also faces a number of challenges and inconsistencies, particularly the overloaded curriculum containing a heavy weighting of subject-related didactics at the expense of the length and quality of actual teaching practice periods.

ITE for lower and higher secondary levels also faces a number of issues. As already mentioned, the current focus of bachelor's courses is generally considered too theoretical, concentrating mainly on acquiring discipline knowledge in pedagogy and the chosen (usually) two subjects that the graduate will teach, with limited teaching practice and study of didactics. The components of subject didactics and some pedagogy disciplines are introduced and developed only at master's level. Though the current Accreditation Committee's prescribed curricula for teacher education do not prohibit higher education institutions from integrating a certain proportion of didactic subjects and teaching practice into their programmes at the bachelor's level, bachelor's graduates are not considered as fully qualified teachers, therefore universities are not obliged to take this approach. Moreover, the autonomy of universities has since become restricted: their study programmes must follow centrally prescribed study programmes that define core and optional subjects as designated by the Accreditation Commission. In practice, this means that teacher education providers can only enact changes within one-third of the curriculum content for a study programme which is stated in the official description of the study field (see Criteria).

The legislation does not restrict HEIs in their range of subject disciplines on offer for teacher education pathways, nor makes them accountable to the employment market and the actual needs of schools. Candidates usually choose a combination of two subjects, a tradition dating back to before 1989. As there is an evident decrease in the number of students applying for teacher education courses, while the number of faculties offering teacher qualifications has increased (Kosová and Tomengová 2015), HEIs compete for candidates by upholding the freedom of applicants to choose their own subject disciplines. In addition, universities have decreased the level of knowledge and motivation required from candidates by abandoning entrance assessments. The only exception is the Pre-school and Primary Education (PPE) study programme, the attractiveness of which seems to be related to the recent growth of the kindergarten business.

The HEIs' strategies to increase student numbers may not be surprising, as the funding formula is tied to student numbers. Additionally and equally, the present quota-based system of state financing does not encourage universities to select students according to their knowledge and abilities when entering the second phase of their studies at master's level (László 2008). However, graduates may find that they are either unemployable in schools, or they need to teach a significant proportion of subjects which they are unqualified for, because the allocation of teaching hours for their chosen subjects in the national curriculum is very low.

CPS—Complementary Pedagogical Study as an Alternative Way to Gain a Teaching Qualification

According to the 2019 Act, and the 2009 Act before it, in order to become a qualified teacher at primary, lower, and upper secondary schools, candidates need to complete a master's degree in the relevant teacher education study programmes. The graduates of the second level of university studies (i.e. master's/engineer level) in non-teaching fields of study (i.e. technical subjects) can complete their studies through complementary pedagogical study (CPS), which will enable them to gain a teaching qualification and to teach at lower and upper secondary level schools.

The full-time study programme lasts for two years and consists of 200 to 240 teaching hours, of which 20 hours are dedicated to the subject didactics and 20 hours to teaching practice. Candidates complete the programme by defending a written thesis and undergoing an oral examination based on their theoretical knowledge of pedagogy, the psychology of learning, and subject didactics. Complementary pedagogical studies, however, have become a lucrative business for HEIs and non-HE providers, since teaching candidates are required to pay for the qualification. In addition, the guarantors of the qualification course do not need to be experts in education, and are only required to hold the title of associate professor, which can relate to the subject as a discipline rather than its didactics. There is, therefore, not a sufficient quality assurance mechanism that would require institutions providing CPS to ensure an appropriate level of support for their candidates with the process of applying/transferring theory in teaching practice. This is an important issue as almost one-third of teachers in upper secondary schools are graduates of CPS (To dá rozum—That makes sense 2016–2020). Kosová's (2012) critique nevertheless aims at all teaching programmes in general. As research findings point out, Slovak trainee teachers feel confident about their subject knowledge, but recognise insufficient preparation for their professional practice in a number of aspects, such as adapting content to the needs of their pupils; having difficulties with differentiation and inclusion; providing feedback; and understanding the administrative aspects of their work (Gadušová and Vítečková 2013, 2014, 2015a, b; Bilíková et al. 2014; Gadušová et al. 2014b; Kosová and Tomengová 2015; Magová et al. 2016; That makes sense 2016–2020; Vítečková et al. 2016).

Continuous Professional Development of Teachers

The legislation brought both a number of benefits and restrictions to teachers. Firstly, it clearly defined the four teaching career stages and linked these to teachers' expert occupation: each has a prescribed number of teaching years, a certain number of credits the teacher must earn, and other indicators (Kubalíková and Kacian 2016). As each stage has a prescribed salary band (i.e. the higher the stage, the higher the salary band), achieving the required number of credits is paramount for teachers. This should not be surprising as, according to OECD reports, teachers' financial rewards are one of the lowest in the EU and OECD countries, though the situation is gradually improving (European Commission 2018). However, in the same vein, the legislation did not enable those teachers who had been involved in different training programmes before 2009 to have these activities accredited as part of their professional development. Secondly, though the legislation distinguished three pathways for teachers' CPD, only formally accredited institutions enable participants to gain formal credits. The other two pathways—that is, mutual expert discourse among teachers (non-formal) and self-education (infor-mal)—do not enable teachers to formally evidence their enhanced profes-sional knowledge, and thus have been marginalised.

The Methodology and Pedagogy Centres are state subsidised or financed via European Social Funds, and can therefore offer CPD training for free. However, there is no accountability or sufficient research into the impact of the CPD course on teacher practice, student learning, and school innovation (Pavlov 2013). As the education sector is underfinanced, teachers and schools have limited access to other providers who might have greater expertise in terms of aiding teachers in their professional growth. Universities, though the main providers of ITE, play a minimal role in the provision of CPD courses since they cannot afford to subsidise them. Lastly, the legislation does not recognise key professional roles engaged in teacher development, such as the role of a mentor or a coach (Jones 2009; Gadušová et al. 2014a; Hanesová 2016), though it simultaneously stipulates that novice teachers must be sup-ported by such a professional during the first year of their teaching career. As a result, the CPD system is viewed as a process of knowledge transmission and related neither to teachers' actual needs nor to the school context in which they work (Pavlov 2013; Kubalíková and Kacian 2016).

Conclusion

State-funded education cannot be separated from politics—from the relation-ships between the public, their political representatives, and those who are expected to exercise pedagogical expertise and implement the required changes (Apple 2004; Freire 2006; Ball 2016). However, education has never been at the centre of party politics in Slovakia (Kosová 2012; Slovenská komora učiteľov 2012–2020). This lack of interest in education can be seen in the fact that there have been 17 ministers of education (including 2 ad interim) since the establishment of Slovakia as an independent nation-state, many of whom have been the initiators of reforms based on the principles of school education in other countries without introducing similar or comparable conditions for their execution. Their proposals, however, have rarely been adopted by their successors and sometimes completely ignored. Slovakia, in contrast to other post-communist countries such as Hungary, the Czech Republic, and Poland, initiated educational reforms later on, while leaving the control over education decisions in the hands of the government (Herbst and Wojciuk 2017). This is evidenced in the steps taken by various governments across different historical periods to formulate and implement seemingly systematic structural and curricular reforms; in the low levels of public spending (Kneuer et al. 2018); in an inadequate education policy regarding defining professional teacher competences, roles, and standardised qualification requirements; and last, but not least, in teacher pay reform (Hajdukova 2013; Kneuer et al. 2018).

Even 30 years since the collapse of the communist regime, Slovak educational experts, academics, and teacher educators—as well as teachers themselves—express deep disappointment with the insufficient transformation of the educational system, with unsatisfactory curriculum reforms and professional teacher education, as well as the low social status of teachers (e.g. Hroncová 1999; Kasáčová 2004; Valica and Pavlov 2007; Slovenská komora učiteľov 2012–2020; Porubský et al. 2014a; Hurajová 2016). These frustrations arise from the realisation that the contradictions and tensions between old and new educational policy and reforms are often expected to be resolved by schools and teachers 'within their situated practice' (Ball 2016, p. 1048) without any real support.

Research has evidenced pre-service and novice teachers' inadequate professional preparation for the scope and complexities of the teaching role. This could also be the consequence of low-quality mentoring on placements (Bilíková et al. 2014). Indeed, the findings from a large-scale, cross-European research project (Jones 2009) suggest that Slovak mentors are not confident with the nurturing aspect of their role: they do not recognise the importance of critically analysing novice teachers' classroom observations; seem to equate the concept of a good teacher with that of a good mentor; and raise the issue of increased workload as mentoring obligations occur in addition to their teaching responsibilities. Other studies likewise confirm that mentors' unmanageable workloads can lead to 'a lack of persistence and professionalism in their mentoring role' (Sandvik et al. 2019, p. 575). Policy-makers and teaching institutions should therefore pay more attention to the specific role of mentors (Jones 2009; European Commission 2015; Sandvik et al. 2019). As quality mentoring of pre-service and novice teachers is paramount for their professional development, mentor education courses should be evaluated to measure their impact on mentors' enhanced knowledge and understanding of novice teachers' individual needs.

Slovakia now has, however, a great opportunity to review and restructure teacher education within the current system of education, as there are a number of evidence-based proposals already at the disposal of the Ministry of Education—drawing on current research and proposals, as reported in the documents on education policy for teachers in the European Union (e.g. Pokrivčáková et al. 2008; Gadušová et al. 2014b; Porubský et al. 2014a; Kosová and Tomengová 2015; Vítečková et al. 2016; Hašková and Pisoňová 2019). Even though researchers comment on teachers' disillusionment, and even apathy and unwillingness to engage in lifelong learning, the authors of this study have observed evidence of untapped enthusiasm and energy in teachers, when given opportunities for self-determination and agency (Bačová 2021). Recent strikes and demonstrations by teachers (Slovenská komora učiteľov 2012–2020; Iniciatíva slovenských učiteľov 2018) also illustrate their willingness to engage in meaningful, well formulated, and carefully planned school and teacher education reforms, as well as their resilience and rich sources of moral capital. From this perspective it is possible to reimagine a new professional identity of the teacher 'as an intellectual, rather than as a technician or as a bundle of skills and competences' (Ball 2016, p. 1056). This would, as Ball strongly argues, put 'the teacher back into the sphere of the political, as an actor who […] looks critically at the meaning and enactment of policy' and who is able to develop their own professional identity within thriving collaborative learning communities (Admiraal et al. 2021). Teachers' dedication to professionalism and the moral purpose of their role should be recognised by policy-makers. Slovakia's teaching workforce, similarly to other European countries (EESC 2008), is clearly ageing, and therefore attracting high calibre young people to the profession is paramount. This will only be possible if educational policy sufficiently addresses teachers' career development, and ensures 'adequate pay and social recognition of the profession' (EESC 2008). Policy implementation should both harness teachers' professional capital and recognise their needs (European Commission 2015). Last but not least, more funding should be allocated to the organisation and management of teaching practice: that is, the subject expertise of trainee teachers could gradually develop and flourish with the support of teacher educators and teaching practice mentors, and the providers of teaching qualifications and CPDs should become accountable to the needs of their graduates and the schooling sector. Taken together, these recommendations would hold the teacher education market responsible to the current and future needs of the teaching profession.

References

Admiraal, W., W. Schenke, L. De Jong, Y. Emmelot, and H. Sligte. (2021). Schools as professional learning communities: what can schools do to support professional development of their teachers? *Professional Development in Education*, 47(4), 684–698.

Apple, M. W. (2004). *Ideology and curriculum*. 3rd ed. New York and London: Routledge.

ASK—Asociácia Susan Kovalikovej. (n.d.). *Vzdelávanie pre 21. storočie* [Education for 21st century]. Retrieved from http://ask21.sk/sk.

APSWŠ—Asociácia priateľov slobodných waldorfských škôl na Slovensku. (n.d.). Retrieved from http://apsws.iwaldorf.sk/.

Bačová, D. (2021). *Exploring L2 teacher motivation to participate in a theatre festival*. ELTJ.

Ball, S. (2016). Neoliberal education? Confronting the slouching beast. *Policy Futures in Education*, 14(8), 1046–1059.

Bilíková, A. et al. (2014). Key competencies of mentor teachers essential for successful mentoring of novice teachers: A research study. *XLinguae: European Scientific Language Journal*, 7(4), 55–74.

Bockaničová, K., A. Butašová, B. Ďuriš, A. Krnáčová, and T. Miklošovič. (2018). *Stav implementácie inovovaných štátnych vzdelávacích programov v oblasti cudzích jazykov do pedagogickej praxe v základných školách* [The level of implementation of innovative curricula of foreign languages into the pedagogical practice at primary and lower secondary schools]. Bratislava: Štátny pedagogický ústav.

Butašová, B. et al. (2017). *Rozvíjanie profesijných kompetencií učiteľov materských, základných a stredných škôl v kontexte zvyšovania úspešnosti reformy systému základného vzdelávania* [The development of professional competencies of early years, primary and secondary school teachers in the context of successful school reform]. Bratislava: Štátny pedagogický ústav.

Commission of the European Communities. (2007). *Improving the quality of teacher education*. Retrieved from http://www.europarl.europa.eu/RegData/docs_autres_institutions/commission_europeenne/sec/2007/0931/COM_SEC%282007%290931_EN.pdf.

CVTI SR. (2020). *Štatistické ročenky—vysoké školy 2016/2017* [Statistical Yearbooks—Universities 2016/17]. Retrieved from http://www.cvtisr.sk/cvti-sr-vedecka-kniznica/informacie-o-skolstve/statistiky/statisticka-rocenka-publikacia/statisticka-rocenka-vysoke-skoly.html?page_id=9596.

Dakowska, D., and R. Harmsen. (2015). Laboratories of reform? The Europeanization and internationalization of higher education in Central and Eastern Europe. *European Journal of Higher Education*, 5(1), 4–17.

EESC. (2008). *Improving the quality of teacher education.* Retrieved from https:// www.eesc.europa.eu/en/our-work/opinions-information-reports/opinions/ improving-quality-teacher-education.

European Commission. (2018). *Education and Training. Monitor 2018 Slovakia.* Retrieved from https://ec.europa.eu/education/sites/education/files/document-library-docs/et-monitor-report-2018-slovakia_en.pdf.

European Commission. (2015). *New priorities for European cooperation in education and training.* Retrieved from https://eur-lex.europa.eu/legal-content/EN/TXT/ PDF/?uri=CELEX:52015SC0161&from=HU.

European Commission. (2014). *2014ET-TEMPUS 1—Trans-European mobility scheme (EEC) for university studies, 1990–1994.* Retrieved from https://cordis. europa.eu/programme/rcn/184/en.

European Parliament. (1998). *Briefing 33. The PHARE programme and the enlargement of the European Union.* Retrieved from http://www.europarl.europa.eu/ enlargement/briefings/33a2_en.htm#5.

Fonodová, I. (1996). TEMPUS in Slovakia, 1990–1995. *Innovations in Education and Training International, 33*(2), 103–111.

Freire, P. (2006). *Pedagogy of the oppressed.* 30th anniversary ed. New York and London: Continuum.

Gadušová, Z. et al. (2014a). *Formovanie kompetencií začínajúceho učiteľa* [The formation of competences of a novice teacher]. Nitra: UKF.

Gadušová, Z., and L. Predanocyová. (2018). Developing teacher competences in a student teacher population. *Education Research & Perspectives: An International Journal, 45,* 98–123.

Gadušová, Z., and M. Vítečková. (2013). Mentors' and novices' perception of teachers' professional career start in Slovakia and in the Czech Republic. In: *INTE 2013: Proceedings Book from The International Conference, Roma June 25–27, 2013* (pp. 105–114). Roma: EduInk.

Gadušová, Z., and M. Vítečková. (2014). International research in the field of novice teachers' induction. In: P.-M. Rabensteiner and G. Rabensteiner (Eds.), *Education. Internationalization in teacher education* (pp. 87–106). Baltmannsweiler: Schneider Verlag Hohengehren GmbH.

Gadušová, Z., and M. Vítečková. (2015a). Vysokoškolské studium učitelství z pohledu začínajícího učitele a identifikace jeho problematických oblastí [University-based teacher education from the point of view of a teacher and the identification of its problems]. *Edukácia: vedecko-odborný časopis, 1*(1), 266–275.

Gadušová, Z., and M. Vítečková. (2015b). Transition of novice teachers into school teaching and their support by mentor teachers. In: *ATEE 2014: 'Transitions in teacher education and professional identities'* (pp. 411–420). Annual Conference Proceedings, Braga 2014 August 25–27. Braga: University of Minho.

Gadušová, Z., M. Vítečková, and M. Garabiková-Partlová. (2014b). Novices' and Trainee Teachers' perspectives on the application of knowledge in practice. In: *ERIE 2014: Proceedings of the 11th International Conference Efficiency and*

Responsibility in Education, Prague June 5–6th 2014 (pp. 869–877). Praha: Czech University of Life Sciences.

Hajdukova, Brown E. (2013). Lessons from Slovakia: Progress with inclusive education. *Preventing School Failure: Alternative Education for Children and Youth*, 57(3), 144–147.

Hanesová, D. (2016). *Teachers under the microscope. A review of research on teachers in a post-communist region.* Bloomington: AuthorHouse.

Hargreaves, A., and D. Shirley. (2012). *The global fourth way. The quest for educational excellence.* London: SAGE.

Hašková, A. (2019). Balancing school autonomy and head teacher' accountability for schools in Slovakia. In: S. Ševkušić, D. Malinić, and J. Teodorović (Eds.), *Leadership in education: Initiatives and trends in selected European countries* (pp. 181–206). Belgrade (Serbia): Institute for Educational Research; Jagodina (Serbia): Faculty of Education, University of Kragujevac; Szeged (Hungary): Hungarian-Netherlands School of Educational Management, University of Szeged.

Hašková, A., and M. Bitterova. (2018). School autonomy and school leadership: Case study of school operation in Slovakia. *Problems of Education in the 21st Century*, 73(3), 299–308.

Hašková, A., and M. Pisoňová. (2019). The competences of school leaders and the impact of school reform on their positions. In: R. V. Nata (Ed.), *Progress in education*, Volume 59 (pp. 103–140). New York: Nova Science Publisher.

Herbst, M., and A. Wojciuk. (2017). Common legacy, different paths: the transformation of educational systems in the Czech Republic, Slovakia, Hungary and Poland. *A Journal of Comparative and International Education*, 47(1), 118–132.

Hroncová, J. (1999). Súčasné problémy učiteľskej profesie na Slovensku [Current problems of teaching profession in Slovakia]. *Pedagogická orientace*, 3, 33–39.

Hurajová, A. (2016). Bilingual education in Slovakia on the background of transformation of education system. *European Journal of Science and Theology*, 12(6), 245–253.

Iniciatíva slovenských učiteľov. (2018). *Aktuality* (News). Retrieved from https://isu.sk/.

Jones, M. (2009). Supporting the supporters of novice teachers: an analysis of mentors' needs from twelve European countries presented from an English perspective. *Research in Comparative and International Education*, 4(1), 4–21.

Kasáčová, B. (2004). Zmeny učiteľskej profesie a kontinuálne vzdelávanie učiteľov [Changes of teachers' profession and the continual teachers' education]. *Sborník prací filozofické fakulty brněnské univerzity*. Brno: Masarykova univerzita, Filozofická fakulta, 87–99.

Kneuer, M., D. Malová, and F. Bönker. (2018). *Slovakia Report. Sustainable Governance Indicators 2018.* Bertelsmann Stiftung. Retrieved from https://www.sgi-network.org/docs/2018/country/SGI2018_Slovakia.pdf.

Kosová, B. (2012). Východiská a súvislosti vysokoškolského vzdelávania učiteľov [Bases and connections of university-based teacher education]. In: B. Kosová,

B. Kasáčová, A. Doušková, Š. Porubský, A. Petrasová, G. Petrová, J. Duchovičová, J. Kmeťová, and K. László (Eds.), *Transformácia vysokoškolského vzdelávania učiteľov v kontexte reformy regionálneho školstva. Záverečná správa a návrhy odporúčan* [Transformation of university-based teacher education in the context of national school reform. Final report and recommendations] (pp. 6–67). Banská Bystrica. Retrieved from https://www.minedu.sk/data/att/1903.pdf.

Kosová, B., and Š. Porubský. (2007). Educational transformation in Slovakia: The ongoing search for a solution. *Orbis Scholae*, 1(2), 109–130.

Kosová, B., and Š. Porubský. (2011a). The development and transformation of the school system in the Slovak Republic after the fall of the totalitarian regime from the aspects of educational policy, educational practice and the level of primary schools, and the university preparation of teachers. *The Educational Review*, 23(1), 19–33.

Kosová, B., and Š. Porubský. (2011b). Slovenská cesta transformácie edukačného systému po roku 1989 na príklade primárneho vzdelávania a prípravy učiteľov [The Slovak journey of change of educational system, illustrated on education and training of primary school teachers]. *Pedagogická orientace*, 21(1), 35–50.

Kosová, B., B. Kasáčová, A. Doušková, Š. Porubský, A. Petrasová, G. Petrová, J. Duchovičová, J. Kmeťová, and K. László. (2012). *Transformácia vysokoškolského vzdelávania učiteľov v kontexte reformy regionálneho školstva. Záverečná správa a návrhy odporúčaní* [Transformation of university-based teacher education in the context of national school reform. Final report and recommendations]. Banská Bystrica. Retrieved from https://www.minedu.sk/data/att/1903.pdf.

Kosová, B., and A. Tomengová (Eds.). (2015). *Profesijná praktická príprava budúcich učiteľov* [Professional practical preparation of future teachers]. Banská Bystrica: Belianum.

Kubalíková, A., and A. Kacian. (2016). Twenty-five years of continuing professional development of teachers in the post-communist era in Slovakia: the story of paths not taken. *Professional Development in Education*, 42(5), 836–853.

László, B. (2008). The impact of the Bologna Process on higher education in Slovakia. *European Education*, 40(2), 46–65.

Magová, L. et al. (2016). *Hodnotenie kompetencií učiteľov v európskom a slovenskom kontexte* [Evaluation of teacher competencies in European and Slovak context]. Praha: Verbum.

Malová, D. (2017). *Transformation experiences in Slovakia*. Bratislava: Fridrich Ebert Stiftung. Retrieved from https://library.fes.de/pdf-files/id-moe/13081.pdf.

Malová, D., and B. Dolný. (2016). Economy and democracy in Slovakia during the crisis: from a laggard to the EU core. *Problems of Post-Communism*, 63(5–6), 300–312.

Ministerstvo školstva a vedy. (1994). *Konštantín. Národný program výchovy a vzde-lávania. Štátna politika výchovy a vzdelávania v Slovenskej republike na obdobie 1995–2015. 1. a 2. diel* [Constantine. The national programme of education and training. The state policy on education and training in Slovak republic for the period 1995–2015. Part one and two]. Bratislava: Ministerstvo školstva a vedy, SR.

OZPSAV SK. (2013). *Odpočet plnenia programu Milénium a následných koncepčných dokumentov pre oblasť regionálneho školstva* [The review of meeting the targets of Millenium programme for schools]. Retrieved from https://www.ozpsav.sk.

Parrish, J. M. (2010). Education, Erasmian humanism and More's *Utopia*. *Oxford Review of Education*, 36(5), 589–605.

Pavlov, I. (2013). Kariérny model profesijného rozvoja učiteľov a jeho inštitucionálne základy [Career model of teachers' professional development and its institutional foundations]. In: M. Lukáč (Ed.), *Edukácia človeka = problémy a výzvy pre 21. Storočie* [Human education = problems and challenges for the 21st century] (pp. 27–33). Prešov: Prešovská univerzita v Prešove, Fakulta humanitných a prírodovedných vied.

Petrová, Z., and O. Zápotočná. (2018). Early literacy education in pre-school curriculum reforms: The case of post-communist Slovakia. *Global Education Review*, 5(2), 145–159.

Pokrivčáková, S. et al. (2008). *Inovácie a trendy vo vyučovaní cudzích jazykov u žiakov mladšieho školského veku* [Innovations and trends in teaching foreign languages primary school pupils]. Nitra: Univerzita Konštantína Filozofa v Nitre.

Porubský, Š., B. Kosová, and I. Pavlov. (2014a). Problém štandardizácie učiteľskej profesie v kontexte profesijného rozvoja učiteľov na Slovensku [The problem of standardisation of teacher profession in the context of teacher professional development in Slovakia]. *Orbis Scholae*, 8(3), 23–46.

Porubský, Š., B. Kosová, A. Doušková, M. Trnka, V. Poliach, P. Fridrichová, E. Adamcová, R. Sabo, Z. Lynch, R. Cachovanová, and L. Simanová. (2014b). *Škola a kurikulum—transformácia v slovenskom kontexte* [School and Curriculum—transformation in the Slovak Context]. Banská Bystrica: Belianium. Retrieved from https://www.pdf.umb.sk/app/cmsFile.php?disposition=a&ID=19736.

Porubský, Š., M. Trnka, V. Poliach, and R. Cachovancová. (2015). Curricular reform in Slovakia regarding the attitudes of basic school teachers. *Pedagogická orientace*, 25(6), 777–797.

Pugsley, J., and G. Kershaw (Eds.). (2015). *Voices from the new democracies: the impact of British English language teaching in Central and Eastern Europe. Milestones in ELT*. British Council.

Rodina a škola. (2002). *Milénium. Koncepcia rozvoja výchovy a vzdelávania v Slovenskej republike na najbližších 15–20 rokov* [Millennium. The conception of education and training in Slovak Republic in 15–20 years]. Retrieved from http://www.skve-larodina.sk/milenium/.

Sandvik, L. V., T. Solhaug, E. Lejonberg, E. Elstad, and K. Christophersen. (2019). Predictions of school mentors' effort in teacher education programmes. *European Journal of Teacher Education*, 42(5), 574–590.

Schleicher, A. (2015). *Schools for 21st-Century learners: strong leaders, confident teachers, innovative approaches.* International Summit on the Teaching Profession. Paris: OECD Publishing.

Slovenská komora učiteľov. (2012–2020). *Bilancia roku 2019* [The Evaluation of the Year 2019]. Retrieved from http://sku.sk/odpovede-sku-pre-tlacove-agentury/.

Škola dokorán—Wide Open School. (n.d.). Retrieved from http://www.skoladokoran.sk/en/.

Tandlichová, E. (2008). Výučba cudzích jazykov na ZŠ vo svetle reforiem [Teaching foreign languages through the lens of educational reforms]. In: S. Pokrivčáková (Ed.), *Inovácie a trendy vo vyučovaní cudzích jazykov u žiakov mladšieho školského veku* (pp. 7–12). Nitra: Univerzita Konštantína Filozofa v Nitre.

To dá rozum—That makes sense. (2016–2020). *Vzdelanie je budúcnosť. Projekt: To dá rozum* [Education is the future. Project: That makes sense]. Retrieved from https://todarozum.sk/#oprojekte.

Turek, I. (Ed.). (1990). *Duch školy* [The Spirit of School]. Retrieved from http://www.skvelarodina.sk/duch-skoly/.

Valica, M., and I. Pavlov. (2007). Kríza učiteľskej profesie a jej koncepčné a legislatívne riešenie na Slovensku [The crisis of teaching profession and its conceptual and legislative solution in Slovakia]. *Orbis Scholae*, 1(3), 27–41.

Vítečková, M., M. Procházka, Z. Gadušová, and E. Stranovská. (2016). Identifying novice teacher´s needs—the basic for novices´ targeted support. In: *ICERI 2016: Proceedings 9th International Conference of Education, Research and Innovation, Seville, Spain, November 14th-16th, 2016* (pp. 7731–7738). Seville: IATED Academy.

Združenie Orava—The Association Orava. (2019). *Evaluation of the project Partners for democratic change 1994–1999.* Retrieved from https://www.zdruzenieorava.sk/archiv/hodnotiaca-sprava-partners-for-democratic-change-slovakia_sk.

Part III

The Balkans

6

Teacher Education in Albania: Reforms and Future Developments

Nikoleta Mita and Livia Nano

The Context of Teacher Education

Albania is a country with a population of 2.8 million (INSTAT, 2020) located in South East Europe, in the Western Balkans. Over the last three decades, Albania has experienced large political, institutional, and socio-economic changes. After the fall of communism in 1990, Albania started establishing a democratic system based on political pluralism and a free market economy. Albania expressed clearly its orientation towards a Western model of national transformation.

Albania is now a parliamentary democracy. The country is a member of many international organizations. Albania became a member state of the Council of Europe in 1995. Albania has been a full member of the Bologna Process/European Higher Education Area since 2003 and has been a NATO member since 2009. In 2009 the Stabilization and Association Agreement of Albania with the European Union entered into force, while the country achieved candidate country status in 2014. The country has become a signatory to a number of international and European covenants, conventions and recommendations directly or indirectly affecting the country's education sector.

The democratic changes that have taken place in Albania over the last three decades have also been reflected in education. After the 1990s Albania embarked on an education system reform aimed at remodelling the education system to meet European standards of education and responding to global

N. Mita (✉) • L. Nano
University of Tirana, Tirana, Albania
e-mail: nikoleta55@yahoo.com

© The Author(s), under exclusive license to Springer Nature Switzerland AG 2023   **137**
M. Kowalczuk-Walędziak et al. (eds.), *The Palgrave Handbook of Teacher Education in Central and Eastern Europe*, https://doi.org/10.1007/978-3-031-09515-3_6

developments in education. The vision of the future of education in Albania is to build and strengthen a modern national education system that supports and promotes sustainable economic development, improves levels of competitiveness in the region and consolidates democracy.

Albania's education system consists of:

1. preschool education for children aged 3–6 years old, which is free but not mandatory;
2. compulsory basic education for children aged 6–16 which consists of elementary education from grades I–V and lower secondary education from grades VI–IX;
3. upper secondary education that is of three kinds: gymnasium that covers grades X–XII, vocational education lasting three and four years, and professionally oriented education;
4. higher education offering a short cycle of vocational studies lasting two years; and
5. bachelor programmes (three years), master programmes (one and two-year), and doctoral programmes lasting three to five years.

All levels of education are provided by both public and private education institutions.

Taking into consideration that teachers play a vital role in the improvement of the quality of education, being aware of the questionable quality of teachers, the Government of Albania, has defined teacher education as one of the priorities of the national education reform. Teacher education in Albania means: initial teacher education or pre-service teacher education that is offered in the higher education institutions; induction that is the process of practising teaching for one year after the graduation as one of the requirements to get a teaching licence; and teacher professional development, in-service education for practising teachers.

From the early 1990s of the last century till 2004, the aim of the Government was the democratization and depoliticization of education at all levels, by drafting a new educational legal framework, drafting a new curriculum, updating the teaching force, and increasing the education budget. Three education strategies on pre-university education and two strategic documents on higher education have been approved and implemented starting from 2004.

The National Education Strategy 2004–2015, the first long-term plan for the sector, identified four priorities: *enhancement of leadership, governance and resource management capacities*, improvement of the quality of teaching and learning, improvement of the education funding scheme, and development of the capacity to implement the strategy.

The National Strategy on Pre-university Education 2009–2013, the second education strategy document approved and used during the transition period, set seven strategic priorities:

* an increase of access to all levels of education;
* reforming and strengthening of policy-making, management, and decision-making capacity;
* improvement of quality of instruction processes;
* improvement of the financial aspects of education;
* capacity building and human resource development;
* development of vocational education;
* expanding preschool education.

This strategy had an elaborated vision on teacher education, focused on teacher's professionalism, professional freedom, professional recruitment criteria, teacher's competences, and teacher's motivation; a merit salary approach; diversification of the professional training market; review of the initial teacher education and teacher training curriculum; improvement of teachers working conditions; offering teaching licence, establishment of the Teacher's Order; creation of the teacher's data system.

The third strategic document approved in Albania for the reformation of education was *The Strategy on Development of Pre-university Education (2014–2020)*. The four strategic priorities were as follows:

* enhancing leadership, governance, and management of resources and capacities;
* inclusive quality learning;
* quality assurance based on standards comparable to those of EU countries;
* contemporary teachers and school principals' professional development and training.

Teacher education was and is part of higher education reform. *The National Strategy on Higher Education 2008–2013* oriented the design of teacher education in line with the Bologna Process model. It also initiated the compilation of a national training catalogue based on identified teachers' needs and the implementation of accreditation procedures for the training quality.

The Final Report for Higher Education and Scientific Research Reform (2014) contains aims and principles of reform and a set of proposals. The Report proposes that initial teacher education must be given national priority. This report presents proposals for the restructuring the initial teacher education study programmes underlining the necessity to keep a national common element for 80% of the curricula according to relevant field of science.

Furthermore, during the three last decades, the Parliament and the Government of Albania have adopted a series of laws and byelaws that have had an effect on the development of the education system in general, and on teacher education in particular.

At the present time, there are a number of legal acts that regulate teacher education in Albania. Law no.10 171, approved on 22 October 2009 *On regulated professions in the Republic of Albania* (amended 2010, 2011, 2014) is the main document for all regulated professions, including the teaching profession. Law no. 69, approved on 21 June 2012 *On pre-university education in the Republic of Albania* (amended 2015, 2018) aims to identify the main principles relating to the structure, functioning and the administration of the pre-university education system in the Republic of Albania. It regulates certain aspects related to the teaching profession, such as: the status of the teacher, education, training, qualification, and professional development; the rights of a teacher; and procedures for hiring and termination of contracts. *Law 80/2015 on Higher Education and Scientific Research in the Institutions of Higher Education (IHE) in the Republic of Albania* stipulates the legal framework for study programmes in teacher education and the right of the IHE to provide the programmes of continuing professional development. Law no. 7961 approved on 12 July 1995 *The Labour Code of the Republic of Albania* (amended 1996, 2003) is the main legal document that regulates issues and matters relating to labour and employment in Albania. This law is applicable to some issues pertaining to the teaching profession. Law no. 10247, approved on 04 March 2010 *On Albanian Qualifications Framework* (amended 2018) determines the structure, objectives, functions, and areas of jurisdiction of the Albanian Qualifications Framework.

Issues and problems related to teacher education are regulated through byelaws and regulations, such as government decisions, administrative orders, and directives. For example, *The Code of ethics of teachers in the public and private pre-university education system* (2012) describes in detail the desired aspirations and ethical principles in schools. The code of ethics offers a model of behaviour that is accepted and required by the populace so that the education system can fulfil its social mission towards forging a stronger democratic society. The objective and the purpose of the code of ethics is to assist teachers and the personnel of the education system to understand, recognize and implement the necessary ethical standards to accomplish its mission and reach decisions towards fulfilling this task. This code presents a series of principles and ethical guidelines grouped in two sections: (a) commitment and devotion to students and the learning and teaching process; (b) commitment and devotion to the profession.

Byelaws regulate issues regarding: the duties and responsibilities of teachers; teacher's workloads; the criteria and procedures for teacher qualification; the functioning of the system of teacher continuing professional development; teaching professional practice; the system of accreditation of training programmes; teacher evaluation; teachers' collective contract; procedures of appointing and removing a teacher from an institution of public education; disciplinary measures against teachers; the adoption of a salary structure for teaching personnel in pre-university education.

Based on the legislation and policies, the teacher education in Albania includes three steps:

1. *Initial teacher education* (pre-service teacher education) that is offered by the institutions of higher education. Initial teacher education refers to the education and preparation that student teachers receive before employment.
2. *Induction* that is intended for those who have already completed basic pre-employment education and preparation. The induction requirement has taken into consideration the need to provide society with an adequate supply of teachers who possess the necessary qualities and who have the required professional knowledge and skills. This programme is conceived as a 'bridge' from student of teaching to teacher of students. During the induction phase, teacher candidates have to complete one school year of teaching practice, to pass the state exam and to get the teaching licence.
3. *In-service training and continuing professional development* are processes that occur during the subsequent career.

Entry into the profession requires some credentials. The Albanian legislation has established basic requirements to enter the teaching profession. The policy, governing entry into preparation for teaching, has taken into consideration the fact that well-prepared teachers, both in their relevant subject and methodologically, are essential for quality education. That is, entry into the teaching profession typically requires a diploma, which is obtained only after completion of a higher teacher education programme, induction period and passage of the state examination. These credentials serve as screening devices. Their rationale is to protect the interests of the public by assuring that teachers hold an agreed level of knowledge and skill, and by filtering out those with substandard levels of knowledge and skill.

A number of institutions and structures within the Albania state administration, at the local and school level, are responsible and work to enforce legislation and policies on teacher education, as follows:

* Institutions in charge of initial teacher education are: the Ministry of Education and Sport, Institutions of Higher Education (IHE), and The Quality Assurance Agency in Higher Education.
* Institutions and authorities in charge of granting the right to exercise the teaching profession and professional development are: The Council of Ministers, The Ministry of Education and Sport, The Centre of Educational Services, The Institutions of Higher Education, The Agency for Quality Assurance in Pre-University Education, the General Directorate for Pre-University Education, The Education Offices, schools, and The Training Agencies.

As a result of demographic changes in the country in the last 10 years (INSTAT, 2020), has changed the number of students and teachers. The number of teachers employed in the preschool education system has increased by the fact that the number of children in kindergartens has increased. The number of teachers in the primary and secondary education systems has fallen, as the number of students in primary and secondary education has decreased (see Table 6.1). The number of teachers with university degrees is on the increase, and this comes because of the need to have better teachers in schools. The majority of teachers in the compulsory education system and high schools are females and not a single male works as a teacher in the preschool education system. The number of students that attend the education programmes at IHE has decreased (see Table 6.2).

Despite efforts to reform, and improvements over the last 30 years, teacher education in Albania continues to face several problems and challenges related

Table 6.1 General data on students and teachers (MOESY 2019)

School years	Total students	Total teacher in preschool education	Total teachers in primary education	Total teachers in secondary education
2006–2007	696,352	3546	26,540	8424
2007–2008	682,285	3651	26,102	8761
2008–2009	666,134	3739	27,724	8046
2009–2010	655,566	3919	27,241	8250
2010–2011	647,207	3825	25,973	8179
2011–2012	636,374	4083	25,584	8473
2012–2013	627,127	4136	25,263	8610
2013–2014	610,459	4144	25,051	8606
2014–2015	581,478	4150	24,777	8671
2015–2016	556,502	4247	25,007	8942
2016–2017	536,412	4178	24,866	9042
2017–2018	500,154	4201	24,790	7687

Table 6.2 Registered students in HEIs according to study fields (MOESY 2019)

No.	Study fields	Academic years					
		2012–2013	2013–2014	2014–2015	2015–2016	2016–2017	2017–2018
	Total	174,855	176,173	162,544	148,339	140,525	131,833
00	Generic programmes and qualifications	747	763	507	419	463	355
01	**Education**	**13,079**	**14,509**	**12,432**	**10,277**	**11,521**	**10,344**
02	Arts and humanities	21,437	20,729	18,223	17,492	16,906	15,332
03	Social sciences, journalism, and information	17,814	18,269	16,175	15,026	13,299	12,354
04	Business, administration, and law	49,186	49,547	44,566	39,154	34,093	31,190
05	Natural Sciences, mathematics, statistics	9627	8617	8416	7855	7451	6444
06	Information and communication technology	7550	8101	8620	8256	8829	8663
07	Engineering, manufacturing, and construction	18,286	18,734	19,075	18,135	18,991	18,949
08	Agriculture, forestry, fisheries and veterinary	8473	7440	7910	6879	5645	4492
09	Health and welfare	24,361	25,673	22,826	21,903	20,140	20,331
10	Services	4295	3791	3794	2943	3187	3379

to: the implementation and enforcement of legislation; lack of supporting mechanisms to implement initiatives; decision-making not based on data, evaluations, and research; poor infrastructure and weak financial support.

Teacher Education Reform in the Last Three Decades in the Light of Global Trends

Global developments in teacher education are having an impact on the manner in which teaching and teacher education are perceived and organized from a cross-cultural perspective. International policy documents have been stressing the global concern on the scope and quality of teacher education, in terms of amending their contents, delivery and effectiveness to the requirements of current societal demands.

As we have indicated, Albania is aiming to develop as a democratic modern country. The country is now a member of a number of the international organizations, is aiming to become the member of the European Union, and thus is aiming to provide a quality education for the citizens and prepare them for a global society. Albania has made many efforts to reform education, has included teacher education in accordance with the EU integration agenda, with the international education agenda, and especially with Sustainable Development Goal 4-Education 2030.

Commenting on the approach Albania is using to implement the EU recommendations on education and Sustainable Development Goal 4-Education 2030, UNESCO (2018, p. 41) mentioned 'Albania is hoping to begin negotiations with the EU regarding the start of accession talks, and the reforms should support a stable transition to EU membership. There are 35 different chapters of the EU acquis (Annex 5), and in July 2017 it was accepted in Albania that there is no conflict between the implementation of the SDGs and the EU acquis'. The global concern today is to provide high-quality education. Education, and with it the issue of good teachers and their professional education, has been given high priority in the Sustainable Development Goals and in a number of European Union documents, such as: The strategic framework for European cooperation in education and *Education and Training 2020*, The European Commission communication from 2008 *New skills for new jobs, The Cohesion programmes and policies of the European Union for 2014–2020, The Draft conclusions of the Council and of the Representatives* of the Governments of the Member States, meeting within the Council, on *Improving the Quality of Teacher Education*, adopted in October 2007.

In the framework of these international and European strategic policies, the interest of Albania in teacher education as the vital factor for the quality of teaching and the learning success of students has increased significantly in the last two decades. The education reform in Albania starting from 2004 has defined teacher education as one of the priorities. From 2006–2013, the World Bank supported the *Education Excellence and Equity Project*. The objective of the project was to support the programme of the Government of Albania to: (a) improve the quality of learning conditions for students; (b) increase registration of students in general secondary education; and (c) start higher education reform.

The Council of the European Union and the Representatives of the Governments of the Member States, also emphasized the need for today's teachers to 'develop new knowledge and be innovative through engagement in reflective practice and research' (European Union 2007). In 2015, the European Commission published a guide on policies to improve initial teacher education. Two of the suggested policy actions are related to teacher research competence. European Commission (2015) recommends:

> To achieve a creative and reflective teaching workforce, policies and actions should encourage student teachers and teachers to use and engage in new research in their learning and practice. While ITE lays the foundations for this, policy actions should foster innovative cultures in schools and ensure they have links with universities and other organisations that support research-informed development of teaching practices.

Action research is suggested, by the European Commission (2015) in this guide, as a mode of finding a valid solution to challenges in classroom practice.

Taking into consideration these recommendations, the education reform in Albania aims to reform the curriculum of initial teacher education, implementing a competence-based curriculum, research-based and practice-based approaches and using the unification model. The approved legislation and some measures taken in the last three years are supporting the actions.

UNESCO's policy development guide on teachers (UNESCO 2015) recommends minimum requirements to enter teacher training, as well as relevant curriculum contents and practicum periods leading to qualification. As was mentioned earlier in this chapter, Albania has recognized a need to enhance the professionalism of its teaching workforce. This has been carried out by recognizing teaching as a regulated profession in Albania which is the best achievement indicator related to this recommendation. The reform aims to increase the professional status of teachers. In particular, a need to assure quality in the teaching profession has been articulated.

The Bologna Process stands out as a highly significant reform that has impacted significantly the higher education, and especially initial teacher education in Albania, through remodelling of the programme structure, restructuring of the curriculum content, integrating the European dimension in the curricula using the ECTS system, increasing cooperation, sharing experiences, mobility, and making diplomas of teacher education comparable. In general, Albania's recent teacher education reform intends to align initial teacher education programmes with the European Bologna Process.

UNESCO (2018, p. 10) remarked:

> In the period from 2000–2015, Albania made significant progress in relation to the Millennium Development Goals (MDGs) toward the levels of basic education enrolment but struggled to achieve similar results in the other two MDG indicators: improving education quality to approach OECD country levels; and increasing the basic spending for education to the level of new EU member states. The shortcomings highlighted in the MDG progress report were then adapted to become part of a new national strategy.

As for teacher development, UNESCO (2018, p. 13) noted, 'According to the Education Policy Review, there has not been sufficient progress in the areas of teacher development: teachers have limited possibility to access relevant training, such as in Information and Communication Technology, through their Continuing Professional Development, and the current attempts to improve this throughout pre-university education are regarded as "fragmented"'.

Despite the impact of the international policies and reform efforts, the current status of the Albanian teacher education system is a transitional one, with modest achievements indicators towards the globalization.

Main Characteristics of the Existing System of Initial Teacher Education

The institutions of higher education offer initial teacher education in Albania. Until 2007, all initial teacher education programmes lasted 4 years but the Law no. 9741, dated 21 May 2007 'On Higher Education in Republic of Albania', amended and replaced the old structure of studies with the three cycles model approved in the framework of the Bologna Process (bachelor, professional master and master of sciences, and doctorate). Later, the Law no.

69/2012 'On pre-university education in the Republic of Albania' was amended and the Law no. 80/2015 'On Higher Education and Scientific Research in Republic of Albania' specified that in order to teach in primary and secondary schools, teachers must obtain a second cycle university diploma.

The Law No. 69/2012 'On pre-university education system in Republic of Albania', article 57, and the Law No. 80/2015 'On Higher Education and Research in the Institutions of Higher Education in the Republic of Albania', article 83, prescribes the required qualifications as follows:

> The teacher that will serve in the educational institutions should possess the following diploma in the field of education or an equivalent diploma to it:
>
> 1. Teachers of preschool education should possess the diploma of the first cycle of university studies, bachelor in preschool education;
> 2. Teachers of elementary education should possess the second cycle diploma of the university studies, professional master in elementary education;
> 3. Teachers of the lower and upper secondary education should possess: second cycle diploma of the university studies, master (120 credits) in a specific subject of teaching.

The teaching profession used to have a high status before the 1990s, but this status has dropped significantly since then (Nano et al. 2019, p. 79). During the last two decades, the government has shown a concern to improve the status of teaching profession, but it still remains low.

In recent years, the government has made efforts to attract qualified applicants to the teaching profession by requiring a GPA 7/7.5/8 as an admission criterion to initial teacher education study programmes and offering scholarships. According to the Decisions of the Council of Ministers (2018, 2020) on setting up the criterion of the average grade, all candidates who have completed upper secondary education and wish to undertake higher education at the Faculty of Education for the academic year 2018–2019 should have a minimum average grade of 7; for the academic year 2019–2020 and 2020–2021 they should have a minimum of average grade 7.5. Furthermore, excellent students choosing to teacher study programmes will be offered scholarships.

Also, during the last two decades, new rules with regard to initial teacher education programmes have taken place. Based on Law no 80/2015 dated 22 July 2015 *On Higher Education and Scientific Research in Republic of Albania*, article 83 'Study programmes in the field of education', the initial teacher education curriculum consists of: (1) general psycho-pedagogical curriculum and (2) scientific subject-oriented curriculum. According to this article, it is determined that the general psycho-pedagogical curriculum constitutes 25% of the entire curriculum in the respective cycle of study. Furthermore, article 83 also stipulates that 80% of curricula in all teacher education faculties will have the same content.

These rules are set as the universities are facing numerous problems in relation to initial teacher education, mainly in terms of curricula, teaching methodology, teaching practice and research. Due to the lack of national standards, curricula offered by various universities have significant differences in terms of development student teachers' competences. Two main policy documents *The National Strategy on Higher Education 2008–2013* and *The Final Report for Higher Education and Scientific Research Reform* (2014) have presented clear guidelines relating to the teacher education curriculum, stressing psycho-pedagogical, research, and practical components.

The process of improvement and unification of the curriculum of initial teacher education is ongoing. In order to fulfil this legal requirement, sixteen working groups have been set up and are functioning in the field, including 164 experts from the Ministry of Education, Sport and Youth, the Agency of Quality Assurance of Pre-university Education, and universities all over the country (Progress Report 2019, p. 5). Firstly, all faculties of education that are offering programmes of the same profile must unify the study programmes of the same profile to the extent of 80% in regard to the content of the curriculum (subjects and learning outcomes). However, the legal obligation to approximate the content of the programmes up to 80% has not yet been fulfilled. Secondly, there is a need to revise the teacher education curriculum taking into consideration the approved teacher standards.

According to our observation on the reform implementation, the universities are not responding quickly to enable student teachers to carry out task related to competency-based curriculum and competence-based learning. Starting from the 2008–2009 academic year, the component of research has been strengthened and emphasized. But referring to some research papers, there is a need to reshape the curricula of the teacher education based on practice-oriented and research-oriented approaches.

The teaching practice in Albania is composed of two kinds of activities: passive observations and active practice. In the framework of the passive observations, students are asked to attend five classes per week in a school. In the framework of the active practice, student teachers are asked to teach five hours per week. Universities sign agreements with the schools for the purposes of the teaching practice. The responsible departments appoint a lecturer as a supervisor for 15–20 students. In most cases, there is no person/tutor appointed by the school/educational setting to guide students while they are practising in that institution. Students remain mainly observers and only in a few cases become active participants in the school/educational setting.

Systematic structures and planned and formalized methods of ensuring a connection between the practice and theory in teacher education programmes do not seem to exist. Usually, the two are disconnected. Educational courses are taught separately with no formal connection for ensuring the student experiences in schools are reflected upon, discussed, shared, and presented to the rest of the class.

Vula et al. (2012, p. 43) in their comparative research on teacher education curricula concluded that it is essential that the educational systems empower teachers to become and remain reflective practitioners throughout their careers so that they can assess and improve their teaching; doing so will also increase teachers' ability to conduct research themselves and co-operate with research institutions on research projects as part of their teaching career. The models of research must be built upon a concept of teaching as praxis and require teachers both to examine critically the theories they espouse in light of their findings in school and in turn to critically examine their findings in light of theory. The teaching practice is a component that should be a tool to connect theory and practice through a systematic, formalized, properly supervised and mentored teaching practice component. We uphold the idea that in the context of the twenty-first century it is no longer sufficient for teachers to be limited in classroom research; it is recommended to connect teacher research, school development and system reform. So, teacher education programmes should reshape the development of research skills based on contemporary approaches.

A very important component in preparing future teachers is induction. The teacher induction programme aims to transform a teacher graduate into a competent career teacher. It is an innovation in the field of education and a challenge at the same time. In addition to initial formal education, professional work typically requires extensive practice (one school year) for new teachers upon entry. Such practice is designed to pick up where pre-service training has left off. While credentials assure that new entrants have a minimum or basic level of knowledge and skill, the induction programme for practitioners is designed to augment this basic level of knowledge and skill. The objectives of such programmes and practices are to aid new teachers in adjusting to the environment, to familiarize them with the concrete realities of schools and also to provide a second opportunity to filter out those with substandard levels of skill and knowledge.

Albanian Coalition for Child Education (ACCE) (2014, pp. 5–6) has concluded that although the legal regulations on teacher induction are relatively comparable with that of other countries, the implementation shows that this innovation is facing various problems, such as the inability to include all candidates in teaching practice, weak-functioning of the mentoring system, lack of professional mentors, low results in the state exam, and an inability to cover the inductees' wage. In terms of providing a bridge from initial teacher education to induction, the system needs:

* to combine both professional and managerial considerations in a balanced whole;
* to make effective the mentoring process;
* to improve the state exam;
* to improve the inductee appraisal system;
* to establish professional bodies that will take the responsibilities given by the law;
* to create a database on induction system; and
* to create and publish resource materials on induction system.

According to the Law No. 80/2015 *On Higher Education and Research in the Institutions of the Higher Education in the Republic of Albania*, article 69, point 2, 'Study programmes that give the right to a regulated profession are offered only as full time studies'. This rule does not allow the possibility of attending part-time teacher education programmes. We consider this to be an obstacle that limits the right to education and to create many problems in practical attendance classes for the teachers that attend master programmes.

Main Characteristics of Existing Systems of Teacher Professional Development

Teacher professional development in Albania is regulated by the Law No. 69/2012 'On pre-university education system in Republic of Albania'. Article 58 stipulates the rules on continuing professional training, while the article 59 indicates three categories of teacher qualifications and the payment benefit from the qualifications. The Law No. 80/2015 *On Higher Education and Research in the Institutions of the Higher Education in the Republic of Albania*, article 81 states that Institutions of the Higher Education can offer continuing education programmes as a form of lifelong learning. The modalities of these programmes can be approved by the IHE or in cooperation with the Ministry of Education for the regulated teaching profession. According to the law, the professional development of teachers can be organized as internal professional development, training sessions, professional networks, advice, short-term and long-term courses.

The education policies of the Albania Government from 2004 to 2020 have specified measures and initiatives to reform teacher professional development, including the improvement and modernization of the curricula on teacher training, introducing incentives and motivation systems based on merit, registration of teachers, diversification of the teacher training offer, assuring a high quality of teacher training.

Teacher training centres, institutions, or agencies in Albania offer in-service training and continuing professional development of teachers. They may be part of universities or non-university institutions. Teacher training centres for in-service teacher training offer short courses and they differ from centre to centre. Due to the fact that training courses are based on the demand-offer system and only serve the ongoing professional development of teachers, not initial training, the content and the skills offered by agencies depend on the demands identified by the designated state institutions, and on the capacities of the agencies to design and develop training courses. In-service courses must be accredited by the Ministry of Education, Sport and Youth. Actually, the process is pending.

Teachers can also obtain further qualifications in the course of their careers. Based on their work experience and training (documented in their professional portfolio) and successful passing of the examination for the respective qualification category, primary and secondary school teachers are eligible for three levels of qualification after 5, 10 and 20 years of teaching. They can be promoted to: *qualified teacher* after at least 5 years of experience; *specialized teacher* after at least 10 years of practice (but a minimum of 5 years after becoming 'qualified teachers'); master teacher after at least 20 years of experience (but a minimum of 10 years after becoming 'specialized teachers').

The continuing qualification is carried out in two stages:

First stage: The preparation of a teacher's personal portfolio that is evaluated by a commission established at the Education Office of the district where the teacher works.

Second stage: Teacher exam. Teachers who have presented their portfolios and have been awarded a number of points above the threshold are eligible for this stage. The tests are carried out based on qualification programmes for teachers in the pre-university education system. The final evaluation depends on accumulated credits and test results.

Analysing the professional development process ACCE (2014, p. 38) concluded that: there is no comprehensive long-term policy on the development of the teaching profession; the systems of teacher evaluation in Albania lack a theoretical model; the state administration is still heavily involved in the teacher evaluation system; the process of testing teachers is unsatisfactory.

Policy Issues and Future Implications for the Future Development of Teacher Education

Based on our review, we can point out four main achievements of teacher education reform in Albania:

1. *A legal framework on teacher education.* The Parliament and the Government of Albania have adopted a series of laws and byelaws that have supported the implementation of the education reform of the education system in general, and teacher education in particular. It is necessary to improve and complete the legal framework, especially byelaws in terms of teachers' status, teachers' recruitment, initial teacher education curricula, teacher professional development, induction mentoring, teacher evaluation, teacher salary and promotion.
2. *The inclusion of the teaching profession in the list of regulated professions* is the best positive indicator of teacher education reform in the last 30 years. This is a guarantee for a better quality of teaching and better teachers. In 2011, the Ministry of Education and Science adopted a new policy on hiring teachers in the education system according to the law *On Regulated Professions.* The adoption of a legislation package on the teaching profession has helped to improve and develop the teaching profession. Although this is a great achievement, the Teacher's Guild, as the organ foreseen by law to act as the independent structure for the profession is not yet created. There is a need to create teacher associations in order to bring a new dimension to the teaching profession. That should make teachers more involved, responsive, and responsive to education issues and they would become key players in decision-making in the education system.
3. *Shaping the initial teacher education based on the Bologna Process recommendations.* The reform is in its early stages and there is a need for more clarity for the curricular approach, student-teacher practice, and competence profile of the teachers entering into the profession.
4. *Recruitment of teaching staff according to professional merit.* The recruitment method used in Albania has some advantages. For example, it:

* ensures that the best possible staff are recruited on the basis of their merits, abilities, and suitability for the position;
* ensures that all job applicants are considered equally and consistently;
* ensures that the school meets its commitment to safeguarding and promoting the welfare of young people by carrying out all necessary pre-employment checks;
* develops transparent and prompt systems to close the information gaps between teachers and schools to ensure an effective functioning of the teacher labour market by: requiring all teaching vacancies to be posted;
* creates websites where the information is centralized;
* establishes a network of agencies to coordinate and foster recruitment activities.

However, teacher recruitment is still a critical policy issue.

Despite the reform efforts and improvements made in 30 years, education in Albania continues to face many problems related to implementation of legislation; lack of support mechanisms for the implementation of the undertaken initiatives; decision-making without an evidence, evaluation, and research; unsatisfactory quality of human resources; poor infrastructure; and low financial support.

From the reports and research that have analysed the impact of the education reform on teacher education during the last three decades, we choose as being the most comprehensive and useful for future development, the following three:

* UNICEF Albania. Appraisal of the Pre-University Education Strategy 2014–2020, Final Report, 2019.
* UNESCO. Albania Education Policy review: Issues and Recommendations. Extended Report, August 2017.
* European Commission. 2013. *Teacher education and training in the Western Balkans.* Final synthesis report.

In summary, these reports show that the main policy issues in the field of teacher education are the following.

1. *Strategy for teacher education*

Albania's education system is currently undergoing significant change. Many of the programmes and policies relating to teachers are relatively new, and their effectiveness will need to be monitored and evaluated. As teacher quality is the most important factor for the quality of education, development of a strategy for teacher education including initial teacher education to reform the university preparation of teachers is essential; induction improvement and teacher professional development of teachers is a necessity. Such developments will make it possible to create a synergy through the collaboration of all stakeholders, policymakers, experts, teachers, principals, and major stakeholders which will be crucial to the success of the teacher education reforms.

2. *Teacher's status*

There is a need to raise the status and increase the attractiveness of the teaching profession, while making strategic financial investments to improve the education system as a whole (UNESCO 2017, p. 122). The factors that have caused the low attractiveness to teaching are several: after the 1990s the teaching profession did not enjoy a valued status; the lack of supportive policies for teachers does not make the profession popular; diversified academic offer in higher education with more employment benefits and rewards has prevented the best students from choosing teaching.

Teacher status can be improved by taking the following actions:

* defining the policy of teaching profession, developing five-year projections on teaching workforce;
* using the effective admission criteria to the initial teacher education programmes;
* offering scholarships to the best student teacher candidates, organizing publicity campaigns and incentives directed towards desired applicants;
* offering competitive salaries, benefits, appealing working conditions and other factors designed to make the teaching profession more attractive.

As for the scholarship policy there are some questions that need answers: Do people who received a loan or signing bonus intend to go into teaching anyway? Do people who take signing bonuses and loan-forgiveness opportunities tend to stay in teaching longer than those who do not? Essentially, do these policies merely pay people to do what they planned to do anyway?

3. *Teacher recruitment*

In Albania, teachers are recruited using candidate lists by applying online through the 'Teachers for Albania' platform. The method of recruitment based on professional merit, is appreciated as a good alternative. But it has been facing some problems: the lack of the theoretical background of the model; selection exam measuring of knowledge, while teaching is science and art; repetition of the state exam in the framework of induction; centralized approach instead of the previous decentralization model; carrying out forward planning on a year-by-year basis only, risking being unable to anticipate longer-term trends and to plan ahead accordingly. Recommendations provide schools with more responsibility for teacher personnel management and grant greater responsibility and accountability to schools for teacher selection. Direct interaction with applicants for teaching posts through personal interviews and school visits shall improve the match between the selected candidate and school needs. There is a need to establish independent appeals procedures to ensure fairness and to protect teachers' rights. So, recruitment policy should be linked with demand and supply of teachers through forward planning. The UNESCO (2017, p. 139) recommendation that in the medium to long term, consideration should be given to introducing more flexible routes into the teaching profession to address teacher shortages, is very useful for the pre-service and in-service teacher education.

4. *Initial teacher education*

Initial teacher preparation should support Albania's education reform efforts and prepare teachers for the realities of classrooms and schools (UNESCO 2017, p. 135). The curriculum of initial teacher education is currently a hot policy issue. Curricular unification and harmonization are an unaccomplished objective. According to the UNESCO review, programmes do not provide sufficient preparation in the pre-university curriculum and that course delivery is still characterized by teacher-centred methodology rather than the student-centred techniques that teachers are now expected to use in the classroom. The establishment of training schools for the professional practices would help students to hone their practical skills and would put an end to ineffective training practices.

Expected outcomes of the teacher education reform can be a reality if the policy-making process and reform implementation will be based on a broad consensus of all parties and stakeholders involved and avoid confusion caused by the frequent changes of the system and if the financial support will be appropriate.

Conclusion

As the result of the education reform, some main achievements have been noted related to teacher education in Albania: adopting a modern framework of legislation, including teaching in the list of regulated professions, the design and implementation of initial teacher education study programmes based on the Bologna Process model, and recruitment of teaching staff according to professional merit. Despite the impact of the reform and international policies for teacher education, the current status of the Albanian teacher education system is a transitional one. In this context, four key issues of teacher education, as: (a) lack of a strategy for teacher education, (b) low standing of the teaching profession, (c) problematic teacher recruitment, and (d) non-consolidated systems of initial teacher education and teacher professional development; can be translated into key priorities for teacher education policy and would make it possible to move to the new phase of development that expected to produce a better quality of the teacher education. The documents of UNESCO: Teacher Policy Development Guide (2015), Strategy on Teacher Education 2012–2015; Recommendation concerning the status of teachers (1996), Extended Report on Albania Education Policy (2017) and the EU Conclusions on improving the quality of teacher education (2007) can be used as references on teacher policy development.

References

ACCE. (2014). Professional development and teacher evaluation in Albania, prepared by E. Haxhiymeri and N. Mita. Retrieved from https://www.acce.al/sites/default/files/download/research/Raport%20Teacher%20Evaluation.pdf.

Code of ethics of teachers in the public and private pre-university education system. (2012). Retrieved from https://arsimi.gov.al/wp-content/uploads/2018/02/dok-0033.pdf.

Decision of Council of Ministers no. 216, dated 20.04.2018. (2018). On setting up the criterion of the average grade for candidates admission to the study programmes of first cycle and integrated studies of the second cycle or student transfer to the intermediated years in the institutions of the higher education for the academic year 2018–2019.

Decision of Council of Ministers no. 436, dated 3.6.2020. (2020). On setting up the criterion of the average grade for candidates admission to the study programmes of first cycle and integrated studies of the second cycle or student transfer to the intermediated years in the institutions of the higher education for the academic year 2020–2021 and 2021–2022 and following.

European Commission. (2013). *Teacher education and training in the Western Balkans*. Final synthesis report. Prepared by A. Duda, M. Golubeva, and T. Clifford-Amos. Publications Office of the European Union. Retrieved from https://ec.europa.eu/assets/eac/education/library/study/2013/teacher-balkans_en.pdf.

European Commission. (2015). *Shaping career-long perspectives on teaching. A guide on policies to improve Initial Teacher Education. Brussels: European Commission.* Retrieved from https://www.schooleducationgateway.eu/downloads/files/Shaping%20career-long%20perspectives%20on%20teaching.pdf.

European Union. (2007). Conclusions of the Council and of the Representatives of the Governments of the member States, meeting within the Council of 15 November 2007, on improving the quality of teacher education. *Official Journal of the European Union*, 12.12.2007, C300/6.

INSTAT. (2020). *Population of Albania*. Retrieved from http://www.instat.gov.al/media/6850/population-on-1-january-2020___.pdf.

Law no. 69, dated 21.6.2012. (2012). *On pre-university education in the Republic of Albania*, amended by the law no. 56/2015 and the law no.48/2018. Retrieved from http://arsimi.gov.al/wp-content/uploads/2017/10/Ligji_Parauniversitar.pdf.

Law no. 7961, dated 12.07.1995. (2003). *The Labour Code of the Republic of Albania*, amended by the law no. 8085, dated 13.03.1996, the law no. 9125, dated 29.07.2003. Retrieved from https://qbz.gov.al/preview/c1c18a6c-5f3e-457d-b931-de505b3c7ed0.

Law no. 80/2015. (2015). *On higher education and scientific research in the institutions of the higher education in the Republic of Albania*. Retrieved from https://www.ascal.al/media/documents/legjislacioni/Law%20no.%2080_2015.pdf.

Law no. 9741, dated 21.5.2007. (2007). *On higher education in the Republic of Albania*, amended by the law no. 9832, dated 12.11.2007, the law no.10307, dated 22.07.2010, and the law no.10493, dated 15.12.2011. Retrieved from https://www.ascal.al/media/documents/legjislacioni/Albania_Law__revised.pdf.

Law no. 10171, dated 22.10.2009. (2009). *On regulated professions in the Republic of Albania*, amended by the law no. 10357, dated 16.12.2010, the law no. 10470, dated 13.10.2011, and the law no. 90/2015, dated 17.97.2014. Retrieved from http://arsimi.gov.al/wp-content/uploads/2017/10/LIGJ_NR_10_171_PRR.pdf.

MOESY. (2019). *Statistical annual report on education, sports and youth 2017–2018 and timely series*. Tirana: MOESY.

Nano, L., N. Kallçiu, and N. Mita. (2019). The Albanian student-teacher perspective on reasons for choosing teaching as a career. In: M. Kowalczuk-Walędziak, A. Korzeniecka-Bondar, W. Danilewicz and G. Lauwers (Eds.), *Rethinking teacher education for the 21st century. Trends, challenges, new directions* (pp. 79–97). Opladen, Berlin, Toronto: Verlag Barbara Budrich.

North Atlantic Treaty Organization Website. Retrieved from http://www.nato.int/cps/ic/natohq/topics_48891.htm.

Progress Report. (2019). Reform of teacher education and training: Albania. Retrieved from https://education.ec.europa.eu/sites/default/files/tt-report-al.pdf.

UNESCO. (1996). *Recommendation concerning the status of teachers*, adopted by the Special Intergovernmental Conference on the Status of Teachers, Paris, 5 October 1966. Retrieved from https://www.ilo.org/wcmsp5/groups/public/%2D%2D-ed_dialogue/%2D%2Dsector/documents/normativeinstrument/wcms_162034.pdf.

UNESCO. (2015). *Teacher policy development guide*. Retrieved from https://unesdoc.unesco.org/ark:/48223/pf0000235272.

UNECSO. (2017). Albania education policy review: Issues and recommendations. Extended report. Editions UNESCO, Paris.

UNESCO. (2018). *Situation analysis of education in Albania: Towards SDG4-Education 2030*. Retrieved from https://unesdoc.unesco.org/ark:/48223/pf0000259245.

UNICEF Albania. (2019). *Appraisal of the pre-university education strategy. Final report, 2014–2020*. Prepared by M. Wort, D. Pupovci, and E. Ikonomi. Retrieved from https://www.unicef.org/albania/media/2031/file/Education%20Sector%20Appraisal%20Document%20Eng.pdf.

Vula, E., B. Saqipi, T. Karaj, and N. Mita. (2012). Moving towards practice-oriented and research-based teacher education. *Excellence in Higher Education*, 3(1), 37–45. Retrieved from http://ehe.pitt.edu/ojs/index.php/ehe/article/view/42/45.

Website of EU delegation to Albania. Retrieved from http://eeas.europa.eu/delegations/albania/eu_albania/political_relations/index_en.htm.

7

Teacher Education in Bosnia and Herzegovina: The Most Significant Changes in Recent Decades for the Initial Education and Professional Development of Teachers

Irma Čehić, Sanela Merjem Rustempašić,
Jasmina Bećirović-Karabegović,
and Izela Habul-Šabanović

Introduction

The complex political system in Bosnia and Herzegovina—with three constituent nations, two entities, one district and 12 ministries and one department of education, and with different levels of jurisdiction—creates a correspondingly complex educational system at all levels of education. Differing educational policies and a lack of clear, unified guidelines pave the way to hurried, inadequate, and incomplete modifications of curricula being enacted in only one entity or canton at a time.

In Bosnia and Herzegovina, there are several state universities which train teachers, with the oldest and most highly ranked being the University of Sarajevo. There are also universities in Tuzla, Zenica, Bihać, Travnik, and two in Mostar, all operating in Bosnian and Croatian. In the Republic of Srpska (an entity within BiH) are the University of Banja Luka and the University of East Sarajevo, with their accompanying faculties in Bijeljina, Foča, and Pale. The number of private universities in BiH is also significant, but they do not generally comprehensively offer teacher education, except for few that are educating both class teachers and subject teachers.

I. Čehić (✉) • S. M. Rustempašić • J. Bećirović-Karabegović • I. Habul-Šabanović
University of Sarajevo, Sarajevo, Bosnia and Herzegovina
e-mail: irma_cehic@yahoo.com

© The Author(s), under exclusive license to Springer Nature Switzerland AG 2023   **159**
M. Kowalczuk-Walędziak et al. (eds.), *The Palgrave Handbook of Teacher Education in Central and Eastern Europe*, https://doi.org/10.1007/978-3-031-09515-3_7

The situation across these institutions is fundamentally complex because there is no State Ministry of Education, therefore all policy decisions are confined to lower levels. Beyond this, some universities are under the socio-political influence of neighbouring countries, especially Serbia and Croatia. Nevertheless, even within such a definitively complicated system, there are numerous examples of good practice and cooperation between the entities and cantons, clearly demonstrating the existence of a desire to improve the education system(s) in BiH.

The reform of primary education, which started in 2003, did not happen throughout the whole state simultaneously. It was followed by staggered transitions into the Bologna system of study, which contributed to the change of teaching curricula and teacher education programmes, with the opening of new departments at the existing universities, as well as with the creation of new cantonal, entity, and private universities. As such, the current system(s) of formal education and professional development of teachers in BiH remains very inconsistent.

The University of Sarajevo offers a full range of programmes for primary and secondary school teachers at their teacher training faculties and in their academic departments: Faculty of Education, Faculty of Philosophy, Faculty of Natural Sciences, Faculty of Sport and Physical Education, and Musical and Art Academy. In addition, the Department of Pedagogy at the Faculty of Philosophy runs a special programme, *Supplementary pedagogical education*, for teachers who have not graduated from teacher training courses, and who teach specialised subjects in vocational secondary schools. Other universities have differing scopes and numbers of teaching faculties. Nonetheless, the obligatory and statutory professional training of teachers is carried out every year. Additionally, there are other forms of training organised by organisations and associations. At state level, the Agency of Preschool, Primary and Secondary Education (APOSO) organises professional training mainly related to the common core and subjects with common contents across all three programmes. The Cantonal Associations of Teachers of Specialised Courses are additionally engaged in professional training oriented around topics that are related to specific subjects. Furthermore, there are several non-governmental organisations involved on a state level in different forms of training, such as the Centre for Education Initiatives (CEI), Step by Step, and Save the Children.

Most professional training is currently related to inclusive education, as teachers are expressing the greatest need for this type of additional education. In the Canton of Sarajevo, several studies have been carried out over the last two years on the quality of professional teacher training, with the participation of all University of Sarajevo teacher training faculties. This research has shown that the quality of vocational education depends on: what content of training courses is offered to teachers regarding the topics of the courses and teachers' interest in them, who are the authors and the lectors, what the financial capacities are (related both to personal and school budget) and what kind of support is provided from the school for professional teacher training, as there must be substitute teachers to replace the teachers undertaking training. In the future, members of the research team plan to make a catalogue of teacher training topics that could be adequately graded and contribute meaningfully to teacher advancement in BiH.

In this chapter, we will present the system of teacher education that existed just before the war (i.e. the period before 1992–1995) when there were very few universities, all of which were state-owned. This period in Bosnia and Herzegovina's history is important because the war and post-war periods represented a period of adaptation. Additionally, we will explore the direction in which the development of teacher training faculties in Bosnia and Herzegovina are heading; the ratios of theoretical to practical training; and the extent to which practice is represented in official programmes of initial education. We will also discuss the involvement of university professors from teacher training faculties in the process of professional teacher training within the faculty itself, as well as in the work of other government and non-governmental organisations, because most of the university professors are included in different programmes of professional development of teachers periodically or continuously. Furthermore, we will examine the main characteristics dominating the development of the teaching profession in BiH. Also, based on the results of different studies conducted during the last few years that we will discuss in this chapter we will recommend ways and solutions to improve teacher initial education as well as the different forms of teachers' professional development.

The Context of Teacher Education

The importance of empowering the teaching profession around the world is becoming a priority. The teaching profession faces many challenges, as we could best see at the time of the pandemic when it was necessary for teachers to quickly adapt to the new circumstances in the real and virtual classrooms. Therefore, it is necessary that the teaching profession gains an adequate status in our society and starts to be adequately paid so that it might become a desirable future vocation for the best and most successful students. At the same time, this would ensure the orientation of future teachers to lifelong learning that would allow them to keep pace with the progress of science and modern technology. After all, in our fast-changing world, it is teachers who need to empower students to successfully pursue occupations in the future that do not even exist at present. Thus, teachers face a real challenge. Donaldson (2013) points out that the importance of school education for individual and collective well-being, as well as for social cohesion and economic progress, is becoming increasingly evident all around the world. Indeed, many governments, that are included in PISA testing are advocating for the kind of innovation in education that they believe will enable their country to be competent in fulfilling the needs and meeting the challenges of its citizens. The Western Balkan countries have, to varying degrees, developed standards for the teaching profession, established teacher licensing procedures, and defined learning outcomes in education and teacher training. Within this diverse context, we believe that the key factors in implementing an education reform are the quality and drive of teaching staff. The present need to improve teachers' initial education, in order to create the conditions necessary for their professional development (and teacher assessment and evaluation), is outlined in the *Strategic Directions for the Development of Education in Bosnia and Herzegovina* (Vijeće ministara Bosne i Hercegovine 2008). The key goals are improving the level of educational standards; updating content and didactical methods of work; teacher achievement evaluation; and continuous professional development of teachers at all levels of the education system. In summary, BiH needs teachers who, along with an in-depth knowledge of their subject matter, possess a robust knowledge of pedagogy and methodology, as well as the skills and competences needed to guide and motivate students.

Educating future teachers in our country does not rest on consistently defined learning outcomes and competences, although the current conditions of market competition, where a large number of faculties offer a different quality of education to future teachers, would require the education sector to develop such competences above all. Rangelov-Jusović et al. (2013, p. 46) point out that

changes in legislation and the development of strategic documents in education have not accompanied significant changes in practice, nor are they accompanied by action plans, education policies or by-laws. This is especially true in the area of teacher professional development and quality assurance. The strategy of teacher education and professional development has not yet been developed and there is no common understanding of the quality of training before entering the service nor while working in-service.

Teacher professional activity has been one of the most prominent topics in the andragogy literature of the last two decades. Deficiencies in teachers' competences—whether 'core', 'basic', 'extended', 'transversal', 'national', and 'transcultural'—pose a challenge to our social and human sciences to think and act 'on the border of their own operational concepts, and to overcome their own boundaries and competences' (Derida 2002). In itself, the development of teacher competency standards implies a particular approach to the teaching profession that emerged in response to the pressure coming from a policy level to raise the quality of education through the provision of 'better teachers'. The central question to this approach regards what the teacher should know and be able to do, with knowledge and skills expressed through measurable characteristics and behaviours. In this context, 'good' and 'better' teachers are those who comply with the requirements set out in policy documents (Radulović 2007). On the European continent, there are clear standards of the teaching profession that have been defined to guide all initial teacher education programmes. National teacher competence standards should, inter alia, serve as a framework for establishing initial and professional educational programmes for teachers via appropriate institutions and their professional development programmes. The analyses of current programmes, both for education and teacher professional development (TPD), testify to the existence of different approaches, mainly due to the lack of a unified national curriculum. Going forwards, the aim of education reform should be to ensure that national standards are as compatible as possible with those of the European Union. Indeed, this should certainly be the first step.

Here we must point out that there is a gap between education strategies worldwide and those in Bosnia and Herzegovina—starting with the beginning of the teacher education process, that is, the selection threshold for prospective teachers entering initial training programmes. With a set of requirements including entrance exams, interviews, and excellence in high school grades, Egyptian authorities have imposed strict conditions for employment in schools. Similarly, in Singapore, candidates for a teaching post will only be considered if they were among the highest academic achievers during their high school education, and in Finland, a country with a long-standing reputation of having one of the most developed and acclaimed education systems in the world, only 10% of those who apply have the opportunity to enter a teacher education and training programme (Stewart 2010). It is noticeable that the entrance exam for future teachers is significantly different now in BiH when compared to the earlier period, but also to the ones that exist in other countries. At the time of the Socialist Republic of Bosnia and Herzegovina (1943–1992), the selection of future teachers was prescribed by the Law on

Pedagogical Academies (Assembly of SR BiH 1968; cited in Smajkić 2004, p. 103), where it was clearly stated that

> [...] only students who have completed the Teacher Education Secondary School or the Grammar School could enroll in the study programme of primary school teaching in the lower grades, and students who have completed other types of four-year secondary schools could be enrolled in other study programmes.

When the studies required for teaching the lower grades of primary school were transformed into a four-year programme in 1998, the Faculty of Educational Sciences in Sarajevo introduced a very detailed entrance exam. It consisted of a written native language essay on a given topic, a general knowledge test, psychological tests, a music culture test (singing), and a physical culture test (exercise), as well as an interview with the candidate. This entrance exam was unfortunately eliminated a few years ago. Nowadays, students enrol based on their success achieved in high school. Concerning the large differences between programmes and assessment criteria from different high schools, this way of student admission to universities is not an example of good selection.

Today there is no selection process of this kind. For example, at the Faculty of Educational Sciences in Sarajevo, the entrance exams covering relevant subject knowledge have not been used for the last 10 years—nonetheless, faculties of education or teacher training elsewhere in the country still have entrance examinations. Indeed, a common link for all other teacher training faculties is the native language entrance exam; but there is no such harmonising of other entrance exam subjects, meaning that there is a range from which candidates are assessed, including mathematics, music culture, or fine arts. Nationwide, candidates who have completed any four-year secondary school programme can enrol to study lower-grade primary school teaching, and some faculties have defined a high-grade point average of 3.5 as part of their criterion. Given that the Faculty of Educational Sciences in Sarajevo does not have the entrance exam, the ranking of prospective candidates is based instead on the number of points awarded to their general success during secondary school education; their specific success in the selected group of subjects in secondary school that line up with the subject/s the candidate would like to teach in the future (i.e. Bosnian, Croatian, and Serbian language and literature; mathematics; history; and geography); and their entrance interview.

Candidates are enrolled based both on quotas set by the Ministry of Education, Science and Youth and on the faculty council's proposal for each faculty. If they have achieved an insufficient number of credits in their secondary school education, and/or in the group of subjects prescribed by the ministry, they are eliminated from the enrolment process. The faculty council's appointed committee then interviews the remaining candidates, and, for successful candidates goes on to determine whether or not there are any obstacles to their entry into the teaching profession (e.g. speech impediments or colour blindness), eliminating only those candidates whose personal obstacles would significantly affect their professional development as a future teacher.

Following their graduation, there is no real community concern given to the graduates of teacher training or education faculties. Indeed, it is not uncommon for the best students (i.e. those with high-grade point averages recognised with gold and silver badges) to unsuccessfully search for employment in the profession for a few years, before quitting. Positioning this loss of well-qualified graduates on a global level, the UNESCO report (2014) states that there is a chronic shortage of trained teachers in the world, projecting a worldwide deficit of as many as 5.2 million teachers by 2030, and recommending that governments employ a range of methods to encourage young people into the teaching profession. Therefore, from all of the above, it is quite clear why students are opting to leave BiH after graduation, as part of a broader trend in which 43.3% of BiH-born citizens now live abroad (2017).[1]

The process of drafting national standards, which we do not yet have, cannot be reduced to rewriting ready-made solutions taken from other countries. Instead, there is a need for a methodology that would provide the means to problematise and rethink potential standards, as well as specific starting points for their development, arising from different theoretical approaches—including the diverse needs and perspectives of direct participants, those who are invested in the teaching profession, and, above all, teachers themselves.

Innovation of teacher education curricula (2004–…) in BiH was modelled on similar curricula in Europe, in accordance with European and world standards of modern education, that is, with regards to quality, new methods of student evaluation (referring mostly to partial exams instead of evaluation at the end of the academic year), student mobility in European countries at all levels of study, and the post-study period—that is, the employment-seeking phase. However, in reality, some of these guidelines are not suitable for practical application. Namely, there are no programmes taught in the English language at teacher training faculties in Bosnia and Herzegovina, which therefore greatly impedes and reduces student mobility. Nonetheless, there is cause for optimism regarding the part of the programme that emphasises the

---

[1] Karta Evropepremabrojuljudikojižive u inostranstvu: BiHapsolutnirekorder—Front Slobode.

importance of in-service practice and training of students for their future profession through: in-service practice in primary school teaching; meeting contemporary needs in the education of primary school teachers to enhance their educational competences; quality training of primary school teaching staff in accordance with the applicable primary education laws; and the organisation of primary school instruction for students from the first to the fifth grades.

The quality and efficiency of the teaching process at the teacher training faculties are regularly monitored and supervised by quality committees: the evaluation sheet for assessing teaching and assistant/associated staff is an element of internal evaluation. However, the most important source of teacher evaluation data is the students themselves, the direct users of teaching services in the teaching process. Student evaluation of teachers' and assistants'/associates' work is not an expert or professional assessment of teacher competences, rather it represents students' perceptions of how teaching goals are met and, thus, to what extent they satisfy the interests of students in the teaching process—above all, those goals related to a better understanding of the teaching subject. Student questionnaires have been created in such a way that takes into account the indicators of the quality of teachers' work, which are valid for all professional profiles included in the teaching process.

Teacher education in BiH strives to match study programme quality and student teachers' acquired knowledge with both the related faculties in the region and in the European/international environment. The completion of first-cycle studies qualifies students for successful work in lower-grade primary school teaching, based on the acquired competences which include (NB all of the following are specific to the lower grades): meeting the contemporary needs of teaching understanding the developmental characteristics of students; understanding the education process; understanding contemporary trends in broader society, in order to familiarise students with basic ethical issues and promote intercultural development in a multicultural environment; understanding basic theoretical knowledge in humanities, science, and arts subjects; understanding didactical and methodological procedures, principles, and strategies in the educational process, as well as their applications in the teaching courses; and taking into consideration the opportunities for lifelong learning in information technologies and their application in teaching practice.

Following this, completing the subsequent second-cycle study confirms successful performance in the field based on acquired competences, including (NB all of the following are specific to the lower grades): fulfilling the contemporary needs of teaching; knowledge of students' developmental characteristics and qualification to work in educational institutions; taking responsibility for one's own professional development and lifelong learning; self-evaluation and evaluation of the education process and their pupils' learning; knowledge of basic scientific and theoretical insights regarding humanities, science, and arts subjects; knowledge and application of didactical and methodological procedures, principles, and strategies; and capacity for lifelong learning in modern information technologies and their applications in teaching practice.

Initial Teacher Education

Bosnia and Herzegovina has existed in a very complex form since the 1995 Dayton arrangement (the General Framework Agreement for Peace in Bosnia and Herzegovina). It is divided into two entities: the Federation of Bosnia and Herzegovina and the Republic of Srpska, along with the Brčko District. In addition, the Federation is divided into 10 cantons, so that a total of 13 education ministries exist in the country, none of which are at state level. Consequently, as mentioned earlier, there is no single education policy at any level of education.

This major fragmentation and decentralisation has led to an educational structure in which each canton is responsible for its own curricula at all levels of education, while the Republic of Srpska is a unique educational area. In such a complicated system, there is no single national curriculum at any level of education, but only a so-called 'Common Core' for subjects that are not 'national' such as mathematics, physics, chemistry, biology, technical culture, and culture of living. On the other hand, the three constituent nationalities—Bosniaks, Serbs, and Croats—have very different educational programmes for their own national group of subjects, specifically their respective languages, literatures, histories, geographies, and religions.

Serving its 3,531,000 residents (2013 census), there are 7 state universities and 19 private universities in the Federation of Bosnia and Herzegovina, and two 2 universities and 7 private universities in the Republic of Srpska. Most of these universities have study programmes for teacher education at primary teaching level. Secondary school teachers (i.e. who teach specialised subjects) are educated at non-teacher-education faculties, but they are required to pass a short series of teacher education exams, usually in pedagogy, psychology, didactics, and teaching methodology. In order to better understand the structure of initial teacher education we need to elucidate some aspects of public universities founded before, during and after the aggression, as well as the foundation of private universities.

BiH's oldest and most prestigious university is the University of Sarajevo, officially founded in 1949, with some faculties founded earlier—the very first, which has not ceased working since its establishment, is the Faculty of Educational Sciences, founded in 1946. At the very beginning, all teachers, including primary school and kindergarten teachers, were educated there on a two-year programme: teachers of language, mathematics, physics, chemistry, biology, domestic science, and so on. With the establishment of other teacher training faculties within the University of Sarajevo, some teachers began to be educated there, and nowadays there are only four departments in the Faculty of Educational Sciences: preschool education, primary school education in the lower grades, culture of living and technical education with informatics, and education and rehabilitation.

Before the war, in addition to the University of Sarajevo, there were also the University of Banja Luka (1975), the University of Tuzla (1976), the University Džemal Bijedić in Mostar (1977), all of them existing today, as well as several faculties of the University of Sarajevo in other cities. Then, during and after the aggression against Bosnia and Herzegovina, other faculties/universities were founded. The Federation of BiH established the University of Mostar (1992), the University of Bihać (1997), and the University of Zenica (2000), and the Republic of Srpska established the University of East Sarajevo (1992). The list of private universities is much longer and, unfortunately, steadily increasing, with most founded in Sarajevo, Banja Luka, and Travnik. Most of the private universities don't even have their own spaces and are located on a single floor in office buildings or even private houses in some cases. While public universities generally have full-time teachers and associates, private universities have a smaller proportion of full-time staff, and most classes are delivered by teachers from state universities or other private universities. This means that condensed (occasional) classes are realised to a lesser extent than provided by law. Given the higher tuition fees paid at private universities (sometimes three times higher than at state ones), private higher education has become a lucrative business, which does not have an adequate selection when enrolling students, but at the same time has a high vertical pass rate of students.

In a country that was very proud of its multiethnicity before the war, now everything is observed through the prism of national affiliation. So it is important to emphasise that the state universities opened during the war were built on territories dominated by a single nationality, and therefore created as mono-ethnic: all educators and students belonged to a single, permitted ethnicity. This, of course, had direct ramifications on which teachers, associates, and students were able to work and study, as well as on the contents of the subjects studied. That ensures better horizontal and vertical mobility of students with universities in neighbouring countries than with those within BiH, as well as lesser employment opportunities for university professors and associates from different parts of BiH. Today, by enrolling students from non-dominant religious affiliations, there is an effort from these universities to achieve multinationality.

In the context of such a historically and ethnically complicated system of higher education, there are currently 15 faculties educating primary school teachers. All universities operate according to the Bologna system of study, but different universities, and therefore the faculties where primary school teachers are educated, can be structured in two different ways regarding the duration of each cycle in years: 4 + 1 + 3 or 3 + 2 + 3. The professional title of the diploma varies significantly among the different faculties: students who have completed three years of the first-cycle study have the title of the professor of primary school teaching in the lower grades, class teacher, that is, which is the same academic title that students of the four-year pre-Bologna study cycle were awarded. At faculties operating on a 4 + 1 + 3 basis, students are assigned the title of the baccalaureate of primary school teaching in the lower grades upon completing the first cycle of study. Differences in the acquired qualification after graduation together with inconsistent employment regulations sometimes give preference to students who have acquired a particular diploma qualification regardless of the length of study. All of this has an impact on students' determination to enrol in those faculties that provide them certain advantages in employment, regardless of the quality of study programmes they have studied. For quality initial education of teachers, it is very important to have quality programmes and quality candidates. As mentioned before, the entrance exam was very detailed and extensive in the period from 1998 to 2011 and it consisted of general knowledge tests, a psychological test, orthography test, an essay in the native language, a task of singing and some exercises in the domain of physical education. Candidates were ranked based on general success (40% points) and entrance exam results (60% points). Nowadays we have a significant reduction of the number of enrolled candidates at all faculties, including those for the education of future teachers. There are two main reasons for this: (1) the large number of faculties and (2) the fact that students born in the wartime and post-war period are now being enrolled in faculties, and those were the periods in which we had low birth rate. Reduction in the number of students to be enrolled in faculties led to modification of the scope and quality of the entrance exam for the Faculty of Educational Sciences in Sarajevo in the last ten years. Now, the entrance exam has only consisted of an interview with the candidate, which also serves as a general knowledge test with the basic function being to detect possible speech difficulties. However, the ranking of candidates is based on their success in high school. The University of Zenica also decides student admissions on the basis of general and individual overall success and the success in individual subjects during the secondary school education. On the other hand, by data provided on their website, the University of Tuzla has a written entrance exam in the form of a general knowledge test in one or more subjects that are crucial for the study and its content is decided each year by the entrance committee.

Much like the admissions processes, the curricula for the education of future teachers also differ significantly across BiH, in terms of the number and scope of both general and professional subjects on offer. At the Faculty of Educational Sciences at the University of Sarajevo, students undertake courses in pedagogy and psychology across all four years of their studies, plus one course within all of the six methodics in the fifth, sixth, seventh, and eighth semesters of the first-cycle studies. Six methodics are the methodics of subjects in the lower grades of primary school: Bosnian, Croatian and Serbian language and literature, Mathematics, Natural and Social Science, Art, Music, and Physical Education. On the other hand, at other faculties the number of courses categorised as pedagogical, psychological, and methodical is significantly reduced. Table 7.1 overviews the total number of courses belonging to these three categories, as well as the corresponding in-service practice.

In the row 'in-service practice' we present the numbers of subjects that include professional practice of students and also whether they are independent or listed within other subjects. The number of professional practice classes was not always specified in curricula for different faculties or programmes, so it was not possible to do a representative analysis of the exact number of hours/classes students have to attend within the professional practice. It is important to note that the representation of courses in the curricula is only given for state universities, in the order in which they were founded, because those for private universities are not listed for all universities that have teacher training or educational faculties. Also, some private universities have dual education for class teachers and subject teachers, for example, teachers of Bosnian, Croatian, and/or Serbian language, Culture of living, and so on, so it was unclear how many in-service practices they have in the lower grades of primary school.

Table 7.1 Quantitative analysis of the representation of first-cycle courses

Faculty name (where lower primary teaching education is offered)	Number of pedagogical and psychological courses	Number of methodical courses	In-service practice
Faculty of Educational Sciences, University of Sarajevo	13	24	22
Faculty of Philosophy, University of Banja Luka	20	18	1
Faculty of Philosophy, University of Tuzla	13	13	4
Teacher Education Faculty, Džemal Bijedić University (Mostar)	11	6	11
Faculty of Science and Education, University of Mostar	14	15	3
Faculty of Education in Bijeljina, University of East Sarajevo	8	12	5
Faculty of Pedagogy, University of Bihać	13	12	2
Faculty of Philosophy, University of Zenica	13	13	n/a

Teacher Professional Development

TPD is realised in three ways that are intertwined: (a) as formal education for master's and doctoral degrees in the same or different area of education, organised in parallel with regular work; (b) as an education through seminars, courses, conferences, and so on; and (c) as sharing of experiences between teachers, like examples of good practice. Like initial training as outlined in the previous sections, teacher professional development in BiH, both formal and informal, is also fundamentally fragmented, especially in the Federation of BiH. With the exception of the Agency of Preschool, Primary and Secondary Education (APOSO), there is no government organisation involved in any form of teacher professional development at state level. Instead, the professional development of teachers, mostly undertaken on a voluntary basis, is facilitated by non-governmental organisations. There is a significant difference in teachers' professional development in two entities in BiH. In the Republic of Srpska, in-service training is delivered through the Republic Pedagogical Institute for all teachers that work in this entity. In the Federation of BiH, there are different cantonal associations that implement different forms of teacher professional training mainly at the cantonal level and they are more or less related to cantonal ministries.

Although the Law of Primary School Education legally necessitates teacher training at all levels, teacher professional development (TPD) is only actually available in select geographical areas, therefore is unequal in practice: indeed, the urban hubs of Sarajevo, Banja Luka, and Mostar are where most TPD opportunities are concentrated. Sarajevo, as the capital of BiH, and the Federation of BiH as well, is the headquarter of most non-governmental organisations involved in informal teacher education. Teachers in Sarajevo therefore have more opportunities for professional development, especially its free forms. At the same time, Sarajevo Canton is the canton with the largest budget, so teachers from this canton are among those with higher salaries, which further facilitates their professional development, especially for the forms of TPDs that must be paid for. Five University of Sarajevo teacher training faculties have participated in the canton-level project, *Guidelines for the development of the teaching profession*. The project that started in 2018 aimed to examine teachers about the forms and availability of in-service training, difficulties, and challenges in organising in-service training within schools and organisations that implement them, the content they need to cover during in-service training, and possible ways to connect more intensively their home faculties and schools they work in so that professional training would be a continuous process, not a periodic one. The research conducted within the project had two phases: examining the opinions of teachers of particular subjects and focus group interviews with teachers selected by the cantonal teachers' association for each subject. So far, these focus groups, consisting of teachers with a variety of profiles, have found that there are significant differences between schools in the same canton regarding the internal and external organisation of TPD as well as the attainability of different TPDs.

There are different ways of organising TPD at the school level. For example, in one primary school, there is an expert commission which has been working continuously for many years, composed of a pedagogue and teachers of different profiles—keeping records and planning the professional development for all teachers in the school. These respondents emphasise that this school-level structure gives them uninterrupted insight into the progress of each teacher, thus meaning that the types of professional development to be implemented are set on an annual basis, in direct accordance with the needs and interests of all teachers in the school. In the majority of other public schools, there is no team or committee that deals exclusively with professional development. Instead, as the respondents pointed out, in the process of professional development, they mostly consult with the school pedagogue and the principal. Furthermore, most of the respondents reported that they did not participate in the creation of professional development programmes themselves, highlighting that it was not always easy to take that kind of initiative. The initiative mainly takes the form of the introduction of changes in the teaching process, within both regular teaching and extracurricular activities.

Contrastingly, in a school that follows the Montessori methodology as one of few private primary schools in the canton, the core TPD is realised in collaboration with coaches from the Montessori Centre in London. All teachers are in obligation to attend it annually and it has the same programme for all teachers within school. Private schools in general have different methodology of work that requires specific TPDs in order to maintain their licence. They are founded by different founders and that fact can directly affect the forms of TPD that may represent the only forms of professional development or be the additional ones to those that are already organised for teachers from public schools.

Although not commonly involved in the design of professional development innovations, many of the teachers in the focus groups stated that they attended TPD organised by the Teacher Association of the Canton of Sarajevo and at the home faculty, where they had lectures on topics relevant to the class they were currently teaching. Participants also stated that they had attended professional trainings organised by the Ministry of Education, but also TPDs they had to finance independently, in accordance with the financial and organisational capacities of their school. Because most schools don't have a budget to finance TPDs for all teachers within the school, so principal or teacher's council usually choose one or more representatives who will attend the professional education. In these cases, teachers who attended education are obliged to train other teachers in their school through lectures or workshops. This is a good example of overcoming financial difficulties in organising TPDs for teachers at school level. It is also a model that can be used for those TPDs that have limited number of participants.

Latest activities in organised TPDs on cantonal or wider area level included: *Learning Outcomes* (series of workshops for planning based on learning outcomes for different subjects), *Dance of Writing* (programme of encouraging development of pre-writing skills and speech development), inclusion of children with disabilities as well as children with additional support needs, *Felting* (common for Waldorf methodology, but used to produce teaching materials and for therapeutic purposes), *Friendship Circuits* (series of workshops for integration of children with disabilities as well as children from minority communities, in this case mostly Roma national minority), and Conferences organised by CEI Step by Step, writing inclusion handbooks, developing the

Corruption handbook, education based on the Montessori methodology in working with children, and so on.

The Education Programme for Learning Outcome Focused Planning for Bosnian, Croatian, and Serbian languages realised in 2017 is one of the few TPD programmes implemented for all teachers in the Canton of Sarajevo. In the first phase, the representatives of teachers and educators from each primary school had four weeks of training with professors and associates of the academic community (outwith the Canton of Sarajevo) and other experts, organised by Save the Children, an NGO. In the second phase, the teachers' representatives implemented modification of the training for the rest of the teachers in schools. This second round of training was carried out during the winter break over an average of two to three days, depending on the school where it was implemented. In a survey (Čehić et al. 2018), based on a sample of 96 lower-grade primary school teachers, it was found that this type of additional professional teacher education had both advantages and disadvantages. These survey participants highlighted that the most significant problem they face is that their teacher education is provided indirectly and not by experts in the field, therefore does not offer them answers to many of the questions they face within their professional practice. Additionally, the participants find this type of TPD to be fragmented, so the lack of holistic approach to learning outcomes focused on planning for all subjects instead of one of them in the lower grades of primary school creates difficulties both in the actual education process and in the evaluation of learning outcomes of TPD.

Moving forwards, the teachers in the focus groups identified the TPD topics necessary for their future professional development in line with the challenges they face within their work. The respondents indicated that these topics had either been addressed insufficiently or been ignored: assertive communication; cooperation of colleagues within the school; communication with parents; assessment of student progress and understanding of assessment by students and parents; assessment of children with disabilities; challenges and guidelines for work in an inclusive class; creation and implementation of Individual Educational Programmes (IEP); informatics; implementation of electronic journals; modern strategies in education such as problem-based learning, project teaching, and research teaching. Listed topics are results of the frequent changes in the curriculum of the primary school teaching in the lower grades (changes in the allocated number of school hours and contents of particular subjects, introduction of new subjects, etc.). One of the biggest difficulties in teacher professional development is the fact that all quality forms of training must be paid for, which leads teachers to choose those which are more affordable. That leads to choosing the forms of TPD that are more accessible and not desirable or necessary.

As a result of their informal education and TPD, teachers are introducing new knowledge and modern strategies in their classrooms in curricular and extracurricular activities. Often, they create new extracurricular activities with specific programmes such as: *Music Playrooms*; *Little Researchers*; *Little Creatives*; *School Bazaar*; *Eat Healthy, Grow Healthy*; and *Friendship Circuits*. CEI Step by Step created an online society: Zajednica inovativnih nastavnika—*Community of Innovative Teachers* (hereinafter referred to as ZIN) for preschool, primary, and high school teachers, and pedagogues. Members of the ZIN are from all over the country and they share online the examples of their good practice, information and applications for education organised by CEI Step by Step, as well as publications and handbooks. In addition to regional teachers' conference that has been held for over 12 years and is the one with most participants in BiH. Since 2016 ZIN has been organising the annual award for the most innovative teachers chosen by all members. The award is at the state level and is only one of this kind in BiH. Its impact on improving the quality of education is already evident as the number of innovative practices that are shared among teachers is increasing every year.

The Legislative and Policy Status of the Education System in Bosnia and Herzegovina

The image of the education sector in Bosnia and Herzegovina is a reflection of the state system as defined by the constitution of Bosnia and Herzegovina, the constitutions of the entities and cantons, and the Statute of the Brčko District. As a result of decentralisation of the country education is mostly financed from the public funds of the entity, as well as cantonal, Brčko District, and municipal budgets, depending on the jurisdiction. In total there are 13 education-specific budgets in Bosnia and Herzegovina, that is, one in each entity, one in the Brčko District, and 10 cantonal budgets. Accordingly, there are two entity ministries of education: the Federal Ministry of Education and Science, the Ministry of Education and Culture of the Republic of Srpska, and, one Department of Education in the Government of the Brčko District. These ministries carry out administrative, professional, and legal tasks related to all levels of education (from preschool through to higher education). Throughout the Federation of Bosnia and Herzegovina, the field of education and science is further divided into 10 cantonal ministries of education, science, culture, and sport, which are each responsible for implementing the associated policies in their own canton.

Therefore, in summary, the education system in Bosnia and Herzegovina is largely decentralised and mainly operates under the jurisdiction of the entities and cantons. However, within the State Ministry of Civil Affairs there is also an education sector responsible for the implementation of policies within the jurisdiction of Bosnia and Herzegovina across the board, as well as the establishment of basic principles for the coordination of previously agreed activities, entity authority plans, and international-level strategies, including for education.

At the national level, four framework laws related to education have been adopted: the Framework Law on Higher Education in Bosnia and Herzegovina; the Framework Law on Preschool Education in Bosnia and Herzegovina; the Framework Law on Secondary Vocational Education and Training in Bosnia and Herzegovina; and the Framework Law on Primary and Secondary Education in Bosnia and Herzegovina. As in any country with a strong level of local government, all laws in the Republic of Srpska, the cantons, and the Brčko District, as well as other regulations in the field of education, must be harmonised with the framework laws of Bosnia and Herzegovina. With this unity in mind, the following agencies have been established at a national level: the Agency for the Development of Higher Education and Quality Assurance; the Centre for Information and Document Nostrification in Higher Education; and the Agency for Preschool, Primary, and Secondary Education.

Since its establishment until recently (2007–…), the Agency for Preschool, Primary and Secondary Education (hereinafter referred to as the Agency) has been critical to the development and improvement of education quality in Bosnia and Herzegovina. Within its mandate, the Agency is responsible for: establishing the standards of knowledge and assessment of the achieved results, as well as developing the common core curricula in preschool, primary, and secondary education. It is also responsible for cooperation with pedagogical institutes and other institutions in: supporting, modernising, and developing of preschool, primary, and secondary education; advising relevant educational authorities on the design and implementation of new programme contents; and providing guidelines in the preparation of training programmes for teachers and other educational experts, that is, related to curriculum implementation and the like.

In addition to the Agency, the above-mentioned pedagogical institutes also play an important role in the processes of quality evaluation and professional supervision of educational institutions, as well as in monitoring and evaluating the work and professional development of employees themselves. In

Bosnia and Herzegovina, there are eight pedagogical institutes plus the Pedagogical Institution at the Education Department of the Brčko District Government. These institutes differ in their legal status in that some are established as administrative organisations or units within the Ministry of Education, while others are independent administrative units or organisations responsible to the cantonal government. However, regardless of their legal status, pedagogical institutes in Bosnia and Herzegovina and the Brčko District Pedagogical Institution generally serve a similar function: to link framework legislation and education policies with educational practices, a linkage which, in turn, directly affects the individual educational institutions (Working Group for Teachers Training 2016, p. 20). As such, pedagogical institutes monitor, assess, and evaluate the quality of educational institutions; establish programmes for teacher professional development; and organise seminars, courses, teacher assemblies, and so on.

Conclusion

The very dynamic movement of the world, accompanied by the availability of information, as well as social, political, and economic changes such as global pandemic, global warming, globalisation, and migrant crises—especially in BiH, poses many challenges for the field of education. In the face of this contemporary reality, educators need to abandon ex-cathedra lecturing strategies, which enshrine the mere presentation of data and facts, and begin to develop strategies more focused on coordination, guidance, direction, encouragement, and motivation. Let us remember what we used to learn ourselves. How much did our education actually prepare us to become effective, critical, and compassionate speakers, communicators, thinkers, researchers, and lifelong learners? If we are honest with ourselves, how much did our education simply prepare us to pass exams?

If we, as present and future educators and policy-makers, are to nurture a generation of learners well-equipped to meaningfully and sustainably deal with the unknown, ever-shifting challenges of the twenty-first century, it is quite clear that our education system in Bosnia and Herzegovina requires fundamental change. Firstly, the large number of teacher education faculties should be reduced: state colleges and faculties within state universities are proven to achieve much better results in initial teacher education, due to their quality programmes and teaching staff. In fact, given the current complex system(s) of education in Bosnia and Herzegovina, we believe that initial teacher education should be provided exclusively at state universities, so that the Agency for the Development of Higher Education and Quality Assurance would have the opportunity to approve and validate undergraduate curricula. That would provide the desired level of quality and representation of compulsory subjects in all programmes such as pedagogy, psychology, didactics, and methodics. Furthermore, it is important that excellent teachers with representative experience in classroom teaching are involved in initial teacher education as practical training teachers in their own classrooms so theory and practice could be interconnected. The curricula should significantly increase the number of pre-service practice hours for all teacher education faculties across the board so that the teaching student, especially in their final years, can spend much more time practising independently in the school environment and, thus, better prepare themself for the job market they will face upon graduation by applying and refining their acquired theoretical and pedagogical knowledge.

Teacher professional development training, on the other hand, should be organised in cooperation with different institutions and organisations. Going forwards, it is very important both that TPD is equally accessible to all educators across Bosnia and Herzegovina and that the TPD topics available are appropriate to the needs of the individual educator. Central to this drive for improved accessibility and cohesion is the space for teachers to share their experiences with colleagues, on regional and national levels, especially those colleagues in the same speaking area, which share long histories of common states and have similar education systems. Indeed, in order to coherently and consistently regulate the systems of teacher professional development across Bosnia and Herzegovina, it is necessary to license training programmes, to create annual catalogues (with exact programmes and lists of credits), and to more intensively connect higher education institutions with schools, and various other organisations. Simultaneously, it would be beneficial to build a promotion system for those teachers who show exceptional results in their TPD work, therefore developing a culture of continuous learning and ever-improving standards of teaching. Underpinning all of the above on a socio-economic level, it is essential to create the necessary material and financial conditions for teachers to afford to be absent from their paid work in order to attend diverse and enriching forms of TPD. Ultimately, as outlined in this chapter, Bosnia and Herzegovina has faced numerous challenges in its education systems before and especially since the end of the aggression. The present, highly complex socio-economic and political situation directly affects all structures of the state, including the education system. Nevertheless, some initial teacher education faculties, as well as their teachers, are achieving extraordinary results, as are some of the internationally renowned organisations facilitating teacher professional development. Although we are not yet progressing at the speed we would like, developments are being made every day and, in mind of the recommendations we made above, we are hopeful about the future of teacher education in Bosnia and Herzegovina.

References

Čehić, I., J. Bećirović-Karabegović, S. Rustempašić, and E. Selmanagić-Lizde. (2018). Ishodi učenja—implementacija i edukacija. *U saZnanj*, 1, 178–185.

Derida, Ž. (2002), *Kosmopolitike*. Beograd: Stubovi kulture.

Donaldson, G. (2013). Profesionalac 21. veka. In: V. V. Vidović and Z. Velkovski (Eds.), *Nastavnička profesija za 21. vek*. (pp. 13–23). Beograd: Centar za obrazovne politike.

Ministarstvo civilnih poslova Bosne i Hercegovine. (2016). *Radna grupa za obuku nastavnika. Izvještaj o inicijalnom obrazovanju i stručnom usavršavanju nastavnika sa preporukama, referentni materijal projekta Razvoj kvalifikacijskog okvira za opće obrazovanje*. Sarajevo: Ministarstvo civilnih poslova Bosne i Hercegovine.

Radulović, L. (2007). Standardizacija kompetencija kao jedan od pristupa profesiji nastavnik—kritički osvrt. *Nastava i vaspitanje*, 56(4), 413–434.

Rangelov-Jusović, R., V. V. Vidović, and M. Grahovac. (2013). Okvir nastavničkih kompetencija—pristup ATEPIE. In: V. V. Vidović and Z. Velkovski (Eds.), *Nastavnička profesija za 21. Vek* (pp. 24–39). Beograd: Centar za obrazovne politike.

Smajkić, S. (2004). *Obrazovanje nastavnika osnovne škole u Bosni i Hercegovini (1946–1986)*. Sarajevo: Pedagoška akademija.

Stewart, V. (2010). Raising teacher quality around the world. Retrieved from https://www.ascd.org/el/articles/raising-teacher-quality-around-the-world.

UNESCO. (2014). *Teaching and learning: Achieving quality for all*. 2013/14 EFA Global Monitoring Report. Retrieved from http://www.unesco.org/new/en/education/themes/leading-the-international-agenda/efareport/reports/2013/.

Vijeće ministara Bosne i Hercegovine. (2008). *Strateški pravac razvoja obrazovanja u Bosni i Hercegovini sa planom implementiranja za period 2008–2015*. Retrieved from http://fmon.gov.ba/Upload/Dokumenti/93c849e5-2b36-4d2e-8cfb-54b062eac6ff_Strateški%20pravci%20razvoja%20obrazovanja%20u%20Bosni%20i%20Hercegovini%20sa%20planom%20implementiranja,%202008.–2015.pdf.

Working Group for Teachers Training (2016). Report on Initial Education and Professional Development of Teachers with Recommendations; Reference Material of the Project: Development of the Qualification Framework for General Education. p. 20.

URL: https://ff.unibl.org/i-ciklus-nastavni-plan/uciteljski-studij (Accessed on 12.11. 2019).

URL: https://ff.unze.ba/razredna-nastava/nastavni-plan-i-program/elaborat-nastavnog-plana-na-odsjeku-za-razrednu-nastavu-2012-god/ (Accessed on 12.11. 2019).

URL: https://fpmoz.sum.ba/index.php?option=com_content&view=category&layout=blog&id=22&Itemid=132&lang=hr (Accessed on 12.11. 2019).

URL: https://pfb.unbi.ba/ (Accessed on 12.11. 2019).

URL: https://www.unmo.ba/ (Accessed on 12.11. 2019).

URL: www.pf.unsa.ba/index.php?option=com_content&view=article&id=339&Itemid=154 (Accessed on 12.11. 2019a).

URL: www.pfb.ues.rs.ba/studije.php (Accessed on 12.11. 2019b).

URL: www.untz.ba/uploads/file/nastava/studijski_prog_I_ciklusa/2018-19/FF_Razredna_natava_studijski_program_I_ciklus_2018_19-1.pdf (Accessed on 12. 11. 2019c).

URL: Evo zašto su 'ozloglašeni' privatni fakulteti u BiH postali popularni među mladima (bh-index.com) (Accessed on 01. 03. 2021a).

URL: Karta Evrope prema broju ljudi koji žive u inostranstvu: BiH apsolutni rekorder—Front Slobode (Accessed on 02. 03. 2021b).

URL: https://inskola.com/ (Accessed on 02. 03. 2021c).

8

Teacher Education in Croatia: Reforms and Challenges

Marija Sablić, Alma Škugor, and Marija Lesandrić

Introduction

Both initial teacher education (ITE) and continuous professional development are of the utmost importance to the education sector in every country
around the world, as the quality of teaching staff is one of the main factors
affecting the outcomes of the whole education process, including students'
achievements. Indeed, to date, initial teacher education (ITE) has been discussed from a wide range of perspectives, regarding its structure and curriculum; field experiences, coursework, and the interplay between them; as well as
the learning experiences of student-teachers (Darling-Hammond et al. 2010).
In Europe, the last decade was marked by education strategy creators' increased
focus on research findings, indicating a highly significant and positive relationship between competent teaching staff and the level of pupils' achievements (Vizek-Vidović and Domović 2013).

This chapter will present an overview of teacher education in Croatia over
a period of 25 years: from the early 1990s to the challenges and complexities
of the twenty-first century. There is a discrepancy within the Croatian education system between, on the one hand, the level of scientific achievements,
experiences, and practices, and, on the other, the transferred European education goals and models, as well as attempts to integrate and adapt various other
education models from around the world. The Europeanisation of Croatian

M. Sablić (✉) • A. Škugor • M. Lesandrić
Josip Juraj Strossmayer University of Osijek, Osijek, Croatia
e-mail: marija.sablic10@gmail.com

education has intensified since the beginning of the new millennium, amplified by the processes involved in attaining full EU membership in 2013. As such, systematic attempts have been made to develop new systems of general, vocational, higher, and adult education, with the effects of the Europeanisation of Croatian education noticeable on a legislative level, as well as in the adoption of the *National Pedagogical Standard for the Primary Education System* (2010) and the *National Pedagogical Standard for the Secondary Education System* (2010), along with their respective support agencies. The Europeanisation of Croatian education is also reflected in the introduction of the State Matura exam, the Bologna Process, and the development of the Croatian Qualifications Framework, with the key objectives of clarity and consistency of qualifications between Croatian and European education frameworks, and with the contemporary labour market. Cumulatively, these, and other, initiatives aim to render Croatia a knowledge society, in which lifelong learning is a key driver in an efficient and competitive economy (as initially stipulated within the 2000 Lisbon Strategy, and the 2010 *Europe 2020* programme). Nonetheless, instead of exclusively meeting European goals and fulfilling European models of education, Croatia's progress depends on being able to adapt European recommendations and templates according to the nation's particular needs, understandings, and realities, developing a coherent model of education from kindergarten to university.

At present, there are many disputes regarding the right solutions most applicable to the contemporary Croatian education system—stemming from the severance which took place in the early 1990s when Croatia declared its independence from the Socialist Federal Republic of Yugoslavia, including its system of education which had been marked by a socialist ideology. Following this declaration, the Homeland War (1991–1995) brought aggression against Croatia from the Yugoslav military, but a democratic transition was ultimately achieved and the independent and sovereign state of the Republic of Croatia was established—forming the foundation for Croatia's democratic contemporary education system. In this chapter, this education system and its reforms will be presented, then discussed together with some challenges and recommendations for the future of teacher education in Croatia.

The Education System in Croatia

The education system in the Republic of Croatia is organised mainly in terms of early and preschool education, primary education, secondary education, and higher education (see Fig. 8.1), comprising state-owned—and, to a much

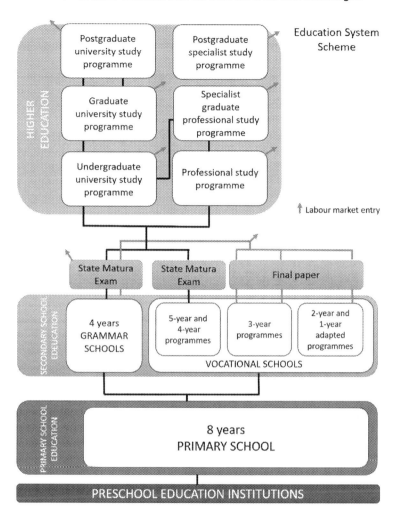

Fig. 8.1   Education system in Croatia

lesser extent, private—kindergartens, schools, and higher education institutions. State-owned kindergartens and schools are secular, and they operate according to the national framework curriculum.

Early and Preschool Education

Early and preschool education includes education, health care, nutrition, and social care programmes implemented in kindergartens in accordance with the *Act on Pre-school Education* (OG 98/19). Kindergartens are public institutions established by the Republic of Croatia, local government, religious communities, and other legal and civic entities. Early and preschool education is intended for children from the age of six months to enrolment in the first grade of primary school; however, only the year before starting the first grade of primary school is compulsory. Parents or guardians pay for day-care services, and their cost, quality, and availability differ on a regional basis. Across the regions, there are significant and systematic differences in the coverage of children in preschool programmes. In 2016, Croatia's coverage of children eligible for day-care programmes ranged from 5.6% to 40.4% and from 24.4% to 82.8% for kindergarten programmes (Central Bureau of Statistics 2017). However, the European Commission's Barcelona objectives (2013) stipulated that 33% of children eligible for attending nursery and 90% of children eligible for attending kindergarten should be covered by early years and preschool education programmes. As such, although Croatia is demonstrating an increasing tendency to include children in early and preschool education programmes, it was nonetheless among the eight EU member states that did not achieve the Barcelona objectives by 2015.

Primary School Education

In accordance with the *Act on Primary and Secondary Education* (2019), which was adopted in line with Croatia's constitution, primary school education lasts eight years (i.e. grades one to eight) and is carried out via regular and special programmes, which are compulsory and free of charge for all children aged six or seven to 15. There is a legal obligation that children who turn six by 1 April, before the beginning of that school year, directly enrol in the first grade of primary school. However, a child may also be enrolled earlier or later in exceptional cases, in accordance with their mental and/or physical needs, as per the request of parents or guardians, and the proposal of an expert panel, ratified by the decision of the state administration office (Act on Education 2019).

Furthermore, those pupils whose nationalities are minoritised in Croatia have the right to primary and secondary education in the language and script of their mother tongue, as formally acknowledged by the *Constitution of the Republic of Croatia*, the *Constitutional Act on the Rights of National Minorities*, and the *Act on Education in the Language and Script of National Minorities*. In practice, there are three education models organising the teaching of these groups of pupils. In Model A, all classes are taught in the language and script of the minority, with compulsory Croatian language classes for an equal number of periods. With this programme, pupils have the right and obligation to learn additional content relevant to their cultural community. In Model B, education is conducted bilingually: the science subjects are taught in the Croatian language, and the humanities subjects are taught in the language of the minority. Model C entails education in the Croatian language, with an additional two to five periods intended for learning and nurturing the minority's language and culture. The choice of model comes from the individual's preference and the resources allocated for implementing that model within the country's mainstream education system (Ministry of Science and Education 2019).

Across the board, primary education is divided into three cycles. During the first (i.e. first and second grades) and most of the second cycle (i.e. third, fourth, and fifth grades), pupils are taught by one teacher who teaches the subjects viewed as knowledge-based—mother tongue language, mathematics, and social science—and the subjects viewed as values-based—fine arts, music, and physical education. From fifth grade onwards, pupils are taught by subject teachers.

Secondary School Education

Upon completion of primary education, pupils have the opportunity to continue their education at a secondary level, although it is not compulsory. All pupils have equal right to enrol in the first grade of secondary school and according to the enrolment quotas passed by the Minister of Education for each school year. Depending on the type of education programme they offer, Croatia's secondary education institutions are divided into grammar schools, vocational schools, and art schools. Grammar schools run a four-year curriculum, and pupils complete their secondary education by passing a State Matura exam. The education of pupils in vocational and art schools lasts between one and five years and is completed by preparing and presenting a final paper. Pupils who have completed vocational education programmes may also take the State Matura exam, as well as gain a higher level of qualification by continuing their education. Grammar schools prepare their students for continuing education, vocational schools train them to enter the labour market (while offering opportunities for continuing education), and art schools allow for the acquisition of knowledge and the development of skills, abilities, and creativity in various artistic fields, with the possibility of continuing education.

Higher Education

The beginning of the twenty-first century was also marked by significant overall changes in Croatia's higher education system, which, in turn, brought changes to the teacher education system. The 2003 *Act on Scientific Activity and Higher Education* indicated the necessity of including Croatia in the European higher education system and the European research area.

Higher education institutions in the Republic of Croatia are universities (with their constituents—faculties and academies of arts), polytechnics, and colleges. Higher education is delivered through university and professional study programmes. Public institutions of higher education are founded by the state, and private universities, polytechnics, and colleges are established by their founders in accordance with legislation. Counties, cities, and municipalities can set up their own colleges contingent upon decisions passed by their representative bodies. In the academic year 2005/2006, reformed study programmes were introduced and students could no longer enrol in pre-Bologna study programmes. Moreover, this law increased the level of university autonomy. University autonomy encompasses independence and agency in terms of internal organisation; establishing educational, scientific, artistic, and professional programmes; finances; and so forth.

In 2001, at the Prague Ministerial Conference, Croatia signed the Bologna Declaration, committing to the now well-known Bologna Process. The main goals of the Bologna Process are fostering a quality assurance system, encouraging the mobility of teachers and students, opening up the possibility of easier diploma recognition, enabling greater flexibility in professional development, linking scientific and teaching work, increasing student competences, and facilitating faster labour market entry. The Bologna Process structures initial teacher education as follows: a two-cycle system of study programmes at some faculties (3 + 2 years of study or 4 + 1 years of study), as well as integrated study programmes (namely, a 5-year study programme at the Faculty of Teacher Education), with a uniform student workload expressed in European Credit Transfer System (ECTS) points and a diploma supplement as a prerequisite for qualitative analysis of the student's achievements and professional orientation (e.g. volunteer work, participation in conferences, sports competitions). In summation, the Bologna Process is characterised by one-term courses, the possibility of monitoring and evaluating the acquired competences via a mid-term exam, evaluating the student's attendance and participation in study programme tasks, more flexible teaching process design, and the student's participation in decision-making.

Education Reforms in Croatia

In Croatia, education system reforms are constant, but rarely have any been carried out systematically and completely. In fact, the majority of such reforms, to date, have not taken place from the bottom up—thus have not recognised the actual roles and needs of teachers, nor have they been truly related to teacher education, proving Barber and Mourshed's (2007) theory that there are no reforms or educational strategies that can succeed without teachers' engagement. Indeed, post-independence, there have been four key, but largely unsuccessful, attempts to reform the education system so far: the Project of the Croatian Education System for the 21st Century (2002–2003), the introduction of the Croatian National Educational Standard for Primary Schools (2005–2009), the Comprehensive Curricular Reform (2014–2016), and the current *School for Life* reform. The latter has been experimentally conducted in grades one and five of primary education and grade seven in biology, chemistry, and physics, as well as in the first grade of grammar schools (all subjects) and the first grade of four-year vocational schools (in general education subjects).

Within the *Project of the Croatian Education System for the 21st Century* (2002–2003), the contemporary situation was analysed and changes to the pre-tertiary education system were announced, with the most important goals being to train students for active citizenship and competitiveness in the labour market. The vision was to replace education based on memorising facts with education that facilitates creativity, problem-solving, knowledge application, and self-directed learning. Particular emphasis was placed on the notion of a learning society, non-formal and informal education, and defining new life-long learning skills such as ICT skills, foreign language skills, technological skills, entrepreneurship, and social skills. This project also proposed the introduction of a nine-year compulsory education programme—primary school (first to sixth grades) and lower secondary school (seventh to ninth grades). The project was intended to provide an extensive list of elective subjects, with evaluation based on the pedagogical concept of 'success for all'. However, despite numerous discussions and a completed proposal for introduction of the changes, the project was not adopted by the Croatian parliament on the basis of insufficient evaluation of the existing situation, low levels of actual reform capacity, and insufficient resources for the reform implementation. The project authors were also criticised for not having reached a consensus on the essential aspects of the proposed change, most notably the introduction of the nine-year primary education programme (Bognar and Lukaš 2016, p. 41).

Following this unsuccessful project, the *Plan for the Education System Development 2005–2010* (2005) was adopted. This document highlighted that Croatia's education system needed to change in order to prepare students for the global changes, such as active inclusion in an increasingly information-based society, easier and faster employment, and harmonisation between particular regions of the Republic of Croatia (e.g. Eastern Croatia was very damaged during the war from 1991 to 1995). Prior to this, in 2004, only 4.3% of Croatia's total GDP had been allocated for education; therefore, in the future financing of education requires monitoring of the actual shares of state budget funds and anticipation of the possibility of increasing total funds for education. The development plan comprised four key priorities: improving the quality and efficiency of the education system, fostering the continued professional development of teachers and other education employees, developing management strategies in the education system, and prioritising social cohesion as a goal. Unlike the previous project, the ministry supported this development plan, and, in 2005, the Croatian National Education Standard (CNES) was drafted as the basis for the change. Committees for each subject were formed, and teachers were involved in public debate. In addition, a cascade model of professional training readying teachers for meeting the CNES was suggested, but it was never fully implemented. Following the experimental application of the CNES, a group of scientists drafted a summary of the stage, but the complete text was never published (Bognar and Lukaš 2016, p. 43). Despite this bureaucratic limitation, there was significant progress in terms of pupils' contentment: pupils attending the schools that were experimenting with the CNES reported being more satisfied with their school and demonstrated greater progress in 8 out of 44 applied measures (Šakić et al. 2006).

However, in 2009, the CNES ceased to be relevant, and, instead, the main topic of the professional dialogues was the Croatian National Framework Curriculum for Pre-school and General Education in Primary and Secondary Schools (NFC), brought into force by the Minister of Education in 2011. Unlike previous plans and programmes, the NFC placed emphasis on competences and learning outcomes and provided teachers with the opportunity to select the content, methods, and conditions for achieving the teaching programme objectives. Preference was given to social constructivism and learner-centred teaching. By the end of 2011, the new government formed a team of experts to prepare a draft of the *Strategy for Education, Science and Technology* (2014), which was adopted following a public consultation. This strategy emphasised the importance of lifelong learning, as well as education based on the eight European competences:

* communication in mother tongue
* communication in a foreign language
* mathematical, scientific, and technological literacy
* digital competence
* learning to learn
* interpersonal, civic competences
* entrepreneurship
* cultural expression.

Following the adoption of the Strategy for Education, Science and Technology, the Comprehensive Curriculum Reform (CCR) started in 2016, supported by working groups comprising 430 experts selected after calls for applications. These expert groups created several thousand pages of curriculum documents. However, after the right-wing victory in the 2016 parliamentary elections, there were problems in implementing the CCR, and all expert group members resigned. Despite this change in government, there remained some political awareness of the need for education reform, which resulted most concretely in the 2019 *School for Life* project. School for Life prioritised curriculum reform and aimed at increasing students' problem-solving competences, their overall satisfaction with their school experience, and the enthusiasm of their teachers. Through these comprehensive curricular and structural changes, the Ministry of Science and Education plans to provide children and young people with a more useful and meaningful education—one which will empower them towards living a twenty-first-century life, entering the world of work, and continuing with education throughout their lives. From a staff perspective, these reforms will provide teachers, as well as other education professionals and employees, the opportunity to improve their professional competences, to enjoy greater autonomy in their work, to explore more creative work, and to be burdened with less administrative work. In turn, parents and guardians would experience a more intensive involvement in their children's education and school life. Since the beginning of the 2019/2020 school year, all of Croatia's elementary and secondary schools have been involved in the *School for Life* project. The first results of the project show that the reform 'School for Life' in its pilot phase has had correspondingly positive effects in relation to the expected changes in the educational system, Principals and teachers welcome autonomy and improvement of their own skills development; parents support independent learning (National center for external evaluation of education 2021).

In his observation of the world's education reforms through a political lens, Schleicher (2018) states that, in real life, there are many good ideas that remain stuck in a political implementation phase due to the fundamentally outcome-orientated nature of the formal political sphere, which, in turn, demands (over-)ambitious reform targets from the educational sphere. In light of this structural blockage, Schleicher states that it is easier to design a reform than to successfully implement it. Indeed, validating this line of thinking, Croatia's teachers have expressed their dissatisfaction with the current situation, that is, where decades of trying to implement education reforms have strictly started and ended with the leading figureheads in the Ministry of Science and Education and, indeed, with changes in government.

Applying an economic lens, Sahlberg (2010) argues that recent education reforms in Croatia have been not only politically motivated but also market-oriented. He argues that some common features of the market and the contemporary education system are standardisation and testing. This standardisation and prioritisation of testing, at the expense of student satisfaction and well-being, lead directly to narrowing the curriculum (i.e. to focus on test material), mandating testing (i.e. to produce uniformly comparable results from all students, regardless of their personalities, interests, and capabilities), increasing class sizes (i.e. to economise financially on teacher to student ratios), and reducing the length of teacher qualification programmes (i.e. to accelerate the supply of teaching graduates to the profession). Unfortunately, marketisation is the direction that the Croatian education system is also turning to, and no education reform has so far resulted in the changes which are most sorely needed—namely, the changes in the teacher education study programmes (information, media, and technology skills, innovation skills, leadership and cooperation) and respect for the needs of today's pupils. In summary, recent reforms have been much more focused on exam results than on students' real needs.

Moving forward, towards reforms better aligned with the actual needs of twenty-first-century students, Sahlberg and Oldroyd (2010) discuss important changes that are urgently required across many education systems in North Europe, such as extending the length of time students spend in education, improving the quality of that education, and tailoring it for entrepreneurship and sustainable economic development. Simultaneously, the teachers of today are responsible for educating young people from a generation defined by economic insecurity caused by austerity, exposure to new and evolving technologies, a need to be literate in peace and active citizenship, and unprecedented diversities of identity. Thus, in order to empower Croatia's young people to play their roles in both future economic sustainability and environmental sustainability, contemporary education policies must be based on a proper understanding of economic and environmental sustainability. Indeed, in any knowledge-based society, people need to be able to work proactively with knowledge, play with new ideas, collaborate with others, and adapt readily to unpredictable situations (Hargreaves 2003). Ultimately, these understandings of changing social life and educational environment should be taken into consideration by the designers of teacher education programmes in order to nurture teachers who will go on to be the key to positive, necessary socio-economic change, with the goal of creating an inclusive and sustainable society both within and outwith Croatia. However, at present, the gaps between policy reformulation, teacher education, and the classroom remain wide.

Teacher Education in Croatia

The current teacher education system in Croatia prepares teachers for working in a range of education institutions—preschools, primary schools, secondary schools, and schools for children with disabilities—and has changed significantly throughout history. With independence and the adoption of the constitution in 1991, numerous legislative changes were introduced, including to the education system, such as democracy, autonomy, decentralisation, and pluralism. Now, there are nine teacher education faculties spread across Croatia's universities, where future kindergarten teachers and future teachers are educated. The admission requirements for undergraduate early years and preschool education and teacher education study programmes are not harmonised throughout the country at present. Students enrol based on their secondary education grades and passing the State Matura exam—in their mother tongue language, foreign languages, and mathematics. At some faculties, prospective students must pass a general knowledge test and additional skills test (i.e. motor skills, artistic and musical skills, and fine arts skills). The cumulative points gained from secondary education grades, the State Matura exam, and the entrance tests give a score which determines the candidates' eligibility for enrolment.

Initial Education of Kindergarten Teachers

Until 1968, Croatia's kindergarten teachers were educated in secondary schools, and, later on, two- then three-year programmes were created. Since the 2012/2013 academic year, these professional study programmes have been run by universities and titled Early and Pre-school Education and

Teaching, which students can attend at undergraduate bachelor's level (three years, 180 ECTS) and graduate master's level (for two years, 120 ECTS). The completion of a university undergraduate programme suffices for working in a kindergarten; in practice, this means that prospective kindergarten teachers can fulfil the same job description and receive the same salary, regardless of whether they have completed a bachelor's degree or a master's degree. Indeed, often, kindergarten founders do not acknowledge the completion of a graduate diploma since it is not technically a requirement for the job, which is likely to be the main reason why the bachelor's programme is more popular. According to Central Bureau of Statistics data, about 500 students have graduated from the preschool education bachelor's programme in recent years, and projections show that by 2030, the system will need an additional 9150 kindergarten teachers if the 2013 Barcelona goals and the 2010 National Pedagogical Pre-school Education Standards are to be met, especially in counties in which the proportion of children covered by the preschool curriculum is currently low (Dobrotić et al. 2018). Therefore, in order to expand the coverage of these preschool programmes, it is essential to significantly increase preschool teacher education programme capacities.

Initial Education of Primary Teachers

The most important change in Croatia's teacher education took place in 1992, when teacher training schools—that is, two-year teacher training schools for subject teachers at the time—were incorporated into the higher education system and became colleges. Consequently, the study programme for subject teachers was extended to four years. This was extended to five years (and 300 ECTS credits) in the 2005/2006 academic year in line with the introduction of the Bologna Process. Higher education institutions have a great responsibility towards teacher training; it must design and implement curricula with, on the one hand, an optimum professional to scientific ratio and, on the other, pedagogical, psychological, didactic, and methodological training (Kostović-Vranješ 2016). Although teacher education programmes differ across Croatia, their common core consists of four components: subject study (e.g. science or literature), study of educational sciences (e.g. psychology, pedagogy, didactics, sociology, and philosophy of education), study of methodologies (e.g. qualitative and quantitative research methods), and professional pedagogical practice (e.g. compulsory time in school). Nonetheless, analysis of the professional and pedagogical practice gained through initial teacher education programmes carried out by Pušić et al. (2019) identifies the mismatch between teacher education and the real needs of students and schools, underpinned by insufficient cooperation between university faculties and education institutions themselves. Although the experience that students gain during their professional pedagogical practice is extremely valuable, especially given that it cannot be attained via any other means, it often remains inconsistent with the rest of their initial teacher education, due to the problem of fundamental gap between the theoretical knowledge taught on their programme and the practical skills learned from school placements.

Most initial teacher education programmes in Croatia are organised according to a simultaneous model that enables students to study professional and educational sciences at the same time. According to Eurydice (2018), a simultaneous model would mean that a student who has enrolled in a five-year integrated teacher education programme will either become a class teacher or become a class teacher with a subject specialism. Croatia's teacher education faculties offer the teacher education programme along with English or German language modules, as well as modules in fields such as fine arts, informatics, educational sciences, sustainable development, and Croatian. Unfortunately, however, these modules are not formally recognised in the labour market; rather, for example, hiring preference is given to a subject specialist in computer science who has completed a computer science education programme at a faculty of science. All the same, in recent years, Croatia's faculties of teacher education have been offering graduate specialist programmes, as well as undergraduate programmes, that teachers have come to recognise as offering a potential avenue for their lifelong learning.

In a situation perhaps unique to Croatia, out of the Central and Eastern European countries explored in this book, the faculty of teacher education in Pula (a coastal city in the very northwest of Croatia, close to the Italian border) offers teacher education in the Italian language. Pula is inhabited by a large number of students whose mother tongue is Italian and who have finished Croatia's Model A general education system for minority language education. Thanks to the definitively intercultural nature of this borderland city, there is a strong possibility that these graduates and future teachers will find employment educating the Italian community in the region.

Initial Education of Subject Teachers

Depending on the subject they will teach, the education of teachers for the upper grades of primary school (i.e. grades five to eight) and for secondary school usually takes place within the teacher education programmes at the faculties of social sciences and humanities and the faculties of science. When the programme for subject teachers was extended from four years to five years in the 2005/2006 academic year, it was split into two cycles. The undergraduate university programme lasts for three years, during which time the student earns 180 ECTS credits and meets the entry requirements for the graduate programme; then the graduate programme lasts for two years, during which time the student earns 120 ECTS credits. The student's time is approximately allocated to the relevant subjects as follows, with variation from university to university: 70–80% for their specialist subject/s; 3–5% for educational sciences; and 7–12% for subject methodologies; leaving 10–12% for other elements. Upon completion of their undergraduate programme, the student acquires their bachelor's title, and upon completion of their graduate programme the student acquires Master of Education title in their chosen specialist subject. However, the bachelor's has proven to be incompatible with the Croatian Qualifications Framework, which does not formally recognise the qualification within the labour market. Therefore, almost all of Croatia's bachelor's graduates also complete the graduate programme in order to find employment in schools. After completing both study programmes, the qualified teachers have the opportunity to continue their studies at postgraduate level.

The Professional Education of Kindergarten and Primary School Teachers

Put simply, professional training commences where initial teacher education ends (Craft 2000). Professional learning can take place on either an individual or a collective basis and, rooted in the school context, contributes to teachers' professional competences through diverse formal and informal learning experiences (Marcelo 2009), including postgraduate programmes. Teachers enrolling in postgraduate programmes in Croatia do not have their new specialisations formally recognised by the Croatian Qualifications Framework. Therefore, completing these study programmes brings them no concrete advantages in terms of seeking employment; rather the benefit is their personal satisfaction with acquiring new competences.

Furthermore, a one-year teacher traineeship is compulsory and considered an introduction into the teaching profession for kindergarten teachers and both primary and secondary teachers (as per the *Act on Pre-school Education* 2019, and the *Act on Primary and Secondary Education* 2019). In the course of the traineeship, the trainee works alongside a mentor (i.e. someone already employed in the role that the trainee seeks to enter)—the purpose is to empower the trainee for their future practical work. Post-traineeship, the trainee takes the licensing exam in order to become a licensed kindergarten teacher or teacher, an employment requirement in the Republic of Croatia.

Lifelong professional development is the last cycle of professional development for teachers in Croatia. The *Ordinance on Promotion of Class Teachers, Teachers, Professional Associates and Principals in Primary and Secondary Schools and Dormitories* (2019) governs this long-term procedure, as well as stipulating the pathway along which the teacher can advance to the position of mentor, advisor, and then outstanding teacher advisor. Teachers can be promoted to a new position if they fulfil the requirements, such as sufficient years of professional experience and sufficient hours of continuous professional development. A teacher can be promoted to mentor after 5 years of professional experience, teacher advisor after 10 years of professional experience, and excellent teacher advisor after 15 years of professional experience. The corresponding licences are renewed every five years. Croatia's teachers make decisions regarding their further professional training independently (Škugor and Sablić 2018), as it is not compulsory and the Ministry of Science and Education does not dictate either promotion or lifelong learning to them.

Professional training for teachers in Croatia mainly takes the form of attending lectures and seminars where teachers and/or scholars present their research findings and discuss education-related topics. Professional development in the form of workshops and teacher networks is much less common. This current situation is unsatisfactory for the teaching population, and Petrović-Sočo (2009), Vujičić (2011), and Miljak (2015) all emphasise the necessity of changing the nation's approach to teacher professional development. Namely, lectures and seminars should be replaced by approaches which will more actively facilitate positive change and growth in teachers' educational practice. Reflection is a vital tool in this regard. With reflection being a driving force in teachers' personal and professional growth (Valenčič Zuljan 2008), it is critical that Croatia's education professionals are encouraged and supported in becoming truly reflexive practitioners—that is, proactive individuals who check and research solutions to practical problems and are characterised by their ability to take an open approach to their work, underpinned by constant consideration and reconsideration of their practice (Šagud 2006, p. 7).

Challenges for the Future of Teacher Education in Croatia

In Croatia and across this part of the world, the structural changes that took place along with the development of a knowledge society and the Bologna Process have ultimately redefined the role of a modern teacher as someone who is no longer the sole source of knowledge for their students. In practical terms, the modern European teacher is expected to possess native and foreign language fluency, computer literacy, mathematical literacy, civic literacy, and entrepreneurial spirit. However, currently, one of the major problems with Croatia's teacher education programmes is their incompatibility with the aforementioned contemporary needs of students and the education system across the board.

With a vision of bridging this gap, as well as building upon recent reforms, Croatia's teacher education faculties are now working towards professionalising the education of educators and teachers in order to reach European standards. Such professionalisation entails building a broad basis of scientifically founded, empirically proven knowledge—regarding learning, teaching, and research methodologies—that fosters learning and teaching processes. This professionalisation guides teachers to act autonomously and competently as critical thinkers, in the best interests of their students, and in accordance with the standards and ethical rules of their profession. In turn, this approach should empower teachers to fulfil their potential as the most powerful drivers of positive change in the field. In practical terms, as mentioned earlier, these goals can be accomplished by increasing the amount of professional-pedagogical practice undertaken by future teachers during their studies and strengthening the cooperation between teacher education faculties and schools.

Going forward, education reform in Croatia must focus not only on education professionals but also on students. Students can be guided and supported so that they not only fulfil their personal goals but also contribute to broader social and economic developments (Croatian education system project for the twenty-first century 2002). A key first step in realising this vision of empowered, proactive students is rendering initial teacher education programmes attractive to highly motivated future teachers (e.g. in the form of modern and engaging course content), as well as rendering the admission process more selective (e.g. through the introduction of entrance exams, as per Finland's system).

None of the challenges or future directions highlighted here can be achieved without sustainable approaches. Indeed, Croatia now faces the dual challenges of motivating the most capable students to choose the teaching profession for their careers, while motivating the most capable current teachers to remain in the profession. This type of long-term approach will allow Croatia's economy and education system to elevate the working conditions, pay, and social status of the teaching profession—understanding that teachers are equal partners in education policy-making, recognised and valued as autonomous, creative, and thought-provoking experts with a wealth of first-hand experience to draw on.

Sustainable and inclusive approaches to policy-making should be matched within the education sector itself by continuously monitoring the quality of undergraduate and graduate programmes for future teachers, involving students in education research, introducing new technologies in teacher education, and providing further possibilities for postgraduate specialist and doctoral studies programmes in the teaching profession—all with a view to ensuring that the education of Croatia's teachers is genuinely lifelong. However, this lifelong learning should not simply depend on the goodwill of teachers themselves. Rather, it should be fully supported by a comprehensive professional licensing system that anticipates and facilitates the conditions for optimum professional development, from the very start to the very end of their careers—so that they can uphold and advance an education system which is truly open, flexible, and inclusive for all those who pass through it.

References

Barber, M., and M. Mourshed. (2007). *How the world's best performing schools come out on top*. London: McKinsey and Company.

Bognar, B., and M. Lukaš. (2016). Ostvarivanje bitnih promjena u nastavi u sjeni reformi obrazovnog sustava [Making significant changes in teaching in the shadow of educational reform]. *Život i škola*, 62(3), 39–53.

Cjelovita kurikularna reform [Comprehensive Curriculum Reform]. (2016). Zagreb: Ministarstvo znanosti, obrazovanja i sporta.

Craft, A. (2000). *Continuing professional development: A practical guide for teachers and schools* (Second ed.). London, UK: Routledge.

Darling-Hammond, L., X. Newton, and R. Chung Wei. (2010). Evaluating teacher education outcomes: A study of the Stanford Teacher Education Programme. *Journal of Education for Teaching*, 36(4), 369–388.

Dobrotić, I., T. Matković, and V. Menger. (2018). *Analiza pristupačnosti, kvalitete, kapaciteta i financiranja sustava ranoga i predškolskog odgoja i obrazovanja u*

Republici Hrvatskoj [Analysis of accessibility, quality, capacity and financing of early and pre-school education in the Republic of Croatia]. Zagreb: Ministarstvo za demografiju, obitelj, mlade i socijalnu politiku.

Državni zavod za statistiku Republike Hrvatske. (2017). *Osnovne škole i dječji vrtići i druge pravne osobe koje ostvaruju programe predškolskog odgoja, kraj šk.g. 2015./2016. i početak šk./ped.g. 2016./2017. Statistička izvješća* [Croatian Bureau of Statistics, Primary schools and kindergartens and other legal entities carrying out pre-school education programmes, end of the school year 2015/2016 and beginning of the school year 2016/2017. Statistical reports]. Zagreb: Državni zavod za statistiku Republike Hrvatske.

Državni pedagoški standard osnovnoškolskog sustava odgoja i obrazovanja [National Pedagogical Standard for the Primary Education System]. (2010). Narodne novine 90/2010.

Državni pedagoški standard predškolskog odgoja i obrazovanja [National Pedagogical Standard for the Pre-school Education System]. (2010). Narodne novine, 90/2010.

Državni pedagoški standard srednjoškolskog sustava odgoja i obrazovanja [National Pedagogical Standard for the Secondary Education System]. (2010). Narodne novine 90/2010.

European Commission. (2013). *Barcelona objectives.* Retrieved from http://ec.europa.eu/justice/gender-equality/files/documents/130531_barcelona_en.pdf.

Eurydice. (2018). *Obrazovanje i osposobljavanje odgojitelja, učitelja i nastavnika* [Education and training of kindergarten teachers, primary school and secondary school teachers]. Retrieved from http://www.mobilnost.hr/hr/sadrzaj/programi/mreze-i-inicijative/eurydice/.

Hargreaves, A. (2003). *Teaching in the knowledge society. Education in the age of insecurity.* New York: Teachers College Press.

Hrvatski nacionalni obrazovni standard [Croatian National Educational Standard]. (2005). Zagreb: Ministarstvo znanosti, obrazovanja i športa.

Kostović-Vranješ, V. (2016). *Inicijalno obrazovanje i profesionalno usavršavanje učitelja usmjereno prema osposobljavanju za promicanje obrazovanja za održivi razvoj* [Initial teacher education and training aimed at training to promote education for sustainable development]. *Zbornik radova filozofskog fakulteta u Splitu, 6–7,* 105–118.

Marcelo, C. (2009). Professional development of teachers: Past and future. *Sísifo. Educational Sciences Journal, 8,* 5–20.

Miljak, A. (2015). *Razvojni kurikulum ranog odgoja. Model Izvor II* [The Early Education Development Curriculum. Model Source II]. Priručnik za odgojitelje i stručni tim u vrtićima. Zagreb: Mali profesor.

Nacionalni centar za vanjsko vrednovanje obrazovanja [The national center for external evaluation of education]. Retrieved from https://www.ncvvo.hr/vanjsko-vrednovanje-odgojno-obrazovnih-ishoda-osnovne-skole/.

Nacionalni okvirni kurikulum za predškolski odgoj i obrazovanje te opće obvezno i srednjoškolsko obrazovanje [Croatian National Framework Curriculum for Pre-school and General Education in Primary and Secondary Schools]. (2011). Zagreb: Ministarstvo znanosti, obrazovanja i sporta.

Nove boje znanja: Strategija obrazovanja, znanosti i tehnologije [New Colours of Knowledge: A Strategy for Education, Science and Technology]. (2014). Zagreb: Ministarstvo znanosti, obrazovanja i športa.

Obrazovanje nacionalnih manjin [Education of national minorities]. (2019). Zagreb: Ministarstvo znanosti i obrazovanja. Retrieved from https://mzo.gov.hr/istaknute-teme/odgoj-i-obrazovanje/obrazovanje-nacionalnih-manjina/571.

Petrović-Sočo, B. (2009). *Mijenjanje konteksta i odgojne prakse dječjih vrtića, akcijsko istraživanje s elementima etnografskog pristupa* [Changing the context and educational practices of kindergartens, action research with an element of an ethnographic approach]. Zagreb: Mali profesor.

Plan razvoja sustava odgoja i obrazovanja 2005–2010 [Plan for the Education System Development 2005–2010]. (2005). Zagreb: Ministarstvo znanosti obrazovanja i športa.

Pravilniku o napredovanju učitelja, nastavnika, stručnih suradnika i ravnatelja u osnovnim i srednjim školama i učeničkim domovima [Ordinance on Promotion of Class Teachers, Teachers, Professional Associates and Principals in Primary and Secondary Schools and Dormitories]. (2019). Narodne novine 68/19.

Priprema, praćenje i evaluacija eksperimentalnog programa cjelovite kurikularne reforme „Škola za život" [Preparation, monitoring and evaluation of the experimental curriculum of the comprehensive curriculum reform "School for Life"]. (2019). Zagreb: Ministarstvo znanosti i obrazovanja. Retrieved from https://skolazazivot. hr/wp-content/uploads/2019/03/Evaluacija-eksperimentalnoga-programa-Cjelovite-kurikularne-reforme-%C5%A0kola-za-%C5%BEivot_final-LK.pdf.

Projekt hrvatskog odgojno-obrazovnog sustava za 21. stoljeće [The project of the Croatian educational system for the 21st century]. (2002). Zagreb: Ministarstvo prosvjete i športa.

Pušić, I., M. Sablić, and A. Škugor. (2019). Comparison of professional-pedagogical practice attended by the Faculty of Teacher Education students in Croatia and Austria. In: M. Kolar Billege (Ed.), *Contemporary themes in education—CTE. Book of abstracts* (pp. 55–56). Zagreb: University of Zagreb, Faculty of Teacher Education.

Sahlberg, P. (2010). Rethinking accountability in a knowledge society. *Journal of Educational Change*, 11(1), 45–61.

Sahlberg, P., and D. Oldroyd. (2010). Pedagogy for economic competitiveness and sustainable development. *European Journal of Education*, 45(2), 280–299.

Schleicher, A. (2018). *World class: How to build a 21st-century school system*. OECD Publishing. Retrieved from https://read.oecd-ilibrary.org/education/world-class_9789264300002-en#page4.

Šagud, M. (2006). *Odgojitelj kao refleksivni praktičar* [Educator as a reflective practitioner]. Petrinja: Visoka učiteljska škola.

Šakić, V., I. Rimac, V. Spajić-Vrkaš, L. Kaliterna-Lipovčan, Z. Raboteg-Šarić, A. Brajša-Žganec, R. Franc, M. Žebec, and T. Babarović. (2006). *Vrednovanje eksperimentalne provedbe Hrvatskog nacionalnog obrazovnog standarda (HNOS)* [Evaluation of the experimental implementation of the Croatian National Educational Standard (CNES)]. Zagreb: Institut za društvena istraživanja Ivo Pilar.

Škugor, A., and M. Sablić. (2018). The influence of experience on pre-service and novice teachers—The Croatian perspective. *European Journal of Teacher Education*, 41(2), 157–168.

Valenčič Zuljan, M. (2008). *Subjektivne teorije—cjeloživotno učenje* [Subjective theories—lifelong learning]. Rijeka: Hrvatsko futurološko društvo.

Vizek-Vidović, V., and V. Domović. (2013). Učitelji u Europi—glavni trendovi, pitanja i izazovi [Teachers in Europe—Major trends, questions and challenges]. *Croatian Journal of Education: Hrvatski časopis za odgoj i obrazovanje*, 15(3), 219–253.

Vujičić, L. (2011). *Istraživanje kulture odgojno-obrazovne ustanove* [Research into the culture of an educational institution]. Rijeka: Sveučilište u Rijeci, Zagreb: Mali profesor.

Zakon o odgoju i obrazovanju u osnovnoj i srednjoj školi [Act on Primary and Secondary Education]. (2019). Narodne novine 98/19.

Zakon o predškolskom odgoju i obrazovanju [Act on Pre-School Education]. (2019). Narodne novine 98/19.

Zakon o znanstvenoj djelatnosti i visokom obrazovanju [Act on Scientific Activity and Higher Education]. (2003). Narodne novine 123/03.

9

Teacher Education in the Republic of Serbia: Challenges, Possibilities, and Directions for Development

Olivera Gajić, Svetlana Španović, Biljana Lungulov, and Branka Radulović

Introduction: Teacher Education in the Republic of Serbia over the Last Three Decades

The end of the twentieth century and the beginning of the twenty-first century were marked by great change in the political and social lives of many European countries, including Serbia and its education system, in terms of the collapse of communist systems in Eastern Europe, an expansion of neoliberalism around the world, the globalisation and political unification of Europe, and the creation of the European Higher Education Area. The core idea was that a common education system could be established across the continent, based on common cultures and values.

Comprehensively analysing the development of the education system in the Republic of Serbia over the past three decades, especially with regard to teacher education and teacher professional development, reveals its underlying characteristics: constant demands for democratisation, alongside the pursuit of values, educational ideals, and a strategic objective. However, the significant evolutions that took place at the European level—such as globalisation, democratisation, knowledge management, and moves to accept diversities—were not the sole influences on the transformation of Serbia's old pedagogical practices, professional identities, and the competences of its

O. Gajić (✉) • S. Španović • B. Lungulov • B. Radulović
University of Novi Sad, Novi Sad, Serbia
e-mail: gajico@ff.uns.ac.rs

leaders, due to numerous social, cultural, economic, and other factors. Indeed, the early 1990s were characterised by tumultuous changes across and within every federal unit after the breakdown of the Socialist Federal Republic of Yugoslavia (SFRY) in 1992. During those years, Serbia underwent a phase of profound reorientation, centred on a series of civil wars and inter-ethnic conflicts, international economic sanctions, hyperinflation, a large-scale influx of refugees and displaced persons, bombing, a devastated economy, widespread poverty, isolation from other countries, a sharp class divide, and a major population decline. This crisis period brought the entire school system, including teacher education, to the point of degradation.

Analysis of the education system during the early 2000s suggested that, in spite of some strengths—such as a developed network of schools, especially primary schools, and solid potential in terms of the people involved in the sector—this was an inefficient system that functioned on the verge of poverty and undemocratically, falling far short of the expected level set by numerous parameters (e.g., UNICEF 2007). Huge social inequalities had emerged and persisted in Serbia, on a bigger scale than the average across Eastern European countries undergoing similar transitions. According to the data for 2007, the Gini coefficient (a statistical measure of wealth inequality between rich and poor, where 0 marks perfect equality of wealth) for Serbia was 29.7—for context, this coefficient was higher only in Romania among European countries (with a Gini coefficient of 31.0) (Gašić-Pavišić 2008). Serbia's Gini coefficient reached 39.6 in 2015.

Against this backdrop of profound wealth inequality, Serbia's education system was extremely centralised, with underdeveloped systems for the planning, management, administration, and monitoring of its functioning and effects. As such, there was both public dissatisfaction with teachers' competences and commitment, and teachers' own dissatisfaction with their socio-economic status and working conditions. This poor quality was largely due to the lack of psychological, pedagogical, and methodical education available via teacher education (Kovač-Cerović 2006).

Teachers, left to fend for themselves and suffering inertia, were thus put in a position where they depended on the conscience and resources of their individual schools to provide the necessary funding; as a result of such a poorly resourced sector, the interest young people took in the teaching profession declined. What marked this as a period of crisis, despite the initiatives of NGOs and international organisations, was the fundamental lack of goals, coordination, and a coherent, systematic policy for teacher professional development within Serbia itself (Gajić 2007). Over the past 30 years, teacher education in this part of the world has been based on traditional pedagogical doctrine. With this predominance of theoretical instruction, students received little pedagogical and methodological practice, and teacher-mentors were neither appropriately prepared nor motivated for this type of work, thus weakening the teacher education system.

As a part of the political and social changes initiated in Serbia since 2000, a number of reform initiatives were undertaken to improve and harmonise the national education system—across almost all segments and at all levels—with contemporary European education policies aimed at the fulfilment of the Lisbon Strategy (2000–2010). However, this transition period in Serbia was characterised by discontinuities in terms of the creation and implementation of the education policy (Vujačić et al. 2011). Numerous changes were initiated with the aim of democratisation, decentralisation, depoliticisation, and the improvement of the quality and efficiency of education, inevitably impacting the teacher education system as well. However, the potential efficiency of such ambitious education reforms was undermined by the rapid pace of new initiatives, as well as chaotic and volatile changes, leading to major professional challenges for teachers, especially regarding the fairness due to lack of transparency, high centralisation, and reduced teacher autonomy in the education system in general (Kovač-Cerović 2006; Gajić 2007).

Considering the discontinuities and volatility marking Serbia's teacher education sector during the early 2000s, including the process of selecting prospective teaching staff, it is perhaps unsurprising that the lack of standard requirements for candidates' education resulted in poor selections of personnel for the teaching profession. As mentioned earlier, these hasty and insufficiently prepared and organised reforms had significant counterproductive effects. First and foremost was a disparity of reforms' outcomes in primary, secondary, and higher education, as well as a confusion between teacher education profiles and their corresponding roles, which resulted in a significant lag, stagnation, and even decline in the quality and efficiency of Serbia's education system (Kamenov 2006).

Aware of the fundamental centrality of teachers to all reforms, education policy-makers sought to take a number of measures to change and innovate the position, competences, and role of teachers. They highlighted possible new directions for pedagogical and developmental activities, professional advanced training, and continuous professional development for preschool teachers, primary school teachers (i.e. classroom teachers), and teachers of various subjects across all educational levels.

Alongside the need for reform came the need to constantly review the quality of future teachers' education and subsequent teacher training, in line with the development of psychological-pedagogical theories, information and communication technologies (Radulović and Gajić 2018; Županec et al. 2018), innovation technologies (Radulović et al. 2016), as well as student achievement (Gagić et al. 2019). Indeed, Rajović and Radulović (2007) noted that the data on students' achievements in Serbia, taken from a number of contemporary national and international evaluations, indicated problems with the type of knowledge teachers acquired throughout their initial professional education. It was clear that many diverse, complex, and changeable tasks were being put before teachers (Radulović and Stojanović 2019), especially in terms of the rapid development of science, and technical and technological innovations.

During the last decade, the education system of Serbia has been increasingly adapting and directing towards European values and tendencies (more inclusive and democratic education environment, student-centred learning and teaching, curricular reform of primary and secondary schools, dual education, and digitalisation), which is reflected in the initial education and especially in the professional development programmes for teachers. In that sense, teacher education in Serbia has gone through various phases over the last 30 years, from traditional and an inert one burdened with social inequalities and ethnic conflicts, through high centralisation, material difficulties, and reduced teachers' autonomy, to promoting, although formally, contemporary pedagogical concepts and approaches to teaching. However, the social status and position of teachers remains unchanged and is still at a significantly low level.

Reforms in Serbia's Teacher Education in Light of Global Trends: Perception of Changes in Practice

As already mentioned, the past three decades were a period marked by processes of social transformation and changes in education policies across Central and Eastern Europe. Mitter (2007) carried out a comparative analysis of the transformation processes in Poland, Hungary, the Czech Republic, and Russia and concluded that while differences were visible in several areas, their common characteristics were the collapse of communist systems and the belief that education policy was the element most responsible for societal progress and development. Nonetheless, there were differences in education policies among the countries of Central and Eastern Europe and Russia, regarding the introduction of market economy principles, the stabilisation of democratic institutions, the emergence of civil societies, and so forth. In Serbia, this period was referred to as a transition period. Beara and Jerković (2015, p. 232) outline how Serbia's transition in the education sector involved the democratisation of schools, changes in funding pathways, and the modernisation of the education process itself: 'the education system can also be seen as a tool of transition, since it is a responsibility of this system to educate young people for the future aspirational society'. Against this backdrop of society-wide change, when turbulent changes occurred in the education sector, especially regarding the decentralisation of school systems, greater school autonomy, structural and programme reforms, initial education, and teacher professional development were crucial.

Entering the twenty-first century, education reform in Serbia experienced a major boom in the first decade, when changes were planned across all levels of education—from designing nine-year primary education in three cycles to a thorough higher education reform in line with the principles of the Bologna Declaration, which Serbia signed in 2003. Indeed, when Jerković et al. (2011) compared the proclaimed and achieved changes in this period, they found that higher education reform was more of a reflection of political efforts to align with the European Union than any internal need for changes. On the other hand, they note that these reforms also brought positive developments to Serbia's education sector: increased competition among teachers, schools, and faculties; more developed awareness of education costs; and a noticeable increase in the interest taken by parents, pupils, and students in their rights.

Despite signing the Bologna Declaration in 2003, genuine reform in Serbia only began in 2005, when the national *Law on Higher Education* was brought in—prescribing the mandatory introduction of three study cycles, accreditation, the quality assurance of study programmes, the European Credit Transfer System (ECTS), and other changes in line with the principles of the Bologna Declaration. However, the law's implementation was characterised by numerous difficulties and criticisms, in particular with regard to the distinct bureaucratisation of the accreditation procedures of study programmes and higher education institutions. In this bureaucratisation, the quality of actual education content was neglected, while the formal transition to meet Bologna demands was prioritised (Antolović 2017).

In 2002, prior to signing the Bologna Declaration, Sombor's faculty of education started the *Teacher Education Development Programme in Serbia—STEP*, which was proposed by the national Ministry of Education and Sports and funded by Finland's Ministry of Foreign Affairs. The aim of the project was to co-develop a modern and transparent curriculum for teacher education in Serbia, drawing on support and collaboration from Finnish teacher education experts. Key focuses included adopting credit points as a course measurement system, fostering respect for the student workload, transition from traditional towards interactive teaching, offering a free choice of advanced studies, integrating studies into professional practice, and affirming elective subjects. The final version of the framework programme generated via this international cooperation was adopted by the University of Novi Sad in 2004 (Tornberg et al. 2005).

Following the transformation of teaching academies with the status of advanced education schools into teacher faculties and faculties of education in 1993, during the subsequent first accreditation cycle, in 2008, these faculties successfully created study programmes following Bologna criteria: one-semester courses, using the ECTS system, balancing the student workload, and so forth. Zlatković and Petrović (2011) examined the compatibility of study programmes across six state-owned faculties and found that there were differences in terms of several parameters. According to their findings, inconsistencies such as differences in the number of offered subjects or differences in the value of ECTS allocated to the same subject across multiple faculties impeded the mobility of students from one faculty to another. Also, differences between faculties were noticed with regard to the number of subjects in certain scientific fields, as one faculty dominated in the fields of mathematics and the natural sciences, while another dominated in the fields of language and literature. Zlatković and Petrović (2011, p. 60) recommended harmonising teacher education programmes across the faculties, in order to establish programmes that would provide more towards the 'creation of the required teacher competences throughout the Republic of Serbia'.

Against this backdrop of the lack of continuity between Serbia's teacher education institutions, recent research has further explored the imbalanced, disjointed nature of teachers' roles in enacting contemporary education reform. The results of research carried out via the Teacher talks for teachers RANON project explore contemporary changes in the education system with striking findings (Pantić and Čekić Marković 2012). The project's data were collected through focus group interviews across 25 groups, cumulatively consisting of teachers and other school staff from 25 Serbian cities, mainly centres of school administrations. The prevailing view expressed was that decentralisation imposed a lot of administrative responsibilities on teachers and that their autonomy remained limited to their work in the classroom. Teachers emphasised that they had not been prepared for the implementation of new trends, as they felt they had been positioned as the implementers of the reforms, while having no influence on decision-making (Pantić and Čekić Marković 2012, p. 11):

There is evidence of apathy and dissatisfaction with the current system and the feeling of teachers that they do not represent a significant link in the decision-making process, while many of them believe that the current educational policies and strategies remain unclear and do not fully understand the entire regulation.

More broadly, between 2000 and 2010, focus groups and individual interviews with teachers, parents, students, principals, experts, and decision makers were key mechanisms for gathering the views of diverse stakeholders regarding changes in the education system. The majority of such research pointed to a worrying trend, which is summed up by Pavlović (2011, p. 93): the high expectations of reform initiatives had 'turned into an experience of saturation and "fatigue of change"'. As noted earlier, teachers reported that the pace of change was too fast and imposed in a top-down manner, meaning that they were not sufficiently prepared and that the appropriate risk assessments were missing. Serbia's teaching community further stated that they were not sufficiently empowered to enact the changes—due to inappropriate initial education and inconsistent vocational training programmes—while professional development policy simply resulted in maintaining the 'status quo in classroom teaching practices and [the] continuous degradation of the teaching profession' (Pavlović 2011, p. 75). These findings highlight the problem of teachers' excessive workloads and insufficient agency during reform trends. However, on a more promising note, this research also pointed to positive developments in Serbia's education policy throughout the first decade of the twenty-first century: foreign language teaching, introduction of elective subjects, greater range of textbooks offered, increased participation of parents in decision-making processes, and so forth.

The Main Characteristics of the Existing Initial Teacher Education System

The Republic of Serbia has a relatively short history of teacher education and training, the beginning of which dates back to the second half of the eighteenth century and the rule of the Habsburg monarchy (Kostić 1974). At the time, teachers took courses aimed at their professional and moral education. Subsequently, however, the poor quality of teaching and education in Serbia's schools during the nineteenth century increased the need for teacher education and advanced training (Gavrilović 1999). The twentieth century brought significant progress for teacher education in Serbia, in the form of the establishment and development of teacher training colleges, which are faculties of education at the country's major universities today.

However, at present, Serbia's teacher training colleges and faculties of education that primarily educate primary school teachers are not yet supplemented by special faculties for subject teacher education for primary- and secondary-level teaching. Thus, future teachers may choose a teaching module within the existing study programmes (e.g. physics and mathematics) or take specific courses in the fields of pedagogy, psychology, and teaching methods within select study programmes. Despite the continuous efforts to improve the competences of future teachers, clarity still seems to be lacking regarding what constitutes 'high-quality' teacher education. Indeed, based on the low number of courses and the abbreviated length of education that can technically be called 'teacher education', it is evident that the field is underdeveloped (Pantić and Wubbels 2010)—mainly limited to a few pedagogical subjects added to other courses not originally developed as an integral part of the teacher education programme itself (Rajović and Radulović 2007).

This insufficiency in the provision of initial teacher education has led to an increasing need for continuous advanced teacher training for in-service teachers, which has resulted in the creation of a professional development system. The reform and promotion of teacher professional development in Serbia began in 2002, when education employees' continuous professional development was made a legal obligation. Subsequently, the process of teacher training has been further developed and improved.

The national document, *Strategy for Education Development in Serbia 2020* (2012), and the corresponding action plan provide, inter alia, strategic policies, measures, and actions aimed at creating a national teacher professional development system for all levels of education. These documents highlight the importance of and the need for a well-suited and well-resourced teacher professional development system, through which teachers can acquire all necessary professional competences for their professional practice. Professional societies support this bid for teachers to enhance and improve their competences by organising specialist conferences, where teachers have the opportunity to learn about contemporary teaching approaches and share their experiences with each other. Indeed, professional societies are a specific and important aspect of contemporary teacher education due to their prevalence throughout the country.

However, there is still no single, uniform answer to the question of what constitutes good-quality teacher education, both in professional circles and among the general public. Most often, proposals for improvement in the education sector are framed as a need to reform the teacher education system, study programmes, and the concept of 'professional development' (Kovač-Cerović 2006). Such an improvement would increase the quality of teachers' initial education, which should be more focused on the contemporary pedagogy, innovative approaches to teaching, and more practice-related education, which will also respect teachers' previous experience and specifics of their work within the professional development. One of the key changes would be the establishment of specialised faculties for the education of subject and vocational teachers, which would significantly contribute to the development of the competences of these teachers and enhance the quality of teaching.

Accreditation of Higher Education Institutions and Study Programmes

At present, internal and external evaluations are carried out in order to check the validity and quality of higher education institutions and programmes at all levels of studies, as stipulated by the *Law on Higher Education* (2018). On the whole, these procedures verify whether or not a higher education institution meets the necessary conditions (e.g. the required number of teachers) to facilitate high-quality education for young people. The external evaluation procedure enables systematic monitoring of the work of higher education institutions. The internal evaluation procedure is carried out by students, who evaluate both the teacher and the teaching process (Radulović et al. 2019). In this way, teachers receive feedback from students at the end of the course, allowing them to improve and develop the quality of their work for the next school year. Taking into account the results of this internal and external evaluation, higher education institutions are offered the opportunity to innovate both course contents and entire study programmes, in order to follow international pedagogical trends and the demands of the labour market.

Forms and Models of Initial Teacher Education in Serbia

According to the *Strategy for Education Development in Serbia 2020* (2012), three basic models for initial teacher education have been developed: simultaneous, consecutive, and transitional. Within the simultaneous model, the future teacher undertakes studies in a field of teaching until they complete master's level, at the same time as gaining pedagogical and other competences important for the teaching profession, in close connection with their chosen field. This is the predominant form of initial teacher education in Serbia, delivered at 36 faculties across six state universities.

Within the consecutive and transitional models, the required competences can be acquired at different points, that is, if a student wants to become a teacher after obtaining a master's degree in a particular profession, they are obliged to acquire an additional 36 ECTS credits in pedagogical, psychological, and methodological fields and school practice. These two initial teacher education models are designed for students of other study programmes, such as technical or technological sciences, as well as for teachers who did not have access to a sufficient number of subjects during their previous education.

Indeed, achieving 36 ECTS has been a legal obligation for every teacher in Serbia since 2009, perhaps an attempt at reducing the great disparities between the faculties that educate teachers. In 1999, Bjekić found that pedagogical-psychological subjects were under-represented in the curricula of teacher education faculties, amounting to, at most, 19% of the total number of subjects, which converts to just 2–10% of course content in terms of number of hours. This under-representation was one of the reasons why the Tempus Foundation (a foundation committed to promoting and implementing EU and other education programmes in Serbia) launched its Master Programme for Subject Teachers in Serbia (MASTS) in 2010, aiming to establish a master's programme for subject teachers at five state-run universities as a means of providing students from non-education faculties with the necessary pedagogical competences during their initial teacher education.

The objectives and curricula of these study programmes were synchronised with both Europe-level regulations (e.g. the *Common European Principles for Teacher Competences and Qualifications*, CEDEFOP 2010) and national-level regulations (i.e. issued within the Republic of Serbia). The primary objective of these study programmes was to provide teaching staff with high-quality professional competences, which would enable them to perform their professional roles independently, create a critical attitude towards their own practice, and develop responsibility for improving both the efficiency of their own work and the work of their education institution more widely. In addition, specific objectives of this study programme included developing cultures of communication, cooperation, teamwork, inclusiveness, professional ethics, and teacher identity; affirming different forms of learning (e-learning, experiential learning, self-directed learning, etc.); and supporting professional development via professional development programmes, and specialist and doctoral studies.

In terms of school practice, the study programme was designed to stimulate students' enthusiasm and aptitude for research, as well as their reflexivity, which are among the core goals of all present and future teacher education programmes in Serbia today. However, reflexivity poses real challenges in practice, as systematic reflection is very demanding for many students, future teachers, and even current teachers. To some extent, these difficulties arise from the sheer complexity of reflection required in taking a holistic approach to solving problems in education settings (Simić 2014). Going forwards, it is worth being mindful of the evidence that reflecting after practice has a greater effect on changing educators' beliefs than reflecting before practice (Tillema 2000), meaning that it is essential for students and teachers alike to gather and reflect on their experiences and implicit biases after school visits during their initial education.

In addition to the aforementioned master's programme, lifelong education programmes have been launched at all universities in the Republic of Serbia, within which it is possible to obtain 36 ECTS credits of pedagogical, psychological, and methodological education and practice, which are also sufficient for those who have already fulfilled the legal requirement of a master's qualification in education.

Problems in Initial Teacher Education

The main problems facing the teaching profession in this part of the world today, most often cited in the literature, are the low socio-economic status of teachers and the low interest of students to become teachers in certain subjects (informatics, psychics, mathematics, etc.). Indeed, according to Leclercq (1996), the contemporary loss of prestige in the teaching profession has a strong influence on the morals and motivation of teachers. Furthermore, a study by Geske et al. (2015) states that only about 1% of parents who were asked wanted their children to become teachers, and the most significant reasons given for such responses were low earnings and occupational stress. As such, it is unsurprising that the country faces a shortage of high-quality prospective teachers. This shortage can be dated back to the 1980s, with the personal values systems of the nation's young people being directed by capitalist and neoliberal ideologies towards more pronounced consumerist and/or materialistic values, as opposed to spiritual, altruistic, and aesthetic values and self-development values (Arsenović-Pavlović et al. 1989). Simultaneously, under late capitalism, teaching is a profession that is allocated a poor level of financial compensation, meaning that many potential teachers either cannot afford such low pay or do not want such low pay for their work, and thus avoid the field.

For those who do enter the teaching profession in Serbia, acquiring competences and job satisfaction are major strengths of the modern reforms in initial teacher education. In fact, various studies (e.g. Beijaard et al. 2000; Cristina-Corina and Valerica 2012; Marušić 2013) have shown that the moral responsibility and social importance of the profession correlate positively with job satisfaction. After all, a sufficiently trained teacher is able to share their knowledge with students in a meaningful way and perhaps pique the interest of students in their taught subject—or indeed in a future of their own in the teaching profession—through well-prepared lessons and interactive teaching methods.

However, a particular problem encountered by the education system in Serbia is that a significantly higher proportion of students are drawn to the role of primary school teacher, while there is a large deficit of teachers in the areas of mathematics, physics, and English. As such, going forwards, seeking ways to right this imbalance and make other teaching roles more attractive and socio-economically viable for prospective teachers is essential for the future sustainability and success of Serbia's teaching profession. Furthermore, special problem is the education of teachers in vocational subjects, which is indicated by the fact that in Serbia there are no higher education institutions where the primary activity is the education of vocational teachers. With a view to tackling these and other challenges, the *Strategy for Education Development in Serbia 2020* (2012) defines the development commitments of higher education, thus more neatly shaping the structure of educational and research activities towards meeting the developmental needs of the economy and society in general. Such a vision of academic development is characterised by the following key features: quality, relevance, efficiency, coverage, internationalisation, student mobility, and modernisation of academic studies—making higher education funding a real investment in the future of Serbia and its young people.

The Main Characteristics of the Existing Teacher Professional Development System in Serbia

Current directions of change in the educational sciences can be characterised by the increasing focus on the society of knowledge (Hargreaves 2003), competency-based education, teaching directed towards learning outcomes (Lungulov 2017), student-centred education, self-regulated learning (Zimmerman 2008), online education, and so forth. These contemporary focuses and directions require the role of the teacher to shift and facilitate accordingly, via the acquisition of new competences. As such, an appropriate initial education and continuous professional development for all teachers is positioned as one of the most important targets for contemporary education policy in many parts of the world (Hargreaves 2001). In addition, the results of contemporary research indicate the profound importance of teachers— including their personalities and professional traits—for students' success in the educational process, as well as for stimulating their motivation, interest, and desire to learn (e.g. Rotgans and Schmidt 2011; Pinker 2014), rather than student characteristics as was previously thought (e.g., Demie 2001).

In Serbia, teacher competences are defined within the *Standard of Competences for the Profession of Teachers and Their Professional Development* (2011) as the roles teachers are socially expected to fulfil, and which form the basis of the contents of their training. This document supports and clarifies Serbia's teacher professional development policy and serves as a framework for teachers' self-reflection and self-evaluation of their own competences. The national standards define four key areas of teacher competences: the teaching area, the subject, and the teaching methods (K1); learning and teaching (K2); support for student personality development (K3); and communication and cooperation (K4). Each of these areas contains competences for teachers to acquire and develop, on the basis of which they will be evaluated: knowledge, planning, implementation, evaluation, and improvement (*Rulebook on Continuous Professional Development and Acquisition of the Title of Teachers, Pre-school Teachers, and Expert Associates* 2017).

Possibilities and Directions for Improving Teacher Professional Development

Teachers in Serbia receive significantly differing initial educations depending on where they study, in the sense that there are currently huge variations in the quality, outcomes, structure, and duration of study programmes that educate future teachers (Kovač-Cerović 2006). Thus, with a view to improving the quality of teacher education Serbia's teachers have access to, the *Law on the Fundamentals of the Education System* (2019) stipulates that all teachers, pre-school teachers, expert associates, and principals employed in education institutions must engage in continuous professional development.

On a national level, professional development policy is defined in the *Rulebook on Continuous Professional Development and Acquisition of the Title of Teachers, Pre-school Teachers, and Expert Associates* (2017), which provides guidance for the following forms of teacher professional development: seminars, trainings, expert conferences, summer and winter schools, and professional trips and study visits. Despite this diversity, in practice, most attention is paid to attending accredited seminars or training programmes, that is, the dominant forms of teacher professional development in Serbia today. National regulations oblige all teachers to fulfil 100 hours of professional development over five years, out of which a minimum of 80 hours must be spent attending accredited seminars and training programmes. All proposed training programmes are reviewed by the Institute for the Advancement of Education, and then those accredited and approved are published in the catalogue listing offerings for the upcoming two to three school years. Teachers and schools have the ability to independently select programmes, contact organisers, and make use of their services (Stanković 2011) in accordance with their own preferences and needs. As an additional form of motivation, teachers are offered instruments for self-evaluating their own professional competences in order to select the seminars most valuable for them.

However, despite their widespread popular use, seminars and trainings are highly 'traditional' forms of teacher development—fundamentally limited in their efficacy by being one-way, sporadic, and detached from both policy reforms and practical implementation (Polovina 2010). Such popular usage may be attributed to the comparative low financial cost incurred in participating. The financing of teacher professional development is not regulated in Serbia, meaning that although education institutions and local governments sometimes fund this vital work, teachers generally fund their training and professional development themselves.

The Challenge of Education Policy

Teacher professional development has become a topical issue in teaching community within the primary and secondary education in Serbia, especially since the start of the century. Since then, numerous laws have been amended; rulebooks have been formulated; centres have been established; professional development programmes have been accredited; and continuous professional development has been made a necessity for all employees working in the education sector. However, despite these indicators of progress in teacher professional development, there are many evident problems and challenges hindering the current system—from the level of teachers themselves to the level of national policy.

Comprehensive research examining the efficiency of teacher professional development programmes and their effect on the quality of teaching and students' learning shows that there is a significant gap between the programmes offered and the real effects in practical work (Pešikan et al. 2010). The same research has identified further shortcomings and limitations in the current system, including the limited competence and experience of programme organisers, the brevity of programme durations, the process of programme accreditation, the inappropriate evaluation of programme implementation, and the inability to monitor the effects of training in teaching practice.

In a similar vein, research by Andelković (2017) found that teachers in Serbia gave the lowest scores to professional development programmes, in terms of rating the sources of their professional knowledge and advanced training. This is to say that teachers find that the professional development programmes offered to them contribute the least to improving the quality of their teaching, when compared to other forms of professional development, such as personal experience and practice, studying literature, and cooperation with colleagues. As such, Andelković (2017) highlighted that many of Serbia's teachers question the practical applicability of the knowledge gained via professional development programmes.

Indeed, striking a balance between theoretical knowledge of academic disciplines and the development of practical professional skills is a continually present topic in contemporary scientific research and professional debates (Domović 2009). Studies on existing teacher education in the region (Zgaga 2006; Rajović and Radulović 2007; Macura-Milovanović et al. 2010) clearly show that existing teacher education largely covers theoretical knowledge and subject-related knowledge, while practical experience of the real classroom instruction is minimal or, in some cases, absent.

Finally, it is important to note here that teachers' opinions have been ignored in the process of defining national standards for teacher competences. Neglecting teachers' opinions in the process of creating standards can lead to their resistance to these standards or to rendering the standards irrelevant to their profession (Radulović et al. 2010). For example, Serbia's teachers highly value knowledge and skills with regard to raising children, but this group of competences is neglected in teacher education and training programmes (Pantić and Wubbels 2010). Fundamental discrepancies like these will only be alleviated by teachers being more frequently invited to be involved in the creation, implementation, and evaluation of their own professional development.

Tensions and Challenges in the Process of Transforming Serbia's Teacher Education Systems

Some of the main challenges influenced by societal changes during the last three decades in Serbia regarding the teacher education mentioned in previous chapters can be summarised into a few crucial conclusions. Serbia's education system still faces serious criticism from both the scientific and professional public for a number of pivotal reasons: insufficient investment in the field, prevailing traditionalism, centralisation, dissatisfaction of teaching staff, and general stagnation or inertia at all levels of the system. Accordingly, the initial and professional education of future teachers faces many challenges. Numerous papers have examined the shortcomings of initial teacher education in Serbia and the region (e.g. Zgaga 2006; Rajović and Radulović 2007; Pantić and Wubbels 2010), with the most commonly identified shortcomings being related to the focus on subject knowledge at the expense of practical experience and the achievement of crucial competences—making personal experience and professional practice the most common ways of developing competences.

The situation is very similar with regard to teacher professional development. Findings from theoretical and empirical research, qualitative analysis, and the evaluation of professional development programmes (i.e. Kovač-Cerović 2006; Rajović and Radulović 2007; Pešikan et al. 2010; Andelković 2017), as well as teachers' personal experiences and observations, point to how the traditional system of professional development remains still dominant in Serbia, despite its neglect of the needs, prior knowledge, experiences, and personal interests of the teachers it exists to serve.

Despite some efforts to create the supportive environments and resources necessary for comprehensive reform management—that is, monitoring the efficiency of applied measures defined by *Strategy for Education Development in Serbia 2020* (2012)—it is essential to make significant efforts towards building institutional and administrative capacities, along with initiating future education strategies. A very serious challenge along this way is the fundamental affirmation of the teaching profession—an essential endeavour given that the neoliberal push to marketise and commodify universities does, and will, lead to deepening the socio-economic stratification of those effectively able to attend, by, among other things, significantly increasing tuition fees for those who do not qualify for state funding. Such gatekeeping will only cause an even greater decline in Serbia's young people's interest in the already undervalued teaching profession.

Implications for the Future Development of Teacher Education in Serbia

At present, education reforms are being implemented very slowly in Serbia, and in order to succeed, it is necessary to shift to a new approach—one where teachers are empowered to act as true bearers of positive change. This goal can be achieved by investing in and fostering the development of competences which allow teachers to take leadership in terms of implementing and facilitating reforms. In particular, reflective competences allow teachers to reorganise their approaches, while continually working on their own professional development (Španović and Vučković 2017, p. 107).

Master's programmes, which are led by teachers themselves, are inspirational and highly contemporary, as they are rooted in the pedagogy of empowerment: that is, organised around creating and leading developmental projects, critical reflections and writing narratives in which theoretical knowledge helps in solving professional problems, organised networking and international engagement, and so forth. Therefore, in Serbia, the aspiration should be to develop a teacher education programme which can 'unleash the potential of [education professionals] to contribute to education reform and thus improve young people's life chances, wherever they may be' (Ball et al. 2019, p. 78).

Simić's (2014) review of the study programmes offered by Serbia's teaching faculties reveals that there is considerable disagreement regarding how much and which psychologies and pedagogies are sufficient, as well as regarding how school practice should be organised. In looking for constructive comparison with another country in Europe, inspiration can be taken from the way that England solved its own iteration of this problem—that is of disjointed teacher education course contents and significant variance in the quality of initial teacher education—by introducing a national curriculum for initial teacher education (Hobson et al. 2010). Given the progress achieved by such unity, perhaps it would be worthwhile to consider a similar model for initial teacher education in Serbia.

As regards the professional development education of teachers in Serbia, while there is currently something of a developed system, including a large number of accredited programmes, there remains a clear gap between the formal objectives stated in the national documents and the reality in practice

(Polovina 2010). On the one hand, rendering teacher professional development a legal obligation offers an answer to contemporary changes and tendencies in education—reflexive teaching practice, changing teachers' role, digitalisation, and so forth—but, on the other hand, it puts teachers in a passive, demotivated position by reducing their professional development to a formality and a 'race' for points.

Going forwards, it is critical that teachers are positioned as equal partners in the planning, organisation, implementation, and evaluation of their own professional development, allowing their voices to be heard in the dual bids to improve the quality of professional development resources and to synchronise them with the needs of actual professional practice (Pešikan et al. 2010). To these ends, Serbia's education policy-makers should more seriously address the issue of establishing a comprehensive teacher professional development system, driven by the needs and goals of teachers themselves, thus creating an environment conducive to them proactively participating and taking responsibility for their professional learning. On a socio-economic level, this endeavour would be best supported by raising the social and material status of the teaching profession (e.g. via economic policies mandating pay increases for education professionals, improved selection process of prospective students), improving working conditions (e.g. via workplace policies that uphold teachers' rights to a safe, supportive work environment, network of professional support to teachers—working with students with disabilities, peer and digital violence, online teaching, etc.), and enhancing conditions for professional development (e.g. via involving diverse and dynamic speakers in running seminars, material support for participation).

The aspirations presented in the *Strategy for Education Development in Serbia 2020* (2012) that, by 2020, there would be at least 38.5% of Serbia's citizens between the ages of 30 and 34 who could be counted as highly educated, and that the national structuring of qualifications would be in line with the needs of the society and economy.

At present, Serbia is a country partly in transition—in the wake of the turbulence outlined at the start of this chapter—characterised by the emigration of young people abroad, population decline, and ageing population. Therefore, the Serbian government faces the challenge of finding popularly accepted solutions to decades-old problems, such as not having access to sufficient numbers of high-quality teaching staff. With these challenges in mind, future academic research will also be directed towards examining teachers' job satisfaction, as well as towards considering students' opinions on the teaching profession.

The Ministry of Education, Science, and Technological Development has outlined directions for the future of Serbia's teacher education system, highlighting the need to reduce the teaching staff deficit for subjects such as mathematics, computer science, and physics; to develop teaching methods, as well as the quality and scope of pedagogical, psychological, and methodological subjects; and to innovate initial teacher education programmes in line with changes in the curriculum for pre-primary, primary, and secondary education. Furthermore, there is no doubt that today's global changes also demand redefining the roles and competences of teachers, as well as those who educate teachers, in order to develop more dynamic concepts oriented towards a new professionalism fit for the twenty-first century.

Ultimately, such further development of Serbia's teacher education requires the establishment of a comprehensive framework for monitoring reform via a coherent information system which includes significant international indicators. In order to be truly impactful and sustainable, defining a strategy for the long-term development of teacher education in Serbia should be the result of a national consensus on gradual, positive changes across all of the education sector, fully upheld by legal and financial support from the state.

Acknowledgements This paper has been created within the scientific research project, *Quality of the Education System in Serbia from the European Perspective* (No. 179010), funded by the Ministry of Education, Science, and Technological Development of Serbia (Grant No. 451-03-2842/2019-14/179010 and Grant No. 451-03-68/2020-14/200125), where all co-authors of this chapter have been or are engaged.

References

Andelković, A. (2017). *Profesionalni razvoj u obrazovanju-pedagoški koncept nastavnika i izazovi školske prakse* [Professional development in education—concept of a teacher and school practice challenges]. Vranje: Pedagoški fakultet.

Antolović, M. (2017). Ka društvu (ne)znanja: O praktičnim implikacijama neoliberalne reforme visokog obrazovanja [Towards (non)knowledge society: Practical implications of neoliberal reform of higher education]. In: N. Branković (Ed.), *Izazovi vaspitanja i obrazovanja u 21. veku* [Challenges of Education in the 21st Century] (pp. 11–23). Sombor: Pedagoški fakultet.

Arsenović-Pavlović, M., V. Rajović-Đurašinović, and V. Stanisavljević-Rakić. (1989). Feminizacija vaspitanja – od savremenosti ka tradiciji [Feminization of upbringing—from modernity to tradition]. *Etnoantropološki problemi*, 6, 67–82.

Beijaard, D., N. Verloop, and J. D. Vermunt. (2000). Teachers' perceptions of professional identity: An exploratory study from a personal knowledge perspective. *Teaching and Teacher Education*, 16(7), 749–764.

Beara, M., and I. Jerković. (2015). Društvene okolnosti i nastavnička profesija [Social circumstances and teaching profession]. *Sociološki pregled*, 59(2), 229–253.

Ball, S., S. Lightfoot, and V. Hill. (2019). Master program koji vode nastavnici [Master program led by teachers]. In: D. Frost (Ed.), *Osnaživanje nastavnika kao nosioca promena: neformalizovan pristup nastavničkom liderstvu* [Empowering teachers as agents of change: a non-positional approach to teacher leadership] (pp. 72–78). Beograd: Centar za obrazovne politike.

Bjekić, D. (1999). *Profesionalni razvoj nastavnika* [Professional development of teachers]. Užice: Učiteljski fakultet.

CEDEFOP. (2010). *Common European Principles for Teacher Competencies and Qualifications*. Retrieved from https://www.cedefop.europa.eu/en/news-and-press/news/common-european-principles-teacher-competences-and-qualifications.

Cristina-Corina, B., and A. Valerica. (2012). Teachers' perceptions and attitudes towards professional activity. *Procedia-Social and Behavioral Sciences*, 51, 167–171.

Demie, F. (2001). Ethnic and gender differences in educational achievement and implications for school improvement strategies. *Educational Research*, 43(1), 91–106.

Domović, V. (2009). Bolonjski proces i promjene u inicijalnom obrazovanju učitelja i nastavnika [Bologna process and changes in initial teacher education]. In: V. Vizek Vidović (Ed.), *Planiranje kurikuluma usmjerenoga na kompetencije u obrazovanju učitelja i nastavnika* [Curricula planning based on competencies in teacher education] (pp. 9–17). Zagreb: Filozofski fakultet.

Gagić, Z., S. Skuban, B. Radulović, M. Stojanović, and O. Gajić. (2019). The implementation of mind maps in teaching physics—educational efficiency and students' involvement. *Journal of Baltic Science Education*, 18(1), 117–131.

Gajić, O. (2007). Standardi obrazovanja nastavnika u svetlu inovacionih promena u reformisanoj školi [Standards of teacher education in the light of innovative changes in reformed school]. In: *Prilozi metodici vaspitno-obrazovnog rada. Diskurs o strategijama obrazovanja i socijalno-pedagoškim temama* [Contribution to methodics of education. Discours about education strategies and socio-pedagogical topics] (pp. 69–89). Novi Sad: Filozofski fakultet.

Gašić-Pavišić, S. (2008). Siromaštvo, dečji razvoj i škola [Poverty, child development, and school]. In: S. Gašić-Pavišić and S. Joksimović (Eds.), *Obrazovanje i siromaštvo u zemljama u tranziciji* [Education and poverty in the transition countries] (pp. 11–31). Beograd: Institut za pedagoška istraživanja.

Gavrilović, N. (1999). *Srpske škole u Habzburškoj monarhiji - U periodu pozne prosvećenosti (1790–1848)* [Serbian schools in the Habsburg Empire—In period of the late Enlightenment]. Beograd: Elit.

Geske, A., K. Kiris, A. Kozlovska, A. Ozola, N. Rečs, and K. Spridzäne (2015). *Skolotäji Latvijä un pasaulē* [Teachers in Latvia and in the world]. Riga: LU. PPMF.IPI.

Hargreaves, D. H. (2001). *Creative professionalism: The role of teachers in the knowledge society*. London: Demos.

Hargreaves, A. (2003). *Teaching in the knowledge society—Education in the age of insecurity*. New York: Columbia University.

Hobson, A. J., P. Ashby, J. McIntyre, and A. Malderez. (2010). International approaches to teacher selection and recruitment, *OECD Education Working Papers*, No. 47. Paris: OECD Publishing.

Jerković, I., V. Gavrilov-Jerković, I. Mihić, V. Mihić, J. Petrović, and M. Zotović. (2011). Dometi reforme obrazovanja u Srbiji [Reach of the higher education reform in Serbia]. In: V. Katić (Ed.), *Trendovi razvoja: "Evropa 2020: društvo zasnovano na znanju"* [Europe 2020: knowledge based society] (pp. 1–4). Kopaonik: Fakultet tehničkih nauka, Univerzitet u Novom Sadu.

Kamenov, E. (Ed.). (2006). *Razvoj sistema vaspitanja i obrazovanja u uslovima tranzicije* [Development of education system in the period of transition]. Novi Sad: Filozofski fakultet.

Kostić, S. (1974). Reorganizacija škola u duhu prosvetiteljskih reformi [*Reorganization of schools in the spirit of Enlightenment reforms*]. In: L. Krneta et al. (Eds.), *Istorija škola i obrazovanja kod Srba* [History of schools and education in Serbia] (pp. 155–216). Beograd: Istorijski muzej SR Srbije.

Kovač-Cerović, T. (2006). National report—Serbia. In: P. Zgaga (Ed.), *The prospects of teacher education in South-East Europe* (pp. 487–526). Ljubljana: Center for Educational Policy Studies.

Law on the Fundamentals of the Education System. (2019). Sl. glasnik RS", br. 88/2017, 27/2018 - dr. zakon, 10/2019, 27/2018 - dr. zakon i 6/2020. Retrieved from https://www.paragraf.rs/propisi/zakon_o_osnovama_sistema_obrazovanja_i_vaspitanja.html.

Law on higher education. (2018). Službeni glasnik RS, br. 88/2017, 27/2018 - dr. zakon, 73/2018 i 67/2019. Retrieved from https://www.paragraf.rs/propisi_download/zakon_o_visokom_obrazovanju.pdf.

Leclercq, J. M. (1996). Teachers in a context of change. *European Journal of Education*, *31*(1), 73–84.

Lungulov, B. (2017). Pedagoški aspekti primene koncepta ishoda učenja u visokoškolskoj nastavi [Pedagogical aspects of learning outcomes concept and its use in higher education]. *Godišnjak Filozofskog fakulteta u Novom Sadu*, 17(2), 243–257.

Macura-Milovanović, S., I. Gera, and M. Kovačević. (2010). *Mapping policies and practices for inclusive education in contexts of social and cultural diversity*. Turin: European Training Foundation.

Marušić, M. (2013). *Sistemi obrazovanja nastavnika i modeli njihovog profesionalnog razvoja – komparativna analiza Srbije i Grčke* [Teacher education systems and models of teachers' professional development]. Unpublished doctoral dissertation. Beograd: Filozofski fakultet Univerziteta u Beogradu.

Mitter, W. (2007). Decenija transformacije i edukacijske politike u Centralnoj i Istočnoj Evropi [A decade of transformation and educational policy in Central and Eastern Europe]. In: A. Pašalić Kreso (Ed.), *Komparativna edukacija: nastavak tradicija, novi izazovi i nove paradigme* [A comparative education: the continuing tradition, new chalenges and new paradigms]. (pp. 75–91). Sarajevo: Connectum.

Pantić, N., and J. Čekić Marković. (2012). Nastavnici u Srbiji: stavovi o profesiji i reformama u obrazovanju [Teachers in Serbia: attitudes about profession and reforms in education]. In N. Pantić and J. Čekić Marković (Eds.), *Nastavnici u Srbiji: stavovi o profesiji i reformama u obrazovanju* [Teachers in Serbia: attitudes about profession and reforms in education] (pp. 7–12). Beograd: Centar za obrazovne politike.

Pantić, N., and T. Wubbels. (2010). Teacher competencies as a basis for teacher education–Views of Serbian teachers and teacher educators. *Teaching and Teacher Education*, 26(3), 694–703.

Pavlović, J. (2011). Predstave o obrazovnim promenama u prošlosti: deset godina našeg života [Representations of educational changes in the past: ten years of our lives]. In: M. Vujačić et al. (Eds.), *Predstave o obrazovnim promenama u Srbiji: Refleksije o prošlosti, vizije budućnosti* [Representations of educational changes in the past: Reflections about past, visions about future] (pp. 63–96). Beograd: Institut za pedagoška istraživanja.

Pešikan, A., S. Antić, and S. Marinković. (2010). Koncepcija stručnog usavršavanja nastavnika u Srbiji: koliko smo daleko od efikasnog modela [In-service teacher training: how far are we from an efficient model?]. *Nastava i vaspitanje*, 59(3), 471–482.

Pinker, S. (2014). *The Village effect—How face-to-face contact can make us healthier, happier, and smarter.* New York: Spiegel & Grau.

Polovina, N. (2010). Supervizija i mentorstvo u obrazovanju: mogućnosti povezivanja teorije i prakse [Supervision and mentoring in education: possibilities for connecting theory and practice]. In: N. Polovina and J. Polovina (Eds.), *Teorija i praksa profesionalnog razvoja nastavnika* [Theory and practice of teacher professional development] (pp. 195–219). Beograd: Institut za pedagoška istraživanja.

Radulović, B., and O. Gajić. (2018). Cognitive scheme as an innovative effective learning strategy. In: D. Karabašić, S. Vukotić, and M. Maksimović (Eds.), *Innovation as an initiator of the development* (pp. 118–137). Belgrade: Faculty of Applied Management, Economy and Finance.

Radulović, B., O. Gajić, S. Španović, and B. Lungulov. (2019). Challenges of initial teacher education in the context of higher education reform in Serbia. *Education and Self Development*, 14(3), 34–39.

Radulović, L., A. Pejatović, and N. Vujisić-Živković. (2010). Profesionalne kompetencije nastavnika [Teacher professional competencies]. *Andragoške studije*, 1, 161–170.

Rajović, V., and L. Radulović. (2007). Kako nastavnici opažaju svoje inicijalno obra-zovanje: na koji način su sticali znanja i razvijali kompetencije [How teachers perceive their initial training: How they acquired knowledge and developed com-petencies]. *Nastava i vaspitanje*, 56(4), 413–435.

Radulović, B., and M. Stojanović. (2019). Comparison of teaching instruction effi-ciency in physics through the invested self-perceived mental effort. *Voprosy obra-zovaniya/Educational Studies Moscow*, 3, 152–175.

Radulović, B., M. Stojanović, and V. Županec. (2016). The effects of laboratory inquire-based experiments and computer simulations on high school students' performance and cognitive load in physics teaching. *Zbornik Instituta za pedagoška istraživanja*, 48(2), 264–283.

Rulebook on Continuous Professional Development and Acquisition of Title of Teachers, Pre-school Teachers, and Expert Associates. (2017). Retrieved from https://www.paragraf.rs/propisi/pravilnik-strucnom-usavrsavanju-napredovanju-zvanja-nastavnika-vaspitaca-strucnih.html.

Rotgans, J. I., and H. G. Schmidt. (2011). The role of teachers in facilitating situa-tional interest in an active-learning classroom. *Teaching and Teacher Education*, 27(1), 37–42.

Simić, N. (2014). *Nastavničke brige i načini njihovog prevazilaženja* [Teacher concerns and coping mechanisms]. Unpublished doctoral dissertation, Beograd: Filozofski fakultet.

Standard of competencies for the profession of teachers and their professional development (2011). *Službeni glasnik RS*, 5/11. Retrieved from http://www.cep.edu.rs/sites/default/files/Standardi_kompetencija_za_profesiju_nastavnika.pdf.

Stanković, D. (2011). Sistem profesionalnog razvoja nastavnika u Srbiji: glavne teme i pravci razvoja [System of teacher professional development in Serbia: the main topics and development]. In: T. Vonta and S. Ševkušić (Eds.), *Izazovi i usmerenja profesionalnog razvoja učitelja* [Challenges and directions of teachers' professional development] (pp. 87–101). Beograd: Institut za pedagoška istraživanja.

Strategy for Education Development in Serbia 2020. (2012). Službeni glasnik RS, 107/2012. Retrieved from http://www.mpn.gov.rs/wp-content/uploads/2015/08/STRATEGIJA-OBRAZOVANJA.pdf.

Španović, S., and Ž. Vučković. (2017). Didaktičke kompetencije nastavnika u novoj paradigmi osnovnoškolske nastave [Didactic competences of teachers in the new paradigm of primary school teaching]. In: N. Branković (Ed.), *Izazovi vaspitanja i obrazovanja u 21.veku* [Challenges of Education in the 21st Century] (pp. 11–23). Sombor: Pedagoški fakultet.

The Lisbon Strategy. (2010). *An analysis and evaluation of the methods used and results achieved.* Brussels: European Parliament. Retrieved from https://www.europarl.europa.eu/thinktank/en/document.html?reference=IPOL-EMPL_ET(2010)440285.

Tillema, H. H. (2000). Belief change towards self-directed learning in student teach-ers: Immersion in practice or reflection on action. *Teaching and Teacher Education*, 16(5–6), 575–591.

Tornberg, A., I. Jerković, D. Grijak, and M. Antolović. (2005). *Rezultati primene novog kurikuluma na Učiteljskom fakultetu u Somboru* [Results of Implementation of the New Curriculum at Teacher Education Faculty in Sombor]. Sombor: Učiteljski fakultet.

UNICEF. (2007). *Stanje dece u Srbiji 2006: Siromaštvo i socijalna isključenost dece* [The situation of children in Serbia 2006: Poverty and social exclusion of children]. Beograd: UNICEF.

Vujačić, M., J. Pavlović, D. Stanković, V. Džinović, and I. Derić (Eds.). (2011). *Predstave o obrazovnim promenama u Srbiji. Refleksije o prošlosti, vizije budućnosti.* [Representations of educational changes in Serbia: Reflections about past, visions about future]. Beograd: Institut za pedagoška istraživanja.

Zgaga, P. (2006). *The prospects of teacher education in south-east Europe.* Ljubljana: Pedagoška fakulteta.

Zimmerman, B. J. (2008). Theories of self-regulated learning and academic achievement: An overview and analysis. In: B. J. Zimmerman and D. H. Shunk (Eds.), *Self-regulated learning and academic achievement—theoretical perspective* (pp. 1–35). London: Taylor & Francis.

Zlatković, B., and D. Petrović. (2011). Inicijalno obrazovanje učitelja u Srbiji: Analiza kompatibilnosti planova i programa učiteljskih fakulteta [Pre-service teacher training in Serbia: the analysis of teacher college curricula compatibility]. *Nastava i vaspitanje*, 60(4), 651–663.

Županec, V., B. Radulović, T. Pribićević, T. Miljanović, and V. Zdravković. (2018). Determination of instructional efficiency and learners' involvement in the flipped biology classroom in primary school. *Journal of Baltic Science Education*, 17(1), 162–176.

10

Teacher Education in Kosovo: Responding to a Challenging Local Context and Converging Towards Good International Practices

Blerim Saqipi

Introduction

Kosovo has a territory of 10,908 square kilometres and is located in the centre of the Balkan Peninsula. Currently estimated to have 1,739,825 inhabitants (KAS 2012), with 47.4% below the age of 25, Kosovo is among the countries with the youngest populations in Europe. Over 92% of the population are ethnic Albanians, and the rest comprise Serb, Bosnian, Turk, Roma, Ashkali, and Egyptian communities. In terms of public spending on education, Kosovo increased its investment from 3.3% of GDP in 2007 to 4.1% in 2012 (World Bank 2015); nevertheless, Kosovo's education expenditure remains lower than the Europe and Central Asia average (4.6%) and the middle- and high-income country average (5%). Of this total expenditure on the education sector as a whole, more than 80% is spent on staff salaries, leaving less than 20% for development purposes. In addition, on a per-pupil basis, Kosovo's education is lower than that of other countries in the same region and income group (World Bank 2014). Overall, the funding practices in Kosovo's education system have been steady, following the same pattern over the last decade without any significant increase.

Underpinning this present reality is important history. Kosovo emerged from an open war in 1999, which, besides human casualties, took a toll on

B. Saqipi (✉)
University of Prishtina, Prishtina, Kosovo
e-mail: blerim.saqipi@uni-pr.edu

© The Author(s), under exclusive license to Springer Nature Switzerland AG 2023
M. Kowalczuk-Walędziak et al. (eds.), *The Palgrave Handbook of Teacher Education in Central and Eastern Europe*, https://doi.org/10.1007/978-3-031-09515-3_10

education, whereby the majority Kosovo Albanian students of all education levels were banned for the duration of the 1990s from the right to education in their mother tongue and forced to study in improvised home schools (Saqipi 2019). Following an interim United Nations administration period (1999–2008) while Kosovo was being established as an independent state—declaring independence from Serbia on 17 February 2008—it engaged in modelling its education system in line with the more formally advanced education systems in Western Europe and North America. Within these education reform efforts, teacher education has been placed at the forefront of the agenda, and teacher education policy discourse has been characterised by continuous policy transfer processes, with the aim of aligning Kosovo's teacher education policies with those of the European Union and the specific country models it deemed appropriate (e.g. Finland).

In the attempt to bridge the gaps caused by the preceding decades of hardship, in 2001, Kosovo launched an ambitious reform in the teaching profession centred on a rapid increase in teacher qualification standards. In 2002, the requirement of a two-year higher education degree was replaced with a requirement of a four-year bachelor's degree—marked also by the establishment of the Faculty of Education at Prishtina's public university. This trend of increasing qualification requirements continued, and, in 2011, Kosovo introduced the minimum requirement of a master's degree for subject teachers and a bachelor's degree (240 ECTS credits) for pre-school and primary teachers. From 2012 onwards, Kosovo opened four new faculties of education across the country's newly established public universities: University of Prizren, University of Gjilan, University of Gjakova, and University of Mitrovica.

This chapter analyses the path Kosovo took in its efforts to upgrade the teacher education system in order to repair the development gaps left behind by the socio-political upheaval of the 1990s. This chapter will also trace the development of the teacher education sector over the last two decades: throughout these years, it was difficult for Kosovo to determine the most effective type and scale of reform to undertake, given the everyday realities on the ground and the pressing need to recover from the losses of the past. Ultimately, this chapter aims to provide a framework of how small and transitioning education systems in other countries can approach teacher education reform, with an orientation towards policy transfer projects.

Between Reinventing and Reforming Teacher Education

Put simply, the last two decades of teacher education development in Kosovo have been intense. Faced with the need to transition away from what was inherited under the post-communist context of former Yugoslavia, and recovering from many years of loss and hardship that resulted in a tragic war in 1999, Kosovo was also obliged to address the professional dimensions of what has generally been agreed upon as poor quality of teaching and learning in schools. Indeed, participation in the 2015 and 2018 PISA assessments confirmed prior observations of poor quality of teaching and learning in schools (as stated in the Kosovo Education Strategic Plan 2017–2021), ranking among the bottom three countries in both assessments. Beyond the limitations of these formal measures, Kosovo's path towards integration into the wider European family necessitated reforming the nation's education system in order to align its policies and practices with the ones at European level.

Against this backdrop, there have been significant reforms in Kosovo's teacher education system over the last two decades. In the teacher education sector, there has been a continuous trend of raising standards and a heavy focus on rewriting national legislation and policies. Alongside the increase in qualification requirements for teachers—in 2002 and 2011, as mentioned earlier—focus was also placed on developing professional standards by mandating a minimum required level of pedagogical training and school training experience within all teacher education programmes. This enforcement of standards onto the teaching profession has been attempted for just under two decades now, and there have been several revisions and reformations of policies at various stages (Saqipi 2014, 2019; Saqipi and Vogrinc 2017). While this imposition of the professional standards through Strategic Framework for Teacher Development in 2017 was expected to push Kosovo's teacher education system to reform current practices, external assessment results and negative societal perceptions expose a dilemma: has the post-war standards-raising movement been producing desired results?

So, it is time to consider an alternative view—a more comprehensive view—of teacher education reform in order to bridge the existing significant gap between present realities and aspirational policy goals. As such, the more substantial elements of teacher education reform must be attended to, including the ways in which teacher education is responding to schools' realities and needs (Saqipi and Vogrinc 2017; Saqipi 2019), the ways in which school placements help student teachers be exposed to the realities of the profession

(Gjelaj et al. 2020), the ways in which the coherence of the teacher education system upholds the continuum of pre-service and in-service teacher education (Murray et al. 2019), and whether or not teacher education is creating teachers as proactive change agents in schools (Berry 2010). These dimensions are examined here in more detail.

The Need for Teacher Education Reform to Be Driven by Demand

When examining teacher education reform, it is important to understand the forces that are driving the system change. Firstly, it is important for policymakers to understand the balance between supply and demand in the teaching profession. Secondly, school reform initiatives need to extend into teacher education—this does not mean that all small reform initiatives should directly impact teacher education programming and content across the board, rather that there should be a general connection between developments and challenges at the school level and at the teacher education level, in both programming and delivery.

As regards the supply and demand balance in the teaching profession, data provided by municipal authorities from the summer 2020 teacher recruitment experience in Prishtina, Kosovo's capital, shows that, in most subject areas, there is a high level of competition for teaching jobs. This varies from profile to profile, but overall the supply exceeds the demand: in fact, for each primary teaching place in Prishtina, there were 30 applicants, and for one mother-tongue teaching position in a lower secondary school, there were about 300 applicants—indicating a profound excess in supply. Nonetheless, in the academic year 2020/2021, Kosovo's faculties of education issued a call for 600 new students for the primary teaching education programme alone, revealing a marked lack of planning and projections accounting for the actual needs schools have for recruiting teachers. Simultaneously, the pre-university student population has continuously been decreasing by about 1000 every year for the last five years (MEST 2016), which in itself speaks to the need for fewer teachers in the system. In sum, the number of new teachers graduating is now higher than the number of teachers retiring. This current imbalance was caused, partly, by the establishment of the four new teacher education institutions over the last decade, as well as high enrolment quotas set by universities in teacher education programmes over the last two decades.

In addition to the challenge of supply and demand balance, Kosovo also faced the ongoing challenge of responding to the complexities of school reform. Over the last 20 years, Kosovo had undergone two major curriculum reforms, shifting away from a traditional, content-oriented, teacher-centred approach and towards a student-centred approach—a shift reflected in the very ambitious competence-based curriculum launched in 2011 and implemented in phases since then (Saqipi 2019b; Tahirsylaj 2021). The debate accompanying this reform has scrutinised the large resulting gap between the ambitions underpinning the curriculum reforms, and the actual capacities of Kosovo's teachers and education system to implement those ambitions in practice.

Indeed, the reality into which Kosovo's curriculum reform, consequently, forced teacher education development raised valid concerns regarding the fundamental discrepancy between the reform visions and the actual capacities to implement them. In some ways, this led to reform fatigue in Kosovo, counterproductively resulting in reduced stakeholder commitment to engage in said reforms (Saqipi 2019b). In addition, teacher education institutions were consistently required to reform their programming in line with the curriculum policy goals, which, in itself, is a legitimate request; however, these demands give rise to concerns over the corresponding narrow, techno-rational view (Saqipi 2019) of teacher education and teacher roles whereby the teacher is imagined to be the curriculum transmitter. Furthermore, Kosovo is yet to gain the understanding that teachers should not be trained on one particular curriculum during pre-service training, but rather that a much broader goal should be the target (Flores 2016). The demand placed on teacher education in Kosovo—and in many countries and cultures around the world too—is to train teachers who can create the curriculum they teach (given the curriculum orientation to leave school role in curriculum design) and lead change processes in their schools. Due to the profound challenges this goal presents, the curriculum reform Kosovo has undertaken in the last decade was simplified on a practical, implementation level. In fact, the significant discrepancy between the implemented curriculum and the intended curriculum is linked to insufficient teacher preparation and lack of support for teachers in the implementation of intended curriculum (Saqipi 2019b).

The Importance of Making Practical Training Relevant

Kosovo has mandated, via secondary legislation, that all teacher education programmes have school placement—otherwise known as practical training in schools—integrated into the programmes. These placements are regulated in terms of minimum ECTS credits points, varying between 10 to 15 ECTS for master's studies and a minimum of 20 ECTS for bachelor's studies. The practical training of student teachers in actual schools is critical for bridging the gap between theory and practice (Gjelaj et al. 2020), ensuring that prospective teachers are trained in line with practice-based approaches (Gjelaj et al. 2020), and allowing prospective teachers to align themselves with both the realities of school life and reform ambitions. In addition to the task of teaching itself, school placements are also now expected to expose prospective teachers to the broader role of teachers both within the school and the profession in general (Hargreaves 2000).

This expanding role of school experience for student teachers concurrently gives rise to the need for school mentors to act on these new, broader demands. However, recent research in the Kosovo context carried out by Gjelaj et al. (2020) shows that school placement mentor teachers are most focused on the core dimensions of the teaching task, such as developing pedagogical competence to meet the basic needs for planning and delivering instruction. While the pedagogical aspect is, indeed, an indispensable part of pre-service teacher education, its dominance reveals that in-service teachers assign less importance to the dimensions of teaching rooted in understanding system requirements, such as knowledge about education legislation and the curriculum, and reflective skills and practices (Gjelaj et al. 2020). However, pedagogy, systems-level, and reflection skills are equally important dimensions in teachers' professional practice and professional identity (Gjelaj et al. 2020), and therefore further development of teacher education in Kosovo must incorporate all three.

Indeed, the onward development of teacher education in Kosovo will need to place greater focus on making the school placement experience as genuinely representative as possible of the actual task of being a teacher, by exposing student teachers to as many of their future expected roles as possible, thus preparing them to face the realities of school life once they transition from pre-service teacher education to employment. This will allow Kosovo's teacher educators to address what research into linking theory and practice in teacher education refers to as a 'wash out' of many of the notions developed during pre-service once the teacher is engaged in in-service practice (Zeichner and Tabachnick 1981; Ballet and Kelchtermans 2008). This is otherwise known as the 'theory-practice gap', whereby the idealistic images of teaching developed during pre-service training are shattered during confrontation with the realities of teaching and school culture (Ostinelli 2009; Darling-Hammond 2017). Hence, going forwards, Kosovo's teacher education will need to face the task of implementing quality pre-service education in terms of both the depth of the task (i.e. addressing the micro-level teaching specifics) and the breadth of the task (i.e. reflecting the broader dimensions of professionalism and the education system).

The Changing Meaning of 'Content'

Teacher education programmes for primary and pre-primary teaching are provided at bachelor's level (240 ECTS credits) and cover academic content, general didactics, subject didactics, and other general education courses. Teacher education for subject teachers is organised as a continuum of bachelor's and master's studies (i.e. the consecutive model), whereby students attend a bachelor's programme in their subject discipline (offered by Kosovo's academic faculties), and then continue to a master's in the pedagogy of their specific subject (offered by Kosovo's education faculties). School placements are mandatory within these programmes for pre-primary, primary, and subject teachers (for the latter, it is planned within the master's programmes).

Within the ongoing debate on teacher education reform, a critical angle is the agreed upon purposes of schooling. Indeed, with the meaning of teaching and learning in the Western world shifting—from transmission to more student-centred approaches (Ostinelli 2009; Werler 2016)—teacher education and teacher professionalism are shifting too. Nowadays, there is a general trend for education policy, both at a national level and further afield, to project teacher education curricula as a forum for addressing knowledge, understanding, skills, attributes, and values (Flores 2016), with the expectation that prospective teachers demonstrate these characteristics themselves, as well as foster them in younger generations.

Teacher education programming in Kosovo does not make a reasonable and justifiable division between courses on academic content (i.e. focused on traditional subjects, such as mathematics, language, science, and arts), general education, and subject pedagogy. Throughout the last two decades, there have been continuous efforts to create a desirable balance between these disciplines. The standards for pre-service teacher education outlined in the *Strategic Framework for Teacher Development* (2017) specify, but do not mandate, the minimum coverage and credit requirements for each of the above disciplines in initial teacher education programmes. The present content of teacher education programmes in Kosovo can be more concretely understood via QATEK 2020 research into how they are currently designed and in what ways they respond to national and international policy reference points. Table 10.1 presents this analysis of the primary teacher education programme (a curriculum

Table 10.1 Summary of the University of Prishtina's current primary teacher education curriculum

Primary teacher education programme components	Findings and analysis from research carried out by QATEK (2020)
Knowledge and understanding	• Courses reflect significant focus on academic content knowledge • Pedagogical knowledge, including knowledge of teaching and learning processes, is addressed to a comparatively lesser extent • Several courses address curricular knowledge, referring to the national curriculum as a framework • Several courses are elective, meaning that this knowledge is not acquired by all students, for example: the contextual, institutional, and organisational aspects of education policies; working in a school as an organisation; and participating in organisational development • Inclusion and diversity are emphasised as important issues to address within courses • Little attention is given to the use of technology in learning, therefore needs more serious consideration going forwards • Group processes and dynamics, learning theories, and motivational issues remain on the margins of programme content and implementation • Evaluation and assessment processes and methods are addressed through a couple of courses

Skills	• A number of courses address aspects of teaching planning, managing, and coordination
	• However, the actual use of teaching materials and technologies is not properly addressed
	• Managing students and groups is not clearly addressed in the programme
	• Research skills development remains at knowledge level and is largely developed through a single course
	• Collecting, analysing, and interpreting evidence and data (e.g. school learning outcomes and external assessment results) for professional decision-making, as well as teaching/learning improvement, remain on the margins of the programme, both in terms of content and implementation
	• Developing analytical and problem-solving skills are not obviously present in the programme
	• Learning through play and learning in nature are emphasised in the programme
	• Several important skills are covered by elective courses:
	  1. collaboration with colleagues, parents, and social services
	  2. negotiation skills: social and political interactions incorporating multiple education stakeholders, actors, and contexts
	  3. future teachers' creativity
	  4. teachers' own metacognitive, interpersonal skills for learning individually and in professional communities
	• Teaching skills honed through transferable skills are hardly present in the course content
	• Courses do not prepare students for adapting to multilevel educational contexts: that is, from macro-level government policies, to meso-level school contexts, and micro-level classroom and student dynamics

Dispositions, attitudes, beliefs, and values	This is the least addressed programme component:
	- A limited number of courses highlight the development of values, beliefs, and attitudes
	- Capacity for change, flexibility, and ongoing learning and professional improvement (including studying and researching) remain on the margins of learning outcomes and course implementation
	- Commitment to promoting the learning of all students (e.g. considering students' additional support needs) is discussed as being valuable, but, in practice, is all but missing in the courses
	- Skills for promoting students' democratic attitudes and practices as European citizens (including the appreciation of diversity and multi-culturality) are neither highlighted nor nurtured by the courses
	- Knowledge-focused courses fail to address the development of self-critical attitudes to teaching (i.e. self-examining, discussing, and questioning practices)
	- Developing empathy is minimally addressed by courses
	- Courses address the skills needed for tolerance (e.g. teamwork, collaboration, and networking) in limited instances
	- Courses make no mention of self-efficacy or growth mindset

review process) at the University of Prishtina's education faculty. In line with the European Competence Framework for teachers (European Commission 2013), the findings are summarised in terms of the programme's constituent courses and learning outcomes.

The problems, lacks, and oversights identified in the table confirm that Kosovo's initial teacher education system is yet to reach an adequate balance between academic knowledge and knowledge about didactics and learning. Nonetheless, this system reflects what can be observed in similar programmes in more advanced education systems if you look at the findings that a large number of teacher competences are reflected also in Kosovo teacher education curriculum. In fact, Kosovo's national accreditation system requires faculties of education to prove that their programmes are aligned with those of at least three Western European universities. Hence, looking forwards, teacher education reform should focus on the quality of programme implementation, rather than the quality of programme design. Indeed, looking backwards to Kosovo's history of teacher education, and given that modern-day Kosovo has inherited a strong tradition of academia-oriented teacher education (Saqipi 2014), the current design of the nation's teacher education programmes can be considered good progress. Furthermore, it is very encouraging that Kosovo has already moved beyond the tradition of a heavy focus on knowledge acquisition (Kaçaniku 2020) and towards a skills-based approach, in the design of teacher education programmes at least.

Simultaneously, this analysis also shows that teacher education programming in Kosovo is presently less responsive to the concepts of attribute and values development. This has implications in two main ways. Firstly, with regards to the teachers themselves, educating teachers who possess the values and attributes needed for nowadays societies—such as empathy, commitment, and a democratic attitude—is crucial for positive teacher behaviour, as well as favourable attitudes towards students and the profession as a whole. Secondly, with regards to the students in their care, contemporary teachers need to ensure that their teaching includes not only knowledge acquisition and skills development but also the nurturing of the aforementioned desired values and attributes in the new generation. In light of this critical balancing act, recent research stresses the increasing complexities and demands placed on the teaching profession, as well as exploring how initial teacher education in Europe has responded to calls to create a brand of teacher professionalism which fulfils contemporary school reforms (see Hargreaves 2000, 2003; Cochran-Smith 2005; Hudson et al. 2010; Biesta 2012; Zgaga 2013; Darling-Hammond 2017).

In this context of demands for a new type of teacher professionalism, teachers seem to be expected to respond to societal phenomena in what Hargreaves (2000) calls the 'post-professional stage'. However, the pressures that come from society and negative phenomena—such as X and Y—are not problems to be solved by individual teachers. Rather, students in Kosovo's schools need to be exposed to processes and practices that help them to develop the values and attitudes their society aspires for new generations—such as democracy and citizenship—and which are prescribed in curriculum policies. However, a prior study (Saqipi 2019a) has shown that teacher education in Kosovo reflects the concepts of democracy and citizenship in a rather contrived manner, that is, primarily addressed within one single course in general teacher education programmes or in a selected number of courses where the programme aims at training teachers to teach civics (Saqipi 2019a). Yet, in reality, students need to truly live democracy for themselves (Dewey 1939, 1966), rather than simply know about it theoretically, and this is what Kosovo's education system needs to prioritise now.

Connecting Pre-service Teacher Education to In-service Teacher Education

Teacher education is a continuous process that starts during initial teacher education, continues into beginning teachers' induction phase, and extends across the course of teachers' careers (Niemi 2015). Thus, any reforming of teacher education should take account of this bigger picture. Continuous teacher professional development is defined as an inclusive process that comprises all formal and informal activities that teachers undertake for professional learning and growth (Sachs 2016). Kosovo started an in-service teacher development system in 2000, initially in the form of a 'training the trainer' model (Saqipi 2014) and later in the form of ad hoc, one-off workshops managed by central authorities. However, the professional development offer for in-service teachers in Kosovo was dominated by donor projects operating with certain time limits and without any sustainability mechanisms built in. In 2008, Kosovo started to decentralise education competences to municipal and school levels, meaning that the responsibility for teacher professional development was decentralised too. That said, the school-based professional development system has not actually been implemented yet, despite sporadic initiatives to do so. Thus, the system has largely continued to be limited to one-off seminars and workshops provided to select groups of teachers, with attendance at in-service professional development made mandatory by law.

The accompanying discussion has, to date, not reached the stage of examining the relevance and impact of in-service professional development; instead, the focus remains on ensuring and expanding the capacities to provide development opportunities for all teachers throughout the country. Hence, the next stage of teacher education in Kosovo should be focused on making in-service teacher education truly teacher-centred and activating its potential to drive positive change in the classroom practices.

This next stage must also involve careful and intentional differentiation between the role of pre-service teacher education and the role of in-service education. At present, Kosovo's in-service professional development is seen by many teachers as supplementing the basics of their profession due to the poor quality of pre-service training. This current lack of quality in Kosovo's pre-service teacher education is despite the fact that a policy was introduced in 2017 to create a standard set of competency profiles for teachers at each stage of their career. This policy, in itself, was a strong idea, but it has not solved the problem immediately, and the ways in which it will influence the teacher education system and teacher professional practice remain to be seen. Presently, the University of Prishtina's faculty of education is preparing to facilitate in-service professional development activities for teachers as a way to bridge the gap between the two levels of teacher education.

Learning from Best Practice or Importing 'Easy' Solutions?

Kosovo has not formally participated in international benchmarking processes, such as OECD TALIS and EU Eurydice; however, it has recently started participating in the OECD-run PISA assessment. Kosovo's participation in PISA in 2015 and 2018 (ranking among the bottom three countries, as mentioned earlier) triggered local debates over the immediate need to reconsider teachers' performance, qualifications, and professional standards. This recent participation in international assessment and the corresponding debates are also an indication that external motivators are important factors driving education reform in Kosovo. Indeed, to date, Kosovo has modelled its teacher education by importing a number of international models and policy reference points, such as the raising of the teaching qualification standard to a master's, an initiative which started in Western Europe more than a decade ago. As such, understood as a country in recovery and transition, as well as aspiring towards European Union integration, Kosovo can be praised for its bid to align its education policy with relevant European reference points and good practice from other countries (Saqipi 2019; Tahirsylaj 2021). This said, Kosovo's tendency to import education policy should be analysed critically, given that it cannot be assumed that policies from abroad will translate well into any given local context (Zgaga 2006; Saqipi and Vogrinc 2017). In fact, there is even a risk that the policymakers will use policy transfer as a cover for what actually needs to be developed via local education reform (Saqipi and Vogrinc 2017). Looking through this critical lens, it is not clear exactly how the education system in Kosovo has been interacting with the policy transfer phenomenon to date, and in what ways teacher education policy reform has contributed to the enhancement of teacher education in practice.

Existing policy transfer literature (e.g., Steiner-Khamsi 2012; Waldow 2012) emphasises the importance of the motivation behind policy transfer, the importance of the policy transfer process, and the importance of the con-textual variables which determine the actual meaning of the transferred policy in practice in the local setting. Indeed, Steiner-Khamsi (2012) differentiates between the cultural, political, and economic motivations behind policy transfer, thus encouraging policymakers and education professionals to have a clear idea of their own motives. However, to date, there has not been any rigorous analysis of what motivations are underpinning Kosovo's policy trans-fer; rather, such motivations seem to have been developed ad hoc and incon-sistently, instead of through any intentional and structured process (Saqipi 2019). Furthermore, at present, there is no documentation of how policies are identified abroad and translated into the local context.

Nonetheless, as a key step towards making future progress, it is useful to understand Kosovo's mixed motivations behind policy transfer projects in teacher education thus far. As mentioned earlier, pre-service teacher education national accreditation standards stipulate that teacher education programmes must be compatible with a minimum of three teacher education curricula in Western European countries, suggesting a socio-political allegiance to recog-nised practices in advanced economies and democracies. As also mentioned earlier, in-service teacher education—and more importantly its design—has been devised and implemented by donor projects which export programmes to Kosovo, managed by organisations and staff from outside of Kosovo, sug-gesting a prioritisation of locally developed and owned initiatives. While such policy transfer projects for both pre-service and in-service teacher education serve short-term political goals, showcasing to the public that education reform is underway, at a professional level they have led to the destruction of the illusion of reform, given that Kosovo had no policy of its own regarding how to engage in policy transfer projects. Indeed, many teachers feel that their concerns have not been addressed in the process of copying reform ideas from elsewhere (Saqipi 2014), and hence their commitment to said reform has never been rallied.

In summation, after two decades of heavy engagement in linear policy transfer projects, it can be inferred that Kosovo's teacher education sector has been primarily motivated by the prospect of finding 'quick', international solutions to import for solving local problems. However, these policy interventions have not yielded the desired changes in teacher professional practice and—more importantly—in student learning. In view of these outcomes, Kosovo now needs to ask whether policy transfer has been carried out with the right motivations, or if it was ultimately used as a problematic shortcut—and, in moving forwards, guidance can be taken from Steiner-Khamsi's (2012) call for viewing policy borrowing less as 'policy transfer' and more as lesson extraction.

Conclusion

Kosovo's teacher education system has been characterised by continuous reforms over the last two decades, driven by the goals of modernising classroom teaching and improving student learning. To date, Kosovo's approach to teacher education reform has primarily been oriented towards translating good policies and practices from elsewhere, in order to demonstrate its inclination towards integration into the wider European family. However, the realities of this policy transfer approach here in Kosovo were that these efforts were largely used as a quick fix in an ultimately ineffectual attempt to solve lasting problems in the education sector, largely focused on the writing and rewriting of legislation. In aspiring towards further European integration, Kosovo should continue to seek a more suitable model of policy transfer— that is, both well-resourced and rooted in meaning-making on a local level.

Modern teacher education reform in Kosovo has been characterised by rapid structural shifts to match the western European raising of teacher education qualification requirements—to a master's—and a 'training more' approach in in-service professional development. However, despite the lack of formal mechanisms for measuring and analysing the extent to which these interventions have actually been enhancing the quality of teacher professional practice, poor or compromised student learning speaks to a need for improved teacher education. Fundamentally reconsidering the approach taken to teacher education at both pre-service and in-service levels will allow Kosovo to move from a 'training more' approach to training for a different purpose, that is, creative teachers who can adequately address the development of knowledge, skills, and attributes in new generations. Thus, it is critical that future teacher education reform moves beyond structural changes, instead focusing on the goals teacher education should serve: educating reflective practitioners and change-leaders. Furthermore, next steps for Kosovo must include transforming the current traditional, techno-rational approach to teacher education into the development of the skills, values, and attributes needed for the twenty-first century, both in the teaching profession and in broader socio-political settings. In tandem, there is a pressing need to agree upon a model which allows for the balancing of academic, didactical, and general education dimensions in initial teacher education programming, therefore securing the foundations of Kosovo's teacher education.

While the current expectation for teachers is to foster innovation both locally and globally, Kosovo's geopolitical context still limits its teachers to the challenges of translating external inputs derived from national policymaking or policy transfer projects, without critically analysing their meaning and use in their own local setting. Therefore, the next stage of Kosovo's teacher education development needs to focus on finding new ways of educating teachers—through a coherent pre-service and in-service system—who do not see their role as following prescribed curricula and ready-made policy reforms that resemble user manuals. Kosovo's experience with teacher education reform to date demonstrates that, in order to bring about successful reform, reform frameworks should include structural dimensions, programme content issues, and tangible links to the challenging realities of teacher professional practice. Ultimately, Kosovo can teach us that the transition processes so inherent in teacher education reform should bring together a balance of comprehensive internal and external inputs in such a way that helps those within the system itself to learn from its development journey.

References

Ballet, K., and G. Kelchtermans. (2008). Workload and willingness to change: Disentangling the experience of intensification. *Journal of Curriculum Studies*, 40(1), 47–67.

Berry, B. (2010). *Teaching 2030: What we must do for our students and our public schools—now and in the future*. New York: Teachers College.

Biesta, G. (2012). The future of teacher education: Evidence, competence or wisdom? *Research on Steiner Education*, 3(1), 8–21.

Cochran-Smith, M. (2005). The new teacher education: For better or for worse? *Educational Researcher*, 34(7), 3–17.

Darling-Hammond, L. (2017). Teacher education around the world: What can we learn from international practice? *European Journal of Teacher Education,* 40(3), 291–309.

Dewey, J. (1939). 'Creative democracy: The task before us' in *John Dewey and the promise of America, Progressive Education Booklet,* No. 14. Columbus, OH: American Education Press. Republished in John Dewey, The Later Works, 1925–1953, Vol. 14.

Dewey, J. (1966). *Democracy and Education.* New York: The Free Press.

European Commission. (2013). *Supporting teacher competence development for better learning outcomes.* European Commission. Retrieved from https://eur-lex.europa.eu/LexUriServ/LexUriServ.do?uri=SWD:2012:0374:FIN:EN:PDF.

Flores, M. A. (2016). Teacher education curriculum. In: J. Loughran and M. L. Hamilton (Eds.), *International handbook of teacher education* (pp. 187–230). Springer.

Gjelaj, M., F. Kaçaniku, and B. Saqipi. (2020). Understanding mentoring role as a step towards improving quality of teacher education: Kosovo experience. *International Journal of Education Economics and Development,* 11(2), 188–203.

Hargreaves, A. (2000). Four ages of professionalism and professional learning. *Teachers and Teaching: History and Practice,* 6(2), 151–182.

Hargreaves, A. (2003). *Teaching in the knowledge society. Education in the age of insecurity.* Open University Press.

Hudson, B., P. Zgaga, and B. Åstrand. (2010). *Advancing quality cultures for teacher education in Europe: Tensions and opportunities.* University of Umeå, Faculty of Teacher Education.

Kaçaniku, F. (2020). Teacher-researcher development? Unpacking the understandings and approaches in initial teacher education in Kosovo. *Center for Educational Policy Studies Journal,* 10(3), 53–76.

Kosovo Agency of Statistics (KAS). (2012). *Kosovo Population and Housing Census 2011—Final Results.* Prishtina: KAS.

MEST. (2016). *Kosovo Education Strategic Plan.* Prishtina (Kosovo): MEST.

Murray, J., A. Swennen, and C. Kosnik. (2019). International research, policy and practice in teacher education. In: J. Murray, A. Swennen, and C. Kosnik (Eds.), *International policy perspectives on change in teacher education: Insider perspectives* (pp. 1–14). Springer.

Niemi, H. (2015). Teacher professional development in Finland: Towards a more holistic approach. *Psychology, Society and Education,* 7(3), 278–294.

Ostinelli, G. (2009). Teacher education in Italy, Germany, England, Sweden and Finland. *European Journal of Education,* 44(2), 291–308.

QATEK. (2020). *Situational analysis on initial teacher education programmes.* UP/QATEK.

Sachs, J. (2016). Teacher professionalism: Why are we still talking about it? *Teachers and Teaching,* 22(4), 413–425.

Saqipi, B. (2014). Developing teacher professionalism and identity in the midst of large-scale education reform—the case of Kosovo" (Doctoral dissertation). Journal of Teacher Researcher 2/2014, Jyvaskyla (Finland): Tuope.

Saqipi, B. (2019). Teacher education policy discourse in the midst of system reorganisation and policy transfer: lessons for small and developing countries. *International Journal of Management in Education*, 13(1), 28–39.

Saqipi, B. (2019a). The evolving concept of democracy in the Kosovo education system: Reflections on the role of teacher education (Chapter 8). In: A. Raiker, M. Rautiainen, and B. Saqipi (Eds). *Teacher education and the development of democratic citizenship in Europe*. London: Routledge.

Saqipi, B. (2019b). Understanding the relation between policy discourse and re-conceptualizing curriculum: Kosovo's perspective on new meaning of context. *CEPS Journal*, 2, 33–52.

Saqipi, B., and J. Vogrinc. (2017). *The prospects of reforming teacher education*. Libri Shkollor.

Steiner-Khamsi, G. (2012). Understanding policy borrowing and lending. Building comparative policy studies. In: G. Steiner-Khamsi and F. Waldow (Eds.), *World yearbook of education 2012: Policy borrowing and lending in education* (pp. 3–17). New York: Routledge.

Tahirsylaj, A. (2021). What kind of citizens? Constructing 'Young Europeans' through loud borrowing in curriculum policy-making in Kosovo. *Comparative Education*, 57(1), 115–129.

Waldow, F. (2012). *Standardization and legitimacy: Two central concepts in research on educational borrowing and lending.* In: G. Steiner-Khamsi and F. Waldow (Eds.), *World yearbook of education 2012: Policy borrowing and lending in education* (pp. 411–427). New York: Routledge.

Werler, T. (2016). Commodification of teacher professionalism. *Policy Futures in Education,* 14(1), 60–76.

World Bank Group. (2015). Country Snapshot-Kosovo. Prishtina: The World Bank Country Office in Kosovo. Retrieved from http://www.worldbank.org/content/dam/Worldbank/document/eca/Kosovo-Snapshot.pdf.

World Bank Group. (2014). Kosovo Public Finance Review: Fiscal Policies for a Young Nation. Prishtina: World Bank.

Zeichner, K., and B. R. Tabachnick. (1981). Are the effects of teacher education washed out by school experience? *Journal of Teacher Education*, 32, 7–11.

Zgaga, P. (2006). *The prospects of teacher education in South-east Europe*. Pedagoska fakulteta.

Zgaga, P. (2013). The future of European teacher education in the heavy seas of higher education. *Teacher Development,* 17(3), 347–361.

11

Teacher Education in North Macedonia: Reforms, Standardisation, and Creating Communities of Lifelong Learners

Majda Joshevska and James M. Underwood

Introduction

This chapter explores teacher education in North Macedonia and looks ahead to possible ways in which teacher development could be improved over the next decade. The first sections address and discuss the situation today, with regard to teacher education, including in terms of the evolution up to this point in time. Firstly, a broad overview is presented, after which the specific context and practices of teachers' ongoing development are addressed. In the later sections of this chapter, it is proposed that models of practice that could develop teachers in North Macedonia should focus on empowerment, autonomy, and the creation of communities which support and enable extended professionals.

M. Joshevska (✉)
Foundation for Education and Cultural Initiatives Step by Step,
Skopje, Macedonia
e-mail: majda.josevska@gmail.com

J. M. Underwood
University of Northampton, Northampton, UK

M. Kowalczuk-Walędziak et al. (eds.), *The Palgrave Handbook of Teacher Education in Central and Eastern Europe*, https://doi.org/10.1007/978-3-031-09515-3_11

Context of Teacher Education in North Macedonia

Teacher education in North Macedonia has been fundamentally affected by the political turmoil so typical of countries of former Yugoslavia, which is also true for most former communist countries. This turmoil, in many ways, still prevails today. This is why North Macedonia, as with other former Yugoslavian member states, almost 30 years after the break-up of the federation (1991–1992), is still often said to be in a transitional period. This affects many facets of life in contemporary North Macedonia, including education. The main characteristic of the education systems in many Western Balkan countries, especially North Macedonia, can be defined as an ongoing struggle to consolidate a traditional and outdated education infrastructure with abruptly changing, often populist, education policies that are rarely based on empirical evidence (Joshevska and Kirandziska 2017).

North Macedonia has had formal teacher education for 75 years. During this time, the model and philosophy of teacher education has changed to reflect the spirit of the times and the needs of the country. In the earliest of these years, the late 1940s, one significant consideration was the amount of time spent in formal education deemed necessary for future primary school teachers, leading to raising the level of teacher education to an academic degree. Up to the late 1950s, teaching was considered to be a vocation, a skill set that could be acquired through a total of two years' study. However, as formal education was made available to more and more people, a need for the greater professionalisation of teaching grew, requiring a more rigorous programme of training. Therefore, 1964 saw the creation of pedagogy academies in Skopje, Shtip, and Bitola.

The reasons for this transformation lay in the need to standardise teacher education in order to ensure the quality of teaching for the then-eight years of primary education. Furthermore, where secondary teachers were concerned, the aim was to elevate secondary education as a means of effective, pre-university-level education, and thus teaching at secondary education level needed to become more subject-specific. Later on, at the beginning of the 1980s, courses that focused on prospective teachers' taught subjects were removed from the curricula at the academies for pedagogy and transferred to subject faculties. From this point on, teachers that taught mathematics at grades 6–8 in primary education, or at secondary level, were educated at the Faculty of Mathematics, rather than at the Faculties of Pedagogy. This contributed to elevating teachers' taught subject knowledge from the level of two years of post-secondary education to the level of a bachelor's degree (Kamberski

2000). The next section explains in detail how lower primary teachers (grades 1–5) and subject teachers (grades 6–8 and secondary education subject teachers) acquire their credentials to teach in primary and secondary education, respectively. The current situation in higher education for teachers, mainly regarding the effects of recent higher education reform and the process of unifying the quality of initial teacher education (ITE), is also summarised.

Initial Teacher Education (ITE)

Since North Macedonia became independent from Yugoslavia in 1991, higher education has generally undergone transformations congruent with the country's complex socio-economic and political circumstances. Teacher education has been no exception. These reform priorities have been marked by qualitative parameters, with the aim of improving education quality and measuring North Macedonia against European standards. Two crucial reforms have characterised the changing status and perception of teachers' initial education in North Macedonia. The first was the implementation of the Bologna reforms to higher education, with North Macedonia signing the accord in 2003, aimed at increasing the transparency and quality of the national education system, as well as international academic mobility (Benelux Bologna Secretariat 2009). The second reform was the introduction of an additional year of primary education, raising the total from eight years to nine years. There is ample research about the benefit of quality early education for better education outcomes and success in later life, especially when it comes to literacy and numeracy skills (i.e. Duncan et al. 2007). However, in North Macedonia, preschool uptake is only 35%, as recorded in 2017, and thus lags behind the EU goal of 95%.[1] As preschool institutions are not equally distributed in the country and preschool is not free, most excluded children are those from rural areas, children with disabilities, and those with lower socio-economic status, such as from the Roma community. This reform aimed to make one year of preschool education mandatory and free for all students[2] in order to provide equal educational opportunities for all school-age children (Miovska-Spaseva et al. 2018).

After the Bologna Declaration was signed in 2003, the country's faculties (departments) started implementation within two to three years of the signing. The idea behind the Bologna Process was to create a singular European standard of higher education through the transference of credits acquired upon passing higher education courses (i.e. the Education Credit Transfer System or ECTS): for instance, in order to be awarded a BA, a student must acquire 240 ECTS credits. The Bologna Process and ECTS standards ensure horizontal (across disciplines) and vertical student mobility (advancement in degrees by transferring credits from one university to another) through pledging unity with EU standards regarding the difficulty level of subjects studied within an academic year. However, in practice, the ECTS is mainly reduced to a mechanical conversion of the number of students' contact hours, rather than any estimation of difficulty level or labour intensity. As such, many of the challenges in initial teacher education (ITE) are partly a consequence of the problematic and reductionist implementation of the Bologna Process, which has created an uneven basis for any comparison of the quality of education provided by different faculties educating teachers.

In an analysis conducted by Miovska-Spaseva et al. (2018), there are differences in the implementation of ITE programmes at different faculties. For example, there are different numbers of contact hours and credits for same subjects at different faculties, as well as differences in subject status (mandatory or elective). Furthermore, there are different pathways to becoming a teacher depending on the grade level and/or taught subject. Primary school teachers are educated in the faculties of pedagogy, but also in faculties in different disciplines (faculties for mathematics and science, of philology, fine arts, etc.). Subject teachers can enter the profession through either direct training to teach (acquiring 240 ECTS credits) or through an additional pedagogical qualification at a faculty that does not specifically train teachers (acquiring 240 + 30 ECTS credits). This second option means that candidates take a few extra exams (i.e. in psychology, pedagogy, and teaching methodology) which qualify them to teach the specific subject at primary and secondary levels. What this ultimately contributes to are differences in the types of competences teachers acquire in the course of their ITE. Subject teachers are better experts in the subject areas that they teach, but have limited pedagogical skills or understanding of teaching methods; conversely, primary school teachers are better at creating a stimulating learning environment, but are not as skilled at all subjects or subject-specific teaching methodologies.

Study programmes for ITE, at both teaching and subject faculties, must be approved by the Board of Accreditation and Evaluation of Higher Education in North Macedonia. There is a series of laws and rules stipulated by the National Gazette of the Republic of North Macedonia to verify whether or not a study programme fulfils the conditions necessary to educate future teachers: the Law for Higher Education, no. 35/8, 103/08, 26/09, 83/09, 99/09, 115/10, 17/11, 51/11, 15/13; the Decree for Norms and Standards for Establishing Higher Education Activity, no.103/10; the Rulebook for the Organisation, Work, Decision-Making Model, Accreditation and Evaluation

Methodology, and other issues under the mandate of the Board for Accreditation and Evaluation of Higher Education Institutions, no. 151/12; the Rulebook for Mandatory Components Required from Study Programmes from the First, Second, and Third Study Cycle, no. 25/11; and Instructions for Criteria and Quality Assurance Method of Higher Education Institutions and Academic Staff in the Republic of Macedonia, no. 67/13. These documents encompass all matters related to ITE, from the technical aspects of providing education (e.g. teaching space, financing, staffing, and programme structures at different study routes) to the curricular aspects (e.g. offered subjects, syllabi, compliance with national curricula across faculties, research opportunities for students, selection and graduation criteria, and programme descriptors).

There are marked structural and programmatic differences between the study programmes that are offered at different subject or pedagogical faculties, at different pedagogical faculties; and between faculties offering the same disciplines/subjects. For example, subjects may have different numbers of planned contact hours, as well as status (i.e. obligatory or elective). Furthermore, some study programmes are focused on a broad, academic exploration of the subject's content, while others focus more on teaching to transfer that content and share the knowledge with pupils. What this ultimately contributes to are differences in teachers' preparedness to tackle the realities of a classroom depending on the type of institution from which they have acquired their qualifications.

From a structural perspective, faculties that implement ITE in North Macedonia face a challenge to unify the study programmes for teachers, as analysed in the *Adjustment of the Education Structure in Europe (Tuning Project)* (2006). This methodology is used by universities to (re)design, develop, conduct, and assess study programmes entering the Bologna process. The 'tuning' serves as a reference platform for different subject areas, in an effort to make study programmes comparable, compatible, and transparent.[3] Firstly, there is ambiguity regarding learning outcomes on both modalities of ITE, therefore making it difficult to formulate the teaching competences students should acquire as part of their studies. Secondly, there is an unrealistically high number of required competences, varying depending on the breadth of the subject curriculum in question, contradictory to the recommendations in the instruments which suggest six to eight competences per subject. Thirdly, there is a lack of correlation between study programmes for teachers and the evaluation of students' competences, making it difficult to specify which model of higher education content delivery would generate the best outcomes for teaching students (specifically in terms of delivering knowledge, understanding, and skills). Lastly, the grading of students' outcomes in subject programmes is conducted through tests, essays/seminar papers, presentations, class participation, and a final exam; however, as this model is based on acquiring points for completion, rather than on the quality of that completion, there is a lack of nuance in terms of the subject mastery attained by students (Miovska-Spaseva et al. 2018).

From a programmatic point of view, another crucial issue with regard to ITE in North Macedonia is the effectiveness of the offered study programmes in terms of providing candidates with the necessary knowledge, skills, abilities, and values to be effective teachers. The *Rulebook for Basic Professional Competence in Primary and Secondary Schools* stipulates professional values, knowledge, understanding, and competences in six areas:

1. Knowledge of subject matter and the education system
2. Teaching and learning (i.e. planning and preparation, implementation, evaluation, and educational differentiation to meet students' individual needs)
3. Creating a stimulating and safe learning environment
4. Social and educational inclusion
5. Communication and cooperation with families and communities
6. Professional development and professional cooperation

The comparative analysis conducted by Miovska-Spaseva et al. (2018), suggests that there are marked differences between the competences taught in the faculties of pedagogy and the competences taught in subject matter faculties. For example, the majority of the content learned by subject teachers at faculties in different subject areas (mathematics, language, etc.) prepares them with the knowledge, such as terminology and theoretical paradigms, and skills required by that subject, but not how to be effective teachers in that specific subject. Indeed, this education-focused component is often under-serviced or lacking altogether, being reduced to learning how to plan and prepare class lessons in accordance with a traditional, rather than innovative or scientifically rooted, teaching methodology to the extent required by law. This rigidity is also apparent in the lack of focus given to teaching prospective teachers how to evaluate and differentiate their own pedagogical approaches in order to meet the needs of the students in their care; instead, faculties tend to offer electives which broadly address educational psychology concepts and docimology.

At pedagogy faculties, the study programmes do address all six areas of competences, albeit with varying quality. For example, through most subjects, teachers learn how to plan their lessons and use different teaching methods depending on content and grade level. However, the creation of a stimulating and safe learning environment is addressed only through two topics: using ICT in education and pedagogical communication. Furthermore, competences for social and educational inclusion are not reflected in the qualification path of subject teachers. These examples suggest that there is a difference between the methodology, type of training, and even the philosophy of how lower primary and subject teachers in primary and secondary schools are prepared. In summation, it is clear that initial teacher education in North Macedonian currently faces many challenges: some are in the form of residual structures and concepts from the system established during the socialist republic (1963–1991), and some are in the form of the demands of a contemporary society that changes rapidly and requires flexible, modern study programmes which follow education science and research. The rest of the problem lies in the existing complex and inert education system which struggles between the two.

Following the implementation of the Bologna Process (post-2003), the second reform that affected not only teacher education but also the country's education system on the whole was the 2007 introduction of a mandatory preparatory year to the beginning of the eight-year primary education structure for all children aged six at the start of term—transforming it into a nine-year programme (Концепција за деветгодишно основно образование и воспитание 2007). Prior to this reform, pre-primary education was not equally accessible to all children in North Macedonia due to lack of infrastructure, socio-economic inequalities, and parents' lack of awareness about the importance of early education and development. This added year is facilitated by lower primary teachers educated in one of the country's four faculties of pedagogy (i.e. Skopje, Tetovo, Bitola, or Shtip). Furthermore, primary schools are given the option for subject teachers to deliver ICT and English language classes, provided that they have been educated in the respective faculties and have completed an additional pedagogical qualification (*Law on Primary Education* 2019).

From a policy perspective, there are five laws which regulate the procedure of acquiring a teaching degree and what that qualifies teaching students to do, stipulated by the National Gazette of the Republic of North Macedonia: the *Law for Higher Education;* the *Law for Primary Education* (no. 103/2008, 33/2010, 116/2010, 156/2010, 18/2011, 42/2011, 51/2011, 6/2012, 100/2012, 24/2013, 41/2014, 116/2014, 135/2014, 10/2015, 98/2015, 145/2015, 30/2016, 127/2016 and 67/2017); the *Law regulating the Teaching Academy;* the *Law for Higher Education of Educators in Pre-school, Primary, and*

Secondary Schools (no. 10/2015, 20/2015, 98/2015, 145/2015, 55/2016 and 127/2016); and the *Law for Primary and Secondary School Teachers* (no. 10/2015, 145/2015, 30/2016, 127/2016 and 67/2017). The *Law for Higher Education* overarches all higher education institutions offering teaching degrees, thus implying comparability of learning standards; however, this is mostly to do with matters such as structural, administrative aspects of the institutions' management, student quotas, and the time frame for applications. In practice, this law does very little with regard to regulating the quality of education that teachers acquire, as this falls, instead, under the autonomy of the higher education institution itself.

Decentralisation, in this sense, allows teaching institutions to create their own programmes, select staff, and award degrees, thus, at least in theory, setting standards for the quality of pre-service training, as well as criteria for the selection of students. However, practice has shown the opposite to be true: most of the students who enrol in the country's education faculties are required to have a C-grade average across all subjects upon graduating high school (i.e. equivalent to a 3.00 in a 5.00-point system), whereas other areas of study require at least a B-grade average. As such, comparatively, the selection criteria for students applying to a teaching degree amount to admitting those with average or below average grades. This situation contrasts strongly with, for example, Finland, where less than a quarter of applicants are admitted to teacher education programmes and teaching any syllabus above preschool level requires at least a master's degree (Paronen and Lappi 2018).

Understood in combination, the low selection criteria for prospective teachers and weak curricular programming in North Macedonia's education institutions—unsurprisingly—yield poor education outcomes for students. In 2015—the first year the country enrolled in the Organisation for Economic Co-operation and Development (OECD) PISA assessment process—students in North Macedonia scored an average of 127 points below the OECD average, being surpassed by students in countries with a similar socio-economic profile, such as Serbia and Bulgaria (OECD 2018). In 2018, when North Macedonia enrolled its 15-year-old students for the second time, the results were slightly better, with an average of 88 points below the OECD average (Education GPS 2019; OECD 2019a). Despite this improvement, these results signify that the country's primary education leaves much to be desired, with the quality of teachers that the teacher education system produces being a key factor.

Faced with this situation, in 2017, the government attempted to establish greater control over standards of teachers' pre-service education by introducing the *Law for regulating the Teacher Academy*, which built upon the five laws mentioned earlier. Based on this new law, the government established a new institution, separate from the teacher education institutions responsible for licensing future teachers: *The Teacher Academy*. The role of the Teacher Academy was intended to examine the competencies of students graduating from the faculties of education, in order to evaluate their eligibility to be employed as teachers in a public school (as stipulated in the Law for Teachers' Academy, Article 41). However, the academic community perceived this act as blatant interference with the autonomy of higher education institutions and an attack on the legitimacy of their teaching programmes (Јаневска 2019). In their view, the creation of a new institution solely for the purposes of selecting candidates and expanding their skills and knowledge in terms of innovative teaching methodologies was impractical. Instead, they argued that any such improvement would need to occur within the existing pre-service education institutions for teachers—to do otherwise would be an expensive and unnecessary exercise. Due to these objections, the 'teacher academy' concept has been frozen.

Professional Development

The poor-quality student outcomes, described in the previous chapter, with regard to OECD PISA results, imply a gap between teachers' pre-service education and the demands of the modern classroom, education trends, and labour market requirements. It has become clear that completing the mandatory four years to acquire a bachelor's degree and the negligible amount of pre-service classroom training offered to prospective teachers are not enough to thrive as a professional educator. As in most professions that closely reflect societal changes, teachers today require continuous professional development and much more flexibility than they did 30 years ago. There is no available data for North Macedonia about how many teachers are leaving the profession, but other data suggest that there is a global trend. For example, according to 2018 US Labor Department statistics, public educators in the US were leaving their profession at a rate of 83 per 10,000 each month, which is the highest rate since measurement commenced in 2001. There are differences between reported attrition rates globally—ranging from 30% to 50% in the first year (in the US, the UK, Norway, Australia, and Sweden), to less than 5% in the Netherlands and Hong Kong (Carlsson et al. 2019). As for attrition rates for teachers in North Macedonia, anecdotal evidence suggests that it is perhaps lower than elsewhere. However, this may be due to the relatively stable status teachers have as public servants, and lenient policies regarding working hours, as opposed to general work satisfaction.

The perceptions of teachers about insufficient learning resources, skills, and knowledge at their disposal to address increasingly diversifying student learning needs are indicative of at least a moderate level of discontent (Power School 2019). One way in which teachers compensate for that which their pre-service education has not prepared them for is to become actively involved in continuous professional development. The European Commission report (2015) specifies the necessity of continuous development for teachers' professionalism, that is, providing learning support structures for teachers, providing career paths, improving teachers' competency levels, and nurturing school learning cultures. The current state of play regarding professional development in North Macedonia is that practising teachers should acquire 60 hours of in-service professional development over three academic years, 40 of which need to be accredited by the Bureau for the Development of Education (BDE) and financed through the national budget (Law for Primary and Secondary School Teachers, published in the National Gazette of the Republic of North Macedonia no. 10/2015, 145/2015, and 30/2016, Article 21). The BDE is a government institution under the Ministry of Education and Science (MoES) that is in charge of devising national curricula and providing support for teachers and their professional development. However, presently, the BDE is very limited in its ability to fulfil this task due to a lack of political independence and staff to meet the professional needs of teachers. Furthermore, there is a lack of congruence between the priorities for professional development identified by the teachers in their everyday work and the BDE's identified areas (OECD 2019b).

North Macedonia's decentralisation process was envisioned as bringing a level of independence for schools to identify their own priorities and offer relevant training to their teachers in line with the specific needs of their students. However, in reality, schools have been left with minimal funding for this purpose as most of the funds available to them, both centrally and locally, are spent on school maintenance and reconstruction, subsidies for students, and salaries for teachers. In fact, the professional development of teachers does not even appear as an expenditure category recognised by the MoES. Therefore, the gap between professional needs and pre-service knowledge is mostly addressed via outside support: the civil society sector and international organisations, informal teachers' networks, and, although much more seldom, self-financed training.

However, throughout the 1990s and 2000s, as the transitional process unfolded in the education system, the agency to choose teacher training topics was reserved for the organisations offering the above-mentioned outside support, most often based on the internal project objectives approved by their funding entity. In this respect, teachers themselves have not had many opportunities to choose the topics of their own professional development. Indeed, more recently, teacher training has become more teacher-guided by, for example, soliciting the priorities they have identified as needing development in order to best serve their classrooms. Furthermore, an increasing number of teachers and practitioners in North Macedonia have become trainers as well, thus enhancing the practicality and accurately localised applicability of the taught skills, as opposed to more theoretical, technical, and abstract types of training.

In 2001, a conflict between the two majority ethnicities living in North Macedonia—Macedonians and Albanians—occurred, revealing underlying interethnic intolerance and division. The conflict was formally put to rest with the Ohrid Framework Agreement, signed that September, although the agreement did little to tangibly improve interethnic relations and increase integration between peoples. Nevertheless, the subsequent reforms in education—especially providing mother tongue learning for Macedonian, Albanian, Turkish, Serbian, and Bosnian students—revealed a need for more teachers to learn how to provide positive learning experiences for students from each cultural background, specifically how to mainstream interculturalism alongside teaching methodologies related to subject matter and/or learning.

External Support for Teachers' Professional Development

The competences gap between what teachers could do once they graduate from university and the requirements of a classroom in transitional and post-conflict North Macedonia have been addressed by donor projects from international institutions that have been aimed at teacher professional development. The first projects that appeared targeted early education and lower primary education. In 1994, the Step by Step Programme supported by the Open Society Institute (New York) and Georgetown University (Washington) was initially implemented and then subsequently transformed into an association of civil society organisations aimed at improving early childhood education and development through holistic intervention in preschool institutions. This meant that preschool educators were trained and mentored in new, child-centred teaching methodologies, and preschool classrooms were equipped and transformed accordingly. The overall programming of the country's educational processes was revised in line with the Step by Step Methodology where the central pillars are interactions; family and community involvement; inclusion, diversity, and democratic values; planning and assessment; teaching strategies; learning environment; and professional development. Indeed, this transformation of North Macedonia's education system was part of the country's overall socio-political transformation post-independence. One of the changes in professional development design was focused on the greater professionalisation of the teaching profession (i.e. improving interactions, planning and assessment, teaching strategies, learning environment, and professional development), and the second included students' experiences and diverse cultural make-up in the learning process (i.e. investing in family and community involvement and inclusion, diversity, and democratic values). Arguably, the holistic design of this programme supported the development of 'extended professionalism' (Hoyle 2008) as a professional profile that seeks continuous improvement and a systematic approach to one's own profession.

While this programme approached teacher in-service education in a holistic way, other projects' objectives were to provide more specific training connected to subject matter or desired competences. For example, the Primary Education Project (PEP) by the United States Agency for International Development (USAID) provided training to more than 16,500 teachers and more than 970 school officials to help improve students' mathematics and science skills. More specifically, the training objectives of this project were to enable teachers to improve students' critical thinking skills, to use modern ICT in order to compete in the labour market, to stimulate inquiry-based learning and creativity, and to improve school-based assessment that supports learning quality.

In the 2013–2018 period, another important project was implemented across North Macedonia: the USAID-funded Readers are Leaders project. The goal of the project was to improve early grade literacy and numeracy skills as key prerequisites for future learning. The project included a comprehensive assessment of literacy and numeracy for lower primary school students, completed in Macedonian, Albanian, and Turkish, based on a sample of more than 6000 students. The assessment results were relatively low compared to international standards. The other components of the project focused on improving teachers' competences via training sessions and workshops. However, the project also incorporated school-based professional development opportunities for teachers, which was quite progressive at the time. Instead of the commonly implemented one-size-fits-all training or workshop model, the learning communities, which will be described later in more detail, provide in-school professional collaboration which is tailored to address the needs of the involved teachers in their schools.

A particular documented area of weakness in teachers' competences is the way they assess their students. The OECD (2018) results indicate an absence of educational standards against which teachers grade their students and provide a realistic picture of students' achievements. Furthermore, these results also indicate a lack of realistic assessment of teaching quality as aiming towards improving students' educational outcomes. This is problematic because numerous studies (e.g. Canales and Maldonado 2018; Lee 2018; Didion et al. 2020) have proven the connection between teaching quality and students' learning outcomes. Consequently, policy changes need to be steered towards a competency-based merit system of teacher appraisal and providing merit-based incentives for teachers' career development, as quality teachers are the best way towards providing quality learning outcomes.

In the 2012–2016 period, USAID supported the project Teacher Professional and Career Development (TCPD), implemented by the Macedonian Civic Education Center (MCEC), which had set out to create a system focused on the professional competences and teaching standards which would serve as the basis for teachers' career advancement. This system additionally envisioned objective, clear, and transparent teacher evaluation, focused on professional development and continuous support for teachers. Among the key findings from this project was that effective appraisal systems also incorporate a learning culture by, firstly, selecting prospective teachers who have solid capacities for teaching to enter the profession, and, secondly, simultaneously providing incentives for in-service teachers to expand their levels of expertise and autonomy throughout their careers (OECD 2019b).

These projects are merely a selection of the many that have been implemented across schools in North Macedonia, so this is by no means an exhaustive list. Each fulfils two important criteria: firstly, they had a wide scope, that is, they included all schools in the country, and, secondly, they relied on cooperation with the education institutions responsible for the quality of teaching (Bureau for Development of Education), the quality of the school (State Education Inspectorate), and assessment (State Examination Centre). This scope and cooperation on an institutional level implies that part of the projects' objectives was to inform policies and practices through the relevant government bodies, as well as to devise instruments, standards, and criteria that include new provisions derived from the projects' objectives—that is, defining education outcomes and standards, assessment standards, teacher appraisal criteria, and so forth.

Additionally, these projects can be said to have had longer-term aims of building on the capacities of the staff working in these institutions to take on the professional development component after the projects had ended. Whether this was successful or not is a difficult question to answer. On the one hand, policies and practices pertaining to teachers have improved in quality and depth, albeit often perceived by teachers as representing too much regulation and additional administrative work (Joshevska 2017). On the other hand, the resources and human capital available in these institutions are insufficient to undertake the tasks mentioned. For example, the insufficient number of BDE advisors prevents them from conducting field visits and teacher supervision as frequently as is realistically required for continuous support. Furthermore, these externally provided projects have allocated funding for the training they conduct, which is often far more than schools or the government in North Macedonia can commit themselves for the professional training of teachers.

Teachers' Roles, Identities, and Professionalism

The structure of education systems in most 'developed' countries today pushes teachers to 'teach to the test', that is, to communicate only the information which is necessary for students to perform well on national or international assessments (Hargreaves 2000). This paradigm causes confusion regarding the role of the teacher and prioritises the uniformity of testing, standards, and outcomes at the expense of the realities and needs of diverse student bodies. In the Global North, the contemporary role of the teacher has changed considerably since the middle of the twentieth century (Hafsah 2017), becoming less of a (sole) source of information and more of a facilitator in the process of creating knowledge and developing skills, such as critical thinking, problem-solving, conflict-resolution, and higher-order thinking skills. As such, teachers today face the challenge of incorporating 'non-cognitive' skills into mainstream education, in the face of unyielding demands to 'show results' (Gabrieli et al. 2015).

These recent and current changes in the role of the teacher—which can also be viewed as an expansion of the role of the teacher as one who not only educates but also promotes students' personal growth beyond that which is entailed in the curriculum, rather than a person who teaches students to be solely good at test-taking which is the other extreme—require a different kind of professional. Specifically, educators must involve a sense of flexibility in their skill sets in order to accommodate the changing needs of both students and the education system. In other words, today's education professionals are asked to commit to the pursuit of constant improvement and diversification of skills beyond pre-service training and beyond compartmentalised training in discrete teaching methodologies. Again, this is where Hoyle's (2008) 'extended professionalism' should be promoted as a favourable teacher profile, guiding them to cope with the dynamics of a modern classroom, the needs of students, and the narrowing of autonomy (Joshevska 2012, 2016; Joshevska and Kirandziska 2017; Underwood and Kowalczuk-Walędziak 2018). For the purposes of explanation, Hoyle (2008, p. 291) made a distinction between the 'extended' and the 'restricted' professional. Although he abandoned this later, it is still useful for making the argument here.

> A restricted professional was construed as a teacher for whom teaching was an intuitive activity, whose perspective was restricted to the classroom, who engaged little with wider professional reading or activities, relied on experience as a guide to success, and greatly valued classroom autonomy. An extended professional was construed as a teacher for whom teaching was a rational activity, who sought to improve practice through reading and through engaging in continuous professional development, who was happily collegial, and who located classroom practice within a larger social framework.

What Hoyle (2008) is describing as an 'extended professional' is a teacher who proactively develops their own learning in a sustained way and consciously views their profession within a broader socio-cultural landscape. In our view, this type of a professional profile is what ITE and policymakers should promote in order to achieve a more holistic learning experience for students that reflects the reality of the society they enter. Indeed, 2012 research interviews with teachers from North Macedonia and England, selected on the basis that they fit the 'extended professional' profile, provided an insight valuable for informing professional development programmes encouraging the development of this type of identity. They highlighted that professional development opportunities have helped them become better and more confident professionals, but that government-imposed controls and formalities restrict their creativity as teachers. In fact, despite the difference in context (English vs Macedonian teachers), most of the teachers in both countries perceive similar conditions to be restrictive in terms of their autonomy and professionalism. For example, both groups of teachers found external evaluations and inspections to be reductionistic and provide no useful information about what they need to do in order to become better teachers (Joshevska 2012).

Indeed, the question of whether or not the current education system supports—or even requires—'extended professionalism', and whether the opposite—the intuitively teaching 'restricted professional'—is the more achievable goal, remains very pertinent. The professionals Hoyle describes as 'restricted' are actually still very reliable and effective teachers; however, they function definitively within the sanctity of the classroom and school environments, seemingly detached from the socio-politics of the outside world and the corresponding proactive, independent investment in professional development. The argument for this latter, broader teacher role rests on a more deliberate investment in self-improvement, which is what professional development and connecting in practitioners' communities aim to achieve, thus providing an avenue towards redefining the teaching profession as a whole. In practice, the way to achieve this would be not only with professional improvement on a personal level, but also with collaborative action from groups of teachers who are connected in communities of practice. The main argument about the benefit of professional learning communities is that it provides a forum for professional inquiry and collaborative learning, which improves practice and teachers' professional confidence (i.e. Laal and Ghodsi 2012; Jones et al. 2013; Joshevska and Kirandziska 2017; Pregner et al. 2019).

In addition to improved practice, belonging to a professional collective arguably strengthens teachers' professionalism, which has been explored in literature at great length and in great depth using various theoretical models and definitions. Before the 1960s, in most of the Western world, the typical teacher primarily resembled an intuitive practitioner (Atkinson and Claxton 2000): isolated in the classroom, passing on knowledge in the form of a lecture, using and having access to limited resources, and focused on classroom management, with students' motivation and mastery of the course content perhaps seen as something of a secondary order (Hargreaves 2000).

As explained before, the education paradigm has changed in the last 60 years, with more student-oriented teaching now expected, which has inevitably expanded the role of teachers beyond that of simply subject matter experts. Contemporary teachers are expected to use interactive and engaging methods to accommodate the learning needs of different types of students, as well as attending to students' social, emotional, and moral needs (Hargreave and Goodson 1996; Hargreaves 2000). However, there is a marked contradiction at play: on the one hand there is the need to expand the teacher's role as outlined earlier and as supported by research (Joshevska 2012; Hauge and Wan 2019), but on the other hand, there are government regulatory systems that focus almost exclusively on students' outcomes in terms of percentiles and international test results. This fundamental contradiction causes an ambiguity regarding the teaching role, as teachers are expected to juggle all of the demands put on them, as well as their own professional goals in the classroom.

In other words, teachers' roles keep expanding beyond being just transmitters of learning content: teachers today are required to have a variety of skills, not only in pedagogy, but also in how to address students' socio-emotional needs, helping students with different learning abilities and/or behavioural problems, counselling families, and so forth. Nevertheless, the governments around the world, pressed to see 'results', increase the demands for the universalisation of education outcomes only by what can be numerically evaluated on an international test. Arguably, this requires a redefinition of teaching quality and teachers' professional identity, critically with the two being separate entities (Joshevska 2012). While quality teaching can be described through a comprehensive list of desirable and research-based competences—such as subject mastery and using a variety of pedagogical devices and interactive methodologies—teacher quality is a much more abstract concept, incorporating personal characteristics beyond teachable competences that can be taught in traditional training models.

Professional Learning Communities

Teachers' professional identities can be strengthened through continuous professional development (CPD). There is a marked positive impact on teachers' competences that comes from effective CPD, with the most effective helping with the improvement of teachers' practice and students' learning; strengthening the social status of the teaching profession, career prospects, and even salary; as well as increasing the retention of quality staff (e.g., Bolam et al. 2005; OECD TALIS 2009; Opfer and Pedder 2010; Frost 2014). The most far-reaching CPD models promote reflection and experimentation as a key for improving practice, emphasise peer support, promote teachers' independent judgements on how to address classroom-specific needs and the achievement of their personal professional goals, encourage the extension and structuring of professional dialogue for the purpose of sharing knowledge, sustain professional development, and enable teachers to implement new knowledge based on their personal capacities (Frost 2012).

Such effective CPD models, however, have not been implemented equally worldwide. In many countries in Southeast Europe, including North Macedonia, CPD has been implemented in a fragmented fashion, covering discrete areas of expertise. One limitation of this disjointed approach is that it focuses mostly on teachers' individual professional needs rather than on directly promoting the co-construction of knowledge and, ultimately, school-level improvement (Frost 2012). This type of approach also overlooks what Bolam et al. (2005) describe as an important need to focus on defining shared values and visions, collective responsibility for learning, reflective professional inquiry, and collaboration as key to the co-creation of knowledge. Indeed, arguably in order to create a learning environment which addresses students' needs and also provides a thriving professional environment for teachers to reflect the needs of a twenty-first-century classroom, North Macedonia needs an approach that promotes the creation of school-based, collaborative associations of teachers which devise and implement tailor-made interventions in order to address the immediate needs of their schools, then use that as the basis for informing policy, from these grassroots upward (Frost 2012).

Teacher Leadership as the Basis of Professional Learning Communities

An alternative to the PD model of training in different skills in a compartmentalised way, where somebody external decides what are the professional needs of teachers, is the concept of 'teacher leadership' as a model of school-based PD (Bangs and Frost 2011, 2012; Frost 2010, 2011, 2012). It is a promising model in that it promotes teachers' personal agency and the following of their own vision regarding classroom practice in order to inform educational reform (Frost 2012). This is an essential type of empowerment that North Macedonia needs to install in order to nurture the type of teacher professionalism that most resembles Hoyle's 'extended professional' identity (2008).

In North Macedonia, during the implementation of the recent USAID Readers are Leaders project, the established learning communities in over 90 primary schools were run on the basis of the teacher leadership methodology outlined earlier. In the context of this project, the concept of teacher leadership recognises the potential of each teacher to be an agent of change in their school, as an expansion of their existing role—that is, there is no need for a position to be specifically created in the school in order to successfully promote positive change. Furthermore, this model relies on the same pillars which underpin the 'extended professional' profile: reflection, professional enquiry, culture of learning, shared responsibility, and personal agency. As part of Readers are Leaders, the teachers were mentored by other, more experienced practitioners who helped them define challenges from their practice and create systematic interventions utilising teacher leadership and action research methods, a combined approach defined as 'teacher-led development work'. In this process, teachers collected evidence and insights from their development projects in development portfolios. More specifically, they carried out a systematic analysis of a specific problem they were facing in their practice, which they were able to resolve through their teacher-led development work and the collaborative processes in their learning community. This practice, over time, creates a large evidence base for a variety of classroom challenges, which is invaluable as a resource to the teacher, a resource for the teaching profession, but also as an argument for substantial, meaningful education reform.

Joshevska's research (2015, 2016) into the perceptions of teachers in North Macedonia reached 341 teachers via an online survey, which enquired into the benefits of belonging to a learning community. Her findings emphasise above all else the importance of improved cooperation. This broad concept, in turn, can be broken down into initiating conversations among teachers about pedagogical practice (64%), an increased sharing of teaching techniques (55%), and an increase in the number of joint projects (43%) (Underwood and Joshevska 2019). In the latter research, teachers spoke positively about their perception of increased empowerment and self-efficacy, with one contributor explaining:

> The project allowed us to feel like leaders, to be able to identify a problem, to research it, to work on it and to think of practical solutions within a certain time. This gave us self-confidence.

Indeed, such a learning community—that is, one based on the principles of teacher leadership—provides a connection between the realities of classroom and school environments, and the knowledge and skills acquired through in-service education. Based on the experiences from implementing professional learning communities in North Macedonia in order to reconceptualise professional development of teachers and make empirically based judgements about 'what works' in their own classroom and school, there are several benefits that are worth mentioning:

* cost-effectiveness: Teacher leadership is underpinned by the idea that teachers are capable, competent, and in a perfect position to lead change as part of their existing role, with schools being in charge of classroom innovation and professional development. Thoughtful restructuring of the teacher's professional profile and area of control would increase the prospects of

sustainability, locating any restructuring within an already existing system rather than inventing new positions or structures with (substantial) financial implications.

* generation of a large evidence base: In North Macedonia, as part of the 2013–2018 Readers are Leaders project, 90 learning communities were established with a total of around 1650 members, making it one of the most widely piloted models of professional development in North Macedonia. In the academic year 2017/2018, teachers' development portfolios generated an enormous evidence base spanning locally relevant, current pedagogical issues and solutions. If these data are taken into consideration when creating new policies regarding teachers' professional development, this would serve two important principles: evidence-based reform—which is presently greatly lacking in North Macedonia—and the bottom-up informing of education policy. Arguably, these principles are the backbone of teacher leadership.

* increased democratic potential of schools: Learning communities largely rely on collaboration and dialogue between practitioners in order to find the best possible solutions to classroom-related issues. Using evidence to inform policy creates a forum for the wider participation of teachers in decision-making; using teachers' experiences and their documented data as a basis for informing reforms both necessitates and confirms the expansion of school-level and national-level capacity for democratic and participatory leadership.

* international networks and co-creation of knowledge: The interaction between community participation, especially in extended communities, and the sharing of knowledge includes a focus on types of knowledge shared and the different values that teachers put upon these. In effective professional learning communities, it is acknowledged that different forms of knowledge are shared, including knowledge of specific classroom strategies, knowledge of approaches to lesson design, and knowledge of underpinning values regarding teaching (Underwood and Kowalczuk-Walędziak 2018). Sharing this knowledge in an ongoing discourse creates and affirms the teaching community and its members.

Concluding Remarks

In this chapter North Macedonia has been presented as a country that has undergone a prolonged and disruptive socio-political transition over the past three decades. There are historic pressures shaping the nature of education in the country and current pressures on teachers to develop and change their professional practice rapidly, all within a context of limited resources on a national level. With the rise of globalisation and the implementation of the Bologna Process, North Macedonia has also been influenced by external trends, including the codification of teaching standards and participation in international league tables (i.e. OECD PISA assessments), even though the results of these are not affirming. Additionally, North Macedonia has relied on the guidance of projects implemented by international aid organisations such as the Open Society Institute, EU Commission, UNICEF, USAID, and World Bank to intervene in education practices and inform education reform to the extent possible. On the one hand, this has brought significant gains in terms of professional development with the most effective affirming teachers and building communities, but, on the other, has risked undermining the potential of teachers themselves to effect change locally. On a discourse level, involvement in teacher-led development work and teacher leadership projects has brought a conversation around empowerment in North Macedonia, with this empowerment reflected in teachers who have embraced the global and local challenges of engaging in an increasingly complex professional role of being a teacher in the twenty-first century. With these developments has also come the generation of a wealth of fruitful data regarding the effectiveness of teacher-led development projects, thus providing a robust basis for future progress.

Going forwards, teacher education in North Macedonia faces distinct challenges. Some of these are the challenges of building an effective education system within an unstable economy, while others are of ensuring education quality during a time of societal, political, and environmental change. Ultimately, the solution we propose—teacher leadership as the basis of professional learning communities—has grown from our own experiences in such projects. Fundamentally, this relies on the concept that each teacher can be the leader of initiatives that answer the specific needs of their classroom or school without the need for creating a special position in the school for classroom innovation, or external expertise for identification of the challenges which are typical for that specific context. For that to work, intervention is needed at the level of central government: giving teachers and schools greater autonomy to define their own needs and to encourage them to collaborate around finding solutions in order to open up a lasting communication channel with the teachers and use that data to inform education reform. This solution is not entirely new and, as this chapter has identified, some existing projects and approaches do just this: handing agency to teachers and schools affirms and empowers them, fully acknowledging their capacity to lead positive change.

Notes

1. https://www.unicef.org/northmacedonia/early-childhood-education.
2. In North Macedonia, preschool is not mandatory and there is a lack of preschool institutions across the country.
3. It is important to note that in the foreword of this document, it is emphasised that the intention of the provided methodology is not to impose uniformity among higher education institutions.

References

Adjusting the Education Structures in Europe (TUNINC PROJECT). (2006). Socrates—Tempus.

Atkinson, T., and G. Claxton (Eds.). (2000). *The intuitive practitioner: On the value of not always knowing what one is doing.* Buckingham: Open University Press.

Bangs, J., and D. Frost. (2012). *Teacher self-efficacy, voice and leadership: towards a policy framework for Education International.* Brussels: Education International.

Benelux Bologna Secretariat. (2009). *Bologna beyond 2010—Report on the development of the European Higher Education Area, Background Paper for the Bologna Follow-up Group.* Leuven/Louvain-la-Neuve Ministerial Conference, 28–29 April 2009. Retrieved from http://www.ehea.info/media.ehea.info/file/2009_Leuven_ Louvain-la-Neuve/91/8/Beyond_2010_report_FINAL_594918.pdf.

Bolam, R., A. McMahon, L. Stoll, S. Thomas, M. Wallace, A. Greenwood, K. Hawkey, and M. Ingram. (2005). *Creating and sustaining effective professional learning communities (EPLC) project. A research report.* Bristol: Departnment for Education and Skills (DfES), University of Bristol.

Canales, A., and L. Maldonado. (2018). Teacher quality and student achievement in Chile: Linking teachers' contribution and observable characteristics. *International Journal of Educational Development*, 60, 33–50.

Carlsson, R., P. Lindqvist, and U. K. Nordänger. (2019). Is teacher attrition a poor cstimate of the value of teacher education? A Swedish case. *European Journal of Teacher Education*, 42(2), 243–257.

Didion, L., J. R. Toste, and M. J. Filderman. (2020). Teacher professional development and student reading achievement: A meta-analytic review of the effects. *Journal of Research on Educational Effectiveness, 13*(1), 29–66.

Education GPS. (2019). *North Macedonia Student Performance (PISA 2018).* Retrieved from https://gpseducation.oecd.org/CountryProfile?plotter=h5&primaryCountry=MKD&treshold=5&topic=PI.

Duncan, G. J., C. J. Dowsett, A. Claessens, K. Magnuson, A. C. Huston, P. Klebanov, L. S. Pagani, L. Feinstein, M. Engel, J. Brooks-Gunn, H. Sexton, K. Duckworth, and C. Japel. (2007). School readiness and later achievement. *Developmental Psychology, 43*(6), 1428–1446.

European Commission. (2015). *Shaping career-long perspective on teaching. A guide on policies to improve initial teacher education.* Report from the ET2020 Working Group Schools Policy 2014–2015. Retrieved from http://ec.europa.eu/dgs/education_culture/repository/education/library/reports/initialteacher-education_en.pdf.

Frost, D. (2010). Teacher leadership and educational innovation. *Zbornik Instituta za pedagoska istrazivanja, 42*(2), 201–216.

Frost, D. (2011). *Supporting teacher leadership in 15 countries. International Teacher Leadership Project Phase 1. A Report.* Cambridge: Leadership for Learning (LfL) at the University of Cambridge.

Frost, D. (2012). From professional development to system change: teacher leadership and innovation, *Professional Development in Education, 38*(2), 205–227

Frost, D. (2015, September). *The role of teacher leadership in the transition to democratic society.* Paper presented at the European Conference on Education Research (ECER), Budapest, Hungary.

Frost, D. (2014, September). *Non-positional teacher leadership: a perpetual motion miracle. Changing teacher professionality through support for teacher leadership in Europe and beyond.* Paper presented at European Conference on Education Research (ECER), Porto, Portugal.

Gabrieli C., D. Ansel, and S. B. Krachman. (December, 2015). *Ready to be counted: The research case for education policy action on non-cognitive skills a working paper.* Retrieved from https://www.casel.org/wp-content/uploads/2016/06/ReadytoBeCounted_Release.pdf.

Hauge, K., and P. Wan. (Reviewing editor). (2019). Teachers' collective professional development in school: A review study. *Cogent Education, 6*(1).

Hafsah, J. (2017). Teacher of 21st century: Characteristics and development. *Research on Humanities and Social Sciences, 7,* 50–54.

Hargreaves, A. (2000). Four ages of professionalism and professional learning. *Teachers and Teaching: History and Practice, 6*(2), 151–182.

Hargreave, A., & Goodson, I. F. (1996). Teachers' professional lives: Aspirations and actualities. In: I. F. Goodson, & A. Hargreaves (Eds.), *Teachers professional lives* (pp. 1–27). London: Farmer Press.

Hoyle, E. (2008). Changing conceptions of teaching as a profession: Personal reflections. In: D. Johnson and R. Maclean (Eds.), *Teaching: professionalization, development and leadership* (pp. 285–304). Netherlands: Springer.

Јаневска, Н. (2019). Академија за насатавници: за и против. Faktor.mk. Retrieved from https://faktor.mk/akademija-za-nastavnici-za-i-protiv.

Jones, L., G. Stall, and D. Yarbrough. (2013). The importance of professional learning communities for school improvement. *Creative Education, 4*, 357–361.

Joshevska, M., and S. Kirandziska. (2017). The rise and rise of teacher leadership in Macedonia. In: D. Frost (Ed.), *Empowering teachers as agents of change: a non-positional approach to teacher leadership* (pp. 79–84). Leadership for Learning: The Cambridge Network.

Joshevska, M. (2012). *An exploration of teachers' professional identity.* MPhil thesis. Cambridge: University of Cambridge.

Joshevska, M. (2016). *The voice of extended professionals: teachers' perceptions about professional identity.* Paper presented at ECER, Dublin, Ireland.

Joshevska, M. (2017). The voice of extended professionals—learning community members. *International Journal for Education, Research and Training (IJERT), 3*(1), 51–58.

Концепција за деветгодишно основно образование и воспитание. (2007). Retrieved from https://www.bro.gov.mk/wp-content/uploads/2019/05/Koncepcija-za-devetgodisno-osnovno-vospitanie-i-obrazovanie.pdf.

Kamberski, K. (2000). *Preschool and primary education in Republic of Macedonia (development, current state and perspectives).* Skopje, Faculty of Philosophy.

Laal, M., and S. M. Ghodsi. (2012). Benefits of collaborative learning. *Procedia—Social and Behavioral Sciences, 31*, 486–490.

Lee, S. W. (2018). Pulling back the curtain: Revealing the cumulative importance of high-performing, highly qualified teachers on students' educational outcome. *Educational Evaluation and Policy Analysis, 40*(3), 359–381.

Miovska-Spaseva, S., D. Iliev, F. Shehu, K. Barbareev, and L. Mehmedi. (2018). *Teachers' education in primary school in Republic of Macedonia: Situation and perspectives.* Skopje: Open Society Foundation—North Macedonia.

OECD. (2018). *PISA 2015 Results in Focus.* Paris: OECD Publishing. Retrieved from https://www.oecd.org/pisa/pisa-2015-results-in-focus.pdf.

OECD. (2019a). *Programme for International Student Assessment (PISA). Results for PISA 2018. Country Note.* Retrieved from https://www.oecd.org/pisa/publications/PISA2018_CN_MKD.pdf.

OECD. (2019b). *OECD reviews of evaluation and assessment in education: North Macedonia, OECD Reviews of Evaluation and Assessment in Education.* Paris: OECD Publishing.

Opfer, D., and V. D. Pedder. (2010). Benefits, status and effectiveness of continuous professional development for teachers in England. *The Curriculum Journal, 21*(4), 413–431.

Paronen, P., and O. Lappi. (2018). *Finish teachers and principals in figures*. Helsinki: Finish National Agency for Education.

Power School (2019, May 6). A teacher professional development overview. Retrieved from https://www.powerschool.com/resources/blog/a-teacher-professional-development-overview/.

Pregner, R., C. L. Poortman, and A. Handelzalts. (2019). The effects of networked professional learning communities. *Journal of Teacher Education*, 70(5), 441–452.

Teaching and Learning International Survey (TALIS). (2009). *Creating effective teaching and learning environments: First results from TALIS*. Paris: Organisation for Economic Co-operation and Development (OECD).

Underwood, J., and M. Kowalczuk-Walędziak. (2018). Professional communities among teachers a summary of a conceptual framework. *Polish Journal of Educational Studies,* 71(1), 123–142.

Underwood, J. & Joshevska, M. (2019). Building communities among teachers: the experiences of teachers from Macedonia of engagement in extended communities. In V. Orlović Lovren, J. Peeters, and N. Matović (Eds.), *Quality of education: Global development goals and local strategies* (pp. 153–170). Faculty of Philosophy. University of Belgrade.

12

Teacher Education in Slovenia: Between the Past, the Present, and the Future

Mojca Peček

Introduction

Teacher education in Slovenia has a long history. Secondary school teacher education was initially offered by lycées or universities; then, after the school reform of 1848/1849 when lycées were discontinued, it was offered only by universities. Basic school teacher education was first provided, in the form of teaching courses, in the second half of the eighteenth century. One hundred years later, in 1869, teacher training schools were founded; in 1947 the first Teacher Training College was established; and in the academic year 1987/1988, the first cohort of students enrolled in a full higher education programme. In recent times, the teacher education system has been deeply affected by Slovenia gaining independence from Yugoslavia in 1991 and by the Bologna Process. Reforms in the teacher education system prior to gaining independence arose from the country's internal needs and corresponding solutions; since its independence, Slovenia has become more integrated into international landscapes. The Bologna reform in particular, issued from the European Union level, introduced common principles relating to the development of higher education that subsequently affected teacher education as well. However, although principles underpinning further development of teacher education at a

M. Peček (✉)
University of Ljubljana, Ljubljana, Slovenia
e-mail: mojca.pecek@guest.arnes.si

© The Author(s), under exclusive license to Springer Nature Switzerland AG 2023   **269**
M. Kowalczuk-Walędziak et al. (eds.), *The Palgrave Handbook of Teacher Education in Central and Eastern Europe*, https://doi.org/10.1007/978-3-031-09515-3_12

European level have been agreed upon, teacher education is still predominantly regarded as the responsibility of national ministries of education and, therefore, the teacher is still predominantly perceived as a teacher in their national context (Zgaga 2008). Slovenia is no exception in this regard. Thus, the teacher education system in Slovenia maintains its own specific features and forms, despite Europe-wide common principles.

Thus, in order to understand how teacher education works in Slovenia today, societal, political, economic, cultural, and historic—as well as education-related—circumstances and shifts should be taken into account. In the following chapter, a short history of these changes and the structure of the contemporary education system in Slovenia will be presented, before discussing the ways in which both the initial teacher education system and the teacher professional development system have been developed and structured. Lastly, this paper will analyse some of the present tensions and challenges, as well as potential directions for the future, faced by teacher education in Slovenia.

Socio-political Context

In 1918, after almost 600 years under Habsburg rule, Slovenia joined the Kingdom of Serbs, Croats, and Slovenes, later renamed as the Kingdom of Yugoslavia. After World War II the Socialist Federal Republic of Yugoslavia was established, in which Slovenia was one of the six republics under the federal parliament and government in Belgrade. In the second half of the twentieth century, interethnic conflicts, deepened by Yugoslavia's economic crisis and disintegration of Yugoslavia, evolved into the demand for independence (Natek et al. 2000, p. 1). On 23 December 1990, 88.5% of Slovenia's population voted to have their own state, and on 25 June 1991, the Republic of Slovenia declared its independence. A ten-day war followed in the summer of that year. Slovenia was officially recognised by the European Union in January 1992 and joined the United Nations in May 1992. Subsequently, Slovenia joined NATO (March 2004), European Union (May 2004), the Eurozone (January 2007), and the OECD (2010).

Slovenia is a small European country in terms of land area (20,273 km^2) and population (2.08 million) (Statistični urad republike Slovenije [SURS] 2019d). Although the number of foreign citizens living in Slovenia has increased in recent years and represented 6.6% of the population in 2019 (SURS 2019d), the country has a relatively homogeneous ethnic structure. According to the 2002 census, 83.1% of the population consider themselves

Slovenian, 1.8% Croats, 2.0% Serbs, 1.6% Muslims (including Bosniacs), 0.3% Hungarians, 0.1% Italians, 2.2% others, and 8.9% of unknown nationality (SURS 2002). The country's official language is Slovenian and, in ethnically mixed areas, the official languages are also Italian and Hungarian; additionally, the Romani language is protected by law. Slovenia is a democratic republic and a social state governed by law, with the state's authority based on the principle of separating powers into legislative, executive, and judicial strands, and a parliamentary system of government.

As part of Yugoslavia (prior to independence in 1991), Slovenia succeeded in maintaining close ties (e.g., economic, cultural, educational) with Central and Western Europe. Since its independence, Slovenia has managed to facilitate a relatively fast and successful establishment of a democratic system. However, like other countries undergoing this type of transition, it has faced numerous problems due to rapid and fundamental changes (e.g., political, economic, cultural, educational)—brought about by the dual competing factors of proximity to the European Union and the heavy burden of a socialist past (Natek et al. 2000, p. 1). In 2008, the global financial crisis halted the progress of economic and social development in Slovenia, and it has been a challenge to find a path back to economic recovery and renewed prosperity since then: GDP per capita was 22,083 euro in 2018 (SURS 2019a). To contextualise government spending on education within that, public expenditure for formal education was 4.8% of Slovenia's GDP in 2017, within which preprimary education accounted for 20.1%; basic education for 43.5%; upper secondary education for 16.9%; and tertiary education for 19.5% (SURS 2017).

Education System

The 1990s—with Slovenia's independence won in 1991—were a turning point in the development of the contemporary education system. In 1995, the *White Paper on Education in the Republic of Slovenia* was introduced, stipulating the current school system's core principles, and new school acts regulating the entire education system (from preschool up to university education) were adopted. This new legislation became the basis for considerable changes on a policymaker level and decision-making processes alike, and established basic governance mechanisms as well as the regulatory framework for the operation of schools. These acts and regulations have been amended several times since, but their core rules have remained more or less the same. On the whole, these reforms were based on the following principles: the right to education; equal opportunities for pupils; the possibility of choice at the level of curricula, school activities, teacher education, schools; fostering excellence in students; increased quality of education; an increase in teachers' and schools' professional responsibility and autonomy of teachers and schools; plurality of cultures and knowledge; and lifelong learning (Krek 1995) (Fig. 12.1).

Preschool Education

Preschool education is part of the education system and is not compulsory (Eurydice 2019; Taštanoska 2019). Children can attend preschool institutions from the age of 11 months until they enter compulsory education at the age of six. Professional staff adhere to the Kindergarten Curriculum, that is, the fundamental programme document adopted in 1999. Kindergarten programmes include education, care, and meals and are subsidised by the state, with parents paying means-tested fees.

In the last decade the number of children in kindergartens has increased by one-third. In the school year 2018/2019, 81.7% of all preschool age children attended preschool education. The proportion of four- and five-year-old children attending preschool education is 93.5% (SURS 2019b; Kozmelj 2019).

Compulsory Basic Education

Basic education is compulsory and state-funded, free of charge for all children whose sixth birthday occurs in the calendar year they enter first grade, is organised as a single-structure, and spans nine years (Taštanoska 2019; Eurydice 2019). It is provided by public and private schools, as well as educational institutions for pupils with special needs and adult education organisations.

The basic school programme is specified by the timetable and curricula of compulsory and optional subjects. Besides, it is specified by guidelines and educational concepts that define methods of working with children and cross-curricular contents to guide the work of education professionals. It is divided into three three-year cycles. In the first cycle pupils have a class teacher for most subjects; in the second cycle, specialist subject teachers are gradually introduced; then during the third cycle pupils are taught exclusively by specialist subject teachers. In grades 1 and 2, teachers assess pupils' progress with descriptive marks, and then from grade 3 onwards with numerical marks from 1 to 5, whereby 1 is negative and the rest are positive. At the end of grades 6 and 9 pupils sit for a national examination.

STRUCTURE OF THE EDUCATION SYSTEM IN THE REPUBLIC OF SLOVENIA

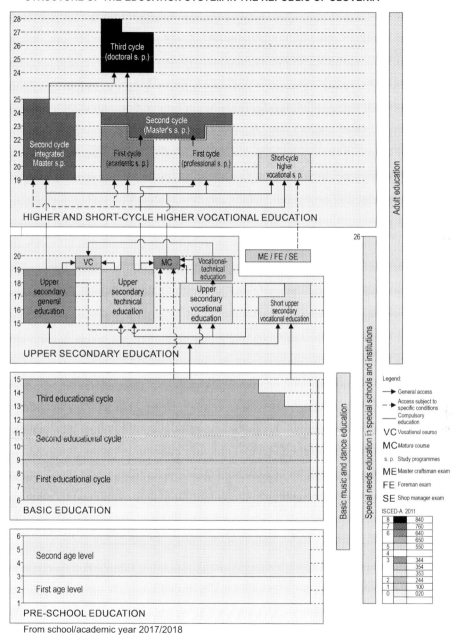

From school/academic year 2017/2018

Fig. 12.1 Structure of the education system in the Republic of Slovenia (2019)

Upper Secondary Education

Successful completion of compulsory education enables pupils, typically aged 15, to proceed to an education programme at a selected upper secondary school, a transition regulated at a national level through the common national application system (Peček 2015; Taštanoska 2019; Eurydice 2019). Upper secondary education is non-compulsory, takes two to five years to complete, and does not carry tuition fees. It is divided into general upper secondary education (different types of four-year *gimnazija* programmes), technical upper secondary education (four years), and vocational upper secondary education (two to three years). *Gimnazija* education ends with the general *matura* and technical education with the vocational *matura*.

It is estimated that all students who have completed their basic school education continue their studies at the upper secondary level. In the school year 2018/2019, 91.2% of the population aged 15–18 were enrolled in upper secondary education: 35% of pupils opted for general education, 46.2% for technical education, and 18% for vocational education (Kozmelj 2019).

Tertiary Education

Like some other EU countries, Slovenia opted for a gradual implementation of the Bologna reform, and since the academic year 2009/2010, only 'post-reform' programmes have been offered. The most important fundamental objectives of tertiary education are high-quality education, employability for students upon completing their studies and mobility for students and staff, fair access to education for students, diversity of institutions and study programmes, and international comparability of study programmes (Taštanoska 2019, p. 39).

The higher education reform of 2004 introduced a three-cycle structure (Peček 2015; Pavlič Možina and Prešeren 2011; Taštanoska 2019; Eurydice 2019). The first cycle has a binary system of academic and vocational study programmes (180–240 ECTS; 3–4 years), leading to a first-cycle degree. The second cycle offers master's degree programmes (60–120 ECTS; 1–2 years). The third cycle covers doctoral study programmes (180 ECTS; 3 years). Long, non-structured master's degree programmes are allowed as an exception. In public higher education institutions, Slovenian students and students from EU member states pay tuition fees for part-time studies, while full-time studies are free of charge. For third-cycle studies, tuition fees are paid by students, but can be subsidised by public funds under certain conditions.

The transition to higher education is managed on a national level. The number of places available is fixed for all study programmes and is announced each year by higher education institutions in the pre-enrolment period. In case the number of applicants exceeds this capacity, candidates are selected from those with a better overall grade in the *matura* examination, higher overall marks in third and fourth years, or marks in individual subjects in upper secondary education (Peček 2015; Pavlič Možina and Prešeren 2011; Taštanoska 2019). Admission requirements include the following: a general *matura* certificate or a vocational *matura* examination and an additional exam for university first-cycle study programmes; a vocational *matura* or a general *matura* certificate for vocational first-cycle programmes; a first-cycle degree in a corresponding field of studies (and additional exams when this is not the case) for master's degree studies; a second-cycle degree for doctoral studies; and additional aptitude test results (e.g., artistic talents, physical skills) are required for certain study programmes.

Over the past 20 years, tertiary education has undergone several legislative and structural changes, rapid institutional development, and a significant increase in student numbers. In 2018/2019, there were 3 public and 3 private universities, 1 independent public higher education institution, and 48 private higher education institutions in Slovenia (Taštanoska 2019, p. 40). Slovenia surpassed the specific target of the *Europe 2020 Strategy* (2013), namely, to have 40% of the population aged 30–34 holding tertiary qualifications (Taštanoska 2019, p. 39). In the academic year 2018/2019 the share of people aged 19–24 participating in tertiary education was 46.1% (SURS 2019c): 75,991 students were enrolled in tertiary education programmes, of which 10,566 were enrolled in short-cycle higher education courses and 65,425 in higher education programmes, including 3089 in doctoral study programmes (Sever 2019).

Education of Children with Special Needs

Education for children with special education needs (SEN) is provided exclusively as a public service, with provision following a multi-track approach and a variety of services offered between mainstream education and special needs institutions (Peček 2015; Taštanoska 2019; Eurydice 2019). A Special Education Needs Guidance Commission coordinates professional and administrative activities that qualify a child for their appropriate educational setting. The majority of children with SEN enrol in programmes with adapted implementation and additional professional assistance provided in mainstream classes.

Recently there has been a decline in the number of children with SEN enrolled in adapted and special programmes offered in special class units, and an increase in the number of children with SEN enrolled in mainstream programmes. There were 9948 children with SEN enrolled in mainstream and adapted basic schools in the academic year 2018/2019, and most of these children (76.5%) were included in mainstream programmes with additional professional assistance, meaning that children with SEN represented 4.1% of all children in mainstream basic compulsory programmes (Kozmelj 2019).

Recent Reforms in Teacher Education

As mentioned in the introduction, teacher education in Slovenia has a long history. The first organised basic school teacher education was established in 1774, on the basis of the General School Ordinance, with prospective teachers attending teaching courses. The third Basic School Act in 1869 led to the establishment of the first four-year teacher training schools. This was increased to five years in 1929 (Cencič 1990, p. 138; see also Janša-Zorn 1997; Peček 1998). As there was a shortage of teachers after World War II, teaching courses were again in place in 1955 when teacher training schools were reintroduced, initially providing four-year and later, once more, five-year programmes (Cencič 1990, pp. 138–139; Janša-Zorn 1997, p. 8).

Upper secondary teacher education followed a somewhat different path. Initially it was offered by lycées or universities; then, after the school reform of 1848/1849 when lycées were discontinued, it was offered only by universities. After World War II, graduates from different universities took to teaching in upper general secondary schools and also in the upper grades of basic compulsory schools (Janša-Zorn 1997, pp. 8–9).

As there was a need for subject teachers in the upper grades of basic school, the Teacher Training College (programme comprising tertiary two-year study and a thesis) was established in Ljubljana in 1947, renamed the Academy of Education in 1964. In 1961 another Academy of Education was founded in Maribor. The main purpose of the transition from the Teacher Training College to the Academy of Education was to ensure that all basic school teachers completed a two-year tertiary education programme: as a result, a class teacher training programme was added to its repertoire in 1964 (Janša-Zorn 1997). In the academic year 1987/1988, the first cohort of students enrolled in a full higher education programme (i.e., a four-year study programme and a thesis). This transition presented many dilemmas. There was broad agreement that subject teachers should be educated via four-year higher education programmes, but there was not the same consensus that this was needed for class teachers. Eventually the decision to include this study programme in higher education prevailed and academies of education became faculties of education with the goal of creating better conditions for high-quality research and higher quality teacher education programmes (Janša-Zorn 1997, p. 28; Zgaga 1997, p. 50). In 2003, a third faculty of education was established within the new University of Primorska in Koper. In 2009, the implementation of the new Bologna study programmes began: all teachers in Slovenia are now required to attain a second-cycle degree, that is, a master's degree or 300 ECTS.

All of these changes dramatically changed the working conditions for faculty of education academic staff, namely forcing them to attain doctoral degrees as quickly as possible and to secure the appropriate accreditation newly required for working in a university. While lecturers at the former teacher training schools were mostly experienced practitioners and textbook writers, at academies of education, and even more so at faculties of education, practical teaching experience ceased to be the decisive factor in securing an employment contract. More lecturers with a sound academic, research-based background were sought in order to ensure the new faculties carried the same weight as other, more established faculties (Razdevšek-Pučko and Peček 2002, p. 217).

In addition to faculties of education, prospective teachers can also currently acquire their degree in other programmes at one of Slovenia's three universities, namely, in courses relevant to the subject they will teach (e.g., the Faculty of Mathematics and Physics for future maths and physics teachers). Traditionally, this type of teacher education ran in parallel with regular studies for specific professions. As a result, there were no significant differences between study programmes for students training to become teachers and those aiming to enter other careers in the field. The only difference was that student teachers were simply required to attend a minimal additional number of prescribed units in methods of subject teaching, as well as in pedagogy and psychology (Razdevšek-Pučko and Peček 2002, p. 218). With the implementation of the Bologna Process there came an intention to change this; however, most faculties made a distinction between their programmes only in second-cycle degree studies. While graduates from faculties of education can work as subject teachers in basic, technical, and vocational upper secondary schools, graduates from other faculties can work as subject teachers in all basic and all upper secondary schools.

According to Hudson and Zgaga (2008, pp. 8–9) international cooperation is traditionally broadly embedded in university studies; however, teacher education is traditionally developed comparatively more within its national boundaries, a contrast which applies both in Slovenia and further afield. Prior to the 1990s, teacher education in Europe was rarely a subject of European and/or international cooperation. However, shifts away from predominantly national focuses began with the Maastricht Treaty in 1992, as well as with cross-border programmes like Erasmus, Socrates, Leonardo, and Tempus which emerged at the end of the 1980s and into the 1990s (Hudson and Zgaga 2008, pp. 8–9). Subsequently, the Bologna Process brought about an even bigger change across Europe in this regard and Slovenia is no exception. International trends did play something of a role in teacher education reforms before Slovenia's independence (e.g., Troha 1992, p. 105; Marentič Požarnik 1992); however, the main issue was always how to educate teachers in such a way as to ensure the provision of high-quality education within the national education system. As such, approaches and solutions mainly followed internal needs for change and pressure from above, that is, the state and its political system. Consequently, the teacher education reform of the 1990s, following Slovenia's independence in 1991, was necessary due to the reformation of basic and upper secondary schools that required a different kind of teachers—teachers that are willing to make their own professional decisions and stand by them (e.g., Peček and Razdevšek-Pučko 2000). Key features of this reform included how it responded to challenges and solutions identified by its users and practitioners, and aimed to find a consensus among different interest groups in the country (e. g. teachers in schools, teacher educators at faculties, student teachers, Ministry of Education, Science, and Sport). The reform was implemented during a time of relatively high university and teacher autonomy (Razdevšek-Pučko and Peček 2002). In contrast, the Bologna reform has since been conducted from the top-down, whereby the 'top' is no longer the state, but rather a new set of standards developed at European Union level—thus, it is not a reform based on the needs identified in Slovenia. Therefore, the Bologna reform has proved hard to accept in Slovenia, especially by academic staff upon whom it was forced, generating a wide range of opposing views which will be further discussed later.

Current System of Initial Teacher Education

Initial teacher education in Slovenia is provided by faculties as well as by higher education institutions, in line with higher education legislation and education regulations regarding requirements for teachers and other education professionals. Slovenian legislation states that preschool teachers must complete a three-year professional study programme (180 ECTS); and all basic and upper secondary school teachers must complete a higher education degree (four years) in the appropriate field (pre-Bologna programmes) or a master's degree (Bologna programmes) (300 ECTS). All teachers should attain appropriate pedagogical education and successfully pass the teaching certification examination (e.g., Pravilnik o izobrazbi učiteljev in drugih stro-kovnih delavcev v izobraževalnem programu osnovne šole 2011; Eurydice 2019; Taštanoska 2019).

Models of Bologna teacher study programmes vary: some follow the 3 years (first cycle) + 2 years (second cycle) model (e.g., in the Faculty of Arts at the University of Ljubljana) and others follow the 4 years (first cycle) + 1 year (second cycle) model (e.g., in the Faculty of Education at the University of Ljubljana); therefore, both are two-cycle programmes. There are also exceptions, for example, 5 years + 0 year programmes (e.g., in the Faculty of Mathematics and Physics at the University of Ljubljana), also referred to as one-cycle programmes.

Initial teacher education for class teachers is based on the integrated or concurrent model, meaning that professional, general, and subject components are inseparably combined. Education for preschool teachers, and subject teachers in basic or upper secondary schools, can follow either the concurrent or the consecutive model. The consecutive model as a pathway towards becoming a qualified teacher can be realised in two ways: on the one hand, the first cycle can provide appropriate knowledge in the taught subject while the second cycle can provide vocational education; on the other hand, experts with work experience in particular fields and an existing degree in a relevant subject (300 ECTS) can complete a supplementary pedagogical-andragogical programme (60 ECTS) (Eurydice 2019). Teachers who teach in special education programmes in special basic schools are educated in study programmes that apply the integrated model. Teachers who teach in the third three-year cycle in special basic schools can be mainstream subject teachers, but they need to obtain a dedicated qualification (of at least 60 ECTS) before working with children with special needs.

Following a completed master's degree, students can enrol in PhD programmes which, in the 2019/2020 academic year, have been extended from three to four years (240 ECTS). The fundamental aim of PhD programmes is to deepen students' understanding of theoretical and methodological concepts in the area of teacher education and educational science.

The admission procedure for teacher education institutions is the same for all students in whatever higher education institution or study programme they enrol. Thus, a condition for entry into teacher education is positive results from the general *matura* or positive results from the vocational *matura*, plus an additional general *matura* subject. For study programmes, like for example art pedagogy or physical education, special aptitude or psychophysical abilities are tested. A higher education institution may limit enrolments where the number of applicants significantly exceeds the number of available places. The selection criteria are academic results at the *matura*, marks from the third and fourth years of secondary school and aptitude test results (if relevant) (*Zakon o visokem šolstvu* 2012). Students who have completed a first-cycle programme in an appropriate discipline, or students who have finished a first-cycle programme in other disciplines then complete bridging study obligations or an extra year (60 ECTS), may enrol in second-cycle programmes (*Zakon o visokem šolstvu* 2012; Eurydice 2019) (Fig. 12.2).

Curricula and syllabi of the study programmes are under the autonomy of the higher education institutions themselves; however, they must meet the requirements as specified by the *Criteria for the accreditation and external evaluation of higher education institutions and study programmes* (Svet Nacionalne agencije Republike Slovenije za kakovost v visokem šolstvu (NAKVIS) 2019). The administrative framework for the development of teacher education programmes used to be stipulated by the *Accreditation criteria for teacher education study programmes* (*Merila za akreditacijo študijskih programov za izobraževanje učiteljev* 2011), but those accreditation criteria are currently no longer valid. At the moment, the NAKVIS Council considers only general criteria for the accreditation of teacher education programmes (NAKVIS 2019) which have no education-specific requirements. Such an accreditation must be confirmed by the Ministry of Education, Science, and Sport. The current practice of the ministry is to confirm those teacher education programmes that meet the currently invalid criteria mentioned earlier (*Merila za akreditacijo študijskih programov za izobraževanje učiteljev* 2011), including whether or not a programme provides a second-cycle master's degree; includes sufficient hours of teaching practice; includes areas that are currently important, such as preparing the candidate to teach children with special needs; ensures the candidate will be employable; as well as what professional title is awarded upon completion of the programme (Adamič Tomič 2019).

The *Criteria for accreditation of teacher education study programmes* (*Merila za akreditacijo študijskih programov za izobraževanje učiteljev* 2011) stipulated that a teacher education programme should include at least 60 ECTS in pedagogical-psychological studies (i.e., psychology, pedagogics, didactics, andragogy, methodology of pedagogical research, etc.), in the humanities and social sciences (i.e., philosophy, sociology, anthropology, etc.), in subject or relevant didactics, as well as at least 15 ECTS of teaching practice.

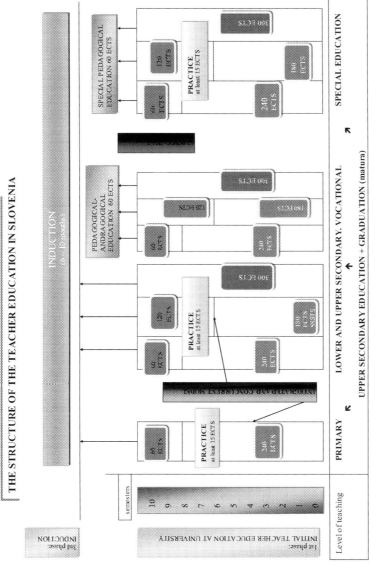

Fig. 12.2 The structure of the teacher education in Slovenia (Peček and Lesar 2011)

Students should attain the following general competences:

– Effective teaching
– Participation in the work and in the social environment
– Ability to undertake professional development
– Management abilities

As already mentioned, the curricula and syllabi of study programmes are under the autonomy of higher education institutions; thus, the structure, number, and length of courses a student must complete vary from programme to programme. For example, the curricula of study programmes at the Faculty of Education, University of Ljubljana, are divided into four basic groups: compulsory general or basic pedagogical courses, compulsory vocational courses, elective courses (general and vocational), and intensive practical training in the first cycle and a master's thesis in the second cycle (Eurydice 2019; Faculty of Education 2019). There is variance from programme to programme in terms of the length of practical training (at least 15 ECTS) and the way it is integrated into the programme (Peček and Lesar 2011). One part of practical training usually includes long (i.e., a few days or weeks), continuous practice in the classroom, and another part consists of observation of individual teaching hours. Some programmes, such as class teaching at the Faculty of Education, University of Ljubljana, provide practical training throughout the course of study. In the first cycle, practical training is offered in the form of continuous classroom practice. Additionally, practice is facilitated in special didactics and other courses, for example, theory of education and psychology. In the second cycle, practical training is an integral part of various courses, but there is no continuous classroom practice. Other programmes (e.g., programmes at the Faculty of Arts, University of Ljubljana) have practical training only in the second cycle, where all teaching-related education is concentrated.

Assessment methods are set separately for each course in the curriculum. Taking into account the diversity of delivery modes for individual courses (i.e., lectures, seminars, tutorials, project and research work, diaries, performances, etc.), various student activities may be separately evaluated and constitute part of the final mark in the course. In general, the traditional methods of assessment (i.e., colloquium [mid-year tests], oral and written examinations, seminar papers, etc.) are supplemented by marked special tasks within individual courses. The assessment scale spans 1–10, where 1–5 are failing marks and 6–10 passing. To complete a study programme, the student must have all courses assessed with a positive mark, and then write and orally defend a master's thesis in front of a panel, with the thesis presenting theoretical and/or empirical research conducted by the student themselves.

Current System of Teacher Professional Development

While teacher professional development in the 1980s was merely a moral obligation, the new legislation adopted at the beginning of the 1990s introduced a system which enabled those who undertook professional training to be awarded higher titles (e.g., mentor, advisor, counsellor) and correspondingly higher salaries. Although teachers were initially generally somewhat critical of this new system—there were very few programmes available and there was an imbalance between themes, not all of which provided an equal opportunity to acquire points—annual internal evaluations of the system up until 2010 show that the quality improved with each new academic year, provided additional career opportunities for all teachers, and resulted in significant and positive motivation for participants (Peček 2008).

The right and obligation of teachers to undertake continual professional development is stipulated by law and the *Collective agreement for the educational sector* (*Kolektivna pogodba za dejavnost vzgoje in izobraževanja v Republiki Sloveniji* 2019), as well as by relevant rules. The *Rules on the selection and co-financing of further education and training programmes for education professionals* (*Pravilnik o izboru in sofinanciranju programov nadaljnjega izobraževanja in usposabljanja strokovnih delavcev v vzgoji in izobraževanju* 2017) issued by the minister responsible for education outlines the organisation and financing of programmes, the responsibilities of decision-making bodies, as well as the award and recognition of points for the career advancement of preschool and school teachers (Eurydice 2019). The aim of this further education is not only the professional development of education staff as individuals, but also the improved quality and efficiency of schools and the education system as a whole.

There are two main types of continuing professional development (CPD) programmes (Eurydice 2019):

– Programmes which qualify teachers for different posts, for teaching a new subject, or for teaching their existing taught subject on a higher level are prescribed by law. Thus, it is both the right and the duty of the teacher teaching a subject for which such a programme is prescribed to undertake this type of training. In the school's annual work plan, the head teacher should prioritise teachers' training via this type of programme and ensure that they are available to undertake such training. The providers of these programmes are higher education institutions which have developed and implemented their programmes in accordance with the rules on higher education.

– Shorter programmes of career development aimed at promoting the vocational and disciplinary development of teaching staff. The providers of these programmes are diverse institutions dealing with education.

The Ministry of Education, Science, and Sport outlines the priority topics and fields for continued professional development on a national level. These themes are defined by the Council of Experts for General Education and in cooperation with the Development and Counselling Institutes. Every year the ministry announces a public call for proposals and co-financing of programmes, with programmes selected by the tender commission and approved by the minister's decision. The chosen programmes are then published in a special catalogue, thus informing schools and teachers of their opportunities.

The *Collective agreement for the educational sector* (*Kolektivna pogodba za dejavnost vzgoje in izobraževanja v Republiki Sloveniji* 2019) specifies the right to up to five days of leave for teacher professional development per annum or 15 days over three years. Teachers may take training during their regular work and get a paid leave of absence. Teachers are free to decide which programmes they want to take; however, training for major curricular changes or other reforms is either compulsory or recommended. The Ministry of Education, Science, and Sport allocates funds to cover the cost of participation in CPD programmes. Teachers are also compensated for any travel and accommodation expenses incurred during training. Additionally, teachers receive a salary increase for acquiring formal higher education qualification or receive points for participating in programmes that count towards their future promotion, offering further motivation for education staff to pursue training (Eurydice 2019).

However, the teacher professional development system in Slovenia is not without its problems. While the state and municipalities do provide some funds to cover the material costs of participation in teacher professional development programmes, the amount given to schools is frequently insufficient, which is the main reason why such opportunities are not fully taken up in practice. Indeed, this was especially the case in the years of recession in the early 2010s. Another issue is each school's ability to cover for teachers' absences while still implementing its core programme of education provision: the head teacher and the teacher who wishes to attend training must find an agreeable solution and, in practice, this most often results in solidarity, with teachers covering classes for one another.

Tensions in Recent Teacher Education Reforms

Teacher education reforms in Slovenia have been accompanied by many challenges, conflicts, and often very heated and prolonged discussions and negotiations. As mentioned before, one of the key questions concerning teacher education reforms after World War II was the level of education required for teachers: is it possible to educate a teacher in a two-year tertiary education programme or is it necessary to do this in a four-year tertiary education programme? This discussion was concluded in 1986 when it was agreed that all teachers needed a four-year education. Since the Bologna reform, this question has lost its potency as it has become clear that all teachers would need to attain a second-cycle master's degree. The only exception to this are preschool teachers—in the past the requirement was a completed two-year tertiary education programme, whereas now the requirement is a completed first cycle, that is, 180 ECTS or three-year programme.

Another question which arises with every reform, including the Bologna reform, is about the study programme model that should be followed: either consecutive (with subject education first, followed by pedagogical education) or concurrent (pedagogical education alongside subject education from beginning to end). Different faculties across the country have always made different decisions, usually in accordance with their own academic traditions and norms.

While teaching practice for students was fairly well organised in teacher training schools, a problem arose with the academic year 1987/1988, when the first cohort of students enrolled in a higher education programme, as those programmes were less ready to provide opportunities for practical work (Cencič 1990). Ever since, the quality and length of teaching practice for students has been one of the key questions underpinning all teacher education reforms in Slovenia, including the Bologna reform (e.g., Razdevšek-Pučko and Peček 2002; Marentič Požarnik 1992).

In terms of the tradition, quality, and length of practical training, there are differences between education programmes at faculties of education and other faculties, and between practical training for class teachers and subject teachers. Practical training at faculties of education, especially in programmes for class teachers, is longer and more integrated into the study process than in other programmes. The Bologna reform led to significantly longer and better quality practical teacher training in all faculties that educate teachers; nevertheless, there are still differences in the length and the method of delivery across study programmes. One of the reasons for this discrepancy came to the fore during the transition from academies of education to faculties of education in 1991: namely, universities found it difficult to avoid explicit or implicit perceptions that practice was 'only an introduction' to the trade/vocation and thus not truly worthy of academic studies at the university level (Marentič Požarnik 1992; Razdevšek-Pučko and Peček 2002). This transition period also uncovered the assumption that teachers working with younger children—and thus dealing more directly with their upbringing—would need more teaching practice than teachers working with older pupils, where formal education and knowledge of the taught subject were assumed to be more important than the methods of teaching or understanding children (Marentič Požarnik 1992; Razdevšek-Pučko and Peček 2002).

These imbalances in perception, and therefore actual provision of teacher education, continue with regard to graduates' types of education: graduates from faculties of education, especially graduates in class education, attain in-depth pedagogical-psychological knowledge, while graduates from other faculties attain more subject-related knowledge and have less developed teaching skills (Janša-Zorn 1997, p. 24). For the former, the emphasis in their studies is on their profession, and for the latter on the relevant scientific field (Zgaga 1997, p. 51)—this particularly applies to teachers who do not attend faculties of education and attain some teaching skills later in their careers, while working towards their second-cycle degree or even after completing their master's degree. As a result, every reform of teacher education in Slovenia is affected by heated debates between advocates for scientific fields (i.e., mathematics, physics, geography, etc.) and proponents of educational courses (i.e., theories of education, didactics, psychology, etc.). The material results of these debates often depend on the balance of power of those advocates at the faculties at the time of each reform. In this process, the need for the right balance between the two extremes is often forgotten (Janša-Zorn 1997; Zgaga 1997, pp. 52, 53).

As mentioned before, the Bologna reform has received much criticism in the education community in Slovenia, as well as many of the other countries in this handbook. Nevertheless, the reform has introduced many changes in teacher education, which fundamentally widen the spectrum of teachers' competences: the inclusion of education for children with special needs; the inclusion of education for marginalised groups of children, such as migrants; and the posing of questions around inclusion, class management, individualisation and differentiation, and interdisciplinary work. It is true that some of these themes have been included in teacher education programmes as electives only, nevertheless, these themes can meet the wider spectrum of needs today's teachers have, as they were met before the reform. Current teacher education programmes also include more interdisciplinary courses, provide more elective subjects, and allow for easier transfers between study programmes, as well as for international comparability. Current teacher education programmes have led to higher levels of student mobility both within and out of Slovenia, with greater international mobility of students and employees as faculties encourage students and their staff to spend at least one semester abroad.

Nonetheless, criticisms of the Bologna reform remain valid and essential. Admittedly, previous reforms were affected by their particular political, social, educational, and professional contexts, but they were always generated within Slovenia itself and included a very wide range of teachers and researchers from the country's own field of education. The same cannot be claimed for the reforms of the last 20 years, in particular the Bologna reform. Recently, the development of the education system as a whole, including teacher education, has become ever more influenced by results from international analyses (TIMMS, PISA, PIRLS, etc.) and international strategic documents, such as the Sorbonne Declaration and the Lisbon Strategy, aimed at reviewing the quality of each country's education system and providing directions for future development. As a result, the Bologna reform is often considered to be a reform that led those who helped draft the strategic guidelines for the development of education in Slovenia to fully adopt Europe-level education policy (Kroflič 2014, p. 10; see also Kovač 2006, p. 104), despite the fact that there were no analyses indicating that changes in the direction dictated by the Bologna reform were necessary or constructive for the future development of tertiary education in the country (Kellermann 2006, p. 34; Kovač 2006, p. 104). Nonetheless, the Bologna reform introduced new concepts, new terminology, and new ways of thinking to teacher education programmes in Slovenia and thus significantly changed the way teachers are educated: a new, performance- and competence-oriented paradigm emerged (Kotnik 2006, p. 85; Tancig and Devjak 2006, p. 9). Indeed, competence is the central concept of the Bologna agreement, yet the term itself, it is often claimed, has a range of meanings, creates confusion, and has no scientific basis (Kotnik 2013).

Another criticism of Bologna reform needs to be mentioned. Although the main focus of the Bologna reform is supposed to be the reform of education content, many ongoing discussions and dilemmas relate to formal issues, such as study programme levels (Medveš 2006, p. 7; Peček and Lesar 2011). While most faculties wanted to maintain uniform, single-cycle studies unchanged, as there were no obvious problems with the former system, the pressure for two-cycle studies prevailed via the question of the employability of graduates from first-cycle degrees (Medveš 2006). Formally, faculties came to terms and provided options for two-cycle studies; in reality, however, graduates of first-cycle degrees in teacher education have remained unemployable, as the required level of education for all teaching positions, according to Bologna reform, is a second-cycle degree or 300 ECTS.

During the implementation of the Bologna reform, it was often said by its critics that it represented a break with the tradition of European universities: instead of seeing knowledge as value in and of itself, the reform frames knowledge as an 'investment', replacing the humanist, European tradition of higher education in the humanities with the economic, utilitarian pursuit of studies as a commodity (Medveš 2006, p. 8). Indeed, Kellermann (2006, p. 34) points out that the Bologna reform is concerned with employability, mobility, and competitiveness, but overlooks the traditional ideals of universities, such as research for the sake of scientific progress and the development of well-educated people. Consequently, the fundamental motivation of students and teachers to pursue their studies from places of questioning, curiosity, and criticism has been replaced with a capitalist motivation based on employability and market value (Kellermann 2006, p. 30). Kotnik (2013, p. 166) comes to similar conclusions, while Kroflič (2014, p. 11) takes this further and claims that in education profession this leads to unprofessionalism and the bureaucratisation of study and research.

Such changes, however, affect not only the pedagogical work of teachers in tertiary education but also their research (Kroflič 2014). In this area too, competitiveness and usefulness of research play their role, leading researchers to non-academic research proposals. By itself this might not be an issue; however, fundamental, theoretical research studies in education are lacking. Due to appointment criteria, teachers in higher education are required to prove the relevance and usefulness of their research internationally, which effectively means that they need to publish more papers abroad than at home. Additionally, Slovenian publications and journals increasingly use English rather than Slovenian as their working language, in an attempt to be more open to international readerships. Again, by itself, publications abroad and English as working language might not be an issue; however, consequently, Slovenian terminology related to education is neglected, as are material issues and questions specific to Slovenian educational system (Lesar and Peček 2009).

Some Possible Futures for Teacher Education

In conclusion, Slovenia currently faces a range of dilemmas and questions—as well as opportunities for future changes—in its teacher education system. At the time when the Bologna programmes were drafted, strong opposition arose to spreading teacher education programmes over a two-cycle degree as it was hard to ensure that graduates from the first-cycle degree would still be employable. Indeed, there are not many jobs available for them, and therefore most students continue their studies to attain a second-cycle degree that provides them with sufficient qualifications to work as teachers. It is thus questionable whether or not a two-cycle degree for a teacher education programme makes sense, given that the second-cycle is effectively essential in any case: perhaps it would be better to have a single-cycle, five-year study programme (300 ECTS). Another reason for questioning the reasonableness of two-cycle teacher education programmes is the mobility between some programmes. A student who wishes to transfer from one study programme to another upon completion of the first-cycle degree can do this by fulfilling additional differential study requirements of up to 60 ECTS. For some second-cycle programmes, however, this is not enough, which puts the fundamental quality of their education under question. This discrepancy is particularly vexing in the class teacher programme since it is very difficult to ensure the comparability of knowledge gained in one year (second-cycle degree), despite the additional 60 ECTS, against students who have completed their first-cycle degree in the class teacher programme (earning 240 ECTS). At this point in time, it looks very likely that class teacher programmes will become single cycle, five-year study programmes at all faculties of education in Slovenia, which might be the best solution for this issue.

Another dilemma relates to the question of entry exams. In order to acquire better quality student teachers, it is urgent that thorough entry exams are introduced which would test not only candidates' knowledge but also their aptitude for working with children (e.g., Ažman et al. 2019). There is an agreement between all three universities in Slovenia which educate preschool teachers to introduce entry exams. Whether or not this will actually happen—and whether or not entry exams will be extended to other teacher education programmes—remains to be seen. There is strong opposition to this proposal by those who claim that the right to education is universal and that it is the responsibility of employers to decide who they employ (more on this topic can be found in Peček and Macura 2019).

Teacher education does not feature in public awareness as frequently as teachers' working conditions, fiercely fought for by teacher unions. Nevertheless, when there are pressing challenges in basic and upper secondary education, civic initiatives often arise to demand better quality education for teachers and better teachers. In particular, they demand that teacher education programmes pay more attention to the development of emotional, social, and spiritual intelligence, plus argue that the ability of teachers to facilitate dialogic co-creation, teamwork, and pupils' upbringing is as important as their technical expertise (e.g., *Civilna pobuda. Kakšno šolo hočemo? (Civil initiative. What kind of school we want?)* 2009).

Professional and scientific conferences and research papers often make calls for a review of the content of teacher education programmes, primarily in terms of what skills and knowledge teachers lack. The list of themes often cited is long (e.g., EADSNE 2012; Messner et al. 2016). However, initial teacher education fundamentally cannot prepare teachers to be fully able to respond to each and every challenge encountered in their teaching career. Challenges change, as do doctrines, and therefore the most appropriate solutions do too. It is thus necessary that the teacher acquires solid and wide-ranging initial knowledge that will enable them to meet emerging challenges confidently and independently. At the same time, initial teacher education must be supplemented by a rich system of continuous education which helps teachers to update and upgrade their skills throughout their careers and in schools the holistic assistance systems such as school counselling services need to be in place to support them.

Some challenges posed to the continuous teacher professional development system, such as funds to cover the material costs of participation in CPD programmes and the ability to cover for teachers' absences, have already been discussed before. It can be added here that this system has become outdated—last reformed in the 1990s and subject to only minor changes since then—and no longer sufficiently motivates teachers towards further professional development (e.g., Ažman et al. 2019). CPD programmes financed by the Ministry of Education, Science, and Sports are, at present, only a minor part of the activities available to teaching staff in Slovenia for their professional development. However, these activities are widely scattered, their funding comes from different sources, and there are no clear methods for measuring their effects in terms of better quality work carried out by teachers and teaching institutions. Going forwards, there is a need for a nation-wide, consistent, and fact-based strategy of teacher education professional development. All training and education activities should be connected in one cohesive system which clearly defines the role and the duty of formal and informal continuous teacher education. Indeed, this is becoming even more important now, when it is under question whether or not the current teacher promotion system tied to continuous professional development remains the right way to motivate teachers for further education.

References

Adamič Tomič, B. (2019). *Sektor za razvoj kadrov v šolstvu* [Sector for professional development in education]. Ministrstvo za izobraževanje, znanost in šport. Phone call—enquiry. 8.7.2019.

Ažman, T., B. Japelj Pavešić, N. Potočnik, and M. Zavašnik. (2019). *Sporočilo konference Učeča se profesionalna skupnost* [Learning professional community—Conference message]. Ljubljana: Ministrstvo za izobraževanje, znanost in šport. Retrieved from http://www.eurydice.si/sporocilo-konference-uceca-se-profesionalna-skupnost.pdf.

Cencič, M. (1990). Dodiplomsko praktično usposabljanje razrednih učiteljev [Undergraduate practical teacher training for class teachers]. In: M. Velikonja, M. Plestenjak, C. Razdevšek-Pučko, M. Resman, and V. Troha (Eds.), *Učitelj, vzgojitelj—družbena in strokovna perspektiva* [Teacher, educator—a social and a professional perspective] (pp. 138–141). Bled: Zveza društev pedagoških delavcev Slovenije.

Civilna pobuda Kakšno šolo hočemo? [Civil initiative What kind of school we want?]. (2009). Retrieved from http://cdk.si/kaksno_solo_hocemo/osn_manifesta07-06-09.html.

EADSNE (European Agency for Development in Special Needs Education). (2012). *Teacher education for inclusion. Profile of inclusive teachers*. Odense, Denmark: European Agency for Development in Special Needs Education.

Eurydice. (2019). *Slovenia*. Retrieved from https://eacea.ec.europa.eu/national-policies/eurydice/content/political-social-and-economic-background-and-trends-77_en.

Faculty of Education. (2019). *Študijski programi* [Study programmes]. Retrieved from https://www.pef.uni-lj.si/studijski-programi.html.

Hudson, B., and P. Zgaga. (2008). Introduction by the Editors. In: B. Hudson and P. Zgaga (Eds.), *Teacher education policy in Europe. A voice of higher education institutions* (pp. 7–15). Umea: Faculty of Education.

Janša-Zorn, O. (1997). Od Višje pedagoške šole do Pedagoške fakultete [From Teacher Teaching College to the Faculty of Education in Ljubljana]. In: O. Janša-Zorn, G. Kocijan, and I. Škoflek (Eds.), *Zbornik ob 50.letnici Višje pedagoške šole, Pedagoške akademije in Pedagoške fakultete v Ljubljani* [Teacher Teaching College, Academy of Education, Faculty of Education in Ljubljani, 50th Anniversary Conference Proceedings] (pp. 7–69). Ljubljana: Modrijan.

Kellermann, P. (2006). Od Sorbone do Bologne in še naprej [From Sorbonne to Bologna and beyond]. *Sodobna pedagogika*, 57(4), 24–37.

Kolektivna pogodba za dejavnost vzgoje in izobraževanja v Republiki Sloveniji [Collective agreement for the educational sector in the Republic of Slovenia]. (2019). Retrieved from http://pisrs.si/Pis.web/pregledPredpisa?id=KOLP19.

Kotnik, R. (2006). Konceptualne dileme implementacije načel bolonjskega procesa [Conceptual dilemmas in implementing the principles of the Bologna Process]. *Sodobna pedagogika*, 57(4), 82–99.

Kotnik, R. (2013). *Nova pradigma v izobraževanju: je manj lahko več?* [A new paradigm in education: can less be more?]. Maribor: Subkulturni azil.

Kovač, M. (2006). Bolonjska reforma kot etnološki fenomen: primer Univerze v Ljubljani [The Bologna Reform as an ethnographic phenomenon: The case of the University of Ljubljana]. *Sodobna pedagogika*, 57(4), 100–111.

Kozmelj, A. (2019). *In 2018/19, too, more basic school pupils and fewer upper secondary school students than in previous years*. Ljubljana: SURS. Retrieved from http://www.stat.si/StatWeb/prikazi-novico?id=8144.

Krek, J. (Ed.). (1995). *Bela knjiga o vzgoji in izobraževanju v Republiki Sloveniji* [White Paper on Education in the Republic of Slovenia]. (1995). Ljubljana: Ministrstvo za šolstvo in šport RS.

Kroflič, R. (2014). Katerim uporabnim interesom služijo bolonjska prenova visokošolskega študija in njeni spremljevalni pojavi [What practical interests serve Bologna reform of higher education and its by-products]. *Vzgoja in izobraževanje*, 45(3), 10–14.

Lesar, I., and M. Peček. (2009). Education (edukacija) versus 'upbringing and teaching/learning' (vzgoja in izobraževanje)—terminological problems and their implications in practice. In: E. Protner, V. Wakounig, and R. Kroflič (Eds.), *Pädagogische Konzeptionen zwischen Vergangenheit und Zukunft: Ambivalenzen, Begriffsverwirrungen und Reformeifer. Erziehung in Wissenschaft und Praxis* (pp. 63–74). Frankfurt am Main: Peter Lang.

Marentič Požarnik, B. (1992). Izobraževanje učiteljev med univerzo, državo in stroke [Teacher education between university, state and the teaching profession]. In: F. Žagar (Ed.), *Kaj hočemo in kaj zmoremo* [What we want and what we can do] (pp. 8–22). Ljubljana: Pedagoška fakulteta.

Medveš, Z. (2006). Bolonjski proces med univerzo in uradništvom [Bologna Process between University and Bureaucracy]. *Sodobna pedagogika*, 57(4), 6–21.

Merila za akreditacijo študijskih programov za izobraževanje učiteljev [Criteria for the accreditation of study programmes for teacher education]. (2011). *Uradni list RS* 94/11 and 21/18. Retrieved from http://pisrs.si/Pis.web/pregledPredpisa?id=MERI41#.

Messner, E., D. Worek, and M. Peček (Eds.). (2016). *Teacher education for multilingual and multicultural settings*. Graz: Leykam.

NAKVIS (Nacionalna Agencija Republike Slovenije za kakovost v visokem šolstvu) [Slovenian Quality Assurance Agency for Higher Education]. (2019). *Merila za akreditacijo in zunanjo evalvacijo visokošolskih zavodov in študijskih programov* [Criteria for the accreditation and external evaluation of higher education institutions and study programmes]. Retrieved from https://www.nakvis.si/akreditacije-in-evalvacije-v-visokem-solstvu/zakonodaja/.

Natek, M., K. Natek, R. Šimec, M. Gabrovec, B. Pavlin, and S. Klasinc. (2000). *Portrait of the Regions, Volume 9, Slovenia.* Luxemburg: Eurostat, European Commission. Retrieved from https://ec.europa.eu/eurostat/documents/3217494/5628980/KS-29-00-779-EN.PDF/3f76edf8-3793-4b3a-a8d4-2b52dea222b3?version=1.0.

Pavlič Možina, S., and P. Prešeren (Eds.). (2011). *Facts about Slovenia.* (8th ed.). Ljubljana: Government Communication Office.

Peček, M. (2015). Slovenia: An overview. In: T. Corner (Ed.). *Education in the European Union: post-2003 member states (Education around the world series)* (pp. 249–268). London: Bloomsbury Academic.

Peček, M., and I. Lesar. (2011). *Governance of educational trajectories in Europe: Teacher education Slovenia: GOETE work package III: country report.* Ljubljana: University of Ljubljana, Faculty of Education; [Frankfurt am Mein]: GOETE, Governance of Educational Trajectories in Europe.

Peček, M., and S. Macura. (2019). Defining the boundaries of inclusion within compulsory education and teacher education. In: P. Zgaga (Ed.), *Inclusion in education: reconsidering limits, identifying possibilities* (pp. 45–69). Berlin: Peter Lang.

Peček, M., and C. Razdevšek-Pučko. (2000). Towards greater faith in teachers' professional authority: restructuring the primary teachers' study programme in Slovenia. *European Journal of Teacher Education*, 23(3), 261–274.

Peček, M. (1998). *Avtonomnost učiteljev nekdaj in sedaj* [Teacher's autonomy in the past and today]. Ljubljana: Znanstveno in publicistično središče, 1998.

Peček, M. (2008). *Responsibilities and autonomy of teachers: Slovenia.* Ljubljana: Eurydice.

Pravilnik o izboru in sofinanciranju programov nadaljnjega izobraževanja in usposabljanja strokovnih delavcev v vzgoji in izobraževanju [Rules on the selection and co-funding of further education and training programmes for educational professionals]. (2017). *Uradni list RS*, (33). Retrieved from http://www.pisrs.si/Pis.web/pregledPredpisa?id=PRAV13060.

Pravilnik o izobrazbi učiteljev in drugih strokovnih delavcev v izobraževalnem programu osnovne šole [Rules on teacher and other professional staff education in the basic school education programme]. (2011). *Uradni list*, (109). Retrieved from https://www.uradni-list.si/glasilo-uradni-list-rs/vsebina/2011-01-4943?sop=2011-01-4943.

Razdevšek-Pučko, C., and M. Peček. (2002). Teacher training in Slovenia: Between academic autonomy and professional competence. In: R. G. Sultana (Ed.), *Teacher education in the Euro-Mediterranean region* (pp. 213–229). New York: Peter Lang.

Sever, M. (2019). *In 2018, 16,680 graduates completed tertiary education, 3.1% fewer than ten years ago.* Ljubljana: SURS. Retrieved from https://www.stat.si/StatWeb/en/News/Index/8146.

Structure of the education system in the Republic of Slovenia. (2019). Retrieved from https://www.gov.si/assets/ministrstva/MIZS/Dokumenti/ENIC-NARICcenter/solske-sheme/STRUCTURE-OF-THE-EDUCATION-SYSTEM-IN-THE-REPUBLIC-OF-SLOVENIA.pdf.

SURS. (2002). *Popis 2002 (Census 2002)*. Retrieved from https://www.stat.si/popis2002/si/rezultati/rezultati_red.asp?ter=SLO&st=7.

SURS. (2017). *Expenditure for Formal Education, Slovenia*. Retrieved from https://www.stat.si/StatWeb/nk/News/Index/7816.

SURS (2019a). *In 2018 the highest growth of GDP in the Osrednjeslovenska region (7.3%) and the lowest in Goriška (3.7%)*. Retrieved from https://www.stat.si/StatWeb/en/news/Index/8567.

SURS. (2019b). *Pre-school Education*. Retrieved from https://www.stat.si/StatWeb/Field/Index/9/83.

SURS. (2019c). *Tertiary Education*. Retrieved from https://www.stat.si/StatWeb/en/Field/Index/9/111.

SURS (Statistični urad republike Slovenije—Statistical office of the Republic of Slovenia). (2019d). *Population, Slovenia, 1 January 2019*. Retrieved June 5, 2019 from https://www.stat.si/StatWeb/nk/News/Index/8062.

Tancig, S., and T. Devjak (Eds.). (2006). *Prispevki k posodobitvi pedagoških študijskih programov* [Contributions for modernisation of educational studies programmes]. Ljubljana: Pedagoška fakulteta.

Taštanoska, T. (Ed.). (2019). *The education system in the Republic of Slovenia 2018/2019*. Ljubljana: Ministry of Education, Science and Sport of the Republic of Slovenia. Retrieved from http://www.eurydice.si/publikacije/The-Education-System-in-the-Republic-of-Slovenia-2018-19.pdf.

Troha, V. (1992). Izzivi sprememb v izobraževanje razrednih učiteljev [Challenges posed by changes in class teacher education]. In: F. Žagar (Ed.), *Kaj hočemo in kaj zmoremo* [What we want and what we can do] (pp. 103–107). Ljubljana: Pedagoška fakulteta.

Zakon o visokem šolstvu (Higher Education Act). (2012). *Uradni list*, (32). Retrieved from https://www.uradni-list.si/glasilo-uradni-list-rs/vsebina/2012-01-1406/.

Zgaga, P. (1997). Izobraževanje učiteljev kot del sistema visokega šolstva [Teacher education as part of the higher education system]. In: K. Destovnik and I. Matovič (Eds.), *Izobraževanje učiteljev ob vstopu v tretje tisočletje* [Teacher education at the beginning of the third millennium] (pp. 46–58). Ljubljana: Pedagoška fakulteta.

Zgaga, P. (2008). Mobility and the European dimension in teacher education. In: B. Hudson and P. Zgaga (Eds.), *Teacher education policy in Europe. A voice of higher education institutions* (pp. 17–41). Umea: Faculty of Education.

13

Teacher Education in Montenegro: The Current State, Challenges, and Future Perspectives

Dijana Vučković, Veselin Mićanović, and Tatjana Novović

Introduction: The Background to Teacher Education in Montenegro

Montenegro is a Mediterranean country in Southeast Europe on the Balkan Peninsula. Montenegro's favourable position at the crossroads of the Mediterranean between Western Europe and Southwest Asia has rendered it the site of turbulent historical circumstances, especially from the Middle Ages to the present day—including during and between the world wars, as well as the shifting of national borders throughout the Balkans at the end of the twentieth century.

For most of the twentieth century, Montenegro was part of a common state of the South Slavic people, formed in 1918 and named the Kingdom of Serbs, Croats, and Slovenes—and later renamed in 1929 as the Kingdom of Yugoslavia. Following World War II, Montenegro was part of the newly formed Federal People's Republic of Yugoslavia, which was then called the Socialist Federal Republic of Yugoslavia from 1963 until its dissolution in the 1990s. After Slovenia, Croatia, Bosnia and Herzegovina, and North Macedonia separated from the federation, Montenegro remained in the state union with Serbia until 2006. That year, in a referendum, the Montenegrin population

D. Vučković (✉) • V. Mićanović • T. Novović
University of Montenegro, Podgorica, Montenegro
e-mail: dijanav@ucg.ac.me

© The Author(s), under exclusive license to Springer Nature Switzerland AG 2023
M. Kowalczuk-Walędziak et al. (eds.), *The Palgrave Handbook of Teacher Education in Central and Eastern Europe*, https://doi.org/10.1007/978-3-031-09515-3_13

decided to withdraw from the state union; thus, in May 2006, Montenegro restored its independence.

This brief overview of the most important changes in terms of state organisation in this part of Southeast Europe, in which Montenegro has been involved for only the last century, clearly demonstrates the region's turbulent history. Nowadays, Montenegro is a community enriched by its multiethnic, multi-faith, and multicultural status (Zvizdojević et al. 2015) and is defined as such by the Constitution of Montenegro (2007).

Montenegro's formal teacher education (TE) system can be traced to 1863, when the theological school in Cetinje began educating future teachers (Backović 2001; Delibašić 2003, 2009; Zorić and Vučković 2019). In 1869, a theological teacher training school was opened, which operated until the beginning of WWI in 1914. Indeed, until that point, teacher education (TE) was mainly entrusted to church schools, and the period between the two world wars marks a visible—although not complete—separation of TE from priesthood education (Delibašić 2009).

After WWII, and up to the 1990s, TE in Montenegro underwent a period of strong and accelerated development, although under the mantle of state-sanctioned communist ideology and socialist mechanisms (Prekić 2016). Such an ideological orientation meant the absolute disconnection of TE from orthodox religion. However, abandoning this religious dimension and introducing a monolithic communist ideology meant, in practice, replacing one powerful doctrine with another, creating an education sector that had very little autonomy, and which was firmly centralised yet had very ambitious goals, meaning that educational programmes were extremely burdensome for students and educators alike (Delibašić 2003). The end of WWII and efforts to return to peacetime life shed light on the lack of formally educated teaching staff in Montenegro (Prekić 2016). After the end of WWII until the 1990s, the teaching profession was gradually developed, which resulted in opening a number of profiles regarding the education of teachers (preschool, class, and subject teachers). Moreover, the duration of teacher education for all groups of teachers has been gradually extended, so, for example, in 1947 class teachers were educated in four-year secondary schools, while from 1951, they were requested to graduate from five-year secondary schools, and since 1967 from higher schools. However, almost all higher educational institutions for TE were developed in the 1990s. TE for class teachers was officially transformed into a four-year higher education study programme at the University of Montenegro (UoM) in 1992, which had been founded in 1974 in Podgorica (known as Titograd 1946–1992), the capital of Montenegro. From this point onwards, Montenegro's TE has been predominantly implemented within this institution. This chapter aims to create a complete picture of TE in Montenegro, as well as to highlight the key obstacles, concerns, dilemmas, and controversies that accompany these processes.

The 2001 Reform Process

From the 1990s until 2001, there were no major or significant changes in Montenegro's education system. Due to radical socio-political upheaval, education systems were not a priority in this part of Europe in the final decade of the twentieth century; thus, the state union of Serbia and Montenegro preserved almost all the frameworks and achievements of the Socialist Federal Republic of Yugoslavia education system. As such, the subject programmes for all levels were content-oriented; the teaching style was mostly traditional, teacher-oriented, and content-oriented; and the education system was fully centralised and under strict state control (Backović 2001).

In the 2001 *Book of Changes* (Backović 2001), the 'big picture' of a new Montenegrin education model was set out—and foundational principles defined—therefore providing a framework for modelling the whole concept of the education continuum, with particular emphasis on decentralisation; inter-culturalisation; equal opportunities; choices offered according to students' individual potential; introduction of European standards; implementation of quality control systems; development of human resources; promotion and development of the continuing education for teachers; coherence of programmes with the level of education, in accordance with National Qualification Framework (NQF), as well the age characteristics of students; and gradual introduction of changes (Backović 2001).

Twenty years on, the aforementioned principles remain valid and applicable. Collectively, they provide a framework for all the constituent aspects of the education system, that is, programmes, the teaching process, pre-school teachers and subject teachers, and ways of involving students. The *Book of Changes* is the contemporary defining paradigm and philosophy of education influencing the way in which teachers undergo professional development and training in Montenegro. Critically, the aforementioned principles uphold a high degree of teacher autonomy, strengthening the professional and pedagogical competences of teaching professionals at all pre-university levels—as per the guidance that 'education should be built in the direction of supporting inclusion and participation activities at all levels and fields of work and activity' (Backović 2001, p. 23).

Underpinned by these principles, the overall professional development of teachers (both pre-service and in-service) in Montenegro is a continuing process of progression. The transition from the transmissive to the transformative curriculum required a more active and motivated approach to knowledge sources, through a co-constructive discourse between all participants (i.e. teachers and learners), resulting in a significant change in the role of the teacher, as well as the quality of the education process (Vonta 2009 cited in Novović 2010). Ultimately, this shift 'was designed to place the child [i.e., the learner] at the centre of the education process' (Šebart and Hočevar 2019, p. 58).

This 2001 reform process—in addition to the aforementioned educational paradigm—was enacted in line with international and domestic documents and regulations, including the UN Universal Declaration of Human Rights (1948), the UN Declaration on the Rights of the Child (1959), the Convention against Discrimination in Education (1960), as well as the Constitution of the Republic of Montenegro (1992). All of these documents were accepted unreservedly by administrators in the education sector, as Montenegro made clear its commitment to European and transatlantic integration, a commitment which has been deepened since 2006 and the restoration of state independence.

After analysing the heritage of TE in Montenegro, reform-makers (Backović 2001) carried out a comparative overview of education models from other European countries, in order to take guidance from those most fitting and relevant to the Montenegrin setting (Backović 2001). For instance, the Finnish model has been generally treated as an ideal systematic approach to education, as the decision-makers estimated that the principles emphasised by the *Book of Changes* are very well set in the Finnish model, and Finnish teacher education is especially emphasised as exemplary, as well as the Finnish model of inclusive education (Backović 2001). Decision-makers pointed to the link between the Finnish model of education and the Slovenian one, as Slovenes emulated Finland during their education reform (Backović 2001), a Slovenia's model was viewed as both exemplary and feasible from a Montenegrin perspective due to common roots in the Socialist Federal Republic of Yugoslavia period. In addition, Slovenia achieved respectable results in education after its separation from The Socialist Federative Republic of Yugoslavia, it ranks well in the PISA results, besides other favourable features in OECD comparisons, such as higher investment in education per student (Gawlicz and Starnawski 2018). For instance, the model of a nine-year primary school organised in three cycles was taken over from Slovenia, as well as the partnership work of pre-school and class teachers in the first grade of primary school (Backović 2001).

The *Strategic Plan for Education Reform for the period 2003–2004* (2003) was drawn from the *Book of Changes* (Backović 2001), with the purpose of creating a more precise operational model from its projected goals and principles. The plan suggested that newly formed institutions should take over some of the ministry's responsibilities. These institutions are the Bureau for Educational Services (responsible for professional questions regarding pre-school education, elementary and grammar school, e.g. creating curricula, teaching quality control, continuous professional development of the working staff, as well as researches in education) and the Centre for Vocational Education (responsible for all professional issues related to vocational education). Besides, three councils were constituted during 2003: the General Education Council, the Vocational Education Council, and the Adult Education Council. Their role is to form a link between the Ministry and the aforementioned institutions.

The most recent *Strategy of teacher education in Montenegro 2017–2014* (2016, pp. 4–5) emphasises that initial and continuing TE should enable several goals. They are given in Table 13.1, with explanations of the areas within which they belong: 'know-what' and 'know-how'. The former encompasses knowledge about teaching/learning content, while the latter combines several areas directly oriented towards pedagogy, psychology, and teaching methodology.

The aforementioned objectives anticipate the complex and multidimensional nature of personality development and learning that enhance students' cognitive, affective, psychomotor, and conative progress. As such, it is an educational rhetoric based on contemporary theories of learning and goals that emphasise creativity; critical thinking; self-determination; student interest; adopting positive attitudes towards oneself, others, and the environment; as well as adopting positive value orientations. In order to fulfil this holistic vision of contemporary education, teachers, as experts in the task of achieving such goals, need to be well educated (Strategy of teacher education in Montenegro 2017–2024, 2016).

Initial Teacher Education

After WWII, class teachers in this part of Europe were educated in vocational high schools, and subject teachers were educated at the Higher Pedagogical School in Cetinje (1947–1961/1962). Then in the 1962/1963 academic year,

Table 13.1 Strategic goals, 2016

Strategic goal	Type of competence
Understanding the subject matter and its practical application	Teaching/learning content (know-what)
Understanding student development (cognitive, social, physical, and emotional)	Developmental psychology (know-how)
Identifying and evaluating diversity as well as the metacognitive strategies that students apply (i.e. how do students learn?), and achieving competences to adapt teaching to these differences	Pedagogy, psychology of learning, and didactics (know-how)
Developing curricula, methods, and forms of work according to the needs of students	Teaching methodology (know-how)
Acquiring and developing pedagogical competences, and using research to improve students' critical thinking and problem-solving skills	Pedagogy, teaching methodology, and research methodology (know-how)
Creating an appropriate environment for the active learning process, for motivating students, and for fostering healthy student relationships	Teaching methodology (know-how)
Development of communication skills which enhance teaching and learning: verbal, non-verbal, written, media, technical, etc.	Transversal skills, communication skills, digital competences, and key competences (know-what and know-how)
Understanding how to evaluate learning outcomes	Pedagogy, teaching methodology, and educational psychology (know-how)
Developing collaboration skills with students, parents, colleagues, and the wider community to advance the learning process	Pedagogy, teaching methodology, and psychology (know-how)

the Pedagogical Academy was formed by merging the Nikšić (Nikšić is a town in the northwestern part of Montenegro) school for teachers and the Cetinje Higher Pedagogical School (Cetinje is the old capital of Montenegro)—for six years, that is, until the end of the 1967/1968 academic year, it educated both class teachers and subject teachers at the same time (Šuković 2003). Subsequently, in the 1967/1968 academic year, the department for subject and class teaching was split. To this day, the class teaching department remains there as a part of the institution where it was originally formed, while the department for subject teaching was gradually separated to allow for the formation of special faculties and academies, namely the Faculty of Mathematics and Natural Sciences (FNM) (in 1978), the Music Academy (in 1980), the Faculty of Fine Arts (in 1988), the Faculty of Sport and Physical Education (in 2008), and, most recently, the Faculty of Philology (in 2016). Independent

Table 13.2 Faculties for teacher education

Faculty	Courses for	Intended teaching career
Faculty of Philosophy	a. Preschool teachers b. Class teachers c. Subject teachers	a. Kindergartens and the first grade of primary school b. First (i.e. grades 1st to 3rd) and second cycle (i.e. grades 4th to 6th) of primary school, teaching all subjects except English c. Teaching history, geography, sociology, or philosophy
Faculty of Natural Sciences and Mathematics	Subject teachers of mathematics, physics, biology, and computer science	Third cycle (i.e. grades 7th to 9th) of primary school, and in grammar and vocational education training (VET) schools
Music Academy	Music teachers	Third cycle of primary school, in grammar and VET schools, and in specialised music primary school and music VET schools
Faculty of Fine Arts	Art teachers	Third cycle of primary school, in grammar and VET schools, and in specialised art VET schools
Faculty of Sports and Physical Education	Physical education teachers	Third cycle of primary school, and in grammar and VET schools
Faculty of Philology	Language and literature teachers (i.e. Montenegrin, Serbian, English, Russian, German, Italian, and French)	Third cycle of primary school, in grammar and VET schools, and in specialised art VET schools

of this, the Department for Pre-school Teacher Education was first established in 1972 and is part of the institution where it was founded, the Pedagogical Academy (now the Faculty of Philosophy), located in Nikšić.

Since the 1990s (and before), there have been two basic types of teacher education offered at the UoM: one covers the education of class teachers and pre-school teachers, while the other covers the education of subject teachers (see Table 13.2).

In secondary vocational schools, classes are taught by experts in specific fields, such as engineers, pharmacists, economists, and lawyers. This category of lecturers does not undergo formal TE, but they are required to take a professional exam consisting of material on pedagogy, psychology, and didactics (*Rulebook on the Professional Exam of Teachers* 2003).

Until the 1990s, with the exception of pre-school TE, all TE programmes lasted for four years. In the 1990s, pre-school TE was realised in the form of a two-year higher education programme. The separation of teaching faculties—which started in 1978 and was completed in 2016, as mentioned before—led to the improvement and development of students' professional competences, that is, that part of knowledge concerning their main field of study, such as mathematics, physics, music, and language, but also marked a gradual separation from the pedagogical-psychological headquarters at the Faculty of Philosophy. Thus, over time, a strong scientific or artistic spirit has developed in almost all of Montenegro's teaching faculties to such an extent that those subjects belonging to the corpus of necessary pedagogical and psychological knowledge have been completely minimised (Vučković and Čalović Nenezić 2014; Strategy of teacher education in Montenegro 2017–2024, 2016).

The curricula of these faculties and their study programmes (see Tables 13.3 and 13.4) testify to the dominant elements within teacher education: content-oriented approaches dominate the education of subject teachers, while a better balance between knowledge of the subject and knowledge of pedagogy, psychology, and appropriate teaching methods is found in the education of pre-school and class teachers (Vučković and Čalović Nenezić 2014).

The teacher education subjects are grouped into five categories: content-oriented (e.g. focused on scientific or artistic content), general academic skills (e.g. foreign languages, computer science, academic writing), pedagogical and psychological disciplines (e.g. general pedagogy, school and family pedagogy, educational psychology, developmental psychology); teaching methodology (teaching and learning methods and techniques, instructional planning, class preparation, methods of assessments), and research methodology (qualitative and quantitative research methods in education, action research).

It should be highlighted that FNM educates not only mathematics teachers but also mathematicians as researchers, so, for the second profile (mathematicians as researchers), content-oriented subjects are those that constitute the

Table 13.3 Subject percentages in class teacher and pre-school teacher education plans in the 1990s and early 2000s

Study programme	Course overview by number of subjects										Total	
	Content-oriented		Academic skills		Pedagogy and psychology		Teaching methodology		Research methodology			
	N	%	N	%	N	%	N	%	N	%	Subjects	%
Class teacher training	11	30.55	5	13.88	7	19.44	12	33.33	1	2.77	36	100
Preschool teacher training	9	45.00	2	10.00	4	20.00	5	25.00	0	0.00	20	100

Curriculum plans 1992–2007 (1992) (bachelor's degree), with N = number of subjects

Table 13.4 Subject percentages in initial teacher education plans in the 1990s until 2007

Study programme		Course overview by number of subjects										Total	
		Content-oriented		Academic skills		Pedagogy and psychology		Teaching methodology		Research methodology			
		N	%	N	%	N	%	N	%	N	%	Subjects	%
Philosophy	Plan 1992	18	62.06	5	17.24	2	6.89	1	3.44	3	10.34	29	100
Sociology	Plan 1992	21	63.63	6	18.18	2	6.06	1	3.03	3	9.09	33	100
History and geography	Plan 2001	34	82.92	3	7.31	2	4.87	2	4.87	0	0.00	41	100
Physical education	Plan 1999	30	75.00	5	12.50	2	5.00	2	5.00	1	2.50	40	100
English lang. and literature	Plan 1992	25	75.75	5	15.15	2	6.06	1	3.03	0	0.00	33	100
Russian lang. and literature	Plan 1999	19	76.00	3	12.00	2	8.00	1	4.00	0	0.00	25	100
French lang. and literature	Plan 2003	18	69.23	5	19.23	2	7.69	1	3.84	0	0.00	26	100
Italian lang. and literature	Plan 1999	17	68.00	5	20.00	2	8.00	1	4.00	0	0.00	25	100
Serbian lang. and South Slavic literature	Plan 1992	26	81.25	3	9.37	2	6.25	1	3.12	0	0.00	32	100
Mathematics	Plan 1992	18	66.66	7	25.92	1	3.70	1	3.70	0	0.00	27	100
Biology	Plan 1993	23	74.19	4	12.90	3	9.67	1	3.22	0	0.00	31	100
Physics	Plan 1994	25	75.75	5	15.15	2	6.06	1	3.03	0	0.00	33	100
Music education	Plan 1995	18	78.26	1	4.34	2	8.69	2	8.69	0	0.00	23	100
Fine arts	Plan 1995	21	84.00	1	4.00	2	8.00	1	4.00	0	0.00	25	100

profession of mathematicians engaged in research, not work in school. The plans presented in Table 13.4 indicate that most of the faculties that educate (and) teachers pay much more attention to scientific or artistic content.

The bachelor's teacher education curricula of the 1990s–2007 included almost no research methodology, which was instead included in master's degree programmes. All bachelor's programmes lasted for four years before the signing of the Bologna Declaration. Most of the bachelor's curricula covered one teaching methodology—for example, methodology of teaching biology (at the study programme for biology) or methodology of teaching English language and literature (at the English language and literature study programme)—with the exception of the two-group programmes (e.g. the two-group programme for history and geography which covered the two teaching methodologies of teaching history and teaching geography). The most numerous subjects in almost all curricula are those content-oriented (know-what), while the majority of programmes comprise two pedagogical and psychological disciplines (e.g. general pedagogy and educational psychology). In contrast, class teachers and pre-school teachers have a much more regular distribution in their class schedules, creating a direct and clear focus on the teaching profession.

Transition to the New Study Programme System (2007 and 2012)

Montenegro signed the Bologna Declaration in 2003, which was then implemented at the UoM with great effort, consideration, and discussion. Even today, the public (experts and laymen alike) have not fully embraced the principles of the Bologna Declaration, so dissatisfaction with education on the whole is expressed as criticism of the declaration—this narrative is upheld by the mainstream media which frequently comments that pre-Bologna education was of a high quality, and that it has since been severely damaged (Perović and Vučković 2019). However, such narratives and criticism fail to acknowledge the unfortunate timing whereby the declaration was adopted at the same time as major public discussions on the quality of the education system began. As such, the accumulated dissatisfaction attributed to the Bologna Declaration is misplaced as it is a document which offers only a framework for the activities of universities, with the goals of improving education and ensuring quality comparability. Therefore, both before and after the declaration, universities have been and are equally autonomous according to national legislation in all matters concerning the organisation of teaching and learning, the issues on which the quality of diplomas largely depends.

When the Bologna Declaration was adopted, the formal prerequisites for introducing a new concept of study were introduced by the Ministry of Education and by the University of Montenegro, facilitating the nation's gradual adaptation to the requirements and principles of the declaration. New documentation was prepared for the introduction of three study cycles—bachelor's, master's, and doctoral degrees—plus rules were developed for individual cycles, precise forms for curriculum design were created, the importance of study programme comparability and ECTS rules was emphasised, and so forth. However, as shown in the *Situation Analysis and Strategic Commitments at the UoM* (2015), the essence of these changes in the Montenegrin context was actually repackaging existing programmes into a new format. Almost all subjects from previous four-year studies have been retained, but a significant number of them were split into two or more semesters (e.g. the two-semester course Educational Psychology was kept in the new plan as two courses—Educational Psychology I and II). When it comes to the internal structure of the curriculum, it has remained almost the same, for example, topics and lessons remained a key part of the curriculum, and with them the curricula list hard-to-achieve and immeasurable goals, as well as extensive literature inconsistent with the accurate students' individual potential. For example, it is not uncommon that a subject is credited with 4 ECTS (which means that a student should study it for 5 hours and 20 minutes per week), with a fund of 2 hours of lectures, one hour of exercises, and a dozen books (mostly textbooks, manuals, monographs) for learning. With such shortcomings in the subject curricula, a very small number of elective courses have been introduced, and not enough attention has been paid in comparison to other related faculties. The preferred model of studying for UoM, supported by the Ministry of Education, was the one made according to 3 + 1 + 1 + 3 scheme (i.e. a three-year bachelor's degree at 180 ECTS + one year of specialist studies at 60 ECTS + a one-year master's degree at 60 ECTS + a three-year doctoral degree at 180 ECTS). Three-year bachelor's and one-year specialist studies together provide a four-year educational degree, exactly as it was before the Bologna Declaration. Within this maximum potential, the required amount of pre-service study is 240 ECTS for class teachers and subject teachers, and 180 ECTS for pre-school teachers. As such, for prospective subject teachers, the necessary education for employment in a school is a completed bachelor's degree plus specialist studies (i.e. 3 + 1). A four-year bachelor studies model, comprising 240 ECTS, has been accredited for class teachers. With the first accreditation from 2007, the first model of one-year master's degree programmes for class teachers was also introduced and developed. Therefore, for the first time, class teachers who are educated in Montenegro have the opportunity to complete master's studies, which we consider important for the development of the profession. The second (re-)accreditation of these programmes occurred in 2012, but similarly almost negligible changes occurred at that time. The individual subject percentages are shown in Tables 13.5 and 13.6 (*Curriculum Plans* 2007), where N refers to the number of subjects.

In addition to the class teacher education programme being offered in the official language—that is, Serbian until 2017, then Montenegrin-Serbian, Bosnian, and Croatian since 2017—an Albanian language programme was formed in 2008, covering the same curriculum as the basic programme, with alterations as regards the language aspects.

As seen in Tables 13.5 and 13.6, in addition to the number of subjects that pre-service teachers study, the ECTS distribution plays an important role in their education. The distribution of subjects and ECTS are evidently far better balanced in the education of pre-school and class teachers, compared to subject teachers. Looking at the overall profiling of preservice teachers, the balance of disciplines is almost the same today as it was in the 1990s. While the methodology of research has been introduced at times, the teaching methods, as well as pedagogy and psychology, remain represented at a very low level. In this context, it is highly questionable that some study programmes can be accredited as serving the educational-pedagogical profession at all if, in most of them, the ECTS credits allocated to pedagogy, psychology, and teaching methods do not exceed 25 of the total 240.

Vučković's 2010 research conducted with students three years after the introduction of the Bologna Process in Montenegro shows that, in Montenegrin higher education, the process of abandoning established habits (e.g. ex-cathedra lectures, reproductive learning, traditional testing and assessment, lack of a practical learning component, and extensive curricula) was (and it still is) very slow and uncertain. It is striking that the students included in this research pointed out almost the very same problems that were identified at the beginning of the century, and even earlier (Delibašić 2003). As such, this situation completely reflects the claim that 'despite the obvious progress, the fact that European countries are jealously clinging to their traditional national systems cannot be neglected today' (Zgaga 2008, p. 14). Indeed, the *Book of Changes* (Backović 2001) mentions throughout, as probably its most central thesis, that the transformation from a school of memorising into a school of critical thinking should be brought to life across every segment of teaching and learning. However, the aforementioned research (Delibašić 2003; Vučković 2010) finds that teachers 'jealously' guard those teaching concept

Table 13.5 Subject percentages in class and pre-school teacher education plans from 2007 to 2016/2017

Study programme	Degree	Course overview by number of subjects and ECTS												Total	
		Content-oriented		Academic skills		Pedagogy and psychology		Teaching methodology		Research methodology		Final exam			
		N	ECTS	N	ECTS	N	ECTS	N	ECTS	N	ECTS	N	ECTS	Subjects	ECTS
Class teacher training	Bachelor's	21	86	7	20	12	54	18	65	2	9	1	6	61	240
		34.42%	35.83%	11.47%	8.33%	19.67%	22.50%	29.50%	27.08%	3.27%	3.75%	1.63%	2.50%	100%	100%
Preschool teacher training	Bachelor's	10	48	9	29	7	43	10	47	1	6	1	7	38	180
		26.31%	26.66%	23.68%	16.11%	18.42%	23.88%	26.31%	26.11%	2.63%	3.33%	2.63%	3.88%	100%	100%
	Specialist	5	30	2	10	2	14	0	0	0	0	1	6	10	60
		50.00%	50.00%	20.00%	16.66%	20.00%	23.33%	0.00%	0.00%	0.00%	0.00%	10.00%	10.00%	100%	100%

Table 13.6 Subject percentages in subject teacher education plans from 2007 to 2016/2017

		Course overview by number of subjects and ECTS												Total	
		Content-oriented		Academic skills		Pedagogy and psychology		Teaching methodology		Research methodology		Final exam			
Study programme	Degree	N	ECTS	N	ECTS	N	ECTS	N	ECTS	N	ECTS	N	ECTS	Subjects	ECTS
Philosophy	Bachelor's	27 56.25%	161 67.08%	12 25.00%	38 15.83%	5 10.41%	20 8.33%	2 4.16%	9 3.75%	1 2.08%	6 2.50%	1 2.08%	6 2.50%	48 100%	240 100%
Sociology	Bachelor's	31 73.80%	144 80.00%	7 16.66%	20 11.11%	1 2.38%	4 2.22%	0 0.00%	0	3 7.14%	12 6.66%	0 0.00%	0	42 100%	180 100%
	Specialist	5 41.66%	30 50.00%	0 0.00%	0	4 33.33%	16 26.66%	2 16.66%	8 13.33%	0 0.00%	0	1 8.33%	6 10.00%	12 100%	60 100%
History	Bachelor's	24 75.00%	156 86.66%	8 25.00%	24 13.33%	0 0.00%	0	0 0.00%	0	0 0.00%	0	0 0.00%	0	32 100%	180 100%
	Specialist	3 25.00%	18 30.00%	2 16.66%	12 20.00%	4 33.33%	16 26.66%	2 16.66%	8 13.33%	0 0.00%	0	1 8.33%	6 10.00%	12 100%	60 100%
Geography	Bachelor's	31 86.11%	167 92.77%	5 13.88%	13 7.22%	0 0.00%	0	0 0.00%	0	0 0.00%	0	0 0.00%	0	36 100%	180 100%
	Specialist	3 25.00%	20 33.33%	1 8.33%	6 10.00%	4 33.33%	16 26.66%	3 25.00%	12 20.00%	0 0.00%	0	1 8.33%	6 10.00%	12 100%	60 100%
Physical education	Bachelor's	28 66.66%	128 71.11%	5 11.90%	12 6.66%	0 0.00%	0	8 19.04%	37 20.55%	1 2.38%	3 1.66%	0 0.00%	0	42 100%	180 100%
	Specialist	3 25.00%	16 26.66%	1 8.33%	3 5.00%	4 33.33%	16 26.66%	2 16.66%	11 18.33%	1 8.33%	5 8.33%	1 8.33%	9 15.00%	12 100%	60 100%
English lang. and literature	Bachelor's	29 76.31%	149 82.77%	7b 18.42%	27 15.00%	0 0.00%	0	0 0.00%	0	0 0.00%	0	2 5.26%	4 2.22%	38 100%	180 100%
	Specialist	6 46.15%	29 48.33%	0 0.00%	0	4 30.76%	16 26.66%	2 15.38%	11 18.33%	0 0.00%	0	1 7.69%	4 6.66%	13 100%	60 100%
Russian lang. and literature	Bachelor's	32 84.21%	156 86.66%	6 15.78%	24 13.33%	0 0.00%	0	0 0.00%	0	0 0.00%	0	0 0.00%	0	38 100%	180 100%
	Specialist	6 46.15%	32 53.33%	0 0.00%	0	4 30.76%	16 26.66%	2 15.38%	8 13.33%	0 0.00%	0	1 7.69%	4 6.66%	13 100%	60 100%
French lang. and literature	Bachelor's	28 80.00%	155 86.11%	6 17.14%	24 13.33%	0 0.00%	0	0 0.00%	0	0 0.00%	0	1 2.85%	1 0.55%	35 100%	180 100%
	Specialist	6 46.15%	32 53.33%	0 0.00%	0	4 30.76%	16 26.66%	2 15.38%	8 13.33%	0 0.00%	0	1 7.69%	4 6.66%	13 100%	60 100%

Subject	Degree	n	%	n	%	n	%	n	%	n	%	n	%	n	%	n	%	n	%	n	%	n	%	Total
Italian lang. and literature	Bachelor's	31	81.57%	151	83.88%	7	18.42%	29	16.11%	0	0.00%	0	0.00%	0	0.00%	0	0.00%	0	0.00%	0	0.00%	38	100%	180
	Specialist	6	46.15%	32	53.33%	0	0.00%	4	30.76%	16	26.66%	2	15.38%	8	13.33%	0	0.00%	1	7.69%	4	6.66%	13	100%	60
German lang. and literature	Bachelor's	27	81.81%	156	86.66%	6	18.18%	24	13.33%	0	0.00%	0	0.00%	0	0.00%	0	0.00%	0	0.00%	0	0.00%	33	100%	180
	Specialist	6	46.15%	32	53.33%	0	0.00%	4	30.76%	16	26.66%	2	15.38%	8	13.33%	0	0.00%	1	7.69%	4	6.66%	13	100%	60
Serbian lang. and South Slavic literature	Bachelor's	39	86.66%	165	91.66%	6	13.33%	15	9.09%	0	0.00%	0	0.00%	0	0.00%	0	0.00%	0	0.00%	0	0.00%	45	100%	180
	Specialist	6	46.15%	32	53.33%	0	0.00%	4	30.76%	16	26.67%	2	15.38%	8	13.33%	0	0.00%	1	7.69%	4	6.67%	13	100%	60
Montenegrin lang. and South Slavic literature	Bachelor's	39	86.66%	165	91.66%	6	13.33%	15	9.09%	0	0.00%	0	0.00%	0	0.00%	0	0.00%	0	0.00%	0	0.00%	45	100%	180
	Specialist	6	46.15%	32	53.33%	0	0.00%	4	30.76%	16	26.67%	2	15.38%	8	13.33%	0	0.00%	1	7.69%	4	6.67%	13	100%	60
Mathematics	Bachelor's	31	88.57%	172	95.55%	4	11.42%	8	4.44%	0	0.00%	0	0.00%	0	0.00%	0	0.00%	0	0.00%	0	0.00%	35	100%	180
	Specialist	8	66.66%	40	66.66%	0	0.00%	2	16.66%	10	16.66%	2	16.66%	10	16.66%	0	0.00%	0	0.00%	0	0.00%	12	100%	60
Biology	Bachelor's	30	88.23%	162	90.00%	4	11.76%	18	10.00%	0	0.00%	0	0.00%	0	0.00%	0	0.00%	0	0.00%	0	0.00%	34	100%	180
	Specialist	6	50.00%	28	46.66%	1	8.33%	5	16.66%	10	16.66%	1	8.33%	8	13.33%	0	0.00%	2	16.66%	9	15.00%	12	100%	60
Physics	Bachelor's	27	75.00%	152	84.44%	3	8.33%	6	3.33%	0	0.00%	0	0.00%	0	0.00%	0	0.00%	6	16.66%	16	8.88%	36	100%	180
	Specialist	4	26.66%	24	40.00%	3	20.00%	10	16.66%	6	10.00%	4	26.66%	10	16.66%	0	0.00%	6	16.66%	10	16.66%	15	100%	60
Music education	Bachelor's	51	83.60%	167	92.77%	4	6.55%	2	1.11%	4	2.22%	4	6.55%	7	3.88%	0	0.00%	0	0.00%	0	0.00%	61	100%	180
	Specialist	10	62.50%	31	51.66%	0	0.00%	0	0.00%	4	6.66%	2	12.50%	22	36.66%	0	0.00%	2	12.50%	3	5.00%	16	100%	60
Fine arts	Bachelor's	29	87.87%	172	95.55%	4	12.12%	8	4.44%	0	0.00%	0	0.00%	7	3.88%	0	0.00%	0	0.00%	0	0.00%	33	100%	180
	Specialist	5	55.55%	52	86.66%	3	33.33%	6	10.00%	0	0.00%	1	11.11%	2	3.33%	0	0.00%	0	0.00%	0	0.00%	9	100%	60

which seem traditional to them. It is clear that entrenched habits are difficult to change, and even very young teachers have been found to undertake a traditional teaching approach (Bešić and Reškovac 2012). Perhaps these patterns and behaviours can be attributed to these two factors, among others: firstly, the comfort and economy that experienced teachers find in preparing repeated sessions that feel very familiar to them, and, secondly, the fact that younger teachers tend to rely more on the way they were taught themselves, rather than on any understanding of what they should do as taught at university.

The 2017 (Re-)accreditation Process

All programmes at the UoM have been officially oriented towards learning outcomes since 2017. A revised version of Bloom's taxonomy for the cognitive domain (Anderson and Krathwohl 2001; Krathwohl 2002) was used to redesign the curriculum and focus it on learning outcomes, as well as the planning of outcomes for developing the affective and psychomotor domains according to the corresponding taxonomies for the two areas (Kennedy 2007). However, the two outcome groups (affective and psychomotor domain) remained largely neglected in the redesigned programmes (Pešikan and Lalović 2017). Practically, learning outcomes have been written almost exclusively for the cognitive domain. Indeed, how much the written outcomes actually changed the orientation and organisation of teaching is difficult to say. Nevertheless, it is important to emphasise that the Montenegrin qualifications framework— that is, the basis upon which learning outcomes and competences are defined—is dominated by the values of a democratic society in which every individual is given the opportunity to be continuously educated and to critically assess and re-examine the learning content (Godoń et al. 2004).

Higher education at the UoM has been free for all students since the 2017/2018 academic year, covering the first two study cycles (i.e. bachelor's and master's studies). Students pay fees only if they fail to meet their scheduled obligations on a regular basis. The status of key competences for lifelong learning, in the context of pre-school and class teachers' education, is defined along two dimensions, as partially confirmed by Pešikan and Lalović's 2017 research:

> Firstly, the initial and continuing education of teachers should prepare them to facilitate the student's acquisition of key competences [...] The second perspec-

tive is based on the assumption that since key competences are to be acquired by every individual, teachers should also acquire them. (Gordon et al. 2009, p. 15)

The other important question here is how much and how well these competences are recognised in the deeper structures of programmes and teaching, as

key competences are not finite and their development should be supported by transversal skills such as critical thinking, creativity, initiative, problem-solving, risk assessment, decision-making and constructive management of feelings. (Gordon et al. 2009, p. 11)

On an organisational level, the new format for class teacher education since 2017 has been 5 + 0, where bachelor's and master's studies are integrated, while other TE programmes use a 3 + 2 model. Legal employment requirements have not changed in recent years, meaning that employment in class or subject teaching requires 240 ECTS and pre-school teaching requires 180 ECTS.

Differences between the education of subject teachers on the one hand and class and pre-school teachers on the other remained obvious even after the introduction of learning outcomes (*Curriculum Plans* 2017). In this regard, in the education of subject teachers, teacher knowledge (i.e. 'know-how' competences, or pedagogy, psychology, and teaching methodology) is neglected compared to subject knowledge (i.e. 'know-what' competences, or knowledge of science that teachers will teach within the subject, such as biology, chemistry, and literature), while this balance is significantly better established in TE for class and pre-school teachers. All outcomes in class and pre-school teacher education programmes are directed towards developing complex teacher competences within the European framework (ETUCE 2008; Caena 2014), while in subject teacher education programmes, just one—or even none—of the outcomes refers to a set of teaching competences (Zorić and Vučković 2019). Such an orientation indicates that the Montenegrin education system depends on the strongly held traditional belief that an individual who is well-versed in a particular field of science or art, at the same time, is automatically a good teacher (Vučković 2010).

As outlined in the tables, Montenegro's subject teacher education programmes, despite the new curricula, lack the disciplines central to teaching: pedagogy, psychology, and teaching methodology. Yet, such minimal knowledge of general pedagogy, general psychology, and teaching methods simply cannot be expected to lead to the development of essential complex teaching competences. Indeed, Montenegro's consistently poor PISA results may, in part, be interpreted as a result of this way in which subject teachers are educated. The most recent results show that subject teacher education faculties do not provide students with subjects for the acquisition of functional knowledge and competences for the implementation of teaching:

> This assessment is very important as it represents the first step in reform efforts to focus the entire education system more on competences than on content, to encourage an orientation towards functional knowledge and increase its representation. (PISA 2018, p. 14)

In complete contrast to Montenegro's subject teacher education system, the pre-school teacher education programme is predominantly directed towards pedagogical, psychological, and didactic-methodological training, with the acquisition of content-oriented knowledge in those particular areas which serve as the backbone of early childhood learning (e.g. understanding speech culture, grasping initial mathematical concepts, and gaining familiarity with natural and social environments). Pre-school pedagogy programmes encompass the study of age-specific developmental characteristics (e.g. through learning about developmental psychology, developmental disorders and difficulties, and speech development), fostering methods such as the Montessori programme and Step by Step. As Novović (2017, 2018) notes, Montenegro's pre-school teachers have been trained to work with interest centres (where children can choose materials and activities that attract them, e.g. manipulative centre, role play centre, and construction), thematic planning (allowing the teacher to connect different contents and activities within one topic), child development (which encourages the holistic development of the child), learning in the spirit of social constructivism (i.e. learning as a process by which an individual through interaction with others constructs knowledge and understanding of reality), and inclusive groups (i.e. where children with different educational needs learn together, in the same groups). The proportion of practical teaching in the overall structure of the programme is 25%, and it exclusively takes the form of teaching practice. Originally organised as an applied course (since 2007), in 2017, Montenegro's pre-school teacher education programme grew into an academic programme, organised as 3 + 2 (180 + 120 ECTS); however, only a bachelor's degree, and not a master's, is required for employment as a pre-school teacher.

From the adoption of the Bologna Declaration in 2003 until 2017, class teacher education was implemented according to the 4 + 1 model (240 bachelor's + 60 master's ECTS), at which point the programme was transformed into the 5 + 0 model (integrated bachelor's and master's 300 ECTS). At present, four years of bachelor's-level studies are required for employment as a class teacher, which is a legal solution that is valid from before. The university developed a five-year integrated study in 2017, but other legislation has not been changed in line with this new model, so harmonisation of legislation is yet to be expected (Eurydice Montenegro 2019). Class teacher education is composed of three basic parts:

* science and arts subjects;
* pedagogical and psychological disciplines;
* didactic and methodological subjects (which are mainly theoretical, with a 25% practical component).

These three groups are widely considered to be the basis for teacher education (ETUCE 2008; Caena 2014; Darling-Hammond 2017; Trippestad et al. 2018; Tatto and Menter 2019), beyond which there are subjects that encourage the development of cross-curricular competences (i.e. transversal competences), such as computer science, technology, and English. There is also a specific option for learning about inclusive teaching in Montenegro's class teacher education programme, but teachers' ability to work in inclusive classes is developed through all methodological disciplines, as well as through actual teaching practice (Novović 2016).

In summary, Montenegro's current class teacher education programme is largely in line with the requirements deemed necessary for future teachers: 'in-depth subject knowledge, advanced pedagogical skills, reflective practices and the ability to adapt teaching to the needs of each individual as well as to the needs of the group of learners as a whole' (ETUCE 2008, p. 8). However, such requirements still need to be further developed, so that the country's teacher education can become more directed towards transversal competences and research, forming teachers as researchers and reflective practitioners, in order to strike a balance between theory and practice (ETUCE 2008, p. 8; Darling-Hammond 2017).

That said, as much as Montenegro's pre-school and class teacher education programmes are focused on teaching competences, Vučković and Čalović Nenezić's analyses (2014, p. 110) show that while:

the teaching is formally student-centred (there are global goals, general methods and learning, forms of testing and evaluation, etc.), [...] in practice it is content-focused—a dominant part of the programme consists of learning contents with a list of basic references.

Indeed, the same situation was previously observed in empirical research where the student respondents reported that their learning outcomes were tailored towards the most dominant methods of assessment (Vučković 2010), which, as with many countries in this part of the world today, are written exams and tests.

In order to unite established content-oriented education approaches with the critical thinking and research skills necessary for the twenty-first century, high-quality teacher education today needs to have 'both strong subject matter and pedagogical preparation, […] that integrates research and practice' (Darling-Hammond 2017, p. 292). Indeed, if this is to be the goal, then the question of research-oriented study for both class teachers and pre-school teachers has not yet been sufficiently addressed in Montenegro. In fact, only a few subjects facilitate, let alone nurture, problem- and research-based learning: students may be introduced to research methodology, but their methodological knowledge is rarely evidenced by research outputs of their own. Besides, a doctoral studies framework has not yet been developed for these pre-school and class teacher education programmes, as doctoral studies frameworks have not yet been developed at all at the UoM in the field of teaching methodology. This fact reveals a great deal about the Montenegrin attitude towards TE—in particular, the long-held, traditional conviction that teaching does not require as high a qualification as a doctoral degree—thus dividing Montenegro's education system from well-developed education systems around the world (Darling-Hammond 2017, p. 292).

The practical dimension of TE is mainly realised through a group of methodological subjects in Montenegro (e.g. methodology of teaching mother tongue and literature in the teacher education programme is studied through three subjects, with the first of these subjects dominated by theory, while the remaining two subjects are dominated by practice, i.e. students under mentorship realise classes in primary school). Although the practical component of teaching is present in the sense that students facilitate classes or activities under the mentorship of existing teachers, covering two or three classes per subject in one semester, and observe about 30 lessons delivered by their classmates (Zorić and Vučković 2019), going forwards this component must continue to expand. All such classes are prepared in cooperation with teaching assistants and tutors from elementary schools, and after the class—which is systematically observed—extensive analysis and detailed feedback are given to students by the professor and teaching assistant, as well as often by the school mentor. Students themselves have evaluated this part of their studies as highly useful, since such activities specifically prepare them for classroom work (Vučković 2010). They believe that through school practice in methodological subjects, they can independently plan, prepare, implement, and evaluate the teaching process. Students find very detailed preparations for teaching and the process of its implementation and evaluation so interesting that they participate in all activities often on their initiative (often volunteer to teach even though the curriculum and the teacher do not oblige them to do so), which inevitably results in a stronger bond between students within the group as they help each other in all phases of work (Vučković 2010).

Enrolment in Study Programmes

In some of the countries Montenegro admires, like Finland, the teaching profession is very well respected and there is considerable interest in enroling in these studies (Darling-Hammond 2017), to the extent that only 10–15% of applicants are successful in enrolling (Rautiainen et al. 2018, p. 421). The situation in Montenegro, however, is very different. Across the board, a prospective student's eligibility for enrolment in initial teacher education is decided by the points allocated to their previous education achievements (up to a maximum of 47 for study programmes for which no entrance exam is taken). Students' achievement are scored by considering (a) general success during all grades of high school, (b) grades from two subjects that are of special importance for the profession (e.g. important subjects for enrolment in the study programme for class teacher education are, particularly, Mother tongue and Mathematics, for enrolment in the study programme for psychology points are Mother tongue and Psychology) from the third and fourth grades, (c) success in the external Matura exam, and (d) *Luča* (diploma awarded in Montenegro for excellent performance in all subjects during all years of schooling) or equivalent diploma. However, although an entrance exam is required for enrolment in the Music Academy, as well as fine arts and physical education programmes, there is no such requirement for other programmes and faculties. Generally speaking, around 30% of candidates get enrolled in pre-school, and 45% get enrolled in class teacher education courses, while around 100% of candidates get enrolled in subject teaching programmes. Compared to Finland, which has very good results in the selection of candidates, pre-school and class teachers in Montenegro are still far from achieving such results, but there is a favourable trend in this regard. This is especially true if we keep in mind the situation before the Bologna Declaration when almost everyone who was interested was enrolled in these programmes (Delibašić 2003). On the other hand, other study programmes have not made progress in the selection of candidates in terms of the number

Table 13.7 Enrolment into education programmes for teachers in Montenegro (bachelor's studies)

Enrolment term	2017/2018			2018/2019			2019/2020		
	1st	2nd	3rd	1st	2nd	3rd	1st	2nd	3rd
Preschool teacher training	NoA = 120 NE = 30 Min = 33.23 Max = 41.59 F = 30 M = 0	–	–	NoA = 116 NE = 30 Min = 33.84 Max = 47 F = 30 M = 0	–	–	NoA = 73 NE = 30 Min = 32.53 Max = 47 F = 30 M = 0	–	–
Primary School Class Teacher Department	NoA = 81 NE = 30 Min = 32.41 Max = 47 F = 29 M = 1	–	–	NoA = 54 NE = 30 Min = 30.43 Max = 47.00 F = 29 M = 1	–	–	NoA = 64 NE = 30 Min = 33.03 Max = 47 F = 27 M = 3	–	–
History	NoA = 32 NE = 32 Min = 12.9 Max = 37.42 F = 4 M = 28	NoA = 12 NE = 8 Min = 25.29 Max = 31.31 F = 6 M = 2	–	NoA = 18 NE = 18 Min = 16.67 Max = 40.19 F = 2 M = 16	NoA = 9 NE = 9 Min = 13.41 Max = 35.01 F = 4 M = 5	NoA = 12 NE = 12 Min = 13.30 Max = 34.91 F = 2 M = 10	NoA = 29 NE = 29 Min = 19.82 Max = 41.68 F = 4 M = 25	NoA = 2 NE = 2 Min = 21.21 Max = 41.05 F = 1 M = 1	NoA = 7 NE = 7 Min = 13.23 Max = 33.08 F = 2 M = 5
Geography	NoA = 39 NE = 39 Min = 14.51 Max = 44.45 F = 19 M = 20	NoA = 20 NE = 11 Min = 25.10 Max = 36.90 F = 8 M = 3	–	NoA = 22 NE = 22 Min = 12.40 Max = 38.51 F = 11 M = 11	NoA = 17 NE = 17 Min = 17.94 Max = 44 F = 11 M = 6	NoA = 2 NE = 2 Min = 44 Max = 44 F = 0 M = 1	NoA = 16 NE = 16 Min = 16.26 Max = 36.31 F = 4 M = 12	NoA = 16 NE = 16 Min = 16.74 Max = 43.85 F = 9 M = 7	NoA = 7 NE = 7 Min = 20.44 Max = 31.80 F = 1 M = 6
Sociology	NoA = 31 NE = 30 Min = 19.83 Max = 36.24 F = 19 M = 11	–	–	NoA = 31 NE = 30 Min = 20.63 Max = 44.77 F = 22 M = 8	–	–	NoA = 29 NE = 29 Min = 17.69 Max = 37.55 F = 18 M = 11	NoA = 32 NE = 11 Min = 30.75 Max = 44.93 F = 10 M = 1	–

Philosophy	NoA = 28; NE = 28; Min = 14.4; Max = 47; F = 11 M = 17	NoA = 9; NE = 2; Min = 31.08; Max = 33.28; F = 2 M = 0	–	NoA = 16; NE = 16; Min = 20.59; Max = 47.00; F = 11 M = 5	NoA = 5; NE = 4; Min = 26.97; Max = 31.15; F = 1 M = 3	NoA = 12; NE = 12; Min = 16.21; Max = 37.79; F = 5 M = 7	NoA = 10; NE = 10; Min = 15.93; Max = 40.34; F = 8 M = 2	NoA = 13; NE = 13; Min = 19.22; Max = 47; F = 10 M = 3
Montenegrin language and South Slavic literature	NoA = 17; NE = 17; Min = 21.67; Max = 41.61; F = 14 M = 1	NoA = 28; NE = 28; Min = 16.27; Max = 37.10; F = 27 M = 1	–	NoA = 23; NE = 23; Min = 18.48; Max = 47.00; F = 20 M = 3	NoA = 14; NE = 14; Min = 19.99; Max = 41.90; F = 11 M = 3	NoA = 3; NE = 3; Min = 22.96; Max = 27.94; F = 3 M = 0	NoA = 14; NE = 14; Min = 18.89; Max = 44.44; F = 11 M = 3	NoA = 9; NE = 9; Min = 20.14; Max = 36.64; F = 7 M = 2
Serbian language and South Slavic literature	NoA = 21; NE = 21; Min = 19.56; Max = 43.02; F = 15 M = 6	NoA = 13; NE = 13; Min = 17.64; Max = 41.60; F = 13 M = 0	NoA = 11; NE = 11; Min = 14.59; Max = 33.13; F = 5 M = 6	NoA = 20; NE = 20; Min = 19.37; Max = 39.17; F = 11 M = 9	NoA = 5; NE = 5; Min = 19.23; Max = 30.55; F = 4 M = 1	NoA = 5; NE = 5; Min = 19.21; Max = 28.97; F = 2 M = 3	NoA = 5; NE = 5; Min = 16.28; Max = 44.20; F = 2 M = 3	NoA = 4; NE = 4; Min = 23.41; Max = 33.94; F = 2 M = 2
English language and literature	NoA = 80; NE = 80; Min = 17.14; Max = 47.00; F = 56 M = 24	–	–	NoA = 86; NE = 80; Min = 23.16; Max = 47; F = 58 M = 22	–	NoA = 74; NE = 74; Min = 19.70; Max = 47; F = 57 M = 17	NoA = 13; NE = 6; Min = 29.80; Max = 44.42; F = 5 M = 1	–
Russian language and literature	NoA = 19; NE = 19; Min = 15.30; Max = 39.56; F = 13 M = 6	NoA = 18; NE = 18; Min = 16.28; Max = 37.06; F = 9 M = 9	NoA = 5; NE = 5; Min = 19.48; Max = 27.58; F = 3 M = 2	NoA = 9; NE = 9; Min = 24.82; Max = 44; F = 8 M = 1	NoA = 6; NE = 6; Min = 20.59; Max = 34.70; F = 4 M = 2	NoA = 4; NE = 4; Min = 22.17; Max = 29.10; F = 1 M = 3	NoA = 13; NE = 13; Min = 19.37; Max = 41.02; F = 12 M = 1	NoA = 3; NE = 3; Min = 23.14; Max = 25.96; F = 2 M = 1
Italian language and literature	NoA = 21; NE = 21; Min = 18.75; Max = 37.45; F = 19 M = 2	NoA = 18; NE = 18; Min = 14.81; Max = 39.00; F = 16 M = 2	NoA = 7; NE = 6; Min = 22.01; Max = 47.00; F = 4 M = 2	NoA = 24; NE = 24; Min = 21.60; Max = 38.38; F = 24 M = 2	NoA = 9; NE = 9; Min = 22.76; Max = 41.02; F = 8 M = 1	NoA = 13; NE = 13; Min = 23.02; Max = 44.84; F = 10 M = 3	NoA = 3; NE = 3; Min = 16.82; Max = 27.29; F = 2 M = 1	NoA = 1; NE = 1; Min = 36.58; Max = 36.58; F = 1 M = 0

(continued)

Table 13.7 (continued)

Subject	Enrolment term	2017/2018			2018/2019			2019/2020		
		1st	2nd	3rd	1st	2nd	3rd	1st	2nd	3rd
French language and literature	NoA	26	13	4	16	2	12	3	12	5
	NE	26	13	4	16	2	12	3	12	5
	Min	17.65	17.91	21.95	19.35	35.78	12.75	21.67	20.57	20.73
	Max	47.00	34.76	34.19	44.84	40.31	40.90	35.59	41.19	39.70
	F / M	F = 21 M = 5	F = 8 M = 5	F = 3 M = 1	F = 11 M = 5	F = 2 M = 0	F = 8 M = 4	F = 1 M = 2	F = 12 M = 1	F = 4 M = 1
German language and literature	NoA	55	–	–	37	5	–	27	8	4
	NE	45			37	3		27	8	4
	Min	27.51			19.82	31.26		17.77	24.53	18.02
	Max	49.00			47	43.08		41.79	41.55	42.62
	F / M	F = 35 M = 10			F = 26 M = 11	F = 2 M = 1		F = 17 M = 10	F = 6 M = 2	F = 4 M = 0
Physical education	NoA	56	34	9	63	10	16	27	63	23
	NE	37	20	3	53	5	2	12	33	7
	Min	37.13	21.24	18.68	34.54	40.07	54.40	35.27	33.20	34.95
	Max	63.12	55.01	22.52	62.53	50.70	58.38	50.72	60.38	50.49
	F / M	F = 8 M = 29	F = 7 M = 13	F = 0 M = 3	F = 6 M = 28	F = 1 M = 4	F = 0 M = 2	F = 0 M = 12	F = 6 M = 26	F = 0 M = 7
Maths	NoA	20	4	2	9	2	6	11	2	1
	NE	20	4	2	9	2	6	11	2	1
	Min	17.13	21.53	19.86	22.45	20.64	21.91	18.61	27.16	18.26
	Max	47.00	41.80	41.80	44.50	30.54	36.35	42.36	33.18	18.26
	F / M	F = 15 M = 5	F = 3 M = 1	F = 2 M = 0	F = 6 M = 3	F = 1 M = 1	F = 4 M = 2	F = 10 M = 1	F = 0 M = 2	F = 1 M = 0
Physics	NoA	15	4	1	12	2	3	6	1	7
	NE	15	4	1	12	2	3	6	1	7
	Min	13.42	20.48	19.47	13.89	20.57	19.04	25.83	44.50	14.27
	Max	47.00	40.36	19.47	41.50	29.67	37.66	44.50	44.50	40.49
	F / M	F = 5 M = 10	F = 1 M = 3	F = 0 M = 1	F = 6 M = 6	F = 0 M = 2	F = 1 M = 2	F = 4 M = 2	F = 1 M = 0	F = 2 M = 5

Biology	NoA = 33 NE = 33 Min = 18.28 Max = 47.00 F = 26 M = 7	NoA = 17 NE = 17 Min = 17.23 Max = 41.92 F = 15 M = 2	NoA = 6 NE = 4 Min = 20.96 Max = 29.83 F = 3 M = 1	NoA = 24 NE = 24 Min = 11.80 Max = 41.98 F = 19 M = 5	NoA = 11 NE = 11 Min = 16.58 Max = 35.65 F = 10 M = 1	NoA = 12 NE = 12 Min = 12.56 Max = 35.31 F = 12 M = 1	NoA = 20 NE = 20 Min = 15.32 Max = 40.61 F = 14 M = 6	NoA = 15 NE = 15 Min = 17.58 Max = 36.23 F = 14 M = 1
							NoA = 17 NE = 17 Min = 10.82 Max = 38.91 F = 10 M = 7	
Music	NoA = 2 NE = 2 Min = 32.24 Max = 33.47 F = 0 M = 2	NoA = 1 NE = 1 Min = 33.73 Max = 33.73 F = 0 M = 1	NoA = 3 NE = 3 Min = 32.58 Max = 45.72 F = 2 M = 1	NoA = 2 NE = 1 Min = 60.31 Max = 60.31 F = 1 M = 0	NoA = 2 NE = 2 Min = 38.68 Max = 69.63 F = 2 M = 0	NoA = 1 NE = 1 Min = 44.37 Max = 44.37 F = 1 M = 0	NoA = 11 NE = 7 Min = 32.82 Max = 64.56 F = 7 M = 0	
Fine arts	NoA = 10 NE = 10 Min = 36.68 Max = 64.50 F = 9 M = 1	NoA = 1 NE = 1 Min = 58.50 Max = 58.50 F = 1 M = 0	—	NoA = 10 NE = 10 Min = 38.07 Max = 61.68 F = 8 M = 2	NoA = 4 NE = 4 Min = 38.70 Max = 55.82 F = 2 M = 2	—	NoA = 11 NE = 11 Min = 40.50 Max = 67.97 F = 9 M = 2	—	—

Abbreviations: *NoA* number of applicants; *NE* number enrolled; *Min* the minimum number of points allocated to enrolled applicants; *Max* the maximum number of points allocated to enrolled applicants; *F* female candidates enrolled; *M* male candidates enrolled of applicants and the number of enrolled students. Table 13.7 illustrates the enrolment data for bachelor's studies in more detail: namely numbers of applicants, numbers of accepted applicants, the range of points in their applications (from minimum to maximum), and their gender.

As noted earlier, this table demonstrates the relationships between the numbers of candidates applying and the numbers of candidates enrolled in bachelor's programmes for teacher education in Montenegro in recent years. The range of points between the first-ranked candidates and those at the end of the ranking list is smaller in those programmes for which there is a larger number of interested candidates (e.g. pre-school, class teachers education, English language and literature), which means that there are more homogeneous groups in these programmes. The groups of students are inhomogeneous in other departments, which significantly complicates the work of teachers. In terms of the popularity of teaching areas, the table also illustrates that programmes for pre-school and primary school class teachers—as well as for English language and literature, German language and literature, sociology, and physical education—garner significantly higher levels of enrolment interest than all other teaching courses. These programmes close their enrolment windows mostly during the first enrolment term (June) and do not take in all candidates—and this rejection rate exists on a broad spectrum whereby the most oversubscribed course, pre-school education, has rejected an annual average of 73 candidates over the last three years, while, at the other end of the scale, the English and German courses have each denied an annual average of just four candidates over the last three academic years. However, there are ongoing problems regarding the measures (or lack thereof) by which candidates are accepted or rejected from the course of their choice—in particular, the absence of rules around the minimum number of points yielded from high school education that candidates must first acquire in order to apply to university. Furthermore, the fact that most of the programmes enrol candidates in order—that is, by enrolment deadline and number of points, without minimum restrictions—means that those with very low numbers of points are accepted. As regards what should or will happen next, it is worth noting that, 10 years ago, students enrolled in class teacher education programmes were already advocating for the reinstatement of the entrance exam, including a general knowledge and a verbal communication test (Vučković 2010). Now, using the Accreditation form of the Faculty of Philosophy (2017), such a qualifying exam is proposed to be reintroduced for those applying to pre-school and class teaching education programmes (re)commencing in the 2020/2021 academic year.

Studies for pre-school teachers and class teachers at the UoM can be attended by candidates who have previously completed a four-year high school programme (i.e. gymnasium or vocational school). Studies for subject teachers—in the form of a master's programme from 2017 onwards—can be chosen after finishing a three-year bachelor's programme. Lastly and critically, Table 13.7 demonstrates that Montenegro's teacher education studies are dominated by women, a true reflection of Montenegro's education sector on the whole (Šišević 2009). The lack of men undertaking such studies is particularly pronounced in the fields of pre-school and primary school education; indeed, not a single man has enrolled himself in a pre-school education programme in the last three years, and just five men have enrolled in a primary teaching programme over the same time period. Female students also currently form a striking majority in the programmes preparing Montenegro's next generation of teachers to educate across all languages and literatures—Montenegrin, Serbian, English, Russian, Italian, French, and German—as well as sociology, philosophy, biology, mathematics, music, and fine arts. Male candidates outnumber their female counterparts only in courses for history, physical education, and physics.

Continuous Professional Development: In-service Teacher Training

In-service teacher training is currently under the jurisdiction of the Bureau for Education Services of Montenegro, where the Department for Continuous Professional Development (CPD) was formed in 2005 based on the Strategic Plan for Education Reform for the period 2003–2004 (2003). CPD is defined as life-long learning and is considered 'a crucial factor for improving teacher quality, schools, and teachers' impact on student learning' (Louws et al. 2017, p. 487). The system of teacher professional development in Montenegro was formed in the period between 2005 and 2009—with teachers, pedagogues, school officials, counsellors, and supervisors from the Bureau for Education, as well as foreign experts, all participating in its development (Popović 2010). Such a system did not exist in this form before. Now, at last, the forms and types of programmes for advanced training (both requested and offered) have been defined, along with the procedure by which they are accredited and posted in the *Catalogue of the Programme for the Advanced Training of Teachers* (of which six have been published to date).

This system of professional development has been gradually introduced into all the kindergartens, elementary schools, and gymnasiums in Montenegro—based on carrying out professional development activities at the kindergarten/school level, as well as creating and upholding a personal plan of professional development. Personal professional development plans are tailored to the needs of the individual, based on the institutional needs of the school where the said individual is employed (Popović 2010). The standards that employees must achieve in order to obtain a work license are defined, and the achievement of these standards for all employees is planned at the school level, thus responding to the needs of the school. In addition, employees can, based on an individual plan, participate in additional activities that enable them to acquire advanced teaching professions, which is a response to their individual needs. CPD activities are carried out by a team for professional development, led by a coordinator.

In accordance with the results of Subotić et al.'s (2009) research, it was found that the implementation of the continuous professional development system supports the teacher's lifelong learning, plus contributes to their reflection on their own work as a basis for planning further learning. Participation in CPD activities is one of the basic requirements for advancing to higher professional positions, as stipulated in the *Guide for internship for teachers* (*Official Journal of Montenegro*, no. 68/03, 2003). The system of professional titles for teachers includes four titles: teacher-mentor, teacher-counsellor, teacher-higher counsellor, and teacher-researcher. The title is awarded based on evidence of attendance at accredited training programmes and engagement in other tasks related to the profession, such as participation in projects and research and in publishing articles (Popović 2010).

In theory, professional development programmes enable the subsequent introduction of innovations in the teaching process (Bitan-Friedlander et al. 2004). However, after implementing such programmes in Montenegro for many years ourselves, we can state with confidence that this training is mostly short-term and abstract (i.e. considering the short duration of training, there is a lack of tangible outcomes), meaning that it has limited effects in regard to the actual changes brought about in the professional habits of teachers (Pešikan et al. 2010). As such, going forwards, longer-term programmes are critical to the success of Montenegro's ongoing teacher education. These types of programmes would aim to provide the conditions for high-quality and efficient innovation of the teaching process through continuously supporting teachers (Vujačić et al. 2017).

Discussion, Conclusions, and Directions for Future Development

The Strategy of teacher education in Montenegro 2017–2024 (2016) was created following contemporary scientific findings in the field, shifting towards a conceptualisation of education whereby teachers are autonomous and creative workers, as well as reflexive practitioners and researchers. However, the realisation of this vision is currently hindered by, among other things, cultural codes developed in the past, among which centralisation takes a prominent position (Gawlicz and Starnawski 2018, p. 394), as well as minimal understanding of the importance and complexity of the teaching profession as evidenced by the content-oriented ('know-what') nature of the curricula for the education of subject teachers in Montenegro to date.

As outlined in this chapter, in practice, the education of teachers in Montenegro can be differentiated into two basic types: the first for pre-school and class teachers, and the second for subject teachers. Technically, as mentioned earlier, a third category includes the experts who teach vocational subjects in vocational education training schools (i.e. economists, engineers, doctors, etc.); however, these educators have not been categorised here as teachers, even though they do teach. We have not specifically analysed them here, since they do not have initial teacher education.

In summary, the first type of TE, for pre-school and class teachers, is the much better balanced of the two in regard to the ratio of content-oriented subjects to pedagogy-oriented subjects. All the same, both types of TE programmes should be more oriented towards transversal skills: key competences for lifelong learning in the twenty-first century. Furthermore, the practical teaching component should be significantly strengthened, in terms of both the type and amount of practical activities students are able to experience before graduating. Additionally, the primary methods of knowledge review and grading at present are written tests and written exams, especially final exams, as is the case in many European countries, meaning that even when students are able to undertake practical activities, they are not adequately recognised through grades. In tandem with increasing access to practical teaching practice, the future teacher as a reflexive practitioner and researcher in the twenty-first century should be trained to proactively improve their own professional practice long-term by carrying out research (Darling-Hammond 2017). Research-skills could help teachers to better identify problems in practice, analyse them clearly and objectively, and find solutions that fit the specific context. In addition, teacher-researchers are focused on continuous monitoring of research published by other researchers, so they are well informed about various aspects of modern knowledge of education.

Ultimately, the efforts made in line with the 2016 Strategy of teacher education in Montenegro 2017–2024 have, as yet, proved insufficient, meaning that greater reform is needed. Given that the various teacher orientations are currently scattered between the UoM's faculties—that is, across the cities of Podgorica, Nikšić, and Cetinje—any sort of harmonisation is prevented. As such, the only real solution seems to be to gather all the teacher orientations under one university unit: a singular teacher faculty that would educate the different profiles of teachers via separate, but united, departments. Under such harmonisation, the existing teacher education faculties could remain in use as units educating non-education experts, such as scientists or artists.

As explained earlier, Montenegro's education sector would benefit from increased numbers of well-suited candidates applying to undertake teacher education. Interest in the teaching profession is directly tied to its socio-economic position, meaning that the status of teachers in society must be improved, since that is the way to motivate good candidates to choose this profession (Darling-Hammond 2017; Gawlicz and Starnawski 2018). Going forwards, enrolment policies should resolve a few vital points, as referred to in this chapter:

* A better gender balance of the candidates is necessary, since children and young people should have guidance from adults across the gender spectrum, and teachers have been their role models (Radović 2007);
* Adding a minimum threshold of points required in order to enrol in undergraduate teacher education courses would create a filter through which candidates with strong academic track records would pass, ensuring that programme places are allocated to those assumed to be best fitted to the course of study. Research show that adolescents who have poorer educational attainment achieve poorer professional outcomes (Reynolds and Johnson 2011);
* It is necessary to provide an entrance exam which would ensure not just a simple evaluation of the knowledge, skills, and abilities of candidates, but also evaluate their personal motivations and interests (Darling-Hammond 2017).

Given the current lack of formal employment in Montenegro available to graduates from fields such as the humanities, many prospective students who would otherwise be interested in careers as, for instance, history or philosophy teachers simply cannot afford to undertake any teacher education programme without the promise of paid work upon graduation. To offset this employment problem, it would be logical and purposeful to consider dual subject teaching models, educating future teachers to give classes in at least two complementary subjects (e.g. biology and chemistry, or sociology and philosophy), thus opening up opportunities for work (Delibašić 2003). There are significant tendencies to connect subjects in educational system nowadays—that is, for interdisciplinary courses such as STEM (science, technology, engineering, and mathematics) or STEAM (science, technology, engineering, arts, and mathematics)—which is an important argument for supporting teacher education for two or more subjects. Besides, some education systems have had joint degrees for years, for example, Scotland (Eurydice Scotland 2021b) and Croatia (Eurydice Croatia 2021a).

Furthermore, as noted earlier, the development of third cycle of studies is essential for Montenegro because the teaching profession would thus get a complete educational vertical which could, at the same time, have a positive impact on the enrolment. Doctoral studies are, by nature, research-oriented, so their development, accreditation, and realisation could significantly fortify the research component of the teaching profession. The research in education must become a part of teachers' everyday routines, for certain, with an aim of improving teaching practice as well as solving problems in education on the basis of empirical data and their analysis, instead of on the basis of personal impressions and impressions.

Looking beyond Montenegrin borders, Linda Darling-Hammond's (2017) study on key factors for education of high-quality teachers who can be considered internationally recognised is a valuable guide/resource for Montenegro because many problems that Montenegrin society has faced in the recent and distant past, and which are current today, can be solved only by quality education, and an important factor of such education is a quality teacher (Bešić and Reškovac 2012). Her framework includes selecting the best candidates for the profession; running high-quality teaching programs; linking theory, practice, and research; employing teacher standards; establishing induction models; supporting continuous professional development; collaborating with colleagues; and investing in capacity building of both teachers and schools (Darling-Hammond 2017, pp. 306–307). The teaching profession is becoming ever more complex through the processes of digitisation and globalisation (Collinson et al. 2009, p. 5), plus classrooms are increasingly diverse, so teachers need to comprehensively develop inclusive pedagogies and social competences in their own education (Ben-Peretz and Flores 2018, p. 209).

Ultimately, it can be concluded that international trends shape national education policies in the Montenegrin context—such as the Strategy of teacher education in Montenegro 2017–2024, 2016—as well as pre-school and class teacher education. On the other hand, the education of subject teachers does not follow these trends, raising critical questions around how much the Montenegrin education system actually functions as a whole. It is obvious that the cultural habits—such as underestimation of the pedagogical, psychological, and methodological component in the education of subject teachers—acquired historically, most especially in the period up to the 1990s, continue to obstruct the development of a modern teacher education system. However, looking to the future, a unified and comprehensive Montenegrin TE system would be relatively simple to establish, given that almost all teachers are currently educated at the same public university. Nonetheless, the success of this endeavour would require a concentrated effort to develop a truly shared understanding of the teaching profession, its complexity, and its importance among the country's decision-makers, as well as other education stakeholders, such as university professors working on initial teacher education and educators in charge of in-service teacher training. There is still work to be done in raising awareness regarding the true importance of high quality TE—that is to say the crucial role of education in the development of an inclusive, equitable, and sustainable society where autonomous and competent teachers play a key role. To close this chapter optimistically, it is worth noting that this work has already begun. It is expected that the Instrument for Pre-Accession II project 'Integration of key competences into the educational system of Montenegro', as well as the national Agency for Control and Quality Assurance of Higher Education established in 2019, and guided by the Strategy of teacher education in Montenegro 2017–2024 (2016) and other documents, will contribute to a better understanding of the fundamental complexities of TE and the necessary changes yet to occur in this vital sector.

References

Accreditation form of the Faculty of Philosophy. (2017). Nikšić: Faculty of Philosophy.

Anderson, L. W., and D. R. Krathwohl. (2001). *A taxonomy for learning, teaching and assessing: A revision of Bloom's taxonomy.* New York: Longman Publishing.

Backović, S. (Ed.). (2001). *Knjiga promjena. [The Book of changes].* Podgorica: Ministarstvo prosvjete i nauke.

Ben-Peretz, M., and M. A. Flores. (2018). Tensions and paradoxes in teaching: Implications for teacher education. *European Journal of Teacher Education, 41*(2), 202–213.

Bešić, M., and T. Reškovac. (2012). *Evaluacija reforme obrazovanja u Crnoj Gori 2010–2012* [Evaluation of the Education Reform in Montenegro 2010–2012]. Podgorica: Zavod za školstvo.

Bitan-Friedlander, N., A. Dreyfus, and Z. Milgrom. (2004). Types of "teachers in training": The reactions of primary school science teachers when confronted with the task of implementing an innovation. *Teaching and Teacher Education*, 20(6), 607–619.

Caena, F. (2014). *Initial teacher education in Europe: an overview of policy issues.* European Commission—Directorate—General for Education and Culture.

Collinson, V., E. Kozina, Y. K. Lin, L. Ling, I. Matheson, L. Newcombe, and I. Zogla. (2009). Professional development for teachers: A world of change. *European Journal of Teacher Education*, 32(1), 3–19.

The Constitution of the Republic of Montenegro [Ustav RCG]. (1992). O.J. of Montenegro, no. 48

The Constitution of Montenegro [Ustav RCG]. (2007). O.J. of Montenegro, no. 1.

Curriculum Plans 1992–2007. (1992 onwards). Podgorica: University of Montenegro.

Curriculum Plans 2007–2012. (2007). Podgorica: University of Montenegro.

Curriculum Plans 2017–2022. (2017). Podgorica: University of Montenegro.

Darling-Hammond, L. (2017). Teacher education around the world: What can we learn from international practice? *European Journal of Teacher Education*, 40(3), 291–309.

Delibašić, R. (2003). *Filozofski fakultet u Nikšiću (1977–2002)* [Faculty of Philosophy in Nikšić (1977–2002)]. Nikšić: Filozofski fakultet.

Delibašić, R. (2009). *Istorija pedagoške misli u Crnoj Gori* [The History of Pedagogical Thought in Montenegro]. Podgorica: CID.

ETUCE. (2008). Teacher education in Europe. An ETUCE Policy Paper. Brussels.

Eurydice. (2019). *Montenegro.* Retrieved from https://eacea.ec.europa.eu/national-policies/eurydice/crna-gora/.

Eurydice. (2021a). *Croatia.* Retrieved from https://eacea.ec.europa.eu/national-policies/eurydice/content/croatia_en.

Eurydice. (2021b). *Scotland.* Retrieved from https://eacea.ec.europa.eu/national-policies/eurydice/content/united-kingdom-scotland_en.

Gawlicz, K., and M. Starnawski. (2018). Educational policies in Central and Eastern Europe: Legacies of state socialism, modernization aspirations and challenges of semi-peripheral contexts. *Policy Futures in Education*, Special Issue: Educational Policies in Central and Eastern Europe, 16(4), 385–397.

Godoń, R., P. Jucevičienė, and Z. Kodeljac. (2004). Philosophy of education in post-Soviet societies of Eastern Europe: Poland, Lithuania and Slovenia. *Comparative Education*, 40(4), 559–569.

Gordon, J., H. Gabor, M. Krawczyk, T. Leney, A. Michel, D. Pepper, E. Putkiewicz, and J. Wiśniewski. (2009). *Key competences in Europe: Opening doors for lifelong learners across the school curriculum and teacher education.* CASE Network Reports No. 87. Warsaw: Center for Social and Economic Research (CASE).

Kennedy, D. (2007). *Pisanje i upotreba ishoda učenja—Praktični vodič* [Writing and the use of the outcome of studying—practical guide]. Beograd: Savet Evrope, Kancelarija u Beogradu.

Krathwohl, D. R. (2002). A revision of Bloom's taxonomy: An overview. *Theory into Practice*, 41(4), 212–218.

Louws, M. L., K. Veen, A. Jacobiene, Meirink, A. and J. H. van Driel. (2017). Teachers' professional learning goals in relation to teaching experience. *European Journal of Teacher Education*, 40(4), 487–504.

Novović, T. (2010). Predškolstvo u kontekstu bolonjskih promjena [Preschool studies in context of changes related to Bologna Declaration]. *Sociološka luča*, IV(1), 106–122.

Novović, T. (2016). The concept of inclusive education in the master's degree. In: N. Gutvajn and M. Vujačić (Eds.), Challenges and perspectives of inclusive education (pp. 173–182). Beograd: Institute for Educational Research, Volgograd: Volgograd State Socio-Pedagogical University, Faculty of Teacher Education, University of Belgrade.

Novović, T. (2017). The preschool educational system in Montenegro: Current state and prospects. *Journal of Contemporary Educational Studies*, 68(3), 172–189.

Novović, T. (2018). The preschool curriculum in the educational context in Montenegro. *Journal of Contemporary Educational Studies*, 69(4), 200–218.

Perović, D., and D. Vučković. (2019). Success in studying at the University of Montenegro: Is there hyper-production of diplomas? *Interdisciplinary Description of Complex Systems*, 17(2-B), 385–402.

Pešikan, A., and Z. Lalović. (2017). *Obrazovanje za život: Ključne kompetencije za 21. vijek u kurikulumima u Crnoj Gor* [Education for life: Key competences for 21st century in curriculums in Montenegro]. Podgorica: UNICEF Crna Gora.

Pešikan, A., S. Antić, and S. Marinković. (2010). The concept of professional development of teachers in Serbia- between the proclaimed and hidden model. *Teaching and Upbringing*, 59(2), 278–296.

PISA Study Results [Rezultati studije PISA 2015]. (2018). Podgorica: Ministarstvo prosvjete.

Popović, D. (2010). Professional development and changed roles of teachers. In: P. Vukotić (Ed.), *Montenegro in the XXI century—in the era of competitiveness: Education* (pp. 239–258). Podgorica: Montenegrin Academy of Arts and Sciences.

Pravilnik o pripravničkom stažu [Guide for internship for teachers]. (2003). Official Journal of Montenegro, 68/03.

Pravilnik o polaganju stručnog ispita nastawnika [Rulebook on the professional exam of teachers]. (2003). In: O.J. of Montenegro, no. 67/2003, pp. 21–26.

Prekić, A. (2016). Komunizam i obrazovanje: iskustva Crne Gore 1945–1955. [Communism and education: The experience of Montenegro 1945–1955]. *Acta Histriae*, 24(3), 527–642.

Radović, V. (2007). *Feminizacija učiteljskog poziva* [Feminisation of teachers' profession]. Beograd: Učiteljski fakultet.

Rautiainen, M., M. Mäensivu, and T. Nikkola. (2018). Becoming interested during teacher education. *European Journal of Teacher Education*, 41(4), 418–432.

Reynolds J. R., and M. K. Johnson. (2011). Change in the stratification of educational expectations and their realization. *Social Forces*, 90(1), 85–109.

Šebart, K. M., and A. Hočevar. (2019). *Delusion of preschool education. Does anyone care about the process quality anymore?* Hamburg: Verlag Dr Kovač.

Šišević, R. (ur.) 2009. *Crna Gora u brojkama* [Montenegro in Numbers]. Podgorica: Monstat—Zavod za statistiku Crne Gore.

Situation Analysis and Strategic Commitments at the University of Montenegro [Analiza stanja i strateška opredjeljenja za reorganizaciju i integraciju Univerziteta Crne Gore]. (2015). Podgorica: Univerzitet Crne Gore, European University Association.

Strategija obrazovanja nastavnika u Crnoj Gori 2017–2024, sa Akcionim planom za 2017. i 2018. godinu [Strategy for Teacher Education in Montenegro 2017–2024, with a Plan of Action for 2017, 2018]. (2016). Podgorica: Ministarstvo prosvjete.

Strateški plan reforme obrazovanja za period 2003–2004. The strategic plan for education reform for the period 2003–2004. (2003). Podgorica: Ministry of Education and Sports.

Subotić, L., and N. Luteršek, et al. (2009). Uticaj primjene sistema profesionalnog razvoja na nivou škole na uključivanje nastavnika u doživotno učenje [Influences of application of the system for professional development of teachers at the level of schools to inclusion of teachers in life-long learning]. *Profesionalni razvoj nastavnika u Crnoj Gori*, 4, 3–16.

Šuković, R. (2003). *Obrazovanje nastavnika u Crnoj Gri (1947–1977). Viša pedagoška škola (1947–1963). Pedagoška akademija (1963–1977)* [The education of teachers in Montenegro (1947–1977). Higher Pedagogical School (1947–1963). Pedagogical Academy (1963–1977)]. Nikšić: Filozofski fakultet.

Tatto, M. T., and I. Menter (Eds.). (2019). Knowledge, policy and practice in teacher education: A cross-national study. London, Oxford, New York, New Delhi, Sydney: Bloomsbury Academic.

Trippestad, T. A., Swennen, A., and T. Werler (Eds.). (2018). The struggle for teacher education: International perspectives on governance and reforms. London, Oxford, New York, New Delhi, Sydney: Bloomsbury Academic.

Vonta, T. (2009). *Organizirana predšolska vzgoja v izzivih družbenih spememb.* Ljubljana: Pedagoški inštitut.

Vučković, D. (2010). Organizacija nastave na Studijskom programu za obrazovanje učitelja [Organization of the teaching process at the program for teacher education]. *Sociološka luča*, IV (1), 146–172.

Vučković, D., and S. Čalović Nenezić. (2014). Pedagogical and psychological foundation of teaching at the University of Montenegro. In: S. Velea (Ed.), *Perspective asupra formării personalalui didactic universitar în domeniul pedagogiei şi psihologiei educaţiei* (pp. 106–116). Timişoara: Universitatea de Vest din Timişoara.

Vujačić, M., R. Dević, and J. Stanišić. (2017). Iskustva učitelja u primeni inovativnih nastavnih metoda u okviru programa stručnog usavršavanja [Experiences of teachers in applying the innovative teaching methods within the programme for professional development]. *Zbornik Instituta za pedagoška istraživanja*, 49(2), 234–260.

Zgaga, P. (2008). Recenzija [Review]. In: N. Pantić (Ed.), *Usaglašavanje programa obrazovanja prosvetnih radnika u zemljama zapadnog Balkana* [Harmonization of the Teacher Education Programs for the Countries of Western Balkans] (pp. 6–9). Beograd: Centar za obrazovne politike.

Zorić, V., and D. Vučković. (2019). Teacher education in Montenegro. In: K. G. Karras and C.C. Wolhuter (Eds.), *International handbook of teacher education* (pp. 473–490). Nikosia (Cyprus): HM Studies and Publishing.

Zvizdojević, J. et al. (2015). *Crna Gora u brojkama* [Montenegro in numbers]. Podgorica: Zavod za statistiku Crne Gore—Monstat.

14

The Professionalisation of Teaching Careers in Romania: Transition Processes from Pre-university Education to Higher Education

Romita Iucu, Anca Nedelcu, and Mirabela Amarandei

Introduction

Over the last three decades, the Romanian educational system has made a transition from an over-centralised Communist philosophy to a more autonomous and decentralised paradigm. For the higher education system, this represented a major shift, bringing significant changes at both the systemic and the institutional levels. Over the same period, the pre-university system has seen many reforms or attempted reforms, due to constant political instability. Whereas the academic arena has remained more stable in terms of legislative changes, pre-university education has been more affected by continuous change.

The Romanian education system is currently legislated by the Education Law 1/2011 and its subsequent amendments. This law brought a shift of perspective in pre-university education, emphasising the quality of education, inclusiveness, and an innovative approach. A paradigm shift was also initiated concerning the focus on students' individual needs. However, many of these changes were never put in place, due to numerous legislative amendments and political instability.

R. Iucu (✉) • A. Nedelcu • M. Amarandei
University of Bucharest, Bucharest, Romania
e-mail: romita.iucu@unibuc.ro

The country reports issued by the European Commission, along with many other studies, emphasise inequalities, educational exclusion, a high percentage of dropouts, and a low level of basic skills and competences among students. According to the European Commission (2019), '[i]n 2017, general government spending on education was equivalent to only 2.8% of GDP, significantly below the EU average of 4.6% and the lowest percentage in the EU'. The European Commission has also pointed out the high level of underachievement in reading, mathematics, and science: the PISA 2015 results show that about 40% of 15-year-olds lack basic competences. However, the Romanian higher education system has seen some remarkable developments, including making the transition from a Communist constricted academic framework to the implementation of the Bologna Process.

The selective system and the restriction of learning opportunities during the Communist period led, after 1990, to expansion and an academic institutional boom, followed by a diversification of institutional profiles, a differentiation of programme types and curricular philosophies, and a growing heterogeneity of students and academic staff. The number of higher education institutions, as well as the rates of participation in higher education, has increased rapidly since 1990. This is a consequence of the massification of higher education. The total number of Romanian public institutions for higher education increased 2.5 times in 10 years, from 48 in 1990 to 121 in 2001 (Curaj et al. 2015). An accompanying significant rise in participation rates shows an improvement in the openness of Romanian higher education: in the 1989/1990 academic year, the tertiary enrolment rate was 8.8% for the 18–22 age group (Szolár 2014), whilst in 2008/2009 it was 63.3% for the 19–23 and above age group (Szolár 2014).

Romania was one of the first countries to sign the Bologna Declaration in 1999. At the institutional level, various measures aimed at implementing the objectives of the Bologna Process were taken from that moment, but the most important step towards systematic change was taken in 2004, with the enactment of specific legislation.

Joining the EHEA (European Higher Education Area, according to the Bologna Process) has generated a series of reforms in Romania, in order to align Romanian universities with the Bologna principles and objectives. This has included introducing the three-cycle system of bachelor's, master's, and doctoral degrees; the mutual recognition of qualifications; and the implementation of a quality assurance system. From the legislative perspective, the years 2004–2005–2006 were some of the most relevant for Romanian higher education reforms.

Since the Education Law 1/2011 was adopted, a number of dimensions have been added to strengthen higher education reforms: the need for excellence in higher education, increasing scientific production and excellence, public funding related to university autonomy and public accountability, access and equity in higher education, and internationalisation.

The national system currently counts 93 higher education institutions, of which 55 are public institutions and 38 are private universities.

There is still a need for measures and actions to increase academic excellence, high quality academic skills, international openness, and access to academic education. A report by the Ministry of Education from 2019—*Report on the state of higher education in Romania,* 2017–2018—shows a decrease in the number of students. In the academic year 2011–2012, approximately 540,000 students were enrolled, whereas in 2017–2018 there were only 410,000 students (Ministry of Education 2019). The decrease is due to the demographic evolution, but also due to the decrease in pass rates for the baccalaureate exam, poverty, and early school leaving. According to the European Commission, the tertiary education attainment for the 30–34 age group in Romania in 2018 was 24.6%, significantly lower than the EU average of 40.7% (European Commission 2019).

The ambitious project by the European Commission—*European Universities Networks*—which aims to build a competitive and resilient European Education Area, represents an opportunity for Romanian universities. After the second call, Romania is now represented within the initiative by 10 academic institutions which are developing in-depth academic cooperation with reputed European universities.

Evolving at the crossroads between national processes and international influences, the Romanian higher education system is striving to improve its reputation and to be more relevant at the international level. The year 2020 was a kind of anniversary for higher education and teacher training systems, since 20 years had passed since the launch and implementation of the Bologna Process, a public policy which significantly impacted the evolution of higher education in general, and the teacher training system in particular. In an analysis developed 10 years ago, at the 10-year anniversary of the Bologna Process, some ideas were noted that are worth keeping in mind. To ensure continuity, they retain a high degree of validity:

> In the field of higher education policy, the European Commission asserts that reforming the teacher education systems by making them more flexible, more coherent and more open to the needs of society is a priority. Reforms are imperative in order to find an answer to the challenges facing the modern world: globalisation and new approaches in the training and retraining of the European labour force. Reforms should qualify the universities to assume a more active

role in building the European knowledge society and in contributing more to the Lisbon Strategy. (Iucu 2009, p. 63)

In accordance with the reform guidelines, as well as with the general lines of the Bologna Process, we can provide an updated representation comprising the main consequences of this process for teacher education systems and practices (Iucu 2009) (see Fig. 14.1).

Indeed, 'For the past twenty years, there has been an increased tendency towards convergence with regard to teacher education. The change in the structure of educational systems, brought about by the implementation of the Bologna Process, had the most significant impact on reforming Initial Teacher Education (ITE)' (Iucu and Iftimescu 2021, p. 24).

The evolution of the Romanian educational system brought about a major challenge in training primary and secondary teaching staff. At the same time, it posed serious difficulties (consisting primarily of anxieties and uncertainties) to the professionalisation of the university teaching staff. Over the last

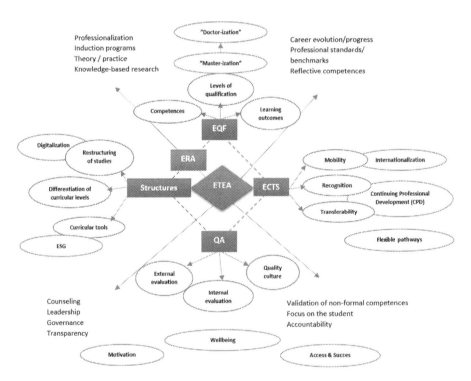

Fig. 14.1 An updated model of the European Teacher Education Area—ETEA, based on Iucu (2009)

couple of years, one of the main problems regarding the training of both higher and pre-university teaching staff was in the separation of the two systems, which sheds no light on the connections and exchanges in the areas of training and professionalisation. Primary and secondary teachers, after all, are the products of higher education. Even so, their degree of professionalisation is insufficient to carry out their noble mission. One of the recurring ideas in the literature on this subject is shaped by the further argument regarding the need for a system of professionalisation for university careers, which is currently not so focused on teaching and learning as it is on research.

We consider this topic to be highly relevant, not only for the Romanian educational system but also for those European educational systems that have failed to deliver the professionalisation experience for the two components of didactic careers (initial education and CPD—continuing professional development). Therefore, our starting point is the analysis of the main challenges that arise when dealing with didactic careers and professionalisation, first presented in *The new professionalisation of the academic career in the context of the European Higher Education Area*, the EUA Expert Voices study:

> (…) moving from a focus on world-class universities to civic universities, a new shift from standardised professions to professions that have not been invented yet, equal access chances are taking a back seat to equal success chances, digital natives are now becoming socially interactive individuals, teachers now do more than teach, they facilitate, there is a shift from learning exclusively based on teaching to learning based on research evidence, an increasing focus on students' well-being has become a reference for studies and research in education, with the aim of designing an environment that motivates and involves students. (Iucu 2019)

The main focus will be on the transition process between the two systems and its defining elements. The aim of our paper is to identify and propose an articulated system of initial and continual training for a well-balanced, professionalised career, in which individual motivation plays an essential role.

The analysis of professionalisation models starts from those instruments that are specific to the initial training, but it is not limited to that. It can be extended to career mentorship and continued professional development. According to the recent *Education and Training Monitor 2019 of the European Commission* (cited in Ro Insider 2019), 'The initial education of local teachers offers very little preparation and practical training, particularly in modern teaching techniques or inclusive pedagogy". The report also notes that 'the certification exam and the tenure exam are used as the main method to screen candidates entering the profession, but this has proved to be less effective than having high entry standards and comprehensive initial teacher education. At the same time, the certification exam tends to assess theoretical knowledge without being an authentic measure of on-the-job competence' (Ro Insider 2019). These arguments lead to a very important idea, namely the professionalisation of the teaching career, underlined in this chapter from a variety of perspectives which, in our opinion, transform the interests and needs associated with professional development into a priority.

We do not aim to argue in favour of a unique model. Instead, our purpose is to support the general need for the system to respect institutional particularities and the imperatives of new pedagogies (including modular learning, problem-based learning, flipped classrooms, collaborative online international learning, education-research interaction, critical thinking skills, and learning analytics). This last perspective, highly comprehensive and epistemologically relevant for our study, provides an alternative to the traditional spectrum described by Hooker in 1997:

> The nineteenth-century model of teaching at higher level still holds sway and teaching has not changed much since. The last 15 years have seen progressive developments in many higher education institutions, but the basic model has not altered significantly, at least not in the majority of institutions. Yet the context in which higher education takes place has changed—and changed dramatically. (Hooker 1997)

The answer to the following question is crucial to further the research on this subject: 'Are the European and national decision-makers aware that any change in the field of education depends on the competences of pre-university and the university teachers, and their rate of professionalisation?'

Longitudinal Perspectives on the Teacher Education System in Romania

The official data presented in the *Report on the State of pre-university education in Romania* (Fig. 14.2) show that, contrary to the regressive trend registered in the past, 'in the 2017/2018 school year, the professional staff capacity in education slightly increased. The number of didactic personnel increased for all education cycles, with the exception of primary and secondary education. The most substantial increase was registered for professional education, as a

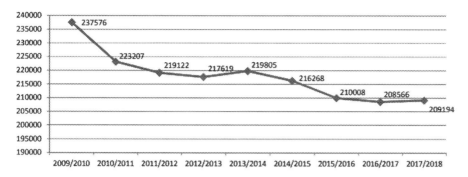

Fig. 14.2 The evolution of pre-university teachers' numbers, based on the *Report on the State of pre-university education in Romania*

result of the rehabilitation of this training route' (Romanian Ministry of National Education 2018).

The same source informs us that, during the 2017/2018 school year, the presence of qualified didactic personnel registered an increase at all levels of educational training and that 'a more substantial presence of qualified didactic personnel is registered in urban areas, at the level of primary and secondary education, but also in pre-university and professional education. For kindergarten and post-high school education, the indicator has a higher value in rural areas' (Romanian Ministry of National Education 2018).

From a public policy perspective, these conclusions regarding the dynamics of didactic personnel and their levels of qualification and professionalisation highlight the need to identify positions that are hard to fill with qualified personnel, but also to evaluate the opportunity of developing programmes designed to attract qualified personnel in schools. 'In spite of this positive perception by teachers, a number of factors have affected the attractiveness of the profession, including low entry requirements for teacher education programmes and traditionally low salaries (OECD 2017). Since 2017, teachers' salaries have been increasing following a new salary grid for public sector employees' (Education and Training Monitor 2019). Besides these elements imported from social policy and social security areas, some financial characteristics are also considered to have a medium-term impact on didactic careers: 'According to the initial 2019 budget, the amount allocated for salaries and other teachers' expenses increased by almost 31%'.

With regard to gender analysis for the same interval of reference, 'the presence of female didactic personnel registered a slight increase in the pre-university education cycle compared with the previous year'. In accordance with the European trend, the situation on each level of study is as follows: 'as the age of children/students decreases, the presence of female didactic personnel increases' (Education and Training Monitor 2019). There is a comparative reference to gender distribution in didactic careers at the European level: 'in general, there is a specific challenge in attracting males to this profession, especially at the primary and kindergarten levels, where the female teaching staff reaches 85% and 96% respectively' (Education and Training Monitor 2019). Other external positions that provide consistency to comparative international analysis regarding the age distribution for didactic staff and the recruitment level for entering a didactic career highlight a series of data that require special consideration: In Romania, less than 30% of schoolteachers are older than 50, compared to an EU average of 37%. This means that raising teaching quality involves working primarily with existing teachers, as the report notes. Furthermore, since the number of teachers is expected to decline in line with the student population, 'any reform of recruitment or initial teacher education will only affect a minority of members of the profession in the next few decades' (Education and Training Monitor 2019).

Beyond the statistics revealed by the reviewed information, aimed at highlighting the problematic elements of the system, we can identify a few problematic areas of a transversal nature. One of these areas is the student load in classrooms (not the didactic norm load, but rather the interactive space of a classroom). In this respect, if we take into account the number of students per teacher, the official report registered slight changes, influenced by reorganisation measures at the system level. Therefore, as a consequence of introducing the preparatory class into primary education, the number of children per kindergarten teacher ratio decreased. Simultaneously, the number of children per teacher ratio increased in primary education (Education and Training Monitor 2019).

One of the most challenging elements for the Romanian didactic training system, but also for the training of trainers, was identified after the publication of the PISA results from 2012, in the OECD report. A series of comments and critical observations were revealed; however, those experts who were able to conduct more nuanced educational analyses were more concerned with one of the items that stands for the collective educational subconscious, especially when it comes to educators, rather than general scores: students' motivation and the grouping of students (OECD 2012). According to this OECD data, in Romania the level of students' motivation for participating in school activities is lower than in any other country that took part in PISA testing. Indeed, this data speaks to the fact that investments need to be made in the systems which train teachers to acquire the transversal skills necessary for providing motivation and emotional support to their students. Only a systemic and integrated intervention would be capable of reforming human resources, and of resuscitating optimism and trust in a training system currently so caught up in a moment of profound instrumental and value-laden reform. A sustained approach in this direction requires not only the will for a public policy that would project and support short-term change, but also a long-term approach that would generate profound reflection on redefining the didactic career and professionalisation (across both pre-university education and higher education). However, there is a paradox: as long as the two education levels—pre-university and higher education—are considered to be separate, they do not communicate or correlate in teacher training. Since there are few synergies between the two, the main beneficiary—the student—finds themself on a journey from school to university, and those who should facilitate this—the teachers—are educated in a manner that does not assure a consistent link between primary, secondary, and tertiary education. Students carry both the information and the motivational and emotional legacy of the system that trained them. This is one of the reasons why systems and career approaches must be correlated. This further confirms the relevance of the argument in this chapter.

One of the programmatic documents, aimed at establishing an evolutionary framework of the Romanian educational system, developed under the coordination of the Romanian Academy, presents a series of ideas oriented towards representative axes centred on the didactic training domain. *The school and education in Romania: From equal access to equality of outcome* (2014) document was meant to define the priorities for reforming Romanian schools, to support policy development, and to identify strategic medium-term directions. According to this document, the current training system has a number of strengths: the existence of a superior-quality primary education, ensured by the quality of teaching and the engaged attitude of the teaching staff from this educational segment; and positive results registered in the continuous training domain through the application of a transferable professional credits system in the didactic career (as a condition for professional evolution and development) (Academia Română 2014).

It seems relevant to mention that the most recent PISA results (2018) present one of the most alarming assessments of the national educational system: Romania has obtained the lowest PISA results over the last 9 years, especially in Maths and Reading. Of course, this is only one perspective on the Romanian pre-university system, but we could also argue that it gives an accurate image of the efficiency and the performance of our teachers.

In a context updated by data generated by international research, it would appear that the public perception of the didactic profession (but not necessarily of the didactic career) has improved slightly:

Although the teaching profession enjoys a positive perception—40.9% of Romanian teachers believe that their profession is valued by society, above the EU-23 average of 17.7%—it is still affected by low entry requirements for teacher education programmes and traditionally low salaries. The report notes that since 2017 the teachers' salaries have been increasing following a new salary grid for public sector employees, reducing from 40 to 25 years the time needed to reach maximum pay and introducing higher bonuses for certain staff. (Editor romania-insider.com, 2019)

Compared to the official European data, investment in education remains low, and funding mechanisms to support equity are weak. In 2017, general government spending on education was equivalent to only 2.8% of GDP, significantly below the EU average of 4.6% and the lowest percentage in the EU (Education and Training Monitor 2019).

Romania is ranked the second last in the world and last in Europe in terms *of the global index of teacher status.* As far as the comparison with other occupations is concerned, respondents in Romania placed the professions of teacher and secondary or high school teacher in 9th and 10th place, respectively. These results are below the average of the other countries in the study, which ranked these professions on average in 7th place. The job of school or high school principal was significantly better ranked, in 4th place. Approximately 33% of respondents said they would encourage their child to become a teacher, an above-average percentage. 'At the same time, only about 8% would definitely encourage the child to become a teacher, a percentage close to the average of all countries in the study. With about 18%, Romania places itself at the bottom of the ranking in terms of student respect for teachers. Only 1% of respondents totally agree with the statement—"Today's students follow their teachers"—the lowest percentage of all countries in the study' (Profesorii in societate [Teachers in the society] 2018).

In Romania, as in other countries, respondents were able to accurately assess the real salary of teachers. Teachers' salaries were the second lowest compared with other countries in the study. With regard to the correlation between teachers' salaries and pupils' performance, 'Romania is ranked last amongst the countries under study. Only about 49% of respondents believe that teachers should be paid according to student performance' (Profesorii in societate [Teachers in the society] 2018). Confidence in the fact that teachers provide a good education for pupils in Romania is placed above the average of the other countries participating in the study. At the same time, the study shows that 'there is no correlation between trust and respect for teachers. In other words, even though respondents were confident that teachers could provide students with a good education, it does not mean they considered the profession as being worthy of the same respect as other professions' in the study (for more in-depth information see the Report *Profesorii in societate* [Teachers in the society] 2018).

Another comprehensive document that is very important and often neglected as a documentation source is the *System Approach for Better Education Results SABER*, a document based on solid empirical evidence and presented by the World Bank. This document embraces the philosophy according to which a systemic approach can deliver comparative data and information about policies and institutions in education 'with the purpose of helping countries to systemically consolidate their educational systems. SABER evaluates the quality of policies in education in comparison with global standards based on empirical evidence, using new tools for problem diagnosis and detailed information regarding these policies' (SABER—World Bank 2017). In relation to the data derived from the extensive lines of inquiry present in the report—policy objectives/policy levers—a final score for each component of the evaluated educational system was reported (one component being the teacher training system). The score varied between the following ratings: advanced, consolidated, emerging, and latent. Our summary of the results indicates that the Romanian system of didactic training has the following characteristics:

1. Establishing clear expectations for didactic staff: This indicator, deployed to analyse the clarity and specificity of expectations for didactic staff, was appreciated by the promoters as **advanced**.
2. Attracting the best graduates towards a career in education: According to this indicator, used to analyse the degree to which the best graduates are retained to work in the educational system, the level of realisation is appreciated as being **consolidated**.
3. Training didactic staff through useful training programmes and relevant practical experience: In accordance with this indicator, used to analyse didactic training through useful programmes and relevant practical experience, the degree of realisation is rated as **emerging**.
4. Correlating teachers' competences with students' needs: The level of realisation for this indicator is rated as **emerging.**

5. Having competent principals to lead the didactic personnel: The level of realisation for this indicator is rated as **emerging**.
6. Monitoring teaching and learning: The level of realisation for this indicator is rated as **consolidated.**
7. Teachers' support for improving teaching and learning: The level of realisation for this indicator is rated as **emerging.**
8. Motivating teachers to achieve superior performances: The level of realisation for this indicator is rated as **emerging**.

An important observation to keep in mind to understand this report, but also to generalise its conclusions, is that the proposed indicators measure the quality of the intention of existing policies, and not how they are implemented. The implementation process can be different for some of the measured objectives (the objectives can be operationalised as indicators with different levels of complexity and generality). However, we estimate that the information offers a comprehensive picture regarding the current state of Romania's didactic training system.

Strengthening continuing professional development is an opportunity to improve teaching quality. 'Unlike many European countries, which will see a significant proportion of their teachers retire within the next 10 years, in Romania less than 30% of school teachers are older than 50 (EU average: 37%). Therefore, raising teaching quality involves working primarily with existing teachers' (Education and Training Monitor 2019). In light of this, the professional development of teachers is a crucial component in the didactic training system. It is also intensely criticised:

> When it comes to professional development, a high percentage of Romanian teachers report taking part in such training, but the content and delivery of the courses is not perceived as sufficiently adapted to their needs. At the same time, 70% of teachers report that participation in continuing professional development is restricted by high costs, compared to an EU-23 average of 44%. Romanian teachers pointed to a high development need in ICT skills for teaching (21.2%), approaches to individualised learning (21.5%), teaching students with special educational needs (35.1%) and cross-curricular skills (22.8%). (Editor romania-insider.com, 2019)

The CPD (continuing professional development) will be a significant priority for the teacher education system in Romania in the near future.

Over the last few years, the Romanian Ministry of Education has implemented a large-scale project called *Relevant Curriculum, Open Education for*

All (CRED 2016), focused on the continuing professional development of teachers in pre-university education. The project, whose goal is curricular empowerment for 55,000 primary and secondary school teachers, ran until 2021 (2017–2021) and had a budget of about €42 million. In order to ensure national coverage, CRED benefits from active partnerships at the local level. 'The training activities will consist of 2,750 groups of teachers in all counties and in the capital. The total number of national training hours is 330,000, involving the contribution of 900 trainers. All 55,000 participants in the training courses will receive a grant of 600 RON. Additionally, 150 teachers who generate good practices will be awarded' (CRED 2016). Eighteen methodological guides covering all disciplines are also provided for in the new framework plans for primary and lower secondary education, and 7200 open educational resources (RED) for all disciplines will be developed. They will be accessible to students and teachers both in open educational resource centres and on an online e-learning platform. At the same time, through the activities included in the CRED, the project aims to increase the quality and relevance of education in schools in vulnerable areas, with the aim of reducing early school leaving by implementing innovative projects focusing on the development of key skills (for more information about the national project, see the CRED *Project—Relevant Curriculum, Open Education for All* website 2016). This is one of the most complex actions for systemic intervention, financed through European funds, with the aim of training and professionally developing teachers in pre-university education. At the time of writing, there is no available report on the degree to which the medium-term project objectives have been met, but the training sessions and the systems for online support are being carried out.

Discussing challenges in a multidimensional way, we can also draw to attention some key elements with historical value for the evolution of the entire educational system in Romania, which preoccupied many policymakers at both central and local levels:

> In addition, the relatively high number of positions filled by staff without proper qualifications remains a challenge, particularly in schools in rural and remote areas. The number of support specialists, such as special education teachers, school counsellors, Roma mediators, is often insufficient. For instance, a school counsellor is expected to work with 800 students, but in practice the student/counsellor ratio is 2.5 times higher. (EC Report 2019)

A series of public policy interventions was identified in the recent history of the Romanian pre-university education, but the success of these interventions was not guaranteed. Although some schools in urban areas benefit from highly trained personnel, schools in rural areas have problems with non-qualified teachers. These are challenges not only in terms of quality education, but also in terms of ensuring that the system is equitable and that the Romanian pre-university system guarantees inclusive quality education for every child. Given that Romania has the highest rate of children at risk of poverty and social exclusion in Europe—38.1%, according to Eurostat, 2020—and the fact that equity and quality education challenges disproportionally affect students from rural and poorer communities, this remains a major issue for national policies.

Having tackled the issue of educational changes and the way in which these have been addressed in Romania in the recent years, we note that the training and professional development for teachers is mainly characterised by the inconsistency of public policies. Since 2002, when the first Integrated National Strategy was promoted for the human resources domain in education, no major events have been registered.

There have been some legislative corrections, transforming the Master of Arts in teaching into a requirement for the initial career training, and a mentoring and coaching process, but none of these measures have been successfully implemented thus far. An additional challenge is the well-known effect of passive resistance of teachers in the classroom, when change comes from the top-down—this lesson was learned by other countries too. Real change in the educational system cannot be achieved without a bottom-up component—this can be overcome by a similar policy proposal, validated and accepted by the main actors in the field of education. Thus, we can observe the bigger picture, with the limitations that generate medium and long-term effects.

Teachers' career policies face significant challenges. Initial teacher education offers very little preparation and practical training, particularly in modern teaching techniques and inclusive pedagogy; in practice, the certification exam and the tenure exam are used as the main method to screen candidates entering the profession (OECD 2017). However, this has proved to be less effective than having high entry standards and comprehensive initial teacher education; in itself, the certification exam tends to assess theoretical knowledge without being an authentic measure of on-the-job competence (ibid). A merit-based allowance tends to encourage teachers to focus narrowly on preparing pupils for tests and academic competitions, rather than encouraging them to improve the outcomes of low achieving students or those from disadvantaged backgrounds (Education and Training Monitor 2019).

We previously referred to the Romanian Academy Report and selected parts of the analysis that gave a poor grade to the Romanian educational system. On a more positive note, we can now turn our attention to what the report identifies as possible solutions and strategic directions for national and international policy:

> Designing national policies based on ex-ante and post-ante analysis for restructuring the teacher training system for the pre-university education level.
>
> Restructuring the teachers; initial education system by introducing gradual training throughout the undergraduate/graduate programmes, to ensure a solid professionalisation.
>
> Consolidating the mentoring system for the teacher career path through the programmes and teacher training centres for mentors at a regional level.
>
> Making the continuous teacher training programme more dynamic by deploying the system of professional credits in a real and incentivising fashion and by extending the number of providers.
>
> Coherent national policies aimed at increasing the payment grid for teaching staff in pre-university education so as to be at least equal with the OECD average. (Academia Română 2014)

We offer these conclusions in order to emphasise that a leading cultural and research institution in Romania took upon itself the task of promoting these ideas at national public policy level. A vision, with its whole spectrum of associated ideas, can be the fundamental factor of evolution based on trust and progress.

Transitions to Teacher Education in the Romanian Higher Education System

In a very interesting study published by Professor Heinz Bachmann from the Pedagogical University of Zurich, tellingly titled *In search of the holy grail*, we found a set of questions that can settle the dimensions aimed at orienting the processes of designing public policies for educational institutions: 'What is needed to be a successful higher education teacher in today's globalised and rapidly changing world? Is it at all possible to define a minimum that is valid for all kinds of teachers?' (Bachmann 2019, p. 1). Without aiming at complete comprehensiveness with regard to answering these questions, Professor Bachman suggests a few small obstacles to overcome in order to achieve a correct understanding of the context of our discussion:

Regarding the diversity amongst different universities, the variety of subjects and backgrounds of teachers and students, one might discard the idea as being presumptuous. On the other hand, there is a need for orientation in the ever-increasing flood of new publications in the field of higher education teaching and learning. (Bachmann 2019, p. 1)

Regarding the elements of the transition to an academic career, its professionalisation, or, more simply put, the initial and continuous education of academic teaching staff in the Romanian higher education system, there are few possible structural and formal references. However, before opening this subject to the applied domain of academic teacher training, we will consider some important data regarding the main challenges in Romanian higher education. Starting with the academic year 2009/2010, under the combined influence of a decrease in birth rates after 1990, the reduction of the number of years necessary for finishing undergraduate studies, brought about by the implementation of the Bologna system since 2005 (with visible statistical effects in 2008 and 2009), and the decrease in the number of high school graduates (a combined effect of school dropouts and the increasing difficulty of the baccalaureate since 2011), have led to an inversion of the trend of massification at the higher education level.

Internal Causes

* an extremely low transition rate from undergraduate to graduate programmes, visibly impacting the rates of youth attainment in graduate education (CNFIS 2019);
* the phenomenon of higher education dropouts, caused by the economic crisis, the lack of sufficient counselling and career orientation services offered by higher education institutions, a decrease in incentives for successfully finishing various study programmes (a master's degree is not perceived as entailing any social or professional benefits);
* the demographic, as well as regional, tank cohort of non-budgeted attainment in Romanian academic programmes has decreased.

External Causes

* Negative demographic developments, although an interesting observation of the CNFIS experts shows that 'the number of students enrolled in the first year of undergraduate studies could rise with an average of 6300 per-

sons/year or 6.1% per year. However, we must take into account the decrease predicted for 2019–2020, based on the decrease in natality observed after 2002' (CNFIS 2019);

* Romania is among the European states (including Spain, Portugal, and Italy) whose economic situation has had a direct impact on the participation in education. Moreover, the gap between Romania and the European average has widened in the last few years (CNFIS 2019);
* Some of the causes of the increasingly lower enrolment rates in higher education, only marginally influenced by the overall number of citizens or the graduation from secondary-level education, are connected to the organisation and implementation of the primary and secondary levels in the national system. The high rates of early school dropout and the low quality of secondary education (at high school and gymnasium levels) are among the factors that negatively impact the rate of enrolment in higher education (CNFIS 2019);
* Another element that can have an impact on these values is the number of Romanian students enrolled in other European universities. According to the statistics publicly reported by Eurostat, approximately 37,000 Romanian citizens were enrolled in undergraduate or graduate study programmes in other states in the European Union in 2019 (CNFIS 2019).

Regarding academic careers, the official data collected at the university level present the following picture. According to the *Romanian National Law of Education 1/2011, Art. 301,* the university professor's recruitment presented the minimum standard for holding a teaching position, which is as follows:

* 'The minimum conditions for holding the teaching position of **university lecturer** are the following: a) holding a PhD diploma; b) compliance with the position-specific job occupation standards, as approved by the university senate of the higher education institution, without imposing any seniority conditions, according to the laws in force; (paragraph 3)' (Romanian National Law of Education 1/2011)'
* 'The conditions that have to be satisfied in order to become a **university senior-lecturer** are the following: a) holding a PhD diploma; b) complying with the minimal standards that are necessary for holding the lecturer's position, [standards] that have been approved as per Art. 219, paragraph (1), letter a); c) compliance with teaching position employment standards, that are specific to every position and that have been approved by the University Senate, without imposing any seniority conditions, according to

the laws in force; (paragraph 4)' (Romanian National Law of Education 1/2011);

* 'The conditions for occupying the **university professor** position are the following: a) holding a PhD diploma; b) holding the habilitation certificate; c) complying with the minimum standards for the occupation of the university professor's position, [standards] that have been approved as per Art. 219, paragraph (1), letter a); d) complying with the teaching position occupation standards, that are specific to that position, and that must have been approved by the University Senate, without imposing any seniority conditions, according to the laws in force; (paragraph 5)' (CNFIS 2019).

Working conditions and salaries in careers in higher education— Throughout a teacher's career, salaries increase according to a matrix-type salary scale. The basic salary is established using a fixed standard value (the value for the multiplication coefficient equal to 1) and multiplication coefficients (bigger than 1). The multiplication coefficients depend on the teaching position and seniority in education and are set in minimum/maximum ranges. The standard value is unique for the entire salary scale and is updated according to the evolution of the consumer prices indicator. The basic salary is calculated as the standard value multiplied by the multiplication coefficient established within the corresponding range from the salary scale.

Career progression—According to the *Romanian Law of Education 1/2011, Article 300,* habilitation involves the following: '(a) Preparing an habilitation thesis; (b) Publicly defending the habilitation thesis in front of a specialty commission assigned by CNATDCU (The National Commission for the Attestation of University Titles, Degrees, Certificates), that should be formed of at least 3 people who should be PhD mentors in Romania or abroad; (c) Admitting the habilitation thesis after being publicly defended; (d) Getting the habilitation certificate'. (1) The habilitation thesis must prove the teaching and research capacities and performances. The thesis should document the professional achievements obtained after getting the PhD; prove the originality and relevance of the academic, scientific, and professional contributions; and be capable of anticipating an independent development of the candidate's future research and/or academic career. (3) Only people who hold a PhD diploma and who are compliant with the minimal standards that are established as per Art. 219, paragraph (1), letter a) may sign up for the habilitation exam. (4) The habilitation application must be submitted to CNATDCU. (5) The habilitation certificate is proposed by CNATDCU and is approved under order of the Minister of Education and Scientific Research (Romanian National Law of Education 1/2011).

This is an analysis that defines the systemic and selectively institutional context regarding a new perspective on the professionalisation of careers in higher education. The question is: how far have we come, relative to the standards of defining professionalisation mentioned in *The Professionalisation of Academics as Teachers in Higher Education:*

> define professional standards for higher education teachers, measure teaching effectiveness and provide constructive feedback for academics, establish the institutional support base for educational development locally, recognise teaching excellence in hiring and promotion decisions, promote the idea of the 'teacher researcher,' recognise research on teaching as a research activity, allocate meaningful funding for educational development, establish a European forum within a currently existing institution that pools and shares resources and existing expertise on educational development across borders. (Committee for the Social Sciences—SCSS 2014)

According to the Romanian perspective, there is only one precondition, one that is also mandatory for pre-university teaching staff: graduating from a psycho-pedagogical module course. Mary McAleese, chair of the EU High Level Group on the Modernisation of Higher Education, which focuses on the issue of academic careers, has stated that:

> We believe absolutely that improving the quality of teaching and learning in higher education can bring about a sea-change for Europe's future. We have almost 4 000 higher education institutions in Europe, of all shapes and sizes. These institutions, for all their differences, share a crucial task and a crucial responsibility—to teach our young (and also our not so young) people, and to teach them to the best level possible. (EU High Level Group on the Modernisation of Higher Education 2014)

Since there is no coherent system with the aim of preparing academic teaching staff in Romania, the aforementioned quote is followed by one whose conclusion entails a strong commitment to opening towards a new process of professionalisation:

> The need for professional training as a teacher at primary and secondary school level is generally taken for granted but remarkably, when it comes to higher education, there seems to be an all too common assumption that such professional teacher training is not necessary, as if it is somehow an idea unworthy of the professional academic. (EU High Level Group on the Modernisation of Higher Education 2014)

Although the concept of professionalisation has not met with unanimous consensus among the European specialists in this domain, the strategic importance of this idea for the public policies regarding higher education cannot be ignored. It is noteworthy that one of the European public policies that has defined the main lines of this domain since 2018, the *Paris Communique*, discussed the problem of the academic career:

> As high quality teaching is essential in fostering high quality education, academic career progression should be built on successful research and quality teaching. It should also take due account of the broader contribution to society. We will promote and support institutional, national and European initiatives for pedagogical training, continuous professional development of higher education teachers, and explore ways for better recognition of high quality and innovative teaching in their career. (Paris Communique; EHEA 2018)

From Teacher Education for Today to Teaching for the Future

> To become a competent teacher is a long-term endeavour and there is always room for improvement. But as in many learning processes, it is helpful to go from the simple to the complex, from the basics to the advanced topics. To define the basics is challenging and at the same time very much appreciated by the learner. (Bachmann 2019)

Teacher education—initial and continuous—now faces multiple challenges, some of them generated by the global context and trends, some by national particularities. These challenges are all interconnected, and none of them can be ignored in a robust process of reshaping and reinforcing the teaching career. Moreover, policymakers should make efforts to ensure that pre-university and academic systems consolidate an open education by building synergies through coordinated processes of initial and continuous teacher education.

In conclusion, we present a few observations and concerns regarding teachers' education in the Romanian framework.

As we can see from the Education and Training Monitor 2019, initial teacher education in Romania offers very little pedagogical and practical training, inclusive education, or training in innovative pedagogies. This has a significant impact both on the professional life of the teacher—difficulties in responding to students' individual needs, questioning their own skills and professional performance—and on the schools' progress and students' performance. At the systemic level, as we have seen, this policy perspective on teacher training generates long-term knock-on effects. The public perception of the teaching profession is not at a satisfying level, and neither is the attractiveness of the teaching profession.

In this situation, we can reflect and ask ourselves: shouldn't the public system, the decision-makers, pay more attention and make more efforts towards a robust initial training, with an emphasis on the pedagogical abilities of the teacher? For many years, we have seen the results of the current teacher training approach, and these are not gratifying. Shouldn't we improve it, shouldn't we experiment?

Today's teachers play a very special role in school life and in their students' life. They are no longer simply providers of information—they are facilitators for learning, for exploration, for self-discovery and evolution. In order to respond to all these needs, they should be equipped with respect for new, efficient, and innovative pedagogies.

The present generation and those to come are digital natives, for whom technology has become a way of life. The competences for the future have been recently reshaped, in a common effort by the EU members states, who have adopted a *Recommendation on Key Competences for Lifelong Learning*. School and teachers should provide knowledge and openness to learning, skills, and attitudes. Literacy, multilingualism, active citizenship, and interpersonal and entrepreneurial skills are among the 2030 skills for lifelong learning. Schools should educate children for a future of uncertainties, with many changes and unprecedented social, economic, technological, and cultural dynamics. The Romanian pre-university education system has a relatively ageing workforce—70% of teachers are under 50 years old—and this means that all reforms or educational policies will be implemented with the current teachers. This imperatively requires a strong concern for the continuous education of teachers, based on criteria and standards established in accordance with new pedagogies and international best practices.

Prospective studies show that in the near future, the global and the domestic labour market will have a strong demand for highly skilled graduates, able to act and be good professionals in a digital economy. The Fourth Industrial Revolution already poses many challenges in terms of competences and skills; the exponential increase of digitalisation in many sectors of the economy will also accentuate disparities and inequities, if national education does not adjust and take action to help younger generations to fulfil their potential. The Bologna Process and its implementation in Romania requires coherent and coordinated actions in the university and pre-university systems to ensure students' successful transition, their openness, and motivation to learn.

Strengthening the knowledge triangle (i.e. the interconnection between research, education, and innovation) in a digital era could open a dynamic dialogue for a higher professionalisation of the teaching career, with a special focus on pedagogies.

Education is continuously being shaped by and for new generations of learners. Even though the educational system is known to be one of the most rigid public systems, given its complexity and scale, disruptive episodes will arise and demand resilience, as for example in the pandemic episode of 2020. Students are at the core of the processes in schools and universities, but teachers are the main facilitators of learning and training. We should therefore ask ourselves whether this interdependency and the need for good professionals and active citizens do not require rapid actions for a complex and correlated professionalisation of teachers' education in pre-university and university systems.

References

Academia Română [Romanian Academy of Science]. (2014). *Scoala și educația în România … de la șanse egale de acces la șanse egale de reușită* [School and education in Romania...from equal opportunities of access to equal opportunities of success]. (pp. 64–67). Bucharest: Editura Academiei Române.

Bachmann, H. (2019). *Minimal teaching skills for higher education teachers—A global debate amongst experts in higher education teaching and learning.* Centre for Teaching & Learning in Higher Education, University of Teacher Education, Zurich (PHZH). Retrieved from https://zenodo.org/record/3484835#. Yc8k5S_US-o.

CNFIS. (2019). *Raport public 2017–2018.* Retrieved from http://www.cnfis.ro/wp-content/uploads/2020/01/Raport_public-CNFIS_2017-2018-integrat.pdf.

Code for Romania. (2019). *Blocaje în pregătirea resurselor umane în educație* [Bottlenecks in training human resources in education]. Retrieved from https://civiclabs.ro/ro/byproducts/blocaje-in-pregatirea-resurselor-umane-in-educatie.

Committee for the Social Sciences—SCSS. (2014). *The professionalisation of academics as teachers in higher education,* Science Position Paper. Retrieved from www.esf.org/social.

CRED. (2016). *Curriculum relevant, educație deschisă pentru toți* [Relevant curriculum, open education for all. National report]. Retrieved from https://www.edu.ro/etichete/cred.

Curaj, A., L. Deca, and C. Hâj. (2015). Romanian Higher Education in 2009–2013. The Bologna Process and Romanian Priorities in the Search for an Active European and Global Presence. In: A. Curaj et al. (Eds.), *Higher education reforms in Romania between the Bologna Process and national challenges* (pp. 1–24). Dordrecht: Springer Science + Business Media.

EHEA. (2018). *Paris Communique.* Retrieved from http://www.ehea2018.paris/.

Iucu, R. (2019). *The new professionalisation of the academic career in the context of the European Higher Education Area.* EUA—Expert Voices. Retrieved from https://eua.eu/resources/expert-voices/79:the-new-professionalisation-of-the-academic-career-in-the-context-of-the-european-higher-education-area.html#.

European Commission. (2019). *Education and Training Monitor 2019, Romania.* Retrieved from https://ec.europa.eu/education/sites/education/files/document-library-docs/et-monitor-report-2019-romania_en.pdf.

EU High Level Group on the Modernisation of Higher Education. (2014). *Report to the European Commission on Improving the quality of teaching and learning in Europe's higher education institutions.* Retrieved from http://ec.europa.eu/dgs/education_culture/repository/education/library/reports/modernisationen.pdf.

Hooker, M. (1997). The transformation of higher education. In: D. Oblinger and S. C. Rush (Eds.), *The learning revolution* (pp. 97–98). Bolton, MA: Anker Publishing Company, Inc.

Iucu, R. (2009). Ten years after Bologna: towards a European Teacher Education Area. In: O. Gassner, L. Kerger, and M. Schratz (Eds.), *ENTEP Ten Years After Bologna* (pp. 13–42). Bucharest: Editura Universității din București.

Iucu, R., and S. Iftimescu. (2021). Twenty years after the Bologna Declaration: From promoter to driver of change. In: D. Worek and C. Kraler (Eds.), *Teacher education: The Bologna Process and the future of teaching* (pp. 17–28). Waxmann Verlag.

Ministry of Education and Science. (2019). *Raport privind starea învățământului superior din România* [Report on the state of Romanian higher education]. Retrieved from https://www.edu.ro/sites/default/files/Raport%20privind%20starea%20%C3%AEnv%C4%83%C8%9B%C4%83m%C3%A2ntului%20superior%20din%20Rom%C3%A2nia_%202017%20-2018.pdf.

RBLS. (2018). *Profesorii-in-societate* [Teachers in the society]. Retrieved from http://www.rbls.ro/wp-content/uploads/2018/03/RaportProfesorii-in-societate.pdf.

Ro Insider. (2019). *EC report points to Romanian teachers' limited initial practical training.* Editor romania-insider.com. Retrieved from https://www.romania-insider.com/education-training-monitor-romania-2019.

Szolár, E. (2014). The Bologna process in Romania. In: T. Kozma, M. Rébay, A. Óhidy, and E. Szolár (Eds.), *The Bologna process in Central and Eastern Europe* (pp. 183–222). Wiesbaden: Springer Science+ Business Media.

World Bank. (2017). *System approach for better education results SABER.* Retrieved from http://saber.worldbank.org/.

OECD. (2012). Education at a Glance, *OECD*, https://doi.org/10.1787/eag-2012-en.

OECD. (2017). Education at a Glance, *OECD*, https://doi.org/10.1787/eag-2017-en.

Ministry of National Education - Romania. (2018). Raport privind starea învățământului preuniversitardin România 2017 -2018, *Ministry of National Education - Romania*, https://www.edu.ro/sites/default/files/Raport%20privind%20starea%20%C3%AEnv%C4%83%C8%9B%C4%83m%C3%A2ntului%20preuniversitar%20din%20Rom%C3%A2nia_2017-2018_0.pdf.

15

Teacher Education in Bulgaria: The Last Three Decades

Viara Todorova Gyurova

Context of Teacher Education

A republic run as a parliamentary democracy, Bulgaria is a small country situated on the Balkan Peninsula (in Southeast Europe), with a territory of 110,993 km². According to 2016 data from the National Statistical Institute, the national population is 5,204,385.

Since the early 1990s, Bulgaria has entered a new stage of national development, characterised by many reforms, including in the fields of education and teacher education. Furthermore, with entry into the European Union in 2007, Bulgaria's borders to other European countries have opened up, bringing new opportunities for Bulgarians to travel, study, and/or work in counties across Europe, and the world. In fact, this opening of borders has enabled them to become real citizens of Europe and of the wider world: more specifically, opportunities for international exchange in the field of education and for financing education activities via European funds have also expanded (Eurydice 2021).

Like all other areas of economic and social life in recent decades, Bulgaria's education system (including teacher education) has been subject to a complex and dynamic context, shaped by both national and global trends. In particular, its development has been influenced by:

V. T. Gyurova (✉)
Sofia University St. Kliment Ohridski, Sofia, Bulgaria
e-mail: viara_gyurova_22@abv.bg

M. Kowalczuk-Walędziak et al. (eds.), *The Palgrave Handbook of Teacher Education in Central and Eastern Europe*, https://doi.org/10.1007/978-3-031-09515-3_15

355

* external factors—that is, the general situation in the country and world-wide in the twenty-first century (including current trends and problems);
* internal factors—for example, the development of education theories (such as the changes in understandings about the specifics of education, school, and learning in the twenty-first century, as well as the teacher's roles therein) and changes across school and university education;
* characteristics and needs of twenty-first-century students;
* characteristics and needs of twenty-first-century teachers.

All of these influences should be understood in the wider context of the definitive role that changes in a country's society and economy have on the education sector, meaning that they serve as external factors for the changes in teacher training.

The most important changes in contemporary Bulgarian education include:

* the introduction of compulsory pre-school education for five- and six-year-old children;
* changes in the aims, structure, and content of school education;
* the decentralisation of school funding, including the introduction of delegated budgets;
* the introduction of the external assessment of students at the end of primary school (4th grade), at the end of junior high school (7th grade), and at the end of the first high school level (10th grade);
* the introduction of state matriculation exams for all students at the end of their secondary education (12th grade);
* the introduction of 19 state education standards, including particular ones related to the status and professional development of teachers, directors, principals, and other educators.

These changes have also had an impact on teacher training and qualification and, to some extent, have been the motive for introducing mandatory qualifications for teachers and other pedagogical specialists, as regulated by the *Pre-school and School Education Act* (2015), *Ordinance No. 12* (2016), and *Ordinance No. 15* (2019). In addition to the creation of these legislative documents, changes in the legal framework for higher education have also impacted teachers' training and qualification in Bulgaria, including the *Higher Education Act* (adopted December 1995 and amended around 50 times, most recently in October 2018 and coming into force since January 2019) and the *Strategy for Development of Higher Education in the Republic of Bulgaria* for the 2014–2020 period.

It is an indisputable fact that the most significant impact on modern education, including on teachers themselves, is technical and technological changes. On the one hand, technical and technological shifts are changing the educational environment and—particularly noticeably—the material and technical bases of education institutions; on the other hand, they are imposing new methodologies (or technologies) of training. It is no coincidence that the use of ICT has been declared a 'key competence' worldwide, that is, a competence crucial for twenty-first-century citizens and for lifelong learning, but also for twenty-first-century teachers and educators (Darling-Hammond 2006; P21 Framework definition 2015; Sharlanova 2018; Gyurova and Zeleeva 2017; Gyurova 2019b). Indeed, educators are now expected to offer a modern learning process based on the use of the latest and ever-changing IC, as well as to create and use electronic resources of their own and, in turn, to motivate and teach their pupils and students to use them too.

In order to keep pace with the time in which they live, and to successfully navigate their profession, contemporary teachers and professors must become digitally competent and maintain a high level of these skills. These new professional roles exist alongside all of the other competences required for their old professional roles, that is, as managers of the class and of the learning process; as educators who form students' skills; and as trainers, but also navigators, mediators, and facilitators of students' learning and self-education. Each of these old and new roles involves performing certain activities, for the success of which teachers need corresponding key competences—for example, managerial, leadership, diagnostic, expert, research, informational, digital, pedagogical, andragogical, heutagogical and paragogical, methodological, psychological, counselling, coaching—and skills—for example, leadership, organisational, communicative, social, research (Gyurova 2018b).

In the *National Strategy for the Development of Pedagogical Staff for 2014–2020*, it is emphasised that, as well as societal changes, the increasing ethnic diversity (ref) and diverse linguistic, behavioural, and everyday needs of the pupils in Bulgaria's schools (ref) require corresponding changes in contemporary teachers' roles and competences. The strategy also points out that, during the first decades of socio-political transitions in Bulgaria, teachers were not active participants in qualification activities. For example, in 2012 only 8% of those employed in the education sector participated in short-term trainings, with that percentage dropping to 1.2% for long-term trainings with a duration of over 60 hours (e.g., specialisations and teacher qualification trainings) (*National Strategy*: 16). Therefore, the Ministry of Education has since introduced the mandatory attestation of teachers every three years and corresponding mandatory (annual) qualifications.

The Global Context of Bulgarian Education Reforms over the Last Three Decades

The mission of teacher education in the twenty-first century is to prepare teachers who are capable of carrying out relevant and up-to-date training for twenty-first-century students. Its form and content are therefore influenced by both national idiosyncrasies and the problems and achievements of humankind across larger communities (e.g., the European Union). In this context, a new element defining teacher education in Bulgaria today is undoubtedly rooted in contemporary trends of globalisation and patterns of migration.

In response to this evolving need for future teachers to master the increasingly global culture of contemporary Bulgaria—including its problems and challenges, intercultural cooperation, and respect for the rights of all people—global literacy subjects (such as Civic Education, Intercultural Education and Training, and Human and Children's Rights) have been introduced into teacher education curricula. Furthermore, the specific problems of humanity defining our era—such as the climate crisis, environmental pollution, and the extinction of species—have been included in the educational content of the disciplines future teachers are to teach in schools. These teachers are expected to transfer up-to-date knowledge, attitudes, and values to their future students. On a policy level, these remits are related to teacher training in compliance with two key 'mandatory requirements for the results in the pre-school and school education system', namely the seventh standard, for inclusive education; and the eighth standard, for civic, health, environmental, and intercultural education (Pre-school and School Education Act, Art. 22 2015).

These standards have been designed in line with contemporary Bulgaria's geopolitics. Due to Bulgaria's geographical position between the SWANA region and Northern Europe, many people migrating from the former pass through the country on their way towards other parts of Europe, in the process of which a small number choose to stay in Bulgaria and make it their home.

In this wider European context, both Bulgaria's adoption of the Bologna Process (1999) and accession to the European Union (2007) necessitated major reforms in terms of the Europe-level trends aimed at achieving coherence between the Bulgarian education system and those of other European countries. These reforms include the introduction of a three-tier higher education structure (and the adaptation of teachers' initial training fitting that new structure), the European Credit Transfer System (ECTS), and the Europass Diploma Supplement to the higher education diploma, as is typical for all EU member states. These changes, as well as the adoption of the

National Qualifications Framework (based on the *European Qualifications Framework*), aim to support the mobility of Bulgaria's citizens, including students in teaching specialties, both within the European Union and around the world.

Much like education in this new century worldwide, a large number of recent changes in teacher training in Bulgaria are related to scientific and technical progress, including the development of ICT. Although not as fast as in other European countries, modern digital technologies and electronic educational resources, educational platforms, and technologies which 'flip' the educational process are definitively entering the education sector and the organisation of the educational process in Bulgaria's schools and universities. For instance, electronic journals and textbooks are now commonplace (though not in all subjects), and the Ministry of Education envisages a gradual replacement of all printed textbooks with electronic ones. These updates are necessarily accompanied by teacher training for the development and use of such resources, which is why, in recent decades, all university curricula for future teachers have included courses related to the use of ICT in education. Furthermore, independent master's degree programmes on the subject have emerged, and the students enrolling in them are predominantly teachers. For example, the Faculty of Pedagogy at Sofia University, St. Kliment Ohridski, offers an *Information and Communication Technologies in Education* programme (in full-time, part-time, and distance formats). The Faculty of Mathematics and Informatics also offers a number of master's degree programmes in the field of modern ICT, such as *e-learning, Technology for Education in Mathematics and Informatics, Information Retrieval and Knowledge Discovery, Technology Knowledge and Innovation, Technology Entrepreneurship and Innovation in Information Technology, Artificial Intelligence, Computer Graphics, Computer Linguistics,* and *Software Technologies.* Furthermore, the university also offers postgraduate courses for teachers in the field of modern technologies.

In the years of transition, the influence of modern educational technologies and innovations in the Bulgarian education system was also manifested in the establishment of distance learning as a form of university education and qualification. However, on an unprecedented level, the COVID-19 pandemic forced Bulgaria's teachers to implement e-learning across the board and immediately, without necessarily having first been trained at a university. As a direct result, school principals needed to organise teacher training for this new form of education very quickly.

The Bulgarian System of Initial Teacher Education

During the years of socialism, the initial teacher education for kindergarten, primary school, and high school teachers in Bulgaria was carried out in two-year courses at pedagogical institutes, while the training of subject teachers (i.e., for high schools and technical schools) was carried out at universities.

Subsequently, Bulgaria joining the Bologna Process (1999) and accession to the European Union (2007) led to the introduction of a three-tier system for higher education, spanning bachelor's, master's, and PhD levels, applicable also to teacher training. Each type of degree requires students to collect a number of credits:

* bachelor's degrees (corresponding to Level 6 in ISCED 2011) are offered in two different formats:

    - bachelor's: a diploma acquired after four years of training at university and successfully meeting the requirements (including at least 240 credits);
    - professional bachelor's: a three-year training period (including at least 180 credits).

* master's degrees (corresponding to Level 7 in ISCED 2011)

    - earned as a minimum of 60 credits after acquiring a bachelor's degree;
    - or a minimum of 120 credits after acquiring a professional bachelor's degree *(Higher Education Act*, Art. 42, para 1);

* PhD degrees (corresponding to Level 8 in ISCED 2011): requires three or four years of training depending on the format of studies (i.e., full-time, part-time, or independent) after acquiring a master's degree, completing 180–240 credits, and a successful PhD thesis defence.

In terms of content, the bachelor's degree provides students with a wide-profile education or specialised professional training in specialisms and professional fields. The master's degree provides students with fundamental education, plus a specialism. The PhD provides students with doctoral programmes, focused on research work and complying with the requirements of the 2019 *Act for the Development of the Academic Staff in the Republic of Bulgaria*.

Admission to all higher education degrees is subject to competition (based on exam results or qualifications), and the number of students able to participate in any form of bachelor's programmes is determined in advance by the Ministry of Education, upon proposal by the respective universities.

Following recent political changes in Bulgaria, subsequent legislation stipulated that all teachers should have a higher education qualification in order to enter the profession (Ordinance on the state requirements 2004). Therefore, teacher institutes were transformed into three-year pedagogical colleges, initially carrying out training for the XXX degree (*Higher Education Act*, 1995, amended and supplemented in 2004, Art. 17, para 6) and, subsequently, the professional bachelor's degree (*Higher Education Act* 1995, amended and supplemented in 2016, Art. 42, para 1a). Students with a professional bachelor's degree can continue to a master's programme within their professional field, in this case pedagogy (*Higher Education Act* 2016, Art. 42, para 6).

In accordance with the three-tier higher education structure, initial training for teachers and educators for all educational levels can be completed within four-year bachelor's programmes. These are programmes preparing kindergarten and elementary school teachers, teachers of different subjects in primary and secondary schools, teachers working with children with special educational need (i.e., children with learning difficulties, health problems, and/or disabilities), assistant teachers in kindergartens, and tutors in education institutions. These curricula include compulsory, elective, and facultative courses; practice hours; and a pre-graduate internship—during which they must acquire the competences (i.e., pedagogical, social, and civic) constituting the professional profile of the teacher, as defined in Annex 2 to Art. 42 of Ordinance 15 (2019).

Requirements for qualifying with a higher education degree for the professional positions of teachers and educators are determined by a state standard. The legislation allows for small exceptions to be made in terms of appointing teachers with a higher education diploma (or, sometimes, without) in subjects taught mainly in vocational or other specialised schools, for which there is a lack of trained staff—including teachers (Pre-school and School Education Act 2015). In these cases, the school management is obliged to work out and implement a plan for the teacher who does not have a teaching qualification so that they can formally acquire the necessary pedagogical competences (Pre-school and School Education Act 2015, Art. 213, para 12).

Teaching candidates can acquire their professional qualification via the higher education system at the same time as training for the relevant professional qualification (in their taught subject or scientific field). In this case, the professional qualification is certified upon graduation by a diploma for higher education, or after graduation by passing a state exam at the end of a post-graduate course and receiving a corresponding certificate.

In line with the national professional qualification requirements, teacher training is both theoretical and practical. Theoretical training includes at least the following compulsory subjects *(Ordinance on state requirements for acquiring the professional qualification of a teacher*, Art. 6):

1. Pedagogy, 60 hours
2. Psychology, 60 hours
3. Teaching methods in taught subject, 90 hours
4. Inclusive education, 15 hours
5. ICT in training, and working in a digital environment, 30 hours.

In addition to these disciplines, teachers-to-be must also complete four elective courses (two from each group), reaching a minimum of 30 academic hours each:

1. Pedagogy, Psychology, and Particular Areas of Didactics (i.e., Methods of Training in a Specific Subject or Subjects) interdisciplinary and applied-experimental—related to key competence training and teachers' professional and pedagogical fulfilment.

Bulgaria's teacher training also requires the compulsory study of at least one facultative discipline for 15 academic hours.

The changes in teacher education in recent years also include an increase in the practical training of future teachers, as carried out in kindergartens and schools in the following forms.

* Supervised observation (30 hours): involves observation and analysis of lessons and classes in a kindergarten setting, and other formats, with children and students, under the direct supervision of a teacher;
* Ongoing pedagogical practice (60 hours): involves attending, observing, and conducting lessons and classes in a kindergarten setting, and other formats—carried out together with a mentor teacher and under the supervision of a qualified teacher, in order to prepare undergraduates for their internship (prior to the state exams);
* Internship practice (90 hours): involves students' independent participation in the educational process as trainee teachers, conducting classes in kindergarten or at school, under the supervision of a mentor teacher and a teacher.

Following the basic bachelor's degree, teachers (including practising ones) can continue their education in one- or two-year master's programmes (i.e., specialised training). If they wish, teachers can also continue to doctoral studies, whereby, after successfully defending their dissertation in front of a specialised jury, the doctoral student receives a higher education and scientific doctoral degree (PhD). Ultimately, initial teacher education in Bulgaria is subject to constant improvement by the pedagogical faculties themselves, in order to prepare competent twenty-first-century teachers (Gospodinov et al. 2018).

Bulgarian Systems of Teacher Professional Development

In recent decades, and especially in recent years, Bulgaria's teachers' continuous professional development (CPD) system has been the subject of serious analysis and changes (Gyurova 2017; Gyurova and Zeleeva 2017; Georgieva 2018; Gyurova 2019a; Sharlanova 2018; Gospodinov et al. 2019; Gyurova and Gyoreva 2019). Simultaneously, the Ministry of Education has launched and implemented several projects to support the qualification and professional development of pedagogical specialists.

As a member of the European Union, Bulgaria endeavours to follow EU-level recommendations regarding teacher education and development, according to which 'the education and development of teachers should be a coherent continuum spanning initial teacher education (with a strong practical component), induction and continuing professional development' (European Commission 2009, pp. 33–34).

In this context, Bulgaria's *National Strategy for the Development of Teaching Staff (2014–2020)* set the strategic goal of having a unified and efficient system of education, training, continuous training, and opportunities for the professional development of pedagogical staff by 2020. The strategy also defines the following operational objectives (with related activities and measures):

1. Developing a system for the preparation and continuing qualification of pedagogical staff
2. Creating a unified legislative framework for state regulation of initial training, continuing qualification, and professional development of teaching staff

3. Developing common and specified standards for pedagogical staff and a system of quality control, differential pay, and professional development
4. Developing a system of special measures for attracting, retaining, and developing pedagogical staff up to the age of 35, plus specialists with a high level of professional training and qualification for working in the secondary education system (National Strategy 2014, pp. 33–34).

Furthermore, a National Council for the Training of Pedagogical Staff was established within the Ministry of Education and Science as a coordinating and advisory body, in order to assist the minister in pursuing state policy regarding the continuing qualification of pedagogical staff.

In accordance with the national strategy, the normative basis for the qualification and development of pedagogical specialists has been updated:

* Ordinance No. 12, on the status and professional development of teachers, school principals, and other pedagogical specialists, was promulgated on 1 September 2016, then later replaced by Ordinance No. 15 on 22 July 2019 (both ordinances set out the state requirements and standards for pedagogical staff, their preparation, and continuing qualification);
* the ordinance on the requirements for acquiring a professional teaching qualification was supplemented (last amended December 2018);
* the ordinance on the uniform requirements for the acquisition of higher education with professional qualification of a teacher was replaced by the ordinance on the state requirements for the acquisition of professional qualification of a teacher (promulgated, issue 89, 11 November 2016, effective since the 2017/2018 academic year);
* amendments to the laws on secondary and higher education have been adopted as well.

In line with these changes, teacher development in Bulgaria can now be viewed via two dimensions: on the one hand, vertically, that is, in terms of the opportunities for migrating upwards to a higher position in the school hierarchy, and, on the other, horizontally, that is, in terms of the opportunities for further education, professional and qualification degrees, and continuing qualification.

Under Article 218 (1) of the Pre-school and School Education Act (2015), teachers' functions, professional profiles, positions, as well as terms and procedure for upgrading qualification, career development, and attestation are determined by the state standard. Ordinance No. 15 sets out the conditions and procedure for upgrading teachers' and educators' qualifications, with the planning, coordination, management, and control of corresponding activities carried out across different managerial levels, namely:

* national: Bulgaria's Ministry of Education and Science annually defines priority areas for continuing qualification
* regional: regional education departments develop plans for the training of pedagogical specialists as part of the annual plan, in accordance with the priorities set by the ministry, regional policy, and the qualification needs of educators in the respective regions
* municipal: municipal administration takes into account the qualification needs of the educators in the respective municipalities
* school: the school, kindergarten, or learning support centre make decisions in accordance with:

  – their own development strategy
  – their individual needs for additional teacher qualifications (including through attestation)
  – their available means of qualification, including any relevant rules
  – opportunities for their teachers to participate in international and national programmes and projects.

After teachers start work at a school (or another educational institution), their professional development and effectiveness are tied to their participation in two main forms of qualification: introductory qualifications (i.e., obligatory for newly appointed pedagogical specialists) and continuing qualifications (i.e., for ongoing professional and personal development). All teachers are required to upgrade their qualifications totalling at least 48 academic hours across each attestation period (i.e., three years), as well as participate in in-service qualifications for at least 16 academic hours, annually.

Over the last decade, there has been a significant increase in the opportunities for teachers to participate in various forms of continuous professional development qualifications in Bulgaria. Forms of continuing qualification include courses, seminars, trainings, workshops, lectures, webinars, master classes, research forums (i.e., scientific and applied conferences, plenary sessions, and round tables), and sharing innovative practices, research, and creative activity. Forms of in-service qualification include lectures, discussion forums (including on pedagogical research and achievements), innovative practice-sharing open lessons, and presentations of creative projects. Teachers receive qualification credits for, firstly, participation in continuous professional development with a duration of 16 academic hours (of which at least eight require attendance); secondly, the preparation, presentation, and publication of a report from a pedagogical forum (international, national, or regional); and, thirdly, publication in a specialised journal issue.

The institutions with the right to carry out teacher training activities include higher education institutions (i.e., colleges and universities), scientific organisations, specialised service units, as well as training organisations whose programmes have been approved by the Minister of Education and Science and entered into the ministry's information register (created 2016). As of December 2017, 2613 approved programmes from 128 organisations were announced on the ministry website.

According to Article 50 of Ordinance No. 15, Bulgaria's teachers can further their qualifications outside the country—in an EU member state or in a third country (i.e., outwith the EU). They may participate in qualification activities organised by organisations and schools or that are part of international programmes and projects. Such qualification must be recognised by the head of the relevant regional education department in Bulgaria.

Although principals are technically required to allocate part of the school budget (at a minimum of 0.8% of the remuneration fund) for qualification activities, in reality many teachers pay for their own participation in such activities. As touched on earlier, in recent years, the Ministry of Education and Science has been seeking opportunities to encourage teachers to actively pursue continuous professional development, including launching their *Qualification for professional development of pedagogical specialists (2018–2022)* project, funded by the *Science and education for smart growth* programme. Within Activity 1, hundreds of teachers participate in short-term training, acquiring one, two, or three qualification credits. Then, Activity 2 provides external funding for pedagogical specialists to acquire fifth to first professional and qualification degrees (PQD), as well as be involved in preparatory courses for the last two degrees (i.e., the highest degrees).

Indeed, these professional and qualification degrees are important for teachers' career development and are associated with an additional monthly remuneration. Applicants for such degrees must meet the following general requirements: to have already acquired the previous professional and qualification degree, to occupy the position of a pedagogical specialist at the time of application, and to be facing no disciplinary sanction. Beyond this, each degree is subject to specific requirements.

The fifth (lowest) professional and qualification degree can be obtained by teachers who have at least two years of teaching experience, a certificate for participation in qualification upgrade trainings for a total duration of at least 16 academic hours, and passed an oral exam with at least a 4.50 grade (i.e., very good). Teachers whose students have earned high national and international honours and awards may also acquire this degree without an exam.

The fourth professional and qualification degree may be obtained by teachers who have acquired the fifth degree, participated in trainings for a total duration of at least 16 academic hours, and passed a written exam on a problem in their professional field with at least a 4.50 grade (i.e., very good).

The third professional and qualification degree can be obtained by teachers who have acquired the fourth professional and qualification degree, completed a one-year professional pedagogical specialisation (with a minimum of 200 academic hours, of which at least 50% require attendance and at least 50% of the disciplines in the syllabus cover pedagogical, psychological, or methodological training), the average grade in their specialisation be at least 4.50 (i.e., very good), and diploma work (i.e., presenting good pedagogical practice).

The second professional and qualification degree may be obtained by teachers who have acquired the third professional and qualification degree, participated in trainings with a total duration of at least 32 academic hours, received a grade of at least 4.50 (i.e., very good) on their written work.

The first professional and qualification degree may be obtained by teachers who have acquired the second professional and qualification degree, taken part in trainings with a total duration of at least 48 academic hours, successfully defended an original written work related to their pedagogical practice or to educational management, and at least two publications in a specialised journal issue on the topic of their written work (within the last attestation period).

Teachers' participation in qualification activities is both a condition and pathway for their career development: according to Ordinance No. 15, Article 2, teachers in schools and kindergartens may successively occupy the following positions:

(a) teacher, including the particular positions of:

* teacher of a full-day group
* resource teacher in a kindergarten, school, or personality development support centre
* teacher of children with special educational needs in a centre for special educational support
* teacher with theoretical training and teacher with practical training in vocational high schools—these positions can be held by someone with the education and qualification necessary for being a teacher (with those

exceptions provided by the law), who are being employed as teachers or educators for the first time and who have no previous teaching experience

(b) senior teacher and, respectively, senior resource teacher, senior teacher of children with special educational needs, senior teacher with theoretical training, and senior teacher with practical training

* This position can be held by someone who (in addition to a higher education degree and the professional qualifications required for the position):

    – has no less than the obligatory qualification credits for each completed attestation period
    – a fifth or fourth professional and qualification degree
    – 10 years of teaching experience
    – from the 2021/2022 academic year onwards, passed their most recent attestation with a rating of at least 'meets requirements'

* Applicants for the position of senior teacher, irrespective of their teaching experience, may also be:

    – teachers who have obtained qualification credits for the attestation period beyond the obligatory requirements
    – a third, second, or first professional and qualification degree
    – from the 2021/2022 academic year onwards, a rating of 'outstanding performance' or 'exceeds requirements' from their most recent attestation.
    – In addition to their daily education and training work with students, senior teachers are also responsible for organising in-service qualifications; assisting other teachers, especially newly appointed and trainee teachers; and participating in the development of the school curriculum and syllabi.

(c) Head teacher and, respectively, head resource teacher, head teacher of children with special educational needs, head teacher with theoretical training, and head teacher with practical training.

* This position can be held by someone who has:

    – a higher educational degree (i.e., master's) and a teaching professional qualification

- a current position as senior teacher or senior educator
- no less than the obligatory qualification credits for their most attestation period
- a third, second, or first professional and qualification degree.

* For this position, it is also envisaged that, from the 2021/2022 academic year onwards, candidates will be appointed if they have a rating of 'outstanding performance' from their latest attestation.
* Head teachers also perform functions related to:

- planning, organising, and reporting qualification activities
- exchanging good pedagogical practices, including teaching for students' acquisition of key competences
- assisting newly appointed teachers and trainee teachers
- providing methodological support for people working as teachers and senior teachers
- developing school documentation (i.e., curricula and syllabi), as well as innovative programme systems.

Lastly, senior teachers and head teachers can both mentor up to two newly appointed and trainee teachers.

Pedagogical specialists work in residential schools and personality development support centres, serving as educators who can occupy, respectively, the positions of educator, senior educator, and head educator. In Bulgaria's preschool and school education systems there are also other pedagogical specialists, such as director or principal (as appointed via competition), deputy director, psychologist, pedagogical advisor, speech therapist, hearing and speech rehabilitator, accompanist, choreographer, sports coach, and head of ICT. These positions require that candidates have the necessary profiles, as defined in Ordinance No. 15 (Section III) and its annexes.

To sum up, in recent years the efforts of the Bulgarian governments and the teams at the Ministry of Education and Science have been directed towards the implementation of the *National Strategy for the Development of Teaching Staff (2014–2020)*: an attempt to put into practice a system for the learning, qualification, and development of Bulgarian teachers, within the context of a continuum of learning throughout their professional lives, as recommended by the European Council.

The Challenges and Difficulties in Reforming Teacher Education and Qualification in Bulgaria

During the 30 years of transition, Bulgarian education and teacher education and qualification have been affected by both external and internal factors. Within that context, there have been and there are a number of typically Bulgarian challenges, namely, poor continuity between the Ministry of Education teams with regard to strategies, policies, and changes in education, including teacher education; continuous changes in the field have created uncertainty for the teachers and school leaders who need to implement them; insufficient government funding for the sector; a shortage of teachers, especially up to the age of 35; as well as generally inefficient staffing across the education system; teachers not being offered motivation for their own development (perhaps linked to the decline in the number of students in recent years, including those dropping out of school–statistics show that over the last decade up to the 5% of students leave before the age of 16); low levels of digital competence among working teachers, especially those who are older; a flawed career development system which does not stimulate competition between teachers and does not motivate pedagogical staff towards career development (in fact, it has been found to even slow down the career growth of teachers under the age of 35); and delayed changes in the curricula and the teacher training programmes with respect to the requirements for twenty-first-century education.

The first years of the new system for the qualification of pedagogical staff highlighted some specific problems within this system.

Firstly, this system has not yet successfully consistently motivated teachers—while most teachers undoubtedly do recognise the need for continuous professional development, many do not necessarily feel motivated to actively pursue it every year. Rather, they believe that such qualifications should be a matter of personal choice, dependent on their needs, motivations, and experience—thus suggesting that Bulgaria's teacher professional development system ought to take these perspectives more fully into account.

Secondly, in many places around the country, teachers themselves do not have a free choice of qualification courses—instead, often directors decide which courses teachers are to attend. However, even assuming the best of intentions, any director risks making the wrong choice among the plethora of courses, trainings, and providers available on the market of teacher education services. Thus, we arrive at the next problem.

Thirdly, while being a positive phenomenon in itself, the huge number of courses on offer can render it difficult to make the right choice.

Fourthly, despite this overall (too) plentiful choice in urban settings, such choice is comparatively very limited in Bulgaria's towns and villages: there are simply not enough specific courses provided for teachers in vocational schools, specifically in terms of the newest developments in the fields in which students are taught.

Fifthly, while legislation is what empowers organisations and institutions to offer qualification courses or trainings in Bulgaria, among them are those which do not meet participants' expectations—in terms of novelty, content, organisation, and trainers.

Sixthly, decisions concerning the choice of trainers are entirely in the hands of the service providers. Often, experts are employed as trainers, despite lacking any previous experience in training or in adult education, meaning that many provide content which is not helpful to the participants.

Lastly, the time limitation on short-term courses (with one qualification credit awarded for an obligatory 16 academic hours) presents a serious problem as these 16 hours can be divided into eight hours of attendance and eight hours for independent work, the former of which, in reality, are only enough to rush through the programme.

Despite such shortcomings, the first steps of the reform in continuous teacher professional development have been made. Indeed, one of its most positive effects to date is that teachers more seriously consider their needs for additional knowledge and skills, and then relate them to future courses as well as to plans for their own development.

Conclusion

The future development of teacher education and qualification in Bulgaria depends largely on the extent to which the experts of the Ministry of Education and Science have a clear vision of what kind of students and young people twenty-first-century schools should prepare. In order to comment on the potential directions for future changes in this field, the interrelated challenges which determine the need for changes in school education in the contemporary world and in Bulgaria, as part of it, should be taken into account: firstly, in terms of the dynamically changing world of the twenty-first century and, consequently, the societal expectations for the outcomes of school education (i.e., what students need to know and be able to do upon leaving school in order to be prepared for the outside world); secondly, in terms of the changed models of school education, whereby the tradition has been combined with the new/the digital, in order to meet societal expectations. Last but not least, must consider Bulgaria's directions for development as a part of the European family and of the world.

If we use the model for effective leadership devised by the British management specialist, John Adair (cited in Chapman 2018), the following factors responsible for managing the future development of teacher education and qualification should be considered:

* The needs of the task: to prepare and continually develop twenty-first-century teachers who are able to teach, educate, and support the development of twenty-first-century students;
* The needs of teachers as the target group: the knowledge (i.e., literacies and competences) and skills teachers need in order to be able to teach, educate, and support the development of twenty-first-century students;
* The needs of the individual teacher: what each teacher needs in order to feel safe in their workplace, confident in what they do, and sure of the direction in which they lead students (all of which are critical for their motivation to stay and progress in the profession).

All of these mean that the Ministry of Education teams should have a clear concept to follow (and corresponding continuity in their actions). Firstly, this concept should be regarding the task (i.e., carrying out the modern training and qualification of Bulgarian teachers) and the means of its achievement (i.e., what higher education institutions need in order to offer the best (most modern) teacher education to future teachers), as well as which organisations are best able to offer up-to-date, useful, and high-quality qualification activities which truly meet the needs of working teachers. Secondly, this concept should be regarding teachers as a professional group, namely under what conditions they work best (i.e., how should schools change so as to offer an educational environment in which teachers and students will achieve the highest accomplishments and feel satisfied with what they do every day?). Thirdly, this concept should be regarding the individual teacher, namely what they need in order to work peacefully and efficiently; what motivates (and demotivates) them at work; where they can get help in case of difficulties; how to overcome or avoid the burnout caused by all the daily stress put on them; and to what extent there are opportunities provided to rest and recover.

In the context of the measures set out in the *National Strategy for the Development of Teaching Staff: 2014–2020*, there can be an expectation of further financial and ICT support to the education system as a whole and to the education and qualification of teachers in particular. This would allow for the creation of better conditions for teachers' professional and career development (including improvement in the quality of education and training services for both future and current teachers), enriched equality and competitiveness between training institutions and organisations (as well as greater control over their activity), and improved socio-economic status for teaching staff.

Considering the constant nature of changes in all spheres of life, including teacher education and qualification, any proposal for a long-term change made today which is too specific may prove to be inadequate over time. Therefore, ultimately, it is more important to know the direction and orientation of change (i.e., tied to awareness of global and national trends), and to implement adequate and flexible strategies for the development of education in general—and of teacher education in particular.

References

Act for the Development of the Academic Staff in the Republic of Bulgaria. (2010, last amend. 26.02.2019). Retrieved from https://www.mon.bg.

Chapman, A. (2018). Action Centred Leadership—John Adair). Retrieved from https://www.businessballs.com/leadership-models/action-centred-leadership-john-adair/.

Darling-Hammond, L. (2006). Constructing 21st-century teacher education. *Journal of Teacher Education,* 57(3), 300–314.

European Commission. (2009). *Council conclusions of November 26, 2009 on the professional development of teachers and school leaders, 2009/C 302/04. Official Journal of the European Union,* C 302/6, Retrieved from https://eur-lex.europa.eu/legal-content/EN/TXT/PDF/?uri=OJ:C:2009:302:FULL&from=EN.

Eurydice. (2021). Bulgaria. *Political, social and economic background and trends.* Retrieved from https://eacea.ec.europa.eu/national-policies/eurydice/content/political-social-and-economic-background-and-trends-12_en.

The Higher Education (HE) Act. (prom., SG, issue 112 of 27.12.1995; amend. and suppl. 2004; amend. and suppl. 2016; last amend. and suppl. 18.10.2018, in force since 20.01.2019). Retrieved from http://lll.mon.bg/uploaded_files/zkn_visseto_obr_01.03.2016_EN.pdf.

Georgieva, S. (2018). Задължителната квалификация на учителите се прави формално [The obligatory qualification of teachers is made formally]. Retrieved from https://www.segabg.com/node/8899.

Gospodinov, B., R. Peycheva-Forsyth, I. Petkova, B. Mizova, and J. Parvanova. (2018). ПРОБЛЕМИ НА ПЕДАГОГИЧЕСКОТО ОБРАЗОВАНИЕ НА УЧИТЕЛИТЕ

[Problems of pedagogical education of teachers]. *Sofia University Journal of Educational Research,* 1, 3–12.

Gospodinov, B., R. Peycheva-Forsyth, and B. Mizova. (2019). *The quality of the continuing qualification of the pedagogical specialists through the perspective of teachers and students.* Sofia University Issue "St. Kliment Ohridski".

Gyurova, V. (2017). За капаните пред качеството на продължаващат Квалификация на учителите [The "traps" on the way to quality continuing training of in-service teachers]. *E-magazine "Pedagogical Forum",* 5(4), 22–29.

Gyurova, V. (2019a). Промени в образованието и квалификацията на учителите в България [Changes in the teacher training and qualification in Bulgaria]. *E-magazine "Pedagogical Forum",* 7(3), 194–203.

Gyurova, V. (2019b). Компетентностно-базиран профил на учителя на 21 век. [Competence-based profile of the teacher of the 21st century]. *Управление и образование,* 15(3), 194–203.

Gyurova, V. (2018a). The role of non-formal education institutions in continuing professional development of teachers in Bulgaria. *Astra Salvensis, Supplement 2/2018: Proceedings of the —IV International Forum on Teacher Education*, 22–24 May 2018, Kazan (Volga Region) Federal University, Russian Federation. VI, 41–48.

Gyurova, V. (2018b). Защо само педагогическа компетентност не е достатъчна за учителя на 21 век? [Why only pedagogical competence is not enough for the 21st century teacher?]. *E-magazine "Pedagogical Forum",* 6(3), 3–9.

Gyurova, V., and R. Gyoreva. (2019). Продължаващата квалификация на педагогическите кадри като критерий и фактор за качество на образованието [Continuing in-service teacher/pedagogical staff training as a criteria and a factor for the quality of education]. *E-magazine "Pedagogical Forum",* 7(2), 3–11.

Gyurova, V., and V. Zeleeva. (2017). The knowledge and skills of the 21st century teachers. *The European Proceeding of Social & Behavioural Sciences EpSBS,* XXIX, 282–291.

National Strategy for the Development of Teaching Staff—2014–2020. (2014). Retrieved from https://www.mon.bg.

Ordinance on the state requirements for the organisation of distance learning in higher education institutions (prom., SG, issue 99 of 09.11.2004). (2004). Retrieved from https://www.mon.bg.

Ordinance No. 12, 2016 on the status and professional development of teachers, principals and other pedagogical specialists (prom., SG, issue 75 of 27.09.2016). (2016). Retrieved from https://www.mon.bg.

Ordinance No. 15 of 22.07.2019 on the status and professional development of teachers, principals and other pedagogical specialists (prom., SG, issue 61 of 02.08.2019, effective since 02.08.2019). (2019). Retrieved from https://www.mon.bg.

P21 Framework definition (2015). Retrieved from https://files.eric.ed.gov/fulltext/ED519462.pdf.

Pre-school and School Education Act. (prom., SG, issue 79 of 13.10.2015, in force since 01.08.2016; amend. 2018). Retrieved from https://www.mon.bg.

Sharlanova, V. (2018). Strengths-based professional and career development of teachers *Astra Salvensis, Supplement 2/2018: Proceedings of the — IV International Forum on Teacher Education*, 22–24 May 2018, Kazan (Volga Region) Federal University, Russian Federation. VI, 59–71.

Strategy for the Development of Higher Education in the Republic of Bulgaria for the period 2014–2020. Retrieved from https://www.mon.bg.

Part IV

The Baltics

16

Teacher Education in Lithuania: Striving for Professionalism

Aušra Rutkienė and Lina Kaminskienė

The Historical and Socio-economic Contexts of Teacher Education in Lithuania

Lithuania regained its independence—from Soviet Russia—in 1990 and became a fully-fledged member of the European Union in 2004. Since the very day it regained its independence, Lithuania has been dedicating human, financial, and political resources to implementing substantial transformations across all sectors, starting with the economy—in tandem, the education, political, and cultural sectors have been working towards recovering—at the same time as developing a new identity as an independent country within the European Union. However, these profound and ongoing transformation processes have been difficult as 50 years living under the Soviet system has left deep imprints in Lithuania's bureaucratic structures and societal mentality. Education, like all other sectors, was centrally controlled from Moscow and all major decisions—concerning changes in curriculum, assessment and examination, education legislation, teacher training, education structure, and so on—were made by the Soviet government, outside of Lithuania's national education system (Želvys 2004).

Thus, one of the first challenges upon regaining independence was to de-ideologise, decentralise, and democratise the national education system

A. Rutkienė (✉) • L. Kaminskienė
Vytautas Magnus University, Kaunas, Lithuania
e-mail: ausra.rutkiene@vdu.lt

© The Author(s), under exclusive license to Springer Nature Switzerland AG 2023
M. Kowalczuk-Walędziak et al. (eds.), *The Palgrave Handbook of Teacher Education in Central and Eastern Europe*, https://doi.org/10.1007/978-3-031-09515-3_16

(Želvys 2004). From 1990 onwards, Lithuania's education sector started to eliminate the influence of the rigid Soviet style and explore its own developmental pathway. One of the first strategic documents guiding this shift was *The General Concept of Lithuanian Education (1992)*. Based on goals, values, and relationships germane to the building of a twenty-first-century democratic society, this document posits four basic principles for Lithuania's education system: humanism; democracy; commitment to Lithuanian culture and plurality enriched by national minorities; and renewal. Three decades on, these core principles remain valid. However, the structure of the general education system changed in the early 1990s and four-year levels were introduced: that is, four years of primary education, four years of lower secondary education, and four years of upper secondary education. This model is still functioning, although debates about re-structuring the general education system are emerging again: Lithuania's politicians are increasingly convinced by potentially promising results evidenced by other EU countries where primary education has a six-year cycle.

The adaptation processes in the education sector spanning from 1990 until 2004, and beyond, have allowed Lithuania to learn from and mould best practices selected from other EU member states, as well as to gain support from such international organisations as the OECD, UNESCO, and the UN. Moreover, growing international cooperation and strengthening networks with education institutions created a strong impetus for systemic comparative research and practical pilots funded by both EU and national programmes. In 1997, the national education reform yielded some successful changes, such as the reviewed and revised curricula and textbooks, which enabled teachers to create more individualised syllabuses and granted schools the right to develop their own curricula, while, at the same time, following a core curriculum defined on the national level (Želvys 2004). As such, in these first decades of the twenty-first century, Lithuania's schools and teachers have successfully started to become more autonomous, taking charge of their own teaching and learning processes.

However, it is critical to locate this review of Lithuania's contemporary education system more concretely within the socio-economic context where these developments and changes are taking place. First of all, a striking majority of Lithuania's teaching staff are women, making teaching a female-led profession. Indeed, in lower and upper secondary schools around 85% of teachers are women, and in pre-school and primary schools around 95% of teachers are women (Statistics Lithuania 2020). Second of all, analysis of Lithuania's socio-economic indicators spanning 2015–2019 demonstrates that the numbers of inhabitants and births have both decreased in recent years (Statistics

Lithuania 2020): the total population decreased by 94,229 (3.26%) and the number of births decreased by 3746 (11.9%).

However, inversely, the number of students in pre-school and primary education has been slightly increasing, in line with the increased birth-rate (and number of inhabitants) prior to 2015; but, simultaneously, the number of students in lower secondary and secondary education, as well as the total number of teachers, are all decreasing (see Fig. 16.1). These dynamics in the number of pupils in education did not well correlate with the decreasing number of teachers.

Within this decrease in Lithuania's teaching population, the average age of teaching professionals is steadily increasing, at last measure (2018) sitting at: 48 years for pre-primary education, 49 years for primary education, 50 years for lower secondary education, and 51 years for upper secondary education (Education Information Management System 2020).

In summary, the demographic trends in Lithuania's teaching profession give rise to caution and concern (Quality and Flexibility of Initial Teacher Education Studies in Lithuania 2020):

* between 2009 and 2018, the number of teachers aged 25 or younger decreased from 828 to 237 (i.e., a decrease of 71%), denoting a very significant drop in the number of young people entering the profession;

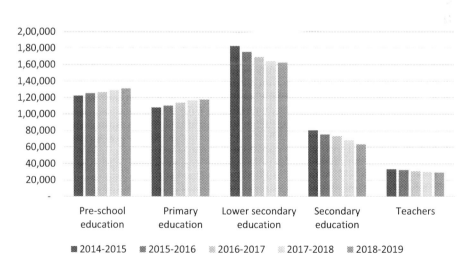

Fig. 16.1 Number of teachers and number of students in pre-school, primary, and secondary education (2014–2019) (Statistics Lithuania 2020)

* between 2009 and 2018, the number of teachers aged 55 or older increased from 7903 to 11,708 (i.e., an increase of 48%), denoting a very significant rise in the number of older people remaining in the profession;
* Furthermore, statistics regarding pupils and schools (Quality and Flexibility of Initial Teacher Education Studies in Lithuania 2020) demonstrate similarly concerning trends:
* between 2001 and 2018, the total number of pupils decreased from 602,643 to 326,041 (i.e., a decrease of 46%), denoting a very significant drop in the overall demand for formal education;
* between 2001 and 2018, the number of schools decreased from 2270 to 1122 (i.e., a decrease of 51%), denoting a very significant drop in the amount of education resources available.

Indeed, Merkys' 2019 study on the demand for teachers records dramatic gaps in the resources available: almost every fourth school currently lacks at least one teacher, and only in every third school does the subject teacher actually teach their own subject on a regular basis, totalling a national shortage of 363 of subject teachers in autumn 2019. If a similar trend in initial teacher education continues, the shortage of teachers can be expected to increase to almost 2000 within the next few years. As such, debates about introducing national support and promotion measures to attract young people towards choosing a career in teaching are more pressing than ever.

The Main Characteristics of Initial Teacher Education in Lithuania

Lithuania's higher education institutions train teachers in the fields of: early childhood education and care; primary and subject education; social and special pedagogy; adult education; and education management. All these types of teachers can work in schools if they have received a teaching qualification at the end of their studies. Colleges provide higher education programmes mainly in the fields of early childhood education and primary education, while universities provide programmes in all fields, ranging from early childhood education to subject pedagogy, via bachelor's and master's degrees. Currently, teacher training in Lithuania is based on two main models: the concurrent model (where disciplinary content knowledge and pedagogical knowledge are taught alongside each other) and the consecutive model (where pedagogical knowledge is taught after disciplinary content knowledge). In addition, some universities offer a parallel model, which allows candidates to gain a teaching qualification in tandem with a qualification in their main study field.

In 2016, two teacher education strategies were developed via consortiums led by Vytautas Magnus University and Vilnius University. Subsequently, a working group to consolidate the varied, and sometimes controversial, views of Lithuanian education scientists and practitioners was formed under the Ministry of Education and Science, and, after an intensive year of consultations, a consensus regarding models of initial teacher education was achieved and formalised in the 2018 Teacher Training Concept, which stipulated, among other things, that

* pedagogical studies cannot be less than 60 ECTS, out of which in-service practice must amount to 30 ECTS;
* higher education institutions should ensure recognition of competences gained through practice and informally;
* one year of pedagogical traineeship is obligatory: after graduation, teachers should spend one year in a school fulfilling a pedagogical traineeship/final 'on-the-job' qualifying phase;
* at least 30% of the teaching staff at higher education institutions which provide teacher training should have professional pedagogical experience in schools and have achieved C1 proficiency level in English.

The adopted *Teacher Training Concept* (2018) created substantial background for changes in the teacher education system. First of all, it made higher education institutions and national authorities to reconsider the recruitment process in order to attract competent candidates to the teacher's profession via several alternative models which ensured a more flexible access to pedagogical studies. Second, teacher education moved to the three excellence centres in Vilnius, Kaunas, and Šiauliai. Third, teacher education in Lithuania is viewed in the international context and thus, research-based teacher education became a priority for the country to raise the quality of teacher education and national education system in general.

Teacher education in Lithuania today faces a variety of challenges, which are related to socio-economic changes in society more widely, including: increasing emigration levels and a decreasing number of inhabitants (Statistics Lithuania 2020); economic and social regional disparities as well as competition between schools for more students (The Report on the Situation of Education in Lithuania 2019); and a growing demand for high quality education from the main stakeholders: that is, policy-makers, students, and parents.

In sum, these challenges put pressure on the teacher education sector from multiple angles, especially with regards to resources, both human and economic. Furthermore, these changes have caused major regional disparities between schools, not only in terms of the number of students in a classroom—ranging from six to 13 students per teacher (Education Information Management System 2020)—but also in terms of their academic achievements, in that students living in regions with greater economic wealth have access to better academic outcomes (Lithuania. Education in the country and regions. 2019. Student achievement gap 2019).

Indeed, the current generation of students in Lithuania is more diverse than ever before—for instance, in terms of learning support needs (The Report on the Situation of Education in Lithuania 2019)—and new ways of teaching are required in order to fully uphold and serve this wide range of backgrounds and needs. The relative number of children with special learning needs has been growing steadily over the past five years—was 11.7 per cent in 2017, 11.9 per cent in 2018, and 12.5 per cent in 2019. Pre-school children with special learning needs in 2016 was 15.7 per cent, in 2017 was 17.5 per cent, and in 2018 19.9 per cent (Education Information Management System 2020). Correspondingly, there is a need for teachers' initial education and continuing professional development to evolve, but current impairments to that progress include: the lack of highly qualified teachers; insufficiently child-centred practices for responding to different learning needs; the low prestige of the profession; the dominance of frontal teaching methods; and limited innovation in the sector.

Transformations in Lithuania's Initial Teacher Education

Lithuania's initial teacher education system has undergone several major transformations since independence, mainly focused on opening up alternative routes to gaining a teaching qualification. In 2003, the historically embedded concurrent model was challenged by the consecutive model, allowing candidates to gain a teaching qualification in one year, that is, a 40 ECTS non-degree programme (extending to 60 ECTS in 2010), after completing a bachelor's degree in their chosen field. These concurrent and consecutive models co-existed as two equals for some years; however, starting from 2010, the concurrent model was used mainly for the education of kindergarten and primary school teachers, while subject teachers were trained in the consecutive model. A 2015 national analysis (The Concept of Teachers Education in

Lithuania 2016) indicated that, during the 2013–2015 period, universities in Lithuania had no students undertaking concurrent pedagogical studies in the fields of chemistry and physics, while the numbers of students undertaking consecutive studies was starting to grow. However, Lithuania's sceptics of the consecutive model refer to studies from other EU countries in order to highlight the issues that they see with this format. For example, Clarke et al. (2012) conducted a five-year study in Ireland on five consecutive teacher education programmes, and found that non-integrated pedagogical studies caused a range of problems for students: most of the graduates indicated that they had not been well prepared for the realities of professional practice, for instance in terms of class management skills and problem-solving skills. According to these graduates, one year is an impossible timeframe for training or re-training an educator.

Nonetheless, on the whole three main directions of initial teacher education can be identified in most EU countries, including Lithuania: (1) the concurrent model, which dominates the training of pre-school and primary education teachers; (2) the concurrent and consecutive models, used for the basic education level teacher training (i.e., for teaching grades 5–8); and (3) the consecutive model, usually used in training teachers for the upper grades (i.e., grades 9–12), which is a compulsory bachelor's + pedagogical non-degree studies + (not obligatory) master's degree. Merkys' 2019 study indicates that over 30 per cent of school principals in Lithuania agree that in response to the growing demand for professional teachers at all levels, the primary school teaching qualification should be gained after completing a university-level studies (i.e., at least four years).

In 2018, regulations defining the quality criteria and competences to be developed during pedagogical study programmes in higher education institutions were approved by the Minister of Education and Science: such as, key and special competences, the introduction of induction period for novice teachers, more flexibility to gain a double specialisation (teaching two or more subjects) and other. These new regulations caused debates regarding the quality of Lithuania's pedagogical studies, as well as potential risks to teachers' professionalism development posed by the recognition of diversified ways to acquire teacher's qualification through several models: a consecutive, a concurrent a parallel. Moreover, an alternative model through the national programme 'Teach for All' was accepted as a part of the national teacher education system. Analysing teachers' professional identity development, Day (2007) notes that the development of subject knowledge and pedagogical knowledge alone are not sufficient. Indeed, professional identity is not simply acquired with a job title, but created and honed through self-realisation and the use of educational philosophy, as well as developing the ability to redefine one's role via self-reflection (Yamin-Ali and Pooma 2012). Thus, it is important that teachers—and those around them—see themselves as educators.

The most recent main transformation in Lithuania's initial teacher education system stems from the government's 2018 decision to establish national teacher e education centres: in Vilnius (Vilnius University), Kaunas (Vytautas Magnus University), and Šiauliai (Šiauliai University) respectively. At this point, all other higher education institutions around the country which had traditionally offered teacher education via their own departments were forced either to stop their study programmes or to establish collaborative models with one of the three centres. The main goal driving this reform was to regulate the number of teacher education programmes on offer—before the reform more than 14 higher education institutions offered various types of pedagogical study programmes—as well to set quality criteria related to studies and research in the field of education.

The Main Characteristics of Teacher Professional Development in Lithuania

In Lithuania, teachers' professional development (TPD) is valued as one of the main components of teacher evaluation. Teachers are legally obliged to undertake professional development and are entitled to five professional development days each year (Shewbridge et al. 2016). The latest regulation adopted by the Minister of Education, Science and Sports, in 2019, indicates that TPD cannot be less than 40 hours per year, and that regional continuous professional development (CPD) providers should collaborate with the three newly-appointed teacher education centres. However, the CPD of teachers in Lithuania is fragmented and scattered, distributed between more than 70 CPD providers across the country.

Research-based teacher education and professional development is closely related to growing demands from the government, parents, universities for the increased professionalism of teachers (Galkienė 2011). However, the concept of teachers' professionalism is multi-layered. Yamin-Ali and Pooma (2012) consider a teacher's professionalism to be their unique teaching philosophy, competence in defining their role and goals, their profound knowledge of the school context, their reflection skills, and their self-efficacy. This said, they do not conceptualise teachers' professionalism as existing in isolation, rather they stress the value of and need for communication and cooperation. Similarly, Jurasaite-Harbison and Rex (2013) highlight the importance of both workplace and informal TPD, all of which takes place both consciously and unconsciously, via adopting and honing both reactive and proactive strategies. With regard to the fundamental aim of TPD, Darling-Hammond et al. (2017, p. 5) note that 'effective professional development is structured professional learning that results in changes in teacher practices and improvements in student learning outcomes.' Still, Borko's (2004, p. 6) description of the myriad of contexts for TPD makes obvious the practical challenges involved in identifying, defining, and measuring teachers' learning:

> For teachers, learning occurs in many different aspects of practice, including their classrooms, their school communities, and professional development courses or workshops. It can occur in a brief hallway conversation with a colleague, or after school when counselling a troubled child. To understand teacher learning, we must study it within these multiple contexts, taking into account both the individual teacher-learners and the social systems in which they are participants.

Indeed, in line with this need to understand the variety inherent in teacher-learners' experiences, Desimone's (2009) model of TPD proposes five key features—(a) content focus, (b) active learning, (c) coherence, (d) duration, and (e) collective participation—all of which are critical to increasing teachers' knowledge and skills, thus improving their practice and, in turn, holding promise for increasing student achievement.

All of this said, it is important to locate TPD within the reality of the career paths presently available to teachers in this part of the world. While other professions have clear and well-established pathways towards promotion and increasing acquisition of wealth and status—for instance, engineers are able to work towards chartered status and lawyers are able to work towards becoming partners—teaching has a comparatively flat career structure with few possibilities for promotion within the bounds of teachers' existing professional practice. Instead, to achieve tangible career progression—that is, a higher salary or increased professional status—teachers are commonly obliged to spend fewer hours in the classroom and more time on administrative and/or management tasks.

All the same, TPD is critical for all teachers and is an ongoing process which spans the entirety of an active professional life: from initial pedagogical traineeship to specialising and/or refreshing professional skill sets until retirement. The main principles regarding TPD in Lithuania were officially adopted in 2012 in the form of the Teachers' Professional Development Concept, which recognised the following forms of professional development:

* individual learning (including scientific activities and research and professional publications);
* collegial knowledge-sharing (including participation in methodological groups and associations of subject teachers; demonstration and reflective supervision of lessons and other educational activities; and coaching, mentoring, and consultation);
* specialised events (including seminars, courses, projects, internships, and trainings)
* academic studies (including higher degree studies; studies in another field; and study programmes aimed at re-training which do not award a degree);
* public activities (including social activities, cultural activities, and artistic expression).

The Concept states that TPD should continue the training received in higher education institutions, while teacher training must provide conditions for future pedagogues to acquire the competences necessary for fulfilling the future teacher's role as education organiser, creative educator, developer of opportunities, coach, adviser, and mediator between the pupil and contemporary information sources. According to the document, the main principles of teachers' continuous development are self-assessment, integration of good practices, motivation, and subsidiarity between the teacher and their school administration.

Regarding teachers themselves, any given teacher's motivation to participate in CPD processes is closely related with their values and other personal motives; nonetheless, this does not mean that external incentives are less important. Lithuania's 2012 Teacher Professional Development Concept suggests that incentives for participation in CPD activities should include

> the teacher's right and opportunity to freely choose the field and form of their professional development in line with the needs of their education institution and the whole country, as well as an opportunity to pursue their career in management after gaining the necessary managerial skills and competence.

The main challenge for TPD in Lithuania, however, remains the quality of provision. While international studies indicate that the higher a teacher's qualification is, the higher the learning achievements of their students are (Sales et al. 2017), data on the quality of general education in Lithuania confirms that students' achievements do not correlate with teachers' professional categories—that is, senior teacher, teacher methodologist, and teacher-expert—and that the education and training quality in schools is only 'average' (National Audit Report 2016), thus bucking the aforementioned international trends. Moreover, the 2016 National Audit reported that teachers' in-service training is both costly and in efficient.

Challenges and Tensions in Transforming Lithuania's Teacher Education: A Quest for a Research-Based and Collaborative Model

At present Lithuania is facing challenges regarding contemporary teacher education approaches, namely in terms of factors such as: reforms in the national curriculum; improving results in PISA and TIMMS surveys; and changes in induction period requirements. Correspondingly, these challenges increase the need to strengthen the country's network of professional communities, so that best practices and insightful experiences from teacher education in other countries can be implemented and consolidated, thus contributing to the internationalisation of Lithuania's teachers' competency frameworks and teacher education programmes—an endeavour best supported by rigorous research.

During the past few decades, research on TPD in Lithuania has lacked a systemic and multi-disciplinary approach, however, on the whole, many researchers have attempted to address the main challenges related the following issues, among others: the decreasing academic results of pupils; the significant regional disparities in education quality; and the lack of strategic visions and school leadership. At the beginning of this chronology, Bulajeva (2000) identified the self-development practices of general education teachers which lead to transformative learning. Similarly, Rutkienė and Zuzevičiūtė (2009) analysed the changing role of the general education teacher specifically in terms of the engagement of the teaching community in the pursuance of more effective learning for their pupils which should lead to more coherent and balanced education.

Moving beyond the immediate or everyday pedagogical setting, Cibulskas and Žydžiūnaitė (2012) developed a model of teachers' leadership development in schools, highlighting that the quality of education mainly depends on teachers' professionalism and leadership. Further, Dromantienė et al. (2013) analysed the institutional, legal, and managerial aspects of Lithuania's TPD system, comparing it to similar systems in other countries, then developing a new career model embedded in principles of quality assurance. On the other hand, Dačiulytė et al. (2013) analysed different models in the upgrading of general education teachers' qualifications, stressing that new models should be implemented placing more responsibility on balancing the school and individual learning needs.

Abromaitienė (2013) analysed the potential of professional supervision as an instrument of TPD, disclosing that the pedagogues who took part in group supervision experienced greater personal and cognitive benefits than those who had no supervision, due to the dual emotional and professional support of the former. Also invested in the prospect of teachers' participation in professional groupings, Česnavičienė and Urnėžienė (2016) researched collegial collaboration as a form of TPD, and found that teachers prefer innovative, rather than traditional, forms of collaboration—especially those that permit the sharing of experience, foster the exchange of innovative teaching practices, and promote co-learning. Lastly, Šedeckytė-Lagunavičienė and Tumlovskaja (2019) analysed the current trends of TPD in Lithuania's general education schools, highlighting the problem of short-term and inefficient courses—as well as the corresponding implications for the quality of education, such as higher academic and personal achievements of pupils.

The latest research in the field of teacher education in Lithuania is largely related to the minimised professional status of teachers. While current national reforms demonstrate a trend towards less centralised control of curricula and teaching methods, levels of trust in teachers' professionalism remain low. Research conducted by Pranckūnienė (2018) reveals the tensions between education policy and practice, as well as the fluctuations of trust in teachers' professionalism while implementing different educational change models. Pranckūnienė's research (2018) found that, in most cases, teachers have limited freedom as to what and how to teach, and that the national education system places more trust to regulations than to teachers. Simultaneous to these restrictions on teachers' freedoms, however, is the growing workload allocated to their remit (Bayer et al. 2009)—both in Lithuania and further afield, including teachers being held increasingly responsible for their students' achievements. Thus, the limits of teachers' professional activity and professionalism become difficult to define, ultimately making the labour expectations put upon Lithuania's teachers too extreme.

Implications for the Future Development of Teacher Education in Lithuania

In 2018 the national initiative *Ideas for Lithuania* articulated the goal of having teaching be a prestigious profession in the country by 2025—giving an official voice to the need for crucial societal transformations related to perceptions of the teachers' role, in particular understanding and accepting the teacher as the leader of the class, as well as a change catalyst. This move has lent momentum to a new wave of discussions around national conceptualisations of teacher education; the diversity of pathways to becoming a teacher; offering high quality, research-based programmes; encouraging more men to enter the women-led profession; and re-thinking teacher professional development, both in terms of its models and its approaches.

Against the backdrop of Lithuania's young people not feeling drawn to pursue a career in teaching, as outlined earlier in this chapter, it is estimated that, in the next few years, the demand for new teachers will be as high as 2000 per year. Current students already enrolled in pedagogical programmes will meet up to half of this demand, meaning that 1000–1500 students per year should be enrolled in initial teacher education programmes going forwards. Besides national incentives to encourage young people to choose the teaching profession and ensure a truly inter-generational sector, Lithuania's newly formed teacher education centres are focused on modernising the programmes they offer. Their goal is to fully develop programmes which are designed to prepare a contemporary teacher who is able to: mould and personalise the curriculum according to the needs of the learners in their care; grasp up-to-date digital technologies; work across disciplines; as well as create and support inclusive classroom environments open to the diverse learners of the twenty-first century.

The debate to centre TPD on research-informed activities is ongoing—and initiatives such as bringing teachers and researchers together via collaborative networks; formalising classroom and action-research as a CPD method; and contributing to research in collaboration with higher education institutions are continuing to gain more and more support from scholars and practitioners alike. Ultimately, however, if any of these initiatives are to become fully-fledged and sustainable realities, Lithuania's policy-makers must uphold rather than hinder the agency of teachers and school leaders—thus giving them space to move beyond the restrictions of the current socio-economic contexts and discourses, and go on to fulfil their potential.

References

Abromaitienė, L. (2013). Supervision as possibility of professional development for pedagogues. *Pedagogika*, 112, 32–38.

Bayer, M., U. Brinkkjær, H. Plauborg, and S. Rolls (Eds.). (2009). *Teachers' career trajectories and work lives*. Springer Science+Business Media.

Borko, H. (2004). Professional development and teacher learning: Mapping the terrain. *Educational Researcher, 33*(8), 3–15.

Bulajeva, T. (2000). Pedagogų profesinis tobulėjimas ir saviugda [Teacher professional development and self-development]. *Acta Pedagogica Vilnensia,* 8, 234–241.

Česnavičienė, J., and E. Urnėžienė. (2016). Mokytojų kolegialaus bendradarbiavimo ypatumai siekiant profesinio tobulėjimo [The peculiarities of teacher collegial collaboration in pursuit of professional development]. *Mokytoju Ugdymas,* 26(1), 15–24.

Cibulskas, G., and V. Žydžiūnaitė. (2012). *Lyderystės vystymosi mokykloje modelis* [A model for leadership development in schools]. Vilnius: ŠAC.

Clarke, M., A. Lodge, and M. Shevlin. (2012). Evaluating initial teacher education programmes: Perspectives from the Republic of Ireland. *Teaching and Teacher Education* 28, 141–153.

The Concept of Teachers Education in Lithuania. (2016). Retrieved from https://www.smm.lt/uploads/documents/Pedagogams/PEDAGOG%C5%B2%20RENGIMO%20KONCEPCIJA-LEU-VDU.pdf.

Dačiulytė, R., L. Dromantienė, V. Indrašienė, O. Merfeldaitė, S. Nefas, D. Penkauskienė, R. Prakapas, and A. Railienė. (2013). *Pedagogų kvalifikacijos tobulinimo Lietuvoje būklė ir plėtros galimybės: mokslo studija.* Vilnius: Mykolo Romerio universitetas.

Darling-Hammond, L., M. E. Hyler, and M. Gardner. (2017). *Effective teacher professional development.* Palo Alto, CA: Learning Policy Institute.

Day, C. (2007). School reform and transitions in teacher professionalism and identity. In: T. Townsend and R. Bates (Eds.), *Handbook of teacher education: Globalization, standards and professionalism in times of change* (pp. 597–613). The Netherlands: Springer.

Desimone, M. L. (2009). Improving impact studies of teachers' professional development: Toward better conceptualizations and measures. *Educational Researcher,* 38(3), 181–199.

Dromantienė, L., V. Indrašienė, O. Merfeldaitė, and R. Prakapa. (2013). Teachers' professional development: the case of Lithuania. *Επιστημονική Επετηρίδα Παιδαγωγικού Τμήματος Νηπιαγωγών, Πανεπιστημίου Ιωαννίνων, Τόμος ΣΤ',* 202–215. Retrieved from https://ejournals.epublishing.ekt.gr/index.php/jret/article/viewFile/760/781

Education Information Management System EMIS (SVIS). (2020). Retrieved from https://www.svis.smm.lt/.

Galkienė, A. (2011) Šiuolaikinio mokytojo vaizdinys: mokinių požiūris [Image of a modern teacher in pupils' perception]. *Pedagogika,* 101, 82–90

Jurasaite-Harbison, E., and L. A. Rex. (2013). Teachers as informal learners: workplace professional learning in the United States and Lithuania. *Pedagogies: An International Journal,* 8 (1), 1–23.

Lithuania. Education in the country and regions. 2019. Student achievement gap. (2019). Retrieved from https://www.smm.lt/uploads/documents/tyrimai_ir_

analizes/2019/B%C5%ABkl%C4%97s%20ap%C5%BEvalga%202019_
GALUTINIS.pdf.

Merkys, G. (2019). *Report on teacher demand in Lithuania* (unpublished).

National Audit Report (2016). Teachers' Qualification Upgrading. State Control. Vilnius: Lithuania. Retrieved from: file:///C:/Users/29230/Downloads/pedagogu-kvalifikacijos-tobulinimas.pdf

Pranckūnienė, E. (2018). Turning points of trust in professional lives of teachers and school leaders. Doctoral dissertation, Kaunas, Vytautas Magnus University.

Quality and Flexibility of Initial Teacher Education Studies in Lithuania. (2020). Retrieved from https://www.smm.lt/uploads/documents/veikla/tarptautinis%20 bendradarbiavimas/Pedagogini%C5%B3%20studij%C5%B3%20 kokyb%C4%97%20ir%20lankstumas.pdf.

The Report on the Situation of Education in Lithuania. (2019). Retrieved from https://www.nsa.smm.lt/wp-content/uploads/2020/07/Svietimo-bukles-apzvalga-2019-web.pdf.

Rutkienė, A., and V. Zuzevičiūtė. (2009). Changing role of the teacher: Engagement of community in pursuance of more effective learning. *Pedagogika*. 95, 53–57.

Sales, A., L. Moliner, and A. Francisco Amat. (2017). Collaborative professional development for distributed teacher leadership towards school change. *School Leadership & Management,* 37(3), 254–266.

Šedeckytė-Lagunavičienė, I., and J. Tumlovskaja. (2019). Mokytojo profesinis tobulėjimas remiantis mokyklų įsivertinimo ir išorinio vertinimo duomenimis [Teacher professional development based on school evaluation and external evaluation data]. Retrieved from http://www.svietimonaujienos.lt/ mokytojo-profesinis-tobulejimas-remiantis-mokyklu-isivertinimo-ir-isorinio-vertinimo-duomenimis/.

Shewbridge, C., K. Godfrey, Z. Hermann, and D. Nusche. (2016). *OECD reviews of school resources: Lithuania 2016. OECD reviews of school resources.* Paris: OECD Publishing.

Statistics Lithuania. (2020). Retrieved from https://www.stat.gov.lt/en.

Yamin-Ali, J., and D. Pooma. (2012). Honing a professional identity: The outcome of a teacher education programme. *Caribbean Curriculum*, 19, 67–90.

Želvys, R. (2004). Development of education policy in Lithuania during the years of transformations. *International Journal of Educational Development*, 24(5), 559–571.

17

Teacher Education in Latvia: Educating Teachers to Become Global Citizens

Mārīte Kravale-Pauliņa, Dzintra Iliško,
Eridiana Oļehnovuča, Ilona Fjodorova, and Inga Belousa

Introduction

Teacher education and understandings of a teacher's professional competence in Latvia have been significantly shaped by the national, social, political, and cultural contexts, as well as the education theories and philosophical foundations characteristic rooted in respective periods of time. Historical studies of teacher education in Latvia indicate that, starting with the First National Awakening in the 1850s, and throughout all stages of state formation, educators have been aware of their professional identity and sought ways of using education to aid the development of the country (Broks 2000; Žukovs 2001; Blūma 2016; Chankseliani and Silova 2018), and to facilitate positive social changes (Krūze et al. 2009).

During the Latvian Republic's first period of independence, 1918–1940, pedagogical competence incorporated elements of idealistic humanism, national romanticism, and tacit authoritarianism. Then, between 1940 and 1990, with Latvia occupied by Soviet military forces, the country's teacher education was subjected to a deconstruction of national ideals, as well as

M. Kravale-Pauliņa (✉) • D. Iliško • E. Oļehnovuča • I. Fjodorova
Center of Sustainable Education, Daugavpils University, Daugavpils, Latvia
e-mail: marite.kravale@du.lv

I. Belousa
University of Latvia, Riga, Latvia

© The Author(s), under exclusive license to Springer Nature Switzerland AG 2023
M. Kowalczuk-Walędziak et al. (eds.), *The Palgrave Handbook of Teacher Education in Central and Eastern Europe*, https://doi.org/10.1007/978-3-031-09515-3_17

immersion in Soviet ideology. During this period, pedagogical competences reflected a normative-oriented paradigm directed towards a behaviouristic, atomistic, and competence-based approach. From 1990, when Latvia re-declared its independence, until the present day, pedagogical competence could be defined as competence-based and identity-based, with both elements present in education discourse (Belousa and Ūzuliņa 2012, p. 90). In general, on the one hand, it is evident that the competence-based perspective serves labour market needs and reflects neo-liberal values. On the other hand, the identity-based perspective is rather compatible with a holistic approach, and recognises the authenticity of a teacher's professional life and identity. Furthermore, this latter perspective creates space for the integration of a civic perspective and citizenship values into the curricula of teacher education.

Appreciating the historical foundations of teacher education in Latvia, this chapter highlights the issue of global citizenship in the implementation of the discipline in the past 30 years. The chapter notes the most significant reforms; examines state planning documents and regulations regarding changes in education policy; and introduces recent scholarship and methodological initiatives that integrate the concept of citizenship into teacher education.

Context of Teacher Education in Latvia over the Past Three Decades

In 1990, Latvia adopted the Declaration of Independence and, looking back at the development of the state and education over the past 30 years, its biggest challenges have been navigating change (Broks 2000; Blūma 2016) and the search for a national identity. After Latvia has regained its independence, the whole education system was in turmoil, as the process of change in education can be slow and controversial, as educators, as well as society more widely, are not always ready or keen to learn from historical mistakes regarding reorganising the education system. As such, the general socio-political situation in post-Soviet Latvia can be characterised by the thought that 'teacher education and the development of professional knowledge and skills were based on pedagogy as a theoretical basis, however, teachers had a negative attitude towards Soviet-era ideological pedagogy. In addition, teachers were not ready to objectively evaluate the Soviet-era educational experience' (Blūma 2016, p. 20).

Along with these fundamental changes in the structure of the state, teachers had to acquire new skills, to embrace diversity and to think critically. During the Soviet time, the role of teachers and teacher educators had been more active than that of learners, as former were required to provide exclusively the 'right' answers and to teach 'correct' behaviour. Teachers were responsible for students' behaviour and within school hours leisure activities. Similarly, in teacher education, higher education institutions were responsible for the quality of pre-service and in-service teacher education (Underwood and Kowalczuk-Walędziak 2018; Peck 2000).

The turn of the century marked a rather challenging time in Latvia with regards to shaping state and education documents and policies. The National Development Plan: 2004–2006 pointed out the incompatibility of the existing education system with the national development goals. Indeed, the quality of higher and vocational education did not yet meet either national needs or European single labour market requirements. Furthermore, the network of education institutions was unbalanced, the number of institutions and the implemented programmes did not meet the demand of the labour market and the development of future skills. The financial resources allocated by the state were insignificant and there was a lack of adequate technological resources, and due to low salaries, the social prestige of the teaching profession was in decline. As a result, these weak and inflexible socio-economic conditions caused a shortage of qualified education professionals, thus negatively affecting the development of newly independent Latvia as a whole (Minister of Special Affairs in Cooperation with International Financial Institutions, 2001; National Development Plan: 2004–2006). Hálasz (2015) argues that the adoption of a lifelong approach to learning has been a major driver in strengthening the role of education in social and economic development, though further efforts are still needed to translate this approach into coherent and effective national policies.

Subsequently, the beginning of the twenty-first century can be considered a time of searching for new approaches and paradigms—identifying and facilitating positive changes in terms of both general quality of life and the education sector was the dual task at the heart of Latvia's contemporary development (Broks 2000, p. 107). Since 2000, new ideas have been integrated into the field of education, and teacher education in particular, including: action research, inclusive approaches, intercultural education, values education, and education for sustainable development. In this shift towards interculturalism and inclusivity, a new aspect has been introduced to the role of the teacher—being a responsible citizen and facilitator of change—and, for teachers in Latvia, involvement in the international community of educators and researchers has helped them to envision themselves as global citizens too.

Officially founded in 1945, UNESCO has long been one of the loudest agencies advocating for global citizenship. Over many decades, these efforts have been strengthened by those of its parent organisation, the United Nations, with a recent culmination in 2015 when the sustainable development goals (SDGs), along with their targets and indicators, were adopted. A few years later, in 2018, the Organisation for Economic Co-operation and Development (OECD) tangibly committed to prioritising global citizenship education (GCE) through its Programme for International Student Assessment (PISA). Both the UN and the OECD have highlighted that education has a crucial role in ensuring global citizenship competence and achieving SDGs.

The Chair of UNESCO's UNITWIN international partnership project at Daugavpils University (DU), Professor Ilga Salīte, notes that two significant stages define teacher education in Latvia since 2000. Firstly, she identifies the five years prior to the UN Decade of Education for Sustainable Development (which itself spanned 2005–2014) when the UNITWIN Chair from Toronto University and the team from DU implemented participatory action research for the reorientation of teacher education towards the aim of sustainable development. Secondly, Salīte identifies the subsequent official UN Decade, when scientific discussions, seminars, and international research initiatives continued providing an open, international network for researchers and leaders in sustainable education from different countries of the world, such as Finland, Canada, Germany, and Australia. Currently, the main work of the UNESCO Chair is based on publishing scholarly journals on teacher education and sustainability, as well as international cooperation.

Thus, networking and cooperation across different fields is a challenge for future teacher education. To find the professional ground in its diversity and to learn together by understanding and becoming a global citizen and acting locally and responsibly, teachers' understanding and experience in the field of global education is crucially important, not only to know but also to act in a civilly responsible way. Global education can be defined and conceptualised from different intellectual perspectives, for example, those of: globalism, internationalism, transnationalism, cosmopolitanism, post-colonialism, and indigeneity. They are anchored in diverse core concepts, such as: justice, equity, diversity, identity and belonging, and sustainable development. Indeed, as Reimers (2020, p. 25) explains in his conceptualisation of global education, it comprises

> both practices guided by a set of purposes and approaches intentionally created to provide opportunities for students to develop global competences, and the theories that explain and inform those practices and their effects. Global competences encompass the knowledge, skills, and dispositions that help students develop, understand, and function in communities which are increasingly inter-

dependent with other communities around the world, and that provide a foundation for lifelong learning of what they need to participate, at high levels of functioning, in environments in continuous flux because of increasing global change.

Reimers highlights the goal of nurturing learners who are able to function at a high level in time of global change, and, indeed, one of the key tasks of teacher education is not only to provide information but also to develop competences which will be useful to the individual throughout their life. The results of the research project, MYPLACE, carried out from 2012 to 2013 studied the phenomenon of youth civic participation and confirmed the low political engagement of young people already mentioned in previous studies (e.g. Mieriņa 2015). Correspondingly, in the domain of teacher education, Šteinberga's 2019 monograph on teachers' professional identity concludes that many social problems could be better addressed if teachers' civic participation increased. With this in mind, it can be argued that the teacher is not only an agent of change but also a guide and a leader to the young people in their care. Thus, in summary, with global citizenship as a key competence for pupils and teachers alike, there is a need to study teachers' professional activity and identity through the multi-faceted prisms of, for instance, professional philosophy, professional knowledge, civic attitude and professional interaction, as well as the socio-economic status of the profession more broadly.

Teacher Education over the Past Three Decades in Light of Global Trends

After the collapse of the Soviet Union and its central planning system, beginning in 1988, Latvia experienced a transition period and underwent many challenges in the areas of economy, society, politics, and education. Indeed, such problems as social inequality, poverty, and economic instability influenced the country's education system and the teacher training process, 'form[ing] the context for the transformations of the higher education sector in Latvia after 1990' (Mhamed et al. 2018, p. 263). Simultaneously, until the end of the 1990s, the process of cultural change and the rise of multiculturalism in education became sensitive and significant issues (Silova 2006). As the national identity of the state was gradually formed towards including Latvia becoming a member of the European Union which, upon accomplishment in 2004, opened the country's access to the internationalisation and globalisation of higher education (Kaša and Mhamed 2013), this gave way to the immediate translation of many new ideas and practices from elsewhere in Europe and around the world—often without a deep understanding of their impact on Latvia's overall education system, including teacher training.

After Latvia regained independence in 1991, higher education became more democratic and national higher education reforms unfolded in line with the Bologna process—which started in 1999 and aimed at creating a European Higher Education Area (EHEA) with academic mobility (Štefenhagena 2012). In line with the development of lifelong learning, the average age of the student population has increased. Collectively and individually, these contemporary shifts in Latvia's education sector have enriched students' communication and cooperation skills, plus contributed to the development of pre-service and in-service teachers' critical thinking skills so significant for educating responsible and engaged citizens (UNESCO 2014, 2015).

With regard to teacher education in particular, in this context of 1990s globalisation, a significant challenge for study programmes was to move to a student-centred approach. This meant changing the educational paradigm, by shifting focus away from teacher activities (i.e. teaching, educating, developing, shaping, and influencing) and towards students' responsibility for their own learning and growth, active learning, cooperation, and development. As was emphasised in the 2001 OECD report, teacher training in Latvia faced many problems in both vocational and non-vocational settings, such as a lack of link between the training itself and the everyday reality of the school work environment; teachers and trainers having little to no opportunities for in-service training via companies; and lack of access to new technologies, hampering the development of digital literacy in education. However, the further development of innovative teacher training strategies, as well as the establishment of cooperation with teachers in neighbouring countries—then, later, in other European countries further afield—fostered students' and teachers' interest and participation in a range of local, national, and international initiatives and projects.

In the Latvian context, DU has a strong track record of teacher training, and, in recent decades, the reorientation of education towards sustainability was addressed at all levels of teacher education by the Faculty of Education and Management. Furthermore, the emphases placed on reorienting programmes towards sustainable development have been much more pronounced than at other Latvian universities. In fact, in reorienting formal teacher education became the key element in the development of a new generation of education professionals committed to education for sustainable development (ESD) in the first decade of the twenty-first century. As such, formal and non-formal educational programmes were designed to integrate ESD, including a wide set of topics such as: holistic education; the impact of globalisation processes on education; the challenges of globalisation; global and local perspectives; human rights; the media; interculturalism; consumer education; the interconnection of tradition and innovation; spiritual intelligence; and engaging teachers in educational action research (Kravale-Pauliņa and Oļehnoviča 2015; Iliško 2016; Laine 2016; Fedosejeva et al. 2018; Kowalczuk-Walędziak 2019). Correspondingly, pre-service and in-service teachers were educated to become 'sustainability change agents' for achieving SDGs in their sector (Iliško et al. 2011), and discussions were promoted around the concepts of social and environmental awareness; holistic approaches to teaching and learning; and responsible, democratic cooperation in education and ethics. Both in tandem with and beyond these discussions, the university implemented some key initiatives, including: the foundation of the Institute of Sustainable Education; the establishment of scholarly journals, such as the *Journal of Teacher Education for Sustainability* and *Discourse and Communication for Sustainable Education* (Pipere et al. 2015; Pipere 2019; Salīte et al. 2020); the establishment of the Earth Charter Centre for ESD; the organisation of annual conferences about sustainable development, culture, and education issues; and involvement in the UNESCO global teacher education network. Indeed, as Belousa and Mičule (2007, p. 161) highlight, DU has 'shown its commitment to be at the forefront of promoting processes of education for sustainable development on a regional and national level'.

Nonetheless, intercultural and global issues have been integrated into many teacher education programmes across Latvia's universities: the University of Liepaja (LiepU) (Liepājas Universitāte 2017), the University of Latvia (LU) (Latvijas Universitate 2018), and DU (Daugavpils Universitāte 2019). The master's in teaching at LU facilitates the cross-curricular competences underpinning ESD, namely: holistic thinking, envisioning change, and achieving transformation, as defined in the 2012 United Nations Economic Cooperation for Europe (UNECE) competence framework, *Learning for the Future: Competences in Education for Sustainable Development.* Indeed, it is expected that the graduates of this programme—teachers—would act as agents of change (Odina et al. 2013, p. 433). In a comparable vein, the DU doctoral study programme in pedagogy has a clear focus on and strategic goal of reorientating research towards sustainable development which aligns with priorities set out in *United Nations Decade of Education for Sustainable Development (2005–2014)* and the *Sustainable Development Strategy of Latvia until 2030 (Saeima of the Republic of Latvia,* 2010*). In both of these frameworks there is an emphasis on* the competences crucial for sustainable development, namely: critical thinking; problem-solving; creativity; initiative; and decision-making.

Iliško et al. (2017, p. 106) emphasise the need for sustainability competences in enabling students 'to participate in the societal process through […] sustainability issues', becoming agents of change themselves. Similarly, Zhukova (2018, p. 101) asserts that there is a need 'to improve the quality of general education in order to prepare students to be productive, successful, socially and environmentally responsible, independent, and confident members of global society'. In summation, Latvia's contemporary pre-service and in-service teacher education programmes locate teaching as a global profession—to fully serve which teachers should be educated for the future, not for the past, via being encouraged to think and act both locally and globally (Odina and Kuzmane 2013).

Description of Teacher Education

The Main Characteristics of Initial Teacher Education

From a global perspective, the changes influencing teacher education systems are related to accelerating social development, as well as the rapid increase in the capacities of science and production (Fadels et al. 2017; Šteinberga 2019). The perpetually shifting dynamics and uncertainties of these fundamental socio-economic processes often give rise to the criticism that teacher educators are unable to ensure the required quality of teacher education, with no changes made in the organisation of course content. However, analysing the quality of teacher education is a complex activity which must take into account not only the education provided, but the learner's own 'internal' potential, as well as the 'external' conditions in which their learning takes place. In turn, the outputs yielded by an education system are then evaluated in line with the social and personal expectations of pupils and their parents; the existing normative regulations; and the requirements of the labour market—moreover, each of these involved parties has its own priorities. At present, the concept of a successful education system centres on the requirement that students acquire knowledge, skills, and abilities which can be applied or transformed in the context of practical, real-life situations. This process is currently conceptualised in terms of competences, thus shifting the emphasis away from knowledge acquisition and towards competence acquisition (Oļehnoviča 2019).

The acquisition of global and civic transversal competences via teacher education programmes is currently set as a goal. However, the question of an adequate system for assessing its accomplishment remains debatable, as objective evaluation requires the long-term gathering of data and corresponding descriptive, multi-factor analysis of the cognitive and creative activity, as well as learning outcomes, underpinning competence development. Only with such a robust analytical process in place can the quality of teacher education be increased at both the quantitative and qualitative level. In Latvia, the scientific substantiation and development of such a measurement system commenced in 2019 with the Ministry of Education and Science national study: *Assessment of higher education students' competences and their development dynamics over the study period.* The dual goals of this study were to ensure the development of the locally-rooted and globally-aware human capital necessary for the development of an inclusive, active, civic, and knowledge-based society in Latvia's economy and, correspondingly, to improve the education quality monitoring system (IZM 2013).

Based on the competence approach, in September 2020, the new state basic education standard (in Latvian: *Noteikumi par valsts pamatizglītības standartu un pamatizglītības programmu paraugiem* 2018) and the state general secondary education standard (in Latvian: *Noteikumi par valsts vispārējās vidējās izglītības standartu un vispārējās vidējās izglītības programmu paraugiem* 2019) were implemented for Grades 1, 4, 7, and 10. Contemporary competence-based education focuses on the development of the key competences and transversal competences necessary for personality development, as well as providing quality education at all levels (i.e. pre-school, primary, secondary, and higher education) and across all types (i.e. general education, vocational education, and academic education). The main pre-conditions for the successful implementation of competence-centred education are the training of teachers for obtaining an initial qualification and the creation of opportunities for professional development. The content of these new study programmes integrates modern scientific principles and industry-specific terminology. Additionally, these programmes aim to ensure that new teachers acquire both digital literacy and media literacy, developing these skill sets through direct experience within the mainstream learning process, rather than as a separate, discrete course. In the new study programmes this is necessary to ensure the acquisition of basic competences of inclusive education and special education for all future teachers. Study programmes should create mechanisms for obtaining regular feedback on the quality of studies from both students and educational institutions (IZM 2018b).

In order to overcome the fragmentation of teacher education programmes and to develop a transition into competence-based teacher education, four of Latvia's higher education institutions (HEIs)—Daugavpils University,

University of Liepaja, University of Latvia, and Rezekne Academy of Technologies (RAT)—have been working in cooperation with education experts from institutions such as National Centre for Education (NCE) and Mission Possible Foundation since late 2018 to design and implement new study programmes. The programmes cover pre-school teaching (i.e. two years full-time); primary teaching (i.e. a professional bachelor's undertaken over four years full-time); a four-year full-time professional bachelor's study programme for the training of primary and general secondary education teachers; and a one-year work environment-based second-level professional higher education programme based on a previously obtained academic bachelor's or master's degree. Based on the teaching profession standard defined by the National Centre for Education (NCE), graduates will obtain their qualification in accordance with the duration of their studies—that is at either the fifth or sixth level of the Latvian Qualifications Framework, which is aligned with the European Qualifications Framework. Furthermore, this restructuring of teacher education included designing a new, work-based study programme for obtaining a teaching qualification after graduating in another field.

Since the 2020/2021 academic year, new teacher education system has been approbated in Latvian higher education institutions in order to make teacher education more qualitative and flexible, specifically in terms of responding and adapting quickly to labour market requirements and technological developments, via providing appropriate opportunities for further education and professional development. This conceptual model envisages two options for obtaining a professional teaching qualification: one is a four-year bachelor's programme for those applicants who choose to become teachers following their secondary education, and the other is a one-year professional programme for those applicants who have obtained a degree in another field.

Admission of students to bachelor's teacher study programmes takes place in accordance with Section 46, Paragraph 3 of the Law on Higher Education Institutions and is based on the results of centralised examinations. However, these results do not fully reflect applicants' readiness and motivation for pedagogical studies. As an additional admission criterion for the programmes, an entrance examination was set for the 2020/2021 academic year, in which the applicant's professional suitability for the teaching profession, motivation to study on programme, as well as any profession-relevant previous skills and experience were assessed. The aim of the entrance examination is to uphold criteria which aid the selection of the applicants most likely to become highly qualified and motivated teachers, as well as to increase appeal and prestige of the teacher's profession on a societal level.

Another significant initiative implemented in 2020 by Latvia's HEIs—in cooperation with the Mission Possible Foundation and the Ministry of Education and Science (MES)—is the development of a new second-level professional study programme, as well as the training of 100 professionals (who already have a degree in a different field) in teaching and, thus, to address the lack of teachers, particularly in the field of languages, mathematics and science in schools. This is a work-based study programme which offers the unique opportunity to simultaneously study at a university and work in a school which is especially important for the Latvian economy, as it ensures the faster entry of qualified specialists into the labour market—moreover, facilitating a new opportunity for professionals to reroute their careers into teaching and acquire pedagogical competence under the guidance of highly qualified teaching staff in just one year. This creates advantages to acquire the specifics of a teacher's work while working at school, combining the knowledge gained at university with examples from the educational environment for the Latvian teacher education system in the context of the European Education Area.

This work-based approach to teacher training is underpinned by the following main principles and components: (1) cooperation between public and non-governmental sectors (e.g. the Mission Possible Foundation and academia); (2) unified communication and selection procedures which are provided by the Mission Possible Foundation for the universities on the basis of a delegation from the Ministry of Education and Science within the framework of the project 'Teaching power'; (3) the study places financed by the Latvian state budget only; (4) the Ministry of Education and Science annually calculates the costs for one study place and allocates the basic financing of the study places to higher education institutions; (5) a unified identification of educational institutions and available vacancies for teachers in Latvia; (6) a unified, nation-wide study programme; (7) additional support for early career teachers; and (8) a common approach to the collection of quantitative and qualitative data for the Mission Possible Foundation by collecting data within the framework of the project 'Teaching power' (IZM 2020a, p. 12). Furthermore, encompassing the specific learning outcomes and competences to be acquired, each student's practice is supervised and evaluated both by a lecturer at the higher education institution, and by a practice supervisor and mentor at the education institution, the latter of whom is to be selected from among the best professionals in the field.

Until now, the strategy for attracting prospective students has mainly centred on marketing Latvia's higher education institutions, not the actual pedagogical education itself. Such an approach did not provide clearly defined entrance criteria or facilitate the selection of the most knowledgeable and motivated candidates suited to pedagogical studies—instead, remaining oriented towards filling the universities' study places for the start of term. The Ministry of Education and Science emphasised that the need to attract applicants better suited to the teaching profession is growing day by day, especially in the context of the newest education reforms by performing a special selection of applicants for universities, which takes place in three rounds and is carried out by the Mission Possible Foundation. Therefore, it is important that the programmes have a sufficient number of suitable applicants and that teacher training programmes are based on unified student selection criteria based on the analysis of the candidate's knowledge and skills, as well as the motivation and professional qualities of the prospective teacher. The most suitable candidates for the teaching career are those who would make a significant contribution to the development of the human capital and national economy in Latvia (IZM 2020a).

The selection of students for the one-year study programme for the academic year 2020/2021 was carried out centrally by the Mission Possible Foundation, which set higher admission quality criteria for the potential students in terms of skills and competences, by creating a three-round selection for 100 study places for more than 600 applicants, of whom 99 students began work-based studies at the University of Latvia, Daugavpils University, and the University of Liepaja. In parallel with their studies, the students started working in schools as teachers for 14 to 21 hours per week. Going forwards, in order to optimise the application system, the Ministry of Education and Science plans to develop and test a teacher supply and demand forecasting tool.

The content of Latvia's new teacher education programmes is linked to the new national curriculum framework for the acquisition of competences. The term 'competence' is understood as the ability of an individual to apply knowledge and skills; express attitudes in a complex way; and solve problems in real-life situations—all within a variety of specific contexts, that is education, work, personal, or socio-political. The term 'mastery' (also termed 'literacy') is used as a synonym for competence, which consists of three key elements: (1) values and virtues, (2) transversal or cross-curricular skills, and (3) understanding and basic skills in seven study areas—language; society and civics; cultural awareness and self-expression via art; natural sciences; mathematics; technology; and health and physical activity. Indeed, any true understanding of a fundamental concept, such as power in the social and civic spheres, will require the input of several subjects or even fields of study (Namsone 2018). Thus, it is expected that pre-service teachers will acquire global civics competence during their own studies, especially in correlation to such values or constructs as life, human dignity, freedom, family, marriage, work, nature, culture, the Latvian language, and the Latvian state—all by developing an evaluative attitude, as well as a sense of responsibility for oneself and one's actions. As such this competence will provide a basis for teachers' richer understandings of the concepts of global citizenship, and for pre-service and in-service teachers to be actively involved in the development of both local and global communities. Concretely, this emphasis on political literacy means that students of teaching are expected to take an active civic position (Kravale-Pauliņa and Oļehnoviča 2015; Iliško 2017; Kravale-Pauliņa et al. 2018). However, such ambitious goals call into question whether or not the Latvian education system has the capacity to achieve such results.

Ultimately, with the introduction of the new teacher education system and education standards in general education, policy-makers in Latvia should create a vision which incorporates learning from both successes and challenges. Indeed, an open dialogue between teachers, professional associations, teacher educators, students, parents, local community, and the non-governmental sector is a compulsory element of learning. Furthermore, it is important to assess the scope of the planned reforms and their impact on the sector over time, as education experts warn that, 'when trying to change a large entity, such as the education system as a whole, we need to understand that not all the necessary changes will happen right away' (Fadels et al. 2017).

The processes of teacher education and pedagogical activity fundamentally require self-reflection, so an important requirement of Latvia's new study programmes is for teachers to develop their pedagogical competence to such an extent that they not only ensure the student's learning but also develop their own ability to solve problems, by enhancing their skills in: (1) contemporary tools and technologies; (2) interpersonal relationships; (3) navigating ethical norms; (4) evaluating personal actions; (5) fulfilling the social role of a citizen; (6) implementing the social role of a family member; (7) choosing a profession and evaluating one's degree of readiness for those choices; (8) self-determination; (9) choosing a lifestyle; and (10) choosing ways to resolve conflicts (Oļehnoviča 2019).

However, if Latvia's education reformers planners fail to assess—in a timely and objective manner—all of the risks which could significantly affect the quality of teacher education and general secondary education in the near future, the gap may widen between the desired and existing professional activities of education professionals, teacher educators, and prospective teachers. In turn, this could potentially increase frustrations in the education profession, as well as create an intellectual and emotional counteraction to the planned innovation process.

The Main Characteristics of Teacher Professional Development

As mentioned earlier, Latvia has undergone many changes in political, social, economic spheres, as well as in teacher education over the past 30 years. Data from the European Commission's European Network on Teacher Education Policy (ENTEP) indicated that understandings of the concept of 'teaching well in general' and the concept of the 'European teacher in the 21st century' have become more significant. The core idea here is that a 'European teacher' should have the same skills and competences that every good teacher has: extensive knowledge of their subject; skills that enable them to teach success-fully; creativity; the capacity to be a mentor in the learning process; and the ability to motivate the learner to succeed in the subject. In Latvia, the MES also developed suggestions for teacher education and in-service training, stat-ing that public understandings of modern and future-oriented educational content should be changed (IZM 2006b).

The *Guidelines for the Development of Education* 2007–2013, 2014–2020, and 2021–2027 show that the development of education in Latvia has been planned in accordance with the processes taking place within the European Union, and by looking for the solutions to education problems on a national scale. The 2007–2013 guidelines took into account the goals and recommen-dations set out in the Lisbon Education Strategy, including those central to the creation of the European Higher Education Area (launched in 2010, on the tenth anniversary of the commencement of the Bologna Process). Furthermore, the 2007–2013 guidelines incorporated the experience of higher education in Europe and improvements across all areas, namely: teacher education; key competences; efficiency of investment; learning of a language; lifelong learning; flexibility of systems; employment of higher edu-cation graduates; and the establishment of a transparent and easily compara-ble qualification structure, in order to make education more broadly accessible, implementing the European School for All guidelines (IZM 2006a).

In order to achieve the goals set out in the *Guidelines for the Development of Education* for 2014–2020 (IZM 2014), it is essential to implement in-depth research on a national level in order to identify the problems and most effec-tive solutions for developing and implementing a support system for teachers and pedagogical assistants. The social partners (e.g. employers and trade union authorities) highlight that teacher education should pay more attention to working with different audiences—that is children with different needs. With this goal in mind, educators need to be able to work with children via diverse methods and the use of technologies, thus ensuring that each child has the opportunity to work at their own pace and to achieve positive results.

The development and improvement of teachers' professional competence is determined by the No. 569 Cabinet of Ministers' *Regulations regarding required education and professional qualification, and development of teachers' professional competences* (in Latvian: *Noteikumi par pedagogiem nepieciešamo izglītību un profesionālo kvalifikāciju un pedagogu profesionālās kompetences pilnveides kārtību* 2018). According to the Regulations, general, professional, and informal education teachers are responsible for the improvement of their own professional competence—investing at least 36 hours over three years, planned in cooperation with the head of their education institution. Higher education teachers are entitled to work outwith this improvement schedule until three years after being certified. Their professional competence development programme will include one of the following topics. The first topic is teachers' general competences: that is innovations and development trends in education; upbringing issues; improvement of civic attitudes; promotion of qualitative, creative pedagogical activity; implementing pedagogical processes according to each students' individual needs; future learning content for promoting future competences; sustainable development and inclusive education; protection of children's rights; health and safety; and recognition and prevention of violence against children and domestic violence. The second topic is educational content and didactics: that is choice of teaching strategies and methods, including literacy; thinking processes; promotion of creativity and innovation; didactic models; traditional, multidisciplinary, and interdisciplinary learning processes; understanding of the concept of competence and transversal skills; innovations in subject and content, and methodology of the subject/field; information and communication technology skills in a modern education environment. The third topic is education management: that is the purposeful, result-oriented organisation of education processes and the implementation of pedagogical processes focused on professional cooperation; leadership; financial skills; administration; school management (including change management); education quality monitoring; and personnel management.

In July 2020, the MES opened public consultation on the draft of education development guidelines for 2021–2027: *Future Skills for the Society of the Future*. The guidelines emphasise that the overarching goal of education development is to provide quality education opportunities to all Latvian residents, in order to promote the growth and realisation of their potential throughout their lives, as well as to expand their ability to change and manage constant socio-economic flux. Objectives have been identified for the implementation of this goal: highly qualified, competent, and excellence-oriented teachers and academic staff; a modern, high-quality education offer focused on the development of skills highly valued in the labour market; support for the growth of all; and sustainable and efficient management of the education system and resources (IZM 2020b).

This vision for the future of Latvia's education sector is characterised by an individualised, personalised approach to education; a balanced set of skills relevant for people's future needs; transformation of education institutions' roles; and a complex education management system. Furthermore, this document identifies key issues that should be prioritised in the next seven years, envisioning that—through strengthening lifelong learning opportunities and developing skills, attitudes, and knowledge—future Latvian society will respond pro-actively to future contexts and challenges. However, these challenges are simultaneously best with behavioural, structural, technological, economic, and labour market aspects. In fact, they betray the assumption that education should serve a technologically advanced economy by providing a highly educated workforce.

The content of the guidelines—including key challenges, objectives, education policy outcomes, and outcome indicators—highlight that economic factors dominate this vision, whereas the social, personal, and emotional purposes of education have either become peripheral or subordinate. Efficiency, accountability, and quality in the context of education are all redefined in market terms, indicating that, for policy-makers, neoliberalism is regarded as the 'common sense' ideology which should drive national education policy for the next seven years.

Education should be centred on the primary purpose of sustaining the development of whole human beings, not creating a workforce—creating spaces for critical citizenship and encouraging social learning processes which enable learners to contribute to sustainable development (UNECE 2012). However, without state support, education reform in these directions will come neither from technological change nor from civic action and voluntary initiatives alone. Instead, teachers need to work with traditional socio-political actors—political parties, trade unions, and cooperative movements—and participate actively in reshaping the direction of education development (Jones 2019). These partnerships have the potential to mitigate neo-liberal agendas and practices in both teaching and learning (Holen et al. 2021). Indeed, what is needed by educators as citizens is an ongoing critical engagement with neoliberalism as part of ongoing efforts to pro-actively and concretely make education more inclusive for a wider range of learners.

In mitigating neoliberalism via education, greater efforts need to be made towards integrating sustainability as a whole-institution approach in educating responsible global citizens. Central to this pursuit of sustainability is the openness of teacher education, in terms of: purpose (reorientation from labour market to civil society); focus (from disciplines and curricula to community); outcomes (from cognitive to holistic); teaching approaches and methods (from lecturing to self-regulating group work); resources (from texts to good practices, life stories, and envisioning); and learning environment (from classrooms to community spaces). These essential shifts can be ensured recognising the wealth of civil society initiatives, then providing the space for them within the domain of teacher education.

Global Citizenship Education Partnership

Civil Society Initiatives to Integrate Global Citizenship Education into Formal Teacher Education

Global citizenship education (GCE) has a clear link with formal education. Yet, civil society organisations (CSOs) with experience in global development, sustainable development, solidarity, peace, and development cooperation are the main contributors to the introduction and furthering of GCE in Latvia, mainly because of their involvement in various global initiatives, activities, and networks. As Hartmeyer and Wegimont (2015, p. 57) highlight, many CSOs work in the field of GCE. Baltic regional seminars on global education illustrate both the rich experience and practical success of Latvian non-governmental organisations (NGOs) in realising GCE-related projects (North-South Centre and LAPAS 2014; North-South Centre and Eesti People to People 2016). As global citizenship transcends geographical, national, cultural, and political borders and is shaped around the human nature, civil society initiatives have broadened the perimeters of the education environment, encouraging educators and students to step beyond their institutions and to recognise their connection to local communities.

Civil society organisations shaping GCE and raising awareness of global issues are shaped by their membership of the Latvian Platform for Development Cooperation (LAPAS)—established in 2004 and now comprising 30 member organisations, plus a GCE working group. Since the beginning of GCE initiatives in Latvia, CSOs have been actively involved in two main ways: firstly, awareness-raising about global and development cooperation issues via public campaigns, roundtable discussions, stakeholder networking and so on; secondly, providing courses and programmes that facilitate knowledge acquisition, skill and attitude development, and value-orientation connected to the global dimension.

Projects and campaigns are the main types of civil society initiatives encouraging the integration of GCE into formal teacher education, as well as shaping conceptual and methodological foundations for further GCE development. A rich contribution to these endeavours comes from the DEAR projects of the EC EuropeAid programme that aim to raise awareness around: responsible consumption; development journalism; sustainable development goals; the climate crisis; tax justice abuse; economic models of solidarity; and so on—targeting education institutions, municipalities, journalists, households, and civil society activists. The first step into structuring the global citizenship field was a 2007 initiative by LAPAS to create the national, multi-stakeholder *Development Education Policy 2008–2015*, with the aim of coordinating public and civic GCE initiatives across both formal and informal sectors. Another remarkable LAPAS initiative was the 2008 study on GCE in the context of national educational standards and curricula, highlighting that, although GCE topics were present on the curriculum, teachers lacked the necessary corresponding pedagogical methodologies and teaching materials. The approach most widely used by formal education is informing students and promoting their understanding, less attention is paid to students' attitude development, and nearly absent from learning experience is students' participation and involvement in the local community. A subsequent study about GCE was conducted by the Education Development Centre describing the presence of the global dimension in social science subjects, as well as the challenges and opportunities found in implementing GCE (IAC 2013a). Thus, in general, the implementation of GCE projects in Latvia has encouraged both the creation and adaptation of a variety of education resources, including in the field of teacher education.

Latvia's first national conference on GCE was organised in 2009 by LAPAS with the support of the Council of Europe's North-South Centre. It provided the first public opportunity to reflect on existing national priorities, achievements, and challenges in the field of GCE, with the main conclusion being that activities sustained by LAPAS were underpinned by hopes that the GCE field in Latvia would be legally acknowledged. However, the *Development Education Policy 2008–2015* was never officially adopted by the government.

Nonetheless, it has served as a key conceptual support for global educators and is used in the non-governmental sector to guide GCE activities.

A further significant initiative in strengthening multi-stakeholders' participation in GCE and the development of cooperation between formal educators and NGOs was the 2013 *NGO Capacity Strengthening in the Process of Policy Development in Development Cooperation and Development Education.* This survey of NGOs identified the most common keywords used by LAPAS members to characterise GCE discourse and experience are: 'glocalisation'; old and new paradigms of development; education for sustainable development; environmental sustainability; intercultural diversity; migration; social justice; fair trade; poverty reduction; cooperation culture; education in a multicultural and multilingual society; and Millennium Development Goals (MDGs) and beyond MDGs (IAC 2013b, c).

The subsequent integration of GCE into formal teacher education has been ensured by the partnership between UNESCO Latvian National Commission and the HEIs that provide teacher education in Latvia. The most successful initiatives in this regard have been the global education weeks—namely *Food security on local and global levels* (2014), *Make equality real* (2015), *You harvest what you plant* (2016), *My world depends on us* (2017), *The world is changing— what about us?* (2018), *Wake Up! This is the final call for the climate* (2019)— and the global action, *The World's Largest Lesson* (2015–2020). This partnership between UNESCO and Latvia's HEIs also provides opportunities to participate in scientific conferences, seminars, and workshops. The further cooperation with the MES in planning the Global Education Enhancement and Innovation Programme and implementing global education projects supported by the Global Education Network Europe (GENE) can be noted as key outcomes of this partnership. Although the current GCE practices are mainly related to young people, teachers, and school administration, LAPAS is now reaching out to the field of formal education through local, community-level initiatives.

Civil society organisations that contribute to GCE are strengthening their capacity through involvement in several global networks. The most significant of these is the European Council North-South Centre (NSC) global education week network. In cooperation with the NSC, two main events are implemented on a national level by LAPAS: annual Baltic region global education meetings, plus the EU and EC programme, *iLEGEND II: Intercultural Learning Exchange through Global Education, Networking and Dialogue (2019–2022).* Latvian CSOs with LAPAS membership are also represented in the European Confederation of Relief and Development NGOs (CONCORD), the Global Alliance of Civil Society Organisations and

Activists (CIVICUS), the Affinity Group of National Associations (AGNA) Network, and the committees of the EC EuropeAid programme DEAR project.

In recent years, the state of GCE in Latvia has been increasingly evaluated in the context of the EU level. Tarozzi and Inguaggiato (2018, p. 14) highlight that GCE partnership, coordinated by LAPAS, ensures a strategic approach to development of global education policy and practices. They observe that GCE in Latvia is rich and varied, with initiatives encompassing national and global activities, research-based activities, and public education events, such as conferences, exhibitions, and campaigns (LAPAS 2018b, 2019)—collectively and individually raising awareness about global social, environmental, and economic challenges and intercultural skill development. Mainly these are short-term or long-term courses and education programmes serving as compensatory activities to cover urgent issues missing in formal—pre-school, school, and teacher training—education. Here GCE has been ensured by actualisation of global challenges, interactive environment, ICT use, guest speakers, etc. The perspective can be marked out as 'a continuum with the awareness-raising approach as one point, and trans-formative global education experiences as a point on the other side of the continuum' (Saleniece 2018, p. 16).

The current practice of the GCE can be characterised by the combination of different educational approaches. Belousa (2016, p. 146) highlights the main education approaches, that introduce the dimension of global citizenship into teacher education: development education, education for sustainable development, intercultural education, human rights education, inclusive education, media education, consumerism education, and peace education. Yet, as the formal education legislation is rather generalised and allows flexible implementation of different GCE topics, regrettably not many of them are widely recognised and applied by educators in practice. Thus, there is a crucial need for richer and more critical integration of GCE in teacher education study programmes (Belousa 2016, p. 147).

In recent years Latvia's teacher education sector has demonstrated noteworthy inter-organisational cooperation (Tarozzi and Inguaggiato 2018, p. 14). Following interaction between stakeholders from the Ministry of Foreign Affairs, the Ministry of Education and Science, LAPAS, UNESCO Latvian National Commission, and the parliament, the government approved the Ministry of Education and Science report: *On Commitment of Additional State Budget Commitments for the Implementation of the Global Education Enhancement and Innovation Program Financial Instrument in Latvia*, authorising the implementation of the Global Education Network in Europe (GENE)

Increase Programme and introducing its budget instrument. The goal of this programme is to enrich formal and non-formal education practice with issues of civic responsibility, understanding of global processes, and active participation in building a just, inclusive, and sustainable society. The Ministry of Education and Science has stated that this programme is important for the gradual introduction of GCE in curricula at pre-primary, primary, and secondary levels, and it will support the curriculum reform, as social competences related solidarity, equality, inclusion, and cooperation are among the key values of the new curriculum (IZM 2018a, p. 1). As a result, formal education teachers in cooperation with non-formal global educators implemented several global citizenship education projects and developed several global education resources for formal and non-formal educators.

Towards Partnerships for Global Citizenship Education

As summarised earlier, global education partnerships are sustainable tools which have encouraged the implementation of global citizenship activities at both local and national levels in Latvia. Involvement in these types of partnership can be characterised as a value-based process of engagement that manifests across a broad range of practices. In turn, both the theoretical concept and the tangible practice of such partnerships have been increasingly integrated into the field teacher education, in line with the democratisation of the mission and values of education institutions (Holen et al. 2021). The fundamental spectrum of possibility for the forms, areas, and implementation of these partnerships (Bovill 2019) challenge normative foundations of the field of education and enrich teacher education through the involvement of diverse players and contexts, thus even mitigating neo-liberal trends in teacher education, such as commodification of education, capitalist measures of student achievement to mention but a few.

Sustained partnerships can be shaped by the involvement of multiple stakeholders that represent all sectors: the state, local governments or municipalities, non-governmental organisations, and the private sector. The key idea is that the main stakeholders—that is UNESCO LNC, LAPAS, and the State Education Quality Service, an institution under the supervision of the MES—understand GCE and their role as complementary (IIC 2019), thus providing a firm foundation for the GCE partnership.

Considering that the aforementioned grouping of stakeholders by sector is a largely neutral process, a form of grouping that both highlights the diversity of stakeholders and indicates the attitudes of stakeholders is applied. The stakeholder grouping has been created based on 'identification' and 'interest', as outlined in Mendizabal's alignment, interest, and influence matrix (2010). With regard to 'identification' the matrix provides a means to define the group's identification with teacher education objectives and conceptual settings (high or low degree of identification). With regards to 'interest' the matrix provides a means to measure the group's willingness or unwillingness to participate in teacher education activities and publicly express their support for the project. Thus, all stakeholders can be divided into four groups, each with its unique interests that shape its participation in the partnership (see Fig. 17.1):

Group A—has a high level of identification with the partnership's objectives, but a low level of interest in participating. The most successful way to involve this group is to take an interest in the partnership's goals and their role in modernising teacher education, improving teacher prestige, and implementing sustainable change, which in turn will generally increase the number of enthusiastic people supporting GCE.

Group B—has a high level of identification with the partnership's objectives and a high level of interest in participating. The most successful way to involve this group is to form a partnership to jointly achieve the partnership's goals. This group includes the most loyal supporters of teacher education, therefore holds significant potential in the development and implementation of new GCE initiatives.

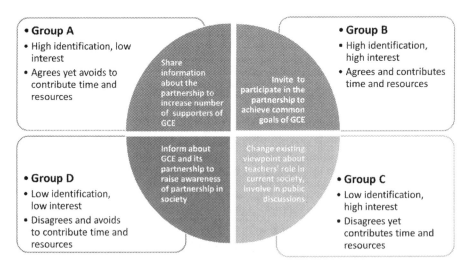

Fig. 17.1 Stakeholder grouping according to their interest and involvement in GCE

Group C—has a low level of identification with the partnership's objectives, but a high level of interest in participating. The most successful way to involve this group is to facilitate discussions to challenge and modify incomplete or negative perceptions of the stakeholders of this group about the global citizenship educator's role and the teaching profession. Representatives of this group are open to communicating and advocating the interests of GCE field.

Group D—has a low level of identification with the partnership's objectives and a low level of interest in participating. This is the most neutral group in relation to GCE, its goals, and its activities, therefore large-scale initiatives involving this group should not be planned. Instead, the most successful way to involve this group is to raise their awareness of the partnership's objectives in general.

This fundamental diversity of stakeholders raises a number of critical considerations in the process of ensuring the sustainability of a cross-sectoral education partnership in Latvia today. The most significant of these is the inclusivity of the partnership and its openness to educators and learners, and other key stakeholders of the sectors: the state, local governments or municipalities, non-governmental organisations, and the private sector: (Saleniece 2018, p. 36). Any partnership should be purposeful, and based on mutual agreements about goals, means, resources, and desired results. Partnership should be designed and executed in line with the profiles and needs of the stakeholders involved, plus the particular GCE purpose/s being targeted. These purposes are conceptualised as a tripartite structure by Biesta (2009, p. 33): qualification (i.e. competence building and knowledge acquisition with a view to being prepared for the job market); socialisation (i.e. the representation of different cultures and learning how to share common human values); and subjectification (i.e. a child learning to exist as a human subject in their own right, not simply as the subject of educational influences), the latter of which Franch (2020) refines as an 'approach centred on a political perspective grounded in social justice and the critical deconstruction of the dominant discourses that shape our understanding and actions'. With this 'critical deconstruction' in mind, perhaps, the use of the very terms 'global citizens' and 'global citizenship' should be clarified considering diverse and nuanced historical, cultural and political contexts of all stakeholders (Saleniece 2018, p. 36).

Cross-sectoral partnerships are also a tool for bridging the gaps between the global and the local, both within and outwith the field of education. Indeed, the process of glocalisation can help create links between global issues and development, and the everyday lives and activities of local communities. This methodology enriches local experience that is characteristic for a particular local Latvian context by reshaping local identities, products, and services of local importance; global experience that is comprehensive for the planet as a holistic entity by reshaping human presences and environments on a large scale to bring advantages to larger parts of the world; and glocal experience that implies relationships between the everyday local lives of people in different places across the globe (Belousa and Pastore 2015).

Latvia's current GCE partnerships can be evaluated in terms of their successes and challenges. The most significant strengths include: an experienced non-governmental sector, especially LAPAS organisations; active involvement of UNESCO LNC; and cooperation between the state and non-governmental sector, including the Ministry of Foreign Affairs and the Ministry of Education and Science. Furthermore, Latvia's GCE successes can also be characterised by the increased integration of global citizenship issues into in-service training seminars; the increased development of GCE information and learning tools available in Latvian; and the increased competence development of educators in the field of GCE (Belousa 2016; Saleniece 2018). However, the challenges that burden GCE in Latvia include: slow progress in moving from the random in-service training of teachers to a systematic and comprehensive integration of GCE into teacher education; the lack of a common database for GCE resources to be used by educators; and the lack of overall GCE evaluation on a national level.

Going forwards, GCE partnerships involving the participation of civil society organisations, UNESCO LNC, and teacher educators from HEIs have huge potential in terms of updating teacher education to serve the needs of an increasingly international Latvia. Initiatives encouraged by existing partnerships have opened up several directions for future development, mainly with regard to the following key aspects of education: time, space, sources of information, learning, and the learner. Reconsidering time entails taking stock of current situations and co-designing visions of hopeful futures. Reconsidering space encourages shifting from individualistic, institution-based learning to communal, locally based learning whereby education institutions are embedded into local communities. Reconsidering the predominant sources of information used in education would create space for a shift towards using alternative sources of information (and inspiration), especially three-dimensional or visual ones, for example personal objects, visualisations, personal development, and change stories. Reconsidering learning means emphasising inductive and personalised approach in order to create a holistic view of personal learning by systemising and prioritising learning experiences, and creating new thematic categories. Lastly, reconsidering the learner necessitates perceiving both students and educators who are involved in formal, non-formal education or everyday learning as an active global citizen and an agent of change.

Current Tensions and Challenges in Teacher Education, Plus Implications for the Future Development of Teacher Education

At present, numerous crises—notably the pandemic—are exposing the need for changes in education, in Latvia and beyond. COVID-19 has radically changed the way that school pupils and university students learn, as well as the role of the educator in the learning process: the sudden closure of schools and universities triggered by the COVID-19 pandemic meant that they were forced to transfer to distance learning and to digitise their learning environment. However, any crisis is a unique opportunity for understanding how education could change in the future. As Heasly (2020, p. 97) asserts, by using respect, resilience, and responsibility for promoting and affirming decisions and actions addressing identifiable crises is enhanced by building a broad spectrum of questions which provide foundations for increased sustainability and securitability for our twenty-first-century world.

A challenge currently facing Latvia's higher education sector is to respond to the needs of today's generation, one, at least hypothetically, born with access to digital devices almost from birth (Chandron et al. 2018) and that requires a learning arrangement differently organised to the traditional one that was 'killed' by the virus. In moving towards these new arrangements of the future, many critical questions must be asked, including the following. Will the generation of teachers qualified under the pre-pandemic, traditional framework be able to maintain the quality of their teaching in a post-pandemic education sector, by both finding clear outcome measures and transforming notions of what quality of education means? On the other hand, by embracing and sustaining the recently accelerated digitisation of education, will Latvia's universities and schools be able to ensure equal education opportunities for all? Digitisation is a process underpinned by the same socio-economic fault lines as any other (modern) education reform Latvia has undergone. Therefore, education policy-makers will need to bear in mind material inequalities, for both students and educators, pertaining to factors such as:

access to devices and software; internet infrastructure and connection quality; digital literacy; socio-economic status; and access to pedagogical resources.

This shift to a new, competence-based approach will push Latvia's schools and higher education institutions to view themselves not as buildings with physical boundaries, but as open learning environments without boundaries (Darling-Hammond and Bransford 2005). Indeed, in line with the Ministry of Regional Development and Local Government's *Sustainable Development Strategy of Latvia until 2030* (2010) equal access to education and education system changes are among long-term priorities. In this process of removing traditional boundaries, education institutions should become open centres for learning and social networking, involving the engagement of all stakeholders—parents, teachers, and learners—as well as wider local communities, including entrepreneurs, industry representatives, and cross-sectoral associations. Furthermore, such outward-looking changes in education will create a smoother connection from school to job market. In turn, these cross-sectoral connections will alter the nature of teachers' work to a large degree, specifically as the traditional approach of teaching subjects as separate from each other will be gradually replaced by a more transdisciplinary learning mode.

By digitising the learning process, schools and universities will be able to provide a more interesting, interactive, and high-quality learning content in a virtual environment. The *National Development Plan* (NAP 2027, 2020) has set Latvia's medium-term priorities for education and science: innovation and higher education, inclusive education, improvement of study content, and developing the education sector in accordance with the trends in the labour market, thus ensuring an access to higher education. As part of the aforementioned national shift towards competency-based education, universities are required to implement digital transformations (learning to use new digital tools and platforms and to create digital content) and adopt innovative practice (make a transition to a student led and autonomous teaching)—as well as to continue the development of mixed (hybrid form of learning including online and face-to-face learning), online learning processes that, to a large extent, were fostered by educators' responses to the COVID-19 pandemic, including their own digital competence development. Among the *NAP 2027* (2020) strategic goals are: social trust; a decent income; and equal opportunities for all. In the context of education, the last of these translates into high-quality education for all, pro-actively including the demographics too often excluded—for instance, via xenophobia, as directed towards Latvia's Roma communities, or via restrictively narrow definitions of 'intelligence', as experienced by those who have additional support needs. Ultimately, a high-quality, pro-actively inclusive, and digitally accessible education is essential in the nurturing of global citizens who can assume an active role, on both local and global levels, in building a more inclusive, tolerant, and safe society.

For the future perspective of the Universities lies the task to educate global citizens who have knowledge and skills to participate in not just their local communities but global ones too. The *Maastricht Declaration—European Strategy Framework* (2015) conceptualises the global citizen as someone who understands the need for a change of current epistemology in envisioning possible futures which opens up the space for national and international debate and requires questioning, thus fostering such values as justice, equality, and human rights for all as necessary aspects in all strands of education and community life. The mandate for the universities is to educate global citizens who have an awareness of global issues and who are engaged in different initiatives in order to improve conditions of the local and global community (Suša 2019). In order for the education to be more globally open, as Franzenburg (2020, p. 22) asserts, education fundamentally cannot be understood as a national project, but as an international one through

> sharing experiences, interpretations, and visions across cultural borders, [education] combines local and global, past, present and future aspects of historical, religious, philosophical, social, political and other issues. This integrates them into a multidimensional, sustainable, interdisciplinary, and intergenerational project of transformation.

Therefore, education can be a vehicle which drives students of teacher education to

> navigate the complexities of global challenges without despair, to develop critical analyses that connect global systems with their local contexts, to experience a sense of interconnectedness, and to work together in ways that open up different possibilities for co-existence in the future. (Suša 2019, p. 23)

Universities should focus on training and preparing the citizens of tomorrow to live in an unpredictable future (e.g. climate crisis, migration, and diseases). Therefore, didactic reorientation refers not only to the renewal of higher education curricula, but also to fully rethinking and transforming teaching strategies and methods with a view to 'supporting the acquisition of competences that enable people to live and act in a sustainable way' in a holistic understanding of the term (Dannenberg and Grapentin 2016, p. 8).

In order for the future of GCE in Latvia to be a successful one, consideration must be given to the practical realities of implementing such a vision, particularly in terms of the people who will be largely responsible for manifesting it in practice: teachers. As such, key challenges for the country's field of teacher education are to diversify new study programmes and teacher professional development programmes, in terms of both their content and quality. Societal changes necessitate that teachers change with them, enriching the content of education and creating new approaches towards teaching. However, realistically, it must be acknowledged that not all people working in schools are readily able to meet these ever-shifting demands, so Latvia's education policy-makers face the pragmatic challenge of ensuring that professional development programmes—and the creation of a new professional support system—truly encompass and serve teachers' actual professional experience and needs. As such, ongoing, work-based learning, plus all kind of support from local authorities and communities are vital for the future development of Latvia's teacher education and, by extension, education across the board.

Every challenge that is experienced in teacher education has a global dimension. This is to say that even if a challenge experienced in the field does not seem overtly global, solutions and responses to it may be found by learning from the best practices all over the world that is reflected in the DU UNESCO Chair international journals (*Discourse and Communication for Sustainable Education* and *Journal of Teacher Education for Sustainability* by local and international scholars).

As outlined earlier, with the contemporary need for problem-solving in this era of plural, intersecting crises, there is a greater need for global competences than ever before. With GCE being the domain of scholarship and practice that facilitates the development of these competences, interest in GCE is growing beyond the domain of formal education: Latvia's non-formal and everyday education sectors also recognise the fundamental importance of GCE—for example in local community development (Belousa and Pastore 2015; LAPAS 2018a), in civil society strengthening (IAC 2013d; LAPAS 2018b, 2019), in youth work (*Attīstības un inovāciju mācību centrs* 2017; Garjāne et al. 2013), and in volunteering (JASMA 2015).

GCE is crucially important in Latvia's ongoing socio-economic recovery post-Sovietisation. One of the main findings of a recent study carried out by the national research programme, 'Innovation and Sustainable Development: Latvia's Post-Crisis Experience in a Global Context' (SUSTINNO), is that Latvia possesses a high level of social alienation, particularly civil and political alienation (*anomie*), which manifests itself in a lack of societal norms, clear convictions, or long-term goals and visions (Zobena and Felcis 2018). In general, such alienation is an extraordinary and abnormal situation that results from the weakening of social ties and identification with shared values, on both individual and community levels. Thus, in the ongoing process of recovering from the regime, civic and political alienation remain profound problems for today's Latvian society.

One of the most ready tools for reducing this civic alienation is GCE. Universities—and teacher education institutes and faculties in particular—are vital centres of education, innovation, and research for both local and global communities. However, the actual learning outcomes—the set of knowledge, skills, and competences that students acquire after successfully completing their study programme—are mostly achieved on university premises, where student teachers' newfound academic confidence is also characterised by a sense of intellectual superiority and alienation from the local community outwith the university. Mindful of this socio-economic stratification somewhat implicit in university teacher education, GCE can provide the tools to build bridges between education institutions, Latvian society, and the local community by bringing sustainability-oriented stakeholders together. Such connections can be formed as quadrilogues, promoting communication and structured cooperation between representatives of at least four stakeholders: governments, parliaments, regional and local authorities, and civil society organisations. Indeed, this is the approach which has been adopted by the Council of Europe in aiming to strengthen policy development and the implementation of GCE. Within quadrilogues, several dimensions of activity are crucial, the most important being an exchange of information and resources between different sectors and participation in GCE-related decision-making that ensures inclusion of all stakeholders, in turn elevating this participation to ownership of the common goals. Lastly, moving forwards to further development, it is important to enrich the GCE experience by integrating the achievements of all major sectors and stakeholders which, in turn, will yield best practices for integrating into teacher education.

Today's learners and, particularly, students of teacher education programmes, are the leaders of the immediate future, where arrogance and alienation have no place in decision-making. Thus, it is the fundamental responsibility of educators to promote sustainable development and active solidarity in future generations of teachers, in order to build a hopeful society, both locally and globally (UNESCO 2015). Educators in twenty-first-century Latvia should (re)build relationships with their local communities; integrate the meaningful experiences of other stakeholders in their teaching; and lead by example in upholding the well-being of their local communities and the cause of global sustainability. Ultimately, via Latvia's educators, GCE has the potential to build bridges: to raise public awareness about the interconnection of global issues and everyday life; to encourage civic participation in local, national, and global communities; and to cure civic and political alienation.

References

Attīstības un inovāciju mācību centrs. (2017). *Jauniešu pilsoniskās līdzdalības veicināšanas programma pilsoniskās kompetences veidošanā: Metodisks līdzeklis* [Youth Civic Participation Programme for the Development of Civic Competence: Methodic Aid]. Ogre.

Belousa, I. (2016). Latvia country policy analysis. In: *Global schools. Global citizenship education in Europe. A comparative study on education policies across 10 EU Countries* (pp. 134–149). Research deliverable issued within the European project "Global Schools", Trento, Italy: Provincia Autonoma di Trento. Retrieved from http://www.globalschools.education/Activities/Research/Research-report-1.

Belousa, I., and I. Mičule. (2007). Experience of the Institute of Sustainable Education. Faculty of Education and Management. In: M. Vilela and K. Corrigan (Eds.), *Good practices in education for sustainable development using the Earth Charter* (pp. 157–161), UNESCO Education for Sustainable Development in Action, Good Practices, No. 3. San Jose, Costa Rica. Retrieved from https://unesdoc.unesco.org/ark:/48223/pf0000217854.

Belousa, I., and A. Pastore. (2015). *Glokalizācijas metodoloģija glokalizācijas izpratnes bagātināšanai un glokālās pieredzes pilnveidei* [Glocalization methodology for enrichment of the understanding of glocalization and improvement of the glocal experience]. Rīga: LAPAS. Retrieved from https://lapas.lv/wp-content/uploads/2015/05/Gloka_06052015_LV.pdf.

Biesta, G. (2009). 'Good education in an age of measurement: On the need to reconnect with the question of purpose in education'. *Educational Assessment, Evaluation and Accountability,* 21 (1), 33–46.

Belousa, I., and S. Ūzuliņa. (2012). Teachers' view on social and emotional aspect of pedagogical competence. *Journal of Social Sciences,* 8(1), 159–165.

Blūma, D. (2016). *Skolotāju izglītība Latvijā paradigmu maiņas kontekstā (1991–2000)* [Teacher education in the context of paradigm shift in Latvia (1991–2000)]. Monogrāfijas sērija "Izglītības pētniecība Latvijā", Nr. 9. Rīga: LU PPMF Izglītības pētniecības institūts.

Bovill, C. (2019). Student–staff partnerships in learning and teaching: An overview of current practice and discourse. *Journal of Geography in Higher Education,* 43(4), 385–398.

Broks, A. (2000). *Izglītības sistemoloģija* [Systemology of education]. Rīga: RaKa.

Chankseliani, M., and I. Silova (Eds.). (2018). *Comparing post-socialist transformations. Purposes, policies, and practices in education.* Oxford: Symposium Books.

Chaudron, S., R. Di Gioia, and M. Gemo. (2018). *Young children (0–8) and digital technology, a qualitative study across Europe.* EUR 29070.

Council of Europe. (2019). iLEGEND II: Intercultural Learning Exchange through Global Education, Networking and Dialogue (2019–2022). Retrieved from https://www.coe.int/en/web/north-south-centre/ilegend.

Dannenberg, S., and T. Grapentin. (2016). Education for sustainable development—learning for transformation. The example of Germany. *Journal of Future Studies*, 20(3), 7–20.

Darling-Hammond, L., and J. Bransford (Eds.). (2005). *Preparing teachers for a changing world. What teachers should learn and able to do?* San Francisco, CA: Jossey-Bass.

Daugavpils Universitāte (DU). (2019). Studiju virziena "Izglītība, pedagoģija un sports" pašnovērtējuma ziņojums par 2018./2019. studiju gadu [Self-evaluation report of the study direction "Education, Pedagogy and Sport, 2018/2019]. Retrieved from https://du.lv/wp-cosntent/uploads/2020/04/Pasnovertejuma_Zinojums_2018_2019_Izglitiba-pedagogija-sports.pdf.

Fadels, Č., M. Bialika, and B. Trinlings. (2017). *Četru dimensiju izglītība: skolēnu panākumiem nepieciešamās kompetences* [Four-dimensional education: The competences learners need to succeed]. Lielvārde: Lielvārds.

Franch, S. (2020). Global citizenship education discourses in a province in northern Italy. *International Journal of Development Education and Global Learning*, 12(1), 21–36.

Franzenburg, G. (2020). Transforming paradigms of sustainable transcultural adult education. *Discourse and Communication for Sustainable Education*, 11, 16–25.

Fedosejeva, J., A. Boče, M. Romanova, Dz. Iliško, and O. Ivanova. (2018). Education for sustainable development: The choice of pedagogical approaches and methods for the implementation of pedagogical tasks in the Anthropocene age. *Journal of Teacher Education for Sustainability*, 20(1), 157–179.

Garjāne, I., L. Žubule, and N. Gudakova. (2013). *Brauksi līdzi? Re, kur FORMULA! Rokasgrāmata jauniešu līdzdalības veicināšanai* [Will you go with us? Look, where THE FORMULA is! Guide for promoting youth participation]. Rīga: Jaunatnes starptautisko programmu aģentūra.

Heasly, B. (2020). Towards an architecture for the teaching of sustainability and securitability. *Discourse and Communication for Sustainable Education*, 11(1), 91–105.

Hálasz, G. (2015). Education and social transformation in Central and Eastern Europe. *European Journal of Education*, 50(3), 350–371.

Hartmeyer, H., and L. Wegimont. (2015). *The state of global education in Europe*. Dublin: Global Education Network Europe, European Union.

Holen, R., P. Ashwin, P. Maassen, and B. Stensaker. (2021). Student partnership: exploring the dynamics in and between different conceptualizations. *Studies in Higher Education*. 46(12), 2726–2737.

IAC. (2013a). *Report on the study about development education aspects in social sciences*. Retrieved from http://www.globalaizglitiba.lv/assets/GlobalaIzglitiba/mateirli/Global-Dimension-A4-gramata2web.pdf.

IAC. (2013b). *Stratēģija NVO kapacitātes stiprināšanai attīstības sadarbības un attīstības izglītības jomās* [Strategy for strengthening NGO capacity for development cooperation and development education]. Retrieved from http://arhive.iac.edu.lv/assets/Uploads/Materiali/STRATEGIJAmaketsjauns.pdf.

IAC. (2013c). *Ceļvedis NVO kapacitātes stiprināšanai attīstības sadarbības un attīstības izglītības jomās* [Guide for strengthening NGO capacity for development cooperation and development education]. Retrieved from http://arhive.iac.edu.lv/assets/Uploads/Materiali/CELVEDIS09.09.2013.pdf.

IAC. (2013d). *Kopā kopjam savu kopienu: Latvijas vietējās kopienas organizāciju pilsoniskās līdzdalības veicināšanas pieredzes stāsti* [Together, for our Community: Stories of the Experience of Promoting Civic Participation of Latvian Local Community Organisations]. Rīga: IAC.

IIC. (2019). *Augstākā izglītība un ilgtspējīga attīstība: Krustpunkti un partnerības. IIC projekta "Globālā pilsoniskā izglītība—tilts uz ilgtspējīgu attīstību" infografika* [Higher education and sustainable development: Intersections and partnerships. Infographics of the project "Global citizenship education—bridge to sustainable development" of the Center of Education Initiatives]. Retrieved from http://iic.lv/wp-content/uploads/2019/07/Infografika_Krustpunkti-un-partneribas.pdf.

Iliško, Dz., S. Ignatjeva, and I. Mičule. (2011). Teacher-carried research as a tool for teachers' professional growth. *Journal of Teacher Education for Sustainability,* 13(2), 87–103.

Iliško, Dz. (2017). Worldview education as a viable perspective for educating global citizens. In: M. de Souza and A. Halahoff (Eds.), *Re-enchanting education and spiritual wellbeing: Fostering belonging and meaning-making for global citizens* (pp. 62–72). New York: Routledge.

Iliško, Dz. (2016). Inquiry-based educational course in higher education towards sustainable communities: A case study. In: W. Leal Filho and P. Pace (Eds.), *Teaching education for sustainable development at university level. World Sustainability Series* (pp. 125–147). Springer, Cham.

Iliško, Dz., Dz. Oļehnoviča, I. Ostrovska, V. Akmene, and I. Salīte. (2017). Meeting the challenges of ESD competency—based curriculum in a vocational school setting. *Discourse and Communication for Sustainable Education*, 8(2), 103–113.

IZM. (2006a). *Guidelines for the development of education for 2007–2013.* Retrieved from http://polsis.mk.gov.lv/documents/2054.

IZM. (2006b). *Proposals for guidelines for improving the quality of teacher education and continuing education.* Retrieved from http://polsis.mk.gov.lv/documents/1913.

IZM. (2014). *Guidelines for the development of education for 2014–2020.* Retrieved from http://polsis.mk.gov.lv/documents/4781.

IZM. (2018a). Informatīvais ziņojums "Par papildu valsts budžeta saistību uzņemšanos Globālās izglītības tīkla Eiropā Globālās izglītības palielināšanas un inovāciju programmas finanšu instrumenta īstenošanai Latvijā" [On commitment of additional state budget for the implementation of the Global Education Network in Europe for enhancement and innovation program financial instrument in Latvia]. Retrieved from http://tap.mk.gov.lv/mk/tap/?pid=40461663.

IZM. (2018b). Informatīvais ziņojums "Priekšlikumi konceptuāli jaunas kompetencēs balstītas izglītības prasībām atbilstošas skolotāju izglītības nodrošināšanai Latvijā" [Informative Report "Proposals for conceptually new competence-based education requirements for ensuring teacher education in Latvia"]. Retrieved from http://polsis.mk.gov.lv/documents/6110.

IZM. (2020a). Informatīvais ziņojums "Darba vidē balstīta studiju programma pedagogu sagatavošanai: īstenošana un attīstība" [Informative report 'Work-based study programme for teacher training: Implementation and development']. Retrieved from http://tap.mk.gov.lv/lv/mk/tap/?pid=40476411.

IZM. (2020b). Izglītības attīstības pamatnostādnes 2021–2027.gadam "Nākotnes prasmes nākotnes sabiedrībai". [Education development guidelines for 2021–2027 "Future Skills for the Society of Future"]. Retrieved from https://www.izm.gov.lv/sites/izm/files/iap2027_projekta_versija_apspriesana_160720201_2.pdf.

IZM. (2013). Viedās specializācijas stratēģija [Smart Specialisation Strategy]. Retrieved from https://www.izm.gov.lv/images/zinatne/IZM_Viedas_Specializ_strategija_2013.pdf.

JASMA. (2015). *Globālā izglītība starptautiskajā brīvprātīgajā darbā* [Young Europeans for Global Development: A Guidebook for Global Education in International Volunteering]. Rīga: JASMA.

Jones, C. (2019). Capital, neoliberalism and educational technology. *Postdigital Science and Education*, 1, 288–292.

Kaša, R., and A. A. S. Mhamed. (2013). Language policy and the internationalization of higher education in the Baltic countries. *European Education*, 45(2), 28–50.

Kowalczuk-Walędziak, M. (2019). Higher degrees by research: Outcomes and challenges for teachers. *Nouva Secondaria*, 10, 165–173.

Kravale-Pauliņa, M., and E. Oļehnoviča. (2015). Human securitability: A participatory action research study involving novice teachers and youngsters. *Journal of Teacher Education for Sustainability*, 17(2), 91–107.

Kravale-Pauliņa, M., E. Oļehnoviča, I. Ostrovska, A. Ivanova, and V. Šipilova. (2018). Youth policy monitoring as a tool for developing social sustainability in local municipality. *Problems of Education in the 21st Century*, 76(3), 350–363.

Krūze, A., I. Ķestere, V. Sirk, and O. Tijūnieliene (Eds.). (2009). *History of education and pedagogical thought in the Baltic countries up to 1940: An overview*. Rīga: RAKA.

Laine, M. (2016). Culture in sustainability in defining cultural sustainability in education. *Discourse and Communication for Sustainable Education*, 7(2), 52–67.

LAPAS. (2007). Attīstības izglītības pamatnostādnes 2008–2015. gadam [Development Education Policy 2008–2015]. Retrieved from http://lapas.lv/wp-content/uploads/2010/04/AI_pamatn_FINAL_latv.pdf.

LAPAS. (2008). Attīstības izglītības jautājumi Latvijas pamatizglītības un vispārējās vidējās izglītības mācību priekšmetu saturā [Development education issues in the content of basic education and general secondary education subjects in Latvia]. Retrieved from http://lapas.lv/wp-content/uploads/2010/04/ai_Lv_izglitibas_sistema.pdf.

LAPAS. (2018a). *Ilgtspējīgas attīstības mērķi: es, kopiena, valsts un pasaule [Sustainable Development Goals: Me, Community, Country and World]*. Rīga: LAPAS.

LAPAS. (2018b). Sustainable development of Latvia: analysis of NGO participation. Spotlight Review on the Report by the Government of Latvia on Implementation of the Sustainable Development Goals in Latvia. Rīga: LAPAS. Retrieved from https://lapas.lv/wp-content/uploads/2018/06/NVOzinojums-EN_v2_final_ar-foto-autoru_18.12.2018.pdf.

LAPAS. (2019). Voluntary National Review: Connector. Case of Latvian CSOs. Retrieved from https://sustainabledevelopment.un.org/content/documents/21422Annex_10.pdf.

Latvijas Universitāte (LU). (2018). Studiju virziena "Izglītība, pedagoģija un sports" pašnovērtējuma ziņojums par 2018./2019. studiju gadu [Self-evaluation report of the study direction "Education, Pedagogy and Sport, 2018/2019]. Retrieved from https://www.lu.lv/fileadmin/user_upload/LU.LV/www.lu.lv/Dokumenti/Julijs_2019/Augusts_2019/IZGLITIBA_PEDAGOGIJA_SPORTS_2018_PUB.pdf.

Liepājas Universitāte (LiepU). (2017). Studiju virziena "Izglītība, pedagoģija un sports" pašnovērtējuma ziņojums par 2015./2016., 2016./2017. studiju gadu [Self-evaluation report of the study direction "Education, Pedagogy and Sport, 2015/2016, 2016/2017]. Retrieved from https://www.liepu.lv/uploads/files/Izglitiba_pedagogija_sports_2016__2017_st_g__ML.pdf.

Maastricht Declaration—European Strategy Framework. (2015). European Strategy Framework. The "Maastricht Global Education Declaration" for Improving and Increasing Global Education in Europe to the Year 2015. Retrieved from https://rm.coe.int/168070e540.

Mendizabal, E. (2010). *The alignment, interest and influence matrix (AIIM) guidance note*. ODI Manual/Toolkit. London: ODI.

Mhamed, A. A. S., Z. Vārpiņa, I. Dedze, and R. Kaša. (2018). Latvia: A historical analysis of transformation and diversification of the higher education system. In: J. Huisman, A. Smolentseva, and I. Froumin (Eds.), *25 years of transformations of higher education systems in post-soviet countries* (pp. 259–283). Palgrave Studies in Global Higher Education.

Mieriņa, I. (2015). Jauniešu pilsoniskās un politiskās līdzdalības formu tipoloģija [Typology of civic and political participation forms of youth]. In: A. Stašulāne (Ed.), *Kultūras studijas: Zinātnisko rakstu krājums. VII: Vēsturiskā atmiņa* [Cultural Studies: Proceedings of Scientific Articles, VII: Historical Memory] (pp. 82–105). Daugavpils: Daugavpils Universitātes Akadēmiskais apgāds "Saule".

Namsone, D. (zin. red.). (2018). *Mācīšanās lietpratībai* [Learning for Mastery]. Kolektīvā monogrāfija. Rīga: LU Akadēmiskais apgāds. Retrieved from https://www.siic.lu.lv/fileadmin/user_upload/lu_portal/projekti/siic/Kolektiva_mono-grafija/Macisanas_Lietpratibai.pdf.

NAP 2027. (2020). Riga: Saeima, approved on 2 July 2020 by decision of the Saeima of the Republic of Latvia No. 418. Retrieved from https://www.pkc.gov.lv/sites/default/files/inline-files/NAP2027__ENG.pdf.

Noteikumi par pedagogiem nepieciešamo izglītību un profesionālo kvalifikāciju un pedagogu profesionālās kompetences pilnveides kārtību [Regulations regarding required education and professional qualification, and development of professional competences of teachers]. Ministru kabineta noteikumi Nr. 569 [Regulations No. 569 by the Cabinet of Ministers] (11.09.2018, pp. 3–4). Retrieved from https://likumi.lv/ta/id/301572-noteikumi-par-pedagogiem-nepieciesamo-izglitibu-un-profesionalo-kvalifikaciju-un-pedagogu-profesionalas-kompetences-pilnveides.

Noteikumi par valsts pamatizglītības standartu un pamatizglītības programmu paraugiem [Regulations regarding samples of the state primary education standards and primary education programmes]. (2018). Ministru kabineta noteikumi Nr. 747. Retrieved from https://likumi.lv/ta/id/303768-noteikumi-par-valstspamatizglitibas-standartu-un-pamatizglitibas-programmu-paraugiem.

Noteikumi par valsts vispārējās vidējās izglītības standartu un vispārējās vidējās izglītības programu paraugiem [Regulations regarding the state standard for general secondary education and general secondary education programme samples]. (2019). Ministru kabineta noteikumi Nr. 416. Retrieved from https://likumi.lv/ta/id/309597.

North-South Centre and Eesti People to People. (2016). *Baltic Regional Seminar on Global Development Education. Concept Paper.* Tallinn: European Commission, North-South Centre.

North-South Centre and LAPAS. (2014). *Report of the Baltic Regional Global Education Seminar "Out of the box: Global education within holistic everyday realities".* European Commission: North-South Centre. Retrieved from https://rm.coe.int/168070ee0.

Odina, I., and L. Kuzmane. (2013). Student mobility to foster the European dimension in teacher education. In: P. M. Rabensteiner and E. Ropo, *European dimension in education and teaching* (pp. 71–101), Volume 7. Schneider Verlag Hohengehren GmgH.

Odina, I., I. Mikelsone, I. Belousa, and L. Grigule. (2013). Implementation steppingstones within sustainability oriented master study program for teachers. *European Scientific Journal*, special edition, 1, 430–442.

OECD. (2001). *Reviews of national policies for education: Latvia.* OECD Centre for cooperation with non-members. Retrieved from https://read.oecd-ilibrary.org/education/reviews-of-national-policies-for-education-latvia-2001_9789264192478-en#pge1.

OECD/Asia Society. (2018). *Teaching for global competence in a rapidly changing world.* Retrieved from https://www.oecd-ilibrary.org/education/teaching-for-global-competence-in-a-rapidly-changing-world_9789264289024-en.

Oļehnoviča, E. (2019). Mācību satura un valodas integrēta apguve kompetenču pieejā: kritiskā diskursa aspekti [Integrated learning of learning content and language in the competence approach: critical aspects of discourse]. In: M. Burima (Ed.), *CLIL jeb mācību satura un valodas integrēta apguve: ietvari, pieredze, izaicinājumi* [CLIL or integrated learning of learning content and language: Frames, experience, challenges] (pp. 19–38). Populārzinātnisku rakstu krājums, Nr. 5. Rīga: Latviešu valodas aģentūra.

Pipere, A. (2019). Journal of Teacher Education for Sustainability after the UN Decade of Education for Sustainable Development: Exploring for the future. *Journal of Teacher Education for Sustainability*, 21(1), 5–34.

Pipere, A., M. Veisson, and I. Salīte. (2015). Developing research in teacher education for sustainability: UN DESD via the Journal of Teacher Education for Sustainability. *Journal of Teacher Education for Sustainability*, 17(2), 5–43.

Peck, B.T. (2000). Change and challenge in education. In: B. T. Peck and A. Mays (Eds.), *Challenge and change in education: The experience of the Baltic states in the 1990's* (pp. 1–93). New York: Nova Science Publishers.

Reimers, F. M. (2020). *Educating students to improve the world*. SpringerBriefs in Education.

Saeima of the Republic of Latvia. (2010). Sustainable Development Strategy of Latvia until 2030. Retrieved from https://www.pkc.gov.lv/sites/default/files/images-legacy/LV2030/LIAS_2030_parluks_en.pdf.

Saleniece, I. (2018). *Global Citizenship in Europe: How Much do We Care*. CONCORD Europe, Brussels, Belgium. Retrieved from https://library.concordeurope.org/record/1917/files/DEEEP-REPORT-2018-006.pdf.

Salīte, I., I. Fjodorova, Dz. Iliško, O Ivanova, and H. Meihami. (2020). JTES for sustainable development: An action research environment for the development and sustainable future of the journal identity. *Journal of Teacher Education for Sustainability*, 22(1), 1–5.

Silova, I. (2006). *From sites of occupation to symbols of multiculturalism: Re-conceptualizing minority education in post-soviet Latvia*. Greenwich, CT: Information Age Publishing.

Suša, R. (2019). Global citizenship education (GCE) for unknown futures. Mapping past and current experiments and debates. A report for the Bridge 47 project. EU: Bridge 47 2019. Retrieved from https://www.bridge47.org/sites/default/files/2019-07/bridge47_gce_for_unknown_futures_report-compressed_0.pdf.

Šteinberga, A. (Eds.). (2019). *Skolotāja profesionālā identitāte*. Salīdzinošais starptautiskais pētījums. Zinātniskā monogrāfija [Teacher's professional identity. Comparative international research. Scientific monography]. Rīga: RTU izdevniecība.

Štefenhagena, D. (2012). Universitātes regulējošais tiesiskais ietvars [The legal regulatory framework of universities]. In: *Universitāšu ieguldījums Latvijas tautsaimniecībā* [The Contribution of Universities to the Economy of Latvia] (pp. 39–49). Rīga: Latvijas Universitāšu Asociācija.

Tarozzi, M., and C. Inguaggiat. (Eds.). (2018). Teachers' education in GCE: Emerging issues from a comparative perspective. Research deliverable published within the European project "Global Schools", Trento, Italy: Provincia Autonoma di Trento. Retrieved from http://www.globalschools.education/Activities/Research/Research-report-2.

UNECE. (2012). *Learning for the future. Competences in education for sustainable Development.* Retrieved from https://www.unece.org/fileadmin/DAM/env/esd/ESD_Publications/Competences_Publication.pdf.

UNESCO. (2014). *Global citizenship education: Preparing learners for the challenges of the 21st century.* Paris: UNESCO.

UNESCO. (2015). *Rethinking education. Towards a global common goal?* Paris: UNESCO Publishing.

Underwood, J., and M. Kowalczuk-Walędziak. (2018). Conceptualising professional communities among teachers. *Polish Journal of Educational Studies,* 1(LXXI), 123–142.

Zobena, A., and R. Felcis. (2018). Ceļā no anomijas uz pašorganizāciju un kolektīvu rīcību. In A. Zobena (zin. red.), *Inovatīvi risinājumi ceļā uz ilgtspēju: Sabiedrība, ekonomika, vide* [Innovative solutions for sustainability: Society, economy, environment] (pp. 144–167). Rīga: LU Akadēmiskais apgāds.

Zhukova, O. (2018). Novice teachers' concerns, early professional experiences and development: Implications for theory and practice. *Discourse and Communication for Sustainable Education,* 9(1), 100–114.

Žukovs, L. (2001). *Pedagoģijas vēsture* [History of pedagogy]. Rīga: RaKa.

18

Teacher Education in Estonia: From the Soviet School System to One of the Best in Europe According to PISA Results

Katrin Poom-Valickis and Eve Eisenschmidt

Historical Overview of Changes and Political Reforms in the Estonian School System

We may divide Estonian educational reforms after the collapse of the Soviet system into three broad periods: (a) from the mid-1980s to the mid-1990s, (b) from 1995 to 2004, and (c) from 2004 to today.

Until 1987 the Estonian education system was part of the Soviet Union's extremely centralised and politicised educational policy system. The common school system for the whole Soviet Union meant limiting to a minimum the so-called local peculiarities and enforcing a uniform education and way of life, from the island of Sakhalin in the east to the Baltics in the west (Ruus and Sarv 2000). At the same time, it should be noted that, despite the foreign power, the Estonian school system and curricula were able to maintain certain essential characteristics in order to preserve the national culture and education during the Soviet occupation. The most essential of these were

* native language education at all levels, including higher education;
* one year longer of secondary school education in comparison to Russian schools (11 years of secondary school until 1984 and 12 thereafter);

K. Poom-Valickis (✉) • E. Eisenschmidt
Tallinn University, Tallinn, Estonia
e-mail: katrinpv@tlu.ee

© The Author(s), under exclusive license to Springer Nature Switzerland AG 2023
M. Kowalczuk-Walędziak et al. (eds.), *The Palgrave Handbook of Teacher Education in Central and Eastern Europe*, https://doi.org/10.1007/978-3-031-09515-3_18

433

* original Estonian textbooks for many subjects (i.e. not only translations of Russian authors, as was common practice in the Soviet Union);
* relatively wide use of active learning methods and supportive methodological materials, for both students and teachers, developed by Estonian education scientists;
* an in-service teacher training system inclusive of all teachers;
* research activities for teachers and an institutionalised teacher support system;
* progressive, humanitarian ideas forming the foundation of Estonian education from the time of Estonian independence before the Second World War: for example, individualisation and differentiated learning were important topics during these times, as they are now (Ruus and Sarv 2000).

A noticeable weakening of the Soviet regime began in the mid-1980s with the so-called perestroika and glasnost enabling greater freedom and exchange of opinions than had been possible before. The country's intellectuals became leaders and drivers of political change in Estonia: indeed, it was at the Congress of Estonian Teachers which took place in March 1987 that the aspiration for independence was officially formulated for the first time. This was both a turning point in Estonian education and the beginning of a comprehensive reform movement. The congress sent a clear message to start secondary education curricular reforms based on 'local' views, not instructions received from Moscow. A new secondary school curriculum was ready by the 1989/90 academic year (Ruus and Sarv 2000).

With the regaining of independence in 1991, a new stage—building an independent state—began. In 1992 the Estonian Law of Education, which became a framework for all subsequent legislative acts in this field, was adopted. In 1996 the Estonian government approved a new national primary and secondary education curriculum that included the description of competences for all school stages. Within this, schools were allowed to compile their own curricula and subject syllabi. This was a period of rapid change in Estonia's educational reform, characterised by teachers' sense of initiative and enthusiasm on the one hand, and by uncertainty on the other. It was challenging for teachers to relinquish deep-rooted, subject-specialist mindsets and evaluate anew what would constitute 'correct' knowledge and ways of teaching. Furthermore, the national curriculum itself retained contradictions: while the overarching vision was forward-looking, not all subject syllabi had managed to embrace the new changes (Ruus and Sarv 2000; Ruus et al. 2008).

In 2002, a revised version of the national curriculum for general education was adopted. The most noteworthy changes in this version were related to more exact definitions of the key and domain-specific competences. Syllabi were also revised, mainly to mitigate learning overload for students, but the relatively strong 'academicism' of the syllabi remained, which may be one of the factors that explain Estonian students' success in TIMSS and PISA reports (Henno and Reiska 2007).

In 2011, a renewed national curriculum addressed student-centred learning processes, where the learner: is an active participant in the learning process; takes part according to their abilities in setting goals for their studies; studies independently and with companions; learns to value their companions and themselves; and analyses and manages their own studies. Additionally, formative assessment, regular development conversations with students, and flexibility to adapt students' learning based on their needs were addressed (Government of the Republic of Estonia 2011).

Milestones in Teacher Education—Reforms and Requirements over the Last Three Decades

During the Soviet regime, initial teacher training (except for pre- and primary schools) was based on academic, university-level education. Then, in 1996 the National Higher Education Standard was established by an Estonian government regulation and preparations to move all initial teacher education to universities started. Alongside this initial education, in-service teacher education was also carefully considered and, in 1998, a regulation to improve teachers' competences was approved (HTM 1998a). The regulation states that in-service training providers can be universities, or other public and private institutions. Schools are responsible for analysing their teachers' professional development needs.

In 1998 Conditions and Regulations for the Certification of Educational Personnel (HTM 1998b) established four consecutive levels of professional qualifications for teachers: junior teacher, teacher, senior teacher, and teacher-methodologist. These levels reflected a range of minimum official requirements regarding teachers' professional competence and the conception of the stages of teachers' professional development. However, a shortcoming of the regulation was a lack of teaching practice content analysis and too high a level of formality.

The most important regulation for teacher education (*Framework Guidelines for Teacher Education*) was accepted in 2000. The framework requirements for teacher education regulate the training of teachers for pre-school institutions; class teachers in basic schools primary level; subject teachers; and special education teachers in basic schools and upper secondary schools; teachers in vocational educational institutions; and teachers in professional higher education schools and universities (Government of the Republic of Estonia 2000). According to the framework, teacher education is treated as an integrated entity consisting of pre-service teacher education, an induction year, and lifelong in-service training to ensure teachers' constant professional growth. To plan further improvements in teacher education, the *National Teacher Education Development Plan for 2003–2010* was approved.

Additionally, in 2002 *The Qualification Framework for Educators* was approved (HTM 2002). This document describes requirements for teachers, principals, and other educational specialists across all educational levels, stating that all teachers should undertake formal pedagogical preparation.

Since 2004, when Estonia became a member of the EU, the Estonian education system has been influenced by different European frameworks and policies. For example, during the compilation of a vision for the European teaching profession— *The Common European Principles for Teacher Competences and Qualifications* (2005)—discussions about teachers' competency models also started to take place in Estonia and the first Estonian teachers' professional standard was adopted. Subsequently, the expectations for teachers were first described in 2005 in the Teachers' Standard, with required competences including planning and management of students' learning, establishing the learning environment, analysis and assessment of learning outcomes, and so on. The standard also requires interpersonal competences, such as communication, cooperation, and motivational skills, and views the teacher as a reflective practitioner and lifelong learner responsible for their own professional development (Ruus et al. 2008).

Due to rapid changes in the teacher education landscape, there was a need to renew the strategy, thus the *Estonian Teacher Education Strategy for 2009–2013* was approved. This strategy aimed to enhance the social status of the teaching profession and to ensure the development of teachers' competences throughout their careers, and provides input on refining and expanding new teacher professional standards. The teacher professional standards established in 2005 were mainly used as a basis for self-evaluation to support teachers who were enrolled in the induction programme during their first years of teaching, but not as a basis for designing initial teacher education programmes, nor to guide teachers' continuous professional learning (Pedaste et al. 2019). Therefore, a new system of three professional levels (i.e. teacher, senior teacher, and master teacher) was introduced in 2013, and these standards have been the basis for the development of all teacher education curricula in Estonian universities since then.

Since 2014, it has been possible to verify teachers' competences and acquire a teacher qualification through professional evaluation by the Estonian Teachers' Association; however, to date only 10% of teachers who enter the profession have used this opportunity (Pedaste et al. 2019) and the primary means to become a teacher is still university graduation.

New strategic focuses of teacher policy have been specified in the *Estonian Lifelong Learning Strategy 2020* (HTM 2014), a document emphasising the need to implement an approach to learning that supports each learner's individual and social-emotional development, the acquisition of learning skills, creativity and entrepreneurship at all levels and in all types of education. Teachers and school leaders are considered to be the key actors in this process. In order to implement the goals specified in the strategy, measures have been provided for making the teaching profession more attractive; for reorganising the continuing education of teachers and school leaders and for providing feedback on teachers' performance; as well as for improving the digital competence of both learners and teachers.

In general, since 2004, the regulations on teacher education in Estonia have been supporting similar goals to the EU's policy documents, plus European Social Funds were used to carry out planned national strategies (e.g. *Eduko, Improving Competencies of Principals and In-service Teachers*, etc.).

Continuity in Teacher Education—From Initial Teacher Education to Workplace Professional Development

The following section overviews initial teacher education and teachers' continuous professional development (see Fig. 18.1).

Initial Teacher Education

Initial teacher education provides basic professional knowledge and skills for working as a professional teacher in pre-schools, basic schools, and vocational schools, as well as upper secondary schools. Currently, the two leading Estonian universities—Tallinn University and the University of Tartu, together with their colleges—provide courses for teacher qualification. According to the 2019 updated *Framework Guidelines for Teacher Education*, teacher education consists of

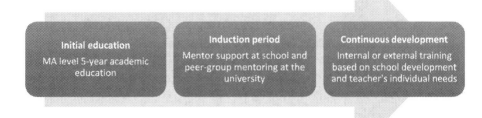

Fig. 18.1 Three phases in teacher education

1. **general studies** focusing on the development of the teacher's overall cultural, communicative, and social competences based on their presumed vocation, profession, and occupation;
2. **subject or speciality studies** aiming at (1) providing subject- or speciality-related knowledge and skills based on up-to-date requirements, and (2) providing a systemic understanding of pupils on a human level and in their socio-cultural contexts, as well as the skill of viewing them from the angle of the teacher's subject or specialism;
3. **professional studies** aiming to ensure the acquisition of the professional knowledge and skills described in the teacher professional standard, to the value of at least 60 credits, including courses on general educational sciences, psychology, subject didactic, and pedagogical research methods, plus at least 10 weeks of supervised practice; and
4. **a graduation thesis or examination** of the corresponding higher education level containing pedagogical research work (*Framework Guidelines for Teacher Education* 2019).

Pedagogical practice plays an essential role in applying the knowledge and skills acquired during theoretical studies. According to the research (Poom-Valickis and Löfström 2019), the most substantial influence on future teachers' perceptions of professional identity is their pedagogical practice. Teacher trainees often start their teacher training with naive ideas about their work, largely based on their personal school experience (Calderhead and Robson 1991). However, during teacher education studies, their perceptions of their role and work become more complex and, by the end of studies, the pedagogical expertise becomes most valued (Poom-Valickis and Löfström 2019).

Other significant political changes which have influenced university curricula development in Estonia after regaining independence relate to the higher education reforms based on the Bologna Process in Europe. The Estonian higher education system was reformed according to the Bologna regulation in 2002 when the 3+2 curricula system was launched. Currently, two teacher pre-service education models are used in Estonian universities: one is a five-year integrated model (class teachers for primary school level), in which subject and educational studies take place concurrently, and the other is a two-phase or consecutive model (for subject teachers and pre-school teachers), in which after graduating from the three-year bachelor-level subject studies, the two-year Master's in teacher education follows. According to Estonian regulations, subject and class teachers in general education schools must be educated at Master's level, and pre-school and vocational teachers at bachelor's level (see Table 18.1).

In the case of the two-phase teacher education model, educational studies (including pre-service school practice) consist of at least 60 credit points (ECTS)—this is equal to one year of studies in Estonian higher education. The curriculum for comprehensive school teachers and upper secondary teachers, as well as those teachers who teach general subjects at a vocational school, is as follows:

* **Pre-school teachers acquire** a Bachelor's degree (180 ECTS) with education as a major (equal to a kindergarten teacher or pre-school teacher's qualification). Those who continue their studies for the Master's degree acquire the early childhood educator and counsellor's qualification.
* **Class teachers acquire** a Master's degree (300 ECTS) with education as a major. This degree provides the class teacher's qualification for practising in a comprehensive school from grades 1 to 6.

Table 18.1 Teachers' education by school level

Students' age	Educational level	Level of teacher education studies
Up to 7	Kindergarten	Pre-school teacher (BA)
7–15	Basic school (9 years): primary school (1–6 forms) and lower secondary (7–9 forms)	Class teacher (MA) and subject teacher (MA)
16–19	Upper secondary school (3 years): 10–12 forms	Subject teacher (MA)
From 16 to adults	Vocational school	Subject teacher (MA) and vocational education teacher (BA)

* **Subject teachers acquire** a Master's degree (300 ECTS) and their major is usually the subject they will go on to teach. A qualified subject teacher must attain a Master's degree and complete teachers' pedagogical studies.
* **Special education teachers acquire** a Master's degree (300 ECTS) in special education. This degree provides the special education teacher's qualification for practising in a comprehensive or specialist school.
* **Vocational school teachers** acquire a degree at a university, higher education institution, or vocational school, and usually work for some years in the labour market before they complete their pedagogical studies at a university.

Starting from 2013, renewed professional standards for teacher education have been issued. According to these standards, the evaluation of teacher competence development takes place during their studies at university. Upon successful completion of initial teacher education studies, the first level teacher certificate is obtained, together with the academic diploma. The first graduates who studied according to these revised curricula were awarded their teaching certificates in 2016 (Pedaste et al. 2019).

The rapid development of ICT, socio-political global and cultural changes, multiculturalism, and the integration of children with special needs into schools are just some of the factors affecting contemporary teachers and teacher education. Because the spectrum of teacher education curricula needs to cover both society's needs and teachers with different competences, teacher education curricula renewal—based on the collected feedback and strategic aims of universities and national teacher education policy—takes place every academic year. To ensure the quality of teaching and learning, curriculum development, resources, and sustainability, an external evaluation of higher education study groups is organised by the Estonian Quality Agency for Higher and Vocational Education.

Admission Requirements for Teacher Education

The pre-condition to starting higher education studies in Estonia is a secondary education certificate. University admission conditions vary but, most often, the results of both national graduation and university entrance examinations are required. Professional aptitude (based on interviews or group discussion), essays, tests (including cultural competency, functional reading, and writing), and practical tests (such as in music and art) may be assessed as well. Admission committees make decisions based on exam content and results of the programme. Master's studies entrance requirements for becoming a subject teacher vary according to programme specifics. In general, however, an applicant must have completed school studies in at least one subject (to a minimum of 45 ECTS) and have a Bachelor's degree. An additional precondition is passing the teachers' professional aptitude tests. The admission threshold, that is, the results required for admission, depends on the relation between the number of candidates, the number of course places available, and of the candidates who exceed the threshold.

Unfortunately, as teaching has not historically been a high-status or high-paying profession in Estonia, teacher education is not currently popular among young adults. Therefore, the recruitment of talented, skilled, and motivated young people into teacher education is challenging.

Induction Year and Continuous Professional Development

In order to support teacher education graduates' smoother transitions from initial education to working life, and ensure that they persist in the teaching profession, the induction year programme was initiated in Estonia in 2004. The purpose of the induction year programme is to support novices' adaptation to the profession and promote the development of their professional skills through constant analyses of practice and learning. The Estonian approach to induction is designed as a period after initial teacher education during which new teachers become fully responsible teachers. This induction is a key part of a teacher's continuous learning in partnership with teacher education institutions and schools (Eisenschmidt 2006).

The induction programme combines two environments: (a) learning and development in the school context with a mentor's support, and (b) quarterly two-day peer meetings at a university during the school holidays. This approach is unique because of the integration of the two types of mentoring: one-to-one mentoring at the school and peer-group mentoring at the university. Universities organised support seminars for new teachers: (1) to help initial teacher education institutions understand what problems new teachers have and to get feedback about the quality of initial education; (2) to discuss problems that new teachers find uncomfortable to discuss at school with their mentors; (3) to support the development of teachers' reflection skills; and (4) to allow new teachers to share their successes and failures in the group sessions and seek solutions together (Eisenschmidt 2006). As such, the university support seminars create a bridge and continuity between initial education and continuing professional development.

Principles and legislation regulating teacher in-service training have also changed during recent decades: teachers are no longer obliged to complete a certain number of in-service training hours over a period of time, but this learning can take place either independently or in in-service training courses. Primary teacher in-service training providers in Estonia are the universities that offer teacher education. The Ministry of Education and Research evaluates the quality and keeps a register of the most extensive (i.e. more than 1 ECTS) courses.

Before 2013, in-service education for teachers was based on a free market model, with all training funds directed straight to the schools, which then decided on the use of those funds themselves. Since 2013, in-service education courses have been ordered centrally, either from the universities or from the in-service teacher training providers. Centrally organised training courses are free of charge for teachers. In-service education funds are also used for supporting teachers' networks, including learning from each other, and a part of those funds is still channelled into schools through local authorities, along with the state education fund. Local municipalities may allocate additional resources for teachers' in-service education and determine the fields in which they may be used. Schools make in-service education decisions based on their own needs and development plans. In fact, it is important to mention that Estonian schools are very autonomous, so one of the key tasks of school leaders is to arrange the professional development of teachers and staff. Teachers' lifelong learning and in-service training are essential components of school development and most schools draft teachers' in-service training plans. Such plans include in-school group training sessions, but teachers are also offered opportunities to attend training courses outwith the school based on their individual training needs. Professional standards for teachers are intended to support them in analysing their professional skills and setting goals for development, and the benefits of teachers' in-service education are assessed annually during teachers' developmental interviews with their school leaders.

Challenges and Future Directions for Teacher Education

Ultimately, the quality of any education system cannot exceed the quality of its teachers. A survey (McKinsey and Company 2007) of the most highly performing school systems suggests that the main driver of student learning in schools is the quality of the teachers. The success of high-achieving school systems is mostly attributable to (a) bringing the right people into the profession; (b) teachers' salary structure; and (c) developing teachers into effective instructors (McKinsey and Company 2007).

Even if Estonians can currently be proud of our PISA results, we must still look critically at the future of our education system. Traditionally, as mentioned earlier, teaching has not been either a high-status or a high-paying profession in Estonia. Since 2000, the country has faced teacher shortages and today only 10% of the teaching workforce in Estonia is under 30 years of age. According to the OECD, more than 50% of Estonian teachers are over 50 years of age (the OECD average is 34%) (OECD 2018), and the majority of them are women. This situation is particularly critical for science and mathematics teachers, as one in five teachers of mathematics, chemistry, geography, and biology and one in four physics teachers are aged 60 or older (Mets and Viia 2018). This means that 20% of our current teachers will need to be replaced upon their retirement in the coming years. At the same time, subject teacher university graduates account for only two-thirds of this need. Thus, we may say that both our greatest successes and most critical problems in the Estonian education system are related to teachers. In order to make teaching an attractive profession, and specifically to reach the 2020 goal of 12.5% of teachers being under the age of 30 set by Estonia's *Lifelong Learning Strategy*, the government must offer competitive salaries and rewarding pay progression for teachers. Even while, in secondary education, teachers' salaries have increased in recent years, they are still sitting at around 89% of the earnings of other tertiary-educated, full-time workers. More competitive salaries could also help improve the profession's gender balance by attracting more men to classroom teaching (OECD 2018).

In order to overcome the shortage of teachers outlined above, and due to the fact that a large proportion of teachers in schools lack the required qualifications, alternative solutions to teacher training are being introduced. For example, the *Teach First* programme provides an educational module for those who have completed university studies in another specialism and are now interested in working in schools as teachers. This two-year programme at Tallinn University includes preparatory studies, observational practice, and 60 ECTS of teacher training—courses are held every two weeks. With this programme, the early career teacher has access to constant help from Tallinn University lecturers/professors, school mentors, and *Teach First* tutors and alumni.

As the number of young people entering teacher education immediately after graduating from their Bachelor's studies is not high, and a large proportion of the people entering teacher training has already started working as teachers, for example, Tallinn University has changed the learning arrangement of teacher education. Subject teacher training was introduced into the cycle of study a few years ago in order to enable existing teachers to acquire higher education qualifications. At the same time, it is essential for the university that the quality of teacher education does not decrease and that all necessary competences described in the teacher professional standards are achieved. Year after year, there is an increase in the number of so-called career-changers, that is, people who already have higher education qualifications and work experience in other fields, but who also want to contribute to society as a whole and opt to enter the teaching profession as a means to do so. This results in much more experienced and older students with very different educational needs to less experienced, younger students undertaking teacher training. Among these students, some do not have pedagogical training but do have a Master's degree, while others have neither a Master's degree nor pedagogical competences. Alongside full-time teachers in Estonian schools, the number of people doing part-time teaching is increasing. These part-time teachers also need support and opportunities to acquire the competences necessary for teaching. Thus, overall, the biggest challenge for Estonia's universities is to better adapt their curricula to fulfil the societal expectations and the changing labour market. In order to provide personalised education pathways, it is necessary to develop solutions for assessing the competences of potential student teachers and to provide more flexible study possibilities considering their professional development needs.

During Estonia's re-independence process, the research basis of Estonian teacher education has strengthened remarkably at two leading universities responsible for teacher education—Tallinn University and the University of Tartu—both of which are research-oriented and aim to follow international research standards. The studies into Estonian teachers and schools conducted over the past decade highlight some shortcomings in our teacher education system that need to be addressed while developing initial and in-service teacher education programmes and designing the national educational policy. These shortcomings are discussed below.

In general, Estonian teachers' pedagogical beliefs show a change from having being subject-focused to being didactic and pedagogy-focused (Poom-Valickis 2003; Poom-Valickis and Oder 2013), as well as an acceptance of social-constructivist beliefs (Lepik et al. 2013; OECD 2014). At the same time, research also reveals that teachers' pedagogical beliefs are not necessarily related to their instructional practices. In the TALIS study (2013), Estonian teachers reported that their most common practices were presenting a summary of recently learned content (80% did this frequently, in all, or in nearly all lessons), followed by checking students' exercise books (71%) and letting students practice similar tasks previously learned and practiced with teacher (68%). Uibu et al. (2011) found that teachers used instructional practices aiming at comprehension, application, and individualisation (related mainly to cognitive constructivism) more than supporting students' independence (according to the social constructivism scale). In a similar vein, TALIS 2018 (OECD 2019) results also point to these same tendencies: Estonian teachers focus on classroom leadership and teaching clarity in order to improve understanding, but less for facilitating learning activities that allow students to take more responsibility for their own learning. Uibu et al. (2016) also analysed the language modelling of class teachers and found that teachers used dialogue in their classes mainly to check their students' knowledge or to transfer knowledge, but rarely to support classroom discussion and shared meaning-making. From the above research, we may infer that although Estonian teachers' beliefs have become more student-centred over the years, their actual teaching practices still seem to be traditional and are slow to change. Interpreting these results, we must also keep in mind that the average age of Estonian teachers is relatively high (compared to the average in OECD countries), with a rather small proportion of young teachers. Thus the pedagogical beliefs and instructional practices of teachers in Estonia might generally be understood to originate from past iterations of initial teacher education—specifically, when a subject-oriented approach prevailed and teachers' autonomy was low. At the same time, as mentioned earlier, this relatively strong, subject-centred approach may also be one of the factors that explain the Estonian students' success in TIMSS and PISA results (Henno and Reiska 2007).

The other worrying tendency revealed by research on Estonian teachers is their low self-efficacy. We know that the impact of collective teacher efficacy on students' learning outcomes is significant, and that collective teacher efficacy is an important mediator between school leadership and students' learning outcomes (Moolenaar et al. 2012; Ross and Gray 2006). In the analysis of the TALIS data, four clusters of Estonian teachers were specified and, of these, two contained teachers with rather low levels of self-efficacy (71%). However, among the teachers with high self-efficacy, only one cluster (17%) of teachers was satisfied with their work and societal position (Loogma and Nemeržitski 2013 cited in Leijen and Pedaste 2018). This lack of teachers' self-efficacy—in an environment with continuously increasing social expectations and political demands—may be related to the teachers' insufficient knowledge and low support in the organisation. We know based on previous research that teacher knowledge and motivational aspects are at the core of the quality of their teaching (Kunter et al. 2013). However, the OECD *Teacher Knowledge Survey*

(Sonmark et al. 2017) revealed that teachers' contemporary knowledge about students' learning and development was modest: furthermore, teachers participating in this research also rated their self-efficacy the lowest in terms of supporting student learning. Interestingly, teachers who had students with additional support needs in their classroom scored more highly on several sub-scales in the knowledge test (Malva et al. 2018). So, from these findings, it seems that teachers who care about their students find a way to improve their own knowledge while facing challenges, but, as learning science (including neurosciences), is developing so rapidly, teachers' knowledge of learning and supporting student development must be constantly updated.

Teachers' satisfaction with their work and willingness to implement educational innovation in their teaching practices is directly linked to school organisational culture, that is, leadership practices and support gained from their colleagues (Vangrieken et al. 2017). Surveys (OECD 2014; Heidmets 2017) show that there is still little cooperation between teachers in Estonia as far as planning, developing, and implementing school innovation is concerned. Moreover, poor collaboration is one of the reasons why subject integration has not been fully achieved, why there is minimal integration of cross-curricular subjects into the learning process, and why there is a lack of systematic development of generic competences. Another problem is that new educational practices are often implemented without adequate prior analyses of their impact and benefits.

Potential Practical Steps

Today's education system is challenged by rapid technological development. Equipping classrooms with technological innovations, and using them meaningfully, are among the challenges in contemporary educational practice. Here, the collaboration between schools and universities in applying and analysing educational innovation is essential. Akkerman and Bruining (2016) have pointed out that school-university collaboration models, co-creation, and crossing borders between different organisations contribute to more systematic teacher professional development. Thus, Tallinn University has also significantly changed its principles of in-service education by implementing collaborative, evidence-based programmes in order to develop schools and school teams as learning communities.

A new Tallinn University in-service training initiative, *Teacher Innovation Lab*, provides teachers with joint learning sessions at the university. During these sessions, teachers develop their teaching practices in subject-/

topic-based learning communities, pilot new solutions, and then apply what they have learned in their classrooms by analysing their experiences and sharing them in the *Teacher Innovation Lab* learning community. University researchers are involved in the process to support the implementation of evidence-based practices and systematic data collection at the *Teacher Innovation Lab*.

In 2017 the first *Future School* programme was launched, aiming to renew Estonia's learning and teaching culture in collaboration between universities and schools. This collaboration model is based on the following principles: leadership, co-creation, and evidence-based development. The renewal means moving towards a school model that supports whole-person development and learner agency, and supports a meaningful action of all parties (Eisenschmidt et al. 2020). Universities also benefit from such collaborative models with schools, as it allows them to explore the effectiveness and impact of science-based methodologies and practices. Therefore, developing new practices, methods, and tools together with schools is a mutually beneficial process to tangibly reduce the gap between theory and practice in educational sciences that has been discussed for decades (Broekkamp and Hout-Wolters 2007).

We predict that strong university-partner schools will increase their role in teacher training in the future. Based on the data collected through university feedback system the workload is currently one of the biggest causes of dropout from teacher training. Increasing the volume of work-based learning would help to alleviate some of the time and burden associated with linking work and study. A national teacher training scholarship for students who already work as teachers would also be an important financial solution in helping reduce workload and allowing individuals to focus on full-time study. However, on the school level, a school leader's support in creating sustainable opportunities to pursue the teaching profession is equally important.

Concluding Remarks and Future Directions for Teacher Education

The quality of teaching is generally considered to be one of the most significant factors impacting students' learning. Thus, the biggest challenge for the Estonian education system is how to overcome the current and future shortage of teachers, and to ensure the quality of teaching so that we can be proud of good PISA results in the future too. Therefore, the universities should actively develop teacher education curricula and establish flexible learning routes for different target groups, in order to guarantee the quality of initial teacher education studies and provide graduates with sufficient knowledge of the subject, pedagogical psychology, and didactics to support the development and learning of every student.

The induction year—originally intended for teachers who had completed their initial teacher education and started their job as teachers—also needs to be restructured, because half of today's teacher education students are already working as teachers during their studies. However, mentor support is needed, especially at the beginning of a career in teaching, and therefore the induction year support programme should be integrated with teacher education studies for teachers who work alongside their studies. School leader awareness also plays an important role: indeed, the primary support which should be guaranteed in a school via mentoring appears to be more efficient in schools where the whole organisation supports new teachers (Eisenschmidt et al. 2008).

In Estonia the implementation of a learning approach that supports the individual and social development of each learner (including teachers) and develops learning skills, creativity, and entrepreneurship is an essential goal in school development (HTM 2014). The challenge is to move towards a more holistic and evidence-based school reform, requiring changes in attitudes, knowledge, and skills. The sustainability of educational innovation depends on the extent to which new teaching methods become part of teachers' daily work. In order to create a critical mass of teachers in schools who collaboratively apply and analyse innovative approaches, school leadership practices, as well the content and organisation of in-service training must change. Teacher agency and leadership—for example, taking the initiative in school improvement, improving one's teaching, and supporting colleagues—and the corresponding professional development should be introduced and supported much more systematically in schools. Thus, development programmes for school leaders should place more emphasis on how to enhance the school's capacity by building a shared commitment to school goals, and creating structures and work conditions that systematically promote teacher collaboration and learning. Universities' in-service training centres can also look for ways to support more effective school development and teacher learning. First experiences of new continuous professional development courses based on university-school partnership models have been promising: here, university researchers and practitioners work together to develop and analyse evidence-based innovative practices to strengthen the teachers' ownership of applied educational changes, and diminish the gap between education research and everyday classroom practice.

In conclusion, we can say that a good education system has been an essential asset for Estonians throughout history. The Estonian education system has developed itself from the Soviet totalitarian education system into one of the most successful, internationally recognised education systems. We are proud of our accomplishments, but we are also aware of our weaknesses and developmental needs. We know that while our contemporary society is constantly changing, our teacher education must keep up with these changes in order to ensure the best quality education for our future generations.

References

Akkerman, S., and T. Bruining. (2016). Multilevel boundary crossing in a professional development school partnership. *Journal of the Learning Sciences*, 25(2), 240–284.

Broekkamp, H., and B. van Hout-Wolters. (2007). The gap between educational research and practice: A literature review, symposium, and questionnaire. *Educational Research and Evaluation*, 13(3), 203–220.

Calderhead, J., and M. Robson. (1991). Images of teaching: Student teachers' early conceptions of classroom practice. *Teaching and Teacher Education*, 7(1), 1–8.

Common European Principles for Teacher Competences and Qualifications. (2005). Retrieved from http://www.pef.uni-lj.si/bologna/dokumenti/eu-common-principles.pdf.

Eisenschmidt, E. (2006). Kutseaasta kui algaja õpetaja toetusprogrammi rakendamine Eestis [Implementation of induction year for novice teachers in Estonia]. *Sotsiaalteaduste dissertatsioonid, 25*. TLÜ Kirjastus.

Eisenschmidt, E., K. Poom-Valickis, and T. Oder. (2008). Supporting novice teachers' professional development: Monitoring the induction year experience in Estonia. In: J. Mikk, M. Veisson, and P. Luik (Eds.), *Reforms and innovations in Estonian education* (pp. 77–92). Peter Lang Publishers House.

Eisenschmidt, E., K. Vanari, and K. Tammets. (2020). Tulevikukool: Eesti kooliuuenduse praktikast [School of the future: About Estonian school reform]. In: M. Heidmets (Ed.), *Haridusmõte 2020 [Educational Thought 2020]* (pp. 508–536). Tallin: Tallinna Ülikooli Kirjastus.

Estonian Teacher Education Strategy 2009–2013 [Eesti õpetajahariduse strateegia 2009–2013]. Retrieved from https://issuu.com/eduko/docs/estonian_teacher_education_strategy.

Government of the Republic of Estonia. (2000). Framework guidelines for teacher education [Õpetajate koolituse raamnõuded]. Retrieved from https://www.riigiteataja.ee/akt/812791.

Government of the Republic of Estonia. (2011). *National curriculum for basic schools*. Retrieved from https://www.riigiteataja.ee/en/eli/524092014014/consolide.

Government of the Republic of Estonia. (2019). *Õpetajate koolituse raamnõuded* [*Framework guidelines for teacher education*]. Retrieved from https://www.riigite-ataja.ee/akt/122082019010.

Heidmets, M. (Ed.). (2017). *Õpikäsitus: teooriad, uurimused, mõõtmine. Analüütiline ülevaade* [*Concept of learning: Theories, research, measurement. Analytical overview*]. Lepingu 16/7.1-5/178 lõpparuanne. Tallinna Ülikool.

Henno, I., and P. Reiska. (2007). Exploring teaching approaches in Estonian science lessons based on TIMSS. In: J. Holbrook and M. Rannikmäe (Eds.), *Europe needs more scientists—The role of Eastern and Central European science educators* (pp. 55–65). Tartu: Tartu University Press.

HTM. (1998a). *Haridustöötajate kutseoskuste täiustamise kord* [Arrangements for upgrading the professional skills of educational staff]. Retrieved from https://www.riigiteataja.ee/akt/22746.

HTM. (1998b). *Pedagoogide atesteerimise tingimused ja kord* [Conditions and Regulations for the Certification of Educational Personnel]. Retrieved from https://www.riigiteataja.ee/akt/103092013037.

HTM. (2002). *Pedagoogide kvalifikatsiooninõuded* [The Qualification framework for educators]. Retrieved from https://www.riigiteataja.ee/akt/193676.

HTM. (2014). *Estonian Lifelong Learning Strategy 2020*. Retrieved from https://www.hm.ee/sites/default/files/estonian_lifelong_strategy.pdf.

Kunter, M., U. Klusmann, J. Baumert, D. Richter, T. Voss, and A. Hachfeld. (2013). Professional competence of teachers: Effects on instructional quality and student development. *Journal of Educational Psychology*, 105(3), 805–820.

Leijen, Ä., and M. Pedaste. (2018). Pedagogical beliefs, instructional practices, and opportunities for professional development of teachers in Estonia. In: H. Niemi, A. Toom, A. Kallioniemi, and J. Lavonen (Eds.), *The teacher's role in the changing globalizing world* (pp. 33-46). BRILL.

Lepik, M., T. Elvisto, T. Oder, and L. Talts. (2013). Õpetajate üldpedagoogiliste uskumuste struktuur ja tüüpprofiilid [The structure and typical profiles of teachers' general pedagogical beliefs]. In: E. Krull, Ä. Leijen, M. Lepik, J. Mikk, L. Talts, and T. Õun (Eds.), *Õpetajate professionaalne areng ja selle toetamine* [*Teachers' professional development and how to support it*] (pp. 248-273). Tallinn: Eesti Ülikoolide Kirjastus.

Malva, L., M. Linde, K. Poom-Valickis, and Ä. Leijen. (2018). *OECD õpetaja pedagoogiliste teadmiste pilootuuringu Eesti raport* [*Report of the OECD Pilot Study on Teacher Pedagogical Knowledge in Estonia*]. Retrieved from https://www.hm.ee/sites/default/files/uuringud/oecd_opetaja_pedagoogiliste_teadmiste_pilootu-uringu_eesti_raport_002.pdf.

McKinsey & Company. (2007). *How the world's best-performing school systems come on top*. Retrieved from https://www.mckinsey.com/industries/social-sector/our-insights/how-the-worlds-best-performing-school-systems-come-out-on-top.

Mets, U., and A. Viia. (2018). *Tulevikuvaade tööjõu- ja oskuste vajadusele: haridus ja teadus* [*Future perspective to the labor force and skills: Education and research*]. Uuringu lühiaruanne. Tallinn: SA Kutsekoda.

Moolenaar, N. M., P. J. C. Sleegers, and A. J. Daly. (2012). Teaming up: Linking collaboration networks, collective efficacy, and student achievement. *Teaching and Teacher Education*, 28(2), 251–262.

OECD. (2019). *TALIS 2018 results (volume I): Teachers and school leaders as lifelong learners*. Paris: OECD Publishing.

OECD. (2018). Estonia. In *Education at a glance 2018: OECD indicators*. Paris: OECD Publishing.

OECD. (2014). *TALIS 2013 Results: An international perspective on teaching and learning*, TALIS. Paris: OECD Publishing.

Pedaste, M., Ä. Leijen, K. Poom-Valickis, and E. Eisenschmidt. (2019). Teacher professional standards to support teacher quality and learning in Estonia. *European Journal of Education*, 54(3), 389–399.

Poom-Valickis, K. (2003). Õpetajate professionaalse arengu uurimine: kuidas muuta eelarvamuslikud tõekspidamised arengupotentsiaaliks [Transforming biased beliefs into development potential]. In: E. Krull and K. Oras (Eds.), *Õpetajate professionaalne areng ja õppepraktika. Õpetajakoolitus IV* [Teacher professional development and student teachers' school practice. Teacher training IV] (pp. 95-109). Tartu: Tartu Ülikooli Kirjastus.

Poom-Valickis, K., and T. Oder. (2013). Õpetajate metafoorides peegelduv arusaam oma rollist [Teachers' metaphors reflecting their perceptions of their roles]. In E. Krull, Ä. Leijen, M. Lepik, J. Mikk, L. Talts, and T. Õun (Eds.), *Õpetajate professionaalne areng ja selle toetamine* [Teachers' professional development and how to support it] (pp. 274-303). Tallinn: Eesti Ülikoolide Kirjastus.

Poom-Valickis, K., and E. Löfström. (2019). 'Pupils should have respect for you, although I have no idea how to achieve this?': The ideals and experiences shaping a teacher's professional identity. *Educational Studies*, 45(2), 145-162.

Ross, J. A., and P. Gray. (2006). Transformational leadership and teacher commitment to organizational values: The mediating effects of collective teacher efficacy. *School Effectiveness and School Improvement*, 17(2), 179-199.

Ruus, V.-R., and E.-S. Sarv. (2000). Changes in Estonian curricula (1987–1999) and some thought on the future. In: B. T. Beck and A. Mays (Eds.), *Challenge and change in education: The experience of the Baltic states in the 1990's* (pp. 141-152). New York: Nova Science Publishers.

Ruus, V.-R., I. Henno, E. Eisenschmidt, K. Loogma, H. Noorväli, P. Reiska, and S. Rekkor. (2008). Reforms, developments and trends in Estonian education during recent decades. In: J. Mikk, M. Veisson, and P. Luik (Eds.), *Reforms and innovations in Estonian education* (pp. 11-26). Peter Lang Publishers House.

Sonmark, K., N. Révai, F. Gottschalk, K. Deligiannidi, and T. Burns. (2017). *Understanding teachers' pedagogical knowledge: Report on an international pilot study*, OECD Education Working Papers, No. 159. Paris: OECD Publishing.

The Qualification framework for educators [Pedagoogide kvalifikatsiooninõuded]. Retrieved from https://www.riigiteataja.ee/akt/193676.

Uibu, K., M. Padrik, and S. Tenjes. (2016). Klassiõpetajate keele- ja suhtluseeskuju hindamine emakeeletunnis struktureeritud vaatluse teel [Linguistic-communicative modelling: Teachers' evaluation based on observation and students' native language skills]. *Eesti Haridusteaduste Ajakiri*, 4(1), 226-257.

Uibu, K., E. Kikas, and K. Tropp. (2011). Instructional approaches: Differences between kindergarten and primary school teachers. *COMPARE—A Journal of International and Comparative Education*, 41(1), 91-111.

Vangrieken, K., I. Grosemans, F. Dochy, and E. Kyndt. (2017). Teacher autonomy and collaboration: A paradox? Conceptualising and measuring teachers' autonomy and collaborative attitude. *Teaching and Teacher Education*, 67, 302-315.

Part V

Eastern Europe

19

Teacher Education in Russia: The Current State and Development Prospects

Roza A. Valeeva and Aydar Kalimullin

Introduction

The system of teacher education in Russia is currently going through a significant transformation, linked to various global, national, and regional challenges, such as globalisation of education, the relationship between research, policy and practice, and neo-liberal approaches to social policy. Against these backdrops, in terms of teacher education in Russia, these transformations and changes are panning out in two main directions. The first is organisational changes, for example, the system-level transformation of the higher education institutions that prepare teachers. The second is the attempt to modernise the content of teacher education study programmes.

Teacher training in Russia has transformed many times since the eighteenth century. Such transformation was the most profound, however, when the country profited from the notable economic growth. With the official end point of the Soviet Union in 1991, the past few decades have marked a pivotal point in Russia's history. Indeed, the 1990s was a turbulent decade for Russia due to the collapse of Soviet socialism, the fall of the Soviet Union, and the development of new political and economic systems. Despite this post-Soviet Union transformation, Soviet teacher training traditions and principles strongly influenced the Russian teacher education system until the early 2000s

R. A. Valeeva (✉) • A. Kalimullin
Kazan Federal University, Kazan, Russia
e-mail: valeykin@yandex.ru

© The Author(s), under exclusive license to Springer Nature Switzerland AG 2023
M. Kowalczuk-Walędziak et al. (eds.), *The Palgrave Handbook of Teacher Education in Central and Eastern Europe*, https://doi.org/10.1007/978-3-031-09515-3_19

(Valeeva and Kalimullin 2019a, b), when Russia co-signed the Bologna Declaration, and shifted from the five-year 'specialist' programme to the new, two-tier degree structure.

These fundamental changes in the political, socio-economic, and cultural aspects of life of Russia in recent decades have, in turn, necessitated a completely new model of teacher education. This model has evolved through key policy documents including the *Conception of Pedagogical Education Development Support* (2013), The Teacher Professional Standard (2013), and the *Comprehensive Programme to Improve the Professional Skills of Educational Institutions' Teaching Staff* (2014). These documents have brought about important changes in teacher education policy with significant consequences in terms of structure and curriculum (Valeeva and Gafurov 2017). The policy initiatives have sought to ensure the necessary conditions for bringing the system of professional teacher education in line with the latest achievements in pedagogical theory and practice in this part of the world, as well as the formation of professional competences in the process of pedagogical training (Menter et al. 2017).

Thus, teacher education in Russia today is a complex system which gives students a chance to enter the teaching profession through a number of different pathways. In light of how the structure of teacher education in Russia has significantly transformed over the past 20 years, as briefly outlined earlier, at present the country's teacher education can be understood as being in a transitional state: from the traditional, Soviet model to training teachers in both traditional and non-pedagogical universities, as is done in many countries throughout the modern world.

This chapter consists of five broad parts. The first will outline the history of teacher education in Russia, before reviewing some of the foundational aspects of the current state and role of teacher education. The second part will provide an introduction to challenges and reforms in the field of teacher education in Russia, with particular emphasis on how it has progressed in recent years. The third will focus on the structure of teacher education in Russia, especially as regards course content in the context of the Federal State Educational Standards. The fourth will overview the current Russian system of teacher professional development in terms of its organisation, its providers, and its financing. The fifth will provide a critical insight into the present tensions and challenges involved in transforming the field for the twenty-first century, as well as suggest directions for the future development of teacher education in Russia.

The Historical Background of Teacher Education in Russia over the Past Three Decades

Teacher training in Russia formally began at the end of the eighteenth century and has transformed many times over the past two centuries (Eskin 1952; Panachin 1979). Throughout the course of its history, the main objective of teacher education in Russia has been the eradication of illiteracy and the improvement of the overall education level of all Russian people, as prompted by key shifts in the country's broader development. The feudalistic social structures of Medieval and Early Modern Europe finally crumbled in the first half of the nineteenth century, then capitalism spread throughout the second half of the nineteenth century and the beginning of the twentieth century. Then teacher education subsequently developed rapidly during the Soviet period (i.e. 1917–1991): indeed, the Soviet Union brought unprecedented education reforms which were aimed at improving education quality while also making education more accessible. However, the collapse of the Soviet Union and the whole socialist system precipitated the birth of new political and economic systems, with corresponding changes in the field of education: setting a course for educational liberalisation; joining the Bologna Process; developing new types of teacher education institutions; introducing fee-based university education; and facing teacher shortages.

From the nineteenth century onwards, teacher training in Russia was carried out via academic universities where special pedagogical institutes were opened at the beginning of the century. Subsequently, on the basis of those institutes, autonomous teacher training institutions were introduced, a tradition which was continued in the Soviet Union (Vasilyev 1966; Shcherbakov 1968; Slastenin 1976; Knyazev 1989; Pletneva 1997), where teacher training was carried out in around 200 teacher training institutes and over 60 universities. Correspondingly, only 5–10% of Soviet Russian teachers were trained in universities and the vast majority were trained in autonomous teacher training institutes. From the 1990s onwards, the number of state teacher training institutes and universities has decreased in Russia: dropping to 96 in the mid-1990s, 70 in 2008, and just 33 today. The fundamental contradiction between educational, research, and technical criteria on the one hand, and the accreditation requirements imposed by the government on the other, is one of the main reasons behind this decline—along with the considerable drop in state support for higher education institutions during the post-Soviet Union economic recession, which caused stagnation. For these reasons, many of them were reformed mainly by merging with academic universities (Bolotov 2001).

Prior to this, however, the necessity for radical changes in the goals, structure, contents, and methodology in teacher education had formally become apparent in December 1988 when the Plenum of the Central Committee of the Communist Party noted the need for an organic unity between: the goals and objectives of education; the diversity of schools; the flexibility of curricula and programmes relying on advanced teaching practice; and innovative methods of teaching and upbringing. There was a need for all of these elements to be better aligned, and this alignment required the transformation of the system responsible for the training and re-training of teaching staff (Isaev 1993).

As a result of the corresponding teacher education theory and practice development in the late 1980s, a comprehensive, targeted programme entitled 'Teacher of the Soviet School' (1987) was adopted. The programme specifically defined the conditions that would facilitate the formation of the Soviet school teacher:

* the unity of pedagogical staff;
* the continuity of the pre-university, university, and postgraduate stages in the teacher's education;
* the admission to teacher training institutions being based on: the generalised model of the prospective teacher's personality; a diagnosis of their professional suitability for pedagogical activity; and a scientifically-based admissions process;
* and the formation of the prospective teacher's holistic attitude to the teaching profession.

The post-Soviet Union reform of teacher education began to grow rapidly throughout the 1990s, following the decision to de-politicise, decentralise, and democratise schools—marking an extremely important new stage in the development of Russian education, including teacher education. As such, the management of education gradually ceased to be politicised, but rather became an object of legislative regulation, that is, the rule of law. The first such law was the Law of the Russian Federation 'On Education' adopted in 1992 which led to some of the country's pedagogical institutes being reorganised into pedagogical universities (Bolotov 2001).

Three stages can be distinguished in the development of teacher education in the post-Soviet period. The first (1991–1998) solved the local-level problems of teacher education institutions—pedagogical colleges and pedagogical institutes—which independently adapted to Russia's new socio-economic conditions. The second (1999–2002) focused on the development of the teacher education system as a whole, as reflected in the *Programme for the Development of Continuing Teacher Education for the period 2001–2010* (2001). The third (2003–2010) centred on the modernisation of the education system, beginning with general education, as reflected in the development and implementation of the *Teacher Education Modernisation Programme* (2003)—approved by the Russian Ministry of Education in April 2003 and hereinafter referred to as *Programme-2003*.

Programme-2003 set out the following tasks for the Russian teacher education system:

* fully orienting towards the functioning and development of its direct consumer—that is, the general education school;
* developing scientific and methodological support for the modernisation processes, both in secondary schools and in the teacher education system itself;
* and expanding the use of state and public mechanisms in managing the functioning and development of teacher education.

Furthermore, *Programme-2003* stipulated directions of development for the theory and practice of teacher education, including

* to develop a system for monitoring and forecasting the pedagogical personnel needs across each of Russia's regions;
* to improve the structure and content of teacher education;
* to bring information technology into teacher education;
* to raising the qualifications of the teaching staff at teacher training universities involved in the field of general education modernisation;
* and to ensure scientific and methodological support for the teacher education modernisation process.

One of the most significant achievements in terms of updating the management of Russia's teacher education system within *Programme-2003* was the creation of conditions for collaboration between the teacher education institutions at the inter-regional level. This was a critical and positive development because, prior to this, up until the early 2000s, despite the increased intra-regional integration of educational institutions, the regional complexes themselves developed separately from each other, resulting in the lack of the continuum of teacher education.

In summation, these reforms in teacher education brought about a wide range of socio-cultural consequences, both positive and negative. For instance, appearance of new values in education led to the new aims and objectives of teacher education, the end of ideology; on the other hand, the teacher education reforms failed to achieve their ultimate goals due to the lack of economic resources and political instability. However, the ongoing need to reform teacher education was recognised at all levels, including by the pedagogical community itself.

The Challenges and Reforms of Teacher Education in Contemporary Russia

By the beginning of the twenty-first century, Russia's teacher education system was based on the principles of continuous development and lifelong learning. This system prepares specialists for work in a variety of education institutions, namely: pre-schools (including specialised pre-schools); primary schools; general secondary education organisations (including lyceums, gymnasiums, and grammar schools); professional education institutions (i.e. vocational and higher education establishments); schools for children with disabilities or additional support needs; and re-training and advanced training organisations. Apart from working in education institutions, educators are also often employed by organisations that have other orientations, for example: social institutions (e.g. adult education, employment services, pension funds, services that provide social and psychological support to child refugees, organisations that work with young people who need behavioural support, juvenile offenders, people who are homeless, and people who have addiction problems); managerial institutions; and family education and development.

Despite these commitments to continuous learning and equipping students to take up a wide range of professional roles, three main groups of problems defined the crisis in Russia's teacher education system at the beginning of 2010. Firstly were the difficulties related to entering the teaching profession: for instance, a large proportion of the school leavers intending to pursue a degree in education had been awarded low grades in their exams, suggesting a lack of the academic aptitude required for entering the field. At the other end of the education process, there was a shortage of job placements in the sphere of education for graduates with a degree in education, thus creating the problem of the so-called double negative selection. Secondly were the problems connected with the inappropriate training received by graduates during their initial teacher education, for example: out-of-date methods of training; insufficient hours of internships or hands-on experience; no activity-based approaches in students' training; no connection between the courses offered to student teachers and the actual needs of the schools in which they were seeking employment; students not being adequately encouraged to undertake research activity; and the under-resourcing of educational programmes. Thirdly were the problems regarding sustainable employment, specifically as connected with: the lack of forecasting in terms of regional demand for educators; the lack of responsibility taken by the regions in terms of not honouring the cap on student numbers and future employment of graduates; ineffectual recruitment methods failing to attract the most talented graduates into teaching careers; the lack of professional support and guidance for beginner teachers; as well as the lack of school vacancies.

Correspondingly, numerous structural problems also arose in the teacher education field. A key example is the definitively reproductive character of teacher education in Russia (Conception of teacher education development support 2013), whereby student teachers are trained to follow instructions, with the primary goal of re-generating the knowledge and practical skills dictated to them. Other fundamental problems included the absence of multi-track teacher training as a means of attracting highly-motivated students to work as teachers, and the lack of a well-targeted political strategy for elevating the socio-economic status of the teacher which would, in turn, motivate school students to become teachers (Bolotov 2014; Margolis 2014).

Collectively, these problems prompted the Russian government to start another reform of teacher education. In the legislative and regulatory acts that came out over the past decade—including the most important of them, the 2012 Federal Law on Education in the Russian Federation—it has been acknowledged that there was a need to modernise education. This legislative decision reflected the political, socio-economic, and cultural changes Russia experienced in the first decade of the twenty-first century, thus defining a completely new model of teacher education. As mentioned in the introduction, this model evolved via key policy documents, including the Conception of Teacher Education Development Support (2013), The Teacher Professional Standard (2013), and the *Comprehensive Programme to Improve the Professional Skills of Educational Institutions' Teaching Staff* (2014).

Firstly, the Conception of Teacher Education Development Support (2013) document located initial teacher training, in-service training, and professional re-training at the heart of the reform. The endeavour to combine the opportunities offered by both general and pedagogical universities created unique and new possibilities for content formation and organisational structure in the teacher education sector.

At the same time, The Teacher Professional Standard (2013) was adopted with the goals of: establishing uniform requirements for the content and quality of vocational education activities; assessing the qualification level of in-service teachers and certification for career planning; devising job descriptions; and developing federal state teacher education standards. *The Teacher Professional Standard* defined everything in the teaching profession: the type, nature, and content of teacher education; teachers' employment contracts; state certification and assignment of the relevant category; labour contracts; and even the value of future pensions.

As The Teacher Professional Standard (2013) is a national framework document, it defines the basic requirements for teachers' qualifications, and may be supplemented by local regulations that take into account the socio-cultural and demographic characteristics of the territory they govern (e.g. the megacity of Moscow, rural areas, and mono-ethnic or multi-ethnic regions). *The Teacher Professional Standard* can also be supplemented by internal standards set by education institutions themselves, in accordance with their own specifics (e.g. schools for gifted children and inclusive schools). Furthermore, the standard makes demands relating to the personal qualities of the teacher, locating them as inseparable from their professional competences, such as a willingness to teach all children, regardless of their inclinations, abilities, and disabilities. Introduction of the new teacher professional standard inevitably entails changes to the standard of their training and retraining in higher education and centres of excellence.

Subsequently, the 2014 *Comprehensive Programme to Improve the Professional Skills of Educational Institutions' Teaching Staff* focused on reforming training for pre-school educators, primary and secondary school teachers, and teachers involved in extracurricular activities. Together, these three documents have provided a unified formal basis for important changes in Russia's education policy with powerful consequences in terms of the structure and curriculum of teacher education (Valeeva and Gafurov 2017)—specifically, seeking to ensure the necessary conditions for bringing the system of professional teacher education in line with the latest milestones in pedagogical theory and practice, as well as, as mentioned in the introduction, formulating professional competences (Menter et al. 2017).

In 2014, a major teacher education modernisation project was launched by Russia's Ministry of Education and Science. This two-stage project (spanning 2014–2017) included 33 small projects aimed at modernising all aspects and main profiles of teacher education. 65 universities from across the Russian regions participated in the project. Its main objective was to provide teacher training in accordance with The Teacher Professional Standard (2013) and the federal state standards for general education (Bolotov et al. 2015). For these four years, the universities participating in the reform project developed and tested new teacher training programmes, assessment tools, models of professional school practice, new technologies, and so on (Margolis and Safronova 2018). Indeed, the project's core tasks illustrate the main trends in teacher education reform in Russia today:

1. developing a competence-based profile for contemporary teachers well equipped to respond to the challenges presented by the twenty-first century, as well as the requirements set by Russia's professional standards for teachers
2. providing multiple, accessible routes to entering the teaching profession
3. implementing an activity-based methodology in teacher training
4. designing educational programmes based on the development of modules that prepare teachers to solve professional problems and puzzles
5. enhancing pre-service teachers' practical training through school-university partnerships
6. implementing new approaches, including the continuous, competence-based model of pedagogical education, as well as developing a corresponding legal framework
7. modernising equipment and facilities at teacher training universities, establishing professional libraries, and devising massive online open courses (MOOCs)
8. scaling up the initial project results:

   (a) other major teacher training universities in Russia will test the newly modernised teacher education programmes
   (b) further advanced training will be given to programme managers and teaching staff
   (c) open access to the results of the project will be provided for all other Russian universities

9. creating online platforms to test the targeted teacher training model in the field of teacher education
10. assessing the quality of the designed programmes through an independent assessment of students' professional competences, following the requirements of The Teacher Professional Standard (2013)

During this reform project, a new model for designing module-based professional educational programmes was successfully tested and implemented, helping to bring an activity-based approach to the teacher training process. The participants of the project also developed and tested 42 new educational programmes to prepare teachers for the main subjects, plus the school practice component was strengthened (Gafurov et al. 2018; Margolis and Safronova 2018).

The priorities driving ongoing teacher training reforms in Russia can be divided into four basic areas. The first regards ensuring that the best-suited students are the ones undertaking teacher education, by eliminating the linear path of learning and creating a direct pathway into the teacher education programmes for diverse groups of students, that is, undergraduates and bachelors, in-service teachers and professionals from other sectors. In addition, bachelor's teacher training programmes as profiling of universal bachelor's programme were developed.

Secondly, the ongoing reforms deal with changes in the content, forms, and methods of teacher training programmes, in order to ensure the implementation of The Teacher Professional Standard (2013), as well as the new standards of school education and practical training, thus strengthening the connections between training content and the actual practical tasks of the profession. The training components exist on subject, psychological, educational, informational, and technical bases. These changes also involve the enrichment of curricula with an extensive system of school-based practices, internships, and training teachers not only to teach different subjects, but in different types of schools and for different groups of students, all via the means of school-university partnerships. Training teachers for a wide range of out-of-school activities and facilitating informal education is also incorporated into these changes.

Thirdly, the reform touches upon improving the efficiency of existing colleges and universities providing teacher training programmes, namely by introducing joint practical training programmes (i.e. the applied bachelor's degree programme), as well as developing master's degree programmes for applicants wishing to start—or continue—a career in education.

Fourthly, the priorities of the reform deal with developing and testing the independent certification of professional teachers who have already received the diploma through various training programmes in order to facilitate the graduates' mentoring system and teachers' career development the establishment of the system of educational programmes' quality assessment (Khromenkov 2015).

At the end of 2017, the results of the two stages of the modernisation programme—2014–2015 and 2016–2017—were presented to the Ministry of Education and Science.

The Structure and Content of Contemporary Teacher Education in Russia

Teacher education in Russia today is a complex system of continuous training which gives students a chance to enter the profession in a number of different ways, as well as maintain their professional skill set throughout the course of their careers. As noted earlier, the structure of teacher education in Russia has significantly transformed over the past 20 years. While in Soviet times, specialised teachers' universities and institutes produced the overwhelming majority (90–95%) of teachers, the picture has now changed and the ratio of pedagogical to non-pedagogical universities providing teacher education has become almost equal. The number of specialised pedagogical universities has decreased, plus non-pedagogical and non-state universities have begun to actively participate in this strand of higher education, applying comparatively liberal requirements for the state accreditation of teacher education programmes. At present, Russia's continuous teacher education takes place across: vocational education institutions, higher education institutions, continuous professional development education institutions, and professional re-training.

As regards Russia's vocational education institutions offering teacher education, in 2017 there were about 430 teacher training colleges and technical schools, catering for more than 110,000 students (MDCC 2018c). Local governments fund most of these institutions and the majority of them are specialised teacher training colleges, from which around 34,000 teachers graduate each year, mainly from pre-school and primary education programmes. These institutions also train the general education school teachers of particular subjects, such as music, drawing, and physical education.

As regards Russia's higher education institutions offering teacher education, the majority were specialised teacher training institutions until the 1990s. Today, the term 'specialised pedagogical universities' has been substituted by the idea of higher education institutions that deliver teacher education through pedagogical programmes (Valeeva and Gafurov 2017). As such, current higher education institutions can be further grouped into:

1. specialised pedagogical universities and institutions
2. traditional, non-pedagogical universities that deliver teacher education through pedagogical programmes
3. specialised universities (e.g. specialising in technical, economic, humanities, linguistic, or agrarian studies) that deliver teacher education through pedagogical programmes
4. Federal, regional, and local universities that were formed as a result of the merger of several universities, including pedagogical universities
5. Private universities that deliver teacher education through select pedagogical programmes

Today, Russia's non-pedagogical universities prepare as many future teachers as the pedagogical universities do (Pletyago et al. 2019). In 2017, teacher education modules were offered at 48 pedagogical universities and 226 non-pedagogical universities, of which 50 universities were not state-funded (MDCC 2018a). The number of students at both types of the universities was almost equal: 115,581 teacher education students attended pedagogical universities and 106,039 teacher education students attended non-pedagogical universities (MDCC 2018a, b).

Within the past decade, small pedagogical universities were merged with large non-pedagogical federal universities to form a completely new type of university which facilitates a large share of Russia's teacher education programmes. Besides, their creation yielded valuable financial benefits, along with highly qualified teaching staff and modern management systems, as the resources of multiple universities were combined. The teacher education units in such universities are commensurate with solely pedagogical universities in terms of the quality of education they provide (UEQM 2017). These new universities are characterised by well-developed infrastructure and efficient educational services, as they incorporate non-pedagogical universities' up-to-date research laboratories serving a range of scientific areas on the one hand, and pedagogical universities' substantial experience in teaching techniques and didactics on the other. One example of such a merger is when, in 2011, two teacher training universities joined Kazan Federal University: now, 10,300 pre-service teachers are studying there—comprising almost 20% of all students at the university—and 9000 teachers take CPD courses there annually. Thus, after the merging of several universities and their resources, a new model of teacher education was implemented (Kalimullin 2014a, b; Valeeva and Gafurov 2017).

A key aspect of Russia's education system is that, in addition to full-time studies, it is also possible to study part-time. This mode became popular during the Soviet period as it meant that students could study and work at the same time. Today, both full-time and part-time students should undertake courses totalling 240 ECTS credits. However, part-time students attend the university for only 40 or 50 days each year, giving them the chance to teach while they study, which is very important for rural regions where teachers are in short supply, and for teachers who plan to change their teacher profiles.

Education Institutions for Continuous Professional Development and Professional Re-training

There are more than 90 institutions for continuing professional development and professional re-training in Russia, with one in every region funded by the local government—teachers should study at these institutions once every three years. It takes 500 hours for those with a higher education degree, but without a teaching degree. These institutions also cater for those teachers who want to change their teacher profiles or broaden their initial qualifications (Gorshunova 2002; Gorbunova 2010).

The types of education institutions in Russia correlate with degree levels. According to article 10 of the law, 'On education in the Russian Federation' adopted in 2012, professional education is divided into the following levels: (1) secondary professional (vocational) education; (2) higher professional education (bachelor's degree); (3) higher professional education (master's degree); and (4) higher professional education (PhDs and post-doctoral degrees).

1. Secondary professional (vocational) education is provided at special teacher training colleges, where school graduates who have completed nine or 11 years at school can study full-time for two or four years.
2. Bachelor's degree programmes take four years and cover 240 ECTS credits, as a rule. If a student has studied at a teacher training college before their bachelor's degree, this is reduced to three years and two months. The bachelor's degree can include up to 15 subject profiles (i.e. for teaching physics, maths, and physical education). There are also double profile bachelor's degree programmes (e.g. for English language and primary school teachers), and these past for five years and cover 300 ECTS credits. All bachelor's degree programmes are taught at higher education institutions: both specialised teacher training universities and traditional, non-pedagogical universities.

3. Master's degree programmes are designed and run by specific universities, depending on the labour market demand—as a rule, it takes two years to complete and covers 120 ECTS credits. The most common form of master's degree is based on the bachelor's degree and begins immediately after completing the latter. Master's degrees of this type involve obtaining a higher degree of education on the same aspect of education or specialism as the bachelor's. However, it is possible to enrol in a master's programme even after graduating from a bachelor's degree in another aspect of education. Either way, a master's student can choose between two routes: to become a highly qualified educator, or to become an educator-researcher. Education at this level is directed towards organising research activities in order to teach future specialists how to conduct research projects, as well as analyse and present their findings. Over the course of their master's studies, students are mainly engaged in independent work supervised by their academic adviser. In comparison to specialist degree programmes, the amount of classroom-based hours is lower, but, instead, students have the opportunity to explore a specific topic or issue within their chosen profession in detail—writing and defending a dissertation that requires academic originality, depth, and independently collected evidence.

4. The highest level of professional education encompasses PhD and post-doctoral degrees, which, like master's level, calls for the writing and defence of an original piece of work. Those who have doctoral and post-doctoral degrees work at universities or at schools as school advisors.

Thus, Russia's pedagogical corps are extremely heterogeneous in terms of the level and quality of their professional training, making it difficult to compose a generalised, national portrait of a teacher. It should also be noted here that the training of vocational school teachers is carried out outside the general system of teacher education. Moreover, these teacher education systems are constantly changing under the influence of market mechanisms and the targeted reform activities of federal and local education authorities.

Earlier, the process of teacher training was completely controlled by central government bodies, which determined not only all the details of training course content and time allotted, but the way the course material was presented. All teacher training schools were required to follow the curriculum which was published by the Ministry of Education every five years. In contrast, the ongoing modern reform is aimed at autonomising and diversifying the higher education institutions that train teachers.

All teacher training universities providing teacher education programmes in Russia follow the Federal State Educational Standards for Higher Education when they develop their own educational programmes—in 2018, the fourth generation of the Federal State Educational Standards for Higher Education (FSESHE 2018a, b) were adopted. The standards for bachelor's programmes in education set 70% of the basic curriculum, and universities can set the remaining 30%. The standards for master's programmes in education set 40% of the basic curriculum and universities can set the remaining 60%. These standards set uniform requirements to the education process.

The FSES set out the range of professional competences which graduates of pedagogical bachelor's programmes in Russia should attain throughout the course of their studies—including eight universal competences (e.g. ability to search, critically analyse and synthesise information, apply a systematic approach to solving assigned tasks; ability to determine the range of tasks within the framework of the goal and choose the best ways to solve them, based on the current legal norms, available resources and restrictions) and eight general professional competences (e.g. ability to carry out professional activities in accordance with the regulatory legal acts in the field of education and the norms of professional ethics; ability to participate in the development of basic and supplementary educational programmes, to develop their individual components (including using information and communication technologies)) (FSESHE 2018a). The graduates of pedagogical master's programmes are expected to attain six universal competences (e.g. ability to carry out a critical analysis of problem situations based on a systematic approach, develop an action strategy; and ability to manage a project at all stages of its life cycle) and eight general professional competences (e.g. ability to carry out and optimise professional activities in accordance with regulatory legal acts in the field of education and the norms of professional ethics; ability to design basic and additional educational programmes and develop scientific and methodological support for their implementation) (FSESHE 2018b). The teacher education curriculum is designed to enable the progressive attainment of these competences.

Furthermore, the structure of a bachelor's degree in education consists of a mandatory, foundational part and a variable part, which makes it possible to fulfil different bachelor's programmes within one orientation. Thus, acquiring a professional teaching qualification happens via a process of mastering disciplines that are grouped into different cycles, among which the professional cycles predominate, occupying three-quarters of all the time assigned to the foundational part of the course. Programmes with different specialisations have almost the same set of foundation disciplines within the natural sciences and social sciences—here, the professional cycle focuses, firstly, on different aspects of culture, education, and social sciences (being three core pedagogical orientations), then, secondly, on subject-specific disciplines that prepare future educators for teaching their chosen subjects.

In its bid for modernisation, the current stage in the development of Russia's teacher education presents the challenge of finding new master's education models. A number of ideas have already been established in national discourse regarding a radical restructuring of teacher training at university level. Firstly, the idea of forming master's programmes of both applied and academic orientations has been fixed in educational standards (FSESHE 2018b). Secondly, there is the idea of different pathways into the teaching profession, including getting a master's degree in education (Artamonova 2011). Thirdly, considerable attention is being paid to the roles of general and additional education organisations in the integral process of teachers' practical training (Glubokova et al. 2015).

The Russian System of Teacher Professional Development, Its Organisation, Providers, and Financing

Approximately 70,000 new teachers enter the Russian education system every year, representing about 5% of the country's total teaching staff (Nikitin 1999). Furthermore, delivering professional reorientation and re-training for in-service teachers within a reasonable time frame also requires significant effort, as more than 1.5 million individuals across the country need these types of teacher education. In Russia, organised professional development for teachers and school principals originated in the nineteenth century with teachers' congresses held in the regions of Russia on the initiative of the pedagogical community (Zubkova 2013). Then, throughout the twentieth century, a system of supplementary professional education was formed. It is through this system that regular work to improve the qualifications and professional knowledge of pedagogical personnel across all categories is undertaken. By the end of the 1980s, Russia's formal professional development system ensured the timely and systematic ongoing education of teachers and school principals (Nikitin 1999).

Russia's teacher education system helps teachers to continue their professional development, in light of their individual education level, qualifications, and teaching experience—indeed, flexibility within this system helps professionals to independently navigate their progress, both horizontally and vertically. For example, a maths teacher who has a bachelor's degree can go on to study a master's degree in order to work at university or at a school for academically gifted children; or a physics teacher can complete another qualification and teach children who need behavioural support; or a clinical psychologist can study to become a speech therapist; or an engineer can study to become a robotics teacher (Valeeva and Kalimullin 2019b).

In Russia, continuous professional development programmes for improving the qualifications of teaching staff must undergo a licencing procedure, and the standard time period for all advanced training programmes is between 72 and 500 academic hours. Long-term training (spanning 216 hours) is intended for: school principals and their deputies; the teachers of selected subjects—for example, computer science and the humanities; and young specialists, that is, graduates of higher teacher education institutions. Short-term training—that is, thematic training, spanning 72 academic hours—is intended for other categories of educators, for example, social pedagogues.

This cumulative system of advanced training and professional re-training for teaching staff is recorded in the student's unified record book, and an individual plan for their professional development is drawn up by an educator to cover a period of three to five years. Such organisation of the course system allows educators to improve their qualifications over one or more years across one or more institutions. The results of interim and final certifications from the advanced training system are also recorded in the student's record book. More formally, to certify the results from the 72+ hours of advanced training, the education institution issues a state document. Professional development is mainly funded by regional budgets. Employees of the education system are guaranteed the opportunity to choose such courses at least once every five years, covering a minimum of 72 hours. Admission to courses is dictated on a budgetary basis by the Department of Education, district departments of education, and methodological centres.

Professional development is a regular pursuit for Russian teachers. According to the 2018 TALIS results, almost every teacher (98%) reported that they had participated in some form of professional development in the past 12 months—regardless of gender, age, work experience, school type, school location, or the proportion of students who were immigrants in the student population. Teachers in Russia participated, on average, in six types of professional development activities—such as reading professional literature; face-to-face courses and workshops; self-observation and/or inviting colleagues to observe their lessons as part of a formal, school-based professional development programme; study visits to other schools; educational conferences; online courses and seminars; participating in the network of teachers—which is one and a half times more than in other countries (TALIS 2019,

p. 12). However, there does appear to be a correlation between the length of professional service and the amounts of training types received, as teachers with more than five years of work experience, on average, mentioned one more type of advanced training more than their less experienced colleagues (TALIS 2019, p. 12).

On the whole, the most popular method of professional development among Russia's teachers is reading professional literature: 91% of Russian teachers used this method in the calendar year preceding the survey—versus 71% among all TALIS member countries (TALIS 2019, p. 12). Face-to-face courses and workshops were also popular (85%), as were self-observation and/or inviting colleagues to observe their lessons as part of a formal, school-based professional development programme (76%). Professional development programmes for teachers are, according to the respondents, most often aimed at: developing competences in the main subject area (89%); improving teaching methods (89%); increasing knowledge in the field of the educational programme (83%); and the practice of assessing students (83%). On the other hand, the least frequently reported vocational programmes included the topics of: school management and administration (28%); communicating with representatives of other countries and cultures (26%); and teaching in a multicultural or multi-lingual environment (24%) (TALIS 2019, p. 13).

In the past two decades, many of Russia's professional development institutions have also become centres for the development of regional education. Within the framework of these institutions, strategies and tactics for the development of regional education are developed and tested; problem areas are identified; transformations are projected; and development resources are formed. They also examine innovations and the effectiveness of project activities aimed at transforming pedagogical realities on a regional level. At the same time, however, these institutions do not lose their basic functions, continuing to provide professional development for teachers.

Overall, the following transition trends have emerged in Russia's present-day teacher professional development education:

* moving towards a variable system that provides teachers with the opportunity to choose an institution for advanced training, including those outside the traditional institutions;
* moving towards students choosing the modules in their educational programme;
* moving towards greater choice of organisational forms of advanced training (e.g. full-time, part-time, part-time via distance learning technologies, and distance learning);

* moving towards training teams of various levels and compositions (e.g. administrative teams, school teams, and innovative municipal teams);
* and moving towards including students in the development of education programme content (Gorshunova 2002; Gorbunova 2010).

In 2014, the *Comprehensive programme for improving the professional level of general education organisation teachers* was adopted—aiming at integrating and improving the efforts of federal and regional education authorities and educational organisations within the framework of implementing state policy in the field. In particular, goals include mastering modern educational technologies, as well as contemporary teaching and upbringing methods, knowledge, skills, and abilities, in order to ensure pro-actively inclusive education for people with disabilities, via the implementation of adapted educational programmes. The programme includes 4 sub-programmes:

* introducing the teachers' professional standard;
* modernising teacher education;
* ensuring the transition to an effective contract system for teaching staff;
* and raising the social status and prestige of the teaching profession.

By order of the Ministry of Education and Science of Russia (No. 703, July 26, 2017), the action plan for the formation and implementation of the *National teacher growth system* was approved, created to regulate the introduction of new teaching positions—teacher, senior teacher, and lead teacher—and to tackle important challenges:

* creating a tool to stimulate teachers' professional growth;
* introducing single sample certification requirements for all teachers in the Russian Federation;
* creating a professional career ladder, where each step reflects the teacher's compliance with the professional standards;
* and introducing new assessment (i.e. certification) methods to check the teacher's compatibility with the position.

Despite the fact that more attention is now paid to the teacher professional development system than before, the concept of re-training still needs to be adjusted. The priority areas within this system should be: training managers; developing curricula; assessing the results of educational work; introducing new teaching methods; and developing activity which promotes the holistic development of the education institution. Ultimately, going forwards, the pedagogical process should be based on the results of scientific research in key reform areas (Action Plan 2017).

Tensions in Transforming Russia's Teacher Education and Directions for Future Development

To date, as outlined in this chapter, major shifts have already taken place in Russia's teacher education system, although the level of training in many educational institutions leaves much to be desired. Recently, weak/turbulent socio-economic conditions, and, above all, the ongoing economic crisis, have had a significantly negative impact on the modernisation process. The funds allocated for teacher education from the regional/national/education sector budget are not enough to cover even the normal functioning of pedagogical universities, let alone for ensuring their development. With the financing of teacher education in such a poor state, its planned modernisation simply cannot be carried out on the required scale. Nonetheless, there are a number of interrelated problems that Russia's teacher education system has faced and continues to face, including:

* inconsistency between modern pedagogical education and Russia's social transformations, causing the necessity of changing the role teacher education from the system of professional training of teachers to the system quickly responding to the changes taking place in education and be of assistance to them;
* the absence of a state-level forecast for personnel training (the currently available forecast does not adequately reflect the demographic trends in the regions);
* limited use of information technologies in education, which, despite significant financial investments, have not yet become embedded in Russia's education culture;
* limited accessibility of pedagogical education on geographical and inclusivity bases;
* the lack of a selection service for applicants to pedagogical education institutions, thus weakening the professional motivation of applicants;
* the exclusion of municipalities from interacting with pedagogical education institutions;
* weaknesses in the scientific development of management and organisational problems with the training of teaching staff;

* and the insufficient funding of the pedagogical sub-industry, for example, the annual expenditures of the Russian budget system on education amounted to only 4.1% of GDP in 2016 (Gokhberg et al. 2020).

These factors are partly caused by the restructuring of Russia's pedagogical university network, including and especially their integration into larger universities, to the extent that their number has decreased by more than a third since the collapse of the Soviet Union. At the same time, teacher training in non-pedagogical universities (and their branches) has expanded. In other words, the modernisation of pedagogical education, thus far, has been aimed at an organisational level to the detriment of the actual content of teacher education courses.

At the beginning of the twenty-first century, the confrontation between university-based and specialised teacher training led to serious competition between pedagogical universities and traditional universities for the priority to offer teacher training. In the traditions of Russian education, there was a peaceful coexistence of these two institutional models of higher pedagogical education; however, on the 15th of 2018, the Ministry of Education and Science, which had carried out all previous reforms, was divided into two separate departments: the Ministry of Education and the Ministry of Science and Higher Education. This structural split contributed to the deepening of this tension, to some extent. Further, according to the Order of the Government of the Russian Federation (April 6, 2020, No. 907-r, 33) pedagogical and socio-pedagogical federal universities were transferred to the jurisdiction of the Ministry of Education of the Russian Federation. The remaining non-pedagogical universities implementing teacher education programmes—numbering more than 200—remained under the jurisdiction of the Ministry of Science and Higher Education. In light of this divide, there is now an acute need to build systemic relations between teacher training programmes in education organisations of different levels, primarily between universities and teacher training colleges, as this will create real opportunities for continuous teacher education and teacher professional growth.

Although critical, these problems related to the organisation and content of teacher education are not exhaustive in Russia's pursuit of a teacher education system built for the twenty-first century. The need to develop the system of lifelong pedagogical education on a foundational level is primarily due to the recent expansion and qualitative change in the scope of teachers' professional activities. Over the past 20 years, the concepts of 'teacher' and 'educator' have fundamentally changed. Now, pedagogical professions that did not exist before have appeared—for instance, tutor and teacher-organiser—and each of them, in addition to general professional skills, requires special skills. However, in Russia's present teacher education system, there is no purposeful teaching of these professions, meaning that there is a real need for the system to adapt and pro-actively include them.

Indeed, as illustrated earlier, education is becoming an increasingly complex system operating within a dynamically changing world, one that makes increasing demands on all participants in the educational process. With this in mind, further modernisation of Russia's teacher education system requires the implementation of the following conditions:

* raising the socio-economic status of the teacher;
* creating the material conditions conducive to boosting teachers' motivation to improve the quality of their pedagogical activity;
* forming an educational environment, within which the teacher, on the one hand, is free to choose the strategy and tactics of their pedagogical activity, and, on the other hand, bears real responsibility for the results of the educational process;
* forming a unified system for monitoring the effectiveness of teacher education, based on analysing the success of graduates' pedagogical activity;
* uniting scientific and pedagogical institutes via real pedagogical practice, by attracting scientists to careers in providing scientific and practical support within general education institutions;
* creating a more robust admissions process that fully familiarises prospective students with the demands of the course they are applying for;
* increasing the proportion of pedagogy students' independent work, as well as their teaching practice in schools;
* and involving practicing teachers who demonstrate excellent pedagogical practice in the teacher education processes.

Thus, the current and recommended transformation processes of Russia's teacher education are in line with international trends (Page 2015; Beauchamp et al. 2016; Menter et al. 2017; Pletyago et al. 2019)—such radical renewal and reform of teacher education are, after all, a necessary response to the challenges of our time.

References

Action Plan ("road map") for the formation and implementation of a National Teacher Growth System. (2017). Retrieved from https://www.garant.ru/products/ipo/prime/doc/71641920/.

Artamonova, E. I. (2011). Peculiarities of organization of multilevel teacher education and its functioning in the framework of the Bologna process. *Pedagogicheskoye obrazovanie i nauka—Teacher Education and Science*, 8, 8–15.

Beauchamp, G., L. Clarke, M. Hulme, M. Jephcote, A. Kennedy, G. Magennis, … G. Peiser. (2016). *Teacher education in times of change.* Bristol: Bristol University Press.

Bolotov, V. A. (2001). *Theory and practice of the teacher education reform in Russia in terms of social change.* Doctoral dissertation. St. Petersburg: Herzen RSPU.

Bolotov, V. A. (2014). Issues of the Reform of Pedagogical Education. *Psikhologicheskaya nauka i obrazowanie*, 19 (3), 32–40.

Bolotov, V. A., V. V. Rubtsov, I. D. Froumin, A. A. Margolis, A. G. Kasprzhak, M. A. Safronova, and S. P. Kalashnikov. (2015). Information analysis products on the first phase results of the project 'Modernization of teacher education'. *Psikhologicheskaya nauka i obrazovanie*, 20(5), 13–28.

Comprehensive programme to improve the professional skills of educational institutions teaching staff. (2014). Retrieved from http://www.consultant.ru/document/cons_doc_LAW_166654/.

Comprehensive target programme 'Teacher of the Soviet School: General Research Concept'. (1987). Moscow: MGPI named after V.I. Lenin.

Conception of teacher education development support. (2013). Retrieved from https://docplayer.ru/38675790-Koncepciya-podderzhki-razvitiya-pedagogicheskogo-obrazovaniya.html.

Eskin, M. I. (1952). *Secondary school teachers' training in pre-revolutionary Russia (XVIII beginning of XX century).* Doctoral dissertation. Yaroslavl: YSPU.

Federal State Education Standards for Higher Education (FSESHE)—bachelor's degree in the specialty 44.03.01 Teacher Education no. 121 as of February 22, 2018. (2018a). Retrieved from http://fgosvo.ru/uploadfiles/FGOS%20VO%203++/Bak/440301_B_3_16032018.pdf.

Federal State Education Standards for Higher Education (FSESHE)—master's degree in the specialty 44.04.01 Teacher Education no. 126 as of February 22, 2018 (3++). (2018b). Retrieved from http://fgosvo.ru/uploadfiles/FGOS%20VO%203++/Mag/440401_M_3_16032018.pdf.

Gafurov, I. R., R. A. Valeeva, A. M. Kalimullin, and R. G. Sakhieva. (2018). Testing practice-oriented master's programme in 'Education and Pedagogical Sciences' (Teacher of Basic General Education). *Psikhologicheskaya nauka i obrazovanie*, 23(1), 25–37.

Glubokova, E. N., S. A. Pisareva, and A. P. Tryapitsyna. (2015). Pedagogical magistracy: standards requirements and new models. *Chelovek i Obrazovanie*, 4(45), 10–18.

Gokhberg, L. M., O. K. Ozerova, E. V. Sautina, and N. B. Shugal. (2020). *Education in Figures: 2020: A Brief Compilation of Statistics.* Moscow: Higher School of Economics.

Gorbunova, L. N. (2010). *Research oriented training of teachers in the context of the modern Russian education development.* Doctoral dissertation. Moscow: APKiPRO.

Gorshunova, L. A. (2002). *Succession in the management of teacher training in the system of continuing education.* Doctoral dissertation. Barnaul: BSPU.

Isaev, I. F. (1993). *Theoretical foundations of the formation of the professional pedagogical culture of the teacher of higher education.* Doctoral dissertation. Moscow: MSPU.

Kalimullin, A. M. (2014a). Processes of reforming teacher training in modern Russia (experience of the Kazan Federal University). *American Journal of Applied Sciences,* 11(8), 1365–1368.

Kalimullin, A. M. (2014b). Improvement of teachers' qualification at Kazan Federal University. *World Applied Sciences Journal,* 30(4), 447–453.

Khromenkov, P. A. (2015). Higher educational teacher education in Russia: Contemporary state and prospects of development. *Sovremennye problemy nauki i obrazowania,* 2–1, 524–524.

Knyazev, E. A. (1989). *Formation and development of the higher teacher education in Russia (1905–1917).* Doctoral dissertation. Moscow: APKiPRO.

Main data-computing center (MDCC). (2018a). Information and analytical materials on the results of monitoring the effectiveness of the activities of universities in 2017. Retrieved from https://monitoring.miccedu.ru/?m=vpo&year=2018/.

Main data-computing center (MDCC). (2018b). Review of higher education in Russia. Retrieved from http://indicators.miccedu.ru/monitoring/?m=vpo.

Main data-computing center (MDCC). (2018c). Characteristics of the system of secondary vocational education in Russia. Retrieved from https://monitoring.miccedu.ru/?m=spo&year=2018.

Margolis, A. A. (2014). Problems and prospects of the development of pedagogical education in the Russian Federation. *Psikhologicheskaya nauka i obrazowanie,* 19(3), 41–57.

Margolis A. A., and M. A. Safronova. (2018). The Project of Modernisation of Teacher Education in the Russian Federation: Outcomes 2014–2017. *Psikhologicheskaya nauka i obrazowanie,* 23(1), 5–24.

Menter, I., R. A. Valeeva, and A. M. Kalimullin. (2017). A tale of two countries—forty years on: politics and teacher education in Russia and England. *European Journal of Teacher Education,* 40(5), 616–629.

Nikitin, E. M. (1999). *Theoretical and organizational-pedagogical basis of development of the extended pedagogical education system.* Doctoral dissertation. St. Petersburg: Institute of Adult Education, Russian Academy of Education.

Page, T. M. (2015). Common pressures, same results? Recent reforms in professional standards and competences in teacher education for secondary teachers in England, France and Germany. *Journal of Education for Teaching,* 41(2), 180–202.

Panachin, F. G. (1979). *Teacher education in Russia. Historical and pedagogical essays.* Moscow: Prosveshcheniye.

Pletneva, I. F. (1997). *Formation and development of higher teacher education in Russia in the XIX century.* Doctoral dissertation. Moscow: MSPU.

Pletyago, T. Y., A. S. Ostapenko, and S. N. Anntonova. (2019). Pedagogical models of mixed education at universities: Review of the Russian and international experience. *Obrazovaniye i nauka*, 21(5), 112–129.

Programme for the Development of Continuing Teacher Education for the period 2001–2010. (2001). Retrieved from http://www.kspu.ru/page-9074.html.

Shcherbakov, A. I. (1968). *Formation of the Soviet school teachers in higher teacher education.* Doctoral dissertation. Leningrad: Herzen LSPU.

Slastenin, V. A. (1976). *Formation of the Soviet school teachers in the process of vocational training.* Moscow: Prosveshcheniye.

TALIS. (2019). *Report on the results of the International research of the teaching staff on teaching and learning TALIS-2018.* Retrieved from https://fioco.ru/Media/Default/Documents/TALIS/%D0%9D%D0%B0%D1%86%D0%B8%D0%BE%D0%BD%D0%B0%D0%BB%D1%8C%D0%BD%D1%8B%D0%B9%20%D0%BE%D1%82%D1%87%D0%B5%D1%82%20TALIS-2018.pdf.

Teacher Education Modernization Programme. (2003). Retrieved from http://docs.cntd.ru/document/901867014 (In Russ.).

The teacher professional standard. (2013). Retrieved from http://www.rosmintrud.ru/docs/mintrud/orders/129/. (In Russ.).

University Education Quality Monitoring (UEQM). (2017). The department of state policy in the domain of higher education. Retrieved from http://indicators.miccedu.ru/monitoring/2017/.

Valeeva, R., and Gafurov, I. (2017). Initial teacher education in Russia: connecting practice, theory and research. *European Journal of Teacher Education*, 40(3), 342–360.

Valeeva, R. A., and A. A. Kalimullin. (2019a). Learning to teach in Russia: A review of policy and empirical research. In: M. T. Tatto and I. Menter (Eds.), *Knowledge, policy and practice in teacher education: A cross-national study.* London: Bloomsbury.

Valeeva, R. A., and A. Kalimullin. (2019b). Teacher education in Russia. In: J. Lampert (Ed.), *Oxford Research Encyclopedia of Education.* New York: Oxford University Press.

Vasilyev, K. I. (1966). *Essays on the history of higher teacher education in the RSFSR (1918–1932).* Voronezh: Centralnoye chernozemnoye knizhnoye izdatelstvo.

Zubkova, N. K. (2013). Development and improvement of the system of professional development of teachers in Russia. *Vestnik TGPU—TSPU Bulletin*, 9(137), 18–25.

20

Teacher Education and Professional Development in the Republic of Belarus: 1990–2020 Overview and Future Prospects

Maria Zhigalova

Introduction

The training and retraining of teachers in Belarus, which is conducted in pedagogical and classical universities, institutes of advanced training and retraining in a multicultural educational University environment, has a certain specificity. It needs to be improved in accordance with the requirements of domestic and international standards, as well as constantly changing society. University graduates are required not only to have a high level of didactic, psychological, pedagogical, and general cultural and professional competence but also socio-cultural and methodological knowledge, which will contribute to the assessment of cultural values of different peoples, and to the development of skills to conduct friendly communication relations aimed at consolidating a multicultural society, which has developed in recent years due to active migration.

The aim of this chapter is to analyse and synthesize how the state of teacher education in Belarus has evolved over the past thirty years. Furthermore, this chapter aims to: (1) formulate a structural, functional, and methodological model for teacher education improvement; (2) strengthen the process of retraining teachers, including at non-pedagogical universities; and (3) enrich the methods of cooperation between classical universities and specialized educational institutions, with the aim of improving the quality of education and

M. Zhigalova (✉)
Brest State Technical University, Brest, Belarus
e-mail: zhygalova@mail.ru

its practice-orientation. In order to explore these issues, two methods are used: the first is document analysis and the second is modelling. These methods enable the consideration of the key issues specified in this chapter in terms of systematic, purposeful, and organized processes. In addition, this chapter is based on the author's own long-term experiences gained during their work in the Belarusian education system in various roles in teaching practice and academic leadership. It also draws on the research results regarding education systems, their structures, organization of teacher training, and experiences of teacher educators, gathered from various other countries, including Austria, Germany, Poland, Russia, and the Czech Republic.

Historical Background

Before we talk about the history of teacher education in Belarus over the past 30 years, we should note:

[T]he adult literacy rate in Belarus has always been high, and now reaches 99.7%. Coverage of basic, General secondary and vocational education is 98%. Belarus has reached the level of the most developed countries in terms of primary and secondary school enrolment. In recent years, the state has allocated at least 5% of GDP to the educational system, which is not inferior to the amount of funding for education in developed European countries. In total, there are more than 8 thousand institutions of basic, additional and special education in the Republic, where the education and upbringing of about 3 million children, students and trainees is provided by more than 400 thousand employees or every 10th person employed in the economy. (Belarus. Facts. *The education system in Belarus*; http://belarusfacts.by/ru/belarus/politics/domestic_policy/education/)

By 2019,

[I]n the ranking on the human development index, Belarus is among the 50 most developed countries in the world among 187 countries on the human development index. Belarus is ranked 21st in the World Education Index, a combined indicator of the United Nations Development Programme (UNDP). In Belarus, the ratio of students to the total population is one of the highest in Europe. The fact that in 2015 the Republic of Belarus entered the European higher education area (the Bologna Process) underlines the high level of quality of education in the country. (Belarus. Facts. *The education system in Belarus*; http://belarusfacts.by/ru/belarus/politics/domestic_policy/education/)

In 1991 the Republic of Belarus began to live in a new socio-political and economic situation associated with the collapse of the USSR. Having become an independent state, it began to create its own national education system based on previous achievements, trying to adapt them to the new conditions. In the Republic of Belarus at the end of the twentieth century and beginning of the twenty-first century, there are studies on a number of important theoretical and methodological problems. Becoming especially significant in the 1990s, have been problems of the formation of professionalism and pedagogical creativity of the teacher (Butkevich 2000; Zhuk and Koshel 2003, Kochetov 1997; Tsyrkun and Punchik 2008), as well as the problem of the quality of pedagogical activity (Kharlamov 2005).

The creation of the national education system was aimed at preserving the positive experience of previous decades, and focused on the ethnic, cultural, and economic characteristics of Belarus, on the one hand, and international educational standards, on the other. The first legal document that defined the manner of this transition was the State programme for the development of the Belarusian language and other national languages in the Belarusian SSR, adopted on the basis of the law of the BSSR *On languages in the Byelorussian SSR* (1990).[1] It provided for the adoption by all educational institutions, especially schools, of Belarusian as the language of instruction by 2000, and the publication of the necessary educational and methodological literature. However, the solution to the problem of switching to the Belarusian language of instruction in the early 1990s was not well prepared for. The necessary conditions for its implementation were not created, and the degree of psychological readiness of society was not taken into account. For four years after the adoption of this Law, most primary schools adopted Belarusian as the language of instruction. As a result, most of the children found themselves in a difficult situation: they entered school from a Russian-speaking environment and were taught in a language that they did not know. This situation was corrected as a result of the 1995 Republican referendum, which confirmed the need to ensure the real right to choose the language of instruction (Russian or Belarusian), guaranteed by the Constitution. Therefore, in 1991, *the Law of the Republic of Belarus On education*[2] was adopted, which set out the basic principles of state policy in the field of education, the goals and objectives of the national education system, its structure, the rights and obligations of teachers, students and students, and the principles of financing. At the same time, a number of important legislative documents and normative legal acts were developed in the field of education, including the Concept of the Development of Pedagogical Education in the Republic of Belarus (2000).[3] These documents set out the new educational policy, and described contemporary problems of education and upbringing of the younger generation. During this period (in the 1990s–2000s) in Belarusian pedagogy there were further development issues of the humanization of education: education of national consciousness and moral ideals of character, value orientations of students (Prokopiev and Mikhalkovich 2002), the development of spiritual strength and abilities of the individual (Kadol 2002), formation of the humanistic system of education (Kabush 2012) and the formation of a pedagogical culture of the family (Chechet 1998).

At the same time, already in the 1990s, the Republic of Belarus actively searched for the most optimal ways to develop general secondary education, developed concepts for the development of national schools, and introduced new legal provisions that justified the status of educational institutions of a new type—high schools, lyceums, higher vocational schools, and colleges.

In the 1990s, the history of Belarusian pedagogical thought was intensively studied (Butrim 2002; Snapkovskaya 2006) and correctional pedagogy received further development (Leshchinskaya 2009). Comparative pedagogy was developed, led by the Kapranova's research (2003). In the 1990s a system of developmental education became widespread and trained about 8000 children in 161 schools. The main features of the experiment were the organization of relations between teachers, children, and parents on the basis of cooperation, rejection of coercion, orientation to the student's personality, and the creation of conditions for its free creative development.

The development of general secondary education was based on the principles of linking the ongoing transformations in accordance with the needs of society, the state, and the individual, to ensure the unity of education and upbringing, relying on the experience, traditions, and achievements of the Soviet school. This took into account the need to eliminate existing contradictions and negative phenomena in the school: students' academic overload, lack of demand for knowledge, the inability of graduates to apply them in practical life, or to quickly adapt to changes in society. In order to bring education closer to the needs of the developing economy, and to meet the educational needs of the individual, the state, and society, an attempt was made to reform the education system in 1994. The goal of the reform was to move from a strictly regulated system of education to a differentiated and variable one in order to ensure the possibility of choosing the content of education and the type of educational institutions in accordance with the individual's life plans. In 1996 the 'Concept of comprehensive school reform' and its corresponding implementation programme were developed and approved,[4] which defined the content of 12 main stages; organizational, managerial, and resource support for the reform; and the strategic directions for the development of general education levels.

Reform of the Education System

The reform of the education system in the Republic of Belarus thus really began in 1998, during which the transition to teaching children from 6 years of age was made. The Belarusian school started the transition to 12-year education, but this was not completed. In accordance with the presidential decree (2008) *On certain issues of general secondary education*,[5] the school kept the 11-year training. All secondary education institutions, including high schools and lyceums, have switched from a five-day school week and a six-day school week. The duration of the school year is 35 weeks. In parallel with the structural reorganization of the school system, the reform was planned to solve a number of challenges. These were: to develop and implement new curricula and programmes; to restore the fundamental character of general secondary education; to ensure broad differentiation of education (profiling) at the senior level of secondary school; to introduce a new system for assessing students' knowledge; to create a school education system based on the formation of patriotism and citizenship among students. To a large extent, these challenges were met. The transition to a new content and technology of education was made, the basic components of general education were defined, providing conditions for the harmonious development of the individual, the organizational structure of secondary schools was changed, and the content of education was revised. In the curriculum, the role of such subjects has increased, aimed at the development and education of the individual as a person and fully realizing the task of humanization. In order to maximize the development of students' abilities and creative potential as well as interest in learning, psychological diagnostics have become widely used, and on this basis, individualization and differentiation of educational and cognitive activities was carried out.

During this period, the reform process also covered the higher education system in the country. Its transformation was based on the *Concept of higher education development in the Republic of Belarus* (1996). The reform that took place in the higher education system of Belarus was primarily aimed at changing the rules of admission to higher education institutions, introducing a multi-level system of training specialists, creating university systems for evaluating the quality of education, testing new learning technologies, and introducing a credit-modular system of training and evaluation of results. The strategic goals of reforming the higher education system were: improving the quality of higher education in the conditions of its mass scale; forming professional mobility of specialists that would ensure the adaptation of graduates to constantly changing conditions of professional activity; education of spiritually, intellectually, and physically developed individuals who are able to actively participate in the economic and socio-cultural life of society. The achievement of these goals assumed in the first place, structural and organizational changes in the educational process: the transition to a two-stage training of specialists (specialist, master); introduction to the pedagogical process and technological innovation; and the creation of the resources (legal, personnel, logistical, and financial) in the provision of training. At the first level (four to five years), specialists with higher education were trained. At the second level, for two years, specialized in-depth professional, research and scientific-pedagogical training of specialists was carried out and the possibility of obtaining an academic master's degree was provided. Educational institutions in Belarus were reorganized into classical and specialized universities. At the same time, universities that provide the academic level of higher education continued to play a leading role in the system of teacher education. They retained the status as the largest educational, scientific-pedagogical, and scientific-research centres. In general, positive trends in the development of education in the 1990s were thus

* the transition to person-oriented learning;
* the development of the differentiation in education;
* updating the content of humanitarian education;
* the emergence of new types of educational institutions;
* the introduction of various training profiles and elective courses;
* the emergence of new trends in the education of young people; and
* the humanization of education.

The development of teacher education in the Republic of Belarus from the beginning of the twenty-first century to the present time is characterised by intensive transformations and changes.

In the 2000s, the legal framework for secondary special and higher education was significantly updated, and educational standards for a number of specialties were developed and put into effect. This contributed to improving the content of education, updating the educational and methodological support of the educational process, and improving the quality of training specialists. Since September 1, 2002, the transition to a 10-point system of assessment of students' knowledge has been implemented. In all subjects and courses,

Norms for evaluating the results of students' educational activities[6] were developed, as well as materials with which the teacher can carry out certification. Since 2002, the legislative and regulatory framework in the field of teacher education has been improved. New documents published included: *The Conceptual framework of ideological-educational work with children, students and studying youth* (2003),[7] laws of the Republic of Belarus *On education of persons with psychophysical development (special education)* (2004),[8] *On higher education* (2007),[9] the *Program for the development of the national education system for 2006–2010* (2006),[10] the *Program for the development of General secondary education in the Republic of Belarus for 2007–2016*,[11] and the educational standard *General secondary education*.[12] The documents were aimed at achieving the main overall goal—creating conditions for the dynamic development of general secondary education that meets the needs of individuals, society, and the state in quality education, taking into account the changing socio-cultural, economic, and demographic situation.

In December 2010, the *Code of the Republic of Belarus on education*[13] was adopted, and entered into force on September 1, 2011, and was aimed at comprehensive and systematic regulation of public relations in the field of education. According to the Code, education is divided into basic education (including pre-school, general secondary, vocational, secondary specialized, higher and postgraduate education), additional education (additional education of children and youth, additional education of adults), special education (learning and training of students who have psychophysical development needs, through the implementation of educational programmes of special education at the levels of pre-school, general secondary education).

Current Educational Provision in Belarus

So it is that today, the national education system of the Republic of Belarus includes: pre-school education; general secondary education; extracurricular forms of education; vocational education; secondary special education; higher education; training of scientific and scientific-pedagogical personnel; professional development and retraining of personnel; independent education of citizens.[14]

The structure of pre-school education includes a network of pre-school institutions that differ by type and profile of work with children. For children under 6 years of age, there are such types of pre-school institutions as a nursery, nursery-garden, kindergarten, and kindergarten-school. According to their profile, they are divided into general purpose institutions with an in-depth focus, sanatorium pre-schools, special pre-schools for children with special psychophysical development needs, and pre-school child development centres.

The modern model of a comprehensive school includes several stages. The first is general primary education. The training period lasts four years, from 1st to 4th grades. The second stage is general basic education (5th to 9th grades). The third stage is general secondary education. It is available to those students who have completed basic school and continued their education in the 10th and 11th grades. Secondary education in Belarus can be obtained in secondary schools and gymnasiums. General secondary education can also be obtained in vocational and secondary specialized educational institutions, which are available after finishing basic school.

In recent years, educational institutions in the Republic of Belarus have adopted a 10-point system for evaluating knowledge. Its introduction is closely related to the work on creating a system of tests and applying a rating assessment of knowledge. Note that in 2002, in accordance with the decree of the President of the Republic of Belarus '[o]n the accession of the Republic of Belarus to the Convention on the recognition of qualifications relating to higher education in the European region',[15] Belarus became a full member of the Lisbon Convention of 1997, prepared jointly with UNESCO and the Council of Europe. This allows for the recognition of diplomas of Belarusian universities, promotes the development of international cooperation, and attracts foreign students to Belarus, the number of whom is planned to increase to 5% of the total number of students. Training of scientific and scientific-pedagogical personnel in the Republic of Belarus is carried out in postgraduate and doctoral programmes of higher education institutions and scientific organizations of the Ministry of Education.

Changes in education in the twenty-first century are dictated by the needs of society and therefore socially constructed. Such education is updated depending on the context. Due to the active migration of the population, the question of teaching Russian as a language of communication to refugees and migrants in order to adapt them to a multicultural society has recently arisen.

In 2012 at the initiative of the Ministry of Education of the Republic of Belarus established the Centre for international cooperation in the field of education of the State educational institution 'Republican Institute of higher school' (hereafter 'the Centre'),[16] which is mandated: to conduct consultations with foreign citizens wishing to study in the Republic of Belarus; to seek foreign partners interested in the selection of candidates for training in the Republic of Belarus of foreign citizens; and to disseminate information about the educational services of Belarusian institutions of higher education for foreign citizens. In addition, the Centre acts as a coordinator of international cooperation between higher education institutions of the Republic of Belarus and other countries. Since 2017, the Center has been organizing distance learning under the advanced training programme 'Methods of teaching Russian as a foreign language'. The purposes of distance learning are to familiarize teachers with modern approaches to the organization of teaching Russian as a foreign language; to introduce the principles, means, methods, and forms of organization of educational activities of foreign students; to introduce Russian as a foreign language course content in the educational system; and to disseminate modern technologies for teaching Russian as a foreign language (Lebedinsky et al. 2019).

Teacher Education in Belarus

Modern continuous pedagogical education in the Republic of Belarus is considered by scientists as a factor in the sustainable development of society (Zhuk 2016). In the *National strategy for socio-economic development of the Republic of Belarus until 2030*, special attention is paid to education as a leading factor in building human potential, where a significant place in the formation of a quality education system is given to the system of training teachers.

The strategic direction of the development of teacher education for the next five years is to ensure continuity in the training of teachers: from specialized training at school to the system of additional adult education.

In 2015, The Minister of Education developed and approved *The Concept for the development of teacher education for 2015–2020*[17] and the Action plan for its implementation. These documents provide for: updating the goals and content of teacher education; modernization of educational process technologies based on strategies of problem-based research, active, and collective learning; improving the training of highly qualified scientific and pedagogical workers, taking into account the current problems of psychological and pedagogical science and educational practice, which will contribute to the improvement of the system of continuous pedagogical education. They also provide for the 'transition to a cluster model of development that ensures the integration of the potential of education, psychological and pedagogical science and effective educational practice, as well as improving the resource provision of the national system of pedagogical education in the information society and increasing the prestige of the teaching profession' (Zhuk 2016, p. 62).

The transition to the cluster form of interaction of its subjects is a mechanism for ensuring the continuity of pedagogical education. For this purpose, the country has created an educational, scientific, and innovative cluster of continuous pedagogical education.[18] The cluster aims to ensure the integration and capacity development of institutions and organizations for training of modern pedagogues, which in the Republic of Belarus is carried out at the following levels: the profile (pre-service) teacher education at the third stage of general secondary education; incomplete higher pedagogical education (teacher training colleges); higher education; postgraduate education; additional education of adults. These levels of teacher training ensure the continuity of teacher education. Since November 2014, this has been a priority task, which solves the problem of reviving specialized teaching in schools by creating 'pedagogical' classes. They are now successfully functioning in Belarus and are considered as a platform for 'a conscious start in the teaching profession and the main mechanism for selecting trained and motivated applicants to pedagogical universities, and in the future—as a guarantee of ensuring the influx of high-quality modern teachers to schools' (Zhuk 2016, p. 64).

Already in the 2015/2016 academic year, more than 100 pedagogical classes and groups were opened in all regions of Belarus, where more than 1500 tenth-graders studied. In the 2017 school year, the number of teacher classes and groups increased from 102 to 319, and the number of students increased from 1600 to 3542. Since 2017, a special procedure for admitting students to universities for pedagogical specialties has been introduced. Thus graduates who were trained in specialized classes and groups of pedagogical orientation mastered the mandatory two-year course of optional classes *Introduction to the teaching profession. Grades 10–11* (lasting 140 hours) and also received a positive characteristic—the recommendation of the school's pedagogical Council,[19] and having good and excellent grades in two profile subjects of at least 8 points (on a 10-point scale), were accepted to the University for pedagogical specialties without exams. In order to provide methodological support for the work of teaching classes at the Belarusian State Pedagogical University (BSPU), the educational and methodological complex *Introduction to the teaching profession—Grades 10–11*, which is published on the BSPU website in the section 'Pedagogical classes' along with workbooks for elective classes for students of 10 and 11 pedagogical classes. According to the Rector of the Pedagogical University, A. I. Zhuk:

> pedagogical tests that simulate situations of pedagogical activity are mandatory for students of pedagogical classes. This includes visiting teachers' lessons, conducting micro-research, organizing games during recess and educational activities, preparing and conducting fragments of lessons, practising in school camps, volunteering, etc. There are prerequisites for the revival of such forms of pre-

professional training as the pedagogical gymnasium and the pedagogical Lyceum. Our goal is to create at least one pedagogical gymnasium in each region. (Zhuk 2016, p. 63)

The system of continuous pedagogical education in Belarus traditionally includes the training of teachers with secondary special education. Twenty-one colleges throughout the country train teachers of pre-school education, primary classes, music education, physical culture and sports, technical labour and drawing, fine arts, and foreign languages. Educational programmes of teacher training colleges and institutions of higher education are interconnected and integrated, and programmes of reduced training are implemented in higher education institutions. Training of teachers with higher education in the Republic of Belarus is currently conducted in 31 specialisms at 12 universities in the country. Since the current socio-cultural situation requires the higher education system to train a competitive specialist with a wide range of academic, socio-personal, and professional competences, including new ones that are in demand in the modern mobile society, since 2016, the country has begun a large-scale project to modernize the structure and content of educational standards, standard curricula, and programmes of higher pedagogical education.

This allowed us to effectively solve one of the priority tasks of the development of teacher education—strengthening the practice-oriented process of training teachers, with maximum immersion of future teachers in the professional environment. In this regard, Belarus has proposed a system for improving the teaching practice of students, giving it a continuous character. The experience of the leading pedagogical University in Belarus, where already in their second year, students were allocated one 'school day' each week, when they are in a school, pre-school, or special educational institution and observe the real educational process, help the teacher in the organization of the lesson and other educational activities, deserves attention. And for first year students, getting pre-professional experience takes place in volunteer groups, the practice of which was organized on the bases of various types of educational institutions: in pre-school institutions; secondary schools, gymnasiums; boarding schools; centres for correctional and developmental education and rehabilitation; centres for social assistance to families and children; and centres for psychological and pedagogical assistance.

Practice-oriented training of teachers provides new opportunities for specialization and a master's degree as the second stage of higher education, which has also undergone certain changes, indicating that it is teachers with a master's degree who will work in specialized classes, gymnasiums, and lyceums, in those institutions where training is conducted at advanced and advanced levels.

Intensive transformations in the economy and socio-cultural development, the emergence of new complex technologies, and transformational processes in the field of education require constant improvement of the qualification of teaching staff. In this regard, the role and importance of the system of additional adult education, which can quickly provide training teachers to work in new conditions, increases.

Today, the country has a network of educational institutions that provide professional development and retraining. Taking into account the principle of life-long education, Belarus has created legal conditions for the implementation of training, retraining, and advanced training programmes. Four hundred educational institutions are implementing additional adult education (vocational training, retraining, advanced training). Every year, about 380 thousand people master the content of educational programmes for additional adult education. Professional development of managers and specialists is organized in all 15 educational profiles, and retraining is carried out in 402 specialties.

Continuous professional training in the professions of workers (employees) is carried out in more than 3500 professions in educational institutions and other organizations (Belarus. Facts. *The education system in Belarus;* http:// belarusfacts.by/ru/belarus/politics/domestic_policy/education/).

It should be noted that the capital's Academy of Postgraduate Education (APE) and regional Institutes of Education Development, as well as Institutes of Advanced Training and Retraining, respond to the requests of institutions of pre-school, general secondary, special, and higher education for the implementation of educational programmes for advanced training, retraining of teachers, and internships. Thus, the Institute of Advanced Training and Retraining of the Belarusian State Pedagogical University (BSPU) has 28 educational programmes of retraining, more than 100 educational programmes of advanced training, with training courses in various areas. And when receiving an educational request from the heads and teachers of specific educational institutions of the Republic, it implements the declared experimental or innovative scientific projects, in which several educational institutions from different regions can participate and use modern technologies for organizing the educational process. The same work is being done in all other regional educational development institutions. These activities formed the basis for determining the strategic directions of fundamental and applied research; experimental and innovative activities in the field of education; as well as for the formation of topics for students' term papers and theses, master's, PhD, and doctoral theses, and research work of departments of all universities that prepare teaching staff.

The Institute for Advanced Training and Retraining of the Brest State Technical University has 22 licenced educational retraining programmes, including a programme on the specialty 'Teaching in English', which allows for the retraining of specialists in technical specialities to work in the conditions of teaching educational subjects for foreigners in English at the Technical University.

Thus, the pedagogical education of the Republic of Belarus is developing today on the basis of the principles of consistency and continuity. In order for this development to be stable and sustainable, appropriate scientific, methodological, and organizational support is needed. In Belarus today, this task is successfully solved in the course of the activities of the educational, scientific, and innovative cluster of continuing pedagogical education. Within its framework, a network of resource centres for practice-oriented teacher education and technology has been created and is successfully operating. Their work is focused on strengthening the continuity and integration of different levels of pedagogical training. Starting from the Republican resource centre for social and pedagogical technologies and ending with regional and school ones, the work is based on regional experience and contributes to the design and implementation of individual educational routes for future specialists in the social and pedagogical sphere, including the implementation of distance learning.

In order to improve the quality of teacher education in our country, a network academy of e-learning pedagogy is being created at BSPU as a leading branch of higher education in the country. As its rector A. I. Zhuk emphasizes:

> [T]he work of the network Academy will allow us to develop our own information and educational environment of pedagogical education as intensively as possible, that is, to switch to the so-called e-learning. It is a modern high-tech scientific and educational platform that will unite teachers, students, scientists not only travel, but also the whole cluster to the professional teaching community in areas such as: didactics network of the lesson; teaching practice in the field of e-learning; network of pedagogical interaction on the basis of the electronic magazine; open lectures, workshops, webinars, IT experienced teachers and the best scholars; formation of the scientific portfolio of a student in education e-learning. (Zhuk 2016, p. 63)

Purposeful work is also being done to increase the prestige of teacher education, create a positive image of the teaching profession in the public consciousness, and, of course, to form a high level of professional competence, citizenship, and general culture of a teacher who is able not only to give, but also to create new knowledge in the field of professional teaching, develop and implement innovative educational programmes and technologies, and constantly improve himself. At present, the focus of modern science is on innovative processes in education. The problems of developing innovative educational technologies in the process of retraining and advanced training, the quality of retraining and advanced training of teachers have been investigated by Zaprudsky (2006), Kashlev (2000), Snopkova (2003), Tsyrkun and Punchik (2008), Zhigalova (2013a, b).

To sum up, we can conclude that today the success of any country on the world stage depends on the speed of implementation of new pedagogical solutions in the education system. This means that a new content of education will be required, which will be based on the convergence of knowledge (mathematics education, humanities education, and natural science education), because the development of education and science, economy, and the social sphere is possible only on an interdisciplinary basis (convergence of knowledge), and with the interaction of science and technology.

Conclusions and Final Reflections

Today, in school education, there is a contradiction between the requirements for interdisciplinarity and convergence of knowledge and the preservation of the subject principle of providing information in school. The convergence of knowledge as the most important mechanism for creating new knowledge is not only a mutual influence but also leads to the interpenetration of various fields of knowledge; when the boundaries between them are blurred, the results arise within the framework of interdisciplinary work at their junction. Therefore, transdisciplinarity as a method of research, as a principle of organizing scientific knowledge, opens up wide opportunities for interaction of many disciplines in solving complex problems of nature and society. In this regard, the new content of education and the organization of the educational process will be based on a system-activity approach, and the formation of the socio-cultural educational environment of the school will ensure the formation of universal educational actions. In turn, the introduction of integrated subjects (meta-subjects) will allow for the continuous updating of content while maintaining the fundamental foundations of knowledge, to ensure the individualization of the learning process. Furthermore, humanitarian education will allow students to form: general cultural and social competences, systematic historical and cultural knowledge; the ability to independently conduct creative work with the content of modern culture and social life as the basis for self-identification of the individual. This will allow us to form moral values and ethics of interpersonal relations, to actualize in the minds of citizens social priorities and ideals, on the basis of which the social climate in society is formed, trust, social solidarity, and a responsible attitude of a citizen to their own life, other people, work, society, and the world around them. This means that the trends in modern didactics will also change. Individualization of training, technical means, and resources will be selected based on the educational needs of individual students. Therefore, differentiation and technical means and resources will be selected based on the educational needs and the group of students, and on the teacher or practitioner (moderator, tutor, developer of educational paths, organizer of project training, coordinator of an educational online platform, mentor of startups, trainer of mind fitness, and developer of tools for teaching states of consciousness will help them in their studies and guide the educational process) (Atlas of new professions 2014). This model will develop the ability to educate independent students who set goals, track progress, and think about learning.

Currently, Belarus has updated research on the problems of multicultural education and upbringing (the development of cultural and educational values, the formation of skills for interaction between different cultures, taking into account ethnic and national characteristics, tolerant coexistence of large and small ethnic groups) by means of literature (Zhigalova 2012, 2017a).

In light of the current dynamic global and national educational transformations, the Belarusian teacher education system should commit to better adapting to these new realities. A number of suggestions for improvements are discussed next.

1. It has long been known that education, including pedagogical education, which is one of the main means of developing a person's personality in social terms, must always keep up with the times, that is, undergo changes and innovations that meet the needs of modern society, taking into account the peculiarities of our Slavic Belarusian mentality. At the same time, we should not forget about the time-tested traditions in education that give results. Taking all this into account, we can only talk about improving the ways of interaction between higher and secondary schools, and about innovations in the field of education in conjunction with national traditions.

2. Since all national educational systems, including the Belarusian one, are united in the world educational space, certain global trends are identified in each system if there is diversity. They are also characteristic of the edu-

cational system in Belarus and include a significant impact of socio-economic factors; striving for higher quality education; study and consideration of international pedagogical experience affecting the improvement of pedagogical education

3. It has already been noted that today in Belarus, as well as in other countries of the world, university education also acquires the features of a multicultural one, so called not only due to the multicultural contingent of students but also due to the diversity of teaching languages. For example, students from China, India, Afghanistan, Pakistan, Eritrea, Nepal, Sri Lanka, Bangladesh, and other countries study at the Brest State Technical University not only at the Faculty of pre-University training, where they study Russian, but also at many faculties of the University, receiving education as a logistician-economist, architect, information technology engineer, and so on. This multicultural educational environment develops the ability of students and teachers to assess and self-evaluate not only their own ethnic professional culture but also the cultures of other ethnic groups developing in a different socio-economic space. All this, of course, contributes to the promotion of Russian scientific intelligence to the world level.

For many years now, our university has been teaching foreign students in several languages (including Russian and English). Therefore, the problem of retraining and teaching staff is acute. In the 2016–2017 academic year, for the first time in the Institute of Advanced Training and Retraining of BrSTU, the specialism 'professional activity in English' was opened, which allowed teachers of technical specialties of our University, without interrupting their main work, to successfully undergo retraining in order to read their academic disciplines in English. Thus, a single educational specific multicultural environment is created, which assumes both the freedom of cultural self-determination of the future specialist, and the enrichment of intelligence and personal development due to diverse and constant intercultural communication.

4. We will also make some judgments about the changes that are taking place in the structure of retraining of teaching staff, especially those who work in technical, medical, agricultural, and other universities. In 2013, a new policy was developed and approved by the Ministry of Education of the Republic of Belarus on 28.03.2013: No 13 'Educational standard' in the specialty 1-08 01 71—'Pedagogical activity of specialists' for retraining of managers and specialists who have higher education, but are not teachers with a diploma. This document establishes the requirements necessary to ensure the quality of education, and defines the content of the educational

programme of retraining and can be used by the employer in solving issues of employment of specialists (Zhigalova 2017b). The document defines a number of requirements: for the educational process and the level of basic education of persons entering to master the content of the educational programme; requirements for forms and terms of education; requirements for the maximum amount of educational load; the organization of the educational process, the results of mastering the educational programme; requirements to a level of preparation; requirements for final certification and maintenance of educational software documentation, to the model curriculum and the model curriculum on the Humanities, social-economic and professional disciplines.

The methodical training of teachers is made up of such disciplines as: foundations of the teaching profession (the essence, content, peculiarities; job analysis of a teacher; teaching morals and teaching ethics lecturer; self-education); educational technology (technology cooperation, full of learning, games technology, collective interaction, modular training, case studies, etc.); pedagogical innovations (methods of innovation, innovative culture); fundamentals of pedagogical measurements (culture of measuring activity in education; methods and technologies of pedagogical assessment, etc.); professional pedagogy (the main trends in the development of the system of professional education, methods, forms and means of professional training, etc.). This structure of courses taught and the system of retraining of University teachers undoubtedly improves the quality of teaching at the University, and therefore increases the quality of professional training of graduates.

5. However, it should be noted that higher education today, as well as secondary education, is going through difficult times. There is a problem of recruiting such domestic and foreign applicants who would be motivated to receive a high-quality education and would be able to effectively assimilate the material of higher education. After all, changes in society and the labour market also change the requirements for the competence of a modern graduate. These include the constant search for and assimilation of new knowledge, which radically changes the educational objectives, values, results, and, above all, the education system as a whole, and therefore the personality of the teacher. The society faces an acute problem of fundamental changes in pedagogical, psychological, philosophical, economic, and other approaches to training not only teachers but also specialists in various fields.

Therefore, the realities of today dictate new requirements for graduates of classical and pedagogical universities, specialists who must be able to study all their lives and be ready for effective socio-economic adaptation. And this is possible only if the graduate teacher is a creative person with deep knowledge, with well-formed professional competences, stable motivation for constant self-education and self-improvement, creative, and professional self-actualization.

All this suggests that today it is necessary to solve the problem of the transformation of pedagogical education, which is associated with changes in both the teacher and the student, as well as the entire pedagogical society.

6. There is also a problem of training specialists of higher education: undergraduates, postgraduates, doctoral students; the problem of the quality of teaching, and in this regard, the quality of retraining of teachers, their internships, including abroad, in order to enrich their professional experience.

7. The entry of our country into the European Bologna system of education in May 2015 has brought to the fore new tasks related to the formation of student qualities such as self-control, self-education, mobility, and the desire for constant self-development, which are not formed simultaneously: they need to be developed from school. That is why educational institutions in Belarus today are focused on developing these qualities. This means that the entire educational process should be aimed at identifying and developing creative abilities of the individual (hence the cooperation of school teachers with professional scientists of higher educational institutions, revived profiling in schools).

8. In Belarus, the University was and remains a link between the Academy of Sciences and secondary schools. Therefore, the issue of training higher school teachers will always be important and significant. It should be noted that Belarusian universities currently employ professors who are members of the Belarusian and Russian Academy of Sciences, the National Academy of Sciences, the Academy of Social and Pedagogical Sciences, and many other public academies. Most of the University teachers take part in the preparation of scientific and methodological complexes, manuals, and textbooks for various types of educational systems, including secondary schools and colleges. Therefore, the problem of quality teaching and the use of innovations in education remain important and significant. We may note some of the innovations used today in the educational and research process of universities. These are essential innovations, which imply the introduction of innovations into the educational system that affect the

very essence of education, but which could not be applied earlier; retroinnovations, that is, the introduction of approaches to teaching that have been forgotten for a long time; combined innovations—the combination of a certain number of educational methods, resulting in a new one; analogue innovations, that is, the addition of a private innovation to an already known method of teaching.

But whatever innovations are used in the educational process, they must necessarily take into account the requirements of modern society and the development of information technologies. In addition, innovations should be applied in four areas: education; training; skill; creativity. It is easy to see that the introduction of innovations is a very serious process that involves a number of theoretical and practical difficulties, as well as a significant share of risk. However, if this is not done, the system may become mired in outdated educational methods for a long time. This threatens to reduce not only the desire of young people to study in educational institutions but also the level of their moral, psychological, ethical, social, and cultural development.

Only some of the problems listed earlier indicate that today' schools, together with secondary and higher education institutions, must jointly solve the following three tasks:

(a) to prepare young teachers for the fact that it is necessary to study throughout their lives, because 'who is behind today for a day, he is behind forever'.
(b) it is necessary to improve the current system of teachers' professional development and retraining. This system should be flexible and responsive to changes and the needs of society and the country as a whole. For it is only possible to implement the large-scale tasks facing the national education, to modernize it, to move in its development to a new technological order, as time demands, based on a high-quality education of a specialist, their mobility and professionalism (Oleks 2009).
(c) in any case, the world today is puzzled by the problem of educating young people as citizens of the entire planet, since the multicultural educational space is in the process of continuous development. And the whole world strives to provide people with a global education strategy that would not depend on the place where people live, or on the current level of their development.

9. The twenty-first century in education may be characterised as a digital universe. Therefore, it is not difficult to assume that the transfer of knowledge from teacher to student and from student to student, from student to

teacher will take place in schools and universities located not only in the building, but also in the virtual network (through the manifestation of mobile devices). This means that educational institutions as places of learning, where students and students are engaged, can be considered as any place equipped for such work. Therefore, the competence of a person in a knowledge society consists of several different components. These are: cognitive (experimental, research activities), informational (consisting of multiple sources, its processing in a limited time), meta-objective (making several decisions simultaneously on the implementation of problems where knowledge from many areas of knowledge is needed), motivational (taking into account the intentions and actions of other people-allies, partners, and opponents), mobile (the ability to make many decisions in a limited time), as well as personal and emotional (the ability to act in conditions of novelty and uncertainty—readiness for different results of their actions, including unexpected ones, social interaction with different people). Such a transdisciplinary approach to the demand, teaching, and meta-subject of knowledge bases will prepare the individual to understand the relationship of processes occurring in a rapidly changing world, self-determination, effective activities, and the formation of an active citizenship. In this regard, the development of the teacher's competence is needed, ensuring the creation and discovery of new knowledge. This will require high-quality databases of educational information that cover not only mandatory programmes, but the world of knowledge as a whole, as well as the collaboration, joint educational space, and interaction time with teachers and classmates, university teachers, and fellow students, necessary for generating ideas, presenting results, feedback and evaluation, is almost limitless. Therefore, this socializing and personalizing component of the educational process is a unique opportunity for cooperation in solving complex problems outside of school time in accordance with the personal interests and needs of students. It provides the creation of new knowledge through the creation of multimedia presentations, animations, digital models, qualitative analysis, expertise, forming the skills and competences of teaching, developing the ability to manage their own knowledge—that is, provides everything that is waiting for today's global economy of the twenty-first century.

Therefore, the education system of the twenty-first century should create conditions for the formation of a graduate who will be ready for successful socialization and career, for learning throughout life. But for such a system of education to develop, it must form a highly moral person who can distinguish good from evil and understand the sophistication of information warfare aimed at separating peoples and destroying civilizational achievements, so as not to become a victim of them. Therefore, today it is very important to teach young people to communicate in reality, not just virtually, to learn to understand the significance of each person on Earth. What will be the future of education in the world and in each individual state depends largely on us, teachers, confident or not in their professionalism and the importance of our joint work, the improvement of which has no limit.

Notes

1. https://studfile.net/preview/10000027/page:82/
2. http://base.spinform.ru/show_doc.fwx?rgn=1922
3. http://docplayer.ru/45286461-Koncepciya-razvitiya-sistemy-pedagogicheskogo-obrazovaniya-v-respublike-belarus.html
4. https://megalektsii.ru/s44860t3.html
5. In accordance with the presidential decree *On certain issues of general secondary education* (2008)
6. https://edu.gov.by/sistema-obrazovaniya/srenee-obr/kontseptsii-standarty-normy-otmetok-po-uchebnym-predmetam/
7. http://docplayer.ru/47898333-Konceptualnye-osnovy-ideyno-vospitatelnoy-raboty-s-detmi-uchashcheysya-i-studencheskoy-molodezhyu.html
8. https://kodeksy-by.com/zakon_rb_ob_obrazovanii_lits_s_osobennostyami_psihofizicheskogo.htm
9. https://studfile.net/preview/2494054/page:7/
10. http://levonevski.net/pravo/norm2013/num31/d31914.html
11. https://pandia.ru/text/77/297/14204.php
12. https://prisno.schools.by/pages/obrazovatelnyj-standart-obschee-srednee-obrazovanie-osnovnye-normativy-i-trebovanija
13. http://www.levonevski.net/pravo/norm2013/num10/d10973.html
14. https://inance.ru/2016/11/obrazovanie-v-belarusi/
15. http://zakonby.net/ukaz/59663-ukaz-prezidenta-respubliki-belarus-ot-04012002-n-5-quoto-prisoedinenii-respubliki-belarus-k-konvencii-o-priznanii-kvalifikaciy-otnosyaschihsya-k-vysshemu-obrazovaniyu-v-evropeyskom-regionequot.html
16. http://studyin.edu.by/
17. https://adu.by/wp-content/uploads/2015/pedklass/koncepciya.pdf
18. http://bspu.by/klaster/informacionnoe-obespechenie
19. http://pedklassy.bspu.by/index.php/pedagogu/fakultativnye-zanyatiya

References

Atlas of new professions (2014). Moscow: Moscow School of Management Skolkovo.

Butkevich, V. V. (2000). *History of pedagogy. The development of primary education and pedagogical thought in Russia in the 19th century.* Mozyr: Belyy veter.

Butrim, G. A. (2002). *Socialization of the personality of the modern schoolboy.* Minsk: Belarus.

Chechet, V. V. (1998). *Pedagogy of family upbringing.* Minsk: Publishing house Krasiko-Print.

Kabush, V. T. (2012). Methods of humanistic education of students. *Akademiya professional'nogo obrazovaniya,* 1–2, 19–27.

Kadol F. V. (2002). *Honor and personal dignity of senior schoolchildren: theory and methodology of formation.* Gomel: Franzisk Skorina Gomel State Universityю

Kapranova, V. A. (2003). *History of pedagogy.* Moscow: Novoye znaniye.

Kashlev, S. S. (2000). *Modern technologies of the pedagogical process.* Minsk: Universitetskoe.

Kharlamov, I. F. (2005). *Pedagogy.* Minsk: Vysshaya shkola.

Kochetov, A. I. (1997). *Educational system: theory, problems, alternatives.* Minsk: Inst. Of professional retraining of educational stuff.

Lebedinsky, S. I., I. S. Rovdo, and M. P. Zhigalova. (2019). *A guide for refugees in the Russian language.* Minsk: Chetyre chetverti.

Leshchinskaya, T. L. (2009). *Education of persons with special psychophysical development in the context of integrated tendencies.* Minsk: NIO.

Oleks, O. A. (2009). Scientific and methodological support of the system of qualification and retraining of personnel in the Republic of Belarus. In: *Adult Education in the CIS member States: experience, priorities and prospects of development. Proceedings of the 2nd International scientific and practical conference. October 29–30, 2009* (pp. 35–45) Mogilev.

Prokopiev, I. I., and N. V. Mikhalkovich. (2002). *Pedagogy. Foundations of general Pedagogy. Didactics.* Minsk: TetraSystems.

Snapkovskaya, S. V. (2006). *History of education and pedagogical thought.* Minsk: BSPU.

Snopkova, E. I. (2003). *Innovative educational technologies for teaching history in secondary school.* Mogilev: Mogilev State University named after A.A. Kuleshov.

Tsyrkun, I. I., and V. N. Punchik. (2008). *Intellectual self-development of the future teacher: didactic aspect.* Minsk: BSPU.

Zaprudsky, N. I. (2006). *Modern school technologies: a guide for teachers.* Minsk: Sir-Vit.

Zhigalova, M. P. (2012). *Ethnoveterinary and multiculturalism in literature: interpretation and analysis.* Saarbrucken: LAP LAMBERT Academic Publishing.

Zhigalova, M. P. (2017a). *Multi-ethnic literature Maloritkin: Interpretation and analysis of the works.* Brest: BrGTU.

Zhigalova, M. P. (2013a). *Modern teaching technologies in adult education.* Brest: BrSU.

Zhigalova, M. P. (2013b). *Theoretical and methodological foundations of the organization of additional education for adults.* Brest: BrSU.

Zhigalova, M. P. (2017b). Training of pedagogical staff in the Republic of Belarus: socio-cultural and methodological aspects. *Nepreryvnoye pedagogicheskoye obrazovaniye: problemy i poiski,* 3(5), 19–31.

Zhuk A. I. (2016). Continuous pedagogical education in the Republic of Belarus—a factor of sustainable development of society. *Nauka i shkola,* 6, 61–67.

Zhuk, A. I., and N. N. Koshel. (2003). *Active teaching methods in the system of professional development of teachers.* Minsk: Propylaea.

21

Teacher Education in the Republic of Moldova: Past and Present Trends

Larisa Kobylyanskaya

Introduction

The process of reforming teacher education in the post-Soviet space has become an important task along with the major changes in the field of education taking place in the Commonwealth of Independent States and Baltic countries. The understanding of the increasing role of a teacher in the modern world is reflected in many international documents of the late 1990s–2000s. Among the main tasks related to the preparation and activities of teachers there are the tasks of ensuring the active participation of teachers in the processes of transformation of education systems.

In the Republic of Moldova, education is a national priority and is the main factor in sustaining human development and building a knowledge-based society. The state ensures by means of its education policy the fundamental right to education necessary for the enjoyment of other human rights, introduction of the fundamental mechanism for the formation and development of human capital, implementation of the educational ideal and educational goals, formation of national consciousness and national identity, promotion of universal values, and aspirations of society for European integration. The educational ideal for the school of the Republic of Moldova includes the formation of a pro-active and self-developing personality, having not only a system of knowledge and the necessary competences needed in the

L. Kobylyanskaya (✉)
Slavic University of the Republic of Moldova, Chisinau, Republic of Moldova

© The Author(s), under exclusive license to Springer Nature Switzerland AG 2023
M. Kowalczuk-Walędziak et al. (eds.), *The Palgrave Handbook of Teacher Education in Central and Eastern Europe*, https://doi.org/10.1007/978-3-031-09515-3_21

labour market but also independence of opinions and actions, openness to intercultural dialogue in the context of national and world values.

The educational process in the education system is carried out in the Romanian language and, within the limits of the educational system, in one of the languages of international communication or in the languages of national minorities. The main educational goal is the formation of a harmonious personality and the development of a system of competences, including knowledge, skills, attitudes and values that enable an individual to actively participate in social and economic life (The Parliament of the Republic of Moldova 2014).

The education system is organized in the form of levels and cycles in accordance with the International Standard Classification of Education (ISCED 2011). Moldova's education system includes a network of educational institutions of various types and forms of ownership, curricula, technologies, and state educational standards of various levels and directions, as well as educational authorities and their subordinate institutions and enterprises. In 2017, based on an in-depth and systematic analysis of the development of all spheres of activity in the Republic of Moldova, the Development Strategy of Moldova until 2025 was developed as a way out of the crisis, aiming for stabilization and modernization of the country (Development Strategy 2017). Thus, it is extremely important today in Moldova to create an education system based on its values and traditions, which would continue to develop in the context of modern educational trends and the globalization of the entire world educational community. The comparison of convergent trends and national features of teacher education systems in the post-Soviet space facilitates a comprehensive assessment of the modern educational policy in the field of teacher training, both from pedagogical positions and in the context of the prospects for geopolitical, economic, and cultural cooperation of the countries that are members of the Commonwealth of Independent States (Kalimullin et al. 2020).

Historical Background

The dialectical approach to the analysis of the development of education in Moldova suggests the need for at least a brief introduction to the state of education and the socio-economic conditions of the development of the region since its accession to Russia. Only this approach makes it possible, on the basis of a comprehensive analysis of the data under consideration, to reveal the patterns and establish the causal relationships of the phenomenon under study.

The struggle of the Moldovan people for freedom and independence has a long history. In the middle of the fourteenth century, an independent Moldavian state appeared on the historical scene, which achieved significant centralization in the second half of the fifteenth century, under Lord Stefan III. From the very beginning, the territorial integrity and sovereignty of the Moldovan state were threatened by Hungarian kings, Turkish sultans, Crimean khans, Polish magnates, and others. At the beginning of the sixteenth century, despite heroic resistance, the country fell under the Turkish yoke. The rule of the Ottoman Empire for almost three centuries greatly hindered the development of the enslaved people.

As a result of the victory won by the Russian Empire in one of the wars with the Turks, the Bucharest Peace was signed on May 16, 1812. Under its terms Bessarabia[1] was annexed to Russia. At the time of the annexation of Bessarabia to Russia, there was no public school system in the province. The only educational institutions were the few monastic schools that operated irregularly and counted a small number of children who came from the most affluent families. As a result, there was continuing illiteracy of the adult population and also of most children (Ivanitsky 1975).

After the annexation, the Moldovans, experienced a political, economic, and national oppression of the Tsarist autocracy. Nevertheless, the economic development of the Dniester-Prut interfluve[2] accelerated. This was also dictated by the fact that the civil legislation of Russia did not apply to Bessarabia. In the special literary sources of that period, we find confirmation of this. Bessarabia received the right to regulate civil legal relations on the basis of local feudal laws (History of the Moldavian SSR 1965).

According to the 1897 census, the average literacy rate in Russia was 24%, and in Bessarabia, it was lower than the national average and accounted for 15.6% of the total population of the province. This difficult situation can be explained by two main reasons: first, the policy of the Tsarist autocracy in relation to the education of the population of the hinterland of Russia; second, the reactionary nature of the Bessarabian provincial zemstvo,[3] its indifference to the needs and demands of the people. The provincial zemstvo council of Bessarabia consisted exclusively of nobles. This undivided rule of the nobility in the zemstvo, the concentration of all the power of the zemstvo institutions in the hands of several noble families contributed to the fact that 'the Bessarabian zemstvo was one of the most reactionary among the 34 provincial zemstvos' (Andrus 1951, p. 13).

In confirmation of the aforementioned context, we will give a number of examples that characterize the state of education of the population of the region and the 'rapid' activity of the provincial zemstvo in this direction. Thus, according to Andrus (1951, p. 13): 'The Zemstvo of Bessarabia from the day of its establishment until 1897 opened only 17 schools', on average, 0.6 schools were built per year. For comparison, according to archival documents, from 1875 to 1877, a total of 52 churches were built in the region (Central State Archive of the MSSR n.d., f. 2991, op. 1, d.225, l. 88).

In practice, the issue of the educational development was not solved, and could not be solved due to the backwardness of the region, which was dragging out a miserable existence in the conditions of a marginal province of Tsarist Russia, as well as due to the inertia and indifference of the provincial authorities to this issue.

On October 12, 1924, the third session of the All-Ukrainian Central Executive Committee decided to establish the Moldavian Autonomous Soviet Socialist Republic (MASSR) as part of the Ukrainian SSR. In April 1925, the First All-Moldavian Congress of Soviets, Workers, Peasants and Red Army Deputies was held in Balta. The Central Executive Committee of the Republic was elected, and a new Constitution of the Moldavian ASSR was adopted, which legislated the creation of the Moldavian Soviet Socialist State (History of the Moldavian SSR 1968).

The new government made some positive changes in the education of the republic. The difficulties faced by the people of the Moldavian Republic in educating the population are eloquently recalled from the report to the Third All-Moldavian Congress (1927) of the Soviets of Workers, Peasants and Red Army Deputies: 'the civil war and the terrible famine of 1922 finally knocked out the economic base from under the entire network of cultural and educational institutions at that time' (Report of the III All-Moldavian Congress 1927, p. 13). The awful conditions in which it was necessary to start work on the education and upbringing of school-age children in the republic were revealed:

> At the time of the organization of MASSR, there were 294 schools with 638 teachers on its territory, that is, approximately 50% of the schools and teachers are necessary for universal primary education. Thus, all the work on the implementation of universal education has become a primary task in the field of public education (Report of the Third All-Moldavian Congress 1927, p. 105)

According to the data of this report, the provision of mass schools for school-age children in the republic was 43% in 1926.

Proceeding from this, the Third All-Poltava Congress (1927) of Soviets of Workers, Peasants, and Red Army Deputies wrote in its resolution:

> Noting the attention that the government paid to the cause of public education, and approving the introduction of universal primary education in those localities where the presence of school buildings made it possible, the Congress instructs the Government to implement the 5-year plan of universal education developed by all measures (Report of the All-Poltava Congress 1927, p. 149)

However, the lack of material resources and the necessary number of teachers did not allow the solution of this problem at that time.

In 1929, at the Fourth Congress of Soviets of Moldova, a five-year plan for the development of the national economy was adopted. According to this plan, starting from the 1930–1931 academic year, universal compulsory education of children from the age of eight was introduced in the Republic. In the following years, the issue of universal seven-year education of children in mass schools was resolved (Andrus 1951).

In March 1918, the territory between Prut and Dniester was reunited with Romania. The Romanian state had resorted to urgent actions to correct the difficult situation in the Bessarabian school. Already in August 1918, a decree was issued that ensured equal rights to education for Bessarabian Romanians and people of other nationalities. In 1919, the Law on Compulsory Primary Education was adopted. Subsequently (in 1928 and 1934), a number of laws were adopted on the organization and improvement of primary, gymnasium, and lyceum education. Thus, secondary education acquired a unitary character. According to statistics, in 1934 in Bessarabia, there were already 40 state and 9 private lyceums, 6 pedagogical schools—a total of 102 state and 13 private secondary educational institutions. After the signing of the Molotov-Ribbentrop Pact and after the Second World War, the education system was reorganized on the 'new' socialist principles, which had previously been tested throughout the USSR and on the left bank of the Dniester.

On August 2, 1940, the seventh session of the Supreme Soviet of the USSR adopted the Law on the Formation of the Moldavian Soviet Socialist Republic. On August 12, 1940, the Council of People's Commissars (CPC) of the Moldavian SSR and the regional Committee of the Communist Party (Bolsheviks) of Moldova adopted a resolution 'On the reorganization of schools in the former Bessarabia' (Chronological Collection of the current legislation of the MSSR 1962–1963, vol. 1, Act 73, p. 205). On the same date the regional Committee of the Communist Party (Bolsheviks) of Moldova adopted a resolution 'On the reorganization of schools in the former

Bessarabia' (Chronological Collection of the current legislation of the MSSR 1962–1963, vol. 1, act 73, p. 205).

This resolution provided for the need of implementing a number of important measures aimed at creating the Soviet system of public education. In the shortest possible time, the system of public education, which had been converted to socialist principles, was radically rebuilt. School-age children were taken into account, a new school network was developed, and the issue of implementing universal compulsory education for children in the republic was raised. For this purpose, more than a thousand different buildings were transferred to become schools. In the 1940/41 academic year, the new school network of the MSSR (including the Left Bank districts) consisted of 1478 primary, 327 lower secondary, and 91 secondary schools, that is, 1896 schools, in which 458,400 children were enrolled. By the beginning of 1941, a total of 10,944 teachers worked in these schools.

Without waiting for the end of the war, the Council of People's Commissars (CPC) of the SSR adopted Resolution No. 726 of June 16, 1944, *On measures to improve mass-political and cultural work and restore public education and health institutions in the regions of the Moldavian SSR* (Andrus 1951, p. 198). In the section 'Issues of schools' it was prescribed:

> 1. To consider as an urgent task of the CPC of the MSSR the fastest restoration of the school network on the territory of the liberated districts of the Moldavian SSR.
>
> 2. To oblige the People's Commissariat of the RSFSR by the beginning of the 1944-45 academic year to:
>
> (i) send 100 teachers of the I-IV classes and 60 teachers of the V-X classes of Russian schools to the Moldavian SSR;
> (ii) allocate and send to the disposal of the People's Commissariat of the Moldavian SSR educational and visual aids and equipment for schools in the amount of 350 thousand rubles;
> (iii) publish in 1944 for schools of the Moldavian SSR 395,000 copies of textbooks in the Moldavian language.
>
> 3. To oblige the All-Union Committee for Higher School Affairs under the USSR Council of People's Commissars to send 6 candidates of sciences—postgraduate studies in 1943–1944 to the pedagogical and teaching institutes of the Moldavian SSR.

After the end of the war, a lot of work was carried out in the MSSR to train personnel and establish a network of mass universal education schools.

The second Congress of the Communist Party (Bolsheviks) of Moldova, which took place in February 1949, was of great importance for the further improvement of culture and well-being. The Congress developed a programme for the development of cultural construction in the Republic, according to which the public education bodies were to ensure the implementation of universal seven-year education in 1950–1951. At the same time, the Congress demanded that the complete elimination of adult illiteracy be considered an urgent task. Thus, from the moment of joining the USSR until the beginning of the 1940s, the Moldavian SSR experienced a flourishing of public education, which had been significantly damaged during the Great Patriotic War.

The beginning of the development of science and education in Moldova dates back to the period after the Second World War, when the Chisinau State University, the Medical and Pedagogical Institute, the Moldavian branch of the USSR Academy of Sciences, and then the Academy of Sciences, a network of branch research institutes, were established. The opening of these institutions ensured the development of the economy, education, culture, and health of Moldova in the Soviet and post-Soviet period. The agricultural branch of the University of Iasi in Chisinau and the Tiraspol Pedagogical Institute, which existed back in the 1930s, also had a certain impact on the subsequent development of the economy, science, and education.

The development of a high level of preschool, general education, vocational, and extracurricular education occurred from the 1950s through to the 1980s. During this period, the Moldavian SSR was a republic with a highly developed diversified industry, intensive highly mechanized agricultural production, good education, and advanced modern culture. With its dynamic development and comprehensive flourishing, the Moldavian SSR clearly demonstrated the success of the new system and the benefits of belonging to the USSR (Krachun 1969; Postovoy 1971).

By the 1980s a third of the MSSR inhabitants studied in 1829 general education schools on the territory of the Republic. From year to year, budget allocations for education grew and made up a quarter of the total budget of the Republic. Significant funds were allocated for the needs of general education schools, and the working and living conditions of teachers were improved.

Educational Reforms of the 1990s

The 1990s were a serious and extremely severe test for Moldova. The rapid implementation of political reforms and the break of relations with Russia aggravated the socio-political and economic situation in the country. This is explained by the fact that Moldova was closely connected with the state and socio-economic structure of the Soviet Union, of which it was a part. In this regard, the problems of the formation of a new Russia somehow influenced Moldova.

The deep global economic crisis of the late twentieth century, and especially the crisis of 1998 that engulfed Russia, had a severe impact on the socio-economic development of all the countries of the post-Soviet space, and Moldova was among them. For quite a long period, the country was affected by a steady deficit in the foreign trade balance, unemployment, political clashes within the country, the foreign policy of countries that undermined the sovereignty of the republic, the aggravation of social and demographic processes, as well as problems of education (Korosteleva 2010; Danii and Mascauteanu 2011; Cantir and Kennedy 2015; Bodishteanu 2020).

It should be noted that the content of the problems of education in Moldova does not differ much from the Russian ones: demographic and personnel (reduction and aging of teaching staff), the quality of education, modernization of all levels of education, ensuring the availability of basic types of education, remuneration of education workers, the weakness of the material and technical base and infrastructure of educational institutions, extremely insufficient allocation of funds for the development of education. The process of reforming teacher education has become an important task, along with the fundamental changes in the field of education taking place in the CIS and Baltic countries.

Among actions triggered by the adoption of the Bologna Declaration entering the European Education Area that took place in Moldova, there are:

* the introduction of a two-stage system of vocational education;
* elaboration and approval by law of the new list of specialties in vocational training in compliance with the Eurostat and ISCED;
* development and introduction of new provisions on curricula and programmes based on learning outcomes and competences (in order to develop the curricular autonomy of universities);
* introduction of uniform criteria for assessing the knowledge, skills, and abilities;

* introduction of the European Credit Transfer System (ECTS);
* providing all graduates with a mandatory Diploma Supplement (also in English) approved by the Ministry of Education; and
* development and approval of the National Qualification Framework in 143 specialties for professional training in higher education. (Annex 5 2011, p. 8)

In 2021, the Republic of Moldova has celebrated the 30th anniversary of its independence. After the adoption of the Declaration of Independence on August 27, 1991, the republic became a sovereign independent state, and a new period in its history began. Over the past three decades, significant changes have taken place in all spheres: political, economic, and social. Of course, they also affected the education system as one of the most important public institutions. The quality of education remains one of the strategic goals of the Republic of Moldova and a priority of many state programmes (Code of the Republic of Moldova 2014; Development Strategy 2017).

Among the most important measures that helped to ensure the effective organization of the educational process is the increase in 2016 in wages for teachers and heads of educational institutions of the country by 8.6%. In addition, a significant area of the Ministry's work was the diversification of educational programmes through the development and approval of ten training programmes in optional disciplines in the field of information technology, career guidance. As for the modernization of higher education, a number of results have been achieved. These are, in particular, the increase of scholarships to students by 4.9%, the development and implementation of new mechanisms for financing of state universities based on performance indicators. Funding was approved with the support of the World Bank for increasing the orientation of higher education programmes towards the labour market and ensuring their quality.

Among the main priorities of the Ministry of Education, Culture and Research of the Republic of Moldova is the development of the *Education Strategy-2030*. The main goals of the new strategy were, first of all, equal access, quality, relevance of training, digitization of education, and professional development of teaching staff in the field of digital technologies. There was also a strengthening of the material and technical base of educational institutions at all levels, and the development of policy documents, ensuring the resilience of the education system to the conditions caused by the pandemic, and in general to various critical situations that may occur.[4]

Higher education in the Republic of Moldova strives to improve the quality of research and teaching, increase student mobility, and strengthen the 'knowledge triangle' (education—research—business environment). Among the key tasks are also improving university management, increasing the attractiveness of universities, and increasing the level of employment of graduates. The strategic goal in the field of education of the country is to ensure its accessibility and the use of modern technologies in the educational process. The development of the infrastructure of educational institutions remains a priority that cannot be postponed in the current conditions. In this regard, the Ministry has set the task of digitizing the educational process in vocational education at the national level. This relates to the organization of training courses for teachers, master instructors on the introduction of information technologies in education, and support for the development of digital educational material and the necessary software. Digitization of vocational education will contribute to the technological development of the country, improve the quality and relevance of training, and also respond to the challenges of the twenty-first century. In addition, it is necessary to unite the efforts of the public and state institutions to improve the level of scientific research in the Republic of Moldova. Today, this is steadily improving due to the accumulation of best practices in this area, and the development of human resources.

Thus, in recent years there have been significant changes at the level of educational policy. Among the most important are the following: giving education a priority status within the framework of the country's socio-economic development; orientation towards the European vector of education development; ensuring the quality of education as the most important factor in the country's economic development; development of the concept of lifelong learning.

Teacher Education System in Moldova

Initial Teacher Education (Pre-service Education)

In the Republic of Moldova, characterized by the desire to integrate into a single European educational space, teacher training is largely determined by the existing standard of training of the European teacher model (European Network on Teacher Policies).

Moldova's teacher education aims at improving the quality of the teacher training process in terms of the principles of continuing education, as well as improving the image of the teacher profession. According to the Ministry of Education, improving the quality of teacher education is an integral part of the overall goal of modernizing the country's education and quality assurance, also in the context of the Bologna Process.

So as to support the teaching profession at different levels and to encourage young people to join the didactic cadres, some governmental initiatives and incentive mechanisms have been developed. These include:

* removing the age limit for full-time studies, including the pedagogical specialties, and allocating an annual budget to fund places to study pedagogy in universities and colleges;
* a support programme for young teachers—graduates of higher and secondary specialized education who were assigned to work in rural areas—that provides them with a number of rights during the first three years of their work, including free housing (for the period of their activity on the countryside), partially paid utilities, and a one-off allowance;
* a system of teacher salaries based on conditions and amounts stipulated by the law, which sets the bonus at a rate of 50% of the salary for the highest educational category, 40% of the salary for the first category, and 30% for the second category;
* a system of advancing teacher qualifications, defined by Articles 54, 28, and 29 of the Law on Education (1995), which provides state-funded, compulsory courses for teachers once every five years; in addition the Concept of Continuing Education has been developed together with the government's position on it, which also regulates the process of advancing teacher qualifications;
* a contest 'Teacher of the Year' takes place on an annual basis, drawing attention to the best teachers in the country and promoting their advancement in the profession and career development.

These changes as well as other policies in the sphere of teacher education are determined by a number of documents adopted on a national level (in addition to the Law on Education, adopted by Parliament in 1995 and other legislative acts):

* The Concept of Education Development in the Republic of Moldova (1994)
* The Concept of Training Pre-university Education Teaching Staff (2003)
* The Concept on In-service Teacher Education of the Teaching and Managerial Staff of Pre-University Education (2004)
* The National Programme for the Development of Education in the period 1999–2005 (implemented in stages: 1999–2001 and 2002–2005)

* The Concept and Strategy for Continuing Education of Pedagogical Cadres (2007)
* Consolidated Strategy for the Development of Education in the period 2011–2015
* The Programme for Long-term Development of the Republic of Moldova (chapter on education)
* Action Plan to implement the Consolidated Strategy for the Development of Education for 2011–2015
* The provisions of the Association Agreement of the Republic of Moldova and the European Union (Annex 5, p. 13)

Initial teacher education in Moldova is carried out at two levels:

1. Secondary vocational education colleges. Colleges enrol graduates from gymnasiums, secondary comprehensive schools, and lyceums who hold school or gymnasium certificates and baccalaureate diplomas. Depending on the educational attainment and chosen field of studies (specialization), they can last from two to four years (four years for gymnasium graduates, two years for graduates from comprehensive secondary school or lyceum). To ensure the necessary level of primary school teacher education at the secondary specialized education (college) level, a curriculum has been developed providing for the study of such subjects as pedagogy (219 hours), psychology (207 hours), and methods of teaching various subjects. Upon passing final exams (and/or defending their graduation project/paper), college graduates can continue their studies in higher education institutions (HEIs). The college diploma qualifies a midlevel specialist in the relevant professional field allowing the graduate to enter the labour market as a preschool educator and primary education teacher. In addition to the diploma of secondary special education, a college graduate can receive a bachelor's degree, successfully passing the relevant exams, and the opportunity to enter the master's program of any profile at the university.

2. Higher education institutes and universities. These train teaching staff for all levels of pre-university education for teaching all school disciplines as well as teachers and administrators for gymnasiums, lyceums, vocational, and secondary specialized education. In addition to studying a professional field, gymnasium graduates are also provided with a lyceum education and a baccalaureate examination (Art. 25 of the Law on Education). According to the provisions of the Bologna Process, all higher education institutions of the Republic of Moldova have introduced the first and second cycles of study. The duration of training in the first cycle is three years and ends with

state examinations and the defence of the diploma for the degree of licentiate. Graduates on the basis of the obtained diploma can enter the labour market or continue their studies at the second cycle—master's degree having a duration of two years.

Primary and secondary school teacher education in Moldova is provided by HEIs in the fields of Teacher Education and Training (in all school disciplines) and Pedagogical Sciences. The field of Teacher Education and Training includes 15 specialties, which correspond to the disciplines taught on the basis of general education. The field of Pedagogical Sciences includes pedagogical, psychological, and psycho-pedagogical specialties.

In order to facilitate the employability of graduates from the pedagogical specialties and implement didactic rules, the national legislation offers the opportunity to train specialists in two related specialties (e.g. physics and mathematics, chemistry, and biology) in the field of the general education, pedagogical sciences. The length of studies is three years in a single specialty (180 credits) and four years for two specialties (240 credits). Such a possibility is particularly helpful for teachers from rural areas, where a limited number of hours for each subject is often insufficient to make a full teaching load.

Education in the field of Pedagogical Sciences can be extended to the second cycle through the programmes of vocational and academic master's degree for a period of 90–120 academic credits. A doctor's degree is also available for holders of master's degree, diploma, or equivalent document recognized by the relevant national authority, who can participate in the enrolment competition.

Basic education in colleges and higher education institutions is carried out in accordance with curricula, defined by the Curriculum Framework. They include disciplines of theoretical and practical education in the area of pedagogy, psychology and teaching methods in the specific specialty. Graduates of higher education institutions of non-pedagogical profile can teach in the education system only after being trained in those subjects (Art. 53 of the Law on Education, 1995).

HEIs are responsible for the content and quality of education within their curricular autonomy. They develop curricula (teaching plans) for each specialty, which are then approved by the Ministry of Education. For the first cycle (licentiate degree), the curriculum includes several mandatory components such as:

* fundamental disciplines (in the amount of 40–60 credits in the programmes of 180 credits and 50–80 credits in the programmes of 240 credits);

* subjects on the specialization (in the amount of 40–70 credits in the programmes of 180 credits and 50–95 credits in the programmes of 240 credits);
* socio-humanities component (in the amount of 18–25 credits in the programmes of 180 credits and 25–35 credits in the programmes of 240 credits);
* a component enhancing communicative skills (up to 10 credits); and
* a practice (15–20 credits in the programme of 180 credits and 20–30—in
the programmes of 240 credits).

In order to ensure a minimum required level of teacher education, the Ministry of Education has developed a standard in a form of psycho-pedagogical module for which 60 academic credit points can be awarded, including 30 credits for theoretical training (the study of psycho-pedagogical disciplines) and 30 for practical training (pedagogical practice), which is being implemented since 2000. The implementation of this module is compulsory for all higher education institutions that provide education in the specialty Education and Training of Teachers. In general, the curricula of the higher education institutions that train teachers do not differ significantly from regulations of the Ministry regarding the psycho-pedagogical module.

Teacher education in both colleges and higher education institutions includes obligatory teaching classroom practices. The conditions of such practices are set by contracts between the teacher education institution and city (district) education departments or pre-university institutions (Annex 5, p. 17).

Continuous Professional Development of Teachers (In-service Education)

The professional development of teachers takes place at different levels (local, regional, and national) according to programmes developed by universities, specialized institutes, centres for continuous education, non-governmental organizations providing continuous professional development, and other institutions approved by the Ministry of Education. Professional development of teachers is regulated by Arts. 54, 28, and 29 of the Law on Education (1995). The advancement of professional, methodical, and psycho-pedagogical qualifications and competences of school teachers (the pre-university education system), as well as education and professional development of administrative employees, is organized and co-ordinated by the Ministry of Education.

As stated by the law, advancement of qualifications of teaching staff is obligatory and should take place at least once every five years to continuously maintain professional qualifications at the level of new conceptual methodological, substantive, and technological advances that take place in education. Retraining or specialization of teachers is carried out according to the needs of both the education system and the individual.

The Regulation on Attestation of Teachers defines their participation in comprehensive training courses for approximately 150 hours, including modular courses on psycho-pedagogy, specific specialty, and technological training, as well as in various short-term (one to three days) courses. The programme of professional development includes basic and optional subjects in three modules: (1) psychology and pedagogy (2) discipline didactics and specialty (3) information and communication technology.

Professional development of teachers throughout the year is based on the level of the institution and at the level city/district. For each school year, the local administration (Department of Education) prepares a work plan that lists all the workshops to be conducted (with an indication, which schools are responsible for their conduct), the seminars and categories of students (e.g. young teachers). For instance, methodical seminars, demonstration lessons, and themed events are organized in schools. Special higher educational institutions—centres of in-service training for the teaching and leadership staff—are responsible for creating programmes of professional development courses and developing forms of teacher assessment.

In Moldova, there have been significant changes at the level of continuing professional education, including:

* adoption of the standards of continuous professional education for teachers;
* adoption of regulations on the certification of teachers on the basis of professional credits, in order to assign a degree;
* inclusion of advanced training, retraining and professional conversion in the system of continuing professional education; development of a draft Concept for lifelong learning;
* development of a draft concept and methodology for the recognition of professional skills acquired throughout life;
* curriculum development for continuing education of teachers, aimed at the formation of professional competences; and
* creation of a material base (modern laboratories of physics, chemistry, and biology) on the basis of the Centre for Pedagogical Excellence, created at the Institute of Pedagogical Sciences and Methodological Support for the introduction of a curriculum on continuing professional education.

In contrast to initial (pre-service) education area, where the possibilities of educational institutions are relatively high, the number of relevant institutions and their capacity to provide continuous education for teaching staff are rather limited. In the field of teachers' re-training, the important role is given to non-governmental organizations, established in the form of public organizations or private educational institutions.

Professional development of teachers and school administrators is carried out at the expense of public funds. Courses financed from the budget are organized by the Department of Training at the Institute of Pedagogical Sciences and at higher education institutions that carry out university level (cycle I) training in the specialty of training 'Education and Teacher Training'. There are also several agencies that provide services to improve the skills of teachers on a fee-paying basis. In this case payments can be made individually, by organizations, institutions, or enterprises (Annex 5, p.19).

Continuing professional education of teachers in Moldova is carried out in the Institute of Pedagogical Sciences and universities, as well as in non-governmental organizations accredited and licensed to provide this type of educational service.

The Institute of Pedagogical Sciences, being an institution of Republican significance, occupies a special place in the system of continuous vocational education, due to the specifics of its bifocal activities: research in the field of pedagogy and psychology and continuous vocational education (professional development of pedagogical personnel, retraining of teachers, professional conversion, psycho-pedagogical education for teachers of universities, colleges, vocational institutions that do not have a teacher's diploma, etc.). In the context of the development and modernization of pedagogical education, the activities of the Republican Centre for the Development of Vocational Education, the Centre for Pedagogical Excellence, and the Centre for the Development of Psychological Assistance in the Education System, which were opened at the Institute of Pedagogical Sciences, are of particular importance.

The symbiosis between science and educational practice, carried out at the Institute of Pedagogical Sciences, gives a good result, given the fact that it was this institution that developed (in 2010) the foundations for the transition of schools to new standards aimed at the formation of competences, and conceptualized the system of their assessment. This reform in the national education system was the impetus for many other transformations in this area.

The largest providers of teacher (pre-service or/and in-service) education in Moldova include:

* Moldova State University;
* 'Alecu Russo' State University from Bălţi;
* 'Ion Creanga' State Pedagogical University;
* Tiraspol' State University (Chisinau);
* The National Institute of Physical Culture and Sport;
* Cahul State University;
* Comrat State University; and
* The Institute of Pedagogical Sciences.

Teacher education is thus provided by a range of public and private educational institutions, whereas the organization of initial teacher education process is funded by the state and extra-budgetary funds (individual contracts, projects, grants, etc.).

Unresolved Problems of Teacher Education

Despite the steps taken in the field of teacher education reform in the Republic of Moldova, there are still some unresolved problems, including:

* non-compliance of the system of teacher training with the provisions of UNESCO and European standards, which provide for the training of these specialists only at the level of higher education;
* the problem of assessing students' knowledge, skills, and competences;
* lack of an external accreditation system for teaching institutions;
* the discrepancy between the demand and supply of teaching staff in the labour market;
* lack of demand by the education system for graduates of pedagogical educational institutions;
* the increasing proportion of teachers reaching retirement age in relation to the total number of specialists in the field of education; and
* the problem of the academic load of teachers, their salaries.

The terms of study at the university should be revised and extended for at least one year by reducing the duration of pre-university education, which lasts in Moldova for 12 years, starting from the age of 7, since at the end of the lyceum education, graduates are already 19 years old.

An urgent problem is the need to improve the quality of practical training of university graduates, so that when they graduate they can immediately engage in teaching at school. In this regard, it is necessary to increase the frequency of practical training, in particular, teaching practice in school. Secondly, it is necessary to increase its duration, for example, by increasing the length of studies at the university. Thirdly, it is advisable to organize a solid pedagogical practice, including a 'Pedagogical Day' in the schedule. Fourthly, it is necessary to have basic applied schools, in which practical training and teaching practice could be organized, and their directors, head teachers, and methodologists would report on the work done to train highly qualified specialists at the councils of the university, faculty, and department. Fifth, it is necessary to involve practitioners of schools in the teaching at the universities. In addressing the issue of employment, a targeted referral to study at universities for the best graduates of lyceums or colleges on the part of institutions, enterprises, and schools that need specialists on a mutually contractual basis could be practised.

There exists also the problem of evaluating knowledge, skills, and competences of students. Under the Bologna education system, the emphasis is, in fact, on the daily preparation of students for seminars, practicum, and laboratory classes and on the constant accumulation of marks for a particular discipline, as the marks obtained are taken into account when calculating the performance indicator, which, in turn, must be at least 60% of the total average semester assessment.

There are some challenges connected with the law concerning languages in the Republic of Moldova. The problem of a political decision to give the Russian language the status of an official language on a par with the Moldovan language in the Republican legislation is also one of the urgent ones. There exist challenges for the preservation and development of Moldovan-Russian and Russian-Moldovan bilingualism. Moldovan and Russian are the official languages in the provinces of Gagauzia and Transnistria. Moldovan, Ukrainian and Russian are the official languages of the two regions of Moldova, which are already established in accordance with local legislation (Gabdulkhakov et al. 2018; Kobylyanskaya 2020).

A very serious problem is the problem of equating (converting) Moldovan higher education diplomas to European diplomas. Ultimately, the principles of the Bologna Declaration had a serious impact on the transformation of teacher education in Moldova, which was largely reflected in the rejection of the specialty system, the introduction of multi-level training, the introduction of the European credit unit transfer system, and so on.

It should be recognized that the problem of full inclusion of Moldova in the single European higher education area persists and includes a number of other problems the degree of which was differentiated by country. A real system of student and teacher mobility, with absolute recognition of diplomas and equal employment, and mass joint training programmes, is required (Duda and Clifford-Amos 2011).

In a number of countries, the reforms of teacher education in the 1990s were marked by the integration of pedagogical institutes with other universities and the creation of regional multidisciplinary universities on this basis. This period is characterized by a decrease in public spending on education, which determined the outflow of teachers and their shortage due to low wages and the deterioration of the material and technical equipment of universities (Valeeva and Kalimullin 2019).

The weak link in the educational systems has become precisely pedagogical universities, which are more focused on the needs of the state, which could not support them sufficiently during the years of economic difficulties. Due to their specifics, pedagogical educational institutions have also shown a low potential for commercialization of their activities. For this reason, a typical solution for some countries (e.g. Kazakhstan and Russia) was the merger of pedagogical institutes and universities with other higher educational institutions. Teacher education is provided by higher educational institutions of various types, differing in specialization (pedagogical, classical, technical, and other universities) and forms of ownership (state, municipal, and private) (Kalimullin et al. 2020).

In general, the transformation of teacher education in Moldova was accompanied by serious political, economic, and social reforms of the transition period from a socialist to a capitalist society. Attempted reforms often ended with mistakes and failures that completely changed the status of education, teachers, and educational institutions. Nevertheless, there was an active search for new models of teacher training, accompanied by various experimental activities. Innovations were manifested in the legislative framework, scientific basis, organization, economy, and content of pedagogical education.

Strategically important is the question of what optimal and effective methods will help to make the transition from the current level of education development to a better one that would meet the needs of citizens, the Moldovan society and the state as a whole. Building a system for training pedagogical personnel in the Republic of Moldova follows the pan-European trends on the basis of international documents adopted by the European and international community. However, it may be concluded that the idea of integrating the European educational system into the Moldovan educational space has not yet been realized, and its implementation has not been well thought out and has sometimes been over-hasty and half-hearted, which has led to some negative results.

Notes

1. Bessarabia is a historical region in Eastern Europe, bounded by the Dniester River on the east and the Prut River on the west. About two-thirds of Bessarabia lies within modern-day Moldova.
2. This is a region between two rivers Dniester and Prut.
3. A zemstvo was an institution of local government set up during the great emancipation reform of 1861 carried out in Imperial Russia by Emperor Alexander II of Russia.
4. https://mecc.gov.md/.

References

Andrus, O. G. (1951). *Essays on the history of schools in Bessarabia and the Moldavian SSR of the first half of the XX century.* Chisinau: Publishing House 'School of Sovetike'.

Annex 5. Study on Teacher Education for Primary and Secondary Education in Six Eastern Partnership Countries. Moldova. (2011). In: A. Duda and T. Clifford-Amos (Eds.), *Study on teacher education for primary and secondary education in six countries of the Eastern Partnership: Armenia, Azerbaijan, Belarus, Georgia, Moldova and Ukraine.* Final report. European Commission, Directorate-General for Education and Culture

Bodishteanu, N. V. (2020). *Republic of Moldova and its Eurasian track of policy: the impact of internal and external factors on the foreign policy formation.* Moscow: HSE.

Cantir, C., and R. Kennedy. (2015). Balancing on the shoulders of giants: Moldova's foreign policy toward Russia and the European Union. *Foreign Policy Analysis*, 11(4), 397–416.

Central State Archive of the MSSR, n.d. f. 2991, on. I, d. 225, l. 88. Local laws of Bessarabia.

Chronological collection of the current legislation of the MSSR, 1962–1963, vol. 1, act 73, p. 205. Chisinau.

Code of the Republic of Moldova dated July 17, 2014 No. 152 On education (with changes and additions as of 09/11/2020). Retrieved from https://online.zakon.kz/Document/?doc_id=34450140.

Danii, O., and M. Mascauteanu. (2011). Moldova under the European neighbourhood policy: 'Falling Between Stools'. *Journal of Communist Studies and Transition Politics,* 27(1), 99–119.

Development Strategy of Moldova until 2025. (2017). Retrieved from https://www.moldovenii.md/en/section/525.

Duda, A., and T. Clifford-Amos. (2011). *Study on teacher education for primary and secondary education in six countries of the Eastern Partnership: Armenia, Azerbaijan,*

Belarus, Georgia, Moldova and Ukraine. Final report. European Commission, Directorate-General for Education and Culture.

Gabdulkhakov, V. F., M. P. Zhigalova, L. I. Kobylyanskaya, Yu. E. Khodynyuk, and M. G. Semenova. (2018). Formation of the cultural code in the minds of teachers of Eastern Europe. *Nepreryvnoye pedagogicheskoye obrazovaniye*, 2(8), 9–14.

History of the Moldavian SSR (1965). Vol. 1: From ancient times to the Great October Socialist Revolution. L.V. Cherepnin (Ed.). Chisinau: Kartya moldovenyaske.

History of the Moldavian SSR (1968). Vol. 2: From the Great October Socialist Revolution to the present day. S.P. Trapeznikov (Ed.). Chisinau: Kartya moldovenyaske.

Ivanitsky, A. I. (1975). *Problems of teaching and social adaptation of the deaf.* Chisinau: Stiinza.

Kalimullin, A. M., M. P. Zhigalova, A. Ibrasheva, L. I. Kobylyanskaya, Y. A. Lodatko, Y. Nurlanov. (2020). Post-Soviet identity in teacher education: Past, present, future. *Education and Self Development*, 15(3), 145–163.

Kobylyanskaya, L. I. (2020). Russian language in the Republic of Moldova in ethnic self-determination in the post-Soviet space. In: M. P. Zhigalova (Ed.), *Ethoses and destinies in modern society: theory and practice* (pp. 55–64). Brest: BrSTU.

Korosteleva, E. (2010). Moldova's European Choice: 'Between Two Chairs'?. *Europe-Asia Studies*, 62(8), 1267–1289.

Krachun, T. A. (1969). *Essays on the history of school development and pedagogical thought in Moldova*. Chisinau: Lumina.

Postovoy, E. S. (1971). *Public education of the Moldavian SSR at a new stage*. Chisinau: Lumina.

Report of the All-Poltava Congress of Soviets of Workers', Peasants' and Red Army Deputies, March 27–April 1, 1927. Balta: Organizational department. Central Executive Committee of the BSSR.

Report of the III All-Moldavian Congress of the Soviets of Workers', Peasants ' and Red Army Deputies (1927). Balta: Organizational department. Central Executive Committee of the BSSR.

The Parliament of the Republic of Moldova (2014). *The Code of the Republic of Moldova on Education No. 152 of July 17, 2014*. Retrieved from https://mecc.gov.md/sites/default/files/education_code_final_version.pdf.

Valeeva, R., and A. Kalimullin. (2019). Teacher education in Russia. In: J. Lampert (Ed.), *Oxford Research Encyclopedia of Education*. New York: Oxford University Press.

22

Teacher Education in Ukraine: Surfing the Third Wave of Change

Olena Shyyan and Roman Shyyan

Introduction

Teacher education (TE) has been the subject of intense political debate in many countries for many decades. At national and international levels, the pressure on teacher education to educate sufficient and highly qualified teachers is increasing (Swennen and Klink 2009, p.1). The process of reforming the education system in general, and teacher education in particular in the post-Soviet countries is extremely complex (Polyzoi et al. 2003; Godoń et al. 2004; Webster et al. 2011; Corner 2017). Ukraine is no exception in this regard. The aim of this chapter is to present an overview and analysis of the educational reforms after Ukraine's independence that was directed on a fundamental change in the tasks of TE, structural transformation of TE network and its entry into the European educational space.

The chapter is structured in the following way: in the first two sections we draw the context of teacher education in Ukraine since independence in 1991to the present and the development of its own education policy from historical analyses in order to identify some of the major tensions of its development that can be divided into three periods (waves). In third section we present teacher education reforms in Ukraine and its specificity that was

O. Shyyan (✉)
Lviv Regional In-service Teacher Training Institute, Lviv, Ukraine
e-mail: olshyyan2@gmail.com

R. Shyyan
Institute of Education Content Modernization, Kyiv, Ukraine

© The Author(s), under exclusive license to Springer Nature Switzerland AG 2023
M. Kowalczuk-Walędziak et al. (eds.), *The Palgrave Handbook of Teacher Education in Central and Eastern Europe*, https://doi.org/10.1007/978-3-031-09515-3_22

directed not only on a fundamental change in the tasks of TE but also on structural transformation of TE network and its entry to the European educational space. Main characteristics of the system of initial teacher education (fourth section) and of existing systems of teacher professional development (fifth section) in Ukraine are described. In the next section we determine and analyse the tensions and challenges that Ukraine faces in transforming teacher education systems. The last section substantiates implications for the future development of teacher education in Ukraine.

The Context of Teacher Education in Ukraine

> The Ukrainian school will be successful if it is joined by successful teachers. They—successful teachers and professionals—will resolve a multitude of issues regarding the quality of teaching, the volume of home assignments, communication with children and school administration. (New Ukrainian School 2016)

Ukraine is a 'young' in terms of its being an independent (since 24. 08. 1991) country of the Central-East Europe. The country of near 42 million people has been struggling its own way from being one of the former Soviet Union' republics to a newly born independent state. Post-communist Ukraine experienced severe structural, institutional and economic crises. Post-communist legacies remained mixed with the multiple external influences both from the East (Russia) and the West (Europe and the USA) (Fimyar 2008). During the 1990s and the first two decades of the twenty-first century, a series of significant state measures were taken in Ukraine. Ukraine's struggle to move closer to the rest of Europe has been ongoing since the 1991 collapse of the Soviet regime, which had imposed artificial barriers while promoting ideas of otherness that contradicted Ukraine's historic sense of European identity. Public support for the country's European trajectory has consolidated significantly since 2014, despite the trauma and turbulence of the past six years (Getmanchuk 2019).

The Revolution of Dignity (*Euromaidan*) created further acute political and economic challenges which led to a broad agenda of structural reforms. Going forward, the old growth model that relied on legacy industries will not deliver Ukraine's aspirations (World Bank 2019). Ukraine is a priority partner for the European Union (EU). The EU supports Ukraine in ensuring a stable, prosperous, and democratic future for its citizens and is unwavering in its support for Ukraine's independence, territorial integrity, and sovereignty. Priority reforms include the fight against corruption, reform of the judiciary, constitutional and electoral reforms, improvement of the business climate and energy efficiency, as well as reform of public administration and decentralization (EEAS 2020).

Like other Eastern European countries, the education system in Ukraine has been undergoing a considerable transformation over the past three decades. Because of its strategic importance for the governmental aims, education was one of the first social spheres to witness frequent (and sometimes chaotic) transformations after the country gained independence (Kutsyuruba and Kovalchuk 2015).

Ukraine faced the challenges coming from the worldwide development of education, especially in regard to a knowledge and information-based economy. The Ukraine Constitution guarantees secondary education free of charge for all citizens of the country and a number of significant changes aimed at solving urgent problems have already taken place (Pukhovska and Sacilotto-Vasylenko 2010).

After Ukraine's independence in 1991, the development of its own education policy and higher education (HE) system was started, while the inherited 'soviet' multilevel education system could not respond adequately to rapid global changes or the new national policy. Such factors as overgrown bureaucracy, residual financing and lack of support to teachers of all levels compromised education's contribution to society and opposed the new development plan towards democracy, knowledge, and information-based society (Stepko 2004). Ukraine's education went through turbulent times, when ministers changed, some initiatives were adopted, others rolled back.

Ukraine has taken steps to become a more open society that is compatible with European education systems (Khustochka 2009). Education, like the Ukrainian society in general, has experienced a focal shift from totalitarian ideology to democracy and pluralism. The new societal realities required profound educational reforms, including the structural organization of secondary schools, universities, curricula, and teacher and educational administrator training programmes at all levels (Koshmanova and Ravchyna 2008). The system of education required profound educational reforms, including structural re-organization of secondary schools, universities, and curricula at all levels (Koshmanova 2007).

The development of the educational system in Ukraine since independence can be divided into three waves. The first two replaced each other 'at the turn of the millennium'. They started in a similar way: from the creation of a strategic document as methodological grounds for further changes. But the similarity is not only in this. In both cases one could observe the contradiction between the declared openness to public discussion and the real tightness of the document preparation. In both cases the documents were preapproved at the *All-Ukrainian Congress of Educators* preceded by the short-term discussion of the project. Then the documents were approved by the central authorities: in the first case, the document was approved by the Cabinet of Ministers, and in the second one by the President of Ukraine. Afterwards it turned out that the effect of the document on the real course of events is much less than expected. Since March 2014 the vector of educational policy in Ukraine radically changed towards Europe. The reforms of the third wave began with a *New Law of Ukraine 'On Higher Education'* adopted In July 2014. Introducing it, Liliya Hrynevych MP, Head of the Parliamentary Committee for Science and Education, said:

> Given the long-term consequences for the country, the adoption of this law is one of the most important, if not the most important, decision made by the Ukrainian Parliament after the Revolution of Dignity … This is the adoption of a democratic, pro-European system … which begins a new era in the development of Ukrainian higher education. One primary purpose is to achieve true quality improvement in higher education … and the transformation of our educational system to become truly competitive in the European Union. (British Council 2015)

It is important to note that the provisions of the new law are underpinned by a democratic and pro-European agenda. This served as a gateway towards greater European integration for Ukraine's extensive network of universities and institutes of higher education. It granted universities enhanced autonomy, decentralized many of the controlling functions previously held by the Education Ministry, launched new regulatory bodies that aligned with the standards of the European Higher Education Area, and paved the way for the fight against academic dishonesty (UNICEF 2019) The Law on Higher Education was the first large systematic reform measure adopted by Ukraine's parliament in the immediate aftermath of the Euromaidan Revolution. But it represented a compromise on the part of many different interest groups, coming on top of years of absence of a clear development strategy for higher education: a policy of nonpolicy! However, it did not address this challenge (World Bank 2019).

The framework Law on Education was passed in 2017. It defines general principles and provides enabling legislation for government subsectors. The law puts in motion some drastic changes to Ukraine's Soviet-era education system, including codifying into law the main elements of the New Ukrainian School (NUS) concept, to be implemented in three phases: phase I

(2016–2018), phase II (2019–2022), and phase III (2023–2029). Elements of the New Ukrainian School concept include modern approaches to: (a) school curricula, focused on twenty-first-century skills and competences; (b) teacher professional development, emphasizing student-centred learning; (c) system management and school administration, emphasizing greater local decision-making powers; and (d) a different role for the central government with a focus on setting and monitoring learning standards (World Bank 2019).

Teacher Education Reforms in Ukraine

General aspects of the teacher education system functioning both in Ukrainian and European environment are discussed in many scientific works, for example, Rolyak and Ohiyenko (2008); Sacilotto-Vasylenko (2008); Pukhovska and Sacilotto-Vasylenko (2010); Silova (2010); Duda and Clifford-Amos (2011); Kutsyuruba and Kovalchuk (2015); and Palaguta (2019). There are studies that represent various aspects of educational development in the context of European integration processes in Ukraine (e.g. Tsvetkova 2019). Difficulties and achievements of the Ukrainian education reforms in this field became the subject of scientific research of both national and foreign scholars (e.g. Holowinsky 1995; Koshmanova and Ravchyna 2008).

During the 25 years of independence, a number of initiatives dealing with Ukrainian higher education in general and teacher education in particular have taken place. Among them are the development and implementation of laws, strategies, initiatives, and policies aiming at fostering a vision of reforming trends and needs in teacher education, such as given here:

* State National Programme 'Education' (*Ukraine of the XXI century*), 1993
* State Programme 'Teacher', 1997, 2002
* Signing the 'Convention on the Recognition of Qualifications concerning Higher Education in the European Region' (1997)
* National Doctrine for Education Development in Ukraine 2002

The last of these included the following statement:

> The training of educators, their professional development is an important condition for the modernization of education. To support educators, to increase their responsibility for the quality of professional activities, the state provides for the development and improvement of the regulatory and legal framework of professional activities of educators; the forecast and satisfaction of the society's

needs for the mentioned educators…; the improvement of the system of motivating the professional development of educators. (National Doctrine for Education Development in Ukraine 2002, p. 14)

In 2002, the introduction of external independent assessment (EIA) started as a complex of organizational procedures aimed at the determination of the level of academic achievements of secondary school-leavers while entering higher educational establishments. This process can serve as an example of fruitful cooperation between state administration bodies with public, international organizations and other interested parties as well as an example of political speculations caused by an intense interest of the public and mass media in the events connected with this large-scale reform.

Following the All-Ukrainian Educational Meeting 'Caring for the teacher is hope for the future', 2005, President's Decree No 1013/2005 *On urgent measures for securing the functioning and development of education in Ukraine* was issued with the purpose of the 'further development of education of Ukraine, its integration in the European educational space as well as the creation of conditions for providing citizens with access to quality education, the strengthening of the high status of educators in the society'.

Joining the Bologna Process in 2005 is among the main steps of second wave towards the integration within the European Higher Education Area. This opened a new stage of the modernization of teacher education in Ukraine. The need to ensure convergence with EU standards and implementation of the principles of the Bologna Process determines the direction of HE reform in Ukraine (Goodman 2013; Kutsyuruba and Kovalchuk 2015). For the first five years in the Bologna Process, Ukraine has already advanced in the implementation of a third cycle for doctoral programmes under the Bologna Process and the European Credit Transfer System for the first and second cycles (Bologna National Report Ukraine 2009). The introduction of the Bologna Process Diploma Supplement, provided greater transparency on higher education qualifications, and the establishment of a Higher Education Reforms Expert Group with EU support with involvement of Ministry of Education and Science of Ukraine and the National Tempus Office (European Commission 2010). Principles of teacher education development declared in the Sectorial Conception of Lifelong Teacher Education (2013) were revised after five years (Conception of the Development of Teacher Education 2018). Another important moment was the creation of the National Agency for Higher Education Quality Assurance (NAQA 2019), modelled on the type of independent institution found in all progressive countries. The key functions of the NAQA included maintaining a degree of quality control within

Ukrainian higher education and reducing the scope for corruption and academic dishonesty. This new institution took on a number of functions previously handled by the Education Ministry, such as the accreditation of educational programmes and the award of scientific degrees.

In 2016, the Ukrainian government launched the New Ukrainian School (NUS) reform initiative in an ambitious bid to radically transform the approach to education in Ukrainian schools and meet the demands of the twenty-first-century economy. This involved a revised curriculum with an emphasis on practical and soft skills, together with extensive teacher training and significant re-equipping of schools. The first Ukrainian schoolchildren to study within the NUS framework entered classes in 2018, meaning that the first NUS graduates are due to complete their school education in 2030. The New Ukrainian School (NUS) is a key reform of the Ministry of Education and Science. With the commitment of national and international partners from across the education landscape, the quality education system needed by the next generation of Ukrainian school leavers is now being shaped. A new competence-based State Standard for Primary Education, 2018, and the State Standard for Basic (lower secondary) Education, 2020, have been developed and introduced. Practical implementation for education through the new State School Standards and further guidance documents, to underpin key-competence-based education in Ukraine and support schools to deliver to their students this approach to learning. There has been an implementation of a competence-based approach to education at different educational levels based on EU key competences frameworks (e.g. EntreComp and DComp) and Competence Potential as the Ukrainian national guidance.

It is important to note that the idea of giving the teacher more freedom to teach (freedom of action—to select educational materials, to improvise and try things out) and freedom to learn is also envisaged by the reform. Therefore, one of the main recent goals is to contribute to teachers' professional and personal growth and to increase their social status (NUS 2016).

The Ukrainian system of teacher training has a long tradition but now is in the process of reorganization following the new global trends and experiences of other states. All the time, the process of teacher training and advanced in-service teacher training was organized in various ways in order to meet the demand of a certain period of time. Reasonably, the aim of training teachers was different. It was not only to prepare educated people who would know the subject and be able to transfer knowledge to the students but also to train them to conduct the main principles of the time and implement the new system in the life of society. These days, teacher training needs to be focused on a new role of the teacher which is based on the modern requirements and life conditions in the country (Gubash 2018).

Accordingly to the World Bank recent review (World Bank 2019), improving the capacity of teachers to deliver the new competency-based curriculum requires a comprehensive and coordinated approach that harmonizes preservice and in-service teacher education and professional development. Current international best practice suggests that doing this in a harmonized way requires a series of instruments and practices being put into place. For instance:

* A teacher competency framework that spells out what teachers should be able to do in several domains (planning teaching, creating conducive learning environments, providing differentiated instruction, teaching the NUS curriculum, assessing learning, etc.) and at different levels of competence (novice, proficient, expert). By defining these abilities, this index of competences serves to define a teacher's proficiencies across their career.
* It is on the basis of this framework and index that preservice and in-service professional development (PD) modules can be developed to be in line with one another (though at different levels).
* Good practice in preservice teacher education includes a set of practicums so that students can progressively learn how to teach in the classroom. It should also be followed by an induction period during which time there is a reduced teaching load and the new teacher has a mentor, usually an experienced teacher, who can coach the new teacher in the first year(s).
* Best practice in in-service PD suggests that the PD must be content-specific, taught mostly in-school, and be relevant to the daily needs of the teacher.

The Main Characteristics of Ukraine's Initial Teacher Education System

Initial teacher education is the first step in ensuring that teachers obtain the skills needed to support student learning. A coherent and comprehensive initial teacher education curriculum covers both content and pedagogical knowledge which are most relevant to twenty-first-century classrooms, and develops practical skills linked to theoretical knowledge (OECD 2019). According to teachers' reports in TALIS 2018, across OECD countries, teachers' initial teacher education most commonly covers subject content, general, or subject pedagogy and classroom practice. Ukraine is not an exception to this (OECD 2019; Palaguta 2019).

As we have already seen, one of the important directions of TE development in recent time in Ukraine is the transition to a new education paradigm—competence-based education as an alternative to more traditional knowledge-based education. The concept of competency is a pillar of efficient teacher training. The approach implies the development of complex capacities that enable pre-service teachers to act effectively in various professional fields of activity and defines personal and professional qualities of a future teacher (Fedorchuk and Mykola 2016).

The pathways to teaching in Ukraine look very traditional and changed slowly. The first main requirement to become a teacher is a completed secondary education (Certificate of Complete General Secondary Education—*atestat*).

The next step is to enter the institute and successfully complete Initial Teacher Education (teacher training in specialized pedagogical institutions) that depends on the chosen pedagogical specialty (result-diploma).

The 'presteps' into the teacher profession in Ukraine are not currently well organized (Rolyak and Ohiyenko 2008). Students do not get any official preparation at public schools to enter teacher training in higher establishments. It is not represented on the governmental and state level, only in some private schools, gymnasiums, and lyceums (Khustochka 2009). Specialized education in the senior classes of upper secondary schools is developed poorly. Some public pedagogical institutes and universities in order to attract students organize entrance programmes and special events ('Day of open doors'). The big number of applicants for each year is explained not by the strong interest in the profession but by the fact that attending a teacher training institution is one way to get higher education free of charge. A lot of secondary school graduates enter the teaching profession when there is no any other opportunity to get higher education (Khobzey 2003) and this tendency is continuing till now.

Although teachers' salaries were recently increased in an effort to improve the social status of the profession, they are lower than the salaries of other tertiary-educated workers in Ukraine. Furthermore, the large share of top-ups reduces the transparency of the overall remuneration package for teachers. These conditions deter many bright students from considering teaching as a profession, unlike in top-performing education systems which consistently attract high-performing students into teacher preparation programmes and the teaching profession. Students entering teacher preparation programmes in Ukrainian pedagogical universities tend to have relatively lower scores on the

EIT than those entering many other fields including sciences, health and welfare, and social sciences, and evidence suggests only a share of those entering teacher preparation programmes will go on to become teachers (World Bank 2019).

The low popularity of the teaching profession has become more pronounced since 2016, when higher education institutions transitioned to their new list of fields and subject areas, distinguishing between classical and pedagogical fields. Since 2016, many universities introduced parallel programmes in which the profession of a subject teacher in general secondary school was defined as a separate subject area. This resulted in the establishment of classical and pedagogical options within a given field, such as 'chemistry' and 'secondary education in chemistry'. Data suggest that for a number of fields, such as chemistry, physics, geography and history, there are many more bachelor's degree students enrolled in the classical field compared to the pedagogical field (a four-fold difference for some fields). This demonstrates the relatively low attractiveness of the teacher profession (World Bank 2019).

Admission to non-university higher education studies is intended for graduates of general secondary schools holding the Matriculation School Certificate 'Atestat'. However, graduates with other secondary school certificates may be accepted. The minimum score/requirement for entry to all higher technical/vocational and professional non-university studies is 'satisfactory'.

For entry to all institutions of higher pedagogical education some form of entrance exam must be taken such as a formal entrance examination, a qualification test, or a qualifying interview for some university-level studies. The marks are determined by each institution or department. Specific ability requirements are set for artistic studies, physical education and architectural preservation studies. A certain age limit is also set. The physical and mental predisposition of candidates to work in a certain professional field must first be ascertained (Ministry of Education and Science 2019).

Selection to initial teacher training in universities is organized on a competitive basis. It is conducted by a special commission which is responsible for the criteria of students' admission for each academic year. The Rector of the educational institution is the head of this commission.

Admission to university teacher education programmes is offered on the basis of the student's average mark in the Certificate of Complete General Secondary Education or Sub-bachelor Diploma, plus the results of the external independent assessment (EIA). All school graduates who want to be admitted to university must undertake the EIA.

Structure and Curriculum Orientation

At present, in Ukraine, there are 40 colleges, 4 academies, 52 universities, 10 institutes which offer teacher education programmes (Teacher Training Higher Education Institutions: Education—Reference Book of Higher Education Institutions 2016). The majority of higher teacher training establishments are public (see www.mon.gov.ua). The first private institutions emerged in 1991–1992 (Holowinsky 1995). In teaching and its content, there is no difference between the private and public programmes of this type (Tomusk 2003).

The degree system was reformed: the old system had only one stage of undergraduate studies, i.e. the degree of 'Specialist', awarded after five years of study. The new system comprises two stages: undergraduate and graduate, with several degree levels. The Magister (Master's degree) is awarded on the basis of a Bachelor's degree or Specialist's qualification generally one to two years after the first degree. Students must pass final examinations and defend a thesis (WHED 2018).

The new Law on Higher Education (2014) changed the legal status of higher educational establishments. Universities got more power in teaching staff issues, finance, determining the minimal and maximal academic staff workload, and other matters. Management of teacher education in Ukraine is still centralized (mainly under the Ministry of Education and Science of Ukraine) but during recent decades, the tendency towards greater HEIs' autonomy can be observed.

In Ukraine initial teacher training is realized on two main levels: Bachelor's and Master's. Teacher education can result in obtaining sub-bachelor (90–120 credits ECTS), bachelor (180–240 credits ECTS), and master (90–120 credits ECTS) degrees.

Pre-primary and primary school teachers get initial training at TE institutions (colleges) and/or Higher educational institutions (HEIs) (institutes and universities). Practical training at kindergarten and primary schools are part of the teacher training programme.

Secondary school teachers are trained by HEIs (institutes and universities), in different faculties (Education, Mathematics and Natural Sciences, Physical Education, etc.). The programme for teachers includes general courses of education and psychology. Practical training at secondary schools is also the part of the teacher training programme.

Bachelor's education is professional training going on four years at the university level. To successfully finish a year a student must acquire 60 credits. During the whole bachelor training students have to complete 240 credits. Future teachers receive a professional bachelor's degree and are competent for teaching at primary school or one subject at secondary one. At the same time it gives the student a proper theoretical background to continue the training immediately or resume it later in a master's degree training.

After training at the Sub-bachelor level, a graduate is assigned the qualification of pre-school or primary school teacher. Bachelor and Master's degrees are obtained in the specialty 'Sciences on Education', 'Pre-school Education', 'Primary school Education', 'Secondary Education (with school subject signification)', 'Special Education', 'Physical Education and Training', indicating the type of professional activity to be undertaken (educator of pre-school children, primary school teacher, secondary school teacher, social pedagogue, and special education needs teacher).

That training at higher educational institutions can be carried out in a form of fulltime (students have regular classes every day, except weekends) and correspondence education (students have to fulfil some academic requirements by taking exams at an institution) or by blending of these two forms. It is possible to take an individual study plan, combining work and studying during the last semesters of training.

According to the Law of Ukraine on Higher Education (2014), universities are entitled to develop educational programmes based on the requirements set by the Law. The main structural elements of the education programme are an appropriate amount of ECTS credits, a list of graduate competences, content of education presented in the form of learning outcomes, forms of assessment (attestation), external quality assurance mechanism, and requirements for professional standards. Fedorchuk and Mykola (2016) noted that beginning from 2015, the standard sets the division on core disciplines (75%) and electives (25%). Not less than 10% of training time takes place in a practicum that is to develop practical skills in assessment, planning and organization of pupils' learning.

Educational practice is a very important part of any Bachelor's or Master's programme in Ukrainian teacher training institutions. Pedagogical activities are included in the curriculum and are meant to be an essential element of teacher education. Traditionally students must fulfil all the stages of pedagogical practice in order to receive a valid Diploma and be qualified to work as teachers. Teaching practice takes place in ordinary schools under usual everyday conditions without any break in the teaching-learning process. Appointed teachers both at schools and from teacher training institutions are responsible for the process of pedagogical practice, guiding students in their work (Khustochka 2009).

Traditionally teaching practice for Ukrainian student-teachers is organized in two forms: active and passive. It starts from the second year of studying as a passive observation of the teaching process. During the last years of studies students take part in the active phase of practice conducting their own lessons. School teachers and appointed university teachers visit lessons to evaluate and guide the students (Rolyak and Ohiyenko 2008).

Updated educational programmes presume gradual increase of individual work of pre-service teachers, research skills, and reflection development. Competence-based initial teacher education entails diverse learning forms and methods. Along with conventional lectures, seminars, and individual tasks, a team-based approach and project work are widely used.

Taking into account the character and peculiarities of pedagogical activities Ukrainian scientists have stressed that modern pedagogical education is only at the starting point in using the competence development concept in the sense that it is used by other European countries (Roliak and Semenyshyn 2018).

The Main Characteristics of Ukraine's Teacher Professional Development System

Modern European educational society shows a great interest in the policy of supporting future teachers' professional development. Consequently, the professional training of a modern teacher should not finish in a pedagogic educational institution. The initial period of teachers' professional socialization is recognized as the most stressful because it is associated with the transition to a new system of social relations (Palaguta 2019). All teachers both newly qualified and experienced face constant needs in continuous development of their competences throughout their teaching careers (Roliak and Semenyshyn 2018).

The issue of advanced teacher training is unpredictable as the teacher functions shift with constant changes in the educational environment. This fact makes researchers deal with the problem taking into consideration the pace of modern life, technological development, and the political and economic state (Folvarochnyi 2011; Gubash 2018).

The whole system of pedagogic education should be structured as continuous professional development (CPD) in such a way as to enable each teacher to regularly update knowledge throughout the period of professional activity (Roliak and Semenyshyn 2018). In Ukraine the creating and functioning of the systems of teacher professional development have a long history but the term 'teacher professional development' is a newly used in Ukrainian education (Pukhovska and Sacilotto-Vasylenko 2010). In particular, the system of in-service teacher training in Ukraine dates back to the 1930s, the time of implementation of a unified model of education, introduction of the unified curricula, programmes, and manuals. Which fully met the requirements for the formation of the administrative and command system totally controlled by the government. This can be effectively promoted by a specially organized in-service teacher training system: the network of *Institutes for Teachers' Improvement*. (Shyyan 1999).

The first wave of changes was observed in the system of public education in the early 1990s. The reforming education processes which were carried out within the framework of economic and political reforms in Ukraine as an independent state, were aimed at the transition to a market economy and an open civil society on the one hand, and were connected with initiatives that came from teachers and educational teams on the other. These processes contributed to the emergence of a variety of educational programmes and institutions, new models of educational content; new pedagogical systems and new cascade model for in-service training suitable for modern society (Shyyan and Shyyan 2003).

At that time, the Institutes for Teachers' Improvement were transformed into the In-service Teacher Training Institutes (ITTIs). Creating the network of ITTIs played and play till now an important role in the development of methodological tools for teaching basic school subjects and allowed for the elimination of gaps in methodological training of teachers.

Participation in advanced training programmes and refresher courses through the state system of advanced training was obligatory for all teachers and had to be taken in to account during the attestation process. Traditionally teachers have to go through the attestation process once every five years. The main state provider of advanced training services leading to the level of qualification (the so-called category) was the ITTI network (one in every region of Ukraine), as well as specialized departments of universities and other HEIs.

With the exception of pre-professional education, some institutions had the right to provide teacher training and further professional development. Teachers also participated in methodological seminars and conferences organized by local educational units, and attended demonstration classes of colleagues as part of their professional development (Slyvka and Shyyan 2010).

Specially organized commissions assign the teacher to one of the four categories based on the results of the attestation: specialist, specialist of the second category, specialist of the first category, or specialist of the highest category. The attained category acknowledges the teacher's qualification level and influences his/her salary (*Ukraine. Teaching Profession* n.d.).

The new challenges of modern society for national education are especially acute in the system of professional training, retraining, and advanced training of teachers for the New Ukrainian School, which acts as a provider of educational reforms at all levels, which is reflected in the key idea of the Concept of the New Ukrainian School: 'New School—a New Teacher'. In particular, changes in the methodology of educational activities, as stated in the Concept of Development of the New Ukrainian School, are a serious challenge for postgraduate pedagogical education (Hrynevych et al. 2016).

Thus, teachers' professional development continuum needs relevant institutional solutions responding on recent wave of change in educational system as a whole (NUS 2016). In 2019 the government approved the Procedure for Professional Development of Pedagogical and Scientific-Pedagogical Workers (Resolution of the Cabinet of Ministers of Ukraine 2019).

The resolution defines that teachers are obliged to constantly improve their skills. New broad opportunities for relevant employees have been identified. They can improve their skills in Ukraine and abroad. Teachers can independently choose specific forms, types, directions and topics of providing educational services for advanced training. Forms of professional development are institutional (full-time, part-time, networking), dual, in the workplace, at work, and so on. Forms of professional development can be combined:

* The number of main types of advanced training has been increased;
* Training in the in-service training programme, including participation in seminars, workshops, trainings, webinars, and master classes;
* Internship;
* Participation in programmes of academic mobility, scientific internship, self-education, obtaining a scientific degree, and higher education may be recognized as advanced training in accordance with this procedure.

It is important to note some peculiarities of advanced training of pedagogical employees. Teachers of preschool, out-of-school, vocational educational institutions improve their skills at least once every five years in accordance with special laws. And for every pedagogical and scientific-pedagogical employee of the institution of general secondary and professional higher education is obligatory to improve their qualification every year.

The main areas of professional development are:

* development of professional competences (knowledge of the subject, professional methods, technologies);
* formation of content common to key competences, defined by part one of Article 12 of the Law of Ukraine 'On Education';
* psychological and physiological features of students of a certain age, the basics of andragogy;
* creation of a safe and inclusive educational environment, features (specification) of inclusive education, providing additional support in the educational process of children with special educational needs;
* use of information and communication and digital technologies in the light process, including e-learning, information, and cyber security;
* language, digital, communication, inclusive, emotional, and ethical competence;
* formation of professional competences in the field; mastering the latest production technologies; acquaintance with modern equipment, equipment, machinery; state and trends in the economy, enterprise, organization, and institution; and requirements for the level of qualification of workers in relevant professions (for employees of professional (vocational) education); and
* development of managerial competence (for heads of educational institutions, scientific and methodological institutions and their deputies) and so on.

In the case of teaching several subjects (disciplines), teachers independently choose the sequence of professional development activities in certain areas within the total amount (duration) of professional development defined by law. The total amount of professional development of a pedagogical or scientific-pedagogical employee of an institution of general secondary, vocational (vocational and technical) education may not be less than 150 hours for five years.

The list of sources of financing has also increased, which includes funds from the state, local budgets, funds of individuals and/or legal entities, other own revenues of the educational institution and/or its founder, other sources not prohibited by law.

Independent financing of advanced training is provided by

* pedagogical and scientific-pedagogical employees of educational institutions who work in such institutions at the main place of work and undergo advanced training outside the plan of professional development of the educational institution; and

* other persons working in educational institutions as pedagogical or scientific-pedagogical workers full-time or part-time.

From January 1, 2020, the heads of educational institutions, after approving the budget of the institution, publish the total amount of funds provided for advanced training. During the next 15 calendar days, each pedagogical and scientific-pedagogical employee who has the right to advanced training submits a proposal to the in-service training plan. At the time of advanced training in accordance with the approved plan with separation from educational process for a pedagogical employee to retain the place of work (position) while maintaining the average salary.

It should be emphasized that a wider vision about who can be a provider of in-service teacher training can be documented. The providers of advanced training may be an educational institution (its structural unit), a scientific institution, another legal person, including several individuals—an entrepreneur who provides educational services for professional development to teachers and / or research and teaching staff. It is expected that this will help create a market for quality educational services.

To date, the NUS professional development (PD) programme has been delivered via blended learning, that is, a combination of face-to-face and online learning. The research evidence suggests that professional development held in specialized centres, like universities or teacher training colleges, leads to greater effectiveness. However, this point requires careful consideration. Very often, on its own, this kind of professional development is ineffective. When used carefully, it does offer some benefits: it allows teachers to get out of the confines of school and provides them some space to reflect on their practice without principals, other teachers, or the pressures of everyday obligations in school, having undue influence. It is in this way that it could be beneficial, especially when combined with on-site, in-school professional development (WB 2019).

Tensions and Challenges

Throughout the last thirty years, in many countries all over the world there have been numerous calls to reform teacher education but there appears to be little change (Polyzoi et al. 2003; Godoń et al. 2004; Aubusson and Schuck 2013). Transformations are always trapped by some challenges and in some cases very difficult to handle them, especially for some developing economies (Demboh and Susanti 2021). Ukraine has the similar examples and experiences in reforming teacher education during the last thirty years.

First two waves of change started in a similar way: from the creation of a strategic document as methodological grounds for further changes. But in both cases one could observe the contradiction between the declared openness to public discussion and the real tightness of the document preparation. Afterwards it turned out that the effect of the document on the real course of events is much less than expected. While efforts to modernize this system were undertaken many of them remained 'on paper'—unfulfilled (Shyyan 2012). Over the twenty-five years since independence, the Ministry of Education in Ukraine has repeatedly emphasized this need for change and has made efforts to modernize both the educational process and the education system as a whole. However, despite some successes and achievements, the quality of education still does not meet the required quality level.

Accordingly to the recent World Bank conclusion (World Bank 2019), there is no clear vision that links higher education to the positive developments for reform in secondary education or to the skills requirements of the labour market. This is a fundamental problem: higher education in Ukraine cannot serve the needs of the people and the economy without clear objectives and a strategy for how to achieve them.

Although the 2014 Law on Higher Education made a major step toward dismantling the centralized structures of the past, it provided more autonomy without the attendant accountability mechanisms or financial flows. Without a strategy for higher education development, individual HEIs use their autonomy to achieve individual goals rather than working to achieve a broader goal for the system and nation. Furthermore, many important decisions governing the sector need to be taken by the Council of Ministers, including any that would lead to changes in funding and because many government agencies oversee subordinate HEIs. This further complicates the lack of a strategic vision.

The vision for higher education in Ukraine needs to prioritize modern approaches to curricula, pedagogical teaching methods, and learning support systems in line with the NUS and labour market needs, while also transforming the system to promote diversity and sustainability.

A strategic vision for higher education should reflect modern approaches to curriculum and pedagogical teaching methods, stronger linkages with employers and the labour market, and greater institutional diversity with larger and more comprehensive HEIs.

Future Development of Teacher Education in Ukraine

Educational reform has been a key component in the national development strategies among most rapidly developing nations (Hallinger 2010; Duda and Clifford-Amos 2011; Zgaga 2013; Hálasz 2015; Darling-Hammond 2017). The many different trends are playing out in different ways in different countries. A report on the future of learning indicates that the drivers that will influence learning and education in the future will include globalization, internationalization, technology, new skills, new ways of teaching and learning, and the labour market (Redecker et al. 2011).

Most of these trends follow the process of education reform in Ukraine. Internationalization is having an important impact on teacher education in our country till now. The year 1997 is renowned for Ukraine making its choice about the foreign-policy vector in the area of education, having signed the *Convention on the Recognition of Qualifications concerning Higher Education in the European Region* (1997). Joining the Bologna Process in 2005 is among the main steps of the second period towards the integration within the European Higher Education Area. The need to ensure convergence with EU standards and implementation of the principles of the Bologna Process determines the direction of HE reform in Ukraine. Introduction of the Bologna Process Diploma Supplement, providing for greater transparency on higher education qualifications, establishment of a Higher Education Reforms Expert Group with EU support with involvement of Ministry of Education and Science of Ukraine and the National Tempus Office (European Commission 2010).

One of the first laws adopted when the third wave of change appeared. The Law of Ukraine on Higher Education (2014) affirmed Ukrainian higher education policy is based upon the principles of democratization, humanism, international integration within the European Higher Education Area (EHEA).

The New Ukrainian School (NUS) is a key ongoing reform of the Ministry of Education and Science. The purpose of the reform is to stop the negative tendencies in the system (outdated didactics, low social status of the teacher and the level of remuneration, lack of motivation for personal and professional growth, etc.) and turn the Ukrainian school on the lever of social equality and cohesion, economic development and competitiveness (NUS 2016).

Significant interest of the world pedagogical community is aroused by teacher training models, an important component of which is the reputation of a highly qualified and valued teaching profession (Sahlberg 2007).

A teacher is the pivotal figure in NUS reform. Therefore, our goal is to contribute to teachers' professional and personal growth and to increase their social status. A teacher who has been given freedom to teach needs to have freedom to learn as well. This kind of freedom is also envisaged by the reform and provided by the new Law 'On Education' (2017).

Ongoing NUS reform implementation, particularly its expanding on upper-secondary level of general education influencing the teacher professional development system and inspiring respective professional communities.

The most visible requirements for teachers' competences here, which could impact both pre-service and in-service curricula, are as follows:

1. A competence-based approach naturally requires particular attitudes from teacher/educators/faculties. In other words, teachers should be entrepreneurial to facilitate students' entrepreneurial skills development, and this is applicable to all key competences, crosscutting skills, and so on.
2. The manner of teachers' learning should be transformed in the direction, which is expected to be introduced into the classroom: a collaborative/ co-operative/ communicative approach focused on soft skills development.
3. New Standards' (National Core Curricula) Implementation requires curriculum development skills as well as the development of a relevant assessment culture.
4. Regarding academic freedom—which is one of the NUS values—a proactive, decisive and simultaneously collaborative teachers' posture will need to be cultivated.

The NUS reform is a matter of many years since it is impossible to quickly change the educational tradition that has been kept up in Ukraine for dozens of years. Teachers' professional development continuum needs relevant institutional solutions responding on a recent wave of change in the educational system as a whole. Yet, the changes are underway and the Ministry of Education and Science does everything to make them irreversible for surfing the third wave. Thus, the evolution of TE should develop in a harmonious interrelation with society as a whole, taking on the role of its guide. During the 1990s and twentieth to twenty-first centuries, in Ukraine, a series of significant state measures were taken. Educational reform in Ukraine was directed not only on a fundamental change in the tasks of TE, structural transformation of TE network, and its entry into the European educational space. These three vectors of educational change define the nature of Ukrainian TE transformation. Although still much has to be done to building the distinctive modern self-sufficient and holistic TE system.

We want to note that the NUS reform has been supported by EU partners, such as the European Training Foundation (ETF), the Finnish Ministry of Foreign Affairs and EU Joint 'Learning Together' Project, Polish Centre for Educational Development (ORE) and the Norwegian-based European Wergeland Centre. These four partners have been of key importance in supporting the implementation of the NUS—the integration of key competences into the new curriculum frameworks. We would like to express our gratitude to the international expert partners who have made a great contribution to making the New Ukrainian School a reality.

A report *The Key Competence Lighthouse. Key-competence-driven reforms in Ukraine and Georgia* by the European Training Foundation (2021, p. 24) highlights the key achievements of the extensive, far-reaching reforms currently taking place in Ukraine under the New Ukrainian School (NUS) initiative:

> It is undertaking the most wide-reaching education reforms of recent times, building on international experiences and innovation among Ukrainian teachers and teacher educators. The latter have been pioneering new approaches to shape an education system that is focused on the needs of the individual learner rather than on delivering uniform knowledge-based lessons.

These reforms should be continued and their positive results supported in order to build a modern system of teacher education, which will have a significant impact on the quality of education of pupils—future citizens of Ukraine.

References

Aubusson, P., and S. Schuck. (2013). Teacher education futures: today's trends, tomorrow's expectations. *Teacher Development*, 17(3), 322–333.

British Council. (2015). *Higher education in Ukraine: Briefing paper.* Retrieved from https://www.britishcouncil.org/sites/default/files/ukraine_he_briefing_paper.pdf.

Conception of the Development of Teacher Education. 2018. Retrieved from https://mon.gov.ua/ua/npa/pro-zatverdzhennya-koncepciyi-rozvitku-pedagogich-noyi-osviti.

Convention on the Recognition of Qualifications concerning Higher Education in the European Region. (1997).

Corner, T. (Ed.). (2017). *Education in the European Union: Post–2003 Member States.* London: Bloomsbury.

Darling-Hammond, L. (2017). Teacher education around the world: What can we learn from international practice? *European Journal of Teacher Education,* 40(3), 291–309.

Demboh, P., and D. Susanti. (2021). Global trends in educational policy implementation and the complexity of quality in education: A Cameroonian perspective. *Integrative Science Education and teaching Activity Journal,* 2(1), 31–43.

Duda, A., and T. Clifford-Amos. (2011). *Study on teacher education for primary and secondary education in six countries of the Eastern partnership: Armenia, Azerbaijan, Belarus, Georgia, Moldova and Ukraine. Final report.* Brussels: European Commission, Directorate-General for Education and Culture.

EEAS. (2020). *EU-Ukraine relations—factsheet Brussels,* 05/10/2020—13:19, UNIQUE ID: 160127_00. Retrieved from https://eeas.europa.eu/headquarters/headquarters-homepage/4081/eu-ukraine-relations-factsheet_en.

European Commission. (2010). *Taking stock of the European neighbourhood policy (ENP)—'Implementation of the European Neighbourhood Policy in 2009. Progress Report Ukraine'.* Brussels.

European Training Foundation (2021). *The Key Competence Lighthouse. Key-competence-driven reforms in Ukraine and Georgia.* Retrieved from https://www.etf.europa.eu/en/publications-and-resources/publications/key-competence-lighthouse-key-competence-driven-reforms.

Fedorchuk, I., and N. Mykola. (2016). Teacher education in Ukraine: Discourses and practice. *IRCEELT-2016,* 165–168.

Folvarochnyi, I. (2011). *Comparative perspective of professional teacher training in Ukraine.* Paper presented at the European Conference on Educational Research, Berlin.

Fimyar, O. (2008). Educational policy-making in post-communist Ukraine as an example of emerging governmentality: Discourse analysis of curriculum choice and assessment policy documents (1999–2003). *Journal of Education Policy,* 23(6), 571–594.

Getmanchuk, A. (2019). *European integration is taking root across Ukraine despite Russia's best efforts.* Retrieved from https://www.atlanticcouncil.org/blogs/ukrainealert/european-integration-is-taking-root-across-ukraine-despite-russias-best-efforts/.

Goodman, B. A. (2013). *Ukraine and the Bologna Process: convergence, pluralism, or both?.* Paper presented at the 12th Berlin Roundtables on Transnationality, Berlin.

Godoń R., P. Jucevičiene, and Z. Kodelja. (2004). Philosophy of education in post-Soviet societies of Eastern Europe: Poland, Lithuania and Slovenia. *Comparative Education,* 40(4), 559–569.

Gubash, O. (2018). The system of advanced training in Ukraine: Retrospective, structural and content analysis. *Народна освіта,* 3(36), 19–24.

Hálasz, G. (2015). Education and social transformation in Central and Eastern Europe. *European Journal of Education,* 50(3), 350–371.

Hallinger, P. (2010). Making education reform happen: Is there an "Asian" way? *Journal of School Leadership and Management,* 30(5), 401–418.

Holowinsky, I. Z. (1995). Ukraine's reconstructive process in education: school reform, teacher education, and school psychology. In: N. K. Shimahara and I. Z. Holowinsky (Eds.), *Teacher education in industrialized nations* (pp. 195–223). New York: Garland Publishing.

Hrynevych, L. et al. (2016). Nova ukrainska shkola. Kontseptualni zasady reformuvannia serednoi shkoly [New Ukrainian school. Conceptual bases for secondary school reforming]. *Kyiv, Ministerstvo osvity i nauky Ukrainy.* Retrieved from https://mon.gov.ua/storage/app/media/zagalna%20serednya/Book-ENG.pdf.

Khobzey, P. (2003). The problem of efficient teacher resource use. In: Ministry of Education and Science of Ukraine, *Reform strategy for education in Ukraine: Educational Policy Recommendations* (pp. 145–169). Kyiv: K. I. S. Retrieved from https://www.irf.ua/files/eng/programs_edu_ep_409_en_ref_strategy.pdf.

Khustochka, O. (2009). *Teacher training in Finland and Ukraine: Comparative analysis of teacher training systems.* Master's Thesis, University of Oslo. Retrieved from https://www.duo.uio.no/bitstream/handle/10852/31154/Master_Thesis.final.pdf?sequence=1&isAllowed=y.

Koshmanova, T. (2007). Teacher preparation in a post-totalitarian society: An interpretation of Ukrainian teacher educators' stereotypes. *International Journal of Qualitative Studies in Education,* 21(2), 137–158.

Koshmanova, T., and T. Ravchyna. (2008). Teacher preparation in a post-totalitarian society: An interpretation of Ukrainian teacher educators' stereotypes. *International Journal of Qualitative Studies in Education,* 21(2),137–158.

Kutsyuruba, B., and S. Kovalchuk. (2015). Stated or actual change in policy terrain? Review of the literature on the Bologna Process implementation within the context of teacher education in Ukraine. *Journal of Ukrainian Politics and Society #1,* 33–57.

Law of Ukraine 'On Higher Education'. (2014). Retrieved from http://erasmusplus.org.ua/vyshcha-osvita-v-ukraini.html.

Ministry of Education and Science (2019). *Admission 2020–2021.* Retrieved from https://studyinukraine.gov.ua/en/admission-2020-2021/.

Ministry of Education of Ukraine. (1992). *Ukraina XXI Stolittya: Derzhavna Nastional'na Prohrama 'OSVITA'* [Ukraine of 21 Century: The State National Program of Education]. Ministry of Education, Kyiv, Ukraine.

NAQA (2019). Retrieved from https://en.naqa.gov.ua.

National Doctrine for Education Development in Ukraine. (2002). Retrieved from http://zakon3.rada.gov.ua/laws/show/347/2002.

New Ukrainian School (NUS). (2016). *New Ukrainian School: foundations of the Standard.* Lviv. https://elibrary.kubg.edu.ua/id/eprint/41546/.

Organisation for Economic Co-operation and Development (OECD). (2019). *TALIS 2018 Results (Volume I): Teachers and School Leaders as Lifelong Learners*, TALIS. Paris: OECD Publishing.

Palaguta, I. (2019). Support to teachers' professional development in Ukraine and England: Evidence from TALIS survey, *Studies in Comparative Education*, 1.

Polyzoi, E., M. Fullan, and J. Anchan (Eds.). (2003). Change forces in post-communist Eastern Europe: Education in transition. London: Routledge.

Pukhovska, L., and M. Sacilotto-Vasylenko. (2010). Perspectives of teacher professional development in Ukraine: discourse and practice. *Порівняльно-Педагогічні Студії*, 3–4, 147–155.

Redecker, C., M. Leis, M. Leendertse, Y. Punie, G. Gijsbers, P. Kirshner, S. Stoyanov, and B. Hoogveld. (2011). *The future of learning: Preparing for change*. Luxembourg: Publications Office of the European Union.

Resolution of the Cabinet of Ministers of Ukraine, No 800 of August 21. (2019). *Some issues of professional development of pedagogical and scientific-pedagogical workers*.

Rolyak, A. A., and E. I. Ohiyenko. (2008). *Comparative analysis of teacher education systems in Ukraine and Scandinavian countries*. Paper presented at the European Conference on Educational Research, Göteborg, Sweden.

Roliak, A. O., and I. V. Semenyshyn. (2018). Continuous professional development of teachers: European context of Ukrainian transformations. *Молодий вчений*, 6(2), 338–341. Retrieved from http://nbuv.gov.ua/UJRN/molv_2018_6(2)__27.

Sacilotto-Vasylenko, M. (2008). *Lifelong learning strategies in teacher education and training: Examples from France and Ukraine*. Paper presented at the European Conference on Educational Research, Göteborg, Sweden.

Sahlberg, P. (2007). Education policies for raising student learning: The Finnish approach. *Journal of Education Policy*, 22(2), 147–171.

Sectorial Conception of Lifelong Teacher Education. (2013). Retrieved from https://zakon.rada.gov.ua/rada/show/v1176729-13#Text

Silova, I. (2010). Rediscovering post-socialism in comparative education. International Perspectives on Education and Society, 14, 1–24.

Shyyan, O. (2012). Educational policy of Ukraine for youth health promotion. Kyiv: National Academy of Public Administration.

Shyyan, O. (1999). *Development of post graduate education teachers of science in West Region of Ukraine (1944–1996)*. PhD Thesis. Kyiv: Academy of Educational Managers.

Shyyan, R., and O. Shyyan. (2003). To create learning community of teachers: Ukrainian edition of cascade model for in-service training. In: *Proceedings of the 28th ATEE Annual Conference (publicação em CD-Rom)*. Malta: Malta University.

Slyvka, Y., and O. Shyyan. (2010). Professional development of teachers of physical education as health educators in Ukraine. In: G. Mészáros, I. Falus, and M. Kimmel (Eds.), *Responsibility, challenge and support in teachers' lifelong professional development: proceedings of the 35th Annual conference of the Association for Teacher Education in Europe*, Budapest.

State National Program "Education" ('Ukraine of the XXI century'). (1993). Retrieved from http://zakon2.rada.gov.ua/laws/show/896-93-п (Pro Derzhavnu natsionalnu prohramu "Osvita" ('Ukraina XXI stolittia').

State Program "Teacher". (2002). Zakon5.rada.gov.ua. Retrieved from http://zakon5. rada.gov.ua/laws/show/379-2002-п (Derzhavna prohrama "Vchytel").

State Standard of Basic secondary education. (2020). Resolution of the Cabinet of Ministers of Ukraine of September 30, 2020 No 898.

Stepko, M. (2004). *Reports from new members of the Bologna Process: Ukraine.* Paper presented at the Conference of European Ministers Responsible for Higher Education, Bergen, Norway.

Swennen A., and M. Klink (Eds.). (2009). Becoming a teacher educator: Theory and practice for teacher educators. Dordrecht: Springer.

Teacher Training Higher Education Institutions: Education—Reference Book of Higher Education Institutions. (2016). Освіта. UA. Retrieved from http://osvita. ua/vnz/guide/search-17-0-0-60-0.html.

Tomusk, V. (2003). The War of institutions, Episode 1: The rise of the private higher education in Eastern Europe. *Higher Education Policy,* 16(2), 213–238.

Tsvetkova, H. (2019). *Professional development of the teacher in the light of European integration processes: collective monograph.* Hameln: InterGING.

The Law of Ukraine on Higher Education. (2014). Retrieved from https://zakon. rada.gov.ua/laws/show/1556-18#Text.

Ukraine State Standard for Primary Education, 27 Feb 2018. Retrieved from https://www.kmu.gov.ua/npas/pro-zatverdzhennya-derzhavnogo-standartu-pochatkovoyi-osviti

Ukraine Law on Education (2017). Retrieved from https://zakon.rada.gov.ua/laws/ show/2145-19/paran186#n186.

Ukraine. Teaching Profession. (n.d.) Retrieved from https://education.stateuniversity.com/pages/1602/Ukraine-TEACHING-PROFESSION.html.

UNICEF. (2019). *Education programme. Challenge.* Retrieved from https://www.unicef.org/ukraine/en/education-programme.

Webster, C., I. Silova, A. Moyer, and S. Mcallister. (2011). Leading in the age of post-socialist education transformations: Examining sustainability of teacher education reform in Latvia. *Journal of Educational Change*, 12(3), 347–370.

World Higher Education Database (WHED). (2018). World Higher Education Database, IAU.

World Bank. (2019). *Review of the education sector in Ukraine: Moving toward effectiveness, equity and efficiency.* Washington, DC: World Bank. Retrieved from http://documents.worldbank.org/curated/en/884261568662566134/ Review-of-the-Education-Sector-in-Ukraine-Moving-toward-Effectiveness-Equity-and-Efficiency-RESUME3.

Zgaga, P. (2013). The future of European teacher education in the heavy seas of higher education. *Teacher Development,* 17(3), 347–361.

Part VI

Conclusion

23

Teacher Education in Central and Eastern Europe: Emerging Themes and Potential Future Trajectories

Ian Menter, Marta Kowalczuk-Walędziak, Roza A. Valeeva, and Marija Sablić

Introduction

In this concluding chapter we are drawing on the accounts of developments in teacher education from 21 countries of Central and Eastern Europe (CEE). We seek to identify both common patterns and differences that emerge. In doing this we, of course, have to give serious consideration to the history, not only of the individual countries but also of the region as a whole. This makes the whole undertaking very complex indeed but also, we believe, deeply fascinating.

In carrying out this analysis we are also influenced by previous comparative work that we have been involved in, for example, the interesting comparison

I. Menter (✉)
University of Oxford, Oxford, UK
e-mail: ian.menter@education.ox.ac.uk

M. Kowalczuk-Walędziak
University of Białystok, Białystok, Poland

R. A. Valeeva
Kazan Federal University, Kazan, Russia

M. Sablić
Josip Juraj Strossmayer University of Osijek, Osijek, Croatia

© The Author(s), under exclusive license to Springer Nature Switzerland AG 2023   **555**
M. Kowalczuk-Walędziak et al. (eds.), *The Palgrave Handbook of Teacher Education in Central and Eastern Europe*, https://doi.org/10.1007/978-3-031-09515-3_23

to be made between teacher education in the Russian Federation and in England (Menter et al. 2017). But we are also building partly on earlier work carried out in the UK, as well as work carried out under the auspices of the World Educational Research Association International Research Network that Teresa Tatto and Ian Menter have led over recent years (Tatto and Menter 2019). In the latter work, via analysis of the approaches and structures to initial teacher learning in 12 countries (i.e. Australia, the Czech Republic, England, Finland, Hong Kong, Israel, Italy, Japan, South Korea, Mexico, Russia, and the USA), we identified a number of themes that reveal a great deal about the nature of approaches to teacher education not only in these countries, but also beyond. At the time this work was carried out, these themes were listed as:

* 'professionalisation and universitisation';
* the relations between research, policy and practice;
* partnership between schools and higher education;
* power and control;
* the rise of 'standards';
* the impact of performativity and accountability; and
* the impact of digitisation (see Menter 2019).

These themes can also be used as a framework via which to describe and potentially to evaluate national teacher education systems around the world. Subsequently, one further theme was added, in order to allow for a focus on the continuum of professional learning for teachers and the links between initial teacher education and continuing professional development. Those eight themes certainly also appear to be important in the 21 settings covered by this handbook, some more so than others, but the analysis has led to the identification of new insights, which will be offered as a summary towards the end of this chapter.

However, this previous project included just 2 of the 21 countries the current text is concerned with—namely, Russia and the Czech Republic. Bearing in mind the complexity and great diversity of teacher education trajectories in CEE countries, as mentioned in the introductory chapter, we apply this framework of eight key themes to this wider range of countries in order to see clearly how issues that manifest in many places around the world are also very present in CEE countries. This framework is also a useful tool in illuminating the mechanisms of the problems in West–East geo-cultural relationships. Indeed, much of the research literature on teacher education reform that has been published in the west partially or completely ignores developments in these countries and is consequently somewhat myopic.

We start by briefly reminding readers of the geographical organisation of CEE. Then, looking across all 21 countries, we offer a summary of how their teacher education systems have changed over the past 30 years. Subsequently, we focus on current developments before looking at the future. So after describing the context, the structure of this chapter is chronological, discussing, in turn, the past, the present, and the future. These sections are followed by some conclusions where we spell out what seem to be the major insights gained from this review.

The Context of Central and Eastern Europe

Our introductory chapter explained how the geography of CEE has long been complex. As a region, CEE can be understood as an ethnically, religiously, linguistically, culturally, and ideologically diverse set of nations and communities—far more than the monolithic, ex-communist block it is all too often reduced to from the outside. With a view to utilising an inherently contemporary lens and creating a text that will be of use for years to come, we have been pragmatic and identified 21 countries that exist independently in 2020 as our focus. We organised these 21 nations into four geo-political groups— the Visegrad Group, the Balkans, the Baltic states, and Eastern European countries—however, even this apparently simple outline of these groups hints at the rich and mixed trajectories towards independence and modernity taken by these nations.

As we noted in Chap. 1, in inviting scholars in each country to prepare a chapter for our book we gave them a list of themes which we hoped would draw out key characteristics in their policies and practices in teacher education, including recent changes, tensions, and influences in policy development, as well as some indications of future lines of development. So in trying to demonstrate what is emerging from this writing we are ordering our analysis into past, present, and future. Once we have summarised each of these, our reasons for identifying the eight emerging themes that seem important, will— we hope—have become apparent.

Histories of Teacher Education in CEE

The political processes that have been underway across these 21 countries for approximately thirty years now are sometimes described under the umbrella term of 'democratisation'. This is an apparently simple term to cover processes of political change in all of these contexts, but even the most cursory review of the particularities of the settings show that there are as many differences as there are similarities. But nevertheless, under this umbrella term, some of the common processes that have brought about changes in education policy are: decentralisation, privatisation, marketisation, pluralisation of approaches, humanisation of teaching and learning processes, and engagement with international assessment programmes such as Programme for International Student Assessment (PISA) and the Bologna reforms of higher education in Europe. However, we cannot assume that the starting point for any of these processes was the same in all 21 countries. Our contributions have demonstrated enormous variation in educational structures and processes, even before the 1990s. Perhaps one of the strongest common features though was the tendency for educational provision to be centrally managed and controlled. Education across the region had always been seen as a key plank of social provision, having had a very important role in creating a national identity and a strong sense of citizenship. Even if this was largely some form of socialist or communist identity, that did not mean that it did not include distinctive cultural and linguistic elements.

In most of the countries concerned, we have seen a sequence of phases in the reform of education and teacher education. The Czech Republic is a good exemplar of this. Following the 'Velvet Revolution' in 1989 and the split from Slovakia, progress in teacher education proceeded in phases. In the first, and relatively short, phase, the emphases were on democratic citizenship, the opening up of private and alternative schools, and the replacement of Russian with English as the compulsory foreign language. In the second phase attention was given to introducing an international and global dimension into the educational environment. The third phase emphasised the management and leadership of schools, with headteachers assuming full responsibility for the quality of their institution's educational processes, as well as much more responsibility for teacher development and training.

In many of the 21 accounts, there was seen to be an issue about the quality of teaching as it was during the 1990s. Because of this, teacher education was very often—but not always—at the forefront of education reform. This was the case a few years later in Kosovo for example, as reform was introduced in an attempt to address what was perceived as the poor quality of teaching and weak professionalism in the teaching workforce. These reforms included efforts to raise the qualification requirements for teachers, thus leading to the enhancement of their professionalism. Here, as in many other countries, policies were commonly based on adopting approaches which were seen as recognised good models elsewhere, often in western countries. Policy borrowing and policy transfer has been recognised as one feature of globalisation in education in many countries (Rizvi and Lingard 2010; Spring 2015) and has certainly been a feature in many CEE countries.

The early stages of reform in education and teacher education were often very turbulent. For example in Ukraine, after independence in 1991, the development of the country's own education policy and higher education system began under an inherited 'Soviet' system that was felt could not respond adequately to rapid global changes and emerging national policy. In attempts to address these shortcomings, the education system went through turbulent and chaotic times: ministers changed, some initiatives were adopted, others were rolled back. Such patterns were not uncommon across the 21 countries.

The earlier conflicts in the Former Yugoslavian Republic (FYR) have led to great complexity in geography, politics, and education in parts of the Balkans. In Bosnia and Herzegovina (BiH), for example, there are 3 constituent nations and 13 ministries of education (each with multiple jurisdiction levels). As such, the development of teacher education in line with the Bologna Process has not been harmonious—rather, there are numerous inconsistencies in legislative, policy, and institutional developments across the country. In fact, the somewhat chaotic expansion of education reforms has led to a more diversified teacher education system, primarily due to the growing role of private and municipal institutions. This is particularly evident in terms of teacher education certification and curricula (especially the number and scope of general and professional subjects available), as well as the providers of teacher development programmes.

In some countries however, it is suggested that the primary attention of policymakers has been towards schools rather than teacher education. In North Macedonia, for example, the first wave of reform post-conflict was the implementation of the Bologna agreement (from 2003 onwards), which aimed at increasing the transparency and quality of the higher education system, as well as international academic mobility. The second wave, however, was the introduction of a nine-year primary education programme with the goal of improving students' educational outcomes. It seems that these reforms may well have improved the social status of teachers and the teaching profession, but they have apparently not had an equivalent positive impact on the quality of initial teacher education and professional development.

Lithuania, after it had won its independence in 1990, drew upon four core principles in reforming education: humanism, democracy, commitment to Lithuanian culture and plurality, and renewal. All of these are interesting terms and equivalent commitments are evident in many countries, including a commitment to supporting a national culture at the same time as plurality (see Saivetz and Jones 1994/2018). Trying to combine both of these can of course be quite challenging. Some forms of nationalism are quite averse to pluralism, after all. The word 'renewal' frequently symbolises a wish to create a sense of reshaping the relationship between education and society, again a common desire in many of these countries.

Nevertheless, in spite of these 'democratising' efforts, several contributors note the continuing influence of communism, most notably in the centralisation of control of education, including teacher education. In practice, regardless of the political leanings of current governments, the teacher education reforms in many of the CEE countries included in this text demonstrate the phenomenon referred to as 'centralised decentralisation' (Chua et al. 2019). This means that although governments may have officially 'decentralised' control over the introduction of changes in the field of education, in truth they retain a tight grip over dominant aspects of such reform and corresponding policy. For example in Hungary, the analysis here of two waves of teacher education reforms, the 2005 Bologna reform followed by the 2013 restoration of the previously undivided ITE programme for subject teachers, led to the conclusion that the reform processes are built on structural and content-focused changes, and, to a lesser extent, are related to changes in learning processes and student-centred approaches. These apparent tensions or contradictions between structure and process are not at all uncommon among our countries. Our Hungarian colleagues also refer to an experience of policy turbulence in the reform of initial teacher education, which has not been offset by attempts to put in place long-lasting and strategic approaches to implementation and evaluation.

Our colleagues from Serbia also confirm that much of the concern in their country in education reform has been directed at trying to adapt the previous Soviet teacher education models to the contemporary political, economic, and social realities of the new Serbia, as well as attempting to address European and international standards. In Croatia it is suggested that educational modernisation processes have been guided by three, sometimes contradictory, rationales, all of which we have encountered elsewhere above. These are cultural and historical values, national identity, and 'European standards' (Fimyar 2010).

So to summarise the ambitions that have guided teacher education reform across our nations since the early 1990s, we can see that there has been a common concern to reshape and modernise structures, systems, and approaches. There was a common desire to learn from good practice elsewhere but also to ensure distinctiveness within each nation in defining national identity and culture and often in ensuring the centrality of the nation's first language as well as recognising diversity. But rarely have the processes of reform run smoothly. Political, historical, and cultural factors have all played a part in providing challenges and sometimes creating barriers, and have also ensured that we cannot look across all 21 countries and make many generalisations about what had been changing, nor about how those changes have happened.

Current Developments

Turning now to the current situation in our 21 countries—how are the processes of reform, modernisation, and democratisation progressing? Our Russian colleagues suggest that teacher education there is in what they describe as a transitional state as the shift is being made from the traditional Soviet model which relied largely on pedagogical institutes towards training teachers in non-pedagogical universities (this is similar to what is happening in many of the countries). Many policy initiatives have already been implemented which aim to bring teacher education in line with the latest pedagogical research in Russia. The reforms have had three elements: (1) improving the structure and organisation of vocational teacher training; (2) improving the content and form of teacher training; and (3) providing scientific and educational support for updating teacher education. By contrast with earlier approaches, these reforms have been characterised by openness, self-organisation, self-determination, and self-development. So although there has been encouragement in Russia from central and regional governments, there is a sense that the reforms are very much locally and professionally, rather than politically, driven (as noted also by Menter et al. 2017). All this said, Russia can be understood as something of an exception among CEE countries in terms of employing research as a key informer of education policy—the authors of the Poland and Croatia chapters, among others, expressed frustration towards political ignorance towards education research, best practice, and day-to-day realities.

Other transitions towards modernisation are underway in Belarus. After the collapse of the USSR and the formation of the independent Republic of Belarus, 1991 marked the beginning of a long period of political, economic, and social transformation, which had a critical impact on teacher education—both in terms of structure and curriculum. The government is paying particular attention to the modernisation of teacher training, viewing this as the key to increasing the quality of the education system, as well as building Belarus' human potential more broadly.

External influences continue to be very evident in most countries. In particular, we are seeing much 'Europeanisation', most notably through 'the Bologna process' of harmonisation of higher education—which has been adopted across 45 countries altogether including all 21 in CEE, and in these CEE countries the process appears frequently to have accelerated the pace of reform. In Moldova, for example, after the signing of the Bologna declaration in 2005, the modernisation of teacher education sped up significantly, specifically in terms of institutional structures, curricula, and assessment and examinations. Furthermore, there have been influential changes to continuing professional education, including the adoption of teacher certification regulations on the basis of professional credits, and also curriculum development for the continuing education of teachers, aimed at developing professional competences. So we can see the influence of the Bologna process is not only directly on higher education but on the teaching profession more widely.

Another external influence that has been significant in several of the countries has been the Programme for International Student Assessment (PISA), carried out by the transnational Organisation for Economic Cooperation and Development. All 21 of our countries are participants in PISA and it has undoubtedly been one of the shaping factors in reform. Estonia, for example, has been very successful in terms of the results that have been achieved. However, even where schools have been successful in international terms there can still be issues of teacher supply. Our Estonian contributors argue that even though the country can be proud of its PISA results, there is still a need to look critically at the future of the education system. For instance, the fact that the average age of a teacher is 49 is particularly worrying, making this one of the oldest teaching workforces in the OECD countries. It indicates an imminent need for an influx of new teaching staff, otherwise, they imply, the next round of results in PISA may be far less pleasing. The supply of teachers is mentioned as a serious concern in several of our countries.

In many countries a distinction had existed between preparation for kindergarten and primary school teaching on the one hand and subject-based teaching in secondary schools on the other. Another effect of the Bologna process has been to bring greater commonality to these programmes, with many countries introducing two cycle programmes, leading to a Master's level award. In Romania there was a similar but different problem. Our colleagues report that in recent years, one of the main problems regarding the training of both higher education teaching staff and school teachers has been the separation of the two systems, severing the connections and exchanges in their mutual training and professionalisation.

The move towards greater participation in mainstream higher education has also had an impact on the research culture of teaching and led to a general upgrading of the profession in many countries. In Slovenia this entailed creating the conditions required to improve the quality of research and teacher education programmes. So, as early as 1991, academies of education became faculties of education within universities. And in 2009, the implementation of new Bologna study programmes began meaning that from that point onwards, all teachers were required to attain a second-cycle degree at master's level. This also occurred in Poland. When Poland joined the European Union in 2004, it began the process of implementing the primary principles of European education. From this point onwards, the previous long-cycle studies for prospective teachers were divided into two basic cycles (3 (BA) +2 (MA)) and teacher education programmes were delivered exclusively via higher education institutions. In most cases these extended programmes are still in the process of implementation.

It is perhaps not surprising that inertia has impeded change in several countries. In Serbia, the majority of the reforms were introduced in a top-down manner, without consultation with teachers or teacher educators. These professionals, therefore, identify themselves more as the executors of reforms rather than their co-creators. In Slovakia it is suggested that the historic reliance on central control has led to a continuation of a commitment to a centralised 'transmission model' in policy processes. This has led to two contrasting phenomena: first, to a diminution of the value and status of education in society. But secondly, it has also created spaces for the development of a significant development of involvement of a range of voluntary networks, and NGOs, which could be described as a kind of 'quasi-privatisation'. This is not dissimilar to what we heard about earlier in Bosnia-Herzegovina.

Language issues continue to be a concern in several countries. Kosovo emerged from an open war in 1999, which besides human casualties had also taken a toll on education. The majority of Kosovo Albanian students at all levels of education had been banned for a decade from the right to an education in their mother tongue and were thereby forced to study in improvised home schools. Language issues continue to create some tensions in many other countries, including the Baltic states, where Russian had been the language of instruction for the whole period of Soviet rule. Now since national languages became the first language of each nation, that has changed, but there are still debates about which other languages should be learned by school students and many families of Russian origin still use the Russian tongue at home (Lieven 1999).

So, to summarise some of the features of current develoments, we see continuing determination to 'shake off the legacy of communism', both in terms of how policy is made and in terms of how education is organised and provided. There are varying degrees of success in relation to this aspiration. In many countries there is an additional concern or tension about the co-existence of populations with varied ethnic and linguistic backgrounds—and, of course, there are continuing movements of populations going on in many of our countries.

Underlying these two overriding concerns in many situations—democratisation and diversity—there is a real struggle for professional autonomy being undertaken as politicians and policymakers continue to feel the pressures of international comparisons. This too connects with the crucial matter of the status of teachers and teaching as a profession within the respective nations and their cultures.

The Future

Finally, what do we learn from our contributors about how the future looks for teacher education in their countries? What are their concerns, hopes, and fears as they look forward?

Undoubtedly the continuing reform of the work of teaching itself is a widespread hope. In both Croatia and Bosnia-Herzegovina (BiH), for example, we hear of continuing desires to move teaching away from a transmission model, based on rote learning and facts towards more creative, enquiring, and participatory approaches. Political challenges arising from the country's history can make this difficult. We have already heard about the complexity of BiH where our contributors recognise the urgent need to rethink current policies in order to unify legislation, as well as to develop teacher competency standards and enhance the quality of teaching in the future. However, they also warn policymakers against a uniform transfer of Western solutions, as they may not necessarily fit well into such a culturally and politically diverse context.

At the same time, we also see hopes for further internationalisation, for the development of sustainability through and within education, as well as for global citizenship. Our Latvian colleagues highlight these priorities and they want to offer a contextual reflection about the process and experience of moving from an emphasis on the national context, education content, values, and development towards the integration of global citizenship competences into the teacher education curriculum.

In Poland there is a desire—at least among teacher educators, teachers, and scholars—to break the tempestuous political character of educational reforms (i.e. fulfilling the manifesto promises of ruling parties) and, instead, to focus more on teachers' needs and expectations, as well as thinking long-term about modernising the education process as a whole.

In reading the accounts we have been given, there is often a balance between optimism and pessimism, as in Slovakia where researchers express a deep disappointment with the insufficient transformation of the education system, that is the lack of progress, but yet there is reason to be optimistic because of teachers' willingness to engage in meaningful, well formulated, and carefully planned education reforms. Indeed, cooperation between teachers, teacher educators, and researchers may be a key element of successful reform strategies. In Croatia it is suggested that the teacher education system can best be renewed by offering new forms of cooperation between schools, universities, authorities, and extracurricular agencies. Thus, our colleagues there argue, there is a need to build on a broad, scientific, empirically proven basis of learning, teaching, and research methodology, in order to foster more effective learning and teaching processes. This, they suggest, will enable teachers to act autonomously and competently as critically engaged intellectuals.

In Montenegro our contributors conclude that the education of future teachers faces many challenges and dilemmas. These include in particular: a lack of orientation towards teacher competences (in the education of subject teachers); discrepancies in teacher education programmes; a lack of transferable skills for the twenty-first century; and insufficient commitment to research. Bulgaria also faces many challenges in the field of teacher education. Examples include constant adjustments to legal acts (instability); low pay for teachers; teachers' feeling a lack of motivation around their own professional development; and delayed changes in both the school curricula and the teacher training programmes, thus failing to meet twenty-first-century needs.

In Lithuania, despite some successes in the reform processes, the country still faces challenges in teacher education, namely: the lack of highly qualified teachers in some regions; insufficiently child-centred practices (failing to accommodate different learning needs); the low social status of the profession; the dominance of 'frontal' teaching; and limited innovations in the field as a whole. Our colleagues there see the following as key to enhancing the teaching profession: the improvement of the social status of the profession; designing teacher education curricula according to the needs of the learners; increasing the use of digital technologies; and creating inclusive classrooms for the diverse learners of the twenty-first century.

In the Czech Republic the most recent trends focus on equality and inclusivity in education. Despite this, colleagues there also highlight a number of challenges that teaching professionals continue to face, including low prestige and salaries, low investment in education, lack of career prospects, and lack of professional support. In Albania, in spite of many positive changes, teacher education still faces many challenges, including: the absence of comprehensive policy to support the development of the teaching profession; excessive government involvement in the modernisation of teacher education; and an insufficient mentoring system for teachers and prospective teachers. Our Albanian colleagues conclude that any further modernisation of teacher education will require a more visionary approach to policy with clearly defined goals and objectives, encompassing all stages of a teacher's career.

Teacher supply issues have been mentioned already and must surely be seen as fundamental in all countries. In Moldova the discrepancy between the supply and demand of teachers in the labour market is causing great concern.

Importantly, in all the accounts the authors express, explicitly or implicitly, concerns regarding the status, roles, and competences of teacher educators—that is, those who support teachers in learning how to teach in complex and diverse twenty-first-century classroom settings. For example, echoing anxieties also impacting many of their neighbours, Polish contributors highlight that there is no national policy or research regarding the status and professional experiences of teacher educators.

As we look ahead therefore we can see that teacher education is likely to continue to be the subject of much attention by policymakers across the region. Three questions arise:

1. To what extent will teachers and teacher educators be able to exert some control over the processes of reform?
2. How can the status of teachers and teaching be raised?
3. To what extent will issues of teacher supply affect the future of the profession?

Each of these questions underlies or permeates the eight thematic conclusions that we present below. Furthermore, as the experience of the Covid-19 pandemic is analysed and reflected upon, we may well see that digital technologies take a new and central place in much education, including teacher education. We may also see significant changes in the ways in which face-to-face classes in both schools and universities are organised (Flores and Swennen 2020; O'Meara and Hordatt Gentles 2020). The extent to which these may be compatible with moves towards the 'humanisation' of pedagogy will be interesting to observe.

Finally, there is little doubt that accountability will continue to be a key theme in all education policy, including teacher education. Again, returning to our first question above, what will be the extent to which the profession can itself take responsibility for these processes rather than leaving them in the hands of external agencies (see Cochran-Smith et al. 2018).

Conclusion

Having offered this overview of developments and trends in teacher education in these 21 countries in Central and Eastern Europe, we hope you can see where the eight themes which follow come from. They are:

1. There is great richness and diversity in the 21 accounts. In particular, we identify a large number of common features, but also a range of fascinating differences.
2. The 21 cases offer a perspective on 'vernacular globalisation' (Rizvi and Lingard 2010). The effects of educational globalisation are clear but yet the individual histories of each nation have their effect, and the lingering influence of a socialist or communist 'legacy' is apparent to some degree in all of the nations. We have also noted that policy borrowing or transfer can create tensions with national cultural traditions.
3. There is sometimes a disjunction between reforms on school education, teacher education, and higher education more generally. Additionally, some reforms focus on structures and organisation, others on curricula and learning.
4. The influence of European integration processes is very apparent in a number of the cases considered. Teacher education across the region is moving towards Master's level programmes.
5. The impact of 'the communist legacy' and the struggle for independence (Chankseliani and Silova 2018) can create further challenges. The complex political geography of CEE, especially since 1989, has had an important influence on subsequent developments and often gives rise to a turbulent policy context. There can be continuing tensions and conflicts in societies going through rapid social transformations.

6. There are links between education development (especially teacher education), economic development, and cultural development (Hálasz 2015). Civic society is sometimes playing an increasing role in teacher education, through voluntary organisations. Education systems, including teacher education, play a crucial role in 'nation-building' and in supporting the development of a national identity (Isaacs and Polese 2016).
7. The importance of cultural and ethnic diversity within many of the countries is apparent and perhaps especially significant are questions around languages.
8. There is great significance in the standing and status of teachers and of teaching as a profession in these 21 settings and the relationship of these with the supply of teachers.

So those are eight insights gained from our synthesising review of the 21 accounts shared by our colleagues. We wish to offer two further points by way of conclusion. First, we want to emphasise the importance of continuing such cross-national and comparative study in teacher education. It really is an invaluable way of making sense of one's own context. Second, one of the most interesting questions to arise from such an ambitious review as we have started here is that key issue of whether policies and practices in teacher education are becoming more or less similar across nations. In other words is there greater evidence of convergence or divergence, or more precisely, what is the balance between convergent and divergent tendencies? In this chapter we have tended to identify aspects of convergence, not least because of the elements of shared history in these countries, but there is certainly also plenty of evidence of differences emerging, as the nation state itself remains—or perhaps in the case of CEE we should say re-emerges—as the key unit of organisation for teacher education across Central and Eastern Europe, as it is around the rest of the world.

References

Chankseliani, M., and I. Silova (Eds.). (2018). *Comparing post-socialist transformations: Purposes, policies and practices in education*. Didcot: Symposium.
Chua, P. M. H., Y. Toh, S. He, A. Jamaludin, and D. Hung. (2019). Centralised-decentralisation in Singapore education policymaking. In: D. Hung, S. S. Lee, Y. Toh, A. Jamaludin, and L. Wu (Eds.), *Innovations in educational change* (pp. 3–21). Singapore: Springer.

Cochran-Smith, M., M. Carney, E. Keefe, et al. (2018). *Reclaiming accountability in teacher education*. New York: Teachers' College.

Fimyar, O. (2010). Policy why(s): Policy rationalities and the changing logic of educational reforms in postcommunist Ukraine. In: I. Silova, *Post-socialism is not dead: Reading the global in comparative education* (pp. 61–92). Bingley, UK: Emerald Group Publishing Limited.

Flores, M. A., and A. Swennen (Eds.). (2020). *European Journal of Teacher Education*, 43, 4. (Special Issue: The COVID-19 pandemic and its effects on teacher education.)

Hálasz, G. (2015). Education and social transformation in Central and Eastern Europe. *European Journal of Education*, 50(3), 350–371.

Isaacs, R., and A. Polese (Eds.). (2016). *Nation-building and identity in the post-Soviet space*. London: Routledge.

Lieven, A. (1999). *The Baltic revolution*. Harvard: Yale University Press.

Menter, I. (2019). The interaction of global and national influences. In: M. T. Tatto and I. Menter (Eds.), *Knowledge, policy and practice in teacher education: A cross-national study*. London: Bloomsbury.

Menter, I., R. Valeeva, and A. Kalimullin. (2017). A tale of two countries—Forty years on: Politics and teacher education in Russia and England. *European Journal of Teacher Education*, 40(5), 616–629.

O'Meara, J., and C. Hordatt Gentles (Eds.). (2020). *Journal of Education for Teaching*, 46, 4. (Special Issue: Teacher education in the COVID-19 pandemic—A global snapshot.)

Rizvi, F., and B. Lingard. (2010). *Globalizing education policy*. London: Routledge.

Saivetz, C., and A. Jones (Eds.). (1994/2018). *In search of pluralism: Soviet and post-Soviet politics*. London: Routledge.

Spring, J. (2015). *Globalization of education*. New York: Routledge.

Tatto, M. T., and I. Menter (Eds.). (2019). *Knowledge, policy and practice in teacher education*. London: Bloomsbury.

Index[1]

A

Academia Română, 339, 345
Academic achievements, 69, 384, 532
Academic community, 174, 251
Academic cooperation, 333
Academic credits, 517, 518
Academic degrees, 33, 244
Academic departments, 160
Academic disciplines, 215, 496
Academic excellence, 333
Academic institutions, 333
Academicism, 435
Academic mobility, 16, 245, 400,
    541, 559
Academic skills, 302, 333
Academic staff, 16, 33, 43, 44, 47, 247,
    277, 278, 332, 360, 410, 537
Academic studies, 212, 286, 388
Academic teachers, 91, 101, 346
Academic traditions and norms, 285
Academic work, 44
Accountability, 13, 61, 63, 72, 88–93,
    125, 155, 333, 410, 544,
    556, 567

Accreditation, 16, 19, 34, 41, 42, 63,
    139, 141, 205, 206, 209, 215,
    234, 237, 246, 247, 277, 280,
    305, 325, 457, 465, 521, 533
Action-research, 42, 43, 145, 261, 302,
    391, 397, 398, 401
Activity-based approaches, 461, 464
Activity-based methodology, 463
Admiraal, W., 127
Albania, 7, 8, 14, 15, 137–156, 566
Amarandei, M., 17
Assessment
    systems, 8, 339
Association for Teacher Education in
    Europe (ATEE), vi, 6, 33, 35

B

Bachelor's programme, 33, 42, 65, 66,
    68, 122, 192, 231, 304, 320,
    321, 361, 404, 464, 469
Bačová, D., 14
Balkans, 4, 7, 8, 13–17, 225, 295,
    557, 559

---

[1] Note: Page numbers followed by 'n' refer to notes.

Baltics, 4, 8, 13, 17–18, 411, 413, 433, 505, 512, 557, 564
Bećirović-Karabegović, J., 15
Belarus, 8, 9, 18, 19, 481–501, 562
Belousa, I., 18, 396, 401, 414, 418, 422
Biesta, G., 61, 84, 97, 100, 234, 417
Bologna agreement, 287, 559
Bologna Declaration, 9, 15, 16, 19, 33, 102, 186, 205, 245, 304, 305, 312, 315, 332, 456, 512, 522, 562
Bologna principles and objectives, 332
Bologna Process, 9, 14, 15, 20, 33, 59, 61, 67, 112, 118, 120–123, 137, 139, 146, 152, 156, 182, 186, 192, 196, 245–247, 249, 263, 277, 278, 306, 332–334, 351, 358, 360, 400, 408, 439, 457, 482, 515, 516, 532, 545, 559, 562–563
Bologna reforms, 13, 65, 245, 269, 274, 278, 285–288, 558, 560
Borko, H., 387
Bosnia and Herzegovina, 7, 14, 15, 159–179, 295, 559

C

Capitalism, 4, 14, 211, 457
Career
    plan, 70
    prospects, 13, 45, 259
    in teaching, 60, 71, 98, 125, 149, 286, 290, 331–352, 382, 391, 405, 461, 539
Čehić, Irma, 15, 174
Central and Eastern Europe (CEE), v, vi, 3–21, 87, 102, 204, 555–568
Černochová, M., 13, 39, 40
Civil society, 204, 252, 253, 411–415, 418, 422, 423, 540
Clifford-Amos, T., 4, 523, 531, 545

Cochran-Smith, M., 54, 234, 567
Cognitive constructivism, 445
Communism, 12, 14, 28, 84, 88, 89, 109, 137, 560, 564
Communist era, 4, 10
Communist identity, 558
Communist ideologies, 19, 27, 29, 30, 114, 296
Communist party, 56, 83
Communist regime, 10, 30, 58, 88, 117, 126
Competence framework, 62, 63, 234, 401
Competence measurement system, 59
Complementary pedagogical study (CPS), 123–125
Continuous professional development (CPD), 45, 61–64, 71–73, 93, 120, 121, 124–125, 127, 146, 162, 181, 195, 203, 208, 213, 214, 251, 252, 257, 259, 260, 283, 284, 290, 291, 299, 321–322, 325, 335, 342, 350, 363, 365, 366, 370, 386, 388, 391, 437, 441–442, 448, 465–471, 518–521, 539
COVID-19, v, 359, 419, 420, 566
Croatia, 6, 7, 14, 15, 160, 181–197, 295, 325, 560, 561, 564, 565
Cross-cultural perspective, 144
Cultural activities, 388
Cultural awareness, 406
Cultural changes, 399, 440, 461
Cultural codes, 323
Cultural contexts, 4, 395
Cultural habits, 326
Cultural traditions, 85, 567
Curriculum
    school-based, 37
    subject-oriented, 148
Czech Republic, 7, 12, 13, 27–49, 112, 125, 204, 482, 556, 558, 566
Czerepaniak-Walczak, M., 96

D

Darling-Hammond, L., 3, 60, 61, 102, 181, 230, 234, 313–315, 323–325, 357, 387, 420, 545
Delibašić, R., 296, 306, 315, 325
Democracy, 4, 17, 28, 32, 58, 85, 110, 114, 137, 138, 191, 235, 237, 355, 380, 529, 560
Democratic administration, 13, 28
Democratic society, 96, 102, 140, 310, 380
Democratisation, 7, 8, 31, 59, 83, 114, 138, 201, 203, 205, 415, 545, 558, 561, 564
Desimone, M. L., 387
Dewey, J., 235
Didactics, 20, 29, 33, 35, 41–43, 46–48, 97, 101, 116, 122, 124, 167, 178, 192, 234, 280, 282, 286, 301, 312, 313, 335–342, 409, 421, 444, 448, 466, 481, 493, 495, 515, 517, 519, 545
Digital competence, 189, 370, 420, 437
Digital era, 352
Digitalisation, 204, 218, 351
Digital literacy, 40, 43, 400, 403, 420
Digital technology, 38–40, 359, 391, 513, 542, 566
Digital violence, 218
Discipline-focussed education, 67
Discourse
    educational, 112, 114
    ideological and philosophical, 114
District examination commissions, 86
District schools, 59
Doctoral degrees, 16, 171, 277, 305, 332
Duda, A., 4, 523, 531, 545
Duschinská, K., 13

E

Eastern European countries, 5, 18, 193, 202, 529, 557
Economic crisis, 84, 270, 346, 474, 512
Economic growth, 49, 60, 455
Economic independence, 60
Economic insecurity, 190
Economic reforms, 113
Economic status, 110, 111
Education
    activities, 290, 355, 416, 462
    competence-based, 68, 69, 403, 533, 535
    faculties, 16, 29, 31, 32, 34, 42, 43, 147, 148, 160, 165, 167, 177, 178, 191, 193, 196, 205, 210, 226, 231, 234, 236, 250, 277, 279, 282, 312, 324, 400
    infrastructure, 244
    institutions, 9, 27, 34, 35, 46, 48, 60, 65, 71, 84, 89, 90, 98, 101, 102, 112, 113, 115–118, 122, 138, 178, 183, 185, 186, 191–193, 205, 206, 209, 210, 212–214, 228, 229, 250, 251, 255, 264n3, 274, 275, 278–280, 282, 284, 332, 333, 336, 346, 347, 349, 357, 361, 366, 372, 380, 382, 383, 385, 386, 388, 391, 397, 403–405, 409, 410, 412, 415, 418, 420, 423, 440, 441, 455, 457–460, 462, 465, 467–471, 473, 474, 476, 485, 488, 489, 491, 499, 516–518, 520, 536, 563
    management, 34, 86, 382, 409, 410
    models, 117, 181, 184, 210, 297, 298, 439, 470, 560
    online, 212

Education (*cont.*)

pedagogical, 89, 279, 285, 405, 463, 474, 475, 489–491, 493, 495, 496, 498, 520, 521, 523, 536, 539, 541

policies, 3–5, 9, 11, 14, 16, 20, 27, 28, 30, 45, 49, 58, 60, 61, 69, 73, 74, 84, 85, 87, 88, 100, 102, 111, 126, 127, 151, 156, 162, 167, 177, 190, 197, 203, 204, 207, 213–215, 226, 231, 237, 244, 262, 287, 325, 390, 396, 410, 414, 456, 462, 505, 527, 529, 558, 559, 561, 567

policy-makers, 218, 419, 422

practices, 110, 263, 415

professional, 144, 173, 194–195, 204, 216, 251, 336, 337, 460, 467, 468, 470, 497, 519, 520, 562

reforms, 5, 8, 9, 13, 14, 16, 18, 19, 31–41, 58–64, 96, 110–125, 138, 144–146, 152–156, 162, 163, 187–191, 196, 203, 205, 206, 217, 226–229, 231, 234, 236–239, 261, 263, 264, 278, 285–288, 298, 358–359, 380, 406, 407, 410, 419, 435–437, 457, 460, 463, 521, 527, 531–534, 545, 547, 556, 558–560, 565

research, 17, 197, 336, 448, 513, 561

sector, 14, 28, 29, 31, 45, 60, 96, 116, 125, 137, 162, 175, 176, 181, 197, 203, 205, 208, 214, 219, 225–227, 238, 296, 298, 321, 324, 356, 357, 359, 380, 384, 397, 400, 410, 414, 419, 420, 422, 462, 474

system, vi, 3, 29, 53, 83, 113, 137, 160, 181, 201, 225, 244, 269, 297, 331, 355, 379, 396, 433, 455, 482, 505, 527, 556

Educational paradigm, 298, 400

Educational philosophy, 386

Educational process, 31, 94, 96, 166, 213, 254, 359, 362, 476, 486, 489, 492, 494, 495, 497–500, 506, 513, 514, 542, 543, 558

Educational tradition, 546

Educational transformations, 11, 495

Eisenschmidt, E., 18, 441, 447, 448

E-learning, 35, 210, 343, 359, 493, 542

ERASMUS mobility, 36

Estonia, v, 8, 12, 17, 18, 433–449, 562

European Commission, 54, 116, 120, 124, 126, 127, 144, 145, 153, 184, 234, 252, 332, 333, 363, 408, 532, 545

European Credit Transfer System (ECTS), 9, 33, 42, 68, 91, 146, 186, 192, 194, 205, 206, 210, 211, 226, 229–231, 245, 246, 274, 277, 279, 280, 282, 285, 288, 289, 305, 306, 311, 312, 358, 383, 384, 439–443, 467, 468, 513, 532, 537, 538

European educational space, 514, 527, 528, 532, 547

European education systems, 529

European Higher Education Area (EHEA), 9, 20, 137, 201, 400, 408, 482, 522, 530, 532, 545

European identity, 528

European integration, 238, 505, 530, 531, 567

European Parliament, 7, 116

European Qualification Framework, 68

European Teacher Education Area (ETEA), 334

European Training Foundation (ETF), 547

Evidence-based practices, 447

Evidence-based programmes, 446
Evidence-based school reform, 448
Evidence-informed policy, 63, 64
External independent assessment (EIA),
    532, 536

F

Federal state teacher education
    standards, 462
Female-led profession, 380
Female students, 321
Female teaching staff, 338
Financial resources, 397
Fjodorova, I., 18
Flores, M. A., 3, 229, 231, 325, 567
Foreign citizens, 270, 488, 489
Foreign language, 35, 36, 87, 89, 90,
    116, 118–120, 187, 189, 191,
    196, 207, 302, 489, 491, 558
Foreign language training, 71
Freedom, 8, 28, 29, 32, 33, 60, 83,
    114, 123, 139, 390, 407, 434,
    496, 507, 533, 546

G

Gadušová, Z., 14, 111, 117, 124,
    125, 127
Gafurov, I. R., 4, 456, 462, 464–466
Gajić, O., 15, 202–204
Gawlicz, K., 83, 87, 298, 323, 324
General education, 70, 90, 92, 187,
    193, 231, 239, 274, 380, 389,
    402, 403, 407, 434, 459, 463,
    473, 476, 485, 511, 517, 546
General education school, 390, 439,
    459, 465, 511
General secondary school, 87,
    276, 536
Global citizenship
    competences, 18, 398
    education, 398, 411–419, 421–423

Globalisation, 4, 5, 11, 146, 177, 201,
    263, 325, 333, 358, 399–401,
    455, 506, 545, 559, 567
Glocalisation, 413, 417
Godoń, R., 4, 310, 527, 543
Gospodinov, B., 363
Graduates, 4, 31, 33, 47, 48, 61, 65,
    67, 89, 91, 109, 115, 122–124,
    127, 149, 165, 190, 192–194,
    197, 253, 276, 277, 286, 288,
    289, 296, 324, 341, 346, 347,
    351, 385, 401, 404, 408, 440,
    441, 443, 448, 460, 461, 464,
    465, 467, 469, 471, 476, 481,
    484, 486, 490, 497, 498, 500,
    513–517, 521, 522,
    533, 535–538
Gyurova, V. T., 17, 357, 363

H

Habul-Šabanović, I., 15
Halász, G., 4, 58–61, 397, 545, 568
Hargreaves, A., 3, 72, 113, 191,
    212, 213, 230, 234, 235,
    256, 258
Higher education
    courses, 31, 245
    degree, 65, 71, 226, 279, 361,
        368, 467
    policy, 60, 333, 545
    reforms, 9, 16, 58, 139, 145, 205,
        245, 274, 332, 400, 439
    sector, 12, 20, 399, 419
    teaching staff, 346, 383
Higher pedagogical education, 475,
    490, 491, 536
Higher pedagogical schools, 89, 299
Hoyle, E., 254, 257, 258, 260
Humanism, 17, 380, 395, 545, 560
Human rights, 13, 28, 401, 414,
    421, 505
Hungary, 7, 13, 53–75, 125, 204, 560

Iliško, Dzintra, 18, 401, 402, 407

Inclusive approaches, 32, 197, 397

Inclusive education, vi, 41, 43, 47, 160, 298, 350, 362, 403, 409, 414, 420, 473, 542

Independence, 7, 8, 16, 17, 19, 84, 89, 109, 117, 182, 186, 191, 226, 252, 269–271, 278, 296, 298, 379, 384, 395, 396, 400, 434, 439, 445, 506, 507, 513, 527–529, 531, 544, 557, 559, 560, 567

Initial teacher education (ITE), 12, 27, 61, 88–93, 112, 138, 163, 181, 207–212, 231, 245–251, 270, 299–304, 334, 360–363, 382, 402–408, 435, 461, 514–518, 528, 556

Innovations in university teacher education, 42

Innovative activities, 492

Innovative approaches, 38, 43, 113, 119, 209, 331, 448

Innovative methods of teaching, 458

Innovative practices, 175, 365, 420, 448

In-service education, 138, 236, 254, 261, 442, 446, 518–521

In-service professional development, 235, 236, 238, 252, 534

In-service teacher education, 15, 28, 45, 71, 101, 155, 228, 235–237, 397, 402, 444, 515, 534

In-service teachers, 237, 401, 435

In-service training, 171, 172, 442, 448, 540

Institutional accreditation, 121

Institutional context, 349

Institutional development, 4, 15, 275, 559

Institutional diversity, 545

Institutional evaluation, 73

Institutional models, 475

Instructional planning, 302

Instructional practices, 444, 445

Integrated subjects, 494

Integrated teacher education programme, 61, 193

Intercultural education, 358, 397, 414

International assessment, 75, 236, 256, 558

International benchmarking processes, 236

International communities, 12, 36, 397, 523

International comparability, 274, 287

International cooperation, 34–36, 206, 277, 278, 380, 398, 488, 489

International Forum on Teacher Education (IFTE), 7

Internationalisation, 33–36, 116, 212, 333, 389, 399, 545, 564
  of teacher education, 17

International mobility, 287

International networks, 36, 116, 262, 398

International organisations, 116, 137, 144, 202, 252, 380, 532

International pedagogical trends, 209

International policy, 144, 146, 156, 231, 345

International research, 27, 340, 398, 444

International standards, 254, 481, 560

International strategic documents, 287

International test results, 258

Internships, 35, 48, 72, 89–91, 361, 362, 388, 461, 464, 492, 498, 541

Interviews, 37, 98, 155, 163–165, 169, 172, 206, 207, 257, 440, 442, 536

Iucu, R., 17, 100, 334, 335

J

Joshevska, M., 16, 256–259, 261

K

Kalimullin, A., 19, 456, 466, 471,
    506, 523
Kálmán, O., 71
Kaminskienė, L., 17
Kazan Federal University
    (KFU), 7, 466
Kędzierska, H., 14, 101
Kelchtermans, G., 230
Kennedy, A., 310, 512
Knowledge
    application, 122, 167, 187
    production, 61
Kobylyanskaya, L., 19, 522
Kopp, E., 61, 68–70
Korzeniecka-Bondar, A., 14, 101
Koshmanova, T., 529, 531
Kosová, B., 110–114, 117, 118,
    120–125, 127
Kosovo, 7, 14, 16, 225–239, 558, 563
Kotnik, R., 287, 288
Kováts, G., 59, 60
Kowalczuk-Walędziak, M., 7, 10, 14,
    20, 21, 86, 93, 95, 100, 257,
    262, 397, 401
Kravale-Pauliņa, M., 18, 401, 407

L

Labour
    contracts, 462
    expectations, 390
    market, 19, 71, 153, 182, 185–187,
        193, 194, 209, 251, 254, 351,
        396, 397, 402, 404, 405, 410,
        411, 420, 440, 444, 468, 497,
        506, 513, 516, 517, 521, 544,
        545, 566
Latvia, 6, 8, 12, 17, 18, 395–423

Leadership
    practices, 446, 448
    staff, 85, 519
Learning
    communities, 45, 48, 73, 127, 254,
        258–263, 446, 447
    conditions, 145
    content, 259, 299, 310, 313,
        409, 420
    cultures, 252, 255
    experiential learning, 210
    face-to-face, 420, 543
    online, 17, 420, 543
    outcomes, 9, 38, 60, 66, 68, 91, 92,
        96, 148, 162, 173, 174, 188,
        212, 234, 247, 255, 310, 311,
        314, 387, 403, 405, 423, 436,
        445, 512, 538
    process, 14, 54, 62, 65, 69–71, 91,
        94, 254, 350, 357, 380, 403,
        408–410, 419, 420, 435, 446,
        494, 538, 558, 560
Lecturer, 119, 148, 277, 301, 347,
    405, 443, 497
Lesandrić, M., 15
Life-long education, 211, 492
Life-long learning, vi, 54, 62, 71, 121,
    127, 150, 161, 166, 167, 182,
    187, 188, 193, 195, 197, 272,
    310, 322, 323, 351, 357, 399,
    400, 408, 410, 442, 460,
    514, 519
Lithuania, 6, 8, 17, 379–391, 560, 565
Local authorities, 85, 422, 423, 442
Local community, 102, 407, 411, 412,
    418, 420–423
Local governments, 58, 85, 86, 176,
    184, 214, 415, 417, 465,
    467, 524n3
Local identities, 418
Local-level problems, 458
Locally-based learning, 418
Lungulov, B., 15, 212

M

Massification of higher education, 332
Massive online open courses
    (MOOCs), 463
Master's degree programmes, 42, 274,
    304–306, 359, 464, 468
Menter, I., 4, 10–12, 20, 63, 100, 313,
    456, 462, 476, 556, 561
Mentoring system for teachers,
    15, 566
Mentors, 45, 125–127, 150, 195, 230,
    283, 314, 322, 345, 348, 362,
    369, 405, 408, 441, 443, 448,
    495, 534
Mićanović, V., 16
Millennium, 38, 58, 115, 118, 120,
    182, 529
Minorities, 173, 184, 185, 193, 338,
    380, 506
Mita, N., 14
Modernisation
    process, 15, 459, 474, 560
    strategies, 19
Moldova, 8, 9, 18, 19, 505–523,
    524n1, 562, 566
Montenegro, 8, 14, 16, 295–319, 565
Multiculturalism, 32, 399, 440
Multi-ethnic regions, 462
Multi-lingual environment, 44, 472

N

Nano, L., 147
National Qualification Framework
    (NQF), 297, 513
Nedelcu, A., 17
Németh, A., 55–57, 61
Neo-liberal agendas and practices, 410
Neo-liberal approaches, 455
Neo-liberal competitions, 11
Neoliberalism, 4, 14, 201, 410, 411
Neo-liberal trends, 415
Neo-liberal values, 396

Networking, 43, 118, 217, 398, 412,
    420, 541
Networks between practice schools and
    universities, 66
New educational practices, 446
New educational programmes, 464
New education law, 85
Non-degree programme, 384
Non-formal educational
    programmes, 400
Non-governmental organisations, 160,
    161, 171, 172, 411, 415, 417,
    518, 520
Non-political research, 100
Non-public institutions, 94
Non-qualified teachers, 344
Non-teaching fields, 123
Non-university institutions, 151
North Macedonia, v, 6–8, 12, 14, 16,
    243–264, 295, 559
Novović, T., 16, 298, 312, 313

O

Oļehnoviča, E., 18, 401, 402, 407
Online platforms, 463, 495
Online resources, 120
Online society, 175
Organisation for Economic
    Co-operation and Development
    (OECD), 28–30, 40, 41, 44, 45,
    47, 48, 54, 60, 61, 95, 100, 101,
    124, 146, 236, 250–252, 255,
    259, 263, 270, 298, 337, 338,
    344, 345, 380, 398, 400,
    443–446, 534, 535, 562

P

Paris Communique, 350
Parmigiani, D., 7, 21
Peček, M., 16, 274–278,
    281–283, 285–289

Pedagogical beliefs, 444, 445
Pedagogical competences, 43, 47, 210, 297, 361, 396, 444
Pedagogical content, 67, 69, 74
Pedagogical courses, 89, 282
Pedagogical educational institutions, 521
Pedagogical faculties, 27, 43, 46, 247, 363
Pedagogical institutes, 19, 71, 176, 177, 360, 457, 458, 476, 523, 535, 561
Pedagogical practice, 34, 42, 43, 90, 192, 193, 196, 201, 261, 362, 367, 369, 438, 476, 518, 522, 538, 539
Pedagogical programmes, 59, 391, 465, 466
Pedagogical research, 42, 48, 280, 365, 438, 561
Pedagogical schools, 89, 509
Pedagogical theory, 19, 112, 203, 456, 462
Pedagogical training, 92, 227, 350, 444, 456, 486, 493
Pedagogical universities, 345, 458, 461, 465, 466, 474, 475, 490, 491, 498, 523, 535
Peer learning, 49
Peer observations, 44
Peer support, 259
Performativity, 13, 556
Pešikan, A., 215, 216, 218, 310, 322
PhD programmes, 279
Poland, v, 6, 7, 12–14, 35, 83–102, 125, 204, 482, 561, 563, 565
Policy-makers, 21, 40, 63, 83, 126, 127, 154, 177, 203, 218, 228, 237, 257, 271, 343, 350, 383, 391, 407, 410, 419, 422, 559, 564, 566
Political changes, 28, 114, 361, 434, 439, 558

Political instability, 331, 460
Political literacy, 407
Political resources, 379
Political system, 10, 28, 58, 59, 112, 159, 278
Poom-Valickis, K., 18, 438, 444
Post-communism, 83
Post-communist legacies, 528
Post-communist transformation, 4
Post-graduate, 92, 194, 197, 359, 362, 458, 487, 488, 490, 498, 510, 541
Post-pandemic education sector, 419
Post-Soviet countries, 527
Post-Sovietisation, 422
Post-Soviet period, 458, 511
Post-Soviet Union transformation, 455
Practical training, 43, 161, 178, 229–231, 282, 285, 335, 344, 350, 362, 367, 368, 463, 464, 470, 518, 521, 522, 537
Practice-oriented process of training teachers, 491
Pre-school children, 384, 538
Preschool classrooms, 253
Preschool education, 138, 139, 142, 147, 168, 182–184, 191, 192, 245, 272, 299, 320, 321, 356, 487, 491, 538
Preschool institutions, 245, 253, 264n2, 272
Preschool teachers, 16, 17, 192, 203, 213, 278, 279, 285, 289, 297, 301–305, 311, 312, 314, 320, 439
Pre-service education, 230, 250–252, 439, 514–518, 520
Pre-service teachers, 10, 306, 534, 539
Pre-service training, 149, 229, 230, 236, 250, 257
Primary education, 16, 40, 56, 66, 160, 166, 182, 185, 187, 205, 244, 245, 249, 250, 253, 338, 339, 380–382, 385, 465, 488, 508, 509, 516, 559

Primary school, 29, 56, 59, 70, 86, 87, 89, 92, 164, 166, 168–170, 172–174, 184–185, 187, 191, 193, 202, 249, 254, 260, 298, 299, 314, 320, 321, 356, 360, 380, 435, 439, 460, 483, 537, 538, 562

Primary school teachers, 33, 41, 42, 56, 57, 66, 118, 122, 166, 169, 174, 194–195, 203, 208, 212, 244, 246, 384, 467, 516, 537, 538

Primary school teaching qualification, 385

Principals, 37, 38, 45, 46, 49, 139, 154, 173, 189, 207, 213, 340, 342, 356, 359, 364, 366, 369, 385, 436, 470, 471, 543

Private educational institutions, 520, 521

Professional development system, 44–45, 208, 212–215, 218, 235, 270, 284, 290, 322, 370, 470, 473

Professionalisation, 12, 17, 47, 60, 61, 74, 75, 196, 244, 254, 331–352, 556, 563

Professionalism, 16, 45, 67, 95, 101, 120–123, 126, 127, 139, 145, 219, 231, 234, 235, 252, 254, 256–260, 379–391, 483, 499, 501, 559

Professional learning communities, 45, 73, 258–263

Professional networks, 151

Professional training of teachers, 160, 256, 474

Programme for International Student Assessment (PISA), 18, 31, 33, 54, 87, 162, 227, 236, 250, 251, 287, 298, 311, 312, 332, 338, 339, 389, 398, 433–449, 558, 562

Prøitz, T. S., 61

Public education institutions, 27

Public education system, 53–55, 60

Public good, 4

Public universities, 28, 102, 167, 168, 226, 326

Q

Qualification programmes, 44, 151, 190

R

Radulović, B., 15, 204, 209

Rapos, N., 61, 64, 68–71

Reflective practitioners, 97, 112, 118, 149, 239, 313, 436

Refugees, 202, 460, 488

Regional authorities, 9

Regional inequalities, 54

Regional teacher education centres, 119

Religious communities, 184

Research
attainments, 98
career, 101
experience, 5, 91
knowledge, 87, 99
project, 42, 116, 120, 126, 149, 263, 399, 468
results, 100, 482

Research-based knowledge, 61, 101

Researchers, 5, 6, 20, 42, 48, 61–63, 65, 85, 100, 117, 127, 177, 287, 288, 302, 313, 322–324, 349, 389, 391, 397, 398, 447, 448, 468, 539, 565

Research-informed activities, 391

Romania, 6, 8, 12, 14, 17, 202, 331–352, 509, 563

Rustempašić, S. M., 15

Rutkienė, A., 17, 289

S
Sablić, M., 15, 20, 195
Sachs, J., 235
Sahlberg, P., 190, 546
Salīte, I., 398, 401
Saqipi, B., 16, 226, 227, 229, 234,
    235, 237, 238
School
    integration, 59
    teachers, 17, 175, 192, 269, 276,
        283, 342, 360, 361, 439, 440,
        465, 468, 498, 518, 539, 563
School-age children, 245, 508, 510
School-based assessment, 254
School-based practices, 464
School-based professional development,
    235, 254, 471, 472
School-university partnerships,
    463, 464
Scientific degree, 533, 541
Scientific institution, 543
Scientific internship, 541
Secondary education
    general, 145, 403, 404, 407, 460,
        484, 485, 487, 488, 490
    lower, 138, 343, 380, 381, 533
    upper, 138, 147, 271, 274, 275,
        290, 380, 381
Secondary school education, 164, 165,
    170, 185, 433
Secondary schools, 27, 39, 40, 56–58,
    67, 86, 87, 91, 98, 115, 118,
    119, 123, 124, 147, 160, 164,
    185, 187, 189, 191, 193, 204,
    228, 249, 274, 276–280, 296,
    349, 361, 380, 433–435, 437,
    459, 482, 485, 488, 491, 495,
    498, 510, 516, 529, 532,
    535–537, 562
Secondary school teachers, 27, 29, 39,
    42, 56, 62, 66, 67, 70, 160, 167,
    269, 279, 343, 462, 517,
    537, 538

Secondary vocational schools,
    29, 301
Serbia, 7, 14, 15, 160, 201–219,
    226, 250, 295, 297, 560, 563
Shyyan, O., 19, 540, 544
Shyyan, R., 19, 540
Silova, I., 4, 5, 9, 10, 395, 399,
    531, 567
Škugor, A., 15, 195
Śliwerski, B., 85, 88, 99
Slovakia, 6, 7, 12–14, 28, 109–127,
    558, 563, 565
Slovenia, 8, 14, 16, 269–291, 295,
    298, 563
Social capital, 113, 115
Social changes, 29, 110, 114,
    203, 395
Social classes, 57
Social cohesion, 162, 188
Social constructivism, 188,
    312, 445
Socialisation, 417, 500, 539
Socialist ideology, 182
Socio-economic development, 4,
    512, 514
Socio-economic trends, 46
Socio-political changes, 54
Soviet communist dictatorship, 56
Soviet government, 379
Soviet ideology, 396
Sovietisation, 56, 57
Soviet military forces, 395
Soviet occupation, 56, 433
Soviet regime, 57, 434, 435, 528
Soviet Russia, 379
Soviet school system, 433–449
Soviet Union, v, 7, 8, 99, 399,
    433, 434, 455, 457, 475,
    512, 528
Španović, Svetlana, 15, 217
Special education, 91, 279, 343, 403,
    435, 440, 482, 487, 491,
    516, 538

Standardisation, 11, 88–93, 99, 190, 243–264

Standards, 9, 34, 61, 83, 137, 162, 196, 203, 226, 245, 278, 297, 336, 356, 403, 436, 462, 506, 530, 556

State-funded education, 125

State-owned kindergartens, 183

State-run public education, 112

State-run universities, 210

State-sanctioned communist ideology, 296

Statistics, 338, 347, 370, 382, 509

Steiner-Khamsi, G., 9, 10, 237, 238

Student-centred approaches, 14, 229, 231, 400, 560

Subject-based teaching, 562

Subject didactics, 29, 42, 43, 46–48, 112, 117, 119, 122, 124, 231, 438

Subjectification, 417

Subject knowledge, 42, 67, 93, 117, 121, 124, 164, 216, 244, 311, 313, 385

Subject-oriented approach, 445

Subject-related pedagogies, 118

Subject-specialist mindsets, 434

Subject-specific disciplines, 470

Subject teachers, 14, 16, 17, 65–68, 70, 159, 170, 185, 192–194, 208, 210, 226, 231, 245, 246, 248, 249, 272, 276, 277, 279, 285, 296, 297, 299–302, 305–307, 311, 312, 321, 323, 326, 360, 382, 384, 388, 435, 439–441, 443, 444, 536, 560, 565

Sustainability
economic, 190
environmental, 190, 413

Swennen, A., 527, 567

Symeonidis, V., 9, 62, 64

Tatto, M. T., 60, 313, 556

Teacher competences, 15, 17, 34, 35, 61, 126, 163, 166, 206, 213, 234, 311, 440, 565

Teacher education
competence-based, 403
courses, 31, 98, 123, 217, 315, 324, 475
curriculum, 18, 117, 118, 147, 148, 232–234, 469, 534–539, 565
market, 127
pathway, 10, 123
policy discourse, 226
reform, 5, 8, 9, 13, 14, 16, 19, 31–41, 58, 60–64, 96, 110–125, 127, 144–146, 152, 154, 155, 226–229, 231, 234, 238, 239, 278, 285, 435–437, 460, 521, 527, 531–534, 556, 560, 561
study programmes, 123, 140, 147, 156, 190, 191, 280, 414, 455

Teacher educators, v, vi, 6, 34, 46–48, 62, 65, 70, 98, 101, 102, 114, 119, 122, 126, 127, 230, 278, 396, 402, 407, 418, 482, 546, 547, 563, 565, 566

Teacher professional development (TPD), 18, 28, 44–45, 47, 86, 87, 95, 101, 138, 150–152, 154, 156, 162, 163, 171–175, 177–179, 195, 201, 202, 205, 208, 212–216, 218, 235, 253, 270, 283–285, 290, 321, 363–371, 386–391, 402–408, 422, 446, 456, 470–474, 528, 531, 539–543, 546

Teacher professionalism, 45, 67, 120–123, 231, 234, 235, 260

Teacher promotion system, 291

Teachers, v, 3–21, 27–49, 53–75,
    83–102, 109–127, 137–156,
    159–179, 181–197, 201–219,
    225–239, 243–264, 269–291,
    295–319, 333, 355–373,
    379–391, 395–423, 433–449,
    455–476, 481–501, 505–523,
    527–547, 555–568
Teacher shortages, 60, 67, 70, 74, 89,
    155, 443, 457
Teachers' salaries, 30, 57, 59, 75, 87,
    100, 337, 340, 443, 535
Teacher training
    courses, 160
    faculties, 38, 160, 161, 164–166,
        168, 172
    system, 19, 333, 341, 345,
        434, 540
Teaching
    community, v, 75, 101, 120, 207,
        214, 262, 389, 493
    methods, 18, 35, 37, 40, 92, 116,
        118, 119, 208, 212, 213, 219,
        246, 249, 302, 306, 311, 362,
        384, 390, 448, 472, 473,
        517, 544
    practice, 42, 70, 98, 109, 114, 117,
        121, 122, 124, 127, 141, 145,
        148–150, 166, 167, 207, 215,
        218, 280, 285, 286, 312, 313,
        323, 325, 390, 435, 445, 446,
        458, 476, 482, 491, 493, 522,
        538, 539
    profession, 4, 14, 15, 18, 19, 34, 41,
        42, 45, 47, 54, 55, 57, 69, 70,
        74, 75, 90–92, 97, 98, 100, 127,
        140–142, 146, 147, 150, 152,
        154–156, 161–163, 165, 172,
        194, 197, 202, 203, 207, 209,
        211, 212, 216–218, 226–228,
        234, 239, 254, 258, 259, 261,
        296, 304, 315, 322–326, 340,
        351, 381, 391, 397, 404, 406,
    417, 436, 437, 441, 444, 447,
        456, 458, 460, 462, 463, 470,
        473, 489, 490, 493, 497, 515,
        535, 536, 546, 560, 562, 566
    qualification, 9, 18, 67, 89, 92, 121,
        123–125, 127, 236, 361, 364,
        382–385, 404, 469
    quality, 48, 255, 259, 299,
        338, 342
    skills, 47, 286
Teaching and Learning International
    Survey (TALIS), 31, 33, 44, 46,
        236, 259, 444, 445, 471,
        472, 534
Technical schools, 360, 465
Transversal skills, 311, 323, 338, 409

U

Ukraine, 8, 9, 12, 18–20,
    527–547, 559
Underwood, J. M., 16, 257, 261,
    262, 397
UNESCO, 19, 114, 144–146,
    153–155, 165, 380, 397, 398,
    400, 401, 413, 414, 423,
    488, 521
Universalisation, 259
Universal values, 85, 505
Universitisation, 9, 12, 556
Upper secondary education, 138,
    147, 271, 274, 275, 290,
    380, 381

V

Valeeva, R. A., 4, 19, 20, 456, 462,
    465, 466, 471, 523
Velvet Revolution, 13, 28–30, 558
Vernacular globalisation, 11, 567
Visegrad countries, 13–14
Vizek-Vidović, V., 181
Vocational higher education, 41

Vocational schools, 86, 87, 91, 92, 185,
187, 321, 371, 437, 439, 440,
468, 484
Vocational teacher training, 19, 561
Vučković, D., 16, 217, 296, 302, 304,
306, 311, 313–315, 320

W

Western European countries, 5, 237
Western European teacher education
systems, 5
Western theories, 5
Workload, 121, 126, 141, 186, 206,
207, 390, 447, 537
World Bank, 145, 225, 263, 341, 513,
528, 530, 531, 534, 536, 544

Y

Young people, 27, 36, 85, 127, 153,
165, 189, 190, 202, 205, 209,
211, 212, 217, 218, 324, 349,
371, 381, 382, 391, 399, 413,
441, 443, 460, 486, 499,
501, 515

Z

Zeichner, K. M., 230
Zgaga, P., 9, 215, 216, 234,
237, 270, 277, 278, 286,
306, 545
Zhigalova, M., 19, 494,
495, 497
Zhuk, A. I., 483, 489–491, 493

Printed in the United States
by Baker & Taylor Publisher Services